Lecture Notes in Artificial Intelligence   10947

Subseries of Lecture Notes in Computer Science

LNAI Series Editors

Randy Goebel
   University of Alberta, Edmonton, Canada
Yuzuru Tanaka
   Hokkaido University, Sapporo, Japan
Wolfgang Wahlster
   DFKI and Saarland University, Saarbrücken, Germany

LNAI Founding Series Editor

Joerg Siekmann
   DFKI and Saarland University, Saarbrücken, Germany

More information about this series at http://www.springer.com/series/1244

Carolyn Penstein Rosé · Roberto Martínez-Maldonado
H. Ulrich Hoppe · Rose Luckin
Manolis Mavrikis · Kaska Porayska-Pomsta
Bruce McLaren · Benedict du Boulay (Eds.)

Artificial Intelligence in Education

19th International Conference, AIED 2018
London, UK, June 27–30, 2018
Proceedings, Part I

 Springer

Editors
Carolyn Penstein Rosé
Carnegie Mellon University
Pittsburgh, PA
USA

Manolis Mavrikis
UCL Institute of Education
London
UK

Roberto Martínez-Maldonado
University of Technology
Sydney, NSW
Australia

Kaska Porayska-Pomsta
UCL Institute of Education
London
UK

H. Ulrich Hoppe
University of Duisburg-Essen
Duisburg
Germany

Bruce McLaren
Carnegie Mellon University
Pittsburgh, PA
USA

Rose Luckin
UCL Institute of Education
London
UK

Benedict du Boulay
University of Sussex
Brighton
UK

ISSN 0302-9743   ISSN 1611-3349   (electronic)
Lecture Notes in Artificial Intelligence
ISBN 978-3-319-93842-4   ISBN 978-3-319-93843-1   (eBook)
https://doi.org/10.1007/978-3-319-93843-1

Library of Congress Control Number: 2018947319

LNCS Sublibrary: SL7 – Artificial Intelligence

Printed on acid-free paper

This Springer imprint is published by the registered company Springer International Publishing AG
part of Springer Nature
The registered company address is: Gewerbestrasse 11, 6330 Cham, Switzerland

Preface

The 19th International Conference on Artificial Intelligence in Education (AIED 2018) was held during June 27–30, 2018, in London, UK. AIED 2018 was the latest in a longstanding series of (now yearly) international conferences for high-quality research in intelligent systems and cognitive science for educational computing applications. The conference provides opportunities for the cross-fertilization of approaches, techniques, and ideas from the many fields that comprise AIED, including computer science, cognitive and learning sciences, education, game design, psychology, sociology, linguistics, as well as many domain-specific areas. Since the first AIED meeting over 30 years ago, both the breadth of the research and the reach of the technologies have expanded in dramatic ways.

For the 2018 conference on Artificial Intelligence in Education, we were excited to have a co-located event, the "Festival of Learning," together with the International Conference of the Learning Sciences (ICLS) and "Learning at Scale" (L@S). The festival took place in London (UK) during June 24–30. Since the days of landmark tutoring systems such as SCHOLAR and WHY decades ago, the fields of artificial intelligence, online learning, and the learning sciences have grown up side-by-side, frequently intersecting, synergizing, and challenging one another. As these fields have grown and matured, they have each experienced trends and waves, and each has seen a recent renewal that we celebrate in this year's conference. In artificial intelligence, the most recent renewal is in the emerging area of deep learning, where advances in computing capacity both in terms of memory and processing speed have facilitated a resurgence of interest in neural network models, with greater capacity than in the last neural network revolution. In the learning sciences, a recent emphasis on scaling up educational opportunities has birthed new areas of interest such as massive open online courses, which are also an important focus for the L@S community. In this year's conference we considered these recent renewals together and asked how advances in artificial intelligence can impact human learning at a massive scale. More specifically we asked how the fields of artificial intelligence and learning sciences may speak to one another at the confluence, which is the field of artificial intelligence in education. Thus, the theme of this year's conference was "Bridging the Behavioral and the Computational: Deep Learning in Humans and Machines."

There were 192 submissions as full papers to AIED 2018, of which 45 were accepted as long papers (12 pages) with oral presentation at the conference (for an acceptance rate of 23%), and 76 were accepted for poster presentation with four pages in the proceedings. Of the 51 papers directly submitted as poster papers, 15 were accepted. Apart from a few exceptions, each submission was reviewed by three Program Committee (PC) members including one senior PC member serving as a meta-reviewer. The program chairs checked the reviews for quality, and where necessary, requesting that reviewers elaborate their review or shift to a more constructive orientation. Our goal was to encourage substantive and constructive reviews without interfering with the reviewers' judgment in order to enable a fair and responsible process. In addition, submissions underwent a discussion period to ensure that all reviewers' opinions would be considered and leveraged to generate a group recommendation to the program chairs. Final decisions were made by carefully considering both scores and meta-reviews as well as the discussions, checking for consistency, weighing more heavily on the meta-review. We also took the constraints of the program into account and sought to keep the acceptance rate within a relatively typical range for this conference. It was a landmark year in terms of number of submissions, so the acceptance rate this year was lower than it has been in recent years, although the number of accepted papers was substantially higher. We see this as a mark of progress – something to be proud of as a community.

Three distinguished speakers gave plenary invited talks illustrating prospective directions for the field: Tom Mitchell (Carnegie Mellon University, USA), Paulo Blikstein (Stanford University, USA), and Michael Thomas (Birkbeck, University of London, UK). The conference also included:

- A Young Researchers Track that provided doctoral students with the opportunity to present their ongoing doctoral research at the conference and receive invaluable feedback from the research community.
- Interactive Events sessions during which AIED attendees could experience first-hand new and emerging intelligent learning environments via interactive demonstrations.
- An Industry and Innovation Track intended to support connections between industry (both for-profit and non-profit) and the research community.

AIED 2018 hosted one full-day and nine half-day workshops and tutorials on the full gamut of topics related to broad societal issues such as ethics and equity, methodologies such as gamification and personalization, as well as new technologies, tools, frameworks, development methodologies, and much more.

We wish to acknowledge the great effort by our colleagues at the University College London in making this conference possible. Special thanks goes to Springer for sponsoring the AIED 2018 Best Paper Award and the AIED 2018 Best Student Paper Award. We also want to acknowledge the amazing work of the AIED 2018 Organizing Committee, the senior PC members, the PC members, and the reviewers (listed herein), who with their enthusiastic contributions gave us invaluable support in putting this conference together.

April 2018

Carolyn Rosé
Roberto Martínez-Maldonado
Ulrich Hoppe
Rose Luckin
Manolis Mavrikis
Kaska Porayska-Pomsta
Bruce McLaren
Benedict du Boulay

Organization

Program Committee

Lalitha Agnihotri	McGraw Hill Education
Esma Aimeur	University of Montreal, Canada
Patricia Albacete	University of Pittsburgh, USA
Vincent Aleven	Carnegie Mellon University, USA
Sagaya Amalathas	UNITAR International University, Malaysia
Ivon Arroyo	Worcester Polytechnic Institute, USA
Roger Azevedo	North Carolina State University, USA
Nilufar Baghaei	UNITEC
Ryan Baker	University of Pennsylvania, USA
Nigel Beacham	University of Aberdeen, UK
Gautam Biswas	Vanderbilt University, USA
Ig Ibert Bittencourt	Federal University of Alagoas, Brazil
Nigel Bosch	University of Illinois Urbana-Champaign, USA
Jesus G. Boticario	Universidad Nacional de Educacion a Distancia
Jacqueline Bourdeau	TELUQ
Kristy Elizabeth Boyer	University of Florida, USA
Bert Bredeweg	University of Amsterdam, The Netherlands
Paul Brna	University of Leeds, UK
Christopher Brooks	University of Michigan, USA
Tak-Wai Chan	National Central University
Mohamed Amine Chatti	University of Duisburg-Essen, Germany
Weiqin Chen	University of Bergen, Norway
Wenli Chen	National Institute of Education, Singapore
Min Chi	North Carolina State University, USA
Sherice Clarke	University of California San Diego, USA
Andrew Clayphan	The University of Sydney, Australia
Cristina Conati	The University of British Columbia, Canada
Mark G. Core	University of Southern California, USA
Scotty Craig	Arizona State University, Polytechnic, USA
Alexandra Cristea	The University of Warwick, UK
Mutlu Cukurova	UCL Knowledge Lab, UK
Ben Daniel	University of Otago, New Zealand
Chandan Dasgupta	Indian Institute of Technology Bombay, India
Barbara Di Eugenio	University of Illinois at Chicago, USA
Vania Dimitrova	University of Leeds, UK
Peter Dolog	Aalborg University, Denmark
Hendrik Drachsler	The Open University
Artur Dubrawski	Carnegie Mellon University, USA

Kristy Elizabeth Boyer	University of Florida, USA
Stephen Fancsali	Carnegie Learning, Inc.
Mingyu Feng	SRI International, USA
Mark Fenton-O'Creevy	The Open University
Carol Forsyth	Educational Testing Service
Albrecht Fortenbacher	HTW Berlin, Germany
Davide Fossati	Emory University, USA
Reva Freedman	Northern Illinois University, USA
Dragan Gasevic	Monash University, Australia
Elena Gaudioso	Universidad Nacional de Educacion a Distancia
Andrew Gibson	University of Technology, Sydney, Australia
Ashok Goel	Georgia Institute of Technology, USA
Ilya Goldin	2U, Inc.
Art Graesser	University of Memphis, USA
Joseph Grafsgaard	University of Colorado Boulder, USA
Monique Grandbastien	LORIA, Université de Lorraine, France
Agneta Gulz	Lund University Cognitive Science, Sweden
Gahgene Gweon	Seoul National University, South Korea
Jason Harley	University of Alberta, Canada
Andreas Harrer	University of Applied Sciences and Arts Dortmund, Germany
Peter Hastings	DePaul University, USA
Yuki Hayashi	Osaka Prefecture University, Japan
Tobias Hecking	University of Duisburg-Essen, Germany
Neil Heffernan	Worcester Polytechnic Institute, UK
Tsukasa Hirashima	Hiroshima University, Japan
H. Ulrich Hoppe	University of Duisburg-Essen, Germany
Sharon Hsiao	Arizona State University, USA
Christoph Igel	DFKI Berlin, Germany
Paul Salvador Inventado	California State University Fullerton, USA
Seiji Isotani	University of São Paulo, Brazil
Sridhar Iyer	IIT Bombay, India
G. Tanner Jackson	Educational Testing Service
Pamela Jordan	University of Pittsburgh, USA
Sandra Katz	University of Pittsburgh, USA
Judy Kay	The University of Sydney, Australia
Fazel Keshtkar	St. John's University, USA
Simon Knight	University of Technology, Sydney, Australia
Kenneth Koedinger	Carnegie Mellon University, USA
Tomoko Kojiri	Kansai University, Japan
Siu Cheung Kong	The Education University of Hong Kong, SAR China
Amruth Kumar	Ramapo College of New Jersey, USA
Rohit Kumar	Spotify
Tanja Käser	Stanford University, USA
Jean-Marc Labat	Université Paris 6, France
Sébastien Lallé	The University of British Columbia, Canada

Nguyen-Thinh Le	Humboldt Universität zu Berlin, Germany
Blair Lehman	Educational Testing Service
James Lester	North Carolina State University, USA
Chee-Kit Looi	NIE, Singapore
Rose Luckin	The London Knowledge Lab, UK
Vanda Luengo	Université Pierre et Marie Curie, France
Collin Lynch	North Carolina State University, USA
Roberto Martinez-Maldonado	University of Technology, Sydney, Australia
Judith Masthoff	University of Aberdeen, UK
Noboru Matsuda	Texas A&M University, USA
Manolis Mavrikis	The London Knowledge Lab, UK
Gordon McCalla	University of Saskatchewan, Canada
Bruce McLaren	Carnegie Mellon University, USA
Agathe Merceron	Beuth University of Applied Sciences Berlin, Germany
Alain Mille	Université Claude Bernard Lyon 1, France
Marcelo Milrad	Linnaeus University, Sweden
Ritayan Mitra	IIT Bombay, India
Tanja Mitrovic	University of Canterbury, UK
Kazuhisa Miwa	Nagoya University, Japan
Riichiro Mizoguchi	Japan Advanced Institute of Science and Technology, Japan
Kasia Muldner	Carleton University, Canada
Kiyoshi Nakabayashi	Chiba Institute of Technology, Japan
Roger Nkambou	Université du Québec à Montréal, Canada
Benjamin Nye	University of Southern California, USA
Amy Ogan	Carnegie Mellon University, USA
Hiroaki Ogata	Kyoto University, Japan
Andrew Olney	University of Memphis, USA
Jennifer Olsen	Ecole Polytechnique Fédérale de Lausanne, Switzerland
Helen Pain	The University of Edinburgh, UK
Ana Paiva	INESC
Luc Paquette	University of Illinois at Urbana-Champaign, USA
Abelardo Pardo	University of South Australia
Zachary Pardos	University of California Berkely, USA
Philip I. Pavlik Jr.	University of Memphis, USA
Mykola Pechenizkiy	Eindhoven University of Technology, The Netherlands
Radek Pelánek	Masaryk University Brno, Czech Republic
Niels Pinkwart	Humboldt-Universität zu Berlin, Germany
Elvira Popescu	University of Craiova, Romania
Kaska Porayska-Pomsta	The London Knowledge Lab, UK
Alexandra Poulovassilis	Birkbeck College, University of London, UK
Luis P. Prieto	Tallinn University, Estonia
Anna Rafferty	Carleton College, Canada
Martina Rau	University of Wisconsin-Madison, USA

Abstracts of Keynotes

What if People Taught Computers?

Tom Mitchell

Carnegie Mellon University, USA
tom.mitchell@cmu.edu

Abstract. Whereas AIED focuses primarily on how computers can help teach people, this talk will consider how people might teach computers. Why? There are at least two good reasons: First, we might discover something interesting about instructional strategies by building computers that can be taught. Second, if people could teach computers in the same way that we teach one another, suddenly everybody would be able to program. We present our ongoing research on machine learning by verbal instruction and demonstration. Our prototype Learning by Instruction Agent (LIA) allows people to teach their mobile devices by verbal instruction to perform new actions. Given a verbal command that it does not understand (e.g., "Drop a note to Bill that I'll be late."), the system allows the user to teach it by breaking the procedure down into a sequence of more primitive, more understandable steps (e.g., "First create a new email. Put the email address of Bill into the recipient field."...). As a result, LIA both acquires new linguistic knowledge that enables it to better parse language into its intended meaning, and it learns how to execute the target procedure. In related work with Brad Meyers we are exploring combining verbal instruction with demonstration of procedures on the phone, to achieve "show and tell" instruction. In work with Shashank Srivastava and Igor Labutov, we are extending the approach to general concept learning (e.g., in order to teach "if I receive an important email, then be sure I see it before leaving work." one must teach the concept "important email."). This talk will survey progress to date, implications, and open questions. This work involves a variety of collaborations with Igor Labutov, Amos Azaria, Shashank Srivastava, Brad Meyers and Toby Li.

Time to Make Hard Choices for AI in Education

Paulo Blikstein

Stanford University, USA
paulob@stanford.edu

Abstract. The field of AI in education has exploded in the past ten years. Many factors have contributed to this unprecedented growth, such as the ubiquity of digital devices in schools, the rise of online learning, the availability of data and fast growth in related fields such as machine learning and data mining. But with great power comes great responsibility: the flipside of the growth of AIED is that now our technologies can be deployed in large numbers to millions of children. And while there is great potential to transform education, there is also considerable risk to destroy public education as we know it, either directly or via unintended consequences. This is not an exaggeration: in recent months, we have indeed learned that the combination of social media, technological ubiquity, AI, lack of privacy, and under-regulated sectors can go the wrong way, and that AI has today a disproportionate power to shape human activity and society.

On the other hand, most schools of education around the world are not equipped – or not interested – in this debate. They either ignore this conversation, or simply attack the entire enterprise of AI in education—but these attacks are not stopping wide dissemination of various types of AIED projects in schools, mainly driven by corporations and fueled by incentives that might not work in the benefit of students (i.e., massive cost reduction, deprofessionalization of teachers, additional standardization of content and instruction).

In this scenario, the academic AIED community has a crucial responsibility—it could be the only voice capable to steering the debate, and the technology, towards more productive paths. This talk will be about the hard choices that AIED needs to face in the coming years, reviewing the history of AI in education, its promise, and possible futures. For example, should we focus on technologies that promote student agency and curricular flexibility, or on making sure everyone learns the same? How do we tackle new learning environments such as makerspaces and other inquiry-driven spaces? What is the role of physical science labs versus virtual, AI-driven labs? How can AIED impact—positively and negatively—equity in education?

I will review some of these issues, and mention examples of contemporary work on novel fields such as multimodal learning analytics, which is trying to detect patterns in complex learning processes in hands-on activities, and new types of inquiry-driven science environments.

The AIED community is strategically placed at a crucial point in the history of education, with potential to (at last) impact millions of children. But the way forward will require more than technical work—it will require some hard choices that we should be prepared to make.

Has the Potential Role of Neuroscience in Education Been Overstated? Can Computational Approaches Help Build Bridges Between Them?

Michael Thomas

University College London/Birkbeck University of London, UK
m.thomas@bbk.ac.uk

Abstract. In the first part of this talk, I will assess the progress of the field of educational neuroscience in attempting to translate basic neuroscience findings to classroom practice. While much heralded, has educational neuroscience yielded concrete benefits for educators or policymakers? Is it likely to in the future? Or is its main contribution merely to dispel neuromyths? In the second half of the talk, I will assess the role that computational approaches can play in this inter-disciplinary interaction. Is neuroscience best viewed as a source of inspiration to build better algorithms for educational AI? Or can neurocomputational models help us build better theories that link data across behaviour, environment, brain, and genetics into an integrated account of children's learning?

Contents – Part I

Full Papers

Contents – Part II

Industry Papers

Young Researcher Papers

Workshops and Tutorials

Full Papers

Investigating the Impact of a Meaningful Gamification-Based Intervention on Novice Programmers' Achievement

Jenilyn L. Agapito[(⊠)] and Ma. Mercedes T. Rodrigo

Ateneo de Manila University, Quezon City, Philippines
jen.agapito@gmail.com, mrodrigo@ateneo.edu

Abstract. Gamification is becoming a popular classroom intervention used in computer science instruction, including CS1, the first course computer science students take. It is being used as a medium to encourage certain student behaviors in anticipation of positive effects on learning experience and achievement. However, existing studies have mostly implemented reward-based game elements which have resulted to contrasting behaviors among students. Meaningful gamification, defined as the use of game design elements to encourage users build internal motivation to behave in a certain way, is contended to be a more effective approach. This concept is founded on the 'Self-Determination Theory', which states that there are three components associated with intrinsic motivation: mastery, autonomy, and relatedness. This study describes the analysis of data collected from an experiment where students of an introductory programming class used a system embedded with elements that map to the components of the Self-Determination Theory: feedback cycles, freedom to fail, and progress to support mastery; control to enable autonomy; and collaboration for relatedness. It looks into whether the experimental group performed significantly better than the control group. It also tries to explore how different user types respond to the different game design elements.

Keywords: Novice programmers · Gamification · CS1

1 Introduction

Computer science educators and researchers are concerned about student retention and attrition [2, 5, 13, 28, 32]. CS1, the first course that computer science students take, has a failure rate of at least 30% across institutions [3, 31]. Students typically enroll in CS1 with little to no background in programming. They are introduced to a fundamental but difficult skill area. This experience shapes their impression of both the course and degree program. However, some researchers speculate that traditional teaching methodologies may not be the ideal choice for programming classes [13, 31]. In particular, it may no longer be effective for students of this generation. Young people these days are attuned to the use of technologies to reinvent social living, communication, and learning, causing their divergent perspective on the dynamics and operations of the world, including the classroom [19].

© Springer International Publishing AG, part of Springer Nature 2018
C. Penstein Rosé et al. (Eds.): AIED 2018, LNAI 10947, pp. 3–16, 2018.
https://doi.org/10.1007/978-3-319-93843-1_1

An approach to instruction reinvention dubbed as gamification has recently become popular. Gamification is defined as adding game-like elements and mechanics to a learning process [7, 10]. It intends to provide users with a more gameful experience and to encourage certain desired behaviors [6] by adding motivational affordances in an environment.

1.1   Gamification in Education

Gamification has become evident in education and classroom design. It is shown to be an effective method to help at-risk students succeed [29]. Several studies focus on gamifying Computer Science subjects [9, 14, 22, 27], including CS1 [12, 20, 30]. They experiment with incorporating game design elements such as badges/reward systems [12, 14, 22, 27, 30], leaderboards [14, 22, 27, 30], point systems and leveling [14], and microworlds [22] into certain aspects of the learning environment (e.g. home works and practical sessions). Students express preference of a gamified strategy over the traditional because it is able to address their need for fun, pleasure, and cooperation [18]. It taps directly into their fundamental desire for recognition, reward, status, competition, collaboration, and self-expression [11].

1.2   Pitfalls of Gamification

Learning environments are commonly gamified by using badges, levels/leaderboards, achievements, and points because they are relatively easy to implement. This practice is referred to as reward-based gamification [24]. However, this is effective in contexts that call for short-term change in behavior and those that can continue to supply the rewards [24]. In the classroom, some students perceived the method enthusiastically and performed well, whereas others felt demotivated and disengaged. Badges can be perceived as an unattractive alternative to grades [27]. Competition-based leaderboards may induce a feeling of embarrassment when made public [17]. Some continue to fight for the top rank while some disengage altogether [23]. They generate uneasiness leading students to dismiss it as a good representation of knowledge [8]. Competition is not fun for some students. Another drawback is when they become too driven by competition that they lose sight of the real purpose, which is to learn [30].

1.3   Meaningful Gamification

Nicholson [23, 24] broadens [7]'s definition of gamification as the use of game design elements to help a user build intrinsic motivation – motivation not triggered by external rewards – to encourage engagement in a specific context [24]. This is referred to as Meaningful Gamification. The theory behind is known as the Self-Determination Theory [4] which states that there are three components associated with intrinsic motivation: mastery, autonomy, and relatedness. Mastery is when one learns to the point of competence; autonomy means having a choice and control of paths; and relatedness is about one's social engagement. There are contentions that gamifying the classroom entails rigorous research and design efforts to maximize its benefits. Otherwise, it will become ineffective because of the potential adverse effects to some students.

1.4 The Gamification User Types Hexad

Personality psychology suggests that two people who seem similar can exhibit different behaviors once subjected to the same situation due to their personality differences [26]. In the case of computerized interactive systems, there are studies indicating that users' idiosyncratic attributes, such as their personalities or motivations, affect their system interactions. Gamification has been used to encourage certain behaviors in anticipation of increasing motivation and engagement. However, experiments reported cases of disengagement and demotivation. Participants have preference of or inclination to varying game design elements. A factor to the results may be their unique personalities or motivations. This, however, is an area that needs to be further studied.

Fig. 1. The gamification user types hexad.

The Gamification User Types Hexad by Marczewski [21] is a framework for user typology that can be aptly used for gamification research. It consists of six user types that characterize people's intrinsic and extrinsic motivations as described by the Self-Determination Theory [9]. These are illustrated in Fig. 1. The four intrinsically motivated user types are Achiever, Free Spirit, Socializer, and Philanthropist. This framework opens up opportunities for better understanding users of gamified environments. Understanding this area can help system designers implement gamified systems that are able to address multiple user types, which has been considered as more effective than a one-size-fits-all approach.

This paper presents the results of a study to explore the impact of gamification on novice programmers' achievement in an introductory programming class. It focuses on the design and implementation of a programming-based activity management system embedded with game design elements based on meaningful gamification. Using data collected while students used the system, we attempt to answer the following questions:

1. Are the scores of a group who used the gamified system significantly higher than a group who used a non-gamified version?
2. How do different user types, as determined by the Gamification User Types, Hexad vary in their response to the different gamification elements?

2 The Gamified System

A gamified programming-based activity management system for introductory programming classes was developed. It is a web-based platform that allows teachers manage assessment activities such as quizzes and laboratory exercises typical of CS1. The questions that may be included in the activities are divided into three categories as in [25]: (1) factual or conceptual; (2) comprehension; and (3) generation questions. Conceptual questions assess if students recall and recognize programming concepts. Activities under this category are multiple choice questions, true or false, and identification. Comprehension questions check if students can read code by determining the output or the values of a certain variable through code tracing. Generation questions cover programming exercises that test the students' ability to write programs.

2.1 Game Design Elements in the System

As discussed, gamifying learning environments do not always achieve the intended outcome. Ineffective implementation could disengage students and in the most serious case, demean and demoralize [23]. Reward-based practices, though easier to employ, do not maximize its potential. In this light, the choice of elements used in the system was anchored on meaningful gamification, purposely mapping them to the three components of the Self-Determination Theory. These elements are (1) control to enable autonomy; (2) feedback cycles, freedom to fail, and progress for mastery; and (3) collaboration to support relatedness.

Autonomy. Giving students options on questions/problems to answer affords them the opportunity to work on something they feel they are good at. This is a modest method of giving students a sense of autonomy. The system allows teachers to include extra items and specify the number of required items. They can choose from the set of questions/problems and answer/solve only up to what is required (e.g. solve 3 out of the 5 problems).

Mastery. The concept of "practice makes perfect" helps support mastery. When a system permits mistakes with no associated high stakes, students are more willing to take risks knowing they can recover. Immediate feedback is also important to help them understand the effects of their actions. These are supported in the system through feedback cycles and freedom to fail. The feedback mechanism includes (1) displaying the score; and (2) marks indicating correct and incorrect items. Still on mastery, progress for various skills is represented as a radar chart to give the students a picture of their headway relative to system-facilitated activities. This is displayed in their "Profile", as shown in Fig. 2, along with other information. The skills tracked by the system are shown in Table 1 with the question types/activities to assess them.

'Debugging' characterizes how students struggle with syntax errors while programming and is evaluated using the Error Quotient (EQ, a quantification of students' compilation behaviors by considering the type, location, as well as frequency of encountered syntax errors [15, 16]. 'Tutoring' represents how students collaborate with other students through peer-mentoring. This is discussed more in the next subsection.

Fig. 2. A student's profile view.

Table 1. Skills represented in the progress chart.

Skill	Question/Activity	In-system name
Knowledge or programming elements	MCQs, true or false, identification	Concepts
Ability to trace code	Code tracing	Tracing
Ability to correct syntax errors while writing a program	Programming	Debugging
Ability to write solutions to programming problems		Programming
Social/collaborative skills	Peer mentoring	Tutoring

Relatedness. Targeting relatedness is the opportunity for collaboration through peer-mentoring. A student may be awarded with "tutor points" by another when the former mentors the latter. They get to decide who they seek for help and whether they will reward them or not.

3 Experiment/User Testing

Two (2) iterations of testing were conducted on different sets of students. The methods were the same for both iterations. However, prior to the second round, the gamified system was modified based on how the first group interacted with the game design elements. This was to test whether the students' response to the system may be attributed to the available game design elements.

The first iteration was conducted on students enrolled in a CS1 class at the Ateneo de Manila University, Philippines. Results of the experiment are discussed in [1]. The second iteration was in Central Bicol State University of Agriculture-Sipocot (CBSUA-Sipocot), a state university in the Philippines. Details are described below.

3.1 Participants

Participants of the second iteration were students of CBSUA-Sipocot. They were taught programming fundamentals using C++. Two sections (1A and 1B) of students aged 18 – 33 participated. They were of varying ages because of open admission and according to their instructor, these students stopped for a number of years after high school before enrolling to college.

Section 1A had 35 students while section 1B had 25. Thirty-two (32) students from 1A completed all the exercises given during the experiment. However, only seven (7) from 1B were able to completely finish. Analysis and discussions in the succeeding sections are on the data involving only these students.

Demographics. The students completed a demographics questionnaire on the first meeting to collect information on their profiles such as age and gender. Section 1A had 15 males and 17 females, while section B had 3 males and 4 females. They were freshmen students taking up a course in information technology.

3.2 Methods

The two classes were randomly assigned as either the control (section 1A) or experimental (section 1B) group. The control group used a non-gamified version of the system, that is, the game design elements described in Sect. 2 were not available in their version. They were not provided with extra items in activities; results were reported to them on the next meeting; students were only allowed one (1) attempt for each activity; and there were no skills tracked.

As stated previously, the features of the gamified system were modified based on how students from the first iteration responded to the different elements. Table 2 shows the features used in the two experiments.

The number of extra items was increased to better provide data on the order in which the items are answered. When a student skips items, it is taken as an indication that he/she picked items he/she is comfortable answering rather than just going through the activity sequentially. A "Display Score" button was added to track if students like to see their scores. Button clicks are logged to indicate this. The number of attempts was decreased from "unlimited" to three (3) – the average number of re-attempts made by students in the first round. As an added metric for progress, a "Display Skill" option was added in their profiles. It allows them to select one of the five skills tracked, ideally their strongest, that will be visible to their classmates. A student choosing to "showcase" his/her preferred skill suggests that the information represented by the progress chart is significant to him/her. As for collaboration, feedback from the first experiment suggests the participants did not know there was such a feature. To make it more visible, a message that emphasizes it was added.

The experiment went on for three days. It was conducted during an arranged schedule which ran for two (2) hours. The questionnaires and activities given are in Table 3. All activities were the same for both the control and experimental groups.

Short quizzes were comprised of ten items each worth one (1) point. The programming exercises had one problem worth five (5) points. Long quizzes came in two parts – an objective and tracing part and a programming part – totaling to twenty-five (25) points.

Table 2. Features of system used by the experimental group.

	Game design element	Iteration 1 features	Iteration 2 features
Autonomy	Control	Extra question in quiz; extra problem in programming exercise	5 extra questions in quiz; 3 extra questions in programming exercise
Mastery	Feedback cycles	Score displayed after submitting an activity; feedback whether each item is correct or wrong may be shown by clicking the 'Show Feedback' button	Score may be displayed by clicking on "Show Score" button; feedback whether each item is correct or wrong may be shown by clicking the 'Show Feedback' button
	Freedom to fail	Unlimited attempts for an activity	3 attempts for an activity
	Progress	Profile which shows radar chart	A "Display Skill" option the profile which makes their chosen skill visible to their classmates
Relatedness	Collaboration	Facility to commend a classmate	A message emphasizing the feature that they can commend a peer

Table 3. Questionnaires and activities given during testing.

Questionnaire/Activity	Day 1	Day2	Day3
Demographics questionnaire	✓		
Gamification user types hexad	✓		
Short quiz	✓	✓	
Programming exercise	✓	✓	
Long quiz			✓
Debriefing questionnaire			✓

3.3 Data Collected

Students' scores in the different activities were collected for both the control and experimental groups. Additional data collected from the version used by the experimental group are the following: (1) number of attempts; (2) if "Show Score" is on; (3) if "Show Item Feedback" is on; (4) question chain (order in which the student answered the questions); (5) number of profile views (the page that has the radar char); (6) if student displayed a skill; and (7) number of tutor points awarded and received.

4   Results

The research questions stipulated previously shall be answered using the data of the students who were able to complete all activities given during the testing.

4.1   Analysis of Students' Scores in Activities

An independent samples t-test was conducted to compare the average short quiz and programming scores and total long quiz scores of the control and experimental groups. Contrary to the first experiment, no significant differences were found in the scores of the two groups: *Short Quiz*: control (M = 5.98, SD = 3.41), experimental (M = 6.07, SD = 2.45), t(10) = 0.129, p = 0.90008; *Programming Exercise*: control (M = 1.41, SD = 1.75), experimental (M = 1.21, SD = 1.57), t(9) = 0.363, p = 0.362; and *Long Quiz*: control (M = 11.69, SD = 22.74), experimental (M = 13.43, SD = 7.95), t(15) = 1.28, p = 0.1098.

4.2   Students' Use of the Different Game Design Elements

As mentioned, the game design elements employed are freedom to fail, feedback, and progress to support mastery; control for autonomy; and collaboration for relatedness.

As determined by the Gamification User Types Hexad, students' user types in the experimental group are shown in Fig. 3.

Freedom to Fail. Freedom to fail is implemented by allowing the students three (3) attempts in a given activity. This gives them the chance to reattempt failed work. See Table 4 for the number of students who took advantage of this. All students reattempted at least one (1) of the six (6) activities. One (1) student made reattempts to five (5) out of the six (6) activities and he was a Philanthropist/Socializer. As in the first experiment, varying numbers for the user types are manifested. The results may show students' tendency to utilize reattempts if available, regardless of user type.

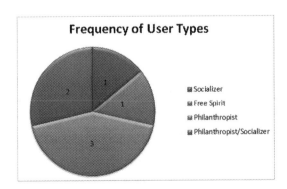

Fig. 3. User types of students in experimental group.

Table 4. Number of students who made re-attempts.

Activity	# of students with 1 attempt	# of students with > 1 attempt	Average # of attempts	Max # of attempts
SQ1	1	6	2	3
SQ2	4	3	2	3
PE1	5	2	1	2
PE2	3	4	3	3
LQpt1	1	6	2	3
LQpt2	5	2	1	2

Feedback. The feedback mechanism implemented in the system used in the second experiments includes (1) a 'Display Score' button that allows a student to view his score; and (2) a 'Show Item Feedback' button that a student can click to display the marks indicating which items are correct and wrong. The system unobtrusively logs when they click on this button to provide data as to whether the feature is being utilized. All seven (7) students clicked the 'Display Score' button for all activities indicating that the score is a vital information to them, regardless of user type. The number of students who utilized the 'Show Item Feedback' feature is shown in Fig. 4.

Consistent with the first experiment, more students clicked on the button for activities comprised of conceptual and comprehension questions (SQ1, SQ2, LQpt1). This may be because there were more items in these activities than the activities with generation questions (PE1, PE2, LQpt2). Hence, feedback is helpful in pointing out which of those items they correctly and incorrectly answered. Additionally, they needed to answer only one (1) problem in PE1, PE2, and LQpt2. Thus, per item feedback may have no longer been useful.

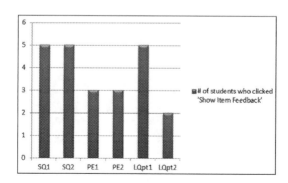

Fig. 4. Number of students who clicked the 'Show Item Feedback' button.

Two (2) students, a Free Spirit and a Socializer, did not show per item feedback for all activities. Two (2) other students, a Philanthropist and a Philanthropist/Socializer showed per item feedback for all activities.

Progress. Aradar chart found in a student's profile represents how they are moving forwards relative to the system-facilitated activities. It includes a summary of the number of activities they have taken, passed, and failed. Views on their profile can be telling that the data shown in the page is notable for them. All seven (7) students viewed their profiles at least once. Two (2) students, a Philanthropist and a Philanthropist/Socializer had the highest recorded profile views count of twelve (12).

An additional metric for progress was a feature to display one's skill so it is viewable by their classmates. Three (3) students utilized this feature, two (2) of them were Philanthropists and one (1) was a Socializer.

Control. The system keeps track of the sequence of items a student answers through a variable called the "question chain". If a student's question chain for an attempt is different from its question sequence, the order in which items were displayed, it could mean the student decided to answer items in the order that he/she is comfortable with. In the previous experiment, students were given an extra item in the quizzes and an programming exercises. They can decide which items to answer and choose to answer the items in the order they prefer. This allows them to skip items they are not ready to answer at the moment. Results showed that question chains tend to differ more on SQ1, SQ2, and LQpt1. Again, the activities comprised of conceptual and comprehension questions and that had more items compared with PE1, PE2, and LQpt2 – activities with generation type questions.

To check whether students actually answer activities non-sequentially, the number of extra items was increased in the second experiment. Quizzes had five (5) extra items and programming exercises had three (3). Figure 5 shows the high number of question chains different from the question sequences of the attempts. Adding more items, especially in the programming exercises, evidenced student's inclination to 'skip' items or answer them in an order different from how they are shown. This may be indicative of their exercise of choice in terms of which items to answer or which items to answer first. This may be observed in spite of students' user types.

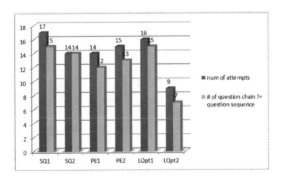

Fig. 5. Number of attempts whose question chains differ from questions sequences.

Collaboration. The system has a commendation facility that seeks to provide an opportunity for collaboration through peer-mentoring. A student may be awarded with "tutor points" by another student when the former mentors the latter. A student has three (3) commends that he/she can award to a peer of his/her choice. Since feedback from last experiment suggested this was not visible, a message highlighting it was added. Out of the seven (7) students, four (4) awarded commends and three (3) received commends. The three students who were awarded with tutor points were all Philanthropists – the user type who likes helping out other people.

5   Limitations

The results of this paper may not be sufficient to make any generalization regarding students' response to gamification because of the sample size, especially of the experimental group. Additionally, implementation of the different elements is limited to those discussed above. Exploring other game elements and their implementations and experimenting with more students may improve results. Nonetheless, the study contributes information that may facilitate further studies in the area.

6   Conclusions

This paper presents the analysis of data on the use of meaningful gamification in an introductory programming class. Data collected from CS1 students were analyzed to determine (1) whether scores of a group who used a gamified system are significantly higher than a group who used a non-gamified version; and (2) how different user types vary in their response to the different gamification elements.

There were no significant differences in the average scores per activity (i.e. short quiz and programming exercise) and total long quiz scores (i.e. sum of long quiz parts 1 and 2 scores) of the two groups. This result is contrary to [1], in which the scores of the experimental group were found to be significantly higher. One factor may be the low number of students who completed all the activities in the second experiment. This can be verified by running further experiments.

Part of the goal was to determine how user types respond to the various game design elements. However, because of the low number of students who finished completely, the results cannot be deemed conclusive. Nonetheless, consistent with the first experiment, students utilize reattempts and take control over items to answer. The score is a vital form of feedback as evidenced by all students clicking on the 'Display Score' for all activities. Feedback per item is also important since it allows them to see which items need to be corrected in later opportunities. All students viewed their profiles at least once. Four (4) of the seven (7) students utilized the commend feature.

The results suggest students utilized the game design elements, particularly freedom to fail (reattempts), feedback cycles, and autonomy/control. However, patterns of students' interactions with the system are assumed to be more observable when the system is deployed in a class for a longer period of time (i.e. one semester) with more participants and activities.

7 Future Directions

Gamification is an interesting layer that can be built into intelligent tutoring systems. If implemented fittingly, its addition could aid in keeping learners motivated and engaged. This study aims to determine how different user types respond to certain game design elements. Patterns on interaction traces can serve as valuable information in characterizing learners. This could aid in developing personalized gamified intelligent systems able to adapt its game design elements to the user's learner type or interaction behaviors. Perhaps learning environments could automatically allow students to reattempt an activity depending on whether or not they passed their most recent attempt. Weaker students, those who do not pass, would most likely appreciate the chance to retake failed activities. Understanding what forms of feedbacks (e.g. score, correct/incorrect marks) are important to learners can aid in designing systems that can intelligently adapt the user interface to display only what seems relevant to its current user. These, among others, may serve as worthy additions to intelligent tutoring systems to support learning.

Acknowledgments. We would like to thank the student participants who signified their voluntary participation in the study. We also like to thank the College of Information Technology, CBSUA-Sipocot, its Dean – Mr. Dennis Gabon, and the CS1 instructors for permitting us to collect data in their school. Much gratitude to the Department of Science and Technology–Engineering Research and Development for Technology (DOST-ERDT) for the scholarship awarded to the student researcher. Lastly, we thank the Ateneo Laboratory for the Learning Sciences (ALLS), Ateneo de Manila University for supporting this study.

References

1. Agapito, J.L., Rodrigo, M.M.T.: Investigating the impact of gamification on novice programmers' achievement and learning experience. Submitted to Research and Practice in Technology Enhanced Learning (RPTEL) (2018)
2. Beaubouef, T., Mason, J.: Why the high attrition rate for computer science students: some thoughts and observations. ACM SIGCSE Bull. 37(2), 103–106 (2005)
3. Bennedsen, J., Caspersen, M.E.: Failure rates in introductory programming. ACM SIGCSE Bull. 39(2), 32–36 (2007)
4. Deci, E.L., Ryan, R.M.: Handbook of Self-determination Research. University Rochester Press, Rochester (2002)
5. Dehnadi, S., Bornat, R.: The camel has two humps (working title), pp. 1–21. Middlesex University, UK (2006)
6. Deterding, S., Björk, S.L., Nacke, L.E., Dixon, D., Lawley, E.: Designing gamification: creating gameful and playful experiences. In: CHI 2013 Extended Abstracts on Human Factors in Computing Systems, pp. 3263–3266. ACM, April 2013
7. Deterding, S., Dixon, D., Khaled, R., Nacke, L.: From game design elements to gamefulness: defining gamification. In: Proceedings of the 15th International Academic MindTrek Conference: Envisioning Future Media Environments, pp. 9–15. ACM, September 2011

8. DomíNguez, A., Saenz-De-Navarrete, J., De-Marcos, L., FernáNdez-Sanz, L., PagéS, C., MartíNez-Herrálz, J.J.: Gamifying learning experiences: practical implications and outcomes. Comput. Educ. **63**, 380–392 (2013)
9. Gibbons, T.E.L COR: a new course framework based on elements of game design. In: Proceedings of the 14th Annual ACM SIGITE Conference on Information Technology Education, pp. 77–82. ACM, October 2013
10. Glover, I.: Play as you learn: gamification as a technique for motivating learners (2013)
11. González, C., Area, M.: Breaking the rules: gamification of learning and educational materials. In Proceedings of the 2nd International Workshop on Interaction Design in Educational Environments, pp. 7–53 (2013)
12. Harrington, B.: TrAcademic: experiences with gamified practical sessions for a CS1 course. In: Proceedings of the 21st Western Canadian Conference on Computing Education, p. 25. ACM, May 2016
13. Hoda, R., Andreae, P.: It's not them, it's us! Why computer science fails to impress many first years. In: Proceedings of the Sixteenth Australasian Computing Education Conference, vol. 148, pp. 159–162. Australian Computer Society, Inc., January 2014
14. Ibáñez, M.B., Di-Serio, A., Delgado-Kloos, C.: Gamification for engaging computer science students in learning activities: a case study. IEEE Trans. Learn. Technol. **7**(3), 291–301 (2014)
15. Jadud, M.C.: An exploration of novice compilation behaviour in BlueJ. University of Kent (2006)
16. Jadud, M.C.: Methods and tools for exploring novice compilation behaviour. In: Proceedings of the Second International Workshop on Computing Education Research, pp. 73–84. ACM, September 2006
17. Kapp, K.M.: Games, gamification, and the quest for learner engagement. T+ D **66**(6), 64–68 (2012)
18. Kim, S.: Effects of the gamified class in engineering education environments. J. Convergence Inf. Technol. **8**(13), 253 (2013)
19. Klopfer, E., Osterweil, S., Groff, J., Haas, J.: Using the technology of today in the classroom today: the instructional power of digital games, social networking, simulations and how teachers can leverage them. Educ. Arcade **1**, 20 (2009)
20. Kumar, B., Khurana, P.: Gamification in education-learn computer programming with fun. Int. J. Comput. Distrib. Syst. **2**(1), 46–53 (2012)
21. Marczewski, A.: User types. In: Even Ninja Monkeys Like to Play: Gamification, Game Thinking and Motivational Design, 1st edn., pp. 65–80. CreateSpace Independent Publishing Platform (2015)
22. Neve, P., Livingstone, D., Hunter, G., Edwards, N., Alsop, G.: More than just a game: improving students' experience of learning programming through gamification. In: STEM Annual Conference 2014 (2014)
23. Nicholson, S.: Exploring gamification techniques for classroom management. Games+ Learning+ Society **9** (2013)
24. Nicholson, S.: A RECIPE for meaningful gamification. In: Reiners, T., Wood, Lincoln C. (eds.) Gamification in Education and Business, pp. 1–20. Springer, Cham (2015). https://doi.org/10.1007/978-3-319-10208-5_1
25. Orji, R., Mandryk, R.L., Vassileva, J., Gerling, K.M.: Tailoring persuasive health games to gamer type. In: Proceedings of the SIGCHI Conference on Human Factors in Computing Systems, pp. 2467–2476. ACM, April 2013
26. Paunonen, S.V., Ashton, M.C.: Big five factors and facets and the prediction of behavior. J. Pers. Soc. Psychol. **81**(3), 524 (2001)

27. Pirker, J., Riffnaller-Schiefer, M., Gütl, C.: Motivational active learning: engaging university students in computer science education. In: Proceedings of the 2014 Conference on Innovation and Technology in Computer Science Education, pp. 297–302. ACM, June 2014
28. Robins, A.: Learning edge momentum: a new account of outcomes in CS1. Comput. Sci. Educ. **20**(1), 37–71 (2010)
29. Ross, P.: Math teacher uses gamification to help at-risk students succeed. Recuperado el **24** (2011)
30. Sprint, G., Cook, D.: Enhancing the CS1 student experience with gamification. In: 2015 IEEE Integrated STEM Education Conference (ISEC), pp. 94–99. IEEE, March 2015
31. Watson, C., Li, F.W.: Failure rates in introductory programming revisited. In: Proceedings of the 2014 Conference on Innovation and Technology in Computer Science Education, pp. 39–44. ACM, June 2014
32. Wortman, D., Rheingans, P.: Visualizing trends in student performance across computer science courses. ACM SIGCSE Bull. **39**(1), 430–434 (2007)

Automatic Item Generation Unleashed: An Evaluation of a Large-Scale Deployment of Item Models

Yigal Attali[(⊠)]

Educational Testing Service,
Rosedale Road, MS-16-R, Princeton, NJ 08541, USA
yattali@ets.org

Abstract. Automatic item generation represents a potential solution to the increased item development demands in this era of continuous testing. However, the use of test items that are automatically generated on-the-fly poses significant psychometric challenges for item calibration. The solution that has been suggested by a small but growing number of authors is to replace item calibration with item model (or family) calibration and to adopt a multilevel approach where items are nested within item models. Past research on the feasibility of this approach was limited to simulations or small-scale illustrations of its potential. The purpose of this study was to evaluate the results of a large-scale deployment of automatic item generation in a low-stakes adaptive testing context, with a large number of item models, and a very large number of randomly generated item instances.

Keywords: Automatic item generation · Item models
Computer adaptive testing · Mathematics assessment

1 Introduction

The advent of internet-based computerized assessment offers many advantages compared to more traditional paper-based assessments, including support for innovative item types and alternative item formats (Sireci and Zenisky 2006), measurement of more complex knowledge, skills, and competencies (Bartram and Hambleton 2005), automated scoring (Shermis and Burstein 2013) which also allows immediate feedback to students (Attali and Powers 2010), and adaptive testing and testing on-demand (van der Linden and Glas 2010).

These advantages have resulted in increased summative as well as formative testing and, as a consequence, the challenge of much higher levels of item development to support these new levels of testing (Downing and Haladyna 2006). One method that may be used to address this challenge is through automatic item generation (Gierl and Haladyna 2013; Irvine and Kyllonen 2002). Automatic item generation (AIG) is based on the notion of item "models" (Bejar 2002), schemas of problems with parameters that can be instantiated with specific values. For example, the model $X + Y = Z$, where X and Y can be any whole numbers in the range 0–9, has two parameters. An item model can be instantiated, using a computer-based algorithm, to display an actual item (in this case, a single-digit addition exercise).

© Springer International Publishing AG, part of Springer Nature 2018
C. Penstein Rosé et al. (Eds.): AIED 2018, LNAI 10947, pp. 17–29, 2018.
https://doi.org/10.1007/978-3-319-93843-1_2

AIG has been used to create items in diverse content areas and formats (see Haladyna (2013) for a historical perspective). From a practical standpoint, the use of item models greatly expands the potential number of items. From a theoretical standpoint, item models provide an opportunity for a construct-driven approach to item development (Embretson and Yang 2006) because they can be tied to a mapping of the construct through an analysis of the cognitive mechanisms related to the item solution and item features that call on these mechanisms (Whitely 1983).

A key aspect of AIG research relates to the psychometric modeling of item models and their instances. In particular, the psychometric properties of automatically generated item instances cannot be known in advance, thus rendering test design and scoring impractical, at least as traditionally construed. The solution that has been suggested by a small but growing number of authors (Cho et al. 2014; Embretson 1999; Geerlings et al. 2011; Glas and van der Linden 2003; Sinharay and Johnson 2008, 2013) is to replace item (or instance) calibration with item model calibration and to adopt a multilevel approach where instances are nested within item models. Typically, the nested instances are viewed as a random effect (e.g., Cho et al. 2014) and any new instance generated from a model does not need to be calibrated; instead, the known item model effect (and optionally, its distribution) can be used for scoring, ignoring the possible instance effect (which is unknown).

Naturally, the feasibility of this approach depends on whether instances are sufficiently similar to each other from a psychometric perspective. Nevertheless, past research has been based on either simulations (e.g., Geerlings et al. 2013) or controlled experiments with small and fixed sets of instances (Arendasy and Sommer 2012; Cho et al. 2014; Geerlings et al. 2011; Sinharay and Johnson 2008). The purpose of this study was to evaluate the results of a large-scale implementation of AIG with a large number of item models and a very large number of randomly generated item instances.

1.1   Current Study

This study is based on *Quick Math*, a practice and assessment system of middle-school mathematics that can be used both to assess (Attali and Arieli-Attali 2015) and strengthen, through periodic practice sessions, procedural and representational fluency with concepts of the number system and operations with numbers. This system is itself part of the CBAL (Cognitively Based Assessment of, for, and as Learning) research initiative to develop assessments that maximize the potential for positive effects on teaching and learning (Bennett 2011). Questions in the system are generated on-the-fly from item models. The use of item models greatly expands the potential number of exercises while at the same time allows repetition, the cornerstone of practice. Models also provide an opportunity for a construct-driven approach to item development (Embretson and Yang 2006). Attali and Arieli-Attali (2017) applied a rational number learning progression to *Quick Math* items and classified students (using a cognitive diagnostic model) to levels of the learning progression.

In this study, we analyzed data from the use of *Quick Math* as a practice tool for test takers that are preparing to take a high-stakes standardized test. The purpose of the analyses was to:

1. Assess the adequacy of the item model parameters from the pilot calibration by (a) comparing them to parameters derived from the study data, and (b) computing and analyzing item and person fit indices between study data and expected performance based on pilot calibration parameters.
2. Explore the results of on-the-fly generated item instances by (a) qualitatively describe the number of instances produced across item models; (b) comparing the size of variance components for the instance effect under the controlled pilot and uncontrolled field data; (c) Explore the relation between variability in performance and number of instances produced for an item model; and (d) delve deeper into the actual instances produced by two item models in an effort to explain variability in performance through an analysis of the instance parameters.

2   Method

2.1   Item Model Calibration

Calibration of item models for the data collection that is the focus of this study was based on data from a previous pilot study of the system (partly reported in Attali and Arieli-Attali 2015). For this pilot study, a total of 822 students from two middle schools participated. The set of items used in this study was comprised of 57 item models with 8 instances for most models and 4 instances for a handful of models, with a total of 400 instances. Instances were generated to cover a representative range of model parameters.

The complete set of 400 items was divided into four non-overlapping sets (or forms), with each set composed of two instances from all item models and each participant was randomly assigned to one of the sets. The forms showed high levels of reliability (Cronbach's alpha of .96) and validity coefficients, with correlations of .80 with state assessment scores.

2.2   Participants

Data for the current study were based on Educational Testing Service's suite of free test preparation tools for the High School Equivalency Test (HiSET®), which can be used to receive high school equivalency credentials. The suite includes interactive practice tests (in all five subtests) as well as additional mathematics resources, including an interactive review book, interactive video lessons, and a version of *Quick Math*. For this study, data from a period of 18 months was analyzed (from June 2015 until December 2016). During this period, 6,005 users of the preparation tools answered *Quick Math* questions.

Note that the calibration sample (middle school students) differs in substantial ways from the study sample. The calibration sample was chosen (in a previous study) because the competencies that are assessed with *Quick Math* are taught by the end of elementary school. However, although its tasks assess core concepts of the number system and operations with numbers that should be relevant to learners from a wide range of developmental levels, the competencies of the older study participants might differ in ways that would adversely impact the quality of the calibration.

2.3   Quick Math Implementation

Users of the HiSET version of *Quick Math* (QM) answer questions that are automatically generated on-the-fly from item models. They receive immediate feedback on the correctness of their answer and are also presented with updated overall feedback in the form of an accuracy score, speed score, and usage points (called XP points), based on the difficulty of items answered correctly (see Fig. 1).

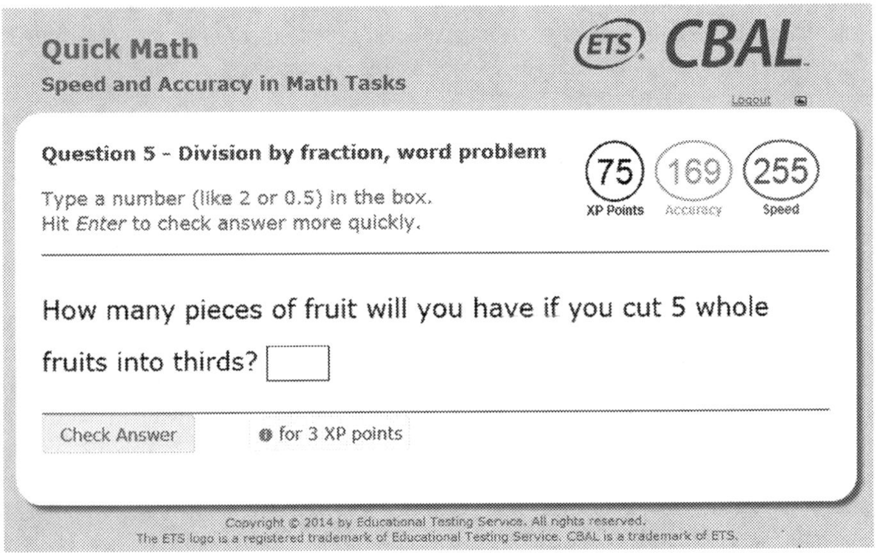

Fig. 1. Quick Math interface and feedback components.

As a formative practice system, item selection was not based on the principle of optimal measurement efficiency, but instead was concerned with two other goals: appropriate challenge for students and distributed practice of different item types. A large body of research has consistently found that the most motivating tasks are those that individuals find moderately challenging (Pintrich and Schunk 2002, Chap. 6). Therefore, an effort is made to assign tasks that are expected to be answered correctly 65% of the time. Similarly, distributed practice is known to more effectively benefit learning than massed practice. Therefore, an effort is made to space the administration of item that test the same competency.

Item Models. A total of 57 item models was used in this version of Quick Math (QM). These models were based on the 50 models used in the school pilot with several models split into separate models. Item instances for these models were generated automatically on-the-fly, as the test was administered to an examinee.

Scoring. To calibrate automatically generated items, the use of a hierarchical model where the item model parameters are treated as random effects has been recommended (Glas and van der Linden 2003; Sinharay and Johnson 2013). This paper uses a simpler version of the model of Glas and van der Linden (2003) that is based on the Rasch model. The model can also be considered to be the Rasch model version of a model used by Janssen et al. (2000) to calibrate items measuring the same criterion.

Based on the pilot data, a latent trait model for accuracy of response, similar to a Rasch IRT model, was developed using a generalized linear mixed model with persons and item models defined as random effects (see Janssen et al. (2004), for a description of this kind of model) and employing the R function glmer in the R package lme4 (Bates et al. 2015). Item model difficulty parameters were set as the random effects from this model. Ability estimates were then computed from these parameters and users' responses using the Expected A Posteriori (EAP) method.

Item Selection. Because the purpose of QM was to engage users and provide them with a practice environment, item models were selected such that expected percent correct would be 65% and that a given item model would repeat only after at least five other item instances were administered. After the item model was selected for administration, a random instance would be generated and presented to the user.

2.4   Analyses

We start by reporting on the distribution of QM use (total items answered) across users and typical time spent answering items.

The main analyses were performed to address two purposes: (1) Assess the adequacy of the item model parameters from the pilot calibration, and (2) Explore the results of on-the-fly generated item instances. To assess the adequacy of the item model parameters from the pilot calibration, we first created a new generalized linear model on the HiSET data with item models and persons treated as random effects and compared the item model parameters to those derived from the pilot data. We then explored item and person fit by employing the residual approach commonly used in Rasch analysis (Wright and Masters 1982, Chap. 5). For each response, a residual is calculated as the difference between the actual response (0 or 1) and the model predicted response:

$$P(Y_{pm} = 1|\theta_p) = \frac{e^{\theta_p - b_m}}{1 + e^{\theta_p - b_m}}$$

Where θ_p is person ability and b_m is item model difficulty parameter.

The residual is standardized by dividing it by its standard deviation. The squared standardized residuals can be averaged across persons for item fit, or across items, for person fit. We have used the variance weighted average index, also called Infit (rather then the unweighted average, or Outfit), because it is less sensitive to extreme person abilities. These mean-square fit indices have an expected value of 1, with reasonable fit indicated by values between 0.7 and 1.3 (Wright and Linacre 1994) and larger values indicating underfit due to excessive randomness in the data. These cutscores are used to flag both persons and items.

To explore the results of on-the-fly generated item instances, we first analyzed the distribution of the number of instances randomly generated across item models. We then estimated generalized linear mixed models with an additional instance random effect (in addition to persons and item models) from both the original pilot data and new HiSET practice data, and the variance components from these models were compared. We continue with an analysis of mean discrepancies (or errors) between expected and observed performance across instances and conclude with analyses of two models with high variability in performance across instances.

3   Results

3.1   Users

During the period that was analyzed, 6,005 users of the HiSET interactive practice tests answered QM questions. As expected from the voluntary use of the assessment, extent of QM use was highly skewed, with a median of 51 questions, 90th percentile of 209 questions, and 99th percentile of 787 questions. Figure 2 presents the distribution (probability density function) of number of questions answered up to the 90th percentile. Also note that the typical QM item is answered relatively quickly: the median response time in this implementation was 15 s. Therefore, a typical user spent 12 min answering items in QM.

Final ability estimates for users with 10 or more items ($N = 4,814$, $M_\theta = -0.70$, $SD_\theta = 1.08$) were associated with low standard errors of measurement ($M_{sem} = 0.28$, $SD_{sem} = 0.14$) and high marginal reliability (0.92).

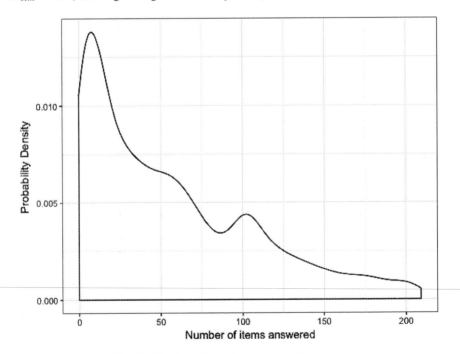

Fig. 2. Number of questions answered by users.

3.2   Item Model Parameters

Recall that item model parameters were based on the middle-school pilot (Attali and Arieli-Attali 2015) with a fixed number of instances per model and a sample-size of around 400 respondents per instance. In contrast, the HiSET data was based on many more randomly generated instances. To evaluate the original item parameters, we first created a new generalized linear model (with the Bernoulli distribution and logistic link function) on the HiSET data with item models and persons treated as random effects. A comparison of the estimated random effects of item models with those from the original pilot showed they were highly correlated, $r(55) = .93$ $(p < .001)$.

To explore item and person fit, Infit values (weighted mean square residuals) were computed (omitting data from users who responded to five items at most) based on the original models. For persons, only 0.5% of users had Infit values greater than the cutoff of 1.3. For items, only two of the 57 item models had Infit values greater than 1.3, and these item models were the most difficult (with 5% correct) and least difficult (90% correct) item models.

3.3   Instances Within Item Models

The item models varied widely in the number of unique instances produced. Figure 3 shows that most item models had less than 100 instances and more than 100 responses per instance (on average), but around 10 of the models had more than 1,000 unique instances and very few responses per instance.

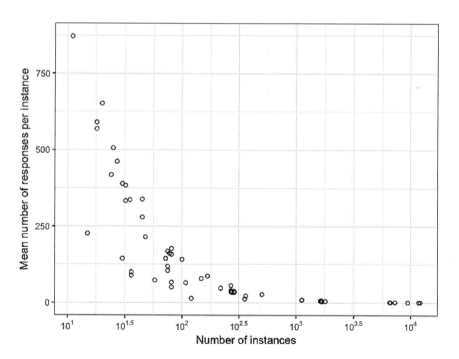

Fig. 3. Instances per model and typical number of responses.

To evaluate how the instance effect played out in the HiSET data, unconditional (no fixed effects included) generalized linear mixed models were estimated with three random effects: persons, item models, and instances (nested within models). The models were estimated separately for the pilot data and the HiSET data. For the HiSET data, only users with at least 10 responses and item models with an average of at least 30 responses per instance were included. Table 1 presents the variance components for these models. The table shows that random components were smaller for the HiSET data as compared with the pilot data, especially for the person effect (32% compared to 41% of total variance), which also indicates that measurement accuracy for the HiSET data was somewhat lower. However, the relative size of the instance effects are similar (11% and 10%), as well as their size relative to the item model effects (20% for both models).

Table 1. Variance components from instance models.

	HiSET			Pilot		
	Variance	%	N	Variance	%	N
Instance	0.43	11	3,976	0.48	10	400
Model	2.20	57	40	2.45	49	57
Person	1.25	32	4,814	2.02	41	822

To get a better sense of the variability in instance scores within item models, Fig. 4 shows (for the 40 item models with a reasonable number of instances) the *SD* and mean of residuals across instances for each model, together with the number of instances for the model. Recall that residuals are deviations between observed and expected performance. Therefore, positive residuals indicate higher than expected performance (easier items). The mean of residuals is in the range of ±0.2 and the *SD* of residuals are between nearly 0 and 0.23. The figure shows a negative relation between mean and *SD* of residuals ($r(38) = -.37$, $p = .020$), as well as a positive relation between *SD* of residuals and number of instances ($r(38) = .31$, $p = .050$), indicating that greater variability across instances is somewhat related to the number of instances.

Finally, to illustrate the variability in instance difficulty, we selected two models with a large variability for further analysis. The first was "Write the number X as a fraction in simplest terms", where the parameter X was a decimal fraction. It had a small number of instances (11) and large variability in errors across instances (.22, with mean errors of $-.15$). The percent correct for all instances is presented in Fig. 5, with the decimal parameter shown along the x-axis. The figure shows that performance on this model varied a great deal, between 20% and 80%. However, most of this variability in performance can be explained by the type of correct answer, namely the denominator of the simplest fraction. Performance is tightly grouped along this continuum, from half (80%), through fourths (78% and 70%) and fifths (47%–35%), to eights (25%–20%).

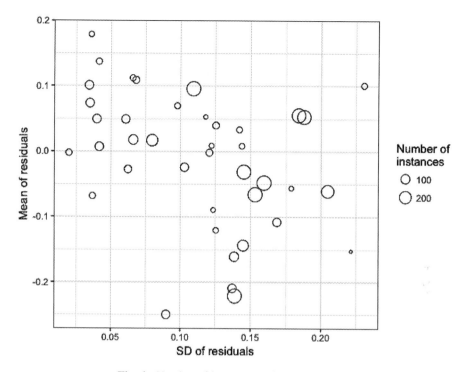

Fig. 4. Number of instances and error summary.

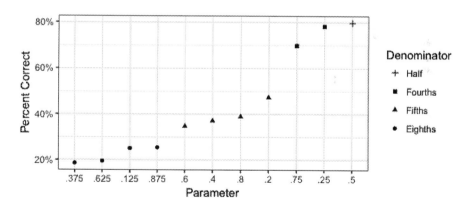

Fig. 5. Instance difficulty for decimal-to-fraction model.

The second model chosen was "The greatest common factor of X and Y is…", where the parameters X and Y are whole numbers in the range 4–75. It had a large number of instances (219) and large variability in errors across instances (.20, with mean errors of −.06). The percent correct for all instances is presented in Fig. 6, with the sum of the two item model parameters (X and Y) shown along the x-axis. In addition, both the size of the correct answer (GCF) is indicated by the size of the bubbles and whether the GCF is a multiple of five or not is indicated by the shading of the bubbles.

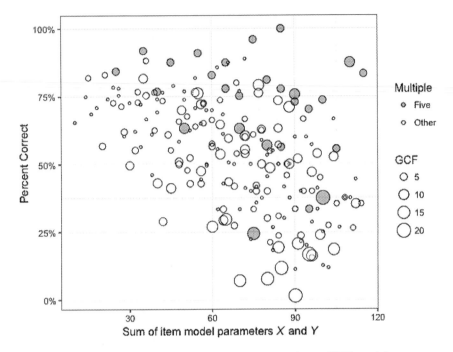

Fig. 6. Instance difficulty for greatest-common-factor (GCF) model.

The figure shows that all three of these factors affect instance difficulty: larger parameters and GCF are associated with harder items, whereas GCF that are multiples of five (5, 10, 15, or 20) tend to be easier. Overall, these three factors account for 46% of the variance in instance difficulty.

4   Discussion

The main practical goal of AIG is to be able to calibrate an item model (or family) once, and then use the instances generated on-the-fly from the model to score examinees without the need to calibrate the items individually. Although research has concentrated on different psychometric models for calibrating the item models, there has not been much empirical work on the success of scoring examinees in situations where a large number of instances is randomly generated and administered.

The purpose of this study was to evaluate the results of a large-scale deployment of AIG in a low-stakes adaptive testing context, with a large number of item models, and a very large number of randomly generated item instances. The measurement model that was used in this implementation was relatively simple. It was based on a multilevel approach where both item models and their nested instances are viewed as random effects, and only item model effects are known in advance. The approach implemented in this study only took into account possible variations in intercepts (or difficulty) across item models and assumed homoscedasticity within models: that is, the model assumed equal instance variance across item models (as did Janssen et al. 2000).

Results supported the adequacy of model scoring and calibration in this large-scale deployment. At the item model level, an analysis of item and person fit found that only 2 of 57 item models showed significant misfit and a very small proportion (0.5%) of users showed significant misfit. In addition, item model parameters between pilot (calibration) and test preparation data were highly correlated.

At the instance level, we found that a multilevel model with an additional instance random effect showed similar variance components between pilot and test preparation data. This is despite the fact that item calibration from the pilot data included a small number of instances (up to eight instances per model) whereas the number of instances generated in the field was very large.

Even though the overall instance effect was small (it accounted for 10% of the variance in the instance model), we found that some item models had large variability in performance across instances. The literature on item models has emphasized two approaches to dealing with instance variance. A focus of one approach (manifested in such names as item cloning and isomorphic items) has been based on the idea that instances should have the same psychometric attributes and, in particular, should have the same item difficulty (Bejar 2002; Glas and van der Linden 2003). In general, however, instances do not have identical psychometric attributes. For example, analyses of the hypothesis of equality of proportion corrects within item models are almost always rejected (Sinharay and Johnson 2008).

A complementary approach to the issue of instance variability has been to understand this variability through cognitive modeling of the item models (e.g., Cho et al. 2014; Embretson 1999). Cho et al. (2014) distinguishes between item model predictive attributes and instance predictive attributes. In a previous study (Attali and Arieli-Attali 2017), the QM item models were analyzed in terms of a rational number learning progression (Arieli-Attali and Cayton-Hodges 2014), which mostly provides item model level prediction of performance: categorization of items in terms of the learning progression reduced item model variance by 62% and instance variance by 23%. In this paper we exemplified the use of instance predictors based on characterizing the numbers used as parameters. This type of cognitive analysis can lead to revision of the item models, as part of an iterative approach to item model design (Graf and Fife 2013).

In the future, we plan to conduct a more systematic cognitive analysis of instance parameters across item models. In particular, an interesting direction to explore is the possibility to create a general prediction model based on the possible numbers that can serve as parameters for a given item model. For example, both the size of numbers and their divisibility are possible important general predictors of instance difficulty. However, the range of possible instance parameters (which can be determined in advance) should provide important contextualization for each item model.

Another future research direction is to compare the psychometric model that was used in this study with more complex models. For example, a model that does not assume equal instance variance across item models and a model that also takes into account possible variations in slope (discrimination) across item models.

References

Arendasy, M.E., Sommer, M.: Using automatic item generation to meet the increasing item demands of high-stakes educational and occupational assessment. Learn. Individ. Differ. **22**(1), 112–117 (2012)

Arieli-Attali, M., Cayton-Hodges, G.A.: Expanding the CBAL™ Competency Model for Mathematics Assessments and Developing a Rational Number Learning Progression. Educational Testing Service, Princeton (2014)

Attali, Y., Arieli-Attali, M.: Gamification in assessment: do points affect test performance? Comput. Educ. **83**, 57–63 (2015)

Attali, Y., Arieli-Attali, M.: Validating predictions from learning progressions: framework and implementation. In: The Annual Meeting of the American Educational Research Association (AERA), San Antonio, TX (2017)

Attali, Y., Powers, D.: Immediate feedback and opportunity to revise answers to open-ended questions. Educ. Psychol. Meas. **70**(1), 22–35 (2010)

Bartram, D., Hambleton, R.: Computer-Based Testing and the Internet: Issues and Advances. Wiley, New York (2005)

Bates, D., Mächler, M., Bolker, B., Walker, S.: Fitting linear mixed-effects models using lme4. J. Stat. Softw. **67**(1), 1–48 (2015). https://doi.org/10.18637/jss.v067.i01

Bejar, I.I.; Generative testing: from conception to implementation. In: Irvine, S.H., Kyllonen, P. C. (eds.) Item Generation for Test Development, pp. 199–217. Erlbaum, Mahwah (2002)

Bennett, R.E.: CBAL: results from piloting innovative k–12 assessments. ETS Res. Rep. Ser. **2011**(1) (2011)

Cho, S.-J., De Boeck, P., Embretson, S., Rabe-Hesketh, S.: Additive multilevel item structure models with random residuals: item modeling for explanation and item generation. Psychometrika **79**(1), 84–104 (2014)

Downing, S.M., Haladyna, T.M.: Handbook of test development. Lawrence Erlbaum, Mahwah (2006)

Embretson, S.: Generating items during testing: psychometric issues and models. Psychometrika **64**(4), 407–433 (1999)

Embretson, S., Yang, X.: Automatic item generation and cognitive psychology. Handb. Stat. **26**, 747–768 (2006)

Geerlings, H., Glas, C.A., van der Linden, W.J.: Modeling rule-based item generation. Psychometrika **76**(2), 337–359 (2011)

Geerlings, H., van der Linden, W.J., Glas, C.A.: Optimal test design with rule-based item generation. Appl. Psychol. Meas. **37**(2), 140–161 (2013)

Gierl, M.J., Haladyna, T.M.: Automatic Item Generation: Theory and Practice. Routledge, New York (2013)

Glas, C.A., van der Linden, W.J.: Computerized adaptive testing with item cloning. Appl. Psychol. Meas. **27**(4), 247–261 (2003)

Graf, A., Fife, J.H.: Difficulty modeling and automatic generation of quantitative items. In: Gierl, M.J., Haladyna, T.M. (eds.) Automatic Item Generation: Theory and Practice, pp. 157–179. Routledge, New York (2013)

Haladyna, T.M.: Automatic item generation: a historical perspective. In: Gierl, M.J., Haladyna, T.M. (eds.) Automatic Item Generation: Theory and Practice, pp. 13–25. Routledge, New York (2013)

Irvine, S.H., Kyllonen, P.C.: Item Generation for Test Development. Erlbaum, Mahwah (2002)

Janssen, R., Schepers, J., Peres, D.: Models with item and item group predictors. In: De Boeck, P., Wilson, M. (eds.) Explanatory Item Response Models, pp. 189–212. Springer, New York (2004). https://doi.org/10.1007/978-1-4757-3990-9_6

Janssen, R., Tuerlinckx, F., Meulders, M., De Boeck, P.: A hierarchical IRT model for criterion-referenced measurement. J. Educ. Behav. Stat. **25**(3), 285–306 (2000)

Pintrich, P.R., Schunk, D.H.: Motivation in Education: Theory, Research, and Applications, 2nd edn. Prentice Hall, Upper Saddle River (2002)

Shermis, M.D., Burstein, J.: Handbook of Automated Essay Evaluation: Current Applications and New Directions. Routledge, New York (2013)

Sinharay, S., Johnson, M.S.: Use of item models in a large-scale admissions test: a case study. Int. J. Test. **8**(3), 209–236 (2008)

Sinharay, S., Johnson, M.S.: Statistical modeling of automatically generated items. In: Gierl, M. J., Haladyna, T.M. (eds.) Automatic Item Generation: Theory and Practice, pp. 183–195. Routledge, New York (2013)

Sireci, S.G., Zenisky, A.L.: Innovative item formats in computer-based testing: in pursuit of improved construct representation. In: Downing, S.M., Haladyna, T.M. (eds.) Handbook of Test Development, pp. 329–347. Lawrence Erlbaum, Mahwah (2006)

van der Linden, W.J., Glas, C.A.: Elements of Adaptive Testing. Springer, New York (2010). https://doi.org/10.1007/978-0-387-85461-8

Whitely, S.E.: Construct validity: construct representation versus nomothetic span. Psychol. Bull. **93**(1), 179 (1983)

Wright, B.D., Linacre, J.M.: Reasonable mean-square fit values. Rasch Meas. Trans. **8**(3), 370 (1994)

Wright, B.D., Masters, G.N.: Rating Scale Analysis: Rasch Measurement. Mesa Press, Chicago (1982)

Quantifying Classroom Instructor Dynamics with Computer Vision

Nigel Bosch[1(✉)], Caitlin Mills[2], Jeffrey D. Wammes[3], and Daniel Smilek[4]

[1] University of Illinois at Urbana-Champaign, Urbana, IL 61820, USA
pnb@illinois.edu
[2] University of British Columbia, Vancouver, BC V6T 1Z, Canada
[3] Yale University, New Haven, CT 06511, USA
[4] University of Waterloo, Waterloo, ON N2L 3G1, Canada

Abstract. Classroom teachers utilize many nonverbal activities, such as gesturing and walking, to maintain student attention. Quantifying instructor behaviors in a live classroom environment has traditionally been done through manual coding, a prohibitively time-consuming process which precludes providing timely, fine-grained feedback to instructors. Here we propose an automated method for assessing teachers' non-verbal behaviors using video-based motion estimation tailored for classroom applications. Motion was estimated by subtracting background pixels that varied little from their mean values, and then noise was reduced using filters designed specifically with the movements and speeds of teachers in mind. Camera pan and zoom events were also detected, using a method based on tracking the correlations between moving points in the video. Results indicated the motion estimation method was effective for predicting instructors' non-verbal behaviors, including gestures (kappa = .298), walking (kappa = .338), and camera pan (an indicator of instructor movement; kappa = .468), all of which are plausibly related to student attention. We also found evidence of predictive validity, as these automated predictions of instructor behaviors were correlated with students' mean self-reported level of attention (e.g., r = .346 for walking), indicating that the proposed method captures the association between instructors' non-verbal behaviors and student attention. We discuss the potential for providing timely, fine-grained, automated feedback to teachers, as well as opportunities for future classroom studies using this method.

Keywords: Instructor non-verbal behaviors · Attention · Motion estimation

1 Introduction

Classroom lecturing can be a daunting task. Presenting the learning material in a meaningful way is only half the battle, as maintaining students' attention and engagement is perhaps equally challenging. One way in which instructors might manage students' attention is through titrating their own behaviors during the lecture (e.g. moving around, altering their volume) in response to their perception of student attentiveness. Indeed, research has shown that an instructor's behavior (e.g., head nodding) is related not only to students' learning [1–4], but also to their characterizations of instructors (i.e. competence

© Springer International Publishing AG, part of Springer Nature 2018
C. Penstein Rosé et al. (Eds.): AIED 2018, LNAI 10947, pp. 30–42, 2018.
https://doi.org/10.1007/978-3-319-93843-1_3

and enthusiasm). To date, however, very little work has focused on quantifying the moment-to-moment dynamics of instructors' behavior in the classroom. Similarly, there is a paucity of work developing tools that can provide live feedback to classroom instructors about their behaviors. The ultimate goal of this work is therefore to fulfill this need and provide automated feedback to instructors regarding their behavioral dynamics in the classroom. A critical first step toward this goal, and the focus of the current paper is to build an automatic quantification system which employs a video-based method in the wild.

Previous research evaluating teachers' non-verbal behaviors has primarily focused on either simulations of instructor behavior by professional actors [5], manual evaluations of behavior [6, 7], human-like avatars of teachers in e-learning [8], or laboratory environments that may not adequately approximate actual classrooms [9, 10]. Although these methods have led to some valuable empirical insights about how instructor behaviors influence learning, they cannot be easily parlayed into feedback systems for instructors. We addressed this gap by creating an automated approach to estimating instructor behaviors (e.g., walking, gesturing, interacting with a presentation) with techniques from artificial intelligence and computer vision. The method we present in this paper also has the advantage that it does not require any specialized sensors, such as depth sensors [10]. Instead, it requires only a video camera. Furthermore, real classroom videos were recorded from a vantage point at the back of the room, thus alleviating privacy concerns related to images of student faces being recorded.

2   Related Work

2.1   Impact of Instruction Behaviors

Instructor behavior is critical to assess given its consistent relationship with various aspects of learning. Witt et al. [2] conducted a meta-analysis of 81 studies including over 24,000 students, and discovered a significant correlation between teachers' non-verbal behaviors and students' self-reported perceptions of how much they were learning ($r = .510$). Furthermore, teachers' non-verbal behaviors were correlated almost as strongly with students' affective learning ($r = .490$), which is a strong indicator of one's enjoyment of the course, and likelihood of enrolling in a future related course.

Computerized learning environments have allowed researchers to precisely manipulate the non-verbal behaviors that (virtual) teachers exhibit and test their influence on students' perceptions. Alseid and Rigas [8] studied the effects of facial expressions (e.g., happy, interested), hand gestures (e.g., pointing, chin stroking), and walking in the context of a computerized learning environment with a virtual teaching agent. Students rated their perceptions of these instructor activities before and after the study. Several of the teacher activities were rated significantly more positively after the study than before, including the two most well-liked activities, pointing (100% positive rating post-study) and walking (98% positive rating post-study). While it is unclear what the impact of these positive ratings would be on learning, it is clear that students develop a preference for particular instructor behaviors, which may in turn foster improved attention or learning.

2.2 Automatic Evaluation of Teaching Behaviors

Multiple efforts have been made to develop automated methods for evaluating teaching and presentation style, including evaluation of non-verbal behaviors. TeachLivE is one example of a software platform designed to capture the behaviors of teachers as they interact with 3D virtual students, and to automatically provide real-time feedback about those behaviors [10]. Participants were 34 teachers in training, half of whom received automated real-time feedback on non-verbal behaviors (specifically, open body postures such as arms hanging down versus arm-crossing and other closed postures) in their first of two sessions with TeachLivE, and half who received feedback in their second session. The participants who received feedback in the first session displayed more open postures in the second session than the other participants, despite receiving no further feedback. This study demonstrated that it is possible to perform real-time assessment of teaching behaviors, and that instructors can modify their behavior based on this feedback. However, TeachLivE requires a close, unobstructed view of the instructor, to allow their behaviors to be tracked with a depth-sensing camera. This is a limitation which would prevent TeachLivE from being broadly applicable in many common lecture hall classroom environments.

Presentation Trainer is another training platform designed to assess non-verbal behaviors and give corresponding feedback to presenters [9]. While it is not specifically intended for teacher training, it does include relevant feedback about the behaviors quantified by TeachLivE (open versus closed posture), as well as stance (shifting side to side, which conveys being uncomfortable). In one empirical investigation of Presentation Trainer, university professionals who received this feedback about behavior self-reported significantly more learning than a matched control group (24.5% more, $p < .05$), indicating that they found the automated feedback helpful for improving their presentations. In a follow-up study, nine students gave presentations to their peers before and after completing a training session with Presentation Trainer [11]. The group of peers rated the quality and frequency of gesture use for both presentations, and ratings were significantly higher *after* training (27.9% improved, $p < .01$). Together, these studies demonstrate that automated evaluation methods exhibit strong potential for the improvement of non-verbal communication skills. However, similar to TeachLivE, Presentation Trainer suffers the shortcoming that it requires a depth-sensing camera and a clear, close and unobscured video of the speaker, both of which are unlikely to be available in typical classroom environments.

2.3 Feasibility of Camera-Based Motion Tracking

Tracking motion in video is a well-studied problem in the field of computer vision. Applications include tracking the movement of people [12], tracking the movement of key visual points (e.g., corners, edges [13]), and background subtraction to find visual changes over time [14]. Camera-based human motion tracking research has typically focused on skeletal tracking and detection of individual body parts [15–17]. However, unobstructed high-quality video of instructors is difficult to acquire, so alternative methods are needed. Kory-Westlund et al. [18] made strides toward this goal with a human motion tracking method that does not require detection of people or individual body parts. Their motion measure correlated quite well with other markers of movement, including posture changes measured by a pressure-sensitive chair (mean $r = .708$), and hand gestures measured by a wrist-mounted accelerometer (mean $r = .720$). This method was optimized for measuring the motions of a person seated in front of a computer with a stationary camera, however, and is unlikely to be capable of effectively tracking more dynamic classroom behaviors.

2.4 Research Questions

We extracted novel estimations of instructor motion, camera pan (rotation back and forth), and camera zoom from classroom videos taken with a standard digital camera. These estimations were then used as features in machine-learned models that detected teacher activities including walking, gesturing, and presentation usage (slide changes). As a proof of concept, we aimed to answer the following research questions: (1) How well can we automatically detect instructors' non-verbal behaviors using only amateur videos taken from the back of a classroom?; and (2) Do the instructor activities detected with this method correspond to student attention in the classroom?

3 Method

We took a multi-step approach to answering the foregoing research questions. We collected classroom videos and manually annotated them for instructors' non-verbal behaviors, then applied methods to estimate motion, camera pan, and camera zoom in the videos.[1] Finally, we applied supervised machine learning methods test whether these estimated features could reliably predict the instructors' non-verbal behaviors. These steps are described in detail below.

3.1 Classroom Videos and Students' Self-reported Attention

Nine classroom lectures were recorded over the span of six days at a Canadian university. There were three videos each of three different instructors, all of whom taught undergraduate psychology classes. The lectures were completely naturalistic and were not manipulated in any way for the study. Lectures included the common elements one might expect: speaking, question answering, referencing presentation slides, and occasionally watching videos on a projector screen. Recordings occurred in two different classrooms, each of which was equipped with a similar setup: a lectern/podium and a stage-like space for the instructor to walk. A researcher started the video camera, which was placed at the back of the classroom, and actively panned and zoomed the camera to keep the instructor and presentation slides in frame.

We also obtained self-reports of attention from the students during the lectures. Students who agreed to participate ($N = 76$) downloaded a thought-probe application to their laptop computers. This application displayed a notification in one corner of the

---

[1] We have made the code for motion, camera pan, and zoom estimation available online at https://github.com/pnb/classroom-motion.

computer screen up to five times per class. The notification prompted students to report their level of attention using a continuous scale ranging from *Completely mind wandering* to *Completely on task*. Students were instructed to introspect about their mental state just before the thought-probe appeared, with *mind wandering* defined to the students as "thinking about unrelated concerns" and *on task* defined as "thinking about the lecture".

3.2   Video Annotation

To determine whether our motion estimation method was associated with the non-verbal behaviors of the recorded instructors, ground truth labels of these behaviors and related events were required. To this end, classroom videos were retrospectively coded to describe instructors' non-verbal behaviors (i.e. gesturing or movement), environmental changes (e.g. lighting or camera pan), and student interaction (e.g. asking or fielding questions). A total of 5,415 annotations were made, of which 24.9% were camera pan, 0.3% camera zoom, 0.7% room lighting change, 0.1% instructor playing video, 3.8% student asking question, and 70.2% other (which were then explained in greater detail in the coder's comments). Because there were relatively few instances of camera zoom, room lighting changes, video playing, and question asking, these annotations were not considered further. We extracted additional annotations from the comments documented by the coder, including 13.1% instructor walking, 33.3% gesturing, and 6.2% presentation slide change. Finally, we expected that camera pan events would be closely related to walking, so we created an additional set of annotations pooling across cases where either the camera panned or the instructor was coded as walking (37.3% of annotations).

Although video annotations were made at the precise moment that a relevant event was observed, the videos were pooled into 30-s segments ($n = 1,431$) to reduce noise for automatic classification[2]. Each 30 s segment was assigned a binary label for each annotation category. For instance, if the first and only camera pan occurred 43 s into a particular lecture, the first 30 s epoch (0–30 s) would be coded as 0, the second (30–60 s) as 1 and the third as 0 (60–90 s). In this manner, we derived a time series of binary ratings at regular intervals, for each possible annotation class. Preprocessing the data this way allowed for automatic classification via supervised machine learning with features estimated from the videos.

3.3   Motion Estimation

We estimated motion in two steps: (1) raw motion detection and (2) human-oriented filtering. Raw motion was detected by applying a background subtraction method which learns a Gaussian mixture model describing the video's pixel values [14]. This method learns descriptive statistics about pixels in the video, and tags pixels with low variance over time as *background*, and those with high variance as *motion* pixels.

---

[2] We experimented with a range of segment lengths from 10 to 60 s, finding that 30–60 s segments provided equivalent results and were consistently better than 10 or 20 s. We thus segmented at 30 s intervals to provide the finest granularity from the 30–60 s range.

Consider the circumstance where the instructor moves across a particular region of the video frame. Intuitively, the pixels the instructor crosses over will change dramatically over time and be correctly labelled as motion. However, other artifacts may be erroneously labelled as motion, so the raw motion data must be filtered.

We observed several different sources of such visual noise in classroom videos (illustrated in Fig. 1), each of which caused background pixels to be incorrectly labelled as motion pixels: (1) electronic noise, causing random pixel variation especially under low-light conditions, (2) camera vibration, caused by brief movements in the camera mount, and (3) intentional camera pan and zoom actions performed to follow the teacher more closely. To combat the first two flaws in particular, we developed a novel filtering approach intended specifically for capturing human motion.

Human motion in the classroom can be distinguished from these sources of noise using the speed and duration of the motion. Morphological filters were developed to distinguish motion at different speeds [19]. Specifically, every pixel where motion was detected was dilated, such that a surrounding circular area with a 5-pixel radius was also labelled as motion. This was conducted with every frame of the video, and the motion label was only upheld if the dilated area overlapped in temporally contiguous frames. By manipulating the length of these time frames (the filter history length), motion with different speeds could be captured. Fast motions were captured with a short filter history length, because even rapid human movements are likely to fall within a five-pixel distance of their position in the immediately prior video frames. Conversely, faster-moving motions were filtered out (leaving only slow motions) by a longer filter history, which would only register a motion occurring in the same area of the video.

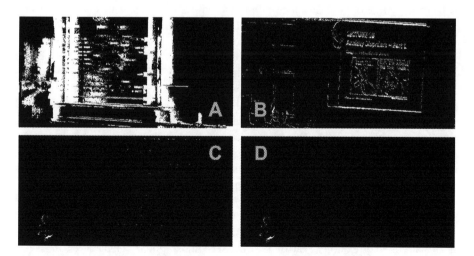

Fig. 1. Examples of three kinds of visual noise in videos: (A) camera pan, (B) camera vibration, and (C) electronic low-light noise. Image D contains an example of smoothed motion from C with lower-left instructor motion preserved and noise visible in the upper-right of C correctly removed (zoom in for detail).

We distinguished instructor motions of different durations by also varying the history length in the background removal process. The background removal history length determines how much time the process considers when calculating the variance of pixels. With a short history length, the background removal process quickly 'forgets' what is moving and what is part of the background. Brief movements will register more strongly with a longer history length, as the background removal process remembers these brief changes for a longer amount of time. If the teacher briefly gestures, the motion pixels from the gesture will only be briefly counted as motion and soon be reabsorbed back into the background (non-motion) pixels. Conversely, a sustained action like walking will continue to register as motion. In practice, we applied filter history lengths of 100 ms and 200 ms, and background removal history lengths of 500 ms, 1000 ms, 2000 ms, and 4000 ms, for a total of [2 filters × 4 background removals] = 8 smoothed motion estimates. We estimated eight values of motion to account for the fact that there are several different types of motion in the classroom, ranging from long and slow (e.g., walking) to short and fast (e.g., a hand wave). Finally, we included unfiltered motion estimates, for a total of 12 estimates.

3.4   Pan and Zoom Detection

For this technique to be effective, we also needed it to detect pan and zoom in addition to motion because the foregoing techniques would label both of these as substantial motion. However, these events are clearly different from, and potentially less informative than, other types of motion (e.g., gesturing). We therefore sought to automatically measure these events so that machine-learned models (Sect. 3.5) could distinguish this type motion from instructor behaviors. For example, a model might learn that brief, high-intensity motion indicates a gesture if and only if a zoom event is not concurrent. Furthermore, camera pan may be an indicator of instructor movement even when walking cannot be detected, so this is an important additional element to track.

To detect these events, we automatically selected 50 salient points to track in the video with a common corner detection algorithm [20]. We then tracked the points (Fig. 2), and computed the correlation between the velocities of salient points in the video (typically known as "optical flow" [13]). Over time some of these points would be lost—for example, when the camera panned so far to one side that a tracked point was no longer in view. When this occurred, we chose a replacement point to track such that it was at least 10 pixels away from another tracked point. The number of tracking points replaced in each video frame was included in the output, since tracking points being lost may be an additional indicator of events such as pan and zoom.

Pan events were captured by measuring the standard deviation (SD) of all tracked points in the preceding one second of video, selecting the middle 50% (25 tracked points) to eliminate outliers, and then measuring the mean SD of those points and the mean pairwise correlation (Pearson's r) between those points. In theory, pan events should have two measurable characteristics: (1) high standard deviations, because the points moved across the video, and (2) large r, because the points moved together as the camera panned.

Zoom events were rare in our data, as noted in Sect. 3.2, but could still be important contextual information, and importantly, will be necessary for applying these techniques to other video sets. To detect zoom events, we measured mean point SD in the same way as pan events, but point correlation was measured differently. In a zoom event, all tracked points appear to move radially, either toward the edge of the frame (zoom in) or toward the center of the frame (zoom out). We thus converted tracked point coordinates from Cartesian to polar coordinates and measured the mean correlation between the point radii. Analogous to pan events, zoom events should have two measurable characteristics: (1) large standard deviation, and (2) radial correlation of points. However, we included the mean SD and mean r values as features for both pan and zoom detection, so that our machine learning methods would not be restricted by certain cutoff values for what qualifies as pan or zoom.

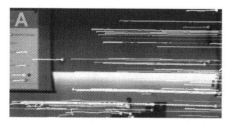

Fig. 2. Example (A) pan and (B) zoom events. In the pan event, most tracked points are moving together to the right as the camera pans left, while in the zoom event points are moving outward radially as the camera zooms in.

3.5   Machine Learning for Prediction of Video Annotations

We created features at the same timescale as the annotations made manually by coders (every 30 s) by calculating the mean and standard deviation of frame-level estimates in each 30-s window, yielding 38 features in total.

We tested the capabilities of our motion estimation methods by training logistic regression models to predict the video annotations. Separate models were trained to detect each annotation type in a one-vs-other scheme: camera pan, instructor walking, gesturing, slide change, and walking + pan combined. Models were cross-validated by training on data from five of the six days of video and testing on the remaining day. This process was repeated six times so that each day's data served as the test-set once. We also applied a forward feature selection process with nested cross-validation to select predictive features [21]. Feature selection took place in training data only, so that features would not be selected based on performance in the testing data.

Model accuracies were measured with Cohen's kappa and area under the receiver operating characteristic curve (AUC), both of which are commonly employed to evaluate predictive models in educational contexts [22–24]. Kappa measures the agreement between two sets of labels; in this case, those labels are the manual video annotations and the automatically predicted annotations. Kappa = 0 represents random chance-level accuracy, while kappa = 1 represents perfect agreement between ground truth and predictions. AUC, on the other hand, measures the tradeoff in accuracy between true positive classifications and false positives across all possible false positive rates, rather than one specific rate. AUC = .5 represents chance-level accuracy, while AUC = 1 represents perfect accuracy.

4   Results

We set out to answer two research questions using these techniques. Below we unpack the results with respect to these two questions.

How well does the proposed method detect teachers' non-verbal behaviors? Table 1 displays the results of supervised classification models trained to predict teachers' non-verbal behaviors and associated classroom activities, from the motion-related features. Overall, models predicted instructor behaviors at levels well above chance, with the exception of slide changes (kappa = .048). Furthermore, predicted rates were similar to the actual base rates present in the video annotations. Thus, we have confidence that these models provide reliable video annotations, and may be applied in authentic classroom settings to examine the role of instructor behaviors (as we have done below).

The models predicted longer-lasting behaviors such as walking with high accuracy, whereas briefer activities were not predicted as effectively (gesture kappa = .298, slide change kappa = .048). Video data and annotations were processed at a 30-s granularity, which may have caused the motion of these briefer events to be lost in the larger period of non-motion. It is possible that with narrower time windows, these finer-grained movements would be detected as accurately. However, we note that our gesture detection models are on par with or superior to previous video-based modeling in classrooms [22].

Table 1. Results of models for automatically predicting video annotations.

Annotation	Kappa	AUC	Base rate	Predicted rate
Camera pan	.468	.768	.419	.460
Gesture	.298	.705	.393	.550
Slide change	.048	.595	.173	.011
Walk	.338	.748	.294	.217
Walk + pan	.397	.683	.516	.549

Do the instructor activities detected with this method correspond to student attention in the classroom? It is also important to establish if predicted instructor behaviors relate to students' self-reported attention. We examined the correlation between the predictions made by the models in Table 1 and students' self-reported levels of attention (see Sect. 3.1). We divided every class lecture into 72 consecutive segments, each of which was 500 s long[3], and calculated the mean self-reported attention level across all students within each segment. We then similarly calculated the mean prediction of each annotation as well as standard deviation (to capture variation in non-verbal behaviors) within each 500 s segment. Finally, we did the same with the ground truth manually-coded annotations to provide a comparison to the automatic method. We thus measured 20 correlations (5 activities × automatic and manual annotation × mean and SD of each) to determine which measures of classroom activity were reliably correlated with student attention. Given the large number of correlations, we applied a post-hoc Benjamini-Hochberg procedure to control for multiple tests [25].

Table 2 contains the correlations that were significant at $p < .05$ after controlling for multiple tests. Two compelling patterns emerge from these results. First, every significant correlation was positive, indicating that increased non-verbal activity from the instructor was generally related to better (not worse) student attention. Second, the automatic annotations were more consistent predictors of attention than even the ground truth manual video annotations.

Table 2. Significant correlations between automatic/manual annotations of instructors' non-verbal behaviors and students' self-reported attention.

Annotation	Method	Pearson's r	N
Camera pan (mean)	Manual	.299	72
Camera pan (SD)	Automatic	.311	72
Gesture (SD)	Automatic	.346	72
Walk (SD)	Automatic	.331	72
Walk OR pan (SD)	Automatic	.303	72
Walk OR pan (mean)	Automatic	.293	72

5   General Discussion

We were interested in automatic evaluation of instructors' non-verbal behaviors as an initial step towards providing useful feedback to instructors. We developed a video-based motion estimation method tailored for classroom videos, and evaluated its effectiveness compared to manual annotations of video, and the ability of these features to predict student attention. In this section we discuss the implications of our findings, as well as limitations and opportunities for future work in this area.

The motion estimation method we proposed was effective for detecting non-verbal activities and related events that had been manually annotated by humans (see Table 1). It shows great promise for teachers who wish to get feedback on their non-verbal behaviors without requiring manual coding, advanced technical tools or professional videographers. It can provide them feedback as to how they might

---

[3] Changing the segment length does not have a dramatic effect on results. Longer segment lengths (e.g., 700 s) produce slightly stronger correlations, but we report our original segment length in this paper (500 s) to avoid overfitting the analysis to desirable results.

improve their lecturing to create a more engaging experience for students. Furthermore, we showed that the automatic assessments of instructors' non-verbal behaviors were significantly correlated with students' self-reported attention in the expected direction (i.e. more activity = more attention). In fact, the automatic annotations of non-verbal behaviors were more strongly related to attention than the manual annotations (which showed only one significant correlation). One possible explanation for this is that the motion estimation method works on every frame of classroom video, whereas humans produced much sparser annotations that may not have been sufficiently fine-grained estimates of non-verbal behaviors in every 500 s segment. The proposed method, being automatic, is also easier to apply frequently and in many classrooms compared to manual annotation – making it suitable for the eventual goal of providing feedback to teachers.

This paper is the first to attempt automatically estimating teacher behaviors from classroom videos taken in the wild. This is a particularly challenging problem because the videos analyzed in this study are from ordinary cameras placed in the back of the classroom, which could pan and zoom at the discretion of the operator. Furthermore, videos were recorded in multiple classrooms with varying designs. Nevertheless, instructor behavior was accurately detected with our methods.

There are two key limitations that should be noted. First, few (i.e. three) teachers were examined in this study. It may be that increased non-verbal activity was related to student attention for these instructors (Table 2), but that replication is warranted since these instructors may not be representative of others' teaching styles. Future work evaluating many more teachers with this method will be able to address this issue by searching for consistent differences in style, and the relationships of these styles with student attention. Furthermore, we will collect data in different classrooms and topics, to measure the robustness of the method across these dimensions and others (e.g., lighting conditions) that might be encountered in classroom applications. Second, certain activities such as slide changes and question answering were not detected as well as motion. Future work with different visual features may be able to capture slide changes, but it is likely that multimodal analysis involving audio will be needed to detect questions effectively [26].

Improving the quality of classroom lectures is a difficult process that can require years of teaching experience to overcome a lack of feedback about one's teaching style. As a step toward ameliorating this difficulty, we developed video-based methods for detecting teachers' non-verbal behaviors and showed that detected behaviors related to student attention. In the future, these methods will enable wide-scale research into assessment for teachers, thus improving the technique of teachers and the learning experiences of students.

References

1. Ambady, N., Rosenthal, R.: Half a minute: predicting teacher evaluations from thin slices of nonverbal behavior and physical attractiveness. J. Pers. Soc. Psychol. **64**, 431–441 (1993)
2. Witt, P.L., Wheeless, L.R., Allen, M.: A meta-analytical review of the relationship between teacher immediacy and student learning. Commun. Monogr. **71**, 184–207 (2004)

3. Babad, E., Avni-Babad, D., Rosenthal, R.: Teachers' brief nonverbal behaviors in defined instructional situations can predict students' evaluations. J. Educ. Psychol. **95**, 553–562 (2003)
4. Pogue, L.L., Ahyun, K.: The effect of teacher nonverbal immediacy and credibility on student motivation and affective learning. Commun. Educ. **55**, 331–344 (2006)
5. Andersen, J.F., Withrow, J.G.: The impact of lecturer nonverbal expressiveness on improving mediated instruction. Commun. Educ. **30**, 342–353 (1981)
6. Allen, J.L., Shaw, D.H.: Teachers' communication behaviors and supervisors' evaluation of instruction in elementary and secondary classrooms. Commun. Educ. **39**, 308–322 (1990)
7. Menzel, K.E., Carrell, L.J.: The impact of gender and immediacy on willingness to talk and perceived learning. Commun. Educ. **48**, 31–40 (1999)
8. Alseid, M., Rigas, D.: Empirical results for the use of facial expressions and body gestures in e-learning tools. Int. J. Comput. Commun. **2**, 87–94 (2008)
9. Schneider, J., Börner, D., van Rosmalen, P., Specht, M.: Presentation Trainer, your public speaking multimodal coach. In: Proceedings of the 2015 ACM on International Conference on Multimodal Interaction, pp. 539–546. ACM, New York (2015)
10. Barmaki, R., Hughes, C.E.: Providing real-time feedback for student teachers in a virtual rehearsal environment. In: Proceedings of the 2015 ACM on International Conference on Multimodal Interaction, pp. 531–537. ACM, New York (2015)
11. Schneider, J., Börner, D., van Rosmalen, P., Specht, M.: Enhancing public speaking skills - an evaluation of the presentation trainer in the wild. In: Verbert, K., Sharples, M., Klobučar, T. (eds.) EC-TEL 2016. LNCS, vol. 9891, pp. 263–276. Springer, Cham (2016). https://doi.org/10.1007/978-3-319-45153-4_20
12. Ramanan, D., Forsyth, D.A.: Finding and tracking people from the bottom up. In: Proceedings of the 2003 IEEE Computer Society Conference on Computer Vision and Pattern Recognition, pp. 467–474. IEEE (2003)
13. Bouguet, J.-Y.: Pyramidal implementation of the Lucas Kanade feature tracker. Intel Corporation, Microprocessor Research Labs (1999)
14. Zivkovic, Z., van der Heijden, F.: Efficient adaptive density estimation per image pixel for the task of background subtraction. Pattern Recogn. Lett. **27**, 773–780 (2006)
15. Yun, X., Bachmann, E.R.: Design, implementation, and experimental results of a quaternion-based Kalman filter for human body motion tracking. IEEE Trans. Rob. **22**, 1216–1227 (2006)
16. Stoll, C., Hasler, N., Gall, J., Seidel, H.P., Theobalt, C.: Fast articulated motion tracking using a sums of Gaussians body model. In: Proceedings of the IEEE International Conference on Computer Vision (ICCV 2011), pp. 951–958 (2011)
17. Rautaray, S.S., Agrawal, A.: Vision based hand gesture recognition for human computer interaction: a survey. Artif. Intell. Rev. **43**, 1–54 (2015)
18. Westlund, J.K., D'Mello, S.K., Olney, A.M.: Motion tracker: camera-based monitoring of bodily movements using motion silhouettes. PLoS One **10** (2015)
19. Maragos, P.: Tutorial on advances in morphological image processing and analysis. Opt. Eng. **26**, 267623 (1987)
20. Shi, J., Tomasi, C.: Good features to track. In: Proceedings of 1994 IEEE Conference on Computer Vision and Pattern Recognition, pp. 593–600 (1994)
21. Guyon, I., Elisseeff, A.: An introduction to variable and feature selection. J. Mach. Learn. Res. **3**, 1157–1182 (2003)
22. Bosch, N., D'Mello, S.K., Ocumpaugh, J., Baker, R.S., Shute, V.: Using video to automatically detect learner affect in computer-enabled classrooms. ACM Trans. Interact. Intell. Syst. (TiiS) **6**, 17 (2016)

23. Paquette, L., de Carvahlo, A., Baker, R., Ocumpaugh, J.: Reengineering the feature distillation process: a case study in detection of gaming the system. In: Proceedings of the 7th International Conference on Educational Data Mining (EDM 2014), pp. 284–287. Educational Data Mining Society (2014)

24. Jeni, L.A., Cohn, J.F., De la Torre, F.: Facing imbalanced data–recommendations for the use of performance metrics. In: Proceedings of the 5th International Conference on Affective Computing and Intelligent Interaction, pp. 245–251 (2013)

25. Benjamini, Y., Hochberg, Y.: Controlling the false discovery rate: a practical and powerful approach to multiple testing. J. R. Stat. Soc. Ser. B (Methodol.) **57**, 289–300 (1995)

26. Blanchard, N., Donnelly, P.J., Olney, A.M., Samei, B., Ward, B., Sun, X., Kelly, S., Nystrand, M., D'Mello, S.K.: Identifying teacher questions using automatic speech recognition in classrooms. In: Proceedings of the 17th Annual Meeting of the Special Interest Group on Discourse and Dialogue (SIGDIAL), pp. 191–201. Association for Computational Linguistics (2016)

Learning Cognitive Models Using Neural Networks

Devendra Singh Chaplot$^{(\boxtimes)}$, Christopher MacLellan, Ruslan Salakhutdinov, and Kenneth Koedinger

Carnegie Mellon University, 5000 Forbes Avenue, Pittsburgh, PA 15217, USA
{chaplot,cmaclell,rsalakhu}@cs.cmu.edu, koedinger@cmu.edu

Abstract. A cognitive model of human learning provides information about skills a learner must acquire to perform accurately in a task domain. Cognitive models of learning are not only of scientific interest, but are also valuable in adaptive online tutoring systems. A more accurate model yields more effective tutoring through better instructional decisions. Prior methods of automated cognitive model discovery have typically focused on well-structured domains, relied on student performance data or involved substantial human knowledge engineering. In this paper, we propose Cognitive Representation Learner (CogRL), a novel framework to learn accurate cognitive models in ill-structured domains with no data and little to no human knowledge engineering. Our contribution is two-fold: firstly, we show that representations learnt using CogRL can be used for accurate automatic cognitive model discovery without using any student performance data in several ill-structured domains: Rumble Blocks, Chinese Character, and Article Selection. This is especially effective and useful in domains where an accurate human-authored cognitive model is unavailable or authoring a cognitive model is difficult. Secondly, for domains where a cognitive model is available, we show that representations learned through CogRL can be used to get accurate estimates of skill difficulty and learning rate parameters without using any student performance data. These estimates are shown to highly correlate with estimates using student performance data on an Article Selection dataset.

1 Introduction

A cognitive model is a computational model of human learning and problem-solving which can be used to predict human behavior and performance on the modeled problems. In this paper, we consider cognitive models in the context of intelligent tutoring systems. A cognitive model that matches student behavior provides useful information about skill difficulties and learning rates. This information often leads to better instructional decisions by aiding in problem design, problem selection and curriculum sequencing, which in turn results in more effective tutoring. A common method for representing a cognitive model is a set of *Knowledge Components* (KC) [1], which represent pieces of knowledge, concepts or skills that are required for solving problems.

© Springer International Publishing AG, part of Springer Nature 2018
C. Penstein Rosé et al. (Eds.): AIED 2018, LNAI 10947, pp. 43–56, 2018.
https://doi.org/10.1007/978-3-319-93843-1_4

Cognitive models are a major bottleneck in intelligent tutor authoring and performance. Traditional ways to construct cognitive models such as structured interviews, think-aloud protocols and rational analysis requires domain expertise and are often time-consuming and error-prone [2]. Furthermore, hand-authored models can be too simplistic and are usually not verified or inconsistent with data.

Cognitive model discovery, sometimes called "KC model discovery" (in Educational Data Mining) or "Q matrix discovery" (in Psychometrics), has been attempted through a number of different methods, but the problem remains an open, important, and interesting one. Some attempts emphasize interpretability and application of the resulting models [3,4], while others have emphasized methods that minimize upfront human effort in feature engineering [5–9].

So far limited attention has focused on more ill-defined domains that are highly visual (e.g., classifying visual inputs) such as learning Chinese characters or non-discrete (probabilistic and/or with lots of exceptions) such as learning English grammar. In this paper, we tackle these ill-defined domains where complex prior perceptual skills and large amounts of background knowledge are required and where the input from the tutor is largely unstructured. We hypothesize that representations learned by machine learning techniques, which capture high-level features, can be used to create a cognitive model of human learning. We propose a novel architecture called *Cognitive Representation Learner* (CogRL) to automatically extract the set of KCs required for each problem in these domains using representation learning (i.e. transforming the raw data input to a representation that can be effectively exploited in machine learning tasks). CogRL does not require any student performance data and works directly on the unprocessed problem content in the tutor. Our contribution in this paper is two-fold: firstly, we show that CogRL architecture is able to identify accurate cognitive models which outperform the baselines in a wide variety of challenging domains such as RumbleBlocks, Chinese Character, and Article Selection. This is particularly useful in domains where a good human-authored cognitive model is unavailable or difficult to construct. Secondly, for domains where a cognitive model is available, we show that learned representations can be used to get accurate estimates of skill difficulty and learning rate parameters without using any student performance data.

2   Datasets

2.1   RumbleBlocks

Prior methods of cognitive model discovery only handle domains with textual problem content. We use data collected from the educational game *RumbleBlocks* [10] to test our system's ability to operate in a domain based on visual inputs. This game tasks students with building tower structures out of blocks in order to teach them basic structural stability and balance concepts. For the purposes of this study, we were less interested in modeling construction skills and more interested in modeling skills for recognizing when towers are more stable. To this end, we used a data set collected for a simplified task [11], where students were shown images of *RumbleBlocks* towers in a randomized order and are asked to classify each tower as either "concept 1" or "concept 2". After each classification, students were provided with correctness feedback. The labels (concept 1 and concept 2) were intentionally kept vague so that students would be unable to use their prior stability and balance knowledge. The data set consists of twenty students classifying thirty towers.

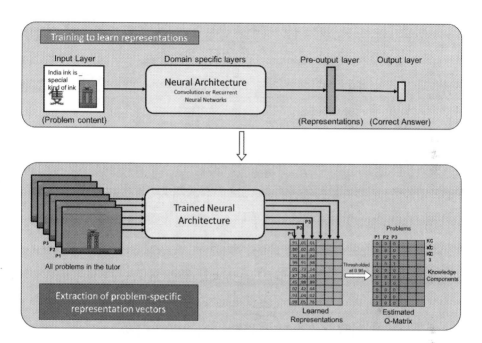

Fig. 1. Architecture of the Cognitive Representation Learner (CogRL) to estimate the Q-Matrix. For each domain, a neural architecture is chosen and trained using the problem content in the tutor and corresponding correct answer. The trained neural architecture is used to produce representation vectors in the pre-output layer for each problem. The resultant matrix is converted to a Q-Matrix by thresholding the values in the representations at 0.95.

2.2   Chinese Characters

For this domain, we use the Chinese vocabulary dataset[1] from the LearnLab Datashop [12]. The problems in the dataset contain 1105 unique Chinese characters with two types of responses, English and pinyin. Pinyin refers to the English character orthography for the Chinese character pronunciation. The dataset consists of 94 students and a total of 61,323 student-item transactions. We extract the set of Chinese characters in the dataset and convert them to 16×16 images for representation learning.

---

[1] https://pslcdatashop.web.cmu.edu/DatasetInfo?datasetId=213.

2.3   Article Selection

For this domain, we use the data from English Article Selection task in the Intelligent Writing Tutor[2]. In this task, each question is a fill in the blank with three options: 'a', 'an' and 'the'. The dataset has 84 unique problems, 79 students with a total of 4,243 student-item transactions. The dataset also provides a human-authored cognitive model with 9 Knowledge Components.

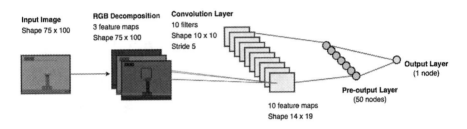

Fig. 2. Architecture of the convolutional neural network used for learning representations for the *RumbleBlocks* dataset. The pre-output layer (Fully Connected Layer) is used as the learned representation for each input image.

3   Methods

3.1   Cognitive Representation Learner

In this subsection, we describe the architecture of the proposed method, Cognitive Representation Learner (CogRL). For each domain, we train a Neural Architecture to predict the correct answer for the given problem in the domain. As shown in Fig. 1, the neural architecture, which is domain-specific, is connected to a fixed size pre-output layer, which will serve as the representations for corresponding problems. The pre-output layer is in turn connected to the output layer which predicts the correct answer for the given input problem. After training the architecture on the problems in the tutor, we use the trained model to compute the representations vectors in the pre-output layer for each problem. These representations are thresholded at 0.95 and used as columns of the estimated Q-matrix. In other words, each dimension of the learned representation constitutes a Knowledge Component in the predicted cognitive model. This cognitive model is evaluated by fitting an Additive Factors Model [13] using the student performance data.

In the *RumbleBlocks* and Chinese character datasets, the problems content is in the form of images. We use convolutional neural networks for these two datasets as they are shown to be effective in learning effective representations from pixel-based image data [14]. For the Articles Selection dataset, the challenge is that the size of the input is variable as opposed to fixed image size in the

---

[2] https://pslcdatashop.web.cmu.edu/DatasetInfo?datasetId=307.

RumbleBlocks and Chinese character datasets. Convolutional Neural Networks can not handle variable input sizes. Recurrent models are suitable for handling variable length input by treating the input as a sequence. Particularly, we use a Long Short-Term Memory Network to learn representations for the Article Selection dataset.

In each of these architectures, we use the pre-output layer of the network as the representations for the corresponding input problem. The size of the representation or pre-output layer is not tuned to optimize the results and kept constant at 50 across all the architectures. These architectures and their training procedure are described in detail in the following subsections.

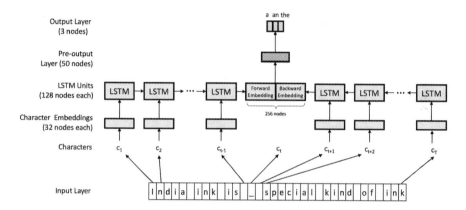

Fig. 3. Architecture of the Long Short-Term Memory (LSTM) network used for learning representations for the Article selection tutor. The pre-output layer (Fully Connected Layer) is used as the learned representation for each input sentence.

3.2 Convolution Neural Networks for RumbleBlocks and Chinese Characters

Convolution Neural Networks [14] are a type of feed-forward neural networks based on the convolution operation, which are typically used for processing visual input. Each convolutional layer consists of a set of learnable filters or kernels, which are convolved across the input image. The output is passed through a nonlinear activation function, such as tanh, and scaled using a learnable parameter. Each element of y_j in the output of a convolution layer is calculated according to the following equation:

$$y_j = g_j \tanh \left(\sum_i k_{ij} * x_i \right) \tag{1}$$

where x_i is the ith channel of input, k_{ij} is the convolutional kernel, g_j is a learned scaling factor and $*$ denotes the discrete convolution operation calculated using the following equation:

$$(x * k)_{ij} = \sum_{p,q}^{R} x_{i-p,j-q} k_{p,q} \tag{2}$$

where R is the kernel size.

The architecture of the convolutional neural network used for learning representations for *RumbleBlocks* is shown in Fig. 2. The input image (75×100) is decomposed into red, green and blue channels which are connected to a convolutional layer consisting of 10 filters of size 10×10 with a stride of 5. The output of the convolutional layer is fully connected to a layer of 50 nodes, which in-turn is fully connected to the output layer predicting whether the configuration of rumble blocks in the input image is stable or not. The network is trained using stochastic gradient descent with a batch size of 32. After training the network, the value of the pre-output layer (50-dimensional) is used as the representation of the corresponding input image. We use the same architecture for Chinese Characters dataset except that the filter size is reduced to 4×4 with a stride 2 to match the size of a smaller 16×16 input image.

3.3   LSTMs for Article Selection

Long Short-Term Memory (LSTM) [15] networks are a type of Recurrent Neural Networks which are suitable for sequential data with a variable size of the input sequence. In addition to the input at the current time step, nodes in a recurrent layer also receive the output of the last time step as input. This recurrence relation makes the output dependent on all the inputs in the sequence seen till the current time step. In addition to the hidden state in a vanilla recurrent unit, LSTM units have an extra memory vector and they can use explicit gating mechanisms to read from, write to, or reset the memory vector. Mathematically, at each LSTM unit, the following computations are made:

$$i_t = \sigma(W_{ii}x_t + b_{ii} + W_{hi}h_{(t-1)} + b_{hi})$$
$$f_t = \sigma(W_{if}x_t + b_{if} + W_{hf}h_{(t-1)} + b_{hf})$$
$$g_t = \tanh(W_{ig}x_t + b_{ig} + W_{hc}h_{(t-1)} + b_{hg})$$
$$o_t = \sigma(W_{io}x_t + b_{io} + W_{ho}h_{(t-1)} + b_{ho})$$
$$c_t = f_t * c_{(t-1)} + i_t * g_t$$
$$h_t = o_t * \tanh(c_t)$$

where h_t is the hidden state at time t, c_t is the cell state or memory vector at time t, x_t is the input at time t and i_t, f_t, g_t, o_t denote the input, forget, cell and out gates at time t, respectively.

The architecture used for learning representations for Article selection is shown in Fig. 3. The input question is split into two parts around the blank. Each character in both the parts has a 32-dimensional embedding. The part before the blank is fed into the forward part of the LSTM sequentially, while the part after the blank is fed into the backward LSTM in the reverse order. At the end of the sequence, both LSTM parts are flattened and combined to a layer of 256 neurons. This layer is fully connected to a pre-output layer with 50 neurons. This layer will serve as the representation for the given input question, which is fully connected to the output layer. The network is trained with all the questions in the English IWT dataset described in Sect. 2 using stochastic gradient descent with a batch size of 32. At the end of the training, for each input question, the pre-output layer embedding is stored as the feature representation of the question.

4   Experiments and Results

Each dimension of the representations learned using CogRL is considered to denote a Knowledge Component (KC). For each problem in a dataset, the representations are thresholded at 0.95, which means that if an element of the representation of a problem is greater than 0.95, then the problem is predicted to require the corresponding KC. This essentially creates a multi-KC Cognitive Model or a Q-Matrix whose rows are the thresholded representations for each problem. This automatically discovered cognitive model is evaluated by fitting the Additive Factors Model to the student performance data. We compare the CogRL cognitive model with two alternative theories of transfer of learning [16]. One, the Faculty Transfer model, is based on faculty theory of transfer that suggests that the mind is like a muscle and generally improves with more experience [17]. The other, the Identical Transfer model, is based on the identical elements theory of transfer that suggest learning transfer occurs across nearly identical stimuli [18]. These models are implemented as follows:

- Faculty Transfer: All the problems require a single common knowledge component.
- Identical Transfer: All the problems require a single unique knowledge component.

The proposed model is also compared with the best human expert cognitive model available with the tutoring system from which the data was collected. We use Item-stratified cross-validation Root Mean Square Error as the metric of comparison. The results shown in Table 1 indicate the CogRL cognitive model outperforms the baselines by a considerable margin, 0.444 vs 0.465 for Chinese Character, 0.449 vs 0.451 for Rumble Blocks and 0.399 vs 0.411 for Article Selection datasets. This indicates that the CogRL architecture is able to learn useful representations which constitute the underlying Knowledge Components for problems in various domains.

We also try to analyze the representation learned by CogRL qualitatively. Figure 4 shows two sets of problem images in the Rumble Blocks domain, which require a common knowledge component. Problem images which have a similar configuration of the blocks are predicted to require a common KC. Note that the exact position of the blocks in all the shown images is very different although they look similar visually.

Table 1. Cross-validated RMSE values for fitting Additive Factors Model (AFM) using various Cognitive Models on three different datasets. The proposed model, CogRL, outperforms the baselines by a considerable margin.

Dataset	Faculty Transfer	Identical Transfer	Best Human Model	CogRL
Chinese Character	0.471	0.493	0.465	**0.444**
Rumble Blocks	0.451	0.537	0.451	**0.449**
Article Selection	0.415	0.522	0.411	**0.399**

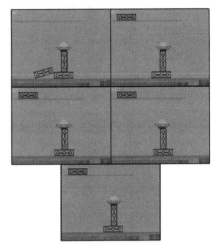

KC 1   KC 2

Fig. 4. Examples of non-identical **RumbleBlocks** problem images in two KCs discovered using Representation Learning. Input images which have a similar configuration of the blocks have a similar representation. Note that the images in one set are not identical, the exact position of the blocks is different in each image, although they look very similar visually.

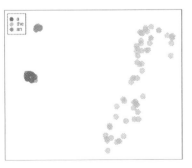
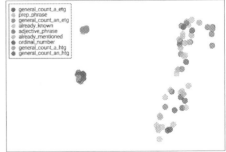

Fig. 5. t-SNE Visualization of Representations learnt for various Problems in the Article Selection dataset labelled using (a) Correct answer, (b) Underlying KC in the best human-authored cognitive model.

The representations learnt for the article selection dataset are visualized using t-Distributed Stochastic Neighboring Embedding (*t-SNE*) [19] in Fig. 5. t-SNE is a popular dimensionality reduction technique well suited for visualizing high dimensional data. The representations of problems are labeled according to the correct answer in Fig. 5(a) and according to the underlying KC in the human-authored cognitive model in Fig. 5(b). As shown in the Fig. 5(a), the representations for problems with the same answer are very similar to each other. However, one problem with answer 'an' is very similar to all problems with answer 'a' rather than other problems with answer 'an'. In Fig. 5(b), we can see that this problem is the only problem in the dataset with KC "general_count_an_htg". The problem is "The salesman is not ___ honest man", which belongs to this KC because the word following the blank starts with a vowel sound but not a vowel character. This makes it very similar to problems where the following word starts with a consonant and have 'a' as the correct answer. Many novice learners confuse problems in this KC to have 'a' as the correct answer. It is interesting to see that automatically learned representations also have this kind of relationship, which suggests that these representations might be indicative of human learning.

5   Extension: Estimating Skill Difficulty and Learning Rates

Intelligent Tutoring Systems are able to improve student learning across a wide range of domains by utilizing student modeling techniques (such as Additive Factors Model [13], Bayesian Knowledge Tracing [20], Performance Factor Analysis [21]) to track the skills students have acquired and to focus practice on unlearned skills. However, student modeling approaches require reasonable initial parameters in order to effectively track skill learning. In prior work, researchers have used pilot studies with fixed, non-adaptive, curriculum to empirically determine the difficulty and learning rates of skills in order to appropriately set the knowledge tracing parameters. In the previous sections, we showed that representation learning using neural architectures can be used for automatic cognitive model discovery, which is especially effective in domains where a good human-authored cognitive model is unavailable. In this section, we show that in domains where a good cognitive model is available (such as article selection), representation learning can be used to estimate the difficulty and learning rates of skills or knowledge components in the given cognitive model. For this task, we leverage the formalism of the Apprentice Learning Architecture [22] to simulate entire classroom studies for Article Selection dataset and demonstrate that empirical estimates of skill difficulty and learning rate parameters from these simulation data have high agreement with the parameters empirically estimated from human data. It is not possible to study the other domains in this context as a human-authored cognitive model is unavailable. The Apprentice learner is trained using the same sequence of problems as received by students in the Articles selection dataset. For each problem, the representations learned by CogRL are passed as input features to the Apprentice Learner. The learner fits a decision tree classifier on seen

problem examples to simulate learning. The data generated using this simulation is fit using Additive Factor Model to get skill slope and intercept estimates.
These estimates are compared to parameter estimates using the original student
performance data.

As a baseline, we also train the Apprentice Learner using human-authored
features defined by domain experts. For the article selection tutor, the domain
experts defined 6 binary features, each of which is true if the following conditions
hold true:

- 'next_word_starts_with_vowel': Whether the word following the blank starts
  with a vowel. This feature approximates whether the noun following the article begins with a vowel sound.
- 'next_word_ending_st_nd_rd_th': Whether the word following the blank ends
  with 'st', 'nd', 'rd' or 'th'. This feature is an approximation of whether the
  next word is an ordinal number or not.
- 'contains_that_where_who': Whether the question contains 'that', 'where' or
  'who'. This feature is an approximation of whether the noun following the
  article is made definite by a prepositional or an adjective phrase.
- 'next_word_already_mentioned': Whether the word following the blank is
  already mentioned elsewhere in the question. The feature is an approximation
  of whether noun that follows the article is already known or mentioned.
- 'next_word_ends_in_s': Whether the word after the blank ends with a 's'. This
  feature approximates if the noun following the article is not a singular count
  noun.
- 'contains_but_comma': Whether the sentence contains 'but' or ','. This feature
  approximates whether the question has two clauses and the noun following
  the article is referred in the first clause and therefore, already known. For
  example, "When I have watermelon, I try not to eat ___ seeds".

Note that the article selection task is fairly complex and it is extremely difficult
to author text-based features that are sufficient to answer all questions in the
dataset correctly. For example, authoring text-based features which recognize
vowel sound in words not starting with vowels like 'honest' is extremely difficult.
The features authored by the experts are shallow and are sufficient to answer
only 75% of the questions correctly.

5.1   Parameter Estimation Results

The parameter estimates for the Article Selection dataset using (1) the original
student performance data, (2) using the simulated data with Human-authored
features, and (3) using the simulated data with CogRL features are shown in
Table 2. As shown in the table, the parameter estimates using CogRL features
have a high correlation of 0.986 for slope, and 0.748 for intercept with the
parameter estimates using the original data. This is considerably higher than
the correlation of parameter estimates using Human-authored features. Most
of the human-authored features are deep and result in very fast learning rate

Table 2. Table showing parameter estimates for the Article Selection dataset using the original student performance data, using the simulated data with Human-authored features, and using the simulated data with Representation Learning features. The parameter estimates using representation learning correlate highly with the parameter estimates using the original data.

| KC Name | Original data | | Apprentice Learner trained using | | | |
| | | | Human-Authored features | | CogRL features | |
	Intercept	Slope	Intercept	Slope	Intercept	Slope
produce_adjective_phrase	0.818	0.093	0.881	0	0.563	0.156
produce_already_known	0.768	0.092	0.547	1.208	0.332	0.202
produce_already_mentioned	0.930	0.044	0.914	16.803	0.721	0.048
produce_general_count_a_etg	0.604	0.066	0.821	0	0.396	0.022
produce_general_count_a_htg	0.202	0.660	0.119	2.627	0.065	2.221
produce_general_count_an_etg	0.670	0.031	0.14	0.882	0.044	0.205
produce_general_count_an_htg	0.467	0.817	0	0	0.037	3.208
produce_ordinal_number	0.783	0.151	0.958	0	0.814	0.003
produce_prep_phrase	0.660	0.138	0.58	0.082	0.348	0.331
Correlation with Original			0.742	−0.187	0.748	0.986

for certain KCs such as 'already_mentioned' and 'already_known', while since they don't cover all features required for learning some other KCs such as 'general_count_an_htg', they have a learning rate of 0. CogRL captures features essential for learning all KCs and seems to better model the struggles that learners are experiencing to acquire deep features. While it would be very difficult to train the Apprentice Learner from raw problem data, CogRL features are able to constitute the right amount of prior knowledge necessary to simulate learning in this domain. Apart from providing accurate parameter estimates without using any student performance data, the CogRL framework also minimizes the amount of human-authoring necessary to conduct simulation studies in this challenging domain.

6 Related Work

There has been a lot of interest in automating cognitive model discovery in the recent past. Learning Factors Analysis is a method for cognitive model evaluation and improvement which semi-automatically refines a given skill set. The improved cognitive model discovered using LFA has been used to redesign an intelligent tutoring system and shown to improve learning gains [4]. However, LFA requires human-provided factors that require some knowledge engineering or cognitive task analysis effort. eEPIPHANY [6] attempts to overcome this limitation by using a collection of data-mining techniques to more automatically improve a human-crafted set of skills. LFA and ePHIPHANY both require a human-crafted set of skills as well as student performance data for cognitive model discovery and improvement.

The requirement of student performance data makes these methods unusable for authoring a cognitive model for a new domain or a tutor with new problems. Li et al. [8] is notable prior attempt at learning a cognitive model without student performance data. Their SimStudent learns a cognitive model by being tutored in the domain through demonstrations of correct actions and yes-no feedback on SimStudent attempts at actions. They show improved cognitive models in various domains such as algebra, stoichiometry and fraction addition [2]. Furthermore, the skill learning in SimStudent was also integrated with feature learning using probabilistic Context Free Grammars (pCFG) to automatically learn features to train the SimStudent [23]. However, as discussed previously, SimStudent requires structured input from the tutor interface and the learning method is mostly applicable in well-defined problem domains where minimal background knowledge is required.

Among approaches using neural networks in educational data mining, Wang et al. [9] train an LSTM to predict student's learning over time using student performance data in programming exercises. The t-SNE visualization of the hidden layer outputs of their trained neural network shows clusters of trajectories sharing some high-level properties of the programming exercise. Pardos and Dadu [24] use contextual representations learnt by a skip-gram model to predict missing skill from a KC model. Michalenko et al. [25] use word embeddings detect misconceptions from students' responses to open-response questions.

In contrast to prior work, we tackle domains where the tutor interface is largely unstructured and problem solving requires complex prior perceptual skills and large amounts of background knowledge. Furthermore, while handling these complex domains, our methods do not require any student performance data which makes them suitable for initializing cognitive models while designing a new tutor. We also provide a method for estimating skill difficulty and learning rate without any student performance data using simulations of Apprentice learner. These estimates can be used as initialization in new tutors to provide a better estimate of mastery for each student.

7   Conclusion and Future Work

We showed that representation learning using neural architectures can be used for automatic cognitive model discovery without using any student performance data, which is especially effective in domains where a good human-authored cognitive model is unavailable or authoring a good cognitive model is difficult. Qualitative analysis of representations learnt by CogRL suggests similarities with human learning. For domains where a cognitive model is available, we show that representation learning can be used to get effective estimates of skill difficulty and learning rate parameters without using any student performance data. In future, the CogRL framework can be modified to make the representations more interpretable and provide constructive feedback for improving instructional design.

References

1. VanLehn, K., Jordan, P., Litman, D.: Developing pedagogically effective tutorial dialogue tactics: experiments and a testbed. In: Workshop on Speech and Language Technology in Education (2007)
2. Li, N., Stampfer, E., Cohen, W., Koedinger, K.: General and efficient cognitive model discovery using a simulated student. In: Proceedings of the Annual Meeting of the Cognitive Science Society, vol. 35 (2013)
3. Cen, H., Koedinger, K., Junker, B.: Learning factors analysis – a general method for cognitive model evaluation and improvement. In: Ikeda, M., Ashley, K.D., Chan, T.-W. (eds.) ITS 2006. LNCS, vol. 4053, pp. 164–175. Springer, Heidelberg (2006). https://doi.org/10.1007/11774303_17
4. Koedinger, K.R., Stamper, J.C., McLaughlin, E.A., Nixon, T.: Using data-driven discovery of better student models to improve student learning. In: Lane, H.C., Yacef, K., Mostow, J., Pavlik, P. (eds.) AIED 2013. LNCS (LNAI), vol. 7926, pp. 421–430. Springer, Heidelberg (2013). https://doi.org/10.1007/978-3-642-39112-5_43
5. González-Brenes, J., Mostow, J.: Dynamic cognitive tracing: towards unified discovery of student and cognitive models. In: Proceedings of the 5th International Conference on Educational Data Mining (2012)
6. Matsuda, N., Furukawa, T., Bier, N., Faloutsos, C.: Machine beats experts: automatic discovery of skill models for data-driven online course refinement. Int. Educ. Data Min. Soc. (2015)
7. Piech, C., Bassen, J., Huang, J., Ganguli, S., Sahami, M., Guibas, L.J., Sohl-Dickstein, J.: Deep knowledge tracing. In: Advances in Neural Information Processing Systems, pp. 505–513 (2015)
8. Li, N., Cohen, W., Koedinger, K.R., Matsuda, N.: A machine learning approach for automatic student model discovery. In: Proceedings of the 4th International Conference on Educational Data Mining (2011)
9. Wang, L., Sy, A., Liu, L., Piech, C.: Learning to represent student knowledge on programming exercises using deep learning. In: Proceedings of the 10th International Conference on Educational Data Mining (2017)
10. Christel, M.G., Stevens, S.M., Maher, B.S., Brice, S., Champer, M., Jayapalan, L., Chen, Q., Jin, J., Hausmann, D., Bastida, N., et al.: Rumbleblocks: teaching science concepts to young children through a unity game. In: 2012 17th International Conference on Computer Games (CGAMES), pp. 162–166. IEEE (2012)
11. MacLellan, C., Harpstead, E., Aleven, V., Koedinger, K.: Trestle: a model of concept formation in structured domains. Adv. Cogn. Syst. **4**, 131–150 (2016)
12. Koedinger, K.R., Baker, R.S., Cunningham, K., Skogsholm, A., Leber, B., Stamper, J.: A data repository for the edm community: the pslc datashop. In: Handbook of Educational Data Mining, vol. 43, pp. 43–56. CRC Press, Boca Raton (2010)
13. Cen, H.: Generalized learning factors analysis: improving cognitive models with machine learning. ProQuest (2009)
14. LeCun, Y., Boser, B., Denker, J.S., Henderson, D., Howard, R.E., Hubbard, W., Jackel, L.D.: Backpropagation applied to handwritten zip code recognition. Neural Comput. **1**(4), 541–551 (1989)
15. Hochreiter, S., Schmidhuber, J.: Long short-term memory. Neural Comput. **9**(8), 1735–1780 (1997)
16. Koedinger, K.R., Yudelson, M.V., Pavlik, P.I.: Testing theories of transfer using error rate learning curves. Top. Cogn. Sci. **8**(3), 589–609 (2016)

17. Nichols, R., Yaffe, G., Reid, T., Zalta, E.N. (eds.): The Stanford Encyclopedia of Philosophy. Winter 2016 edn. Metaphysics Research Lab, Stanford University (2016)
18. Thorndike, E.L.: The Principles of Teaching: Based on Psychology, vol. 32. Routledge, Oxford (2013)
19. Maaten, L.: Learning a parametric embedding by preserving local structure. In: van Dyk, D., Welling, M. (eds.) Proceedings of the Twelth International Conference on Artificial Intelligence and Statistics. Volume 5 of Proceedings of Machine Learning Research. Hilton Clearwater Beach Resort, Clearwater Beach, Florida USA. PMLR, pp. 384–391, 16–18 April 2009
20. Corbett, A.T., Anderson, J.R.: Knowledge tracing: modeling the acquisition of procedural knowledge. User Model. User-Adap. Inter. 4(4), 253–278 (1994)
21. Pavlik, P.I., Cen, H., Koedinger, K.R.: Performance factors analysis -a new alternative to knowledge tracing. In: Proceedings of the 2009 Conference on Artificial Intelligence in Education: Building Learning Systems That Care: From Knowledge Representation to Affective Modelling, pp. 531–538. IOS Press, Amsterdam (2009)
22. MacLellan, C.J., Harpstead, E., Patel, R., Koedinger, K.R.: The apprentice learner architecture: closing the loop between learning theory and educational data. In: Proceedings of the 9th International Conference on Educational Data Mining (2016)
23. Li, N., Matsuda, N., Cohen, W.W., Koedinger, K.R.: Integrating representation learning and skill learning in a human-like intelligent agent. Artif. Intell. **219**, 67–91 (2015)
24. Pardos, Z.A., Dadu, A.: Imputing kcs with representations of problem content and context. In: Proceedings of the 25th Conference on User Modeling, Adaptation and Personalization, pp. 148–155. ACM (2017)
25. Michalenko, J.J., Lan, A.S., Baraniuk, R.G.: Data-mining textual responses to uncover misconception patterns. stat. **1050**, 30 (2017)

Measuring the Quality of Assessment Using Questions Generated from the Semantic Web

Ricardo Conejo[✉], Beatriz Barros, and Manuel F. Bertoa

University of Malaga, Malaga, Spain
conejo@lcc.uma.es

Abstract. This article describes a new feature of the adaptive assessment system SIETTE that allows for the static and dynamic generation of questions from tables of data for knowledge assessment. Almost the same approach can be used to generate questions from data collected in a spreadsheet, a database query, or a semantic web query using SPARQL. The main problem faced with question generation is ensuring that the questions are valid for assessment. For this reason, most of the existing systems propose to use this mechanism only for low-stakes assessments. In this paper, we propose a methodology to control question generation quality and measure the impact of potential invalid instances on the final score as well as recommend some strategies to overcome these problems.

Keywords: Question generation · Semantic web
Automatic assessment

1 Introduction

Question generation from databases [1], and questions from linked open data (LOD), in particular, are a potential source of an unlimited number of questions for a wide variety of uses. For example, Le et al. [2] distinguish between knowledge/skills acquisition, tutorial dialogues, and knowledge assessment.

This article focus on question generation for knowledge assessment, especially when the questions are generated from semantic web sources, like Wikidata or DBPedia. There are already a number of systems that have identified this potential use [3–5]. However, the messy structure and the number of invalid instances that are generated among the valid ones, implies that most of these systems only aim at recreational or self-assessment use [6–8].

We face the problem of using generated questions for high-stakes knowledge assessment in SIETTE, defining a methodology to reduce the number of incorrect instances, measuring the impact of potential invalid instances on the assessment score, and defining some strategies to correct and reduce these problems.

© Springer International Publishing AG, part of Springer Nature 2018
C. Penstein Rosé et al. (Eds.): AIED 2018, LNAI 10947, pp. 57–69, 2018.
https://doi.org/10.1007/978-3-319-93843-1_5

2   Question Generation in SIETTE

SIETTE is a general-purpose, domain-independent assessment environment (see [9,10]). The system incorporates item banking, test building, analysis, delivery and result presentation. It supports classical test theory (CTT), item response theory (IRT), and computer-adaptive testing (CAT). Three main types of item models are supported: (1) multiple choice, single answer questions (MCQ-SA); (2) Multiple choice, multiple answer questions (MCQ-MA); and (3) short answer questions (SAQ). These are just the three internal models that SIETTE uses. Any other type of question that SIETTE can deal with (like sorting, correspondence, drag and drop, etc.) are represented by one of the item models.

The first two item models are simpler to evaluate, but the third one requires an engine that recognizes the student's answer and assigns it into a given pattern solution. SIETTE provides different types of patterns for different uses. The most commonly used are regular expression patterns. For instance, a question could be *"Who is the composer of the Moonlight Sonata?"*. The pattern "{Ludwig {van}} Beethoven" will accept answers like *Beethoven* or *Ludwig van Beethoven*. Multiple patterns can be used for the same question. Additionally, at a teacher's option, patterns can ignore case, accented characters, white spaces, and/or punctuation symbols. They can also includes numerical ranges, magnitudes, and more. If the response of a question is a number, SIETTE allows the construction of patterns that include a variable range. For instance, the SIETTE pattern "[3,14%1]" will accept any number close to π, and the SIETTE pattern [1450#1500] will accept any number between this range. Magnitudes can be added to numerical ranges to recognize different expressions, meaning that [72 km/h%1] will also recognize 20 m/s. Questions might have several correct answer patterns, and even patterns to recognize common incorrect answers, in order to provide accurate feedback.

In some ways, it is easier to generate good SAQs than good MCQs. For the first type, it is necessary to generate a pattern that recognizes the response, which is very easy with numerical values and single-word text. In the second case the main difficulty is to generate alternative options (often called distractors) that are plausible. We will revisit this issue later.

On the other hand, SIETTE can generate questions from templates written in JSP, or any other server-side script language. For instance, a question template that generates two numbers between 0 and 5 and asks for their sum could be:

```
<%
    int x    = Math.abs( siette.util.Random.nextInt() % 5 ) + 1;
    int y    = Math.abs( siette.util.Random.nextInt() % 5 ) + 1;
    int z    = x+y;
%>
What is the result of this operation:<br/>
<center> <%= x %> + <%= y %> </center>
```

An important detail is that SIETTE uses its own *Random* class, that is fixed by setting a seed, for each question according to the question and assessment session id, so the template will always generate the same random instance each time it is called by the same test session. This is important because: (1) there is no need to save the instance itself, just the question template and the seed; and (2) each time the question is posed or reviewed in a test session, the same instance is generated, allowing a user to go back and forth during an assessment. It also allows the teachers to review the assessment session without changing the originally posed instance. On the other hand, this approach has the drawback that if the structure of the question template is changed after the student responds, the instances might differ. However, this is easily solved by locking the question templates once they are posed.

In the simpler cases, the templates generates random numbers or strings that are inserted in the question. A first extension of this technique is the generation of questions from tables containing a data set. To illustrate this implementation, we introduce the example of the periodic table. Suppose we have a spreadsheet containing 103 rows corresponding to the first 103 chemical elements. Columns are labeled NAME, SYMBOL, ATOMIC NUMBER, and so on. From this spreadsheet, it is possible to generate multiple questions, for instance, the symbol of a given element:

```
<%@page import="siette.util.corpus.Table"%>
<%
    Table table = new Table("demo/periodic-table.xls");
    String[] element = table.select();
    String name = table.get( element, "NAME" );
    String symbol = table.get( element, "SYMBOL" );
%>
What is the symbol for the chemical element "<i><%= name %></i>"?
```

There are many other possible question templates that can be generated from the same table. The easiest way is to generate SAQs, but other types are also possible, like *Which of these three elements has the lowest atomic number?* (MCQ-SA question) or *Select from among these six, all the elements that have a density greater than lead* (MCQ-MA question).

The following extension is to read data from a database, rather than from a spreadsheet. As an example, we have used the database from project TREE [11], that contains 32 tables with information about 322 European tree species, including images labeled with metadata that describes them.

```
<%@page import="siette.util.corpus.DatabaseTable"%>
<%
    String query = "SELECT S.BINOMIAL, S.COMMON_NAME, P.IMG "
                 + " FROM SPECIES S JOIN PHOTOS P ON P.SPECIE = S.SPECIE "
                 + " WHERE P.FEATURE='Leaf' "
                 ;
    DatabaseTable table = new DatabaseTable("demo/tree.properties", query);
    String[] plant = table.select();
    String img = table.get( plant, "IMG" );
    String binomial = table.get( plant, "BINOMIAL" );
    String plant_name = table.get( plant, "NOMBRE" );
%>
Write the scientific name of the specie that have this leaf:
<center> <IMG SRC='<%= img %>'> </center>
```

In this case, the accepted pattern might be the binomial scientific name or the common name, although in this case the query should be more complex to cover all possible responses.

The next step is the extension to query from the semantic web using SPARQL. The idea is similar to the previous implementation, but the data source is broader. As an example, the following query from DBpedia generates questions about the flag of a given country.

```
<%@page import="siette.util.corpus.WebTable"%>
<%
String query = "SELECT DISTINCT ?nombre ?name ?population ?flag ?img "
+"WHERE { "
+"    ?country a dbpedia-owl:Country ; rdfs:label ?name ; dbo:flag ?flag . "
+"    ?country ?hasPopulation ?population ; dbo:thumbnail ?img . "
+"    ?country dct:subject dbc:Member_states_of_the_United_Nations "
+"    FILTER (langMatches(lang(?name), \"en\")) "
+"    FILTER (?population > 1000000)   "
+"} "
;
    WebTable table = new WebTable("http://dbpedia.org/sparql",query);
    String[] country = table.select();
    String name = table.get( country, "name" );
    String img  = table.get( country, "img" );
%>
<center>
Which is the country of this flag? <br/>
<center><IMG src="<%= img %>"/><br/></center>
```

Notice that the query has restricted the set of countries to those that are members of the United Nations, and have more that 1 million inhabitants.

In the same way, it is possible to generate questions like *Who is the painter of this picture? (+image)* or *Who is the composer of this musical work? (+sound).* Most of the current approaches to question generation from the Semantic Web generate MCQs [4,12,13]. This approach makes it easier to recognize the correct student response, but it makes it much more difficult to generate appropriate questions. The key point is that options should be plausible. To accomplish this, these systems define a distance between possible responses based on the amount of metadata that matches both the correct answer and the alternatives and other ontology distance measures. Practical results are not always satisfactory. Moreover, generating SAQs usually involves just a single record from the database, while generating multiple choices involves multiple records. Reducing the number of records decrease the potential problems for generating an invalid question (see next section). Nevertheless, deep question generation may involves multiple records and relations [14,15].

Additionally, it is possible to generate hints or feedbacks by selecting some important feature and displaying one or two of the first sentences from the rdfs:comment field. For instance, in a case of where the correct answer is Beethoven, the hint could be ___ *was a German composer and pianist. A crucial figure in the transition between the Classical and Romantic eras in Western music art; he remains one of the most famous and influential of all composers.* Of course, this requires removing any text that matches the correct response pattern. Later paragraphs might give less obvious hints, like *His best known compositions include 9 symphonies, 5 piano concertos, 1 violin concerto, 32 piano sonatas, 16 string quartets, his great Mass the Missa solemnis, and 1 opera.* Another way to generate hints is by selecting other similar records. For instance, if we are asking for a composition by Beethoven, a hint could be *This other piece was composed by the same musician (+sound)*, which is easily obtained with a complementary query.

It is not possible to guarantee that the pattern will match 100% of students' responses. However, SIETTE includes a simple mechanism that displays all student responses on a single page, allowing for modification and reassessment of the pattern (see Fig. 1). This final step achieves 100% correction of actual student's responses, but implies an assessment review, which as we will see, is also necessary when dealing with invalid instances (see Subsect. 4.2)

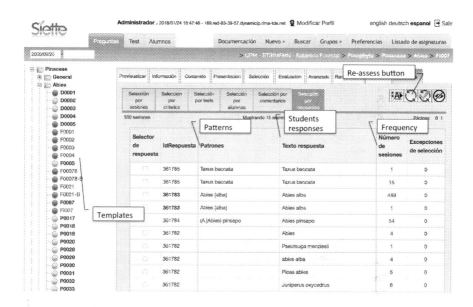

Fig. 1. Listing of all patterns and students' answers for a botany question

3 Problems with Generated Questions

The previous section outlined the technicalities involved in question generation from tables. However, the main problem is not generating the question but ensuring its quality and validity. The technical procedure is the same in the three cases, but there are differences between using a spreadsheet, database or semantic web data. In the first case, the table is uploaded by the teacher to the SIETTE environment. It is commonly constructed for assessment purpose, has a relatively low fixed number of rows, and can be edited by the teacher in case a mistake is detected. In the second case, the database is bigger and the data are mostly correct, but it might not be under the teacher's control. In the last case, the database is huge but there are a significant number of potential problems with data that are not correctly labeled.

Of course, a trivial solution for the problem of generating questions from uncontrolled sources is to create local dumps, that is, generate a spreadsheet or a database from a semantic web query and manually review each record. Another trivial solution (which is also implemented in SIETTE) is to produce a set of static (fixed) instances from a template question, add them to the item bank as normal questions, and review them one by one. These trivial approaches also have its drawbacks because the dynamic behavior is lost, and future changes in the database do not affect the generated questions. Moreover, it might require larger space to store the generated questions, with possible implications for system efficiency. Consider a small number of queries that produce a large number of instances. In this case, the item bank will be filled up with several copies of similar questions. This fact might reduce, for instance, the efficiency of adaptive item selection process. On the other hand, manually reviewing of a huge number of generated questions would be a very tedious task.

In the rest of the paper, we will focus on the problem of dynamic question generation using semantic web queries, which is the most challenging feature. Techniques for detecting and correcting low-quality items can be applied in the three cases, but there are different sources of problems. As a result, we face different problems when questions are generated from semantic web queries, like those detailed below:

1. The first problem is that the databases might not be completely correctly labeled. We have tried DBpedia data with toy examples like the composer of a musical work and found some mislabeled pieces. However, this source of problems is rare.

2. Another source of problems is missing content. For instance, when we tried the query about flags described in the previous section, the link to the Swiss flag was broken. This problem can be avoided at run time by checking the link previously and generating a different instance if there is a broken link.

3. A third type of failure is related to "undesired" or "unexpected" content. This happens, for instance, with a first version of the flags question, when the query in the template generated a question for the flag of *Prussia* or the flag of *Faeroe Islands* which is, in fact a country within Denmark, or for the flag of *Nuaru*, which is a very small island in Micronesia.

4. Another source of problems is the incompleteness of the response pattern in some particular cases. This occurs when the general procedure of constructing the pattern fails for a given instance. For instance, the pattern {United States of} America which is constructed for country names does not recognize the simpler answer *USA*. This type of problems can be avoided by carefully refining the SPARQL query and adding some alternative patterns by using redirection and/or disambiguating properties (for instance, by using the property skos:altLabel to gives name variations). The debug of this problem is done by random approaches, which is generating random test cases until a wrong case appears, correcting the query in that case, and then continuing with the debugging. However, this procedure does not guarantee complete success.

4   Measuring the Quality of Assessment

Depending on the desired use of the question templates, problems that arise can be more or less important, and the procedures to correct them should be more or less sophisticated. Suppose there is a test with n questions coming from n different templates that comes from queries that generating valid instances with a probability p. Further, the test is used for fun or for self-assessment. For high values of p (i.e., for $p > 0.90$) there is no need for further refinement. The user will notice the missing content and skip that question without further consequences.

If the question belongs to a high-stakes assessment, a similar precision might not be acceptable, because for a large population of students, there would be cases in which a relevant number of instance questions will be invalid, and the final score may be affected. In this case, we have to consider not just the average case, but the worst case that might occur among the total number of students. What differentiates these cases is the concept known as "test and score reliability". Informally speaking, test reliability refers to the degree to which a test is consistent and stable in measuring what it is intended to measure. Score reliability refers to the confidence interval in which the true score of a subject is included.

CTT has proposed several definitions of test reliability [16], and one of the most commonly used is based on the concept of a parallel test, meaning that if a test is repeated with a similar question composition, the results should be the same. There are many statistics proposed to estimate the internal consistency reliability, commonly shortened as $\rho_{xx'}$. The most familiar are the Spearman-Brown, Guttman-Flannagan's λ_4, Kuder-Richardson's KR-20 or KR-21, and Cronbach's α. Test reliability varies from -1 to 1. Even in the most carefully manually prepared test, test reliability is not 1. Values over 0.70 are considered good enough.

The true score confidence interval can be estimated assuming normal error distribution as $X \pm z_{\alpha/2}\sigma_x\sqrt{1 - \rho_{xx'}}$, where X is the score obtained in the test, α is the confidence level, and σ_x^2 is the variance of the whole test. If a test contains an invalid question, the student will always fail it, so test reliability will be reduced and variance will increase and, likewise, the interval will also increase.

However, if the number of incorrect questions is small compared to the number of questions in the test, the final reliability might not be compromised.

The research interest at this point is to be aware of the advantages and drawbacks of question generation, quantify the problem, and establish limits of acceptance as in any other engineering activity, implementing quality control procedures previous to the application of the test (see Sect. 4.1). Fortunately, even in high-stakes exams, there are no irremediable consequences, and an assessment can be reviewed. We are also interested in procedures to automatically or semi-automatically detect failures, correct them and reassess (see Sect. 4.2).

4.1   Preliminary Question Analysis

Question generation from huge databases is a kind of industrial production process, and thus, the same quality measurements should be taken. We distinguish two separate phases: software testing and statistical testing.

First, the template query should be proved and refined as much as possible to avoid undesirable results. We call this phase software testing, because software modification techniques are used to improve the question quality. However, as was exemplified in the previous section, query refinement reduces but does not eliminate all potential errors. Moreover, the successive refinements might introduce new invalid instances or impose unnecessary limits on potential instances candidates. To sum up, there is a limit in what can be obtained with software testing.

The first step of the statistical testing phase is to establish a desired confidence level and quantify the expected errors. As was suggested in the previous section, confidence level depends on the assessment goal. Suppose a test with n questions coming from n templates that comes from queries where each one generates a valid instance with probability p, the probability of having a maximum of w wrong instances in the test can be obtained by the cumulative binomial distribution

$$p_w = Pr(X \leq w) = \sum_{i=0}^{w} \binom{n}{i} p^n (1-p)^{n-i}$$

If m students take the test, the probability of having all sessions with less than w wrong instances is p_w^m.

In the next section, we will see that wrong instances can be removed and the test can be reassessed, but there would be a side effect in test reliability, so it is desirable to keep w below the acceptable limits, thus ensuring that p, which is not known, is below a threshold.

Proceeding in the opposite direction, assuming the value of w is desired to be less than a given number (fixed according to the maximum acceptable proportion of wrong instances in any test), the confidence level would be p_w for a single session and p_w^m the confidence level that it is not going to occur in any of the m test sessions. For instance, in a test on $n = 30$ questions, the probability of that any of the $m = 250$ includes less than $w = 3$ invalid instances (less than the 10%) would be $p_w^m \geq 0.945$ if the probability of a single failure is $p \leq 0.01$. Another way of viewing the situation is to predict the number of sessions with w errors. In this case, 73.9% of the cases will have no incorrect instance; 22.4% will include just one failure; 3.2% will include 2 failures; 0.3% will include 3 failures; and only 0.0012% sessions will include 4 or more.

4.2   Posterior Question Analysis

Achieving 100% accuracy in all cases is almost impossible, even with manually generated static questions. For this reason, SIETTE includes a review procedure that allows for editing of the assessment setting and reassessing all assessment sessions according to the given responses. The procedure is easy and can be done with a few clicks.

This procedure is initiated if the teacher or any student detects a failure in the test and request for an assessment review. To facilitate this task, SIETTE can optionally include a comment box beneath each question to collect during-test comments from the student for the posed question. All student comments are displayed together for the same question, so the teacher can evaluate if that question has some kind of misbehavior. There is also built-in automatic detection of incorrect questions that will be explained later. There are two possible cases of incorrect questions: (1) questions with a correct answer different from the one that is set for MCQ, or questions that have an incorrect or incomplete responses pattern for SAQ; and (2) questions that have a problem with the stem and could not be answered correctly. In the first case, the solution is to change the correct answer to the right one or provide a new or better pattern, but in the second, the only remedy is to remove that question from the assessment and reassess according to the remaining $(n - k)$ questions, supposing k items should be removed. The reduction in test reliability can be obtained by applying the Spearman-Brown prophecy formula

$$\rho^*_{xx'} = \frac{R\rho_{xx'}}{1 + (R - 1)\rho_{xx'}},$$

where R is the ratio between assessment lengths, that is, $n/(n-k)$. Table 1 shows the impact on reliability according to the percentage of items lost. Table 2 shows the percentage of variation of the confidence interval.

Table 1. New reliability $\rho^*_{xx'}$ as a function of original reliability and percentage of invalid questions

$\rho_{xx'}$	50%	40%	30%	20%	10%	5%	2.5%
0.70	0.538	0.583	0.620	0.651	0.677	0.689	0.696
0.75	0.600	0.643	0.677	0.706	0.730	0.740	0.746
0.80	0.667	0.706	0.737	0.762	0.783	0.792	0.797
0.85	0.739	0.773	0.799	0.819	0.836	0.843	0.847
0.90	0.818	0.844	0.863	0.878	0.890	0.895	0.898
0.95	0.905	0.919	0.930	0.938	0.945	0.948	0.949

A reduction in reliability implies that the standard error increases, and so does the confidence interval for a given confidence level α. The variation is given by the ratio $\sqrt{1 - \rho^*_{xx'}}/\sqrt{1 - \rho_{xx'}}$. Table 2 indicates the ratio for different combinations of original reliability and percentage of items lost. According to these tables, the number of test items, and the assessment application, it is possible to decide which is the maximum number of items that eventually might be invalidated. For instance, if an assessment is composed of 30 items, and has a reliability of 0.80, removing three items will imply that the confidence interval of the final score will increase 4.3%. Of course, the decision can be the other way around, that is, increasing the assessment length 10% (see [16] for further details about reliability and quality of test scores).

Table 2. Ratio of standard errors before and after removing a given percentage of questions

$\rho_{xx'}$	50%	40%	30%	20%	10%	5%	2.5%
0.70	1.240	1.179	1.125	1.078	1.037	1.018	1.007
0.75	1.265	1.195	1.136	1.085	1.040	1.019	1.008
0.80	1.219	1.213	1.147	1.091	1.043	1.021	1.008
0.85	1.319	1.231	1.159	1.098	1.045	1.022	1.009
0.90	1.348	1.250	1.170	1.104	1.048	1.023	1.009
0.95	1.380	1.270	1.183	1.111	1.051	1.025	1.010

The detection of incorrect instances can be done automatically using psychometric item analysis tools that are already integrated in SIETTE. There are three simple measures that allow for early detection of invalid instances. The *difficulty index* is defined as the proportion of students who answered the item correctly $p = \frac{C}{N}$ where C is the number of student that have answered the item correctly, and N is the total number of students. The *discrimination index* is defined as the difference between the ratio of hits of the first (p_{1q}) and fourth quartiles (p_{4q}). That is, the whole sample is divided into four parts according to the final score obtained in the assessment. The difficulty index is computed for the highest and lowest score parts, and the discrimination index is the difference between both: $D = p_{4q} - p_{1q}$. The point biserial correlation between the response and the item's total score is a good indicator of the item quality. IRT parameters can also be used for instance analysis.

An invalid instance will have a difficulty index and a discrimination index equal to zero (or very close to zero if we consider random responses). The discrimination index will help to identify not only invalid instances, but also those instances that are not valid for assessment, meaning those that do not relate to the knowledge we are measuring with the assessment.

Once the invalid items or instances have been detected, they are marked as *canceled* in the item pool. The test session is reassessed, and those questions marked as *canceled* are considered to have not been posed in every session where they might have appeared. Notice that if the percentage of invalid questions generated by a given template is small, this process will still significantly reduce that figure because the instances marked as *canceled* will be avoided in future assessment sessions. Figure 2 shows the indicators obtained for all the instances of a given template, the cancel slider and the reassess button.

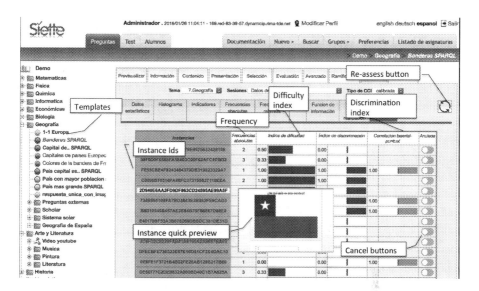

Fig. 2. Listing all instances' indicators to allow canceling of incorrect instances

Measuring difficulty and discrimination indexes is just one of many easy ways to control item quality. SIETTE also includes IRT procedures to calibrate the item bank, obtaining the IRT parameters. To use them, it is also a good idea to use anchor items, which are items that appears in every session and that can be used to establish a common ground.

The dynamic analysis might also suggest that the question generation template produces items with very different IRT item parameters; that is, instances generated by the same template that behave differently. In this case, the best strategy is to split the original template into two or more templates to guarantee fully isomorphic items.

5   Conclusions

Using public databases and the semantic web as source for question generation has a high use potential. However, current applications are restricted to low-stakes assessments. In order to use them for high-stakes assessments, we should be aware of for implications and establish quality control measures and review procedures to ensure the assessment validity and reliability. Following these rules, it is perfectly possible to use this immense source of knowledge for any type of assessment. We plan to apply this technique to generate questions for botany courses at Madrid Polytechnic University.

To sum up, the conclusions of this article can be summarized as follow: (1) generating SAQs reduces the number of invalid questions; (2) invalid questions can be detected manually or automatically by using item analysis techniques; (3) canceling invalid questions and re-assessing guarantees a valid assessment; and

(4) the effect of using invalid questions can be measured and acceptance limits can be established. We have implemented extensions of the SIETTE authoring tool that make it easier to accomplish these tasks. The system can be accessed at http://www.siette.org, where some sample tests, in Spanish and English, can be found in the Demo area.

References

1. Chaudhri, V.K., Clark, P.E., Overholtzer, A., Spaulding, A.: Question generation from a knowledge base. In: Janowicz, K., Schlobach, S., Lambrix, P., Hyvönen, E. (eds.) EKAW 2014. LNCS (LNAI), vol. 8876, pp. 54–65. Springer, Cham (2014). https://doi.org/10.1007/978-3-319-13704-9_5
2. Le, N.-T., Kojiri, T., Pinkwart, N.: Automatic question generation for educational applications – the state of art. In: van Do, T., Thi, H.A.L., Nguyen, N.T. (eds.) Advanced Computational Methods for Knowledge Engineering. AISC, vol. 282, pp. 325–338. Springer, Cham (2014). https://doi.org/10.1007/978-3-319-06569-4_24
3. Unger, C., Bühmann, L., Lehmann, J., Ngonga Ngomo, A.C., Gerber, D., Cimiano, P.: Template-based question answering over RDF data. In: Proceedings of the 21st International Conference on World Wide Web, WWW 2012, pp. 639. ACM Press, New York (2012)
4. Tamura, Y., Takase, Y., Hayashi, Y., Nakano, Y.I.: Generating quizzes for history learning based on wikipedia articles. In: Zaphiris, P., Ioannou, A. (eds.) LCT 2015. LNCS, vol. 9192, pp. 337–346. Springer, Cham (2015). https://doi.org/10.1007/978-3-319-20609-7_32
5. Foulonneau, M., Ras, E.: Using educational domain models for automatic item generation beyond factual knowledge assessment. In: Hernández-Leo, D., Ley, T., Klamma, R., Harrer, A. (eds.) EC-TEL 2013. LNCS, vol. 8095, pp. 442–447. Springer, Heidelberg (2013). https://doi.org/10.1007/978-3-642-40814-4_36
6. Cablé, B., Guin, N., Lefevre, M.: An authoring tool for semi-automatic generation of self-assessment exercises. In: Lane, H.C., Yacef, K., Mostow, J., Pavlik, P. (eds.) AIED 2013. LNCS (LNAI), vol. 7926, pp. 679–682. Springer, Heidelberg (2013). https://doi.org/10.1007/978-3-642-39112-5_87
7. Bühmann, L., Usbeck, R., Ngonga Ngomo, A.-C.: ASSESS — automatic self-assessment using linked data. In: Arenas, M., et al. (eds.) ISWC 2015. LNCS, vol. 9367, pp. 76–89. Springer, Cham (2015). https://doi.org/10.1007/978-3-319-25010-6_5
8. Vega-Gorgojo, G.: Clover Quiz: a trivia game powered by DBpedia. Semantic-Web-Journal.Net
9. Conejo, R., Guzmán, E., Millán, E., Trella, M., Pérez-de, J.L.: SIETTE : a web based tool for adaptive testing. Int. J. Artif. Intell. Educ. 14(1), 1–33 (2004)
10. Conejo, R., Guzmán, E., Trella, M.: The SIETTE automatic assessment environment. Int. J. Artif. Intell. Educ. 26(1), 270–292 (2016)
11. Rios, A., Millán, E., Trella, M., Pérez-de-la Cruz, J.L., Conejo, R.: Internet based evaluation system. In: Artificial Intelligence in Education, vol. 64 pp. 1896–1898 (1999)
12. Bongir, A., Attar, V., Janardhanan, R.: Automated quiz generator. Adv. Intell. Syst. Comput. 683, 174–188 (2018)

13. Alsubait, T., Parsia, B., Sattler, U.: Generating multiple choice questions from ontologies: how far can we go? In: Lambrix, P., et al. (eds.) EKAW 2014. LNCS (LNAI), vol. 8982, pp. 66–79. Springer, Cham (2015). https://doi.org/10.1007/978-3-319-17966-7_7

14. Jouault, C., Seta, K.: Content-dependent question generation for history learning in semantic open learning space. In: Trausan-Matu, S., Boyer, K.E., Crosby, M., Panourgia, K. (eds.) ITS 2014. LNCS, vol. 8474, pp. 300–305. Springer, Cham (2014). https://doi.org/10.1007/978-3-319-07221-0_37

15. Olney, A., Graesser, A., Person, N.: Question generation from concept maps. Dialogue Discourse 3(2), 75–99 (2012)

16. Wainer, H., Thissen, D.: How is reliability related to the quality of test scores? what is the effect of local dependence on reliability? Educ. Measure. Issues Pract. 15(1), 22–29 (1996)

Balancing Human Efforts
and Performance of Student Response
Analyzer in Dialog-Based Tutors

Tejas I. Dhamecha[(✉)], Smit Marvaniya, Swarnadeep Saha, Renuka Sindhgatta,
and Bikram Sengupta

IBM Research, Bangalore, India
{tidhamecha,smarvani,swarnads,renuka.sr,bsengupt}@in.ibm.com

Abstract. Accurately interpreting student responses is a critical
requirement of dialog-based intelligent tutoring systems. The accuracy
of supervised learning methods, used for interpreting or analyzing student responses, is strongly dependent on the availability of annotated
training data. Collecting and grading student responses is tedious, time-
consuming, and expensive. This work proposes an iterative data collection and grading approach. We show that data collection efforts can be
significantly reduced by predicting question difficulty and by collecting
answers from a focused set of students. Further, grading efforts can be
reduced by filtering student answers that may not be helpful in training
Student Response Analyzer (SRA). To ensure the quality of grades, we
analyze the grader characteristics, and show improvement when a biased
grader is removed. An experimental evaluation on a large scale dataset
shows a reduction of up to 28% in the data collection cost, and up to 10%
in grading cost while improving the response analysis macro-average F1.

Keywords: Student Response Analysis · Dialog based tutor
Data annotation and collection cost · Question difficulty
Student ability · Grader agreement

1 Introduction

Student Response Analysis (SRA) [8] is the task of assessing and grading a student response in comparison to a reference answer for the given question. It is
an integral component of any dialog-based Intelligent Tutoring System (ITS),
specifically to enable Socratic tutoring [19]. Such ITS often asks focused questions prompting student to provide short answers. Therefore, the SRA task is
equivalent to short-answer grading. SRA is often modeled as a classification
problem. Obtaining an adequately labeled dataset to train classifiers for SRA is
a critical step in building any dialog-based tutoring system. The collection of a
dataset for this purpose involves creating questions, creating reference answers,
collecting student answers, and having the responses graded by subject matter experts. This overall process is human-effort intensive, time consuming, and

C. Penstein Rosé et al. (Eds.): AIED 2018, LNAI 10947, pp. 70–85, 2018.
https://doi.org/10.1007/978-3-319-93843-1_6

expensive. We observe that there is a scope for reducing and/or directing human-efforts, without reducing the classification performance.

Table 1. Characteristics of the large scale industry dataset.

Domain	Psychology
Number of questions	483
Number of students	1,164
Number of student responses	17,023
Number of words per response	Min: 1, Max: 198, Mean: 15.4, Std: 12.6
Number of graders	9
Number of grades per response	3
Number of grades	51,069
Grade categories	CORRECT, PARTIAL, INCORRECT, NON-ANSWER

In the process of building an SRA for an ITS in the psychology domain, we obtained a large scale industry dataset. The characteristics of this dataset are reported in Table 1. The dataset contains 17,023 answers collected from 1,164 students for 483 questions. Each student answer is graded by exactly 3 graders; with the categories of grade being CORRECT, PARTIAL, INCORRECT, and NON-ANSWER. Each student answered about 17 questions randomly selected by the system. A large portion ($\sim$70%) of students answered 13–20 questions. On an average, 34 answers were collected for each question.

Based on the analysis of the characteristics of data for SRA, this paper aims to present an iterative approach for efficient data collection. We experimentally validate the effectiveness of each stage of the proposed approach and show that significant human-effort can be reduced while improving classification performance.

The SRA is designed as a three-class (CORRECT, PARTIAL, and INCORRECT) classification task. For all our experiments, we choose majority vote of the three graders as the ground truth. The experiments are performed using a deep learning based sentence embedding approach, called InferSent [7][1] that reports state-of-the-art results on various Natural Language Understanding tasks. We generate the InferSent sentence embeddings for question (q), reference answer (r), and student answer (a), to obtain the feature representation $(|q - r|, |r - a|, |q - a|, q * r, r * a, q * a)$ of a sample and then train a 3-class multinomial logistic regression. The next section discusses the related work and details our contributions.

---

[1] https://github.com/facebookresearch/InferSent.

2   Related Work

In the context of existing literature, we position our work along different aspects of obtaining relevant training data. These can be broadly classified into three categories - (i) reducing labeling effort, (ii) reducing labeling cost by using non-experts, and (iii) removing or rectifying noisy labels.

1. **Reducing labeling effort:** Semi-supervised learning techniques rely on clustering to select a subset of student answers for labeling [3,11,25]. Only the cluster centroids are labeled, and all the answers within the cluster are given the same label. Brooks et al. [6] proposed an efficient tool using a similar approach of forming clusters and labeling cluster centroids. They show that the tool improves the teacher's efficiency by grading multiple students answers and providing feedback to them at once. As stated by the authors in one of the recent studies [25], clustering does not result in significant reduction of annotation effort if the responses are long, and is effective for very short student responses. Gweon et al. [10] proposed a two-stage approach where initially the text is automatically graded and then the grades are manually verified. Thus, the annotation task is transformed into a verification one, improving the efficiency of labeling efforts. Active learning (AL) based approaches [1,2,21] help in reducing the labeling efforts significantly by iteratively selecting a subset of samples to annotate. However, AL methods rely on the availability of large amount of unlabeled data and require the supervised model prior to data collection. AL based approaches need that the same classification pipeline is used during training data collection and for the final task. For many complex tasks, such as SRA, it is unlikely that the whole classification pipeline would be fixed beforehand due to its dependence on domain content. In other words, experiments with various choices of modules in the classification pipeline need to be performed; with the prerequisites of availability of data.
2. **Reducing labeling cost by using non-experts:** Instead of using the expert annotators only, one can employ a combination of expert and non-expert annotators to reduce the cost. The research in this direction involves reducing negative impacts of using non-experts while significantly lowering the cost. Snow et al. [23] proposed an approach to control the biases of non-expert annotators on Amazon Mechanical Turk crowdsourcing platform. In recent studies in crowdsourcing [14–16], various multi-stage annotation processes [4,15,16] are proposed to ensure the quality of annotation. The approaches in this category are limited to reducing the labeling cost and seldom focus on the content collection cost.
3. **Removing or rectifying noisy labels:** Research studies involving identification of noisy labels, either remove [9,20] or rectify [17,18,24] them. Techniques are proposed to improve the quality of labeled samples and the quality of the model built from labeled data via repeated labeling [22]. As the noisy labels can be, at times, attributed to certain annotators; Hsueh et al. [12] show that removing these annotators helps in improving the quality of the labels. A typical hypothesis behind this direction of research is that removal or

rectification of noisy labels is critical to training a classifier. We also present an approach to identify noisy labels and a set of unlabeled data points to reduce labeling effort.

There is a sizable amount of research work pertaining to efficient and cost-effective labeling/annotation, in various domains of machine learning. In the context of dialog-based tutoring systems, much of the work has focused on reducing the annotation effort [3,11,25]. Our work considers the inter-dependence of various characteristics of the dataset and focuses on a comprehensive method of iteratively collecting, labeling, and refining data. The difficulty of the question and associated reference answer influences selection of relevant students to collect adequate student responses. Therefore, we believe that the literature pertaining to efficient labeling is inadequate to make the overall human efforts cost effective for the problem presented.

To this end, this paper makes the following contributions to reduce human efforts for content creations and grading without affecting the classification performance.

- An iterative data collection approach for reducing human efforts pertaining to the content creation and grading.
- Automated approach to predict question difficulty.
- Approach for selecting questions and students iteratively to obtain a representative dataset.
- Approach for reducing the grading effort by filtering some of the student answers.

Further, we propose techniques to identify some of the content issues, pertaining to question difficulty, student proficiency, student answers, and grader bias. The next section details the iterative data collection approach.

3   Proposed Data Collection Approach

Each instance of training data for SRA consists of a question, a reference answer, a student identifier, a student answer, and a set of grades that different graders provide. As shown in Fig. 1a, the traditional procedure of creating training data involves following steps.

1. Questions (Q) and their reference answers (R) are created by subject matter experts.
2. Students (S) are chosen.
3. Answers (A) for the questions are collected.
4. Graders evaluate correctness of student answers and provide grades (G).

The ith sample of the dataset, represented as $(q_i, r_i, a_i, s_i, g_i)$, consists of the question (q_i), reference answer (r_i), student identifier (s_i), student answer (a_i), and grades (g_i). The joint distribution for a generative model of M such samples can be mathematically expressed as following:

$$P(Q, R, S, A, G) = \prod_{i=1}^{M} p(q_i, r_i, s_i, a_i, g_i)$$

$$= \prod_{i=1}^{M} \underbrace{p(g_i|q_i, a_i, r_i, \theta^g)}_{\text{Grading}} \underbrace{p(a_i|q_i, s_i)}_{\substack{\text{Student} \\ \text{Answer}}} \underbrace{p(s_i|\theta^s)}_{\substack{\text{Student} \\ \text{Selection}}} \underbrace{p(r_i|q_i)p(q_i|\theta^q)}_{\substack{\text{Question and} \\ \text{Reference} \\ \text{Answer creation}}} \quad (1)$$

where θ^g, θ^s, and θ^q are the parameters governing the characteristics of the graders, students, and questions, respectively.

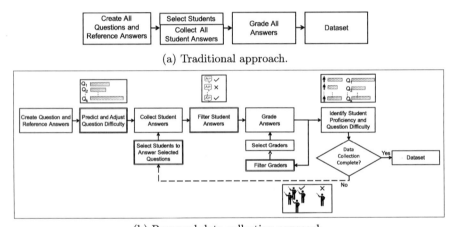

(a) Traditional approach.

(b) Proposed data collection approach.

Fig. 1. As opposed to the traditional monolithic data collection approaches, we propose a more involved iterative data collection approach with four intervention points: adjusting questions based on machine predicted difficulty, refining collected student answers, refining graders and identifying appropriate set of students and questions for successive iterations.

On analyzing the dependencies of the variables, it can be seen that if a question is poorly created, it can affect all the successive steps. Similarly, if a non-representative set of students is selected, the collected answers and therefore, the grades may provide limited information for training SRA. Ideally, the grades should be dependent on the question, reference answer, and student answer only; however, in real-world, the subjectivity of the graders also affect the grades.

To address these challenges, we propose a data collection approach as illustrated in Fig. 1b. It shows an iterative approach with intervention points for each of the four stages of data collection. The correspondence of these stages with components of generative models is shown in Eq. 1s. The boxes outlined with double lines in the figure denote these four stages where our proposed approach improves upon the existing methodology of data collection by minimizing the annotation cost and effort. The process starts at the question creation stage where we automatically predict the question difficulty. The next step involves collecting a subset of student answers consisting of $m < M$ responses (e.g. $m = \frac{M}{2}$). Further, some student answers are filtered out based on certain techniques. In the following step, the remaining student answers are graded. Based on graders' characteristics, some graders' annotations are discarded. Although this last stage does not yield any cost saving in the iteration, it is useful in maintaining quality of grades. Finally, using the tuple information of <Question, Student, Grade>, each student's proficiency and question's difficulty is estimated. These estimates are used for selecting students to answer specific questions in successive iterations to collect additional samples. This iterative approach thus enables focused answer collection activity, wherein students of certain proficiency are asked to provide answers for questions of certain difficulty only. This procedure helps in ensuring that the data set for training is balanced.

In the remaining part of this section, we quantify the overall cost involved in the data collection process and how our proposed approach is based on addressing the different cost components of data collection and annotation process.

3.1   Cost Estimation

Let n^q, n^a, and n^g be the number of questions, number of student answers collected per question, and number of grades obtained per student answer, respectively. Also, let c^q, c^s, and c^g be the costs of creating a question, collecting student answer for a question, and grading a student answer by a grader, respectively[2]. The total cost is given by:

$$\text{Total Cost} = \underbrace{n^q c^q}_{\text{question creation}} + \underbrace{n^q n^a c^s}_{\text{answer collection}} + \underbrace{n^q n^a n^g c^g}_{\text{grading}} \quad (2)$$

If a question is poorly formed, the corresponding student answers as well as the grades are not useful. Similarly, if the students are selected poorly, the n^a responses may not provide the adequate spread of answer variations. Each of such student responses costs $c^s + n^g c^g$. If a grader is biased, it affects all the student answers graded by him/her, thus incurring cost in multiples of c^g.

By using the proposed approach in Fig. 1b, if we can filter out p questions in the difficulty prediction stage, followed by a reduction of m answers by focused student selection, and finally, remove k answers by filtering a selected set of answers, it will yield an overall cost reduction of $p\left(c^q + (k+m)\left(c^s + n^g c^g\right)\right)$. The stage pertaining to filtering graders, may not result in cost saving as the graders are filtered only after the answers are graded. However, it is important to ensure the quality of grades. Additionally, based on graders' performance,

---

[2] For simplicity, we assume that the costs of question creation, answer collection and answer grading are uniform across questions and answers.

grader training may be directed in a more optimized way for future; which can be useful to organizations with large annotator workforce. The few next sections provide details and experimental evaluations of the claims pertaining to each stage of our approach on a large industry data set.

4   Predict and Adjust Question Difficulty

The first step of content creation is correctly formulating the questions. The questions should have carefully attuned difficulty levels. As an extreme case, having all the questions easy may not trigger complex thinking and, having all the questions difficult may discourage students from attempting. This part of question creation corresponds to $p(q_i|\theta^q)$ of the generative model in Eq. 1.

We want to predict question difficulty at the time of question creation, as this would ensure the desired mixture of question difficulty in the dataset. Although, the actual question difficulty is subjective and is relative to student proficiency, we observe that absolute question characteristics such as factoid/non-factoid, clarity of expression, and preciseness of the question play important role in defining its difficulty. Table 2 shows example questions with varying difficulties. These characteristics can be captured using natural language processing approaches. We propose a technique to learn the function f given by

$$f : question \rightarrow \beta \tag{3}$$

where, β is the question difficulty [13]. This is one of the first attempts at predicting question difficulty prior to answer collection. The proposed technique involves a deep learning based feature extraction method followed by classification using multinomial Logistic Regression. Given a question, its embedding is computed using InferSent [7], a state-of-the-art deep learning framework for computing sentence embeddings. These question embeddings are subsequently used as features for the difficultly prediction task. InferSent is trained on the Stanford Natural Language Inference data and the sentence embeddings are computed using a bidirectional Long Short-Term Memory (LSTM) network over the pre-trained word embeddings. InferSent's pre-trained model has been shown to work well for computing embeddings in various NLP classification tasks. Thus, we also use InferSent to obtain a $4,096$ dimensional embedding for each question.

Table 2. Examples of question difficulty. As we move from easy to difficult question, there is a transition from objectivity to subjectivity, factoid to non-factoid, and preciseness to broadness.

Difficulty	Question
Easy	What are the two types of intelligence?
Medium	What is crystallized intelligence, and how does middle age impact it?
Difficult	How do older adults perform in intelligence activities?

To obtain the true question difficulties β, Item Response Theory (IRT) [13] is used. It estimates a question's difficulty based on the grades of the student responses. In a broad sense, a question is considered difficult if it is likely to be answered correctly by high proficiency students. In this work, we used the Two-Parameter Logistic Model of IRT. The Two-Parameter Logistic Model [5] specifies the probability of a correct answer as a logistic distribution in which the items vary in terms of their difficulty and discrimination. It is typically applied to multiple choice or short response items that are scored either correct or incorrect, and do not allow for guessing.

While the question difficulty values (β) are more precise, the buckets or categories of difficulties are sufficient for assisting the question creation procedure. Therefore, we convert the problem into a prediction task where a given question is categorized as easy, medium, or difficult. β is uniformly divided into three intervals as shown below

$$\text{Difficulty Label} = \begin{cases} \text{Easy} & \text{if } -2 \leq \beta < -2/3 \\ \text{Medium if } -2/3 \leq \beta < 2/3 \\ \text{Difficult if } \quad 2/3 \leq \beta \leq 2 \end{cases}$$

We train a 3-way Logistic Regression classifier and employ 5-fold cross-validation. Thus, for each sample, a difficulty label is predicted. Based on the predictions, the class-wise precision, recall, and F1 metrics are reported in Table 3. With our preliminary approach, we are able to identify easy and difficult questions with a reasonable recall of greater than 55%. This suggests that, to an extent, the proposed approach can assist humans in identifying question difficulties, thereby helping to ensure a desired mixture of difficulty levels. In a traditional approach, the content creators themselves can be asked to provide the difficulty levels.

However, it results in additional human-effort related cost. Additionally, we experimented with reference answers, independently and in conjunction with the question, to predict the difficulty. On this dataset, the reference answers did not improve the results. However, our proposed data collection approach does not rule out reference answers' utility.

Table 3. Classification performance of question difficulty prediction in terms of precision, recall, and F1.

	Precision	Recall	F1
Easy	49.12%	**55.63%**	52.17%
Medium	43.41%	35.90%	39.30%
Difficult	54.86%	**57.14%**	55.98%

5   Selecting Students for Answering Selected Question

Selection of students is an equally important aspect of the data collection process. The dataset may get biased towards correct class if the large portion of high proficiency students is selected. The classifier will thus end up not seeing enough samples of PARTIAL and INCORRECT classes, leading to a class imbalance problem. This will eventually lead to a very strict SRA. Therefore, it is important to select students carefully. The aspect of student selection corresponds to the term $p(s_i|\theta^s)$ in the Eq. 1.

It is well understood in the education research community that question difficulty and student proficiency are interdependent. Item Response Theory (IRT) [13] is used to estimate question difficulty and student proficiency jointly. The goals of the analyses of the question and student aspects of content creation are as follows:

- Organizing students into 3 proficiency categories (low, medium, and high) and the questions into 3 difficulty categories (easy, medium, and difficult), to direct the data collection process such that the eventual answer distribution is uniform/representative across the categories.
- Understanding overall characteristics of students and questions can be useful in refining their selection and creation processes, respectively.

Figure 2 shows the question difficulty (QD) and student proficiency (SP) distributions. The more uniform the distributions, the better balanced are the selected questions and students. Some key observations with the large scale industry dataset are discussed below.

- **Medium proficiency heavy student selection:** The student proficiency distribution is non-uniform with significant mass concentrated in the middle. Thus, the students are not selected in a balanced approach. However, this distribution should be uniform to be able to collect the variety of answers.
- **Easy question:** There are about 8% questions which are very easy with β close to -2. Easy questions, in general, tend to have less variability in both the reference and student answers, making SRA training easier. Thus, less number of student answers for such questions should suffice for training.

Once a student set is selected, there is little that one can do to improve the student proficiency distribution as it is students' intrinsic property. Further, it is difficult to exhaustively collect answers for each question from all students in a large scale data collection. Often, each question is answered by only a subset of students. Randomly allocating some students to answer a question may not lead to enough answer variants. This effect can amplify if all the students assigned a question are of similar proficiency. A potential mitigation strategy is to control how often a student with certain proficiency is asked a question of certain difficulty. For example, if there are more medium proficiency students, they should be asked a question less often as compared to low and high proficiency students. In this way, an imbalance of question difficulty and/or student proficiency can be prevented from reflecting in the answer distribution. Table 4a shows the distribution of the answers from the whole dataset, if collected without consideration of question difficulty and student proficiency. Note the imbalance in the distribution, specifically in terms of student proficiency. 44% answers are given by medium proficiency students. Particularly, SP:Low × QD:Easy is most affected. If the data is collected iteratively, this analysis can be useful in selecting the next set of student-question pairs. This assisted student answer collection form the basis of the iterative collection approach, as illustrated in Fig. 1b.

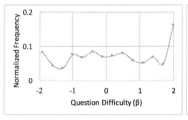 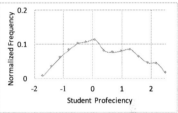

Fig. 2. (Left) Question Difficulty, where higher β corresponds to higher difficulty. (Right) Student Proficiency distribution.

Table 4. Distribution of student answers.

(a) Answers collected without considering question difficulty and student proficiency.

		Question Difficulty Bucket			
		Difficult	Medium	Easy	
Student	Low	11.03%	9.27%	**6.83%**	27.13%
Proficiency	Medium	15.88%	14.71%	13.69%	44.28%
Bucket	High	8.30%	9.12%	11.17%	28.59%
		35.20%	33.10%	31.70%	100.00%

(b) Answers collected in iteration-I.

		Question Difficulty Bucket			
		Difficult	Medium	Easy	
Student	Low	8.90%	7.20%	7.75%	23.85%
Proficiency	Medium	17.72%	11.51%	13.76%	42.99%
Bucket	High	10.93%	9.51%	12.71%	33.16%
		37.56%	28.22%	34.22%	100.00%

In the proposed data collection approach, the answers are collected in an iterative manner. In the first iteration $n^{a\prime}$ ($< n^a$) answers are collected from a random selection of students. At the end of the iteration, the answer distribution, as shown in Table 4a, is computed. The less represented QD × SP pairs are identified. This is followed by selecting students and questions belonging to desired SP and QD categories, respectively. The answers, thus collected, are cumulatively added to the overall dataset. The collection process is terminated after enough samples are collected and/or representativeness criteria of the dataset is satisfied.

To experimentally evaluate the effectiveness of the approach, we select $n^{a\prime} = 17$ randomly selected answers for each question in the first iteration. This results in selecting ∼50% answers, as there are ∼35 responses per question on average. Student proficiency and question difficulty are estimated from this subset. Table 4b shows the observed distribution of the answers. For the next iteration, we select answers from only the following category combinations

{SD:Low × QD:(Easy, Medium, Difficult), SD:High × QD:Medium}, as these categories are least represented in the collected answers. This way we add a total of 2,225 samples from the selected categories. At the end of each iteration, a classifier is trained and evaluated on a held-out test set. The classification results are reported in Table 5. We remove 681 NON-ANSWER responses from our entire dataset to create a 80-20 train-test split. *Base* represents the classifier performance after training on those 80% (13,169) samples. The number of samples after iteration-1 and iteration-2 are 7,245 and 9,470, respectively. Iteration-1 can be seen as a random subsample of the base set, whereas Iteration-2 benefits by inclusion of carefully chosen samples. After two iterations, the size of the dataset is 28.1% smaller than the base set; however, the macro-average F1 and weighted F1 are better than that of the base set.

Table 5. Results of utilizing the proposed iterative student selection approach. The data collected in proposed iterative approach is 28.1% smaller than the whole set. Results are reported in macro-average F1 and weighted F1 metrics.

Accuracy	Training size	Macro-F1	Weighted-F1
Base	13,169	57.39%	63.81%
After 1 iteration	7,245	56.39%	63.25%
After 2 iterations	9,470	**58.03%**	**64.20%**

6   Filter Student Answers

In a typical data collection setup, student answers are graded and then used as training samples. However, one can imagine that there may be outlier answers, which are not useful or, at times, misleading too. If we can automatically detect such answers *prior* to grading, corresponding human efforts can be saved. We propose following two approaches.

6.1   Automatically Detect Relatively Less Useful Answers

The NON-ANSWER responses (e.g. 'I don't know', 'no idea') are not useful for training a classifier. Further, we find that student answers, even when incorrect, often tend to be from the same domain as the reference answer. Thus, we can filter out student answers that do not contain any domain keyword or terms in the corpus such as the textbook or relevant text material, yielding similar or better classifier model. When applying this filter on a combined set of 13,169 samples (*Base*) and 681 NON-ANSWER responses, we are able to filter out 785 responses, saving grading cost on 5.6% answers.

6.2   Very Small and Very Long Answers

A student answer which is too small is likely to miss out on most key aspects of the answer. Similarly, a very long answer may be the outcome of the student not knowing the exact answer. Both these types of answers are not likely to help significantly in training the classifier. Therefore, we propose to filter them out before grading to reduce the human efforts.

For each question, we generate the distribution of the student response lengths and remove the samples not contained within $\mu \pm 2\sigma$, μ and σ being the mean and standard deviation of the student response lengths respectively. Using per question mean and standard deviation statistics allows us to preserve question specific characteristics, as different questions can expect answers of different lengths. Using this approach, we are able to filter out 620 student responses from the *Base* training set (13,169 answers), leading to 4.7% reduction in grading cost.

Table 6 shows that the classification performance improves by individually rejecting the student answers based on their lengths as well as their differences from reference answers.

Table 6. Effect of discarding 5.6% training samples that are significantly different from reference answer; and, effect of length based pruning of 4.7% student answers; individually.

	Macro-F1	Weighted-F1
Base	57.39%	63.81%
– less useful	**60.02%**	**65.59%**
– $\|len - \mu\| \geq 2\sigma$	**59.12%**	**65.04%**

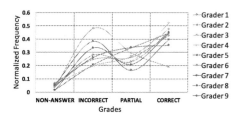

Fig. 3. Distribution of grades given by individual graders.

7   Filtering Graders

The graders grade student answers (a_i) in comparison to the reference answer (r_i) in context of the question (q_i). All the student answers pertaining to a specific question are assigned to exactly three graders; with each grader grading all those student answers. Thus, each student answer is given exactly three grades.

We aim to examine if there is any noticeable aspect (e.g. bias) in any grader's assessments. Figure 3 shows the distribution of grades given by graders. The typical pattern is that the fraction of CORRECT grades is highest followed by INCORRECT and, then, by PARTIAL grade. Note that, a different pattern is exhibited by Grader–2 and Grader–8. Table 7 reports Pearson correlations pertaining to all grader pairs. Similar trends are observed for Cohen's Kappa and F1 metrics too, however they are not shown in this paper due to space constraints.

- Grader–2 has a significantly different grade distribution, with a peak at INCORRECT. Also, the CORRECT grade is at ∼20% which is at least 15% less than all the other graders. Analyzing Table 7 reveals that Grader–2 has a very low agreement with other graders. It suggests that Grader–2 is a peculiarly strict grader. Perhaps, using the corresponding grades as labels can turn out to be misleading/noisy labels while training a classifier.
- Grader–8 appears to have a differently peculiar characteristic, with a relatively flat (INCORRECT: 26%, PARTIAL: 33%, and CORRECT: 35%) grading distribution. However, his/her agreement with other graders is not low. This suggests that Grader–8 may have been assigned easy-to-correctly-answer questions. The chance of observing such unintentional bias may be rooted in question difficulty distribution and question assignment strategy.

Based on this analysis, we discard the grades given by Grader–2. Thus, the ground truths for the answers graded by Grader–2 are calculated as the majority vote of the other two graders. This led to the change of ground truths in 1,184 samples in the train set and 232 samples in the test set. Table 8 shows the experimental results. We test with two configurations - pruning Grader–2 grades from only train set and from both train and test set. Results show that while both lead to improvements in the test set Macro-average F1s, the latter performs significantly better.

Table 7. Inter-grader agreement in terms of Pearson Correlation. Each question is graded by three graders. For each grader pair, their mean agreement over the common set of assigned questions is reported.

	Grader 1	Grader 2	Grader 3	Grader 4	Grader 5	Grader 6	Grader 7	Grader 8	Grader 9
Grader 1				0.7514	0.6358	0.5965		0.6632	0.6811
Grader 2			0.6019	0.5353	0.5495		0.6432		
Grader 3		0.6019		0.6539		0.6533		0.6677	
Grader 4	0.7514	0.5353	0.6539		0.5630	0.6375		0.7827	0.6861
Grader 5	0.6358	0.5495		0.5630		0.6243	0.6257	0.6723	
Grader 6	0.5965		0.6533	0.6375	0.6243		0.7302	0.6362	
Grader 7		0.6432			0.6257	0.7302			
Grader 8	0.6632		0.6677	0.7827	0.6723	0.6362			0.6648
Grader 9	0.6811			0.6861				0.6648	

Table 8. Effect of discarding Grade–2's grades.

	Macro-F1	Weighted-F1
Base	57.39%	63.81%
After pruning Grader-2 (from only train set)	58.14%	63.60%
After pruning Grader-2 (from train and test sets)	**62.35%**	**66.13%**

8   Conclusion

This paper focuses on reducing the human-efforts while collecting dataset for training student response analyzer. We begin by outlining the stages of data collection, its generative modeling, and the cost associated. Unlike many tasks where the cost of dataset creation is mostly related to labeling, the dataset creation for student response analyzer includes the significant cost for question creation and student answer collection along with labeling. We propose an iterative approach to significantly reduce the human-efforts, while improving the classification performance. That leads us to first proposing a deep learning based approach to predict question difficulty prior to answer collection. To ensure a good spread of collected data, we also propose a technique to select students to answer certain questions; and, thus enabling a focused data collection. Further, we show that a significant portion of student answers can be filtered out saving the cost of grading them while improving the classification performance by up to 2% in macro-average F1. By pruning out poor quality graders, our classification result improves up to 5% in macro-average F1. Finally, our focused answer collection approach saves up to 28% in answer collection cost and answer filtering saves ∼10% of grading cost.

References

1. Arora, S., Nyberg, E., Rosé, C.P.: Estimating annotation cost for active learning in a multi-annotator environment. In: Proceedings of the NAACL-HLT Workshop on Active Learning for Natural Language Processing, pp. 18–26 (2009)
2. Baldridge, J., Osborne, M.: Active learning and the total cost of annotation. In: Proceedings of the Conference on Empirical Methods in Natural Language Processing (2004)
3. Basu, S., Jacobs, C., Vanderwende, L.: Powergrading: a clustering approach to amplify human effort for short answer grading. Trans. Assoc. Comput. Linguist. **1**, 391–402 (2013)
4. Bernstein, M.S., Little, G., Miller, R.C., Hartmann, B., Ackerman, M.S., Karger, D.R., Crowell, D., Panovich, K.: Soylent: a word processor with a crowd inside. Commun. ACM **58**(8), 85–94 (2015)
5. Birnbaum, A.: Some latent train models and their use in inferring an examinee's ability. In: Statistical Theories of Mental Test Scores, pp. 395–479 (1968)
6. Brooks, M., Basu, S., Jacobs, C., Vanderwende, L.: Divide and correct: using clusters to grade short answers at scale. In: Proceedings of the ACM Conference on Learning@ Scale Conference, pp. 89–98 (2014)

7. Conneau, A., Kiela, D., Schwenk, H., Barrault, L., Bordes, A.: Supervised learning of universal sentence representations from natural language inference data. In: Proceedings of the Conference on Empirical Methods in Natural Language Processing, pp. 670–680 (2017)

8. Dzikovska, M.O., Nielsen, R.D., Brew, C.: Towards effective tutorial feedback for explanation questions: a dataset and baselines. In: Proceedings of the Conference of the North American Chapter of the Association for Computational Linguistics: Human Language Technologies, pp. 200–210 (2012)

9. Guan, D., Yuan, W., Ma, T., Khattak, A.M., Chow, F.: Cost-sensitive elimination of mislabeled training data. Inform. Sci. **402**, 170–181 (2017)

10. Gweon, G., Rosé, C.P., Wittwer, J., Nueckles, M.: Supporting efficient and reliable content analysis using automatic text processing technology. In: Costabile, M.F., Paternò, F. (eds.) INTERACT 2005. LNCS, vol. 3585, pp. 1112–1115. Springer, Heidelberg (2005). https://doi.org/10.1007/11555261_117

11. Horbach, A., Palmer, A., Wolska, M.: Finding a tradeoff between accuracy and rater's workload in grading clustered short answers. In: International Conference on Language Resources and Evaluation, pp. 588–595 (2014)

12. Hsueh, P.Y., Melville, P., Sindhwani, V.: Data quality from crowdsourcing: a study of annotation selection criteria. In: Proceedings of the NAACL-HLT Workshop on Active Learning for Natural Language Processing, pp. 27–35 (2009)

13. Johnson, M.S., et al.: Marginal maximum likelihood estimation of item response models in R. J. Stat. Softw. **20**(10), 1–24 (2007)

14. Jurgens, D.: Embracing ambiguity: a comparison of annotation methodologies for crowdsourcing word sense labels. In: Proceedings of the Conference of the North American Chapter of the Association for Computational Linguistics: Human Language Technologies, pp. 556–562 (2013)

15. Kittur, A., Smus, B., Khamkar, S., Kraut, R.E.: CrowdForge: Crowdsourcing complex work. In: Proceedings of the ACM Symposium on User Interface Software and Technology, pp. 43–52 (2011)

16. Kulkarni, A., Can, M., Hartmann, B.: Collaboratively crowdsourcing workflows with turkomatic. In: Proceedings of the ACM Conference on Computer Supported Cooperative Work, pp. 1003–1012 (2012)

17. Nicholson, B., Sheng, V.S., Zhang, J.: Label noise correction and application in crowdsourcing. Expert Syst. Appl. **66**, 149–162 (2016)

18. Nicholson, B., Zhang, J., Sheng, V.S., Wang, Z.: Label noise correction methods. In: Proceedings of IEEE International Conference on Data Science and Advanced Analytics, pp. 1–9 (2015)

19. Rosé, C.P., Moore, J.D., Vanlehn, K., Allbritton, D.: A comparative evaluation of socratic versus didactic tutoring. In: Proceedings of the Annual Meeting of the Cognitive Science Society, vol. 23 (2001)

20. Sánchez, J.S., Barandela, R., Marqués, A.I., Alejo, R., Badenas, J.: Analysis of new techniques to obtain quality training sets. Patt. Recogn. Lett. **24**(7), 1015–1022 (2003)

21. Settles, B., Craven, M., Friedland, L.: Active learning with real annotation costs. In: Proceedings of the NIPS Workshop on Cost-Sensitive Learning, pp. 1–10 (2008)

22. Sheng, V.S., Provost, F., Ipeirotis, P.G.: Get another label? improving data quality and data mining using multiple, noisy labelers. In: Proceedings of the ACM International Conference on Knowledge Discovery and Data Mining, pp. 614–622 (2008)

23. Snow, R., O'Connor, B., Jurafsky, D., Ng, A.Y.: Cheap and fast–but is it good?: evaluating non-expert annotations for natural language tasks. In: Proceedings of the Conference on Empirical Methods in Natural Language Processing, pp. 254–263 (2008)
24. Valizadegan, H., Tan, P.N.: Kernel based detection of mislabeled training examples. In: Proceedings of the SIAM International Conference on Data Mining, pp. 309–319 (2007)
25. Zesch, T., Heilman, M., Cahill, A.: Reducing annotation efforts in supervised short answer scoring. In: Proceedings of the NAACL-HLT Workshop on Building Educational Applications, pp. 124–132 (2015)

An Instructional Factors Analysis
of an Online Logical Fallacy
Tutoring System

Nicholas Diana$^{(\boxtimes)}$, John Stamper, and Ken Koedinger

Carnegie Mellon University, 5000 Forbes Avenue, Pittsburgh, PA 15213, USA
{ndiana,koedinger}@cmu.edu, john@stamper.org

Abstract. The proliferation of fake news has underscored the importance of critical thinking in the civic education curriculum. Despite this recognized importance, systems designed to foster these kinds of critical thinking skills are largely absent from the educational technology space. In this work, we utilize an instructional factors analysis in conjunction with an online tutoring system to determine if logical fallacies are best learned through deduction, induction, or some combination of both. We found that while participants were able to learn the informal fallacies using inductive practice alone, deductive explanations were more beneficial for learning.

Keywords: Informal logic · Instructional factors · Analysis
Online tutoring systems · Argumentation · Ill-defined domains

1 Introduction

In late November of 2016, Ipsos Public Affairs surveyed Americans about the accuracy of various real and fake news headlines. They found that respondents rated fake news headlines as "somewhat" or "very" accurate 75% of the time [19]. Given the fact that most (62%) of adults get their news from social media outlets where fake news is most rampant [9], the need for a citizenry capable of evaluating evidence and arguments is more crucial than ever. We propose that educational technology provides an opportunity for accessible, evidence-based instruction on these essential critical thinking skills. To test this claim, we built an online tutoring system designed to teach people how to identify informal logical fallacies.

The recognized importance of critical thinking skills is not new. In 1972, a study conducted by the American Council on Education found that 97% of the 40,000 faculty members interviewed considered fostering critical thinking skills to be the most important goal of undergraduate education [16]. Over two decades later, a similarly large study by Paul et al. [17] of 66 colleges and universities found that 89% of faculty saw critical thinking as a primary objective of their instruction. Note that these faculty members are reflecting on a world

© Springer International Publishing AG, part of Springer Nature 2018
C. Penstein Rosé et al. (Eds.): AIED 2018, LNAI 10947, pp. 86–97, 2018.
https://doi.org/10.1007/978-3-319-93843-1_7

where "fake news" was an article about lizard people in the National Enquirer. Citizens can no longer simply consume information, assuming that a wide distribution or high production value implies a certain level of legitimacy. Being an informed citizen, the foundation of civic engagement, requires evaluating sources of information and recognizing poorly constructed arguments.

The ability to recognize when an argument is built upon a faulty premise is a key facet of critical thinking. In the Common Core Standards for English Language Arts & Literacy, the ability to identify fallacious reasoning or distorted evidence is listed alongside basic communication skills like "evaluating a speaker's point of view" and "[their] use of evidence and rhetoric" as key measures of a student's career or college readiness. The same standards suggest that the cost of failing to adequately teach these kinds of reasoning skills is high. In the introduction to the standards, the authors stress that the importance of these skills extends well beyond the students' academic lives, arguing that students must "reflexively demonstrate the cogent reasoning and use of evidence that is essential to both private deliberation and responsible citizenship in a democratic republic" [12].

There is, unfortunately, little evidence to suggest these aspirational goals are met in practice. In the same study of 66 colleges and universities, Paul et al. [17] found that only a small percentage of faculty members (9%) were teaching for critical thinking on a daily basis. Even then, these generally underwhelming efforts to teach critical thinking skills are only available to students attending colleges and universities. Few opportunities for learning these skills exist for citizens not receiving a post-secondary education. Citizens lack accessible, evidence-based ways to learn critical thinking skills. We propose that educational technology (e.g., educational games, intelligent tutoring systems, etc.) may play a role in filling that vacuum.

Unfortunately, most research and interventions that utilize intelligent tutoring systems focus on well-defined domains such as math and science [7]. This bias towards well-defined domains may be due to an increased cultural focus on STEM education [10], or simply due to the fact that problems in well-defined domains tend to have solutions that are (generally) clear-cut and therefore more amenable to interpretation by a computer system. That said, there has been some work demonstrating that intelligent tutoring systems can be effective learning tools in ill-defined domains. For example, Ashley and Aleven [3], have demonstrated that intelligent tutoring systems can be used to teach law students to argue with cases. Similarly, Easterday et al. [8] has shown that educational games can be used to teach skills such as policy argumentation. With respect to argumentation specifically, research has shown the effectiveness of digital argument diagramming tools on teaching argumentation [18], and fostering critical thinking skills [11].

That is not to say that building educational technology for ill-defined domains does not present unique challenges. In their review of research on intelligent tutoring systems for ill-defined domains, Lynch et al. [15] describe how characteristics such as a lack of formal theories or the inability to verify "correct" solutions make designing systems to teach these domains challenging. In our domain of informal logic, for instance, it would be problematic to simply ask participants if an argument is fallacious because an infinite number of factors could contribute to whether or not a participant considers an argument is valid. Take the following argument for example:

I was just outside; it's raining.

This incredibly innocuous statement would rarely elicit a critical thought in normal conversation. However, in the context of a tutoring system designed to test critical thought, even this mild statement might be met with critiques like: *How long have you been inside? Maybe it stopped raining. It may be raining there, but it's not raining everywhere. How do you define raining? Maybe it's just misting.*

To overcome some of these challenges and make teaching informal logic more tractable, we narrow our focus to the relatively more structured but under-investigated area of informal logical fallacies. By focusing on fallacies, we can avoid the problems associated with focusing on how valid an argument is, and instead focus on teaching learners to identify specific patterns of faulty argumentation. Instead of asking if an argument is fallacious, we can ask if the argument contains a specific fallacy. This unfortunately does not solve the problem of ambiguity completely. Even the presence or absence of a specific fallacy in an argument can be debatable if the argument is sufficiently nuanced. We mitigate this concern by making the arguments we present as unambiguous as possible, albeit at the potential expense of authenticity (see [4]).

In addition to examining the feasibility of teaching informal logical fallacies using an online tutoring system, we also demonstrate the utility of tutoring systems as a platform for researching how students learn to identify patterns of faulty reasoning. Most textbooks teach informal fallacies with a combination of general definitions and specific examples. However, the relative effectiveness of these two different kinds of instruction is unclear. The inclusion of a definition for the fallacy seems intuitive, but it may be the case that students can learn to identify fallacies simply by seeing many different examples (i.e., through induction alone). Note that the Common Core Standards called for these reasoning skills to be *reflexive*, suggesting an automaticity that corresponds to inductive skills. We frame our investigation using the Knowledge-Learning-Instruction (KLI) framework [13], which suggests that the best instruction for teaching a specific skill depends on the type of process used to learn that skill. With respect to the current study, we ask whether identifying informal fallacies is primarily an inductive process or a deductive, sense-making process.

In this work we utilize the agile nature of online tutoring systems to explore how people learn to identify logical fallacies. We tested five different instructional designs. Each design shares some instructional features with one or more of the others. Rather than compare these designs directly, we can leverage the degree to which the different designs overlap by using an instructional factors analysis. The instructional factors analysis determined the relative effectiveness of each of the three main instructional components (inductive practice, expert-explanations, and self-explanations) present in different combinations across the five designs. We found that:

1. We can successfully teach the Appeal to Ignorance fallacy using an online tutor.
2. Participants could learn the fallacy through inductive practice alone.
3. However, deductive explanations (via Expert-Explanations) were more effective than inductive practice.

The main contribution of this work is the use of an instructional factors analysis to determine the relative impact of two traditional types of instruction on teaching logical fallacies. Our results will inform the design of future informal fallacy tutoring systems, and demonstrate the usefulness of intelligent tutoring systems for teaching and researching informal logical fallacies.

2   Methods

A total of 86 participants were recruited using Amazon Mechanical Turk [5]. Participants were required to be located in the United States and were compensated at a rate of $10 USD/hour to participate in the experiment. Demographic information was collected during a post-test questionnaire. Of all participants, 45% were female, 46% were college-educated, and the average age was 31 years old. 77% of participants identified as Caucasian, 8% as Black or African American, 8% as Asian, 3% as Hispanic, and 2% did not identify with the listed options or identified with more than one. None of these demographic factors were significant predictors of performance.

2.1   Informal Logical Fallacies

Informal logical fallacies are patterns of bad argumentation, where the premises fail to support the conclusion. Informal fallacies are distinct from formal fallacies, which are errors in the *form* of an argument (e.g., If P then Q; Q; Therefore P). In contrast, informal fallacies more often contain errors in the content of the argument (e.g., mischaracterizing an opponent's argument). While there are many types of informal fallacies, some are more common than others. Ad Hominem (attacking the person rather than their argument), for example, has become mainstream enough to be mentioned by name during U.S. Presidential Debates. Because prior knowledge and conceptions of well-known fallacies might impact our results, for this work we chose to focus on a lesser known informal fallacy: Appeal to Ignorance.

The Appeal to Ignorance Fallacy. Appeal to Ignorance is an informal logical fallacy that involves using the absence of evidence as evidence itself. For example, if I were to argue, "Bigfoot exists because nobody has proven he doesn't exist"

I would be employing the Appeal to Ignorance fallacy. While this simple example is illustrative, in reality use of the Appeal to Ignorance is often more subtle. During one of his witch hunts in the 1950 s, Joseph McCarthy produced a list of 81 names of people he claimed to be Communists working inside the State Department. When asked about one of the names on the list, McCarthy infamously said:

> *I do not have much information on this except the general statement of the agency that there is nothing in the files to disprove his Communist connections.*

As with most informal logical fallacies, the boundary of what is and isn't fallacious is also often less clear in the real world. For example, the justice system in the United States operates under the assumption of innocence until proven guilty. While this assumption appears to be directly at odds with evidence-based logic, the distinguishing feature here is the thorough, methodical investigation that (at least theoretically) is present in every case. Tindale [20] suggests that we can distinguish an Appeal to Ignorance by asking if there has "been a reasonable effort to search for evidence, or is the absence of evidence for or against something really negative evidence arising from the attempts to show otherwise?" As mentioned previously, we deliberately avoided these kinds of subtleties when designing the problems used in the tutoring system to make the correct answer as clear and unambiguous as possible. Examples of the kinds of arguments implemented in the tutoring systems can be seen in Figs. 1, 2, and 3.

2.2   The Fallacy Tutor

In order to test the relative effect of different kinds of instruction on teaching logical fallacies, we built a simple online tutoring system for teaching one kind of fallacy (Appeal to Ignorance). The online tutoring system was built using the Cognitive Tutor Authoring Tools (CTAT) [1], and hosted on TutorShop, a web-based learning management system. Log data was sent from TutorShop to DataShop [14] for storage and analysis.

Inside the tutor, participants could encounter three types of problems: Fallacy/No Fallacy problems, Expert-Explanation problems, or Self-Explanation problems. The number of each type of problem the participant encountered was determined by the experimental condition the participant was assigned to. We tested five different instructional designs, each with a different number of each problem type (see Table 1).

Fallacy/No Fallacy Problems. Fallacy/No Fallacy (FNF) problems involved presenting the participant with an argument, and asking whether the argument contains an Appeal to Ignorance or not. After selecting an answer, participants received correctness feedback (i.e., correct or incorrect). Unlike the other kinds of problems (Expert-Explanation and Self-Explanation), FNF problems did not provide an explanation of why the argument does or does not contain an Appeal to Ignorance. Explanations and definitions were intentionally omitted from FNF problems, as they were designed to promote inductive rather than deductive reasoning.

Table 1. Number of problem types for each condition

Condition	Instruction	Practice
Baseline	6 Fallacy/No Fallacy	6 Fallacy/No Fallacy
4EE 2SE	4 Expert-Explanation, 2 Self-Explanation	6 Fallacy/No Fallacy
2EE 2SE	2 Expert-Explanation, 2 Self-Explanation	6 Fallacy/No Fallacy
4EE	4 Expert-Explanation	6 Fallacy/No Fallacy
2EE	2 Expert-Explanation	6 Fallacy/No Fallacy

Expert-Explanation Problems. Some participants received either two or four Expert-Explanation problems (depending on condition). Expert-Explanation problems involved presenting the participant with an argument, indicating that it does or does not contain an Appeal to Ignorance, and then providing an explanation as to why it does or does not. In the context of our tutor, these Expert-Explanations provided direct instruction and were designed to promote deductive reasoning.

Self-Explanation Problems. In addition to Expert-Explanation problems, some participants received two Self-Explanation problems (depending on condition). Requiring students to check their understanding by providing an explanation in their own words has been shown to be an effective instructional practice [2]. In our tutor, Self-Explanation problems involved presenting the participant with an argument, indicating that it does or does not contain an Appeal to Ignorance (as additional scaffolding), and then asking them to explain why it does or does not contain an Appeal to Ignorance. After providing their explanation, they were given an expert explanation that they could compare their explanation to. Participants received no correctness feedback from the system about their explanation.

2.3   Instructional Factors Analysis Model

To determine the relative effectiveness of these different types of problems, we generated an Instructional Factors Analysis Model (IFM). IFM is a cognitive modeling approach that is useful for modeling student performance when more than one instructional intervention is used. IFM has been shown to outperform other cognitive modeling approaches such as Additive Factor Models (AFM) and Performance Factor Models (PFM) when multiple instructional interventions were involved [6].

Appeal to Ignorance

Here is an argument, choose whether it contains an Appeal to Ignorance or not.

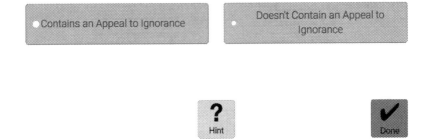

Jim says he's not a spy, but I think he is. Afterall, there is no evidence to prove he's not a spy.

> Contains an Appeal to Ignorance

> Doesn't Contain an Appeal to Ignorance

? Hint

✔ Done

Fig. 1. Screenshot of the tutor interface during a Fallacy/No Fallacy problem. After selecting an answer, participants will be given correctness feedback only.

In our case, the instructional factors of interest are the three different types of problems participants may see in the tutoring system. The general goal of this model is to discover which types of problems are the most beneficial for learning. More specifically, we were interested in whether problems that promote deductive reasoning (Expert-Explanation and Self-Explanation problems) are more effective than inductive practice (Fallacy/No Fallacy problems). This approach has two key advantages. First, if we compare the conditions to one another directly, we fail to account for any instructional overlap across conditions. Instead, an IFM model deconstructs each condition into the relevant features, giving us more detailed insights into which instructional factors are effective, regardless of condition. Second, IFM does not require that a direct observation of student performance is generated from each instructional intervention. This is crucial because both Expert-Explanation and Self-Explanation problems (as they are presently implemented) do not generate direct observations of student performance.

To implement an IFM, we first generated a table where each row corresponded to a student's attempt at a problem (see Table 2 for an example). The columns of the table corresponded to the factors of a mixed-effect model. Our fixed effects were the number of prior opportunities of each of the three kinds of problems (Fallacy/No Fallacy, Expert-Explanation, and Self-Explanation). We used *student* as a random effect. To calculate our outcome variable (Error Rate) we first calculated the Assistance Score, which is equal to the number of incorrect

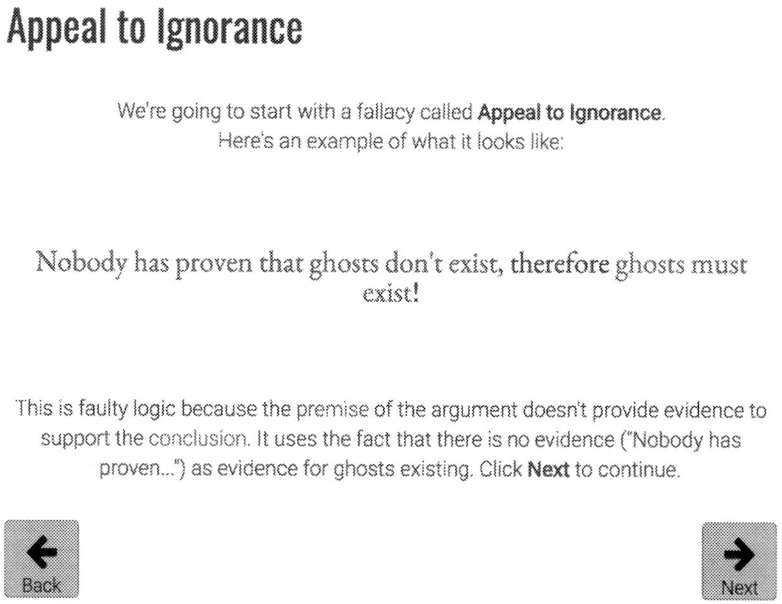

Appeal to Ignorance

We're going to start with a fallacy called **Appeal to Ignorance**.
Here's an example of what it looks like:

Nobody has proven that ghosts don't exist, therefore ghosts must exist!

This is faulty logic because the premise of the argument doesn't provide evidence to support the conclusion. It uses the fact that there is no evidence ("Nobody has proven...") as evidence for ghosts existing. Click **Next** to continue.

Fig. 2. Screenshot of the tutor interface during an Expert-Explanation problem which indicates whether an Appeal to Ignorance is present and explains why.

attempts and hint requests for a particular FNF problem. The Assistance Score is then divided by the total number of attempts and hint requests to produce the Error Rate.

We then implemented the model using the Python library *StatsModels* using the following formulation:

$$mixedlm(Error\ Rate \sim FNF + EE + SE + Error(student)) \tag{1}$$

where FNF, EE, and SE represent the number prior FNF, EE, and SE problems. The term *Error(student)* represents our inclusion of the variable *student* as a random effect. Note that our IFM implementation is slightly different from the implementation reported in [6] in that we use linear regression (rather than logistic regression) to accommodate our continuous outcome variable (Error Rate).

3 Results and Discussion

In order to determine which problem type was most effective for learning, we generated an instructional factors analysis model (IFM). Controlling for the time spent in the tutor, we found that the number of prior Fallacy/No Fallacy (FNF) problems and the number of prior Expert-Explanation (EE) problems were significant predictors of performance ($p < .001$), while the number of prior Self-Explanation (SE) problems was not. Though both FNF and EE problems seem

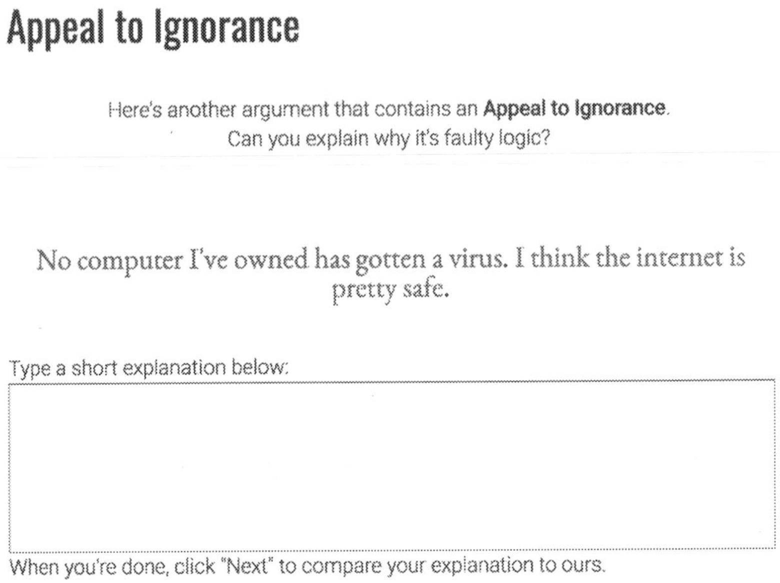

Appeal to Ignorance

Here's another argument that contains an **Appeal to Ignorance**.
Can you explain why it's faulty logic?

No computer I've owned has gotten a virus. I think the internet is
pretty safe.

Type a short explanation below:

When you're done, click "Next" to compare your explanation to ours.

Fig. 3. Screenshot of the tutor interface during a Self-Explanation Problem.

Table 2. Excerpt of data inputed into the IFM. Here students 1, 2, and 3 represent students in the Baseline, 4EE 2SE, and 2EE 2SE conditions, respectively.

Student	Problem	Prior FNF	Prior EE	Prior SE	Error Rate
Stu_1	1	0	0	0	.5
Stu_1	2	1	0	0	.75
Stu_2	1	0	4	2	0
Stu_3	1	0	2	2	.6

to be instructional, EE problems had more than twice the impact ($\beta = -0.034$) on reducing Error Rate than FNF problems ($\beta = -0.015$). These results seem to suggest that instruction aimed at promoting deductive reasoning is more effective than inductive practice. While true in this case, the relationship between deductive and inductive instruction is likely different for different fallacies. Fallacies that are difficult to articulate may be more easily taught through inductive examples. In our future work, we plan to expand the tutoring system to include many different kinds of informal fallacies. This serves the dual purpose of discovering the best kind of instruction for each fallacy, while also potentially revealing the features of a fallacy that inform the kinds of instruction that should be prioritized when teaching it.

It is possible that we did not see an effect for Self-Explanation problems because of the constraints of the experimental design. Because Self-Explanation problems require participants to have a working definition of the fallacy, they must come after Expert-Explanation problems. In each of the conditions with Self-Explanation problems, participants will have seen at least two Expert-Explanation problems before they are required to explain the faulty logic themselves. It may be the case that the novelty of testing one's own understanding does not outweigh the diminishing returns of seeing another explanation of the fallacy. One can imagine a (frustratingly difficult) design that begins with Self-Explanation problems, asking participants to explain why an argument contains an Appeal to Ignorance without any explanation of what an Appeal to Ignorance is. In this hypothetical case, we may see Self-Explanation problems having a measurable, positive effect similar to or greater than that of Expert-Explanation problems. This is an avenue of research for future work.

We have demonstrated that both the deductive EE problems and the inductive FNF problems are effective instructional interventions. What remains to be seen is if participants can learn Appeal to Ignorance in the absence of any general definitions or explanations (i.e., through inductive practice alone). Our Baseline condition was specifically designed to answer this question. Recall that the Baseline condition contains only FNF problems. Participants in this condition never received a definition of Appeal to Ignorance or any explanations of why it was or was not present in an argument. The only feedback they received was whether or not they answered the problem correctly. If it is possible to learn Appeal to Ignorance through inductive practice alone, we would expect the number of prior practice opportunities to predict performance in the Baseline condition, and we found that this is indeed the case. If we consider only participants in the Baseline condition, the number of prior FNF problems is a significant predictor of performance ($p < .001$). This suggests that while deductive instruction may be more beneficial for learning, participants were still able to learn Appeal to Ignorance through inductive practice alone.

3.1   Limitations and Future Work

The ultimate goal of this work is to develop a tutor that could be deployed to late high school classrooms and freely accessible via the web for older adults. While Amazon's Mechanical Turk is a great resource for testing various implementations of the tutor, there are quality limitations that make collecting data from a classroom preferable. In our future work, we plan to expand the tutor to include many more types of informal fallacies. From this variety we hope to uncover the hidden features that make a fallacy more easily learned through either induction or deduction. Another simple, but important addition to our experiment is a measure of enjoyment. It may be the case that you can learn a fallacy through induction alone, but that the act of blindly searching for a pattern is frustrating.

4   Conclusion

The online tutoring system presented here is an initial foray into the vast and complex domain of informal logic. Nevertheless, this relatively simple system has allowed us to gain several key insights: First, it is possible to teach at least one kind of informal fallacy in an online tutoring system. Second, it is possible to learn Appeal to Ignorance using only inductive practice. However, the results from our instructional factors analysis suggest that instruction aimed at promoting deduction is more valuable than inductive practice. These insights are not only useful for the development of future tutoring systems, but offer a promising glimpse into the role that educational technology can play in creating accessible, evidence-based critical thinking instruction.

References

1. Aleven, V., McLaren, B.M., Sewall, J., Koedinger, K.R.: The Cognitive Tutor Authoring Tools (CTAT): preliminary evaluation of efficiency gains. In: Ikeda, M., Ashley, K.D., Chan, T.-W. (eds.) ITS 2006. LNCS, vol. 4053, pp. 61–70. Springer, Heidelberg (2006). https://doi.org/10.1007/11774303_7
2. Aleven, V.A., Koedinger, K.R.: An effective metacognitive strategy: learning by doing and explaining with a computer-based cognitive tutor. Cogn. Sci. **26**(2), 147–179 (2002)
3. Ashley, K.D., Aleven, V.: Toward an intelligent tutoring system for teaching law students to argue with cases. In: Proceedings of the 3rd International Conference on Artificial Intelligence and Law, pp. 42–52. ACM (1991)
4. Boudry, M., Paglieri, F., Pigliucci, M.: The fake, the flimsy, and the fallacious: demarcating arguments in real life. Argumentation **29**(4), 431–456 (2015)
5. Buhrmester, M., Kwang, T., Gosling, S.D.: Amazon's mechanical turk. Perspect. Psychol. Sci. **6**(1), 3–5 (2011). PMID: 26162106
6. Chi, M., Koedinger, K.R., Gordon, G.J., Jordon, P., VanLahn, K.: Instructional factors analysis: a cognitive model for multiple instructional interventions (2011)
7. Corbett, A.T., Koedinger, K.R., Hadley, W.: Cognitive tutors: from the research classroom to all classrooms. In: Technology Enhanced Learning: Opportunities for Change, pp. 235–263 (2001)
8. Easterday, M.W., Aleven, V., Scheines, R., Carver, S.M.: Using tutors to improve educational games. In: Biswas, G., Bull, S., Kay, J., Mitrovic, A. (eds.) AIED 2011. LNCS (LNAI), vol. 6738, pp. 63–71. Springer, Heidelberg (2011). https://doi.org/10.1007/978-3-642-21869-9_11
9. Gottfried, J., Shearer, E.: News Use Across Social Media Platforms 2016. Pew Research Center (2016)
10. J. Handelsman and M. Smith. Stem for all—whitehouse.gov, February 2016. https://obamawhitehouse.archives.gov/blog/2016/02/11/stem-all. Accessed 28 Sept 2017
11. Harrell, M.: Assessing the efficacy of argument diagramming to teach critical thinking skills in introduction to philosophy. Inq. Crit. Thinking Across Disciplines **27**(2), 31–39 (2012)
12. Common Core State Standards for English Language Arts & Literacy in History/Social Studies, Science, and Technical Subjects (2010)

13. Koedinger, K.R., Corbett, A.T., Perfetti, C.: The knowledge-learning-instruction framework: bridging the science-practice chasm to enhance robust student learning. Cogn. Sci. **36**(5), 757–798 (2012)
14. Koedinger, K.R., Stamper, J.C., Leber, B., Skogsholm, A.: LearnLab's DataShop: a data repository and analytics tool set for cognitive science. Topics Cogn. Sci. **5**(3), 668–669 (2013)
15. Lynch, C., Ashley, K., Aleven, V., Pinkwart, N.: Defining ill-defined domains; a literature survey. In: Proceedings of the Workshop on Intelligent Tutoring Systems for Ill-defined Domains at the 8th International Conference on Intelligent Tutoring Systems, pp. 1–10 (2006)
16. Milton, O.: Will that be on the final? (1982)
17. Paul, R.W., Elder, L., Bartell, T.: California teacher preparation for instruction in critical thinking: research findings and policy recommendations (1997)
18. Reed, C., Walton, D., Macagno, F.: Argument diagramming in logic, law and artificial intelligence. Knowl. Eng. Rev. **22**(01), 87 (2007)
19. Silverman, C., Singer-Vine, J.: Most Americans who see fake news believe it, new survey says. BuzzFeed News (www.buzzfeed.com) (2016). https://www.buzzfeed.com/craigsilverman/fake-newssurvey
20. Tindale, C.W.: Fallacies and Argument Appraisal, vol. 23. Cambridge University Press, Cambridge (2007)

Using Physiological Synchrony as an Indicator of Collaboration Quality, Task Performance and Learning

Yong Dich, Joseph Reilly, and Bertrand Schneider[✉]

Harvard University, Cambridge, USA
ydich@college.harvard.edu,
josephreilly@g.harvard.edu,
bertrand_schneider@gse.harvard.edu

Abstract. Over the last decade, there has been a renewed interest in capturing 21st century skills using new data collection tools. In this paper, we leverage an existing dataset where multimodal sensors (mobile eye- trackers, motion sensors, galvanic skin response wristbands) were used to identify markers of productive collaborations. The data came from 42 pairs (N = 84) of participants who had no coding experience. They were asked to program a robot to solve a variety of mazes. We explored four different measures of physiological synchrony: Signal Matching (SM), Instantaneous Derivative Matching (IDM), Directional Agreement (DA) and Pearson's Correlation (PC). Overall, we found PC to be positively associated with learning gains and DA with collaboration quality. We compare those results with prior studies and discuss implications for measuring collaborative process through physiological sensors.

Keywords: Biosensors · Collaborative learning · Physiological synchrony
Electrodermal activity · Galvanic skin response wristbands · Motion sensors
Multimodal

1 Introduction

There has been a renewed interest in leveraging new data collection tools for capturing students' learning processes that go beyond the acquisition of conceptual knowledge. With an ever-increasing ease of access to information, educational researchers are more and more interested in teaching "21st century skills [1]. Those skills include (but are not limited to) students' curiosity, critical thinking, collaborative skills, grit, persistence or creativity. Having accurate and reliable tools for capturing them can pave the way for new kinds of instruction (for example by displaying levels of mastery to teachers through dashboards; by designing awareness tools for students [2]; or by providing real-time, just-in-time, personalized feedback). To reach this goal, educational researchers are starting to use multimodal sensors and learning analytics to richly capture students' behavior (i.e., through Multimodal Learning Analytics, MMLA; [3]). The goal of this project is to make a first step in this direction by exploring how various kinds of sensors, such as eye-trackers, motion sensors, galvanic skin response wristbands, can capture proxies of 21st skills during learning activities. In this paper, we focus on capturing productive social interactions using

© Springer International Publishing AG, part of Springer Nature 2018
C. Penstein Rosé et al. (Eds.): AIED 2018, LNAI 10947, pp. 98–110, 2018.
https://doi.org/10.1007/978-3-319-93843-1_8

physiological measures from motion sensor and galvanic skin response wristbands data. More specifically, we computed various metrics of physiological synchronization and correlated them with a coding scheme for assessing collaboration quality in dyads.

The paper is structured as follows: first, we review prior work that has used electrodermal activity for studying collaborative processes. We then describe the study where the data was collected, our preprocessing procedure and analyses. We conclude with a discussion of our findings and future work for this line of research.

2   Literature Review

2.1   Electrodermal Activity (EDA) in Educational Research

Electrodermal Activity (EDA) is any electrical change measured at the surface of the skin whenever the skin receives innervating signals from the sympathetic nervous system. The sympathetic system is activated in case of an emotional activation like physical exertion or cognitive workload. The electrical conductance increases as the pores begin to fill below the surface with sweat. EDA is generally considered to be a reliable way of measuring sympathetic activation, because the skin is the only organ that is innervated just by the sympathetic nervous system [4].

In educational research, EDA has been used to capture students' affective state. As an example, [5] used data from four different sensors (camera, mouse, chair, and wristband) to predict students' affects in a school setting and was able to explain 60% of the variance of their emotional state when interacting with intelligent tutors. What is of interest to us, however, is the use of physiological sensors to predict students' social interactions. Prior work has identified various indicators of physiological synchrony and correlated those measure with outcome measures. [6], for example, used Signal Matching (SM), Instantaneous Derivative Matching (IDM), Directional Agreement (DA) and Pearson's correlation Coefficient (PC). We describe these measures in more details below, but the idea is that SM captures the difference between two EDA time-series; IDM the rate of change; DA the direction of those changes; and PC the linear relationship between them. The paragraph below and Table 1 summarize some results found by prior work.

Table 1. Summary of Results from prior studies (reproduced and modified from [6]).

Dependent measure	Indicators	Study
Team performance	SM, IDM, DA, PC	[7, 8]
Collaboration, task performance, learning	SM, IDM, DA, PC	[6]
Team work	PC	[10]
Interaction	PC	[9]
Completion time	PC	[11]
Conflicting interactions	PC	[12]

[7] found those indicators of physiological synchrony to be associated with task performance for pairs of participants in a multitask environment under varied task and technology conditions; more specifically, [8] 's findings suggest that PC and DA were the most useful indicators to differentiate between low and high performers. In a collaborative problem-solving task (i.e., designing a healthy, appropriate breakfast for an athlete training for a marathon), [6] found that IDM best predicted collaborative interactions and DA was positively associated with learning. In a collaborative game, [9] collected physiological data in dyads of learners and found that PC was correlated with participants' interaction and self-reported social presence. In a continuous tracking-task simulating teleoperation, [10] reported that PC was a significant predictor of completion time in two-person teams. In a four-persons team, they found that PC was also associated with teamwork effectiveness during real planning meetings [11]. Finally, [12] compared cooperative and competitive play and found that PC was correlated with conflicting interactions.

In summary, there is ample evidence that indicators of physiological synchrony are associated with outcomes of interest to educational researchers (social interactions, learning, task performance). However, most prior work has only looked at PC and there is not a clear understanding of the difference between the four physiological indicators considered in this paper (PC, DA, IDM, SM). In the next section, we present the study where the data was collected, describe our measures of physiological synchrony and correlate them with our dependent measures (task performance, learning gains, collaboration quality).

3 The Study

In this study, participants with no prior programming knowledge were paired and given 30 min to program a robot to autonomously solve a series of increasingly difficult mazes. Two different interventions were designed and used to support collaboration: an informational explanation of the benefits of collaboration and a visualization showing relative verbal contributions of each participant. Participants were given a pre- and post-survey on computational thinking skills and were asked to self-assess their collaboration at the end of the activity. Researchers coded the quality of the collaboration, the progress of the participants, and the quality of their final code. During the study, two mobile eye-trackers captured where participants were looking, a motion sensor captured gross motor movement and position, and two wearable technology bracelets captured EDA.

Fig. 1. The material used in the study: the robot that participants had to program (left image), one maze (middle image) and the Kinect-based speech visualization (right side).

3.1   Design

The study employed a 2×2 between-subjects design to measure the effects of the interventions. A quarter of the dyads received neither intervention (Condition #1, "No Explanation, No Visualization"), a quarter received solely the visualization (Condition #2; "No Explanation, Kinect Visualization"), a quarter received solely the informational intervention (Condition #3; "Explanation, No Visualization"), and the final quarter received both interventions (Condition #4; Explanation, Kinect Visualization") Assignment to conditions was done randomly prior to participant sign-up.

The informational collaboration intervention consisted of the researcher verbally informing the participants about several research findings related to collaboration such as equity of speech time predicting the quality of a collaboration. Dyads not assigned to conditions with this intervention received no such information. The visualization intervention used audio data from the motion sensor to display what proportion of total talk came from each participant over the past 30 s. The proportion of the screen filled with a certain color represented the relative contribution to total talk time (Fig. 1, right side).

The task asked participants to use a block-based programming language to program a robot through a series of mazes (Fig. 1, middle). The robot came equipped with a microcontroller, two DC motors connected to wheels, and three proximity sensors on the front, left, and right (Fig. 1, left). Participants were first shown a tutorial video to illustrate the basic concepts of how to use a block-based programming language to program the robot. Following the video, participants had five minutes to write a simple program to move the robot past a line two feet ahead of it. Data collected during this tutorial activity is not included in our analysis.

After this initial activity, a second tutorial video showing more advanced features such as using prewritten functions to turn and checking the values of the proximity sensors was shown to participants and a printed reference sheet covering the material from the video was provided. The main activity asked participants to spend 30 min attempting to get their robot through the increasingly more difficult mazes. As soon as a robot could solve a maze twice in a row, the next maze was provided. Participants did not know the layout of the mazes ahead of time and were encouraged to write code that could work for any maze. During this main activity, identical hints were given at five-minute intervals to all groups regarding common pitfalls that could lead to stuckness.

3.2   Methods

Forty-two dyads participated in the study ($N = 84$), and forty groups were used in the final dataset. Participants were recruited from a study pool at a university in the northeastern United States. 62% of participants self-identified as students and ages ranged from 19 to 51 years old. 60% identified as female. Participants were compensated $20 per 90-min session of the study. No participants previously knew each other.

In addition to a variety of other sensors (Fig. 2), an Empatica E4 wrist sensor tracked several physiological markers from each participant, including electrodermal activity (at 4 Hz), blood volume pulse (at 64 Hz), and XYZ acceleration (at 32 Hz).

During the 30-min session, roughly between 7,200 to 115,200 data points were generated for each participant per measure, depending on the sampling rate.

Fig. 2. The various measures collected during the study: top left shows the eye-tracking data; bottom left the motion data generated from the Kinect sensor; top right the block-based environment used to program the robot; bottom right the physiological data from the Empatica wristbands.

Learning of computational thinking skills in abstract was assessed by a pre- and post-test consisting of four questions assessing knowledge of computer science principles such as looping, conditional statements, and interpreting code (adapted from [13, 14]). These questions required near-transfer and application of skills learned in the activity. Researchers evaluated the completeness of answers and how well answers demonstrated understanding of computational thinking skills. The sum of the scores were used to generate pre, post, and gains scores for each individual.

While participants worked on the task, the researcher assessed their collaboration and task behaviors. The dyads' collaboration was assessed on nine scales adapted from [15] on a −2/+2 scale: sustaining mutual understanding, dialogue management, information pooling, reaching consensus, task division, time management, technical coordination, reciprocal interaction, and individual task orientation (see [15] for a definition of those dimensions). Two graduate students from the Harvard Graduate School of Education rated video recordings of the sessions using this coding scheme. The task behavior measures were task performance (number of mazes solved), task understanding (use of computational thinking concepts), and improvement over time (evidence of increased conceptual or technical understanding during the task). To calculate inter-rater reliability, a second researchers double coded 20% of the sessions from videos collected during the session and achieved an inter-rater reliability of 0.65 (75% agreement).

After the post-test, participants filled out a self-assessment of their collaboration experience during the activity (also adapted from [15]) that aligned with the researcher coding scheme as well as a demographic survey. Following the conclusion of the activity, the final block-based code each dyad created was evaluated to determine in abstract how well the code could successfully solve different types of mazes. The rubric aligned with the measures used to assess "Task Understanding" in the live coding to act as a check that no hardware or other issues had impacted the code's performance.

4 Data Preprocessing

We collected the following data from the Empatica wristbands: accelerometer, blood volume pulse (BVP), interbeat intervals (IBI), electrodermal activity (EDA), heart variability (HR), tag numbers to different sections in each session. All of this was accessible through Empatica's web portal. In this paper, we focus more specifically on electrodermal activity (EDA).

EDA is measured in a variety of ways: skin potential, resistance, conductance, admittance, and impedance. The wearable we used, Empatica E4 [16], captures electrical conductance (inverse of resistance) across the skin. It passes a minuscule amount of current between two electrodes in contact with the skin in units of microSiemans (μS). In the section below, we describe how we preprocessed the data for our analyses.

4.1 Cleaning the Data

The EDA data from the Empatica E4 comes in the following format: starting Unix time, frequency at which EDA was collected, and the EDA values. The first step was to synchronize the EDA's values. During the study, we asked participants to synchronize their sensors by pressing the button on the wristband before/after each step, which generated a tag in our dataset. By aligning those tags, we were able to synchronize the data from each participant and select one subset of the data (i.e., completing the maze task).

Before calculating our indicators of physiological synchrony, we had to clean the data by removing any extra noise. This noise or "artifacts" can be introduced whenever an individual adjusts the sensor, knocks the wearable against something or place pressure on the device. We used EDA Explorer [17], which is a machine learning classifier, focusing mainly on using support vector machines, that detects noise with 95% accuracy to remove artifacts.

In the paragraph below, we describe the four physiological coupling indices we explored in this paper: Pearson Correlation, Directional Agreement, Signal Matching, and Instantaneous Derivative Matching.

4.2 Computing Indicators of Physiological Synchrony

Each physiological compliance index was coded in the Python language following the mathematical descriptions below this paragraph. To render the data in the Empatica CSV files, Python's Pandas library was utilized to preprocess/clean, format, and analyze the data via dataframes. Other common libraries for mathematical analysis and visualization were used (seaborn, matplotlib, numpy, scipy).

Pearson's Correlation (PC): Pearson's correlation looks for a linear relationship between the EDA level of each participant. For example, a strong correlation means that both participants were likely to be physiologically activated, if positive, (or not, if negative) at similar times. As a sanity check, we looked at the scatter plots, correlations, and line graphs between two dyads, namely group 7 and group 8. According to our coding of collaboration and task performance, group 7 was judged to be a group that demonstrated poor performance and collaboration and success while group 8 was judged to be a good performing group. Figure 3 shows a slight positive correlation in EDA signals for group 8 individuals and a negative correlation in EDA signals for group 7, which is was we would expect. Directional agreement (DA) is identifying whether within each dyad the individuals' signal data points increase or decrease at the same time steps. In Python, each individual's data point at a time step was subtracted with a data point that occurred right before it [8] to determine the change in signal. We then compared both individuals' data points' change: increasing or decreasing. If any points are null, the change in signal calculated would also become null, automatically excluding both individuals' EDA data points at that specific time step. If both data points were indicated as increasing or both were decreasing, then this pair of points would mean both individuals were in "directional agreement" and then the counter variable named "tracking" would increase by 1. DA would be the ratio of the total directionally agreeing pairs of points out of the total number of pairs of data points compared.

Signal matching (SM) was used to look at the differences in area between the data curves of team members [8]. There is an inverse relation with greater area between the curves meaning less synchrony between the signals while less area between the curves meant closer synchrony or higher physiological synchrony. Thus, a negative correlation between a SM value and a qualitative measure would indicate that a small SM value means higher synchrony (and vice versa). Since individuals have different characteristics affecting their EDA signals, their signals need to be normalized to be compared on an equal scale. We normalized those values using z-scores. Once the absolute differences were calculated between the data points of each individual, the overall mean difference of each team was recorded.

Instantaneous Derivative Matching (IDM) also used the same normalized z-scored data. IDM calculates the level of matching between slopes of the two individual's physiological signal curves [8]. The slopes are calculated as the difference between the current point and the one ahead of it. Then these slopes or derivatives calculated for each individual's EDA signals were calculated by subtracting a data point at a time from a data point that's a time step ahead. These differences between the individuals' slopes were summed up and divided by the total time range observed. The following equation was used to compute IDM:

$$\frac{1}{T} \sum_{t=0}^{T-1} |(a_{t+1} - a_t) - (b_{t+1} - b_t)|$$

4.3   Filtering Outliers

Before correlating our four measures of physiological synchrony (DA, SM, IDM, PC) with our dependent measures, we looked for outliers in our dataset. Three groups were missing EDA data due to Empatica wearable malfunctions. The left side of Fig. 3 shows that each measure (except SM) has an outlier that was beyond two standard deviations of the mean. The right side of Fig. 3 shows the percentage of data that was removed after removing noisy artifacts. For our analyses, we removed those outliers because the data was either missing, too noisy or drastically different from other participants (which likely indicates that the wristband did not function properly).

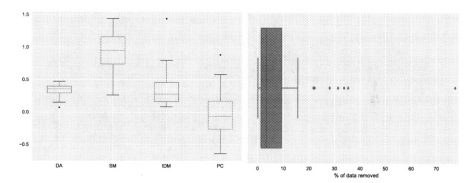

Fig. 3. Left side: boxplots for our 4 measures of physiological synchrony. We can see three outliers (one for DA, one for IDM and one for PC) and one group for which more than 50% of the data was removed.

5   Results

We first briefly summarize the main results of the study (described in detail in [18]). The quality of dyad collaboration (as coded by researchers) revealed significant differences between the two conditions that received the informational intervention to support collaboration (3&4) versus those that did not (1&2): dyads in condition 3 scored 7.1 points higher than those in condition 1 ($p < 0.001$), both of which did not receive the Kinect-based visualization intervention; dyads in condition 4 scored 4.8 points higher than those in condition 2 ($p = 0.03$), both of which did receive the Kinect intervention. Our coding of collaboration was significantly positively correlated with the quality of produced code (r = 0.52, p < 0.001) as well as all three performance metrics: task performance (r = 0.35, p < 0.001), task understanding (r = 0.53, p < 0.001), and improvement over time (r = 0.54, p < 0.001). Participants gained an average of 19.8% points on the survey of computational thinking principles ($t = 6.18$, $p < 0.001$). Learning gains did not differ significantly by condition, individual gender, the gender makeup of the group, or level of education. The quality of the final block-based code dyads produced was significantly correlated with the number of mazes completed (r = 0.45, p < 0.001), task understanding (r = 0.45, p < 0.001), and improvement over time (r = 0.54, p < 0.001).

The main contribution of this paper are the findings from the EDA analysis (not included in [18]). Results are presented visually in Fig. 4. We found that PC was positively correlated with learning gains: r(30) = 0.35, p < 0.05; DA was positively correlated with Dialogue Management: r(30) = 0.35, p = 0.063, Reaching Consensus r (30) = 0.36, p < 0.05 and Reciprocal Interaction r(30) = 0.470, p < 0.001. PC was also negatively correlated with Information Pooling: r(30) = −0.35, p < 0.05.

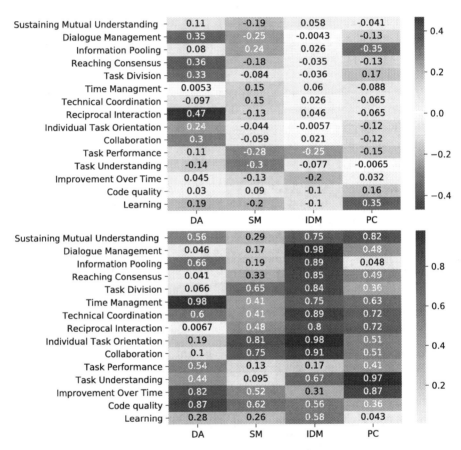

Fig. 4. Correlations between our dependent measures (collaboration, task performance and learning) and the four indicators of physiological synchrony. The heatmap on the top shows Pearson's correlation coefficients and the heatmap on the bottom shows p values.

Because we saw an effect of our intervention on participants' collaboration (but not on learning gains), we hypothesized that it also impacted their physiological synchrony. To check this assumption, we broke down the correlation matrix by condition (Fig. 5). By visually inspecting the heatmaps, we found that the groups in the "No Explanation" condition exhibited negative correlations with our indicators of physiological synchrony (e.g., DA and PC for the Kinect Visualization group and SM and PC for No Visualization). This is represented by dark blue columns in Fig. 5 below. We focus on

DA in our next analyses (first column of Fig. 5), because this measure was significantly correlated with participants' quality of collaboration.

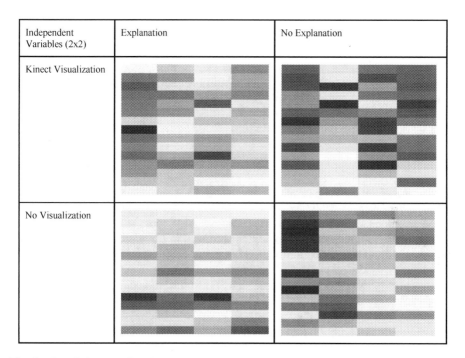

Fig. 5. Correlations matrices between our dependent measures (collaboration, task performance and learning) and the four indicators of physiological synchrony for each experimental condition. See Fig. 4 for the horizontal/vertical labels.

For DA, the experimental condition that saw the Kinect Visualization but received No Explanation was found to have negative correlations with most dependent measures (1st row, 2nd column of the heatmaps). Because this group of participants seemed to behave differently from the other experimental conditions (at least for DA), we explored whether removing it from our sample would produce different results. We found the following significant correlations with those three conditions grouped together (Kinect with Explanation, No Kinect with Explanation, No Kinect with No Explanation – 1st column and 1st row of Fig. 5):

- DA - Sustaining Mutual Understanding: $r(25) = 0.436$, $p = 0.023$
- DA - Dialogue Management: $r(25) = 0.597$, $p = 0.001$
- DA - Information Pooling: $r(25) = 0.551$, $p = 0.003$
- DA - Reaching Consensus: $r(25) = 0.555$, $p = 0.003$
- DA - Task Division: $r(25) = 0.381$, $p = 0.050$
- DA - Reciprocal Interaction: $r(25) = 0.605$, $p = 0.001$
- DA - Individual Task Orientation: $r(25) = 0.395$, $p = 0.042$
- DA - Collaboration: $r(25) = 0.582$, $p = 0.001$

Here, DA is significantly and positively correlated with most dimensions of our rating scheme for assessing collaboration quality. PC is significantly correlated with Learning. Interestingly, SM and IDM are negatively correlated with task performance:

- SM - Task Performance: $r(25) = -0.387$, $p = 0.046$
- IDM - Task Performance: $r(25) = -0.491$, $p = 0.009$
- PC - Learning: $r(26) = 0.410$, $p = 0.030$

By removing participants in the first condition (No Kinect, No Explanation), all correlations become non-significant - except Learning gains with PC ($r(24) = 0.398$, $p < 0.05$).

6 Discussion

In summary, we found that for our entire sample PC seems to be positively correlated with learning gains. When looking at task performance, it was surprising to see that our indicators were generally negatively correlated with how well participants completed the task. This is at odd with prior research. We plan to reexamine how our metrics of performance were coded, and how they relate to our other dependent measures. Finally, DA was associated with our dyads' quality of collaboration, especially when removing the experimental condition where participants saw the Kinect Visualization (but did not receive an explanation about the importance of working together). This suggests that seeing how much each person was talking - but no knowing how to use this information - had a distracting effect on our participants. DA, for example, became negatively correlated with participants' quality of collaboration. This suggests that groups that worked well together were more likely to be unsynchronized; it might be that in those groups, participants paid attention to the visualization (which increased their physiological activation) but each participant might have done it at different times. Those "spikes" lowered participants' scores on our measures of physiological synchronization - when in fact it meant that they were potentially aware of unbalanced levels of participation. This interpretation will be checked in future work through video analyses and log data from the Kinect sensor (i.e., the data can tell us if the participants were looking above the maze, where the visualization was presented).

Finally, it should be noted that our correlations did not agree with prior research. In other studies [6], team performance was found to be positively correlated with SM, IDM, DA and PC. Teamwork and interaction were also positively correlated with PC, and learning gains with DA. In this paper, we found collaboration quality to be associated with DA, task performance to be negatively correlated with IDM, and SM and PC to be positively associated with learning gains. Some of those differences are likely caused by how the constructs were operationalized. [6], for example, used self-report scales for capturing social interactions while we applied a validated rating scheme in the learning sciences [15]. Task performance and learning gains also depend on the task that participants have to complete and can vary widely in their measures (e.g., completion time, success, factual knowledge, transfer questions, etc.). But it is striking to see that our four measures of physiological synchronization seem to be sensitive to different outcomes measures compared to prior work.

7 Conclusion

In conclusion, this paper successfully identified predictors of task performance, collaboration quality and learning gains from physiological sensors. Those results are encouraging, especially in the context of developing real-time, just-in-time, personalized feedback to students. We also plan to leverage those measures to develop dashboards for teacher and awareness tools for students [2].

There are few limitations that are worth mentioning. In order to control the quality of the EDA signal, the study followed recommended recording conditions based on maximum signal-to-noise ratio: subjects were seated at a table which limited their movement. However, since they were manipulating the robot it generated some noise in the data. This required us to remove some participants from our sample. Additionally, new findings show too that EDA should not just be measured on the non-dominant side. There were also 3 groups removed from the dyad data set due to an Empatica wearable or user malfunction because not all of the EDA data was collected, inhibiting proper clean up and analysis.

In terms of future work, we want to consider the more specific characteristics of EDA: tonic versus phasic changes. Tonic skin conductance level is the smooth underlying slowly changing levels in the absence of external stimuli. This is also known as skin conductance level (SCL). Phasic skin conductance response is identified by the rapidly changing peaks which are associated with short term events and occur in the presence of external stimuli (sight, sound). These peaks or abrupt increases in the skin conductance are referred to as Skin Conductance Responses (SCRs).

In conclusion, our next step is to compute those indicators in real-time and test out the effectiveness of displaying this information to learners and teachers in order to promote self-regulation, real-time monitoring, data analysis, and provide the opportunity to give formative feedback.

References

1. Dede, C.: Comparing frameworks for 21st century skills. In: 21st Century Skills: Rethinking How Students Learn, vol. 20, pp. 51–76 (2010)
2. Buder, J.: Group awareness tools for learning: current and future directions. Comput. Hum. Behav. **27**, 1114–1117 (2011)
3. Blikstein, P., Worsley, M.: Multimodal learning analytics and education data mining: using computational technologies to measure complex learning tasks. J. Learn. Anal. **3**, 220–238 (2016)
4. Dawson, M.E., Schell, A.M., Filion, D.L.: The electrodermal system. In: Handbook of Psychophysiology, vol. 2, pp. 200–223 (2007)
5. Arroyo, I., Cooper, D.G., Burleson, W., Woolf, B.P., Muldner, K., Christopherson, R.: Emotion sensors go to school. In: AIED (2009)
6. Pijeira-Díaz, H.J., Drachsler, H., Järvelä, S., Kirschner, P.A.: Investigating collaborative learning success with physiological coupling indices based on electrodermal activity. In: Proceedings of the Sixth International Conference on Learning Analytics and Knowledge (2016)

7. Montague, E., Xu, J., Chiou, E.: Shared experiences of technology and trust: an experimental study of physiological compliance between active and passive users in technology-mediated collaborative encounters. IEEE Trans. Hum. Mach. Syst. **44**, 614–624 (2014)

8. Elkins, A.N., Muth, E.R., Hoover, A.W., Walker, A.D., Carpenter, T.L., Switzer, F.S.: Physiological compliance and team performance. Appl. Ergon. **40**, 997–1003 (2009)

9. Järvelä, S., Kivikangas, J.M., Kätsyri, J., Ravaja, N.: Physiological linkage of dyadic gaming experience. Simul. Gaming **45**, 24–40 (2014)

10. Henning, R.A., Boucsein, W., Gil, M.C.: Social–physiological compliance as a determinant of team performance. Int. J. Psychophysiol. **40**, 221–232 (2001)

11. Henning, R., Armstead, A., Ferris, J.: Social psychophysiological compliance in a four-person research team. Appl. Ergon. **40**, 1004–1010 (2009)

12. Chanel, G., Kivikangas, J.M., Ravaja, N.: Physiological compliance for social gaming analysis: cooperative versus competitive play. Interact. Comput. **24**, 306–316 (2012)

13. Brennan, K., Resnick, M.: New frameworks for studying and assessing the development of computational thinking. In: Proceedings of the 2012 Annual Meeting of the American Educational Research Association, Vancouver, Canada (2012)

14. Weintrop, D., Wilensky, U.: Using commutative assessments to compare conceptual understanding in blocks-based and text-based programs. In: 11th Annual ACM Conference on International Computing Education Research, ICER 2015 (2015)

15. Meier, A., Spada, H., Rummel, N.: A rating scheme for assessing the quality of computer-supported collaboration processes. Comput. Support. Learn. **2**, 63–86 (2007)

16. Garbarino, M., Lai, M., Bender, D., Picard, R.W., Tognetti, S.: Empatica E3—A wearable wireless multi-sensor device for real-time computerized biofeedback and data acquisition. In: 2014 EAI 4th International Conference on Wireless Mobile Communication and Healthcare (Mobihealth) (2014)

17. Taylor, S., Jaques, N., Chen, W., Fedor, S., Sano, A., Picard, R.: Automatic identification of artifacts in electrodermal activity data. In: 2015 37th Annual International Conference of the IEEE Engineering in Medicine and Biology Society (EMBC) (2015)

18. Starr, E., Reilly, J., Schneider, B.: Using multi-modal learning analytics to support and measure collaboration in co-located dyads. In: The 13th International Conference on the Learning Sciences

Towards Combined Network and Text Analytics of Student Discourse in Online Discussions

Rafael Ferreira[1,2(✉)], Vitomir Kovanović[3], Dragan Gašević[2,4], and Vitor Rolim[1]

[1] Federal Rural University of Pernambuco,
Rua Dom Manuel de Medeiros, Recife, Brazil
{rafael.mello,vitor.rolim}@ufrpe.br
[2] University of Edinburgh, Old College, South Bridge, Edinburgh EH8 9YL, UK
{rafael.ferreira,dragan.gasevic}@ac.ed.uk
[3] University of South Australia, 160 Currie Street, Adelaide, SA 5000, Australia
Vitomir.Kovanovic@unisa.edu.au
[4] Monash University, 19 Ancora Imparo Way, Clayton, VIC 3800, Australia
dragan.gasevic@monash.edu

Abstract. This paper presents a novel method for the evaluation of students' use of asynchronous discussions in online learning environments. In particular, the paper shows how students' cognitive development across different course topics can be examined using the combination of natural language processing and graph-based analysis techniques. Drawing on the theoretical foundation of the community of inquiry model, we show how topic modeling and epistemic network analysis can provide qualitatively new insight into students' development of critical and deep thinking skills. We also show how the same method can be used to investigate the effectiveness of instructional interventions and its effect on student learning. The results of this study and its practical implications are further discussed.

Keywords: Community of inquiry model
Epistemic network analysis · Content analysis
Instructional interventions · Online discussions

1 Introduction

Asynchronous online discussions represent one of the most commonly used tools for supporting social interactions within online and blended courses [3]. With the increased shift towards social learning models and constructivist pedagogies, there is a rising need to understand how asynchronous online discussions can be used to foster learning and knowledge (co-)construction by the group of learners. In this regard, the Community of Inquiry (CoI) model [13] represents one of the most widely used and researched pedagogical models which tries to

C. Penstein Rosé et al. (Eds.): AIED 2018, LNAI 10947, pp. 111–126, 2018.
https://doi.org/10.1007/978-3-319-93843-1_9

understand how asynchronous online communication impacts student learning and cognitive development. Using the CoI model, a large body of research examined the effect of different instructional approaches to student engagement and learning outcomes [15]. However, the majority of research evidence provides a high-level overview of student learning by focusing solely on the *learning process*, with insufficient understanding of how it relates to *learning content*. Moreover, there is limited evidence on how various instructional interventions affect the development of positive learning outcomes concerning different components of both learning processes and learning content.

In this paper, we show how the combination of network-based analysis and natural-language processing (NLP) techniques [24] can be used to provide more detailed insights into student learning in asynchronous online discussions. Using the data from six offers of a fully-online graduate-level course in software engineering, we show how a combination of Epistemic Network Analysis (ENA) [32] and Latent Dirichlet Allocation (LDA) [7], can provide rich insights into the effect of instructional scaffolding on student learning of particular course topics. Study results and practical implications are further discussed.

2   Background

2.1   The Community of Inquiry Model

While numerous models and approaches to understanding students' online learning have been proposed, the Community of Inquiry (CoI) model represents arguably the most widely-used and researched theoretical framework that outlines the important facets of students' online learning [15]. The CoI model defines three dimensions (called presences) that together provide a holistic overview of online learning experience: (1) *Cognitive presence*, which captures the development of desirable learning outcomes such as critical thinking, problem-solving, and knowledge (co-)construction [12,14,17], (2) *Social presence*, which models the social climate within learners' group (i.e., cohesion, affectivity, and open communication) [28], and (3) *Teaching presence*, which concerns the instructors' role before (i.e., course design) and during (i.e., facilitation and direct instruction) the course [4].

To assess the levels of CoI presences, researchers can use either a set of coding schemes for content analysis of discussion transcripts [13] or a 34-item survey instrument by Arbaugh et al. [5]. The CoI model and its instruments have been extensively used and validated in a large number of studies, both in traditional online [15], and MOOC contexts [21]. Finally, there has been some research focusing on the development of automated tools for identification of cognitive presence phases [18,22,35] which show the potential of data mining and natural language processing (NLP) techniques for assessing students' learning within communities of inquiry.

From the standpoint of the present study, the most important construct is the cognitive presence, which captures the development of critical and deep-thinking skills [13,14]. Rooted in the inquiry-based conceptions of learning of Dewey [9] and

Lipman [23], cognitive presence is operationalized using a four-phase inquiry process: (1) *Triggering event*, where a problem or dilemma is identified and conceptualized, (2) *Exploration*, in which students' explore and brainstorm potential solutions to the issue at hand, (3) *Integration*, during which students (co-)construct new knowledge by synthesizing the existing information, and (4) *Resolution*, in which students evaluate the newly-created knowledge through hypothesis testing or vicarious application to the problem/dilemma that triggered the learning cycle [14]. The four phases of cognitive presence are theorized as being differentiated across two orthogonal dimensions: (1) *perception-awareness* dimension, which captures the differences between early and late stages of cognitive presence, and (2) *deliberation-action* dimension, which differentiates between phases that primarily occur in the shared world of student discourse (triggering event and resolution) and the ones that happen in the private world of reflection (exploration and integration).

The recent studies of the CoI model recognised self-regulated learning (SRL) [36], metacognition [2] and computer-supported collaborative learning (CSCL) [33] as central to understanding students' online learning. For example, Gašević et al. [16] examined the use of role assignments – a key CSCL technique for fostering student deep and collaborative learning [11] – in combination with externally-facilitated regulation [6] as a scaffolding for student discussion participation. What Gašević et al. [16] results show is that give clear instructions of discussion participation, and role assignments increased students' cognitive presence, as evidenced by the higher percentage of their contributions showing the presence of later stages of inquiry cycle, namely integration and resolution phases.

2.2   Research Questions

It should be noted that the CoI model focuses on the *learning process*, (rather than learning outcomes) and how different course designs and interventions affect students' learning experience, such as the one by Gašević et al. [16]. However, there has been limited research that tried to examine how students' cognitive presence develops concerning different course topics, or how different instructional interventions affect students' cognitive development around the different course topics. We suspect that this is primarily due to the very time-consuming and labour-intensive work required to assess cognitive presence on such fine-grained level. However, with the rapid development of sophisticated NLP, text mining, and graph analysis techniques, there is a potential to use them to identify different course topics and levels of cognitive presence [22,35] (semi-)automatically and examine how they relate to each other. In this paper, we utilized LDA, a popular NLP method [32], and ENA, a graph analysis technique [7], to provide insights into students cognitive presence development with regards to different course topics. As such, our first research question is:

RESEARCH QUESTION 1:
What is the relationship between students' cognitive presence and different course topics? Can we use the proposed NLP and graph-based method to uncover cognitive presence development with respect to different course topics?

In addition to examining the overall relationship between cognitive presence and the course topics, we are interested in exploring whether the proposed approach can provide additional insights into the effects of externally-scaffolded interventions such as the one presented in Gašević et al. [16] study. While Gašević et al. [16] provide general evidence of the effectiveness of the role-assignment scaffolding, it is essential to examine how the intervention affected the cognitive presence development in relation to different course subjects. As such, our second research question is:

RESEARCH QUESTION 2:
What is the effect of instructional scaffolding intervention on students cognitive presence of particular course topics? Can we use the proposed model to assess the effectiveness of role assignment intervention on the development of students' cognitive presence?

By addressing proposed research questions, the paper contributes to the existing body of knowledge in the literature on the CoI model and provides a novel method for assessing students' communities of inquiry through the data-informed lenses.

3 Method

3.1 Data and Course Design

The analysis presented in this paper builds upon the same dataset used in the Gašević et al. [16] study. The primary benefit of using the same dataset is that it makes it simple to directly compare the "traditional" analysis and the proposed approach based on a graph- and text-mining. The data encompasses six offerings of a masters level research-intensive course in software engineering offered entirely online at a Canadian public university between 2008 and 2011. The course covers 14 different topics related to software requirements, design, implementation, evolution, and process which are grouped into six modules (Table 1).

The course consisted of four tutor marker assignments (TMA1–4) which accounted for 15% (presentation of a published peer-reviewed paper), 25% (literature review paper), 15% (project proposal), and 30% (project) of the final grade, respectively. Discussion participation in the course accounted for the remaining 15% of the grade [for further details on the course design, see 16]. As part of the TMA1, students were required to select one research paper on a software engineering topic, record a video presentation, and post a URL to a new course

Table 1. Course topics by weeks.

Module	#	Section	Label
Software engineering scope	1	Introduction	`intro.scope`
Software requirements	2	Introduction	`reqs.intro`
	3	Methods	`reqs.meth`
Software design	4	Introduction	`desig.intro`
	5	Structure, architecture and quality	`desig.qual`
	6	Methods and strategies	`desig.meth`
Software construction approaches	7	Introduction	`const.intro`
	8	Languages	`const.lang`
	9	Component-based and product-line engineering	`const.meth`
Software maintenance	10	Introduction	`maint.intro`
	11	Reverse engineering and knowledge management	`maint.manag`
Software engineering process	12	Introduction	`proc.intro`
	13	Stages	`proc.stages`
	14	Key issues	`proc.issues`

online discussion, where other students would engage in the debate around their presentation. During the first two offerings of the course, student participation was primarily driven by the extrinsic motivational factors (i.e., course grade), with limited scaffolding support. In our study, this group – referred to as *control group* – consisted of 37 students who produced 845 messages (Tables 2 and 3). After the first two course offers, the scaffolding of discussion participation through role assignments and clear instructions were implemented. In total, 44 students – referred to as *treatment group* – were exposed to this instructional intervention, and produced the total of 902 messages (Tables 2 and 3).

Table 2. Distribution of cognitive presence phases in control and treatment groups.

ID	Phase	Messages					
		Control		Treatment		*Total*	
0	Other	71	8.40%	69	7.56%	140	8.01%
1	Triggering event	196	23.19%	112	12.10%	308	17.63%
2	Exploration	390	46.15%	294	33.39%	684	39.15%
3	Integration	152	17.98%	356	39.26%	508	29.08%
4	Resolution	36	4.28%	71	7.69%	107	6.13%
	Total	845	100%	902	100%	1,747	100.00%

Table 3. Number of students and messages across the two study conditions.

Condition	Course offering	Students	Messages
Control	Winter 2008	15	212
	Fall 2008	22	633
	Total	37	845
Treatment	Summer 2009	10	243
	Fall 2009	7	63
	Winter 2010	14	359
	Winter 2011	13	237
	Total	44	902

The complete study dataset consists of 1,747 discussion messages produced by 81 students that were coded by two expert coders using the content analysis instrument for cognitive presence [14]. The coders achieved an excellent level of agreement (percent agreement = 98.1%, Cohen's κ = 0.974) with a total of only 32 disagreements which were resolved through discussion. The distribution of cognitive presence phases for both control and treatment groups are shown in Table 2, while the details about course offerings are shown in Table 3. While both conditions produced a similar number of messages, the difference in the distribution of four phases of cognitive presence is clearly visible, in particular relating to the higher number of integration messages and a lower number of triggering event and exploration messages for the treatment group.

3.2 Analysis Procedure

Natural Language Processing. As the first step of our analysis, we used NLP techniques to detect topics from student discussion messages. In particular, we used Latent Dirichlet Allocation (LDA) [7], a widely used NLP method for topic modelling, which uses a statistical approach to discover prominent themes in the document corpora. More precisely, through the analysis of word co-occurrences, LDA models *topics* as statistical distributions across all words in the corpora (i.e., model vocabulary) and *documents* (i.e., posts) as distributions across all identified topics. LDA has been extensively used in social sciences [26] and humanities [1], including education [cf. 19], where it has frequently been used for problems such as the detection of topics in students' discussions [37], course evaluations [27], and public media discussions [20].

Before applying LDA, we pre-processed the dataset to enable for a more accurate topic detection, as commonly done in NLP [24]. We (1) converted all words into lowercase, (2) removed *stop words*, which were the words with little or no value for topic detection (e.g., prepositions, articles), (3) removed all words shorter than three characters and numbers, and (4) adopted a stemming algorithm to remove the derivational affixes of words [10].

It is important to mention that LDA requires the number of topics specified in advanced. While there are several methods to identify the optimal number of topics [34], since we analysed the corpus of manageable size (1,747 messages) from a well-designed course (see Sect. 3.1), it allowed us to evaluate several models with the number of topics close to the number of topics defined in the course syllabus (Table 1). In the end, 15 topics were identified as optimal, which corresponded to 14 content-related topics from the syllabus and one additional topic related to course logistics (gen.com). The output of LDA algorithm was a $1,747 \times 15$ matrix, with each row containing the relevance of all 15 topics for a given discussion message.

3.3   Epistemic Network Analysis

After we identified prominent topics in the discussion corpus, we examined the relationship between students' cognitive presence and course topics through Epistemic Network Analysis (ENA) [32]. ENA is a graph-based analysis technique which can be used to examine rich relationships between a set of concepts. In educational settings, ENA is typically used to examine the relationships between different elements in a coded dataset, such as coded discourse transcripts. For example, ENA can be used to examine students' cognitive connections during problem-solving [25], or the dynamics and interactions in students' group discourse [31]. Building on the theory of epistemic frames [29], ENA can be used to model complex domains as networks of connections among relevant constructs [30]. Unlike other network analysis tools, ENA was primarily designed for problems with a relatively small set of concepts characterized by highly dynamic and dense interactions. It can also be used to compare the differences between different groups of analysis units – such as between the control and treatment groups in the present study.

Within ENA, the connections among the different concepts (i.e., codes) are derived for each *analysis unit* (e.g., study subject) based on the concept co-occurrences in data subsets called *stanzas* (e.g., sentence, paragraph, document). From code co-occurrences, ENA first creates a high-dimensional representation, called *analytic space*, of all analysis units. The analysis units are then projected in a lower-representational space, called *projection space*, which is derived from analytic space through single-value decomposition. It should be noted that besides binary codes that represent presence/absence of a particular code, ENA can also be used for codes that represent strength or probability of a given code. In this case, the analytic space is not constructed from code co-occurrence, but the weighted product of codes' values; the weighting can be done as (1) direct product (*direct product* method), (2) square root of the direct product (*square root* method), or (3) natural log of the direct product (*natural log* method). In the end, the output of ENA is a series of graph models which capture the relationships between different coding categories [31], in our case four cognitive presence phases and course topics.

In the present study, each discussion message was coded with four binary codes capturing presence/absence of cognitive presence phases and fifteen codes representing the relevance of all extracted topics (0.00–1.00). Both units of analysis and stanzas were students (i.e., all student messages) within control and treatment groups. The use of students as units of analysis enabled us to see for each student his connections between phases of cognitive presence and the different topics, as well as between different phases of cognitive presence. Since our codes for topics were ratio variables measuring the presence of each topic in every message, we examined all three types of weighting (direct product, square root, and natural log) and conducted the statistical comparison between control and treatment groups in all three cases. However, given the space limitations, in the next section, we report only the network models created with the direct product weighting method. The results obtained with other two weighting methods were comparable.

4   Results

Figure 1 shows the projection of individual students' networks with relationships between cognitive presence and course topics. The analytic space was created using the *direct product* method (see Sect. 3.3) while visualisation was done using svd_1 and svd_2, which accounted for 30 and 18% of variability between students' network models, respectively. The differences between the students in the treatment and control groups can be observed visually, with the key difference along

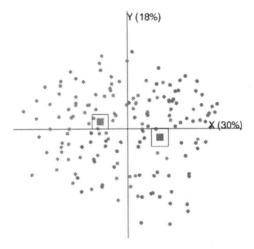

Fig. 1. ENA projection of students' networks between cognitive presence and course topics. The model is created using *direct product method* and shows first (svd_1) and second (svd_2) singular values, respectively axis X and Y. Networks of students from control (red) and treatment groups (blue) are shown as colored circles, while their group means are shown as colored squares (95% CI are outlined around the group means). (Color figure online)

the X-axis which represents the first singular value of the analytic space. The circles represent students in control (red) and treatment (blue) groups, while rectangles represent group-average networks (95% CI are also outlined). The group-average graphs for all students (Figs. 2a and b) indicate that svd_1 primarily distinguishes between students focusing more on early phases (triggering event and exploration) or later phases (integration and resolution) of cognitive presence. The exploration phase is especially related to the topic of software construction methodology, indicating the unique importance of this topic in the course and is primarily captured by the Y-axis.

The visual comparison of the graphs of the control and treatment groups (Figs. 2c and e) shows that the exploration phase was the principal focus of student discourse before the intervention in the course, whereas the discussion shifted towards the integration phase after the role-based and externally-facilitated regulation scaffolding was introduced. Not surprisingly, this is well aligned with the results reported by Gašević et al. [16] on the same dataset. The abbreviated network models for two groups (i.e., with the top 25% of the strongest edges, Figs. 2d and f) reveal the shift towards the integration phase more clearly, with far more topics being connected to the integration phase than before the intervention. Interestingly, in both abbreviated models, the resolution phase got removed, indicating smaller differences between the two groups with regards to the resolution phase. Finally, Fig. 3 which shows the subtracted graph (i.e., the difference between the two networks) and indicates the far more connections of the topics to the integration and resolution phases in the treatment group than in the control group; likewise, there is a higher number of links to the triggering event and exploration phases for the control group than in the treatment group.

In addition to visual examination of the differences between network models for control and treatment groups, we examined the statistical difference between network models for control and treatment groups using all three weighting methods for constructing analytic space (Table 4). Thus, independent-samples t-tests were conducted to compare the differences in students scores among the X and Y axes, using each of the three weighting methods. With respect to X-axis, there were statistically significant differences between the control and treatment groups using all three weighting methods ($p < .001$) with the average effect sizes of 1.56 Cohen's d which is considered a large effect size [8]. These findings suggest that there is on average 1.56 standard deviation a higher number of connections among cognitive presence and course topics in the treatment group than in the control group. With regards to Y-axis, the differences between the control and treatment groups were significant for the direct product and natural log methods $p < .05$ and with effect sizes of 0.43 and 0.35 Cohen's d, respectively. The observed differences can be considered small to medium effect sizes [8].

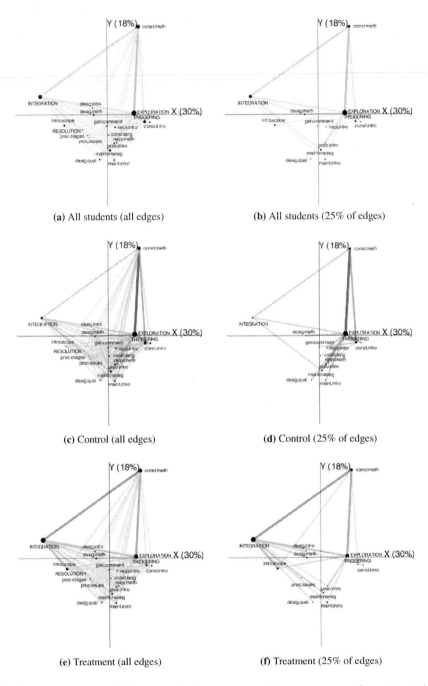

(a) All students (all edges)

(b) All students (25% of edges)

(c) Control (all edges)

(d) Control (25% of edges)

(e) Treatment (all edges)

(f) Treatment (25% of edges)

Fig. 2. Group-average ENA networks between cognitive presence and course topics. (Color figure online)

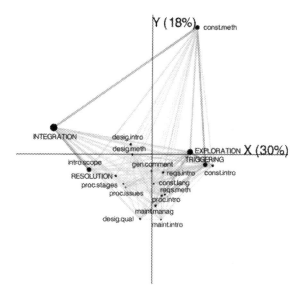

Fig. 3. Differences between control (red) and treatment (blue) group-average networks of cognitive presence and course topics. (Color figure online)

5 Discussion

5.1 Discussion of the Results in Relation to Research Questions

Based on the study results presented in the paper, we can see that the proposed approach provides important and novel insights into the development of cognitive presence with regards to the different course topics, answering the first research question. As expected, exploration and integration are the most prominent cognitive presence phases; this finding aligns well with their distribution (Table 2). However, the direct associations between triggering event and exploration phases and between exploration and integration phases provide additional qualitatively new insights into the students' cognitive presence development which are above the message-level which is provided by CoI content analysis instrument. While cognitive presence has been typically evaluated by looking at number of messages in each phase, the presented approach provides richer insights into the cognitive presence development, by showing the relationship between different cognitive presence phases that reveal the *quality* of the learning process and not its outcome (i.e., number of messages in each phase).

In terms of course topics, we see that software engineering construction methods were particularly well-represented in the data, while other topics received less attention. General course logistics also showed on the graph (Fig. 2a), primarily relating to triggering event phase. This is not surprising since they are typically procedural questions relating to course organization, expectations and activities.

Table 4. Comparison of networks models between control and treatment groups.

Weighting method	X-Axis (svd_1)			Y-Axis (svd_2)		
	Control N = 73	Treatment N = 90	Cohen's d	Control N = 73	Treatment N = 90	Cohen's d
Direct product	0.179**	−0.151**	1.580	−0.047*	0.039*	0.428
Square root	−0.153**	0.129**	1.546	−0.003	0.003	0.031
Natural log	0.158**	−0.133**	1.555	0.033*	−0.028*	0.348

Note: * indicates $p < .05$, ** indicates $p < .001$

Figure 2 shows that the X-axis primarily differentiates between early and later phases of cognitive presence. This is well aligned with the conceptualisation of cognitive presence [14] provided in Sect. 2. In this regard, the X-axis primarily differentiates across the deliberation-action dimension of the practical inquiry model that underlies the conceptualization of cognitive presence, while the Y-axis differentiates across the perception-awareness dimension. However, we can see that differences in this second dimension were much smaller than on the first one, which explains the higher portion of variability (30%).

As posted in the second research question, an essential aspect of our analysis focused on the effect of instructional scaffolding intervention on the students' cognitive presence development in different course topics. Our results showed the effect instructional intervention had, not just on an overall cognitive presence level, but also on particular course topics. The observed effect sizes for svd_1 (X-axis) differences were substantial, suggesting significant differences, in particular, relating to the frequencies of exploration and integration messages.

It should also be noted that with the move towards the integration phase, students also substantially changed the topics of their discussion. For example, process issues, software engineering scope, and introduction to design methodologies appear more prominently in the treatment group, whereas software construction process, software engineering requirements, and construction languages being more common before the intervention. Given that students had a choice of papers to present and discuss, the differences in topics are probably unsurprising. However, the navigation through the course and course expectations could be affected by the intervention. Indeed, messages related to the topic of course logistics were more prominent before the intervention, signalling that the instructional intervention was associated with the reduction of the students' need to seek help regarding course practicalities. Similar findings were also shown using subtracted network model (Fig. 3 albeit in a more condensed form).

5.2 Study Limitations

While this proposed approach shows a promise in addressing significant issues in the research around communities of inquiry, there are some important limitations of the present study which should be acknowledged. First, while we used the data from six-course offerings, the data is still from a single course at a single institution which can negatively affect the broader usability of the presented approach and the generalizability of our study findings. Second, it is possible that the generalizability of the findings from the present study is somewhat limited, given the specifics of the adopted course design and instructional intervention. Finally, as most data mining analysis involves making many methodological decisions, such as deciding on various algorithm tuning parameters, it might be that the findings in our study would be different with a different set of tuning parameters.

5.3   Study Contributions and Conclusions

The primary contribution of the present study is a novel analytical method for assessment of cognitive presence concerning different course topics. Through NLP and graph-based analysis techniques, we showed how it is possible to provide more in-depth insights into students cognitive presence development with regards to different course topics. Moreover, by examining cognitive presence on the student level instead of the message level, we were able to gain rich understanding of students' cognitive presence development which goes beyond simple message counts. In practical terms, the presented method can be used to enable instructors better facilitation of students' course participation by analysing cognitive presence concerting different key course topics. Moreover, the tool can be used to assess the quality of students inquiry-based learning by examining students' connections between different cognitive presence phases.

Another substantial contribution of the present study is the examination of the effects of instructional scaffolding through externally-facilitated regulation and role assignment on students' cognitive presence of different course topics. While the general benefits of this instructional scaffolding in the same dataset were already explored by Gašević et al. [16], the present study shows how it impacted students' cognitive presence of different course topics. This and similar types of analyses have a strong potential to provide relevant research evidence on the benefits of different instructional interventions in social learning environments, where participation in asynchronous online discussions represents a principal learning activity.

Finally, there are some important ways in which this work can be extended and improved. In the future, we intend to investigate the trajectory shift from triggering phase to integration phase by exploring additional analytic features available in the epistemic network analysis. Using a similar approach as presented in this study, we also aim to examine social and teaching presences as well as their relationships. By doing this, we hope to provide a comprehensive analysis of student online learning experience which builds upon the potentials provided by the collected educational data.

References

1. Blei, D.M.: Topic modeling in digital humanities. J. Digit. Humanit. **2**(1) (2012). Special Issue
2. Akyol, Z., Garrison, D.R.: Assessing metacognition in an online community of inquiry. Internet High. Educ. **14**(3), 183–190 (2011). https://doi.org/10.1016/j.iheduc.2011.01.005
3. Anderson, T., Dron, J.: Three generations of distance education pedagogy. Int. Rev. Res. Open Distance Learn. **12**(3), 80–97 (2010). http://www.irrodl.org/index.php/irrodl/article/view/890/
4. Anderson, T., Rourke, L., Garrison, D.R., Archer, W.: Assessing teaching presence in a computer conferencing context. J. Asynchronous Learn. Netw. **5**, 1–17 (2001)
5. Arbaugh, J., Cleveland-Innes, M., Diaz, S.R., Garrison, D.R., Ice, P., Richardson, J.C., Swan, K.P.: Developing a community of inquiry instrument: testing a measure of the community of inquiry framework using a multi-institutional sample. Internet High. Educ. **11**(3–4), 133–136 (2008). https://doi.org/10.1016/j.iheduc.2008.06.003
6. Azevedo, R., Moos, D.C., Greene, J.A., Winters, F.I., Cromley, J.G.: Why is externally-facilitated regulated learning more effective than self-regulated learning with hypermedia? Educ. Technol. Res. Dev. **56**(1), 45–72 (2008). https://doi.org/10.1007/s11423-007-9067-0
7. Blei, D.M., Ng, A.Y., Jordan, M.I.: Latent dirichlet allocation. J. Mach. Learn. Res. **3**, 993–1022 (2003). http://dl.acm.org/citation.cfm?id=944919.944937
8. Cohen, J.: The analysis of variance. In: Statistical Power Analysis for the Behavioral Sciences, pp. 273–406. L. Erlbaum Associates, Hillsdale (1988)
9. Dewey, J.: My pedagogical creed. Sch. J. **54**(3), 77–80 (1897)
10. Feldman, R., Sanger, J.: The Text Mining Handbook: Advanced Approaches in Analyzing Unstructured Data. Cambridge University Press, Cambridge (2007)
11. Fischer, F., Kollar, I., Mandl, H., Haake, J.M.: Scripting Computer-Supported Collaborative Learning: Cognitive. Computational and Educational Perspectives. Springer Science & Business Media, New York (2007). https://doi.org/10.1007/978-0-387-36949-5
12. Garrison, D.R.: Cognitive presence for effective asynchronous online learning: the role of reflective inquiry, self-direction and metacognition. Elem. Qual. Online Educ. Pract. Dir. **4**(1), 47–58 (2003)
13. Garrison, D.R., Anderson, T., Archer, W.: Critical inquiry in a text-based environment: computer conferencing in higher education. Internet High. Educ. **2**(2–3), 87–105 (1999). https://doi.org/10.1016/S1096-7516(00)00016-6
14. Garrison, D.R., Anderson, T., Archer, W.: Critical thinking, cognitive presence, and computer conferencing in distance education. Am. J. Distance Educ. **15**(1), 7–23 (2001). https://doi.org/10.1080/08923640109527071
15. Garrison, D.R., Anderson, T., Archer, W.: The first decade of the community of inquiry framework: a retrospective. Internet High. Educ. **13**(1–2), 5–9 (2010). https://doi.org/10.1016/j.iheduc.2009.10.003
16. Gašević, D., Adesope, O., Joksimović, S., Kovanović, V.: Externally-facilitated regulation scaffolding and role assignment to develop cognitive presence in asynchronous online discussions. Internet High. Educ. **24**, 53–65 (2015). https://doi.org/10.1016/j.iheduc.2014.09.006
17. Heo, H., Lim, K.Y., Kim, Y.: Exploratory study on the patterns of online interaction and knowledge co-construction in project-based learning. Comput. Educ. **55**(3), 1383–1392 (2010). https://doi.org/10.1016/j.compedu.2010.06.012

18. Kovanović, V., Joksimović, S., Gašević, D., Hatala, M.: Automated cognitive presence detection in online discussion transcripts. In: Proceedings of the Workshops at the LAK 2014 Conference Co-located with 4th International Conference on Learning Analytics and Knowledge (LAK 2014), Indianapolis, IN (2014). http://ceurws.org/Vol-1137/

19. Kovanović, V., Joksimović, S., Gašević, D., Hatala, M., Siemens, G.: Content analytics: the definition, scope, and an overview of published research. In: Lang, C., Siemens, G., Wise, A., Gašević, D. (eds.) Handbook of Learning Analytics and Educational Data Mining, pp. 77–92. SoLAR, Edmonton (2017). https://doi.org/10.18608/hla17.007

20. Kovanović, V., Joksimović, S., Gašević, D., Siemens, G., Hatala, M.: What public media reveals about MOOCs: a systematic analysis of news reports. Br. J. Educ. Technol. **46**(3), 510–527 (2015). https://doi.org/10.1111/bjet.12277

21. Kovanović, V., Joksimović, S., Poquet, O., Hennis, T., Čukić, I., de Vries, P., Hatala, M., Dawson, S., Siemens, G., Gašević, D.: Exploring communities of inquiry in massive open online courses. Comput. Educ. **119**, 44–58 (2018). https://doi.org/10.1016/j.compedu.2017.11.010

22. Kovanović, V., Joksimović, S., Waters, Z., Gašević, D., Kitto, K., Hatala, M., Siemens, G.: Towards automated content analysis of discussion transcripts: a cognitive presence case. In: Proceedings of the Sixth International Conference on Learning Analytics & Knowledge (LAK 2016), pp. 15–24. ACM, New York (2016). https://doi.org/10.1145/2883851.2883950

23. Lipman, M.: Thinking in Education. Cambridge University Press, Cambridge (1991)

24. Manning, C.D., Schütze, H.: Foundations of Statistical Natural Language Processing, vol. 999. MIT Press, Cambridge (1999)

25. Nash, P., Shaffer, D.W.: Mentor modeling: the internalization of modeled professional thinking in an epistemic game. J. Comput. Assist. Learn. **27**(2), 173–189 (2011). https://doi.org/10.1111/j.1365-2729.2010.00385.x

26. Ramage, D., Rosen, E., Chuang, J., Manning, C.D., McFarland, D.A.: Topic modeling for the social sciences. In: NIPS 2009 Workshop on Applications for Topic Models: Text and Beyond, Whistler, Canada (2009)

27. Reich, J., Tingley, D., Leder-Luis, J., Roberts, M.E., Stewart, B.: Computer-assisted reading and discovery for student generated text in massive open online courses. J. Learn. Analytics **2**(1), 156–184 (2014). http://epress.lib.uts.edu.au/journals/index.php/JLA/article/view/4138

28. Rourke, L., Anderson, T., Garrison, D.R., Archer, W.: Assessing social presence in asynchronous text-based computer conferencing. J. Distance Educ. **14**(2), 50–71 (1999). http://www.ijede.ca/index.php/jde/article/view/153

29. Shaffer, D.W.: Epistemic frames for epistemic games. Comput. Educ. **46**(3), 223–234 (2006). https://doi.org/10.1016/j.compedu.2005.11.003

30. Shaffer, D.W.: Epistemic frames and islands of expertise: learning from infusion experiences. In: Proceedings of the 6th International Conference on Learning Sciences, ICLS 2004, pp. 473–480. International Society of the Learning Sciences, Santa Monica (2004). http://dl.acm.org/citation.cfm?id=1149126.1149184

31. Shaffer, D.W., Collier, W., Ruis, A.R.: A tutorial on epistemic network analysis: analyzing the structure of connections in cognitive, social, and interaction data. J. Learn. Analytics **3**(3), 9–45 (2016). https://doi.org/10.18608/jla.2016.33.3

32. Shaffer, D.W., Hatfield, D., Svarovsky, G.N., Nash, P., Nulty, A., Bagley, E., Frank, K., Rupp, A.A., Mislevy, R.: Epistemic network analysis: a prototype for 21st-century assessment of learning. Int. J. Learn. Media **1**(2), 33–53 (2009). https://doi.org/10.1162/ijlm.2009.0013

33. Stahl, G., Koschmann, T., Suthers, D., Sawyer, R.K.: Computer-supported collaborative learning: a historical perspective. In: The Cambridge Handbook of the Learning Sciences, pp. 409–426. Cambridge University Press, Cambridge, New York (2006)

34. Wallach, H.M.: Topic modeling: beyond bag-of-words. In: Proceedings of the 23rd International Conference on Machine Learning, ICML 2006, pp. 977–984. ACM, New York (2006). https://doi.org/10.1145/1143844.1143967

35. Waters, Z., Kovanović, V., Kitto, K., Gašević, D.: Structure matters: adoption of structured classification approach in the context of cognitive presence classification. In: Zuccon, G., Geva, S., Joho, H., Scholer, F., Sun, A., Zhang, P. (eds.) AIRS 2015. LNCS, vol. 9460, pp. 227–238. Springer, Cham (2015). https://doi.org/10.1007/978-3-319-28940-3_18

36. Winne, P.H., Hadwin, A.F.: Studying as self-regulated learning. In: Hacker, D.J., Dunlosky, J., Graesser, A.C. (eds.) Metacognition in educational theory and practice. The Educational Psychology Series, pp. 277–304. Lawrence Erlbaum Associates Publishers, Mahwah (1998)

37. Yang, D., Wen, M., Rose, C.: Towards identifying the resolvability of threads in MOOCs. In: Proceedings of the 2014 Conference on Empirical Methods in Natural Language Processing (EMNLP), pp. 21–31 (2014). http://www.aclweb.org/anthology/W/W14/W14-41.pdf#page=28

How Should Knowledge Composed of Schemas be Represented in Order to Optimize Student Model Accuracy?

Sachin Grover[(✉)], Jon Wetzel, and Kurt VanLehn

Arizona State University, Tempe, AZ, USA
{sachin.grover,jwetzel4,kurt.vanlehn}@asu.edu

Abstract. Most approaches to student modeling assume that students' knowledge can be represented by a large set of knowledge components that are learned independently. Knowledge components typically represent fairly small pieces of knowledge. This seems to conflict with the literature on problem solving which suggests that expert knowledge is composed of large schemas. This study compared several domain models for knowledge that is arguably composed of schemas. The knowledge is used by students to construct system dynamics models with the Dragoon intelligent tutoring system. An evaluation with 52 students showed that a relative simple domain model, that assigned one KC to each schema and schema combination, sufficed and was more parsimonious than other domain models with similarly accurate predictions.

1 Introduction

In a recent review of the student modeling literature, Pelánek [21], pointed out that there are two major problems addressed by the field. One is to estimate a student's mastery of a set of knowledge components (KCs) given the student's performance on a set of items and a Q-matrix. The Q-matrix maps items to the knowledge components involved in responding correctly to the item. In one common formulation, the rows of the Q-matrix correspond to items, the columns correspond to KCs, and there is a 1 in a cell if that KC is involved in generating a correct response to that item. The Q-matrix is determined by the task domain alone. It is not a function of a student's knowledge or behavior.

The second problem addressed in the student modeling literature, and in this paper, is referred to as *domain modeling* by Pelánek [21]. An algorithm is given a large set of student responses to items, and it defines KCs, finds a Q-matrix and estimates the mastery for each student of each KC. Although there are methods for solving the domain modeling problem when posed in this fashion [1,8], the resulting KCs are hard to interpret. The only information about them is the Q-matrix. This makes it difficult to use the resulting profile of student mastery to guide instructional decision making.

© Springer International Publishing AG, part of Springer Nature 2018
C. Penstein Rosé et al. (Eds.): AIED 2018, LNAI 10947, pp. 127–139, 2018.
https://doi.org/10.1007/978-3-319-93843-1_10

Thus, the more common version of the domain modeling problem assumes that an expert defines both the KCs and the initial version of the Q-matrix, and then student response data are used to improve the Q-matrix. This has the advantage that the set of KCs is not changed, so it is as interpretable and useful for decision-making as the expert can make them. Several methods have been developed to solve this version of the domain modeling problem [5–8,18].

Yet another version of the domain modeling problem is to manipulate the granularity of the KCs. One starts with an initial set of KCs, then either combines KCs to form large grained KCs, or splits KCs to form finer-grained KCs [2]. Other contributions to the study of KC granularity have compared several different domain models that differ in the granularity of their KCs [10,16].

All these domain modeling approaches make a convenient assumption: When students practice an item involving a certain set of KCs, only the KCs associated with that item (i.e., the 1's in that step's row of the Q-matrix) are affected by the practice. All other KCs maintain their same probability of mastery. Let us call this the KC independence assumption.

This KC independence assumption colors our way of thinking about learning. For example, when trying to see how competence grows, we can graph the probability of mastery of a KC over time. This is called a learning curve. The KC independence assumption means that the time-axis of the learning curve only needs to have the steps where that KC was involved. By assumption, its probability of mastery cannot change during other steps, so they can be left off the time-axis.

The KC independence assumption would seem natural to behaviorist who view all "knowledge" as a stimulus-response rules; each such rule is a KC. It would also seem appropriate to early information-processing psychologists who viewed all knowledge as production rules; each production is a KC. Information-processing psychologists who viewed knowledge as semantic nets could assume that most types of links in the network were KCs.

However, cognitive psychology today recognizes that people organize much of their knowledge into larger structures, often called schemas, scripts or frames. The key idea of such larger structures is that they are activated all at once. Thus, for instance, when students were read an algebra word problem slowly, as soon as they heard "A river boat is traveling upstream at 5 mph..." they activated an algebraic word-problem schema that not only contained the key equations but could even predict what the rest of the problem would say [19]. Similarly, when you hear a story that begins, "Roger asked the maître-de for a table near the window..." then you'll activate your restaurant schema, which predicts events such as ordering food and objects such as waiters and the bill.

After some rocky initial controversies, AI now accepts that schemas can be represented as production systems or semantic nets. For example, one can represent the river-current schema by using two kinds of productions: Some fire when a schema should be activated and dump an element such as "river-current-schema" into working memory. Other productions match that working memory element and dump a plan or other information into working memory that tell the agent how to enact the schema. It may take dozens or hundreds of production rules to represent a single schema. Similarly, it make take dozens of hundreds of semantic network links to represent a single schema.

Although schemas are activated all at once, they might be too big and complex to be learned all at once. Thus, it might be inaccurate to treat each schema as a KC. If we want to use a domain model based on a Q-matrix, then perhaps we need to decompose schemas into pieces such at that each piece can be learned independently of the others.

This particular problem hasn't been addressed in the student modeling literature [20, 21, 23, 24]). Nonetheless, we had to face it when trying to develop a student model for the Dragoon intelligent tutoring system [14, 27–29]. We evaluated several different mappings of KCs to schemas. Like most explorations of domain models, our evaluation was based on the fit of the model to student data. We describe first Dragoon, then its schemas, then the domain models and finally the evaluation and its results.

2 Dragoon

Dragoon is a step-based tutoring system for teaching students how to construct mathematical models of systems that change over time. Although such models are often represented with differential equations, Dragoon use a node-link representation that was pioneered by Stella [9, 22]. Figure 1 (which appears later), shows a screen capture of a simple problem and its model.

Dragoon has three types of quantities: parameter, accumulator and function. A parameter (diamond shaped node) is a quantity whose value is given as part of the problem statement and its value does not change over time. The other two types of quantities have values that can vary over time. Time is discrete. If a quantity is an accumulator (square shaped node), then its value at the next time is its value at this time plus the sum of its inputs. That is, it accumulates its inputs (which may be negative, so its value can go down). A function (circular node) is just a mathematical function of its inputs.

Students construct a model by adding nodes, one at a time, to a canvas. To define a node, they fill out a form. The form allows the user to specify properties of the node. Besides the name of the node, there are five properties:

- Description: A phrase describing the quantity
- Type: Either parameter, accumulator or function.
- Value: Parameter nodes have a numeric value. Accumulator nodes have an initial value. Function nodes do not have a value.
- Units: Some quantities have units, such as meters or kg.
- Expression: Function nodes have an algebraic expression for calculating their value. Accumulator nodes have an algebraic expression for calculating the increment to their value. Parameter nodes do not have an expression.

Students must type or click in the Expression. The other property values are selected from menus. Specifying one of these properties is the smallest unit of user interface behavior that can be interpret as contributing to the solving of the problem. Thus, specifying a property is a step. As usual when dealing with multi-step problems, the Q-matrix maps KCs to step instead of items. This is a name change only. Just like items on a test, the student's responses to steps are assumed to be conditionally independent given the student's mastery of knowledge. From now on, we will refer only to steps instead of items.

Like many step-based tutoring systems, Dragoon colors a step green if the student enters a correct response and red if the entry is incorrect. If the student fails several times, Dragoon fills in the step correctly and colors it yellow. It has other features as well, but they are not relevant to this paper.

This section has introduced the syntax of the Dragoon notation for models. The concepts of node type (parameter, accumulator and function) and node properties (name, description, type, value, units and expression) will be important later, when we describe how to define domain models.

3   Schemas

In mathematics, electronics, physics, computer programming and many other task domains, there is evidence that experts and competent novices know many schemas [25, 26]. For instance, when physicists notice that an object is flying through the air and that air friction can be ignored, they know its trajectory is a parabola, and they know equations for its horizontal and vertical positions over time. When programmers need to count something, then they know to define a variable, initialize it to zero, and increment it for each item counted.

Schemas have been extensively investigated for arithmetic and algebra word problems. For instance, Mayer [17] found that a mere 90 schemas sufficed to solve almost all the algebra word problems in 10 algebra textbooks. Author's in [4] provide a list and brief review of hundreds of relevant studies. Constructing a Dragoon model when given a succinct description of a system, such as the text shown in Fig. 1, is nearly the same as solving a mathematical word problem. In both cases, one must understand the text and generate a mathematical model of the system described by the text. Thus, we assume that a Dragoon student's knowledge can be represented as schemas. Each schema has a part that matches the system description and a template that generates the model. The template consists of a set of nodes, but the properties of the nodes have only been partially filled in or constrained. Typically, the type and expression properties of the template nodes have been filled in, but the other properties have not. To apply a mentally held schema, the student notices that it can be applied, enters the appropriate nodes into Dragoon, and then fills in the missing information.

Although earlier studies with Dragoon used a variety of schemas, the study described here uses only three: linear, exponential and acceleration. These schemas are explicitly taught in system dynamics courses.

For example, the model shown in Fig. 1 is an instance of the exponential schema. The only difference between the schema and the model of Fig. 1 is that the model has specific information from the problem entered into the name, description, unit and value properties. A linear schema has only an accumulator node and a parameter node, because the accumulator's value changes by a constant amount with each time step.

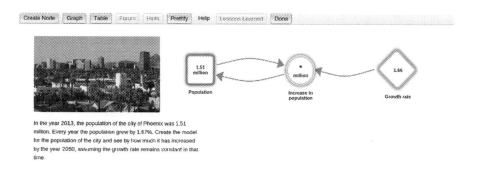

Fig. 1. Completed model in Dragoon showing *Exponential* schema for population growth

3.1 Representing Schema Mastery with KCs

Our domain models are all based on Bayesian Knowledge Tracing (BKT). We use the original [3] version, were every KC has four parameters: slip, guess, learning rate and initial mastery. Forget is always set to 0.

Our first domain model, assumes that each schema corresponds to a KC for BKT. That is, to model a student, we could use just one number per schema, and that is the probability that the student has mastered the schema. For example, when the student creates the model shown in Fig. 1, the student must fill in 5 properties for the "Population" node, 4 properties for the "Increase in population" node, and 4 properties for the "Growth rate" ode. That is, there are 13 steps in solving this problem. If we assume that each schema is a KC, then all 13 steps are mapped by the Q-matrix to the same KC, named Exponential. Let us call this the schema-only domain model.

However, we have observed informally that students find accumulator nodes to be quite confusing. On the other hand, parameter nodes seem more easily understood than the other node types. This suggests that we assigned different KCs to the different nodes of the schema's template. By having different KCs for the same schema, we can assume that the BKT parameters are different. For example, the exponential schema would be represented with three KC: Exponential_accumulator, Exponential_function and Exponential_parameter. Now we can express the conjecture mentioned earlier because the learning rate parameter for Exponential_parameter could be larger than the learning rate parameter for Exponential_accumulator. With the schema-only domain model, there is only one learning rate parameter for the whole schema. In our example of a student creating the model of Fig. 1, the Q-matrix would map the 5 steps for defining the "Population" node to the Exponential_accumulator KC. It would map the 4 steps for defining the "Increase in population" to the Exponential_function KC, and it would map the 4 steps for defining the "Growth rate" node to the Exponential_parameter KC. Let us call this the schema-type domain model.

The main goal of this study presented later is to determine which of these two domain models provides a more accurate assessment of students' learning. However, there is a complexity that needs to be discussed first.

3.2   Representing Compound Schemas

Some problems require applying more than one schema, and in most cases, the schema applications are linked by a shared node. Figure 2 is an example. It shows the solution to this problem:

A bus fleet starts with 105 operational buses. Technicians can repair only 6 buses a week, but 9% of the bus fleet fails each week. Graph the number of bus in service each week for 100 weeks.

The "6 buses per week" part of the problem matches a linear schema. The "9% of the buses fail each week" matches the exponential schema. They share the quantity "number of buses in service" since both schemas affect it. Studies suggest that students have extra trouble when combining schemas to solve a problem. In particular, they can solve single-schema problems with high reliability, thus indicating mastery of the schemas, but fail miserably at solving a problem that combines the two schemas [13,15]. This suggests that more KCs are needed than those mentioned so far.

Several researchers have suggested that there is no generic skill for combining schemas, but instead students learn compound schemas [26]. A compound schema is itself a schema, but it is larger. For instance, a single compound schema would match the bus fleet problem of Fig. 2. However, this solutions doesn't make sense for Dragoon. A student who has already mastered the linear and exponential schemas can easily construct three of the nodes in Fig. 2; it is only the shared node, "bus fleet," that will cause them trouble. To put it differently, if we were using the schema-only domain model and we assigned all the steps of Fig. 2 to the compound schema – let's call it exponential_linear – then the domain model would predict that students would make lots of errors on the nodes that are not shared. This seems unlikely to us.

Our solution is to map only the shared nodes to the KC representing the compound schema. Table 1 shows how the Q-matrix maps KCs to the steps required for constructing the model of Fig. 2. It shows both domain models. Notice that only the accumulator, "Bus fleet," is mapped to the KCs representing the compound schema. The Q-matrix maps the other nodes to the same KCs as the single-schema problems.

3.3   Representing Node Properties

The format of a step can make a big difference to the guess and slip parameters of BKT. For instance, if a step is a menu that has only 3 items, and the student has not mastered the knowledge involved in answering that step, then the chance of a guessing correctly is probably about 1/3. If the step requires typing in an algebraic formula, then the chance of a lucky guess is quite low, and the chance of a slip is quite high. Thus, the format of steps affects the guess and slip parameters of BKT.

As mentioned earlier, when defining a node, the student must enter five properties: its description, type, value, units and expression. The expression is an algebraic expression that is typed or clicked in, but the others are entered by selecting from a menu. With both domain models, schema-only and schema-type, there is a single guess and slip parameter for all 5 properties. This is not likely to yield accurate predictions of error rates given the disparity in step formats.

Table 1. KCs associated with steps of nodes in Fig. 2.

Node	Schema-only domain model	Schema-type domain model
Buses fixed each week	Linear	Linear_parameter
Bus fleet	Exponential_linear	Exponential_linear_accumulator
Buses failing each week	Exponential	Exponential_function
Proportion of buses that fail	Exponential	Exponential_parameter

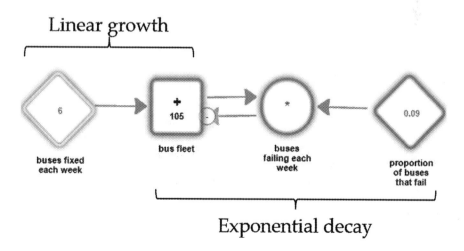

Fig. 2. Schema overlap for a node in Dragoon problem - *Bus Fleet*

One possible solution is to decompose the KCs, reducing their granularity even further. Thus, we would replace, say, linear_accumulator with 5 KCs, such as linear_accumulator_units, which would represent mastery of entering the units property of the accumulator node of a linear schema. Unfortunately, this may make the KCs overly independent. It predicts, for example, that someone could master linear_accumulator_value but have low mastery of linear_accumulator_units. This seems unlikely.

A better solution is to use a combination of BKT with logistic modeling. The basic ideas is to use functions to replace the slip and guess parameters, which in standard BKT have constant values per KC. Each function outputs a value between 0 and 1, which is the range of the slip and guess parameters. The input to the functions are details about the steps, such as whether the step is a menu or a type-in box. If it is a menu, the number of menu items could also be an input to the function. This would allow the functions to compute more values for the chances of a guess or a slip that are sensitive to the details of the step and thus likely to be more accurate than constant values. Logistic regression equations are often used for this purpose. They combine the inputs with a polynomial, then use a logistic function to compress the value of the polynomial, which can be any real number, into the 0.0 to 1.0 interval. They are called regression equations because calibration methods use regression to find values for the coefficients of the polynomial.

All logistic regressions have a constant term as well as one term for each input. The constant term is used to represent the dependence among details, such as the properties. For example, consider a logistic regression for the slip parameter of the linear_accumulator KC. Suppose we want it to be sensitive to the properties of steps. Since there are 5 properties, the polynomial part of the equations would be:

$$C_0 + C_1 * Descr + C_2 * Type + C_3 * Value + C_4 * Unit + C_5 * Expr \qquad (1)$$

The inputs are the variables $Desc$, $Type$, $Value$, $Unit$ and $Expr$. If the step is selecting from the description menu, then $Descr = 1$ and the others are 0, so the value for the slip parameter is the logistic function of $C_0 + C_1$. Similarly, if the step is typing in an algebraic expression, then $Expr = 1$ and the others are zero, so the value for the slip parameter is the logistic function of $C_0 + C_5$. Thus, the constant C_0 represents the portion of the slip parameter that is intrinsic to this KC, linear_accumulator, and the other coefficients represent the portions of the slip parameter that depend on the format/property of the step.

This version of BKT is called FAST [12]. Although it allows a domain model where every BKT parameter is replaced by a logistic regression equation, González-Brenes and other researchers found that replacing just the slip and guess parameters gives the best performance. We tried several ways of using FAST, and we too found that replacing only the slip and guess parameters gave the best performance. Our domain models thus assume that the other two BKT parameters, initial mastery and learning rate, are constants.

We also tried all logical combination of inputs to the regression equation. Thus, we ended up with 6 domain models, shown in Table 2. The first column shows the two KC models discussed earlier, schema-only and schema-type. It also includes a simple KC model, which assumes that the domain has just 3 KCs, one for accumulators, one for functions and one for parameters. It serves as a baseline; all the schema-based domain models should fit better, if the schema idea has merit. The second column indicates what kinds of terms, if any, are included in the polynomial part of the logistic regression equations for slip and guess. If the column says "none" then the slip and guess parameters are constants, as in the standard BKT domain models. Otherwise, it lists the way steps are represented to the polynomial. The Parameters column lists the number of parameters in the domain model. The AUC columns present results from fitting these domain models to data from a study, which is described next.

Table 2. Domain models and their fit to the data. AUC is the mean over ten datasets with the standard error value.

Serial number	KC model	Polynomial terms	Parameters	AUC
1	Node-type	Node properties	25	0.805 ± 0.01
2	Schema-type	Node types	47	0.699 ± 0.006
3	Schema-type	Node properties	87	0.826 ± 0.0041
4	Schema-only	Node types	44	0.685 ± 0.012
5	Schema-only	Node properties	64	0.826 ± 0.0053
6	Schema-only	Node types & properties	108	0.833 ± 0.035

4   Evaluation: The Study

We conducted a study to gather data that could be used to test which of the domain models fit best. The study simply had students solve Dragoon problems while log data were collected. We were only interested in how competence increased due to learning the two schemas that were taught, linear and exponential. Thus, we wrote problems that avoided or equated many known sources of difficulty with word problems [4]:

- The problems did not contain clue words, such as linear and exponential.
- The problems did not contain extraneous, irrelevant quantities.
- All problems contained about the same amount of imagery and details. The problem of Fig. 1 is typical.
- The problems all contained moderately complicated numbers. They avoided simple numbers such as small whole numbers and they avoided complicated numbers, such as 0.0021379.

Participants: Participants were a mix of undergraduate and graduate students with at least high school algebra mathematics background. They were not asked about their background in modeling dynamic systems, as we have found in previous studies that very few students know anything about dynamic systems. 52 students took part in the study.

Procedure: Students came to our lab for one session where they finished 14 Dragoon problems. There was no upper limit to the time it would take. On average, students completed the problems in 2 h 11 min. Students were compensated with money.

Materials: Two online workbooks were created to teach dynamic system modeling to students. The first workbook introduced Dragoon's interface to students along with a few basic concepts about modeling. There were three Dragoon problems in this workbook, with some multiple choice questions as well. The second workbook introduced students to the concept of schemas and then gave students 10 Dragoon problems to solve. The order of the first 7 problems was random. By randomly ordering the problems, we avoided a known problem with embedded assessments: competence is hard to detect when problems increase in difficulty [12]. The last 3 problems were always given in a fixed order and were quite difficult. This allowed us to compare the predictions of the models across students. Two of the problems included a novel schema, acceleration, which had not been taught to students.

4.1 Results

As stated earlier, two different kinds of models were fit and parameters were learned using FAST algorithm [11]. Data were fit using 5 fold cross validation (with 42 students for training and 10 students for test data) and results are presented as an average of the folds. Table 2 shows the average AUC values achieved for the test data. A higher value means a better fit.

5   Discussion

There is a clear pattern in Table 2, which is that a good fit requires that the node property be a part of the model. This makes sense, given that slip and guess are likely to be much different for menus than for typing in an algebraic expression. If that difference is ignored by the domain model, then the AUC is less than 0.7. If that difference is included in the domain model, then the AUC is around 0.8. In retrospect, this is a rather obvious finding. However, it does not seem to have been quantified in the literature before.

One of our main goals was to compare the fits of the schema-only domain model and the schema-type domain model. Table 2 shows that as long as the domain model include node properties, then the fits are very close. The best schema-type model had an AUC of 0.819 and the best schema-only model had an AUC of 0.833. Such close fits are common in educational data mining. If taken at face value, they say that the schema-only model is better than the schema-type model.

Among the 4 domain models that include node properties, the three that include schemas (models 3, 5 and 6) have higher AUCs than the AUC of the first domain model, which ignores schemas entirely. This vindicates including schemas in the domain model.

Now we are down to considering just three domain models (3, 5 and 6). They all have about the same prediction accuracy (AUC). However, model 5 (schema-only with a linear regression that includes node properties) has the fewest parameters. Thus, parsimony suggests it is the best model for these data.

This ambiguity points to a familiar problem: there may have been too little data to distinguish the models empirically. Even though the students generated 9336 steps, our schema-based domain models had over many parameters.

Moreover, the problems may have been too easy. Overall, students responded correctly on their first attempt to 85% of the steps. Even on steps in the problems involving the acceleration schema, which was not taught explicitly, students averaged 77% correct on their first attempt.

Nonetheless, if we take the results at face value, then a rather simple domain model emerges as the best fit to the data: Assign one KC to each schema; Assign one KC to each nodes shared by two schemas, and include node properties in the logistic regression equations for slip and guess.

Somewhat ironically, it appears that not only are schemas activated all at once, perhaps (again, taking the result at face value) these schemas are also learned all at once. Or at least, assigning one KC per schema is a good approximation for student modeling purposes.

Acknowledgments. This research was supported by NSF IIS-1628782, NSF IIS-1123823, ONR N00014-13-C-0029, ONR N00014-12-C-0643 and US Army, W911NF-04-D-0005, Delivery Order No. 0041.

References

1. Barnes, T., Stamper, J., Madhyastha, T.: Comparative analysis of concept derivation using the q-matrix method and facets. In: Workshop at Educational Data Mining at AAAI 2006, pp. 21–30 (2006)
2. Cen, H., Koedinger, K., Junker, B.: Learning factors analysis – a general method for cognitive model evaluation and improvement. In: Ikeda, M., Ashley, K.D., Chan, T.-W. (eds.) ITS 2006. LNCS, vol. 4053, pp. 164–175. Springer, Heidelberg (2006). https://doi.org/10.1007/11774303_17
3. Corbett, A.T., Anderson, J.R.: Knowledge tracing: modeling the acquisition of procedural knowledge. User Model. User-Adap. Inter. **4**(4), 253–278 (1994)
4. Daroczy, G., Wolska, M., Meurers, W.D., Nuerk, H.C.: Word problems: a review of linguistic and numerical factors contributing to their difficulty. Front. Psychol. **6**, 348 (2015)
5. De La Torre, J.: An empirically based method of Q-matrix validation for the dina model: development and applications. J. Educ. Meas. **45**(4), 343–362 (2008)
6. DeCarlo, L.T.: Recognizing uncertainty in the q-matrix via a bayesian extension of the dina model. Appl. Psychol. Meas. **36**(6), 447–468 (2012)
7. Desmarais, M., Beheshti, B., Xu, P.: The refinement of a q-matrix: assessing methods to validate tasks to skills mapping. In: Educational Data Mining 2014 (2014)
8. Desmarais, M.C., Naceur, R.: A matrix factorization method for mapping items to skills and for enhancing expert-based Q-matrices. In: Lane, H.C., Yacef, K., Mostow, J., Pavlik, P. (eds.) AIED 2013. LNCS (LNAI), vol. 7926, pp. 441–450. Springer, Heidelberg (2013). https://doi.org/10.1007/978-3-642-39112-5_45

9. Doerr, H.M.: Stella ten years later: a review of the literature. Int. J. Comput. Math. Learn. **1**(2), 201–224 (1996)
10. Feng, M., Heffernan, N., Mani, M., Heffernan, C.: Using mixed-effects modeling to compare different grain-sized skill models. In: Educational Data Mining: Papers from the AAAI Workshop. AAAI Press, Menlo Park (2006)
11. Gonzalez-Brenes, J., Huang, Y.: Your model is predictive-but is it useful? Theoretical and empirical considerations of a new paradigm for adaptive tutoring evaluation. In: Proceedings of the 8th International Conference on Educational Data Mining. University of Pittsburgh (2015)
12. González-Brenes, J., Huang, Y., Brusilovsky, P.: General features in knowledge tracing to model multiple subskills, temporal item response theory, and expert knowledge. In: The 7th International Conference on Educational Data Mining, pp. 84–91. University of Pittsburgh (2014)
13. Heffernan, N.T., Koedinger, K.R.: The composition effect in symbolizing: the role of symbol production vs. text comprehension. In: Proceedings of the Nineteenth Annual Conference of the Cognitive Science Society, pp. 307–312 (1997)
14. Iwaniec, D.M., Childers, D.L., VanLehn, K., Wiek, A.: Studying, teaching and applying sustainability visions using systems modeling. Sustainability **6**(7), 4452–4469 (2014)
15. Koedinger, K.R., Nathan, M.J.: The real story behind story problems: effects of representations on quantitative reasoning. J. Learn. Sci. **13**(2), 129–164 (2004)
16. Koedinger, K.R., Yudelson, M.V., Pavlik, P.I.: Testing theories of transfer using error rate learning curves. Topics Cogn. Sci. **8**(3), 589–609 (2016)
17. Mayer, R.E.: Frequency norms and structural analysis of algebra story problems into families, categories, and templates. Instr. Sci. **10**(2), 135–175 (1981)
18. Nižnan, J., Pelánek, R., Řihák, J.: Mapping problems to skills combining expert opinion and student data. In: Hliněný, P., Dvořák, Z., Jaroš, J., Kofroň, J., Kořenek, J., Matula, P., Pala, K. (eds.) MEMICS 2014. LNCS, vol. 8934, pp. 113–124. Springer, Cham (2014). https://doi.org/10.1007/978-3-319-14896-0_10
19. Paige, J.M.: Cognitive processes in solving algebra word problems. Problem solving (1966)
20. Pavlik Jr., P.I., Brawner, K., Olney, A., Mitrovic, A.: A review of student models used in intelligent tutoring systems. In: Design Recommendations for Intelligent Tutoring Systems, pp. 39–68 (2013)
21. Pelánek, R.: Bayesian knowledge tracing, logistic models, and beyond: an overview of learner modeling techniques. User Model. User-Adap. Inter. **27**(3–5), 313–350 (2017)
22. Richmond, B.: STELLA: software for bringing system dynamics to the other 98%. In: Proceedings of the 1985 International Conference of the System Dynamics Society: 1985 International System Dynamics Conference, pp. 706–718 (1985)
23. Shute, V.J., Kim, Y.J.: Formative and stealth assessment. In: Spector, J., Merrill, M., Elen, J., Bishop, M. (eds.) Handbook of Research on Educational Communications and Technology, pp. 311–321. Springer, New York (2014). https://doi.org/10.1007/978-1-4614-3185-5_25
24. VanLehn, K.: Student modeling. In: Polson, M., Richardson, J. (eds.) Foundations of Intelligent Tutoring Systems, vol. 55, p. 78. Erlbaum, Hillsade (1988)
25. VanLehn, K.: Problem solving and cognitive skill acquisition. In: Foundations of Cognitive Science, pp. 527–579. MIT Press (1989)
26. VanLehn, K.: Cognitive skill acquisition. In: Spence, J.T. (ed.) Annual Review of Psychology, vol. 47, pp. 513–539. Annual Reviews Inc. (1996)

27. VanLehn, K., Chung, G., Grover, S., Madni, A., Wetzel, J.: Learning science by constructing models: can dragoon increase learning without increasing the time required? Int. J. Artif. Intell. Educ. **26**(4), 1033–1068 (2016)
28. VanLehn, K., Wetzel, J., Grover, S., van de Sande, B.: Learning how to construct models of dynamic systems: an initial evaluation of the dragoon intelligent tutoring system. IEEE Trans. Learn. Technol. (2017)
29. Wetzel, J., VanLehn, K., Butler, D., Chaudhari, P., Desai, A., Feng, J., Grover, S., Joiner, R., Kong-Sivert, M., Patade, V., et al.: The design and development of the dragoon intelligent tutoring system for model construction: lessons learned. Interact. Learn. Environ. **25**(3), 361–381 (2017)

Active Learning for Improving Machine Learning of Student Explanatory Essays

Peter Hastings[1(✉)], Simon Hughes[1], and M. Anne Britt[2]

[1] School of Computing, DePaul University, Chicago, IL, USA
peterh@cdm.depaul.edu
[2] Psychology Department, Northern Illinois University, DeKalb, IL, USA

Abstract. There is an increasing emphasis, especially in STEM areas, on students' abilities to create explanatory descriptions. Holistic, over-all evaluations of explanations can be performed relatively easily with shallow language processing by humans or computers. However, this pro-vides little information about an essential element of explanation quality: the structure of the explanation, i.e., how it connects causes to effects. The difficulty of providing feedback on explanation structure can lead teachers to either avoid giving this type of assignment or to provide only shallow feedback on them. Using machine learning techniques, we have developed successful computational models for analyzing explana-tory essays. A major cost of developing such models is the time and effort required for human annotation of the essays. As part of a large project studying students' reading processes, we have collected a large number of explanatory essays and thoroughly annotated them. Then we used the annotated essays to train our machine learning models. In this paper, we focus on how to get the best payoff from the expensive annotation process within such an educational context and we evaluate a method called Active Learning.

1 Introduction

There is an increasing emphasis at the educational policy level on improving students' abilities to analyze and create explanations, especially in STEM fields [1,2]. This puts pressure on teachers to create assignments that help students learn these skills. On such assignments, teachers could provide several different kinds of feedback, including identification of spelling and grammatical mistakes, overall holistic evaluations of explanation quality, and detailed analyses of the structure of the explanation — what parts of a good explanation were present and how they were connected together, and what parts were missing. It is much

The assessment project described in this article was funded, in part, by the Institute for Education Sciences, U.S. Department of Education (Grant R305G050091 and Grant R305F100007). The opinions expressed are those of the authors and do not represent views of the Institute or the U.S. Department of Education.

easier for teachers (and computers using shallow processing techniques) to provide the first two types of feedback [3]. Deep analysis of explanation structure is much more challenging, but it is necessary for helping students truly improve the quality of their explanations. Holistic and shallow evaluations may help students fix local problems in their explanations, but they do not help students create better chains from causes to effects that are the core of good explanations.

An AI system for analyzing the structure of explanations could be used in a variety of ways: as the back-end of an intelligent tutoring system that would help students write better arguments, as an evaluation system to provide formative assessment to teachers on their students' work, or as the basis of deeper summative assessments of the writing [3].

In educational contexts, as in many others, there is growing availability of large amounts of data. That data can be leveraged by increasingly sophisticated machine learning techniques to evaluate and classify similar data. The bottleneck in many such situations is that most machine learning techniques require a significant amount of labeled data — i.e., data that has been annotated by human coders at high cost of time and money — in order to be effective. A large number of texts may be collected, but what is the best strategy for annotating enough of those texts to produce an automated system that can effectively analyze the rest? That is the research question that we address in this paper.

For several years, we have been working as part of a project aimed at studying students' *reading* processes. To assess how much students understand from what they have read, we collected over 1000 explanatory essays dealing with a scientific phenomenon. Over the course of six months, expert annotators identified the locations of conceptual information and causal statements in these essays. This has provided us with an excellent data set on which to evaluate our research question about how to get the necessary sample size of annotated data for adequate performance; we simply assume that most of the data is unlabeled and try to identify methods that allow machine learning to most quickly create a model that will accurately classify the rest.

This paper focuses on one method called Active Learning in which you start with a small set of labeled data for training. Based on the uncertainty of classification of the rest of the data, you select another batch of data to be labeled, and continue this process until acceptable performance is achieved. The paper describes the specifics of the educational context that our data came from and how the essays were collected and annotated. Then we describe related research and the experiments we performed. We conclude with a discussion of our experiments and results and implications for future research.

2   Student Explanatory Essays

The essays used in this research were scientific explanations generated by 9th grade biology students in 12 schools in a large urban area in the United States. During a 2-day, in-class activity, students were given 5 short documents that included descriptive texts (M = 250 words), images, and several graphs that the student could use to understand the causes of a scientific phenomenon, coral bleaching. Each document was a slightly modified excerpt from an educational website and was presented on a separate sheet with source information at the bottom of the text. In collaboration with our science educators, we co-created all materials and the idealized causal model, shown in Fig. 1, which depicts the ideal explanation that students could make from the documents. The students were told to read the documents and "explain what leads to differences in the rates of coral bleaching." They were told to use information from the texts and make connections clear. They were allowed to refer to the documents while writing their essays.

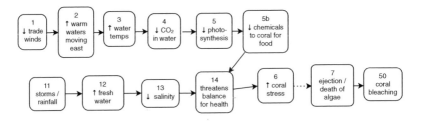

Fig. 1. Causal model for coral bleaching

As mentioned above, the primary goal of the larger research project was to study the students' reading and to try to learn how to help them read more deeply. In support of this goal, all of the essays were closely annotated to determine what the students did and did not include in their explanations. The brat [4,5] annotation tool was used for the annotation process. The mean length of the students' essays was 132 words (SD = 75). The mean number of unique concepts from Fig. 1 in the essays was 3.1 (SD = 2.2) and the mean number of causal connections was 1.3 (SD = 1.7). (See [6] for more details.)

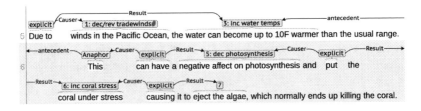

Fig. 2. Annotation with brat

Figure 2 shows two sentences of one (relatively good) student essay in brat, where an annotator has marked the locations of the concepts from Fig. 1 and the causal connections between them. In the first sentence, the annotator has identified a reference to concept code 1, *decreased trade winds*, and a reference to concept code 3, *increased water temperatures*. The annotator has also identified an explicit causal connection from code 1 to 3. The next sentence has an (anaphoric) causal connection from code 3 to code 5, and further connections to codes 6 and 7. Although brat significantly sped up the annotation, and although the essays were relatively short, it still took trained annotators 15–30 min to annotate each one — a significant manpower cost.

3   Related Research

Along with increased emphasis on standardized testing has come an increased emphasis on creating automatic mechanisms for evaluating written essays or responses. Although these Automatic Essay Scoring systems [7] are becoming increasingly sophisticated, they generally use shallow language analysis tools like lexical and syntactic features and semantic word sets [8,9] to provide a single holistic score for the essay rather than a detailed analysis of the contents of the essay [10]. The holistic-score approach has been criticized for its failure to identify critical aspects of student responses [11] and for its lack of content validity [9,12]. The appeal of the holistic-score approach is partly due to the tasks for which these systems are being used, but also due to the difficulty of performing a deeper analysis. Causal connections in text have been very difficult to identify, with two recent systems getting F_1 scores of 0.41 and 0.39 [13,14].

Our previous research has been more successful at identifying causal connections, producing F_1 scores of 0.73 [15]. We have some advantages however. We know what the students are basing their essays on: documents from a narrowly-defined topic. We also have a large amount of training data that we use to train classification models: 1128 annotated student essays. Recent refinements are producing even higher performance [16]. To identify concept codes, we use a window-based tagging approach, creating a separate classifier for each concept and for both causal connection types (*Causer* and *Result*) based on a sliding window of size 7 of unigrams and bigrams along with their relative positions in the window [15]. We use stacked learning [17] to identify specific causal connections from the results of the window-based tagging models. We view this level of performance as acceptable for the creation of formative feedback on the explanations. The point of this research, however, is to ascertain whether similar performance can be achieved using fewer annotated essays, and if so, what is the best method for choosing essays to annotate.

There has been a wide range of previous work aimed at reducing the amount of training data needed to produce an effective classification model. One approach was to ensure a broadly representative sampling of data, but it was found to be no better than random selection [18]. Other research has applied Active Learning (AL) to various tasks [19–21], but they have generally been concerned with predicting a single class for each instance, have often produced results not significantly better than random sampling [22], and there has been little focus on applying AL to text-based tasks [22], especially multi-class tasks like ours.

One exception [23] aimed to classify newswire articles into one of 10 different categories. In contrast to our situation, however, that was a whole-text task. We have a large set of conceptual and causal codes that we want to identify *within* the students' essays, from which we can infer the structure of their explanations.

The research reported in [24] did focus at a sub-document level, namely on temporal relations between two specified events within the text. In this case, the authors were attempting to identify which of 6 temporal relations (e.g., *Before*, *Simultaneous*) held between the two events. This was also applied to newswire texts, which tend to be longer and less error-ridden than student texts. They combined measures of uncertainty, representativeness of a new instance with previously classified instances, and diversity of the entire set to choose the next items to classify, with the first two having a larger effect than the third.

A related technique to AL is Co-training [25] which could further reduce the requirement for annotated data by applying the predictions of the current model to unlabeled data, then assuming that the instances about which the model was most certain were correctly classified, and adding some portion of those instances to the training set. It requires, however, that the model is trained with two sets of features which are conditionally independent of the target class, and performance can be degraded if the predictions were wrong.

4   Experiments

This section describes the method that we used to evaluate different variants of AL on the explanatory essays, including the overall algorithm that was used, the different selection strategies, the measures used to evaluate performance, and the two experiments that we ran.

4.1   Algorithm

Our dataset consisted of 1128 explanatory essays collected as described above. We used a variant of cross validation described below, 10-fold for the first experiment, and 5-fold for the rest:

1. Randomly select 10%[1] of the essays and put them in the initial training set, and put another 10% into the validation set.[2] The rest of the essays were put in the pool of "unlabeled" essays. (In our case, of course, these essays were actually labeled, but those labels were not used until the essays were selected for inclusion in the training set.)

---

[1] The percentages are all parameters to the model. These were selected because they allowed us to see the performance of the models at a reasonable granularity. It should be noted, however, that in our case, 10% of the total set represents over 100 additional essays. In real-world settings, a smaller increment would likely be used due to the cost of annotation.

[2] We used a validation or holdout set to provide a consistent basis on which to judge the performance of the models.

2. Repeat until 80% of the essays are in the training set (with 10% of the essays in the validation set and 10% in the remainder pool):

   (a) Train the model on the training set using Support Vector Machines (SVMs) [26, 27] to create a classifier for each concept code and each causal connection code. The features for the SVM came from the window-based tagging method described above. The 7-word window was dragged across all the texts. Each training instance consisted of the 7 unigrams and 6 bigrams along with their relative positions in the window. The target class was the code of the word in the middle of the window, and its annotation indicated if that instance was a positive or negative instance of the class.

   (b) For each line in each essay in the remainder pool, calculate the predicted confidence for each code. Because we used SVMs, the decision boundary was at 0, so a positive confidence value was a prediction that the code was present. Negative values were predictions that the code was not present. The higher the absolute value, the more confident the model was that the code was or was not there.

   (c) Calculate Recall $(= Hits/(Hits + Misses))$ and Precision $(= Hits/ (Hits + FalseAlarms))$ for each code at the sentence level in the validation set. (Codes rarely occur more than once per sentence.)

   (d) Sort all the essays in the remainder pool based on the average absolute confidence per sentence according to the selection strategy. Selection strategies are described below.

   (e) Move the next 10% of essays from the sorted remainder pool to the training set.

4.2   Instance Selection Strategies

In the AL literature, an Instance Selection Strategy refers to the technique for choosing the next item(s) to have labeled or annotated. Common strategies are based on the uncertainty of classifying the instances, the representativeness of the instances, "query-by-committee", and expected model change [19, 21]. Because our instances are complex, containing many different classes (i.e., the codes from the causal model), in this work we focused on the simplest type of strategy, *uncertainty sampling*.

Although the default approach for uncertainty sampling is to prefer to select the least certain items for labeling, researchers have also evaluated other variants of this [20]. We evaluated three: the default (i.e., *Closest to margin*, the least certain), the most certain (*Farthest from margin*), and interleaving certain and uncertain items. These were implemented by sorting the remaining essays in step (d) of the algorithm above based on this criterion. Specifically, because we used SVMs to classify the codes, and because their decision boundary (the threshold between positive and negative predictions) is 0, we took the absolute value of the confidence in the prediction (i.e., the distance from the SVM's marginal hyperplane), and averaged that over all the sentences in the essay. For the different strategies, we used the lowest average confidence, the highest average confidence, and interleaving of the two, respectively. We compared these methods with a control condition: randomly selecting the next items to be added to the training set.

For each of these (non-random) strategies, we also evaluated two different methods for aggregating the confidences for each sentence. In our first experiment, we simply added all of the scores for the 51 different codes that our models were predicting: 13 codes for concepts in the causal model, and 38 codes for the "legal" connections in the model (i.e., those that respected the direction of the arrows, but potentially skipped nodes, e.g., $1 \rightarrow 2$ and $1 \rightarrow 3$, but not $2 \rightarrow 1$). We called this the *Simple Sum* method. Because the causal connection codes are so much more numerous than the concept codes, we also evaluated an aggregation method, which we called the *Split Sum* method, that normalized the confidence scores by the two sets of codes. In other words, we added the confidence scores for all of the concept codes and divided that sum by 13, then added it to the sum of the causal codes divided by 38. The intuition behind using this approach was that we wanted to avoid biasing the selection decision too much toward the (numerous but relatively rare) causal connection codes.

4.3   Measures

As mentioned above in the section describing the algorithm, we calculated Recall and Precision for each concept code and causal connection code in the validation set. From these, we calculated two averaged F_1 scores that could be used to judge the overall performance of the model. F_1 is defined as:

$$\frac{2 * Precision * Recall}{Precision + Recall}$$

The two different ways of combining the F_1 scores for all the codes in the validation set are the mean F_1 and the micro-averaged F_1. The mean F_1 is simply the average across the F_1 scores for all of the 51 different codes. The micro-averaged F_1 is derived from the Precision and Recall from the whole validation set. In other words, the overall Precision and Recall are based on the *Hits*, *Misses*, and *FalseAlarms* from the whole validation set. As a result, micro-averaged F_1 scores are sensitive to the frequency of occurrence of the codes in the set, and mean F_1 scores are not. Micro-averaged scores are representative of how the model performs *in practice*. Mean F_1 scores give equal weighting to each code to take into account rare codes as much as it does frequent ones.[3] Averaging F_1 scores can be seen as a way of evaluating a learning method in an "ideal" situation, when all frequencies are balanced. Micro-averaging evaluates the model based on its overall performance on natural data with imbalanced code frequencies. Thus, it is useful to take both into account.

---

[3] For what it's worth, these are analogous to the U.S. House of Representatives and Senate, respectively, with one giving more weight to more "populous" (i.e., frequent) entities, and the other giving "equal representation" to each entity.

4.4   Experiment 1: Absolute Confidence Values

As mentioned above, in our first experiment, we combined the uncertainty (or confidence) values by adding all of the absolute values of the predicted confidences for the individual codes, averaged over the number of sentences in the essay. Figures 3 and 4 show the mean F_1 scores and micro-averaged F_1 scores respectively. Each chart shows the percentage of the essays that were in the training set at each iteration on the X axis, and the resulting F_1 score on the Y axis. Each line represents one of the different methods described in Sect. 4.2 for choosing which essays to "label" (move the annotated essay to the training set).

Note that each of the evaluations presented here ends with 80%, or about 900 essays included in the training set. One reason for this is that, at this point, the remaining essays are least typical of the selection method. For example, with the high-uncertainty selection strategy, there would only be the most certain instances remaining. The more significant reason is that in a real world situation where the cost of annotation is high, you would typically want to annotate a much smaller number of items. So data in the left sides of each of the charts are more applicable to practical scenarios.

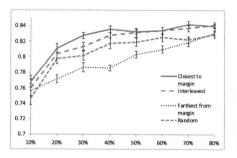

Fig. 3. Absolute mean F1s

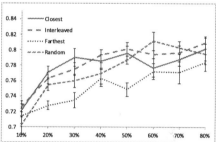

Fig. 4. Absolute micro-averaged F1s

For the mean F_1 scores, the default high-uncertainty/low-confidence/closest-to-marginal-hyperplane method always resulted in the best (or equivalent) scores on the validation set. In other words, one should choose the next set of essays to annotate by selecting those that the classifiers are least sure of. The clear "loser" was the farthest-from-marginal-hyperplane/highest-confidence method. Adding instances which the model was already predicting with high confidence resulted in much slower increase in classification performance.

For the micro-averaged F_1 scores, the results were more mixed. The closest-to-hyperplane method performed best initially, but its performance actually went down with 40% of the essays in the training set. At 60 and 70%, the best scores were produced by the random selection method. However, as mentioned above, results with lower percentages of items in the remainder pool are less indicative of what would be found in practical applications.

While this experiment gave interesting initial results, it also raised some questions. First, we noted that the scores on the randomly selected initial set (at 10%) were higher for the closest-to-hyperplane method, so we wondered what effect that might have on performance. Second, what could be the effect of the frequency of occurrence of the codes (classes) on the overall performance. The codes follow a Zipfian distribution. The most frequent code (50, which is the one the students are asked to explain) occurs in 55% (only!) of the essays. The subsequent frequencies are 12%, 4.7%, 4.2%, and so on. Forty of the 51 codes occur in less that 1% of the essays. While this is the "natural state of affairs" for this set of essays (and for many other natural multi-class situations), we hypothesized that this frequency imbalance would have a differential effect on the mean and micro-averaged F_1 scores. A model could achieve higher mean scores by performing relatively well on very infrequent codes and not so well on more frequent codes. With the micro-averaged scores, the same model would not perform as well. Because of this issue, we wanted to evaluate a method for combining the confidence scores which would take this frequency imbalance into account. We addressed these issues in Experiment 2.

4.5   Experiment 2: Performance Gain, Scaled Confidences

The first question resulting from Experiment 1 was: How does the performance of the initial training set affect increases in performance via AL. To address this question, we additionally calculated the simple performance gain for each method, which we defined as $F_{gain} = F_1@N\% - F_1@10\%$. In other words, we subtracted the method's initial absolute F_1 score from all the F_1 scores for that method. This allowed us to more easily compare performance because each one started at 0. Because the initial training sets were all chosen randomly without regard to the selection strategy, the initial absolute F_1 scores tended to be close anyway. In the results presented in the rest of this paper, we display the simple performance gain values. The initial *absolute* mean F_1 scores were all in the 0.62–0.64 range, and micro-averaged F_1 scores were between 0.70 and 0.73. These values are already relatively good for this complex task — i.e., they classify the components of the essays with sufficient certainty that beneficial feedback could be given, assuming the stakes were not too high, but the focus here is on how to improve the performance of the models most quickly.

The second question raised by Experiment 1 was about the effect of unbalanced frequencies of the codes, and we hypothesized that mean and micro-averaged F_1 scores would be affected differently. To address this question, we scaled the confidence ratings (absolute distance from the marginal hyperplane) for each code in each sentence by dividing by the log of the frequency of the code in the corresponding remainder pool.[4] We assigned a minimum code frequency of 2 to account for rare codes.

---

[4] Alternatively, we could have used the frequencies from the training set. We used frequencies from the remainder pool because they would be more accurate, especially at the earlier stages. In a real-life setting where the items in the remainder pool would be unlabeled, those frequencies would, of course, be unknown.

Simple Sum Confidence Combination. Figures 5 and 6 show the mean and micro-averaged F_1 gain scores for the Simple Sum combination method described above, which calculates the prediction certainty for a sentence by adding the certainties for all the codes. In Experiment 2, however, the values were scaled by the log frequency of occurrence of the codes before they were summed.

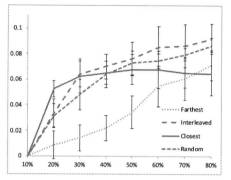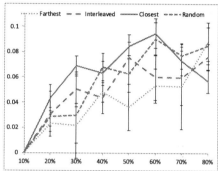

Fig. 5. Simple sum mean F1 gains   **Fig. 6.** Simple sum micro F1 gains

These charts make it more obvious that in the first iteration (i.e., going from 10% to 20% of the essays in the training set), choosing the least certain (closest to the marginal hyperplane) items most quickly improves the performance of the models, both for the mean and micro-averaged scores. Conversely, choosing the most confidently-classified items (farthest from the marginal hyperplane) still provides the slowest growth in model performance. The rest of the story is more subtle but supports our hypothesis about differential effects on the mean and micro-averaged F_1 scores.

In the mean F_1 scores in Fig. 5, it is clear that the closest-to-hyperplane approach plateaued, and actually decreased slightly, while the interleaved and random selection strategies kept improving. This provides some support for the idea raised in related research [20] that including a broader range of examples is beneficial, at least later in the training. The behavior of the closest-to-hyperplane selection strategy could be due to the F_1 scores for the whole set of codes not increasing, or, because the mean F_1 score evenly weights all codes, it could be that some subset goes up, and the rest go down. (Even though the weights are scaled by code frequency, the scaled values are all added together in this combination scheme.) Another factor may be that at some point, there are only high-confidence essays in the remainder set, so adding them to training does not improve overall performance.

The micro-averaged F_1 chart in Fig. 6 gives some insight. Here, the closest-to-hyperplane is always the highest, except in the last two iterations, and, by a small amount, at the fourth. This indicates that this method is, in fact, increasing performance on the most-frequent codes (because the micro-average is more sensitive to code frequency). This presumably happens because we are scaling the confidence values by frequency. With this form of scaling, we are discounting the certainty on the more frequent codes. By biasing the selection strategy further toward essays that have low confidence on frequent codes and away from essays that have low confidence on infrequent codes, we have improved the micro-averaged F_1 scores, but at the expense of the mean F_1 scores on the later iterations. Or, to put it another way, using a frequency-scaled AL combination strategy effectively increases the overall performance of the classifications given natural distribution of the classes.

Split-Sum Confidence Combination. Figures 7 and 8 show the mean and micro-averaged F_1 gain scores for the Split Sum combination method described above, which calculates the prediction certainty for a sentence by adding the average of the certainties for the concept codes with the average of the certainties for the causal codes. As above, the values were scaled by the log frequency of occurrence of the codes before they were averaged and summed. To reiterate, the concept codes identify the particular factors or events that students might identify in their explanations. The causal codes identify explicit connections between them, like "X led to Y." The rationale for the Split Sum combination method is to afford equal weight to the *set* of concept codes and the *set* of causal codes.

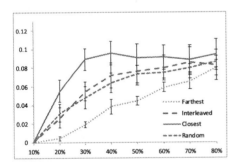
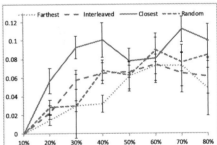

Fig. 7. Split sum mean F1 gains   Fig. 8. Split sum micro F1 gains

In the early stages, these charts also show advantages for the closest-to-hyperplane selection strategies in both the mean and micro-average scores, but the advantages appear more pronounced. By the end of the second iteration, the closest-to-hyperplane strategy performs significantly above the others. As before, the performance of the strategy plateaus on the mean F_1 scores, but only at the point at which it is already well above the others, and it maintains its advantage. Comparison with Fig. 5 shows that it outperforms all of those models as well. Performance on the micro-averaged F_1 was also superior across the board, with the exception of one iteration. This method of combining the average of the conceptual codes with the average of the causal codes, along with the frequency-based scaling, produced a model that learned quickly and outperformed the other selection strategies.

5   Discussion, Conclusions and Future Research

The overall goal of our research project is to develop methods for analyzing the causal structure of student explanatory essays. This type of analysis could be provided to teachers to reduce the demands on them, or it could become the foundation of an intelligent tutoring system that will give students feedback on their essays and help direct the focus of their learning. From the limited number of connections included in the essays that we collected, students clearly have a need for additional practice with specific, focused feedback.

Machine learning approaches can create models for performing detailed analyses of texts but require a large amount of relevant *labeled* training data. This paper has provided an evaluation of Active Learning to determine how effectively it can improve accuracy of the machine learning analysis models while minimizing the costs of annotation. Overall, we found that, especially in early iterations, it was best to choose items that the model was least certain of.

These results suggest some directions for future research. Because the closest-to-hyperplane strategy was initially very good, but later plateaued, we would like to evaluate a hybrid model which initially chooses the least certain instances, then at some point, switches to choosing a mixture of more and less certain items. There are also many other instance selection strategies that could be explored. These have previously been applied to tasks in which, unlike ours, there is a single target classification for items [19]. We would like to explore some of the others that have been used for natural language processing [28].

The co-training approach described above could also be another fruitful way to improve model performance with an even lower cost in terms of additional annotation. It should be noted, however, that at its worst, this might be equivalent to a "dumbed down" version of the farthest-from-hyperplane strategy evaluated here; it would take its predictions (which may be noisy) on the highest confidence items. The advantage of co-training would come from the use of complementary feature sets. The trick would be finding feature sets that are conditionally independent of the target classes.

Finally, all of the methods we have evaluated in this paper assume that entire essays would be annotated and added to the training set. To select an essay for annotation, however, we first evaluate the certainty of the predictions at the sentence level, which is, in turn based on predictions at the word level. Instead of selecting entire essays to add to the training set, we could instead select sentences, phrases or words. This could obviously significantly reduce the additional annotation time. The question is how effective it would be at improving model performance.

References

1. Osborne, J., Erduran, S., Simon, S.: Enhancing the quality of argumentation in science classrooms. J. Res. Sci. Teach. **41**(10), 994–1020 (2004)
2. Achieve Inc.: Next generation science standards (2013)
3. Hastings, P., Britt, M.A., Rupp, K., Kopp, K., Hughes, S.: Computational analysis of explanatory essay structure. In: Millis, K., Long, D., Magliano, J.P., Wiemer, K. (eds.) Multi-Disciplinary Approaches to Deep Learning. Routledge, New York (2018). Accepted for publication
4. Stenetorp, P., Pyysalo, S., Topić, G., Ohta, T., Ananiadou, S., Tsujii, J.: brat: a web-based tool for NLP-assisted text annotation. In: Proceedings of the Demonstrations Session at EACL 2012, Avignon, France, Association for Computational Linguistics, April 2012
5. Stenetorp, P., Topić, G., Pyysalo, S., Ohta, T., Kim, J.D., Tsujii, J.: BioNLP shared task 2011: Supporting resources. In: Proceedings of BioNLP Shared Task 2011 Workshop, Portland, Oregon, USA, Association for Computational Linguistics, pp. 112–120, June 2011
6. Goldman, S.R., Greenleaf, C., Yukhymenko-Lescroart, M., Brown, W., Ko, M., Emig, J., George, M., Wallace, P., Blaum, D., Britt, M.: Project READI: Explanatory modeling in science through text-based investigation: Testing the efficacy of the READI intervention approach. Technical Report 27, Project READI (2016)
7. Shermis, M.D., Hamner, B.: Contrasting state-of-the-art automated scoring of essays: analysis. In: Annual National Council on Measurement in Education Meeting, pp. 14–16 (2012)
8. Deane, P.: On the relation between automated essay scoring and modern views of the writing construct. Assessing Writ. **18**(1), 7–24 (2013)
9. Roscoe, R.D., Crossley, S.A., Snow, E.L., Varner, L.K., McNamara, D.S.: Writing quality, knowledge, and comprehension correlates of human and automated essay scoring. In: The Twenty-Seventh International Flairs Conference (2014)
10. Shermis, M.D., Burstein, J.: Handbook of Automated Essay Evaluation: Current Applications and New Directions. Routledge (2013)
11. Dikli, S.: Automated essay scoring. Turk. Online J. Distance Educ. **7**(1), 49–62 (2015)
12. Condon, W.: Large-scale assessment, locally-developed measures, and automated scoring of essays: Fishing for red herrings? Assessing Writ. **18**(1), 100–108 (2013)
13. Riaz, M., Girju, R.: Recognizing causality in verb-noun pairs via noun and verb semantics. EACL **2014**, 48 (2014)
14. Rink, B., Bejan, C.A., Harabagiu, S.M.: Learning textual graph patterns to detect causal event relations. In: Guesgen, H.W., Murray, R.C. (eds.) FLAIRS Conference. AAAI Press (2010)
15. Hughes, S., Hastings, P., Britt, M.A., Wallace, P., Blaum, D.: Machine learning for holistic evaluation of scientific essays. In: Conati, C., Heffernan, N., Mitrovic, A., Verdejo, M.F. (eds.) AIED 2015. LNCS (LNAI), vol. 9112, pp. 165–175. Springer, Cham (2015). https://doi.org/10.1007/978-3-319-19773-9_17
16. Hughes, S.: Automatic inference of causal reasoning chains from student essays. Ph.D. thesis, DePaul University, Chicago, IL (2018)
17. Wolpert, D.H.: Stacked generalization. Neural Netw. **5**(2), 241–259 (1992)
18. Hastings, P., Hughes, S., Blaum, D., Wallace, P., Britt, M.A.: Stratified learning for reducing training set size. In: Micarelli, A., Stamper, J., Panourgia, K. (eds.) ITS 2016. LNCS, vol. 9684, pp. 341–346. Springer, Cham (2016). https://doi.org/10.1007/978-3-319-39583-8_39

19. Settles, B.: Active learning literature survey. Computer Sciences Technical Report 1648, University of Wisconsin-Madison (2009)
20. Sharma, M., Bilgic, M.: Most-surely vs. least-surely uncertain. In: 13th International Conference on Data Mining (ICDM), pp. 667–676. IEEE (2013)
21. Ferdowsi, Z.: Active learning for high precision classification with imbalanced data. Ph.D. thesis, DePaul University, Chicago, IL, USA, May 2015
22. Cawley, G.C.: Baseline methods for active learning. In: Active Learning and Experimental Design Workshop in Conjunction with AISTATS 2010, pp. 47–57 (2011)
23. Tong, S., Koller, D.: Support vector machine active learning with applications to text classification. J. Mach. Learn. Res. 2, 45–66 (2001)
24. Mirroshandel, S.A., Ghassem-Sani, G., Nasr, A.: Active learning strategies for support vector machines, application to temporal relation classification. In: Proceedings of 5th International Joint Conference on Natural Language Processing, pp. 56–64 (2011)
25. Blum, A., Mitchell, T.: Combining labeled and unlabeled data with co-training. In: Proceedings of the Eleventh Annual Conference on Computational Learning Theory, pp. 92–100. ACM (1998)
26. Vapnik, V.N.: The Nature of Statistical Learning Theory. Springer, New York (1995)
27. Joachims, T.: Learning to Classify Text Using Support Vector Machines - Methods, Theory, and Algorithms. Kluwer/Springer, New York (2002)
28. Olsson, F.: A literature survey of active machine learning in the context of natural language processing. Technical Report T2009:06, Swedish Institute of Computer Science (2009). http://eprints.sics.se/3600/1/SICS-T-2009-06-SE.pdf. Accessed 8 Feb 2017

Student Learning Benefits of a Mixed-Reality Teacher Awareness Tool in AI-Enhanced Classrooms

Kenneth Holstein[(⊠)], Bruce M. McLaren, and Vincent Aleven

Carnegie Mellon University, Pittsburgh, PA 15213, USA
{kjholste, bmclaren, aleven}@cs.cmu.edu

Abstract. When used in K-12 classrooms, intelligent tutoring systems (ITSs) can be highly effective in helping students learn. However, they might be even more effective if designed to *work together* with human teachers, to amplify their abilities and leverage their complementary strengths. In the present work, we designed a wearable, real-time teacher awareness tool: mixed-reality smart glasses that tune teachers in to the rich analytics generated by ITSs, alerting them to situations the ITS may be ill-suited to handle. A 3-condition experiment with 286 middle school students, across 18 classrooms and 8 teachers, found that presenting teachers with real-time analytics about student learning, metacognition, and behavior had a positive impact on student learning, compared with both business-as-usual and classroom monitoring support without advanced analytics. Our findings suggest that real-time teacher analytics can help to narrow the gap in learning outcomes across students of varying prior ability. This is the first experimental study showing that real-time teacher analytics can enhance student learning. This research illustrates the promise of AIED systems that integrate human and machine intelligence to support student learning.

Keywords: Real-time analytics · Classroom orchestration
Teacher-in-the-loop · Human-AI hybrid · Intelligent tutors · Dashboards
Classroom evaluation

1 Introduction

When educational technologies are used in K-12 classrooms, human teachers play critical roles in mediating their effectiveness [33, 37, 41]. The term *classroom orchestration* has been widely used to describe the planning and real-time management of classroom activities [15]. Supporting teachers in orchestrating complex, but effective, technology-enhanced learning has been recognized as a critical research and design challenge for the learning sciences [16, 39, 43].

In recent years, several real-time teacher awareness tools have been designed and developed to address this challenge (e.g., [1, 5, 19, 30, 31, 40, 43]). These tools are often designed to augment teachers' "state awareness" during ongoing learning activities [39, 43], for example, by presenting teachers with real-time analytics on student knowledge, progress, metacognition, and behavior within educational software.

© Springer International Publishing AG, part of Springer Nature 2018
C. Penstein Rosé et al. (Eds.): AIED 2018, LNAI 10947, pp. 154–168, 2018.
https://doi.org/10.1007/978-3-319-93843-1_12

The design of such tools is frequently motivated by an assumption that enhanced teacher awareness will lead to improved teaching, and consequently, to improved student outcomes. Some prior work has found evidence for positive effects of real-time teacher analytics on student *performance* within educational software (e.g., [30]). Yet there is a paucity of empirical evidence that a teacher's use of real-time awareness tools (e.g., dashboards) can improve student *learning*, and scientific knowledge about the effects such tools have on teaching and learning is scarce [32, 39, 44].

In the present work, we investigate the effects of a real-time awareness tool for teachers working in K-12 classrooms using intelligent tutoring systems (ITSs), an important but underexplored area of AIED research. Intelligent tutors are a class of advanced learning technologies that provide students with step-by-step guidance during complex learning activities. ITSs have been found, in several meta-reviews, to significantly enhance student learning compared with other learning technologies or classroom instruction (e.g., [25]). When used in K-12 classrooms, ITSs allow students to work at their own pace, while also freeing up the teacher to spend more time working one-on-one with students [41]. A common intuition is that, in many situations, human teachers may be better suited to support students than ITSs alone (e.g., by providing socio-emotional support, supporting student motivation, or flexibly providing conceptual support when further problem-solving practice may be ineffective). Yet ITSs are not typically designed to work together with teachers, in real-time, to take advantage of these complementary strengths [7, 19, 35, 45]. ITSs might be even more effective if they were designed not only to support students directly, but also to amplify teachers' abilities to help their students (cf. [7, 21, 38]).

We present *Lumilo* [19]: mixed-reality smart glasses, co-designed with middle-school mathematics teachers, that tune teachers in to the rich analytics generated by ITSs (cf., [10]). By alerting teachers in real-time to situations the ITS may be ill-suited to handle on its own, *Lumilo* facilitates a form of mutual support or *co-orchestration* [35] between the human teacher and the AI tutor. We conduct an in-vivo experiment using *Lumilo* to investigate the effects of this form of teacher/AI co-orchestration on the ways teachers interact with students during in-school lab sessions with ITS software, and how, in turn, students learning processes and outcomes are affected. We test whether students measurably learn better when their teacher has access to real-time analytics from an ITS, compared to current practice with ITSs (where the teacher does not use a real-time awareness tool), and compared to a simpler form of *classroom monitoring* support [39], common in widely-used classroom-management systems (e.g., [11, 18, 26]).

2   Methods

2.1   Linear Equation Tutor

We investigate the effects of a teacher's use of a real-time awareness tool in the context of middle school classrooms using *Lynnette*, an ITS for linear equations. *Lynnette* is a rule-based Cognitive Tutor that was developed using the Cognitive Tutor Authoring Tools [3]. It has been used in several classroom studies, where it has been shown to significantly improve students' equation-solving ability [27, 28]. *Lynnette* provides step-by-step guidance, in the form of hints, correctness feedback, and error-specific messages as students tackle each problem in the software. It also adaptively selects problems for each student, using Bayesian Knowledge Tracing (BKT) to track individual students' knowledge growth, together with a mastery learning policy [13]. Students using *Lynnette* progress through five levels with equation-solving problems of increasing difficulty. These range from simple one-step equations at Level 1 (e.g., $x + 3 = 6$), to more complex, multi-step equations at Level 5 (e.g., $2(1 - x) + 4 = 12$).

2.2   Real-Time Teacher Awareness Tool

We created a real-time support tool for K-12 teachers who use ITSs in their classrooms. To this end, we adopted a participatory design approach [17] in which we directly involved teachers at each stage, from initial needs-finding [19, 21] to the selection and tuning of real-time analytic measures through iterative prototyping [19, 20]. The prototype that emerged from this iterative co-design process (described in greater detail in [19–21]), was a pair of mixed-reality smart glasses called *Lumilo*.

Lumilo tunes teachers in to the rich analytics that ITSs generate: It presents real-time indicators of students' current learning, metacognitive, and behavioral "states", projected in the teacher's view of the classroom (Fig. 1, left). The use of transparent smart glasses allows teachers to keep their heads up and focused on the classroom, enabling them to continue monitoring important signals that may not be captured by the tool alone (e.g., student body language and looks of frustration [19, 21]). The smart glasses provide teachers with a *private* view of actionable, real-time information about their students, embedded throughout the classroom environment, thus providing many of the advantages of ambient and distributed classroom awareness tools (e.g., [1, 5]), without revealing sensitive student data to the entire class [5, 19].

Over the course of the design process, *Lumilo's* information displays shifted towards strongly minimalistic designs (with progressive disclosure of additional analytics only upon a teacher's request), in accordance with the level of information teachers desired and could handle in fast-paced classroom environments. *Lumilo* presents mixed-reality displays of three main types, visible through the teacher's glasses: student-level indicators, student-level "deep-dive" screens, and class-level summaries (as shown in Fig. 1). Student-level indicators and class-level summaries are always visible to the teacher by default, at a glance. Student-level indicators display above corresponding students' heads (based on teacher-configurable seating charts), and class-level summaries can display at teacher-configurable locations throughout the classroom [19]. As shown in Fig. 1(bottom-left), if a teacher glances at a student's indicator, *Lumilo* automatically displays a brief elaboration about the currently displayed indicator symbol (i.e., how long the alert has been active and/or a brief explanation of *why* the alert is showing). If no indicators are currently active for a student, *Lumilo* displays a faint circular outline above that student (Fig. 1, top-left). If a teacher clicks on a student's indicator (using either a handheld clicker or by making a 'tap' gesture in mid-air), *Lumilo* displays "deep-dive" screens for that student. As shown in Fig. 1(right), these screens include a "Current Problem" display, which supports remote *monitoring*, showing a live feed of a student's work on their current problem. Each problem step in this feed is annotated with the number of hint requests and errors the student has made on that step. In classroom observations, we have found that because *Lumilo* enables monitoring of student activities from a distance (i.e., across the room), teachers using *Lumilo* often interleave help across students: While helping one student at that student's seat, the teacher might provide quick guidance to a struggling student across the room (Fig. 2, right).

Fig. 1. Teacher's point-of-view while using *Lumilo*. Top row: illustrative mock-ups; Bottom row: screenshots captured through *Lumilo* (taken after the end of a class session, to protect student privacy) [19]. Left: Teacher's default view of the class through *Lumilo*. Right: Deep-dive screens that pop-up if a teacher 'clicks' on a student's indicator.

The deep-dive screens also include an "Areas of Struggle" screen, which displays the three skills for which a student has the lowest probability of mastery. For each skill shown in "Areas of Struggle", the student's estimated probability of mastery is displayed, together with a concrete example of an error the student has made on a recent practice opportunity for the skill. In addition, in the current study, a class-level summary display was available to the teacher: the "Low Mastery, High Practice" display (illustrated on the left, in the top row images of Fig. 1). This display shows the three skills that the fewest students in the class have mastered (according to BKT), at a given point in the class session, out of those skills that many students in the class have already had opportunities to practice within the software [19].

The student indicators displayed by *Lumilo* (Fig. 2, left) are ideas that were generated by teachers in our design studies [19, 21] and implemented using established

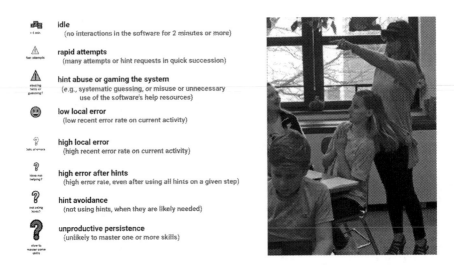

Fig. 2. Left: Indicators displayed by *Lumilo* [20]. Right: Teacher using *Lumilo* during class.

student modeling methods (e.g., [2, 4, 9, 13, 14, 23]). The analytic measures and their corresponding visual alerts were iteratively refined based on prototyping feedback from teachers [19], as well as causal data mining of teacher and student process data from classroom pilots using *Lumilo* [20]. The resulting prototype updates real-time student indicators based on the outputs of sensor-free detectors, including detectors of student hint abuse and hint avoidance [2, 4], gaming-the-system [8], rapid/non-deliberate step attempts or hint requests [2], and unproductive persistence or "wheel-spinning" [9, 23]. In addition, *Lumilo* indicates when a student has been idle for two minutes or more and may be off-task (cf. [6]), when a student has been exhibiting a particularly "low" or "high" recent error rate (less than 30% or greater than 80% correct within the student's most recent 10 attempts) (cf. [23, 34]), or when a student is making errors on a given problem-solving step, despite having already exhausted all tutor-provided hints for that step [2]. By directing teachers' attention, in real-time, to situations the ITS may be ill-suited to handle, *Lumilo* is designed to facilitate productive mutual support or *co-orchestration* [35] between the teacher and the ITS, by leveraging the complementary strengths of each (cf. [22, 35, 38, 45]).

2.3   Experimental Design, Participants, and Procedure

In this study, we investigated the hypothesis that real-time teacher/AI co-orchestration, supported by real-time analytics from an ITS, would enhance student learning compared with both (a) business-as-usual for an ITS classroom, and (b) classroom *monitoring support* without advanced analytics (a stronger control than (a), as described below).

To test these hypotheses, we conducted a 3-condition experiment with 343 middle school students, across 18 classrooms, 8 teachers, and 4 public schools (each from a different school district) in a large U.S. city and surrounding areas. All participating teachers had at least 5 years of experience teaching middle school mathematics and had previously used an ITS in their classroom. The study was conducted during the first half of the students' school year, and none of the classes participating in this study had previously covered equation-solving topics beyond simple one-step linear equations (e.g., $x - 2 = 1$).

Classrooms were randomly assigned to one of three conditions, stratified by teacher. In the Glasses+Analytics condition, teachers used the full version of *Lumilo*, including all displays described above. In the business-as-usual (noGlasses) condition, teachers did not wear *Lumilo* during class, and thus did not have access to real-time analytics. We also included a third condition (Glasses) in which teachers used a reduced version of *Lumilo* with only its monitoring functionality (i.e., without any of its advanced analytics). This condition was included because prior empirical findings suggest that students' mere awareness that a teacher is monitoring their activities within an ITS may have a significant effect on student learning (e.g., by discouraging, and thus decreasing the frequency of maladaptive learning behaviors such as gaming-the-system) [22, 42]. In the Glasses condition, teachers only retained the ability to "peek" at students' screens from any location in the classroom, using the glasses (although without the line-by-line annotations present in *Lumilo*'s "Current Problem" screen). All of *Lumilo*'s student indicators were replaced by a single, static symbol (a faint circular outline) that did not convey any information about the student's state. Further, the "Areas of Struggle" deep dive screens and the class-level displays were hidden. Our aim in providing this stripped-down version *of Lumilo* was to encourage teachers to interact with the glasses, thereby minimizing differences in students' perceptions between the Glasses+Analytics and Glasses conditions. The Glasses condition bears some similarity to standard classroom monitoring tools, which enable teachers to peek at student screens on their own desktop or tablet display (e.g., [11, 18, 26]).

All teachers participated in a brief training session before the start of the study. Teachers were first familiarized with *Lynnette*, the tutoring software that students would use during the study. In the Glasses+Analytics and Glasses conditions, each teacher also participated in a brief (30-min) training with *Lumilo* before the start of the study. In this training, teachers practiced interacting with two versions of the glasses (Glasses and Glasses+Analytics) in a simulated classroom context. At the end of this training, teachers were informed that, for each of their classes, they would be assigned to use one or the other of these two designs.

Classrooms in each of the three conditions followed the same procedure. In each class, students first received a brief introduction to *Lynnette* from their teacher. Students then worked on a computer-based pre-test for approximately 20 min, during which time the teacher provided no assistance. Following the pretest, students worked with the tutor for a total of 60 min, spread across two class sessions. In all conditions, teachers were encouraged to help their students as needed, while they worked with the tutor. Finally, students took a 20-min computer-based post-test, again without any assistance from the teacher. The pre- and posttests focused on procedural knowledge of equation solving. We used two isomorphic test forms that varied only by the specific numbers used in equations. The tests forms were assigned in counterbalanced order across pre- and post-test. The tests were graded automatically, with partial credit assigned for intermediate steps in a student's solution, according to *Lynnette*'s cognitive model.

In the Glasses and Glasses+Analytics conditions, we used *Lumilo* to automatically track a teacher's physical position within the classroom (cf. [36]), relative to each student, moment-by-moment (leveraging *Lumilo*'s indicators as mixed-reality proximity sensors [19, 20]). Teacher time allocation was recorded per student as the cumulative time (in seconds) a teacher spent within a 4-ft radius of that student (with ties resolved by relative proximity). Given our observation that teachers in both of these conditions frequently provided assistance remotely (i.e., conversing with a student from across the room, while monitoring her/his activity using the glasses), teacher time was also accumulated for the duration a teacher spent peeking at a student's screen via the glasses. In the noGlasses condition, since teachers did not wear *Lumilo*, time allocation was recorded via live classroom coding (using the *LookWhosTalking* tool [29]) of the target (student) and duration (in seconds) of each teacher visit. In addition to test scores and data on teacher time allocation, we analyzed tutor log data to investigate potential effects of condition on students' within-software behaviors.

3   Results

Fifty-seven students were absent for one or more days of the study and were excluded from further analyses. We analyzed the data for the remaining 286 students. Given that the sample was nested in 18 classes, 8 teachers, and 4 schools, and that the experimental intervention was applied at the class level, we used hierarchical linear modeling (HLM) to analyze student learning outcomes. 3-level models had the best fit, with students (level 1) nested in classes (level 2), and classes nested in teachers (level 3). We used class track (low, average, or high) as a level-2 covariate. Both 2-level models, (with students nested in classes) and 4-level models (with teachers nested in schools) had worse fits according to both AIC and BIC, and 4-level models indicated little variance on the school level. We report r for effect size. An effect size r above 0.10 is conventionally considered small, 0.3 medium, and 0.5 large [12].

Effects on Student Learning. To compare student learning outcomes across experimental conditions, we used HLMs with test score as the dependent variable, and test type (pretest/posttest, with pretest as the baseline value) and experimental condition as independent variables (fixed effects). For each fixed effect, we included a term for each comparison between the baseline and other levels of the variable. For comparisons between the Glasses+Analytics and noGlasses conditions, we used noGlasses as the condition baseline. Otherwise, we used Glasses as the baseline.

Across conditions, there was a significant gain between student pretest and posttest scores ($t(283) = 7.673, p = 2.74 * 10^{-13}, r = 0.26, 95\%$ CI $[0.19, 0.34]$), consistent with results from prior classroom studies using Lynnette [27, 28], which showed learning gain effect size estimates ranging from $r = 0.25$ to $r = 0.64$. Figure 3 shows pre-post learning gains for each condition. There was a significant positive interaction between student pre/posttest and the noGlasses/Glasses+Analytics conditions ($t(283) = 5.897$,

$p = 1.05 * 10^{-8}, r = 0.21, 95\%$ CI $[0.13, 0.28]$), supporting the hypothesis that real-time teacher/AI co-orchestration, supported by analytics from an ITS, would enhance student learning compared with business-as-usual for ITS classrooms.

Decomposing this effect, there was a significant positive interaction between student pre/posttest and the noGlasses/Glasses conditions ($t(283) = 3.386$, $p = 8.08 * 10^{-4}$, $r = 0.13$, 95% CI $[0.02, 0.23]$), with a higher learning gain slope in the Glasses condition, indicating that relatively minimal classroom monitoring support, even without advanced analytics, can positively impact learning. In addition, there was a significant positive interaction between student pre/posttest and the Glasses/Glasses+Analytics conditions $(t(283) = 2.229$, $p = 0.027$, $r = 0.11$, 95% CI $[0.02, 0.20]$), with a higher slope in the Glasses+Analytics condition than in the Glasses condition, supporting our hypothesis that real-time teacher analytics would enhance student learning, above and beyond any effects of monitoring support alone (i.e., without advanced analytics).

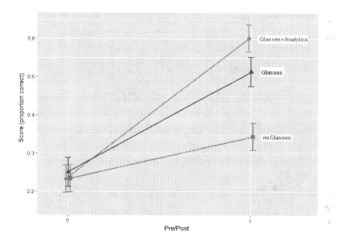

Fig. 3. Student pre/post learning, by experimental condition. Error bars indicate standard error.

Aptitude-Treatment Interactions on Student Learning. We next investigated how the effects of each condition might vary based on students' prior domain knowledge. *Lumilo* was designed to help teachers quickly identify students who are currently struggling (unproductively) with the ITS, so that they could provide these students with additional, on-the-spot support. If *Lumilo* was successful in this regard, we would expect to see an aptitude-treatment interaction, such that students coming in with lower prior domain knowledge (who are more likely to struggle) would learn more when teachers had access to *Lumilo's* real-time analytics [19, 20].

We constructed an HLM with posttest as the dependent variable and pretest and experimental condition as level-1 covariates, modeling interactions between pretest and condition. Figure 4(top) shows student posttest scores plotted by pretest scores (in standard deviation units) for each of the three conditions. As shown, students in the Glasses condition learned more overall, compared with the noGlasses condition, but the disparity in learning outcomes across students with varying prior domain knowledge remained the same. For students in the Glasses+Analytics condition, the posttest by pretest curve was flatter, with lower pretest students learning considerably more than in the other two conditions. There was no significant interaction between noGlasses/Glasses and student pretest. However, there were significant negative interactions between student pretest scores and noGlasses/Glasses+Analytics ($t(46) = -2.456$, $p = 0.018$, $r = -0.15$, 95% CI [-0.26, -0.03]) and Glasses/Glasses+Analytics ($t(164) = -2.279$, $p = 0.024$, $r = -0.16$, 95% CI [-0.27, -0.05]), suggesting that a teacher's use of real-time analytics may serve as an equalizing force in the classroom.

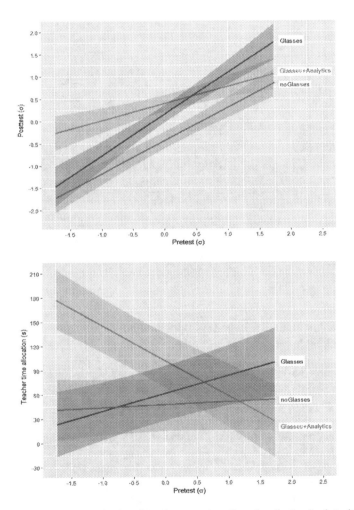

Fig. 4. Student posttest scores (top) and teacher attention allocation (bottom), plotted by student pretest scores, for each experimental condition. Shaded regions indicate standard error.

Effects on Teacher Time Allocation. As an additional way of testing whether the real-time analytics provided by *Lumilo* had their intended effect, we fit an HLM with teacher time allocation, per student, as the dependent variable, and student pretest score, experimental condition, and their interactions as fixed effects. Figure 4 (bottom) shows teacher time, plotted by student pretest, for each condition. As shown, in the Glasses+Analytics condition, teachers tended to allocate considerably more of their time to students with lower prior domain knowledge, compared to the other conditions. There was no significant main effect of noGlasses/Glasses on teacher time allocation ($t(211) = 0.482$, $p = 0.63$, $r = 0.03$, 95% CI [0, 0.14]), nor a significant interaction with pretest. However, there were significant main effects of noGlasses/Glasses+Analytics ($t(279) = 2.88$, $p = 4.26 * 10^{-3}$, $r = 0.17$, 95% CI [0.06, 0.28]) and Glasses/Glasses+Analytics ($t(278) = 2.02$, $p = 0.044$, $r = 0.12$, 95% CI [0.01, 0.23]) on teacher time allocation. In addition, there were significant negative interactions between student pretest and noGlasses/Glasses+Analytics ($t(279) = -2.88$, $p = 4.28 * 10^{-3}$, $r = -0.17$, 95% CI [−0.28, −0.05]) and Glasses/Glasses+Analytics ($t(275) = -3.546$, $p = 4.62 * 10^{-4}$, $r = -0.23$, 95% CI [−0.33, −0.11]).

We also investigated how teachers' relative time allocation across students may have been driven by the real-time analytics presented in the Glasses+Analytics condition. Specifically, we examined whether and how teacher time allocation varied across conditions, based on the frequency with which a student exhibited each of the within-tutor behaviors/states detected by *Lumilo* (i.e., *Lumilo*'s student indicators, described in Sect. 2.3). We constructed HLMs with teacher time allocation as the dependent variable, and the frequency of student within-tutor behaviors/states, experimental condition, and their interactions as fixed effects. Row 3 of Table 1 shows relationships between student within-tutor behaviors/states and teacher time allocation across students, for the Glasses+Analytics vs. noGlasses (GA v. nG) comparison. As shown, teachers' time allocation across students appears to have been influenced by *Lumilo*'s real-time indicators. Compared with business-as-usual (Row 3, Table 1), teachers in the Glasses+Analytics condition spent significantly *less* time attending to students who frequently exhibited low local error, and significantly *more* time attending to students who frequently exhibited undesirable behaviors/states detected by *Lumilo*, such as unproductive persistence (or "wheel-spinning").

Table 1. Estimated effects of condition (rows) on teachers' allocation of time to students exhibiting each within-tutor behavior/state (columns). Cells report estimated effect sizes: *** $p < 0.001$, ** $p < 0.01$, * $p < 0.05$, $\sim 0.05 \leq p < 0.07$

	High local error	Hint abuse or gaming	Hint avoidance	High error after hints	Idle	Low local error	Rapid attempts	Unproductive persistence ("wheel-spinning")
G v. nG	n.s.	n.s.	n.s.	n.s.	n.s.	0.13$\sim$	n.s.	n.s.
GA v. G	**0.20***	**0.17***	**0.19***	**0.18***	**0.22****	**−0.51*****	n.s.	**0.35*****
GA v. nG	**0.16****	0.10$\sim$	**0.14***	0.11$\sim$	**0.17****	**−0.23*****	n.s.	**0.24*****

Rows 1 and 2 of Table 1 show estimates for Glasses vs. noGlasses (G v. nG) and Glasses+Analytics vs. Glasses (GA v. G), respectively. As shown, there were no significant differences in teacher time allocation due to the introduction of the glasses themselves, suggesting *Lumilo*'s overall effects on teacher time allocation may result primarily from teachers' use of the advanced analytics presented in the GA condition.

Effects of Classroom Monitoring Support and Real-Time Teacher Analytics on Student-Level Processes. To investigate potential effects of experimental condition on the frequency of student within-tutor behaviors and learning states detected by *Lumilo*, we constructed HLMs with students' within-tutor behaviors/states as the dependent variable, and pretest score and experimental condition as fixed effects. Row 3 of Table 2 shows estimated effects of classroom condition on the frequency of student within-tutor behaviors/states, for Glasses+Analytics vs. noGlasses (GA v. nG).

Table 2. Estimated effects of condition (rows) on the frequency of student within-tutor behaviors/states (columns): *** $p < 0.001$, ** $p < 0.01$, * $p < 0.05$, $\sim$ $0.05 \leq p < 0.07$

	High local error	Hint abuse or gaming	Hint avoidance	High error after hints	Idle	Low local error	Rapid attempts	Unproductive persistence ("wheel-spinning")
G v. nG	**−0.36** **	**−0.21****	**−0.32****	n.s.	**0.23***	**0.34****	n.s.	n.s.
GA v. G	−0.12~	n.s.	n.s.	n.s.	n.s.	n.s.	n.s.	−0.20~
GA v. nG	**−0.47****	**−0.28****	**−0.41****	**−0.30****	**0.26***	**0.42***	**−0.34****	**−0.15***

Compared with business-as-usual, students in the Glasses+Analytics condition exhibited less hint avoidance or gaming/hint abuse, were less frequently detected as unproductively persisting or making rapid consecutive attempts in the tutoring software and exhibited less frequent high local error. In addition, students in the Glasses+Analytics condition were more frequently idle in the software, and more frequently exhibited low local error. Row 1 of Table 2 suggests that that the introduction of the glasses, even without real-time teacher analytics, may have had a considerable influence on students' behavior within the software. By contrast, there were no significant differences between the Glasses+Analytics and Glasses conditions. These results suggest that, despite the ostensible positive effects of real-time teacher analytics on student learning outcomes, some of the *largest* effects of *Lumilo* on students' within-tutor behavior may result primarily from teachers' use of the monitoring support provided in the Glasses condition, rather than from a teachers' use of advanced analytics.

4   Discussion, Conclusions, and Future Work

We conducted a 3-condition classroom experiment to investigate the effects of a real-time teacher awareness tool on student learning in ITS classrooms. Our findings indicate that teachers' use of *Lumilo*, a real-time awareness tool, resulted in higher learning gains with the ITS. In addition, presenting teachers with real-time analytics about student learning, metacognition, and behavior at a glance had a positive impact on student learning with the ITS, above and beyond the effects of monitoring support alone (without any advanced analytics). The real-time analytics provided by *Lumilo* appear to have served as an equalizing force in the classroom: driving teachers' time towards students of lower prior ability and narrowing the gap in learning outcomes between students with higher and lower prior domain knowledge.

Interestingly, part of *Lumilo's* overall effect on student learning appears to be attributable to monitoring support alone. Follow-up correlational analyses suggested that a teacher's use of the glasses, with monitoring support (i.e., support for peeking at a student's screen remotely), but without advanced analytics, may reduce students' frequency of maladaptive learning behaviors (such as gaming/hint-abuse) without significantly influencing teachers' time allocation across students. These results suggest that the observed learning benefits of monitoring support may be due to a motivational effect, resulting from students' awareness that a teacher is monitoring their activities in the software (cf. [22, 42]), and/or due to a novelty effect. It may also be that the monitoring support provided in the Glasses condition had a positive effect on teacher behavior that is not reflected in the way they distributed their time across students (e.g., an effect upon teachers' verbal or non-verbal communication). Future work is needed to tease apart these explanations.

Although much prior work has focused on the design, development, and evaluation of teacher analytics tools, very few studies have evaluated effects on student learning [24, 32, 39, 44]). The current study is the first experimental study to demonstrate that real-time teacher analytics can enhance students' learning outcomes, within or outside the area of AIED and intelligent tutoring systems.

We see several exciting directions for future work. The current study involved teachers with at least five years of mathematics teaching experience. However, our prior design work with teachers indicated that less-experienced teachers may often struggle to generate effective on-the-spot help, in response to real-time analytics from an ITS [19, 22]. Thus, a promising direction for future design research is to investigate differences in needs for real-time support across teachers with varying levels of experience. In addition, while the current study was conducted over a single week of class time, future longitudinal studies may shed light on whether and how the effects of real-time teacher analytics and monitoring support may evolve over longer-term use (c.f. [32]). More broadly, an exciting direction for future work is to better understand and characterize the complementary strengths of human and automated instruction, to explore how they can most effectively be combined (cf. [21, 35, 38]).

In sum, this research illustrates the potential of AIED systems that integrate human and machine intelligence to support student learning. In addition, this work illustrates that the kinds of analytics already generated by ITSs, using student modeling techniques originally developed to support adaptive tutoring behavior, appear to provide a promising foundation for real-time teacher awareness tools.

Acknowledgements. This work was supported by NSF Award #1530726, and IES Grant R305B150008 to CMU. The opinions expressed are those of the authors and do not represent the views of NSF, IES or the U.S. ED. Special thanks to Gena Hong, Octav Popescu, Jonathan Sewall, Mera Tegene, Cindy Tipper, and all participating students and teachers.

References

1. Alavi, H.S., Dillenbourg, P.: An ambient awareness tool for supporting supervised collaborative problem solving. IEEE TLT **5**, 264–274 (2012)
2. Aleven, V.: Help seeking and intelligent tutoring systems: theoretical perspectives and a step towards theoretical integration. In: Azevedo, R., Aleven, V. (eds.) International Handbook of Metacognition and Learning Technologies, pp. 311–335. Springer, New York (2013). https://doi.org/10.1007/978-1-4419-5546-3_21
3. Aleven, V., McLaren, B.M., Sewall, J., Koedinger, K.R.: A new paradigm for intelligent tutoring systems: example-tracing tutors. IJAIED **19**(2), 105–154 (2009)
4. Aleven, V., Roll, I., McLaren, B.M., Koedinger, K.R.: Help helps, but only so much: research on help seeking with intelligent tutoring systems. IJAIED **26**, 205–223 (2016)
5. Alphen, E.V., Bakker, S.: Lernanto: using an ambient display during differentiated instruction. In: CHI EA (2016)
6. Baker, R.S.: Modeling and understanding students off-task behavior in intelligent tutoring systems. In: CHI, pp. 1059–1068 (2007)
7. Baker, R.S.: Stupid tutoring systems, intelligent humans. IJAIED **26**(2), 600–614 (2016)
8. Baker, R.S., Corbett, A.T., Roll, I., Koedinger, K.R.: Developing a generalizable detector of when students game the system. UMUAI **18**(3), 287–314 (2008)
9. Beck, J.E., Gong, Y.: Wheel-spinning: students who fail to master a skill. In: Lane, H.C., Yacef, K., Mostow, J., Pavlik, P. (eds.) AIED 2013. LNCS (LNAI), vol. 7926, pp. 431–440. Springer, Heidelberg (2013). https://doi.org/10.1007/978-3-642-39112-5_44
10. Bull, S., Kay, J.: Open learner models. In: Nkambou, R., Bourdeau, J., Mizoguchi, R. (eds.) Advances in Intelligent Tutoring Systems, pp. 301–322. Springer, Heidelberg (2010). https://doi.org/10.1007/978-3-642-14363-2_15
11. Chromebook Management Software for Schools. https://www.goguardian.com/
12. Cohen, J.: A power primer. Psychol. Bull. **112**(1), 155–159 (1992)
13. Corbett, A.T., Anderson, J.R.: Knowledge tracing: modeling the acquisition of procedural knowledge. UMUAI **4**(4), 253–278 (1995)
14. Desmarais, M.C., Baker, R.S.: A review of recent advances in learner and skill modeling in intelligent learning environments. UMUAI **22**(1–2), 9–38 (2012)
15. Dillenbourg, P., Jermann, P.: Technology for classroom orchestration. In: Khine, M., Saleh, I. (eds.) New Science of Learning, pp. 525–552. Springer, New York (2010). https://doi.org/10.1007/978-1-4419-5716-0_26
16. Dillenbourg, P.: Trends in classroom orchestration. STELLAR **1**, 5 (2011)
17. Hanington, B., Martin, B.: Universal methods of design: 100 ways to research complex problems, develop innovative ideas, and design effective solutions. Rockport (2012)
18. Hapara | Making Learning Visible. https://hapara.com/
19. Holstein, K., Hong, G., Tegene, M., McLaren, B. M., Aleven, V.: The classroom as a dashboard: co-designing wearable cognitive augmentation for K-12 teachers. In: LAK, pp. 79–88. ACM (2018)
20. Holstein, K., McLaren, B.M., Aleven, V.: Informing the design of teacher awareness tools through causal alignment analysis. In: ICLS (in press)

21. Holstein, K., McLaren, B.M., Aleven, V.: Intelligent tutors as teachers' aides: exploring teacher needs for real-time analytics in blended classrooms. In: LAK, pp. 257–266. ACM (2017)
22. Holstein, K., McLaren, B.M., Aleven, V.: SPACLE: investigating learning across virtual and physical spaces using spatial replays. In: LAK, pp. 358–367. ACM (2017)
23. Kai, S., Almeda, V.A., Baker, R.S., Shechtman, N., Heffernan, C., Heffernan, N.: Modeling wheel-spinning and productive persistence in skill builders. In: JEDM (in press)
24. Kelly, K., Heffernan, N., Heffernan, C., Goldman, S., Pellegrino, J., Soffer Goldstein, D.: Estimating the effect of web-based homework. In: Lane, H.C., Yacef, K., Mostow, J., Pavlik, P. (eds.) AIED 2013. LNCS (LNAI), vol. 7926, pp. 824–827. Springer, Heidelberg (2013). https://doi.org/10.1007/978-3-642-39112-5_122
25. Kulik, J.A., Fletcher, J.D.: Effectiveness of intelligent tutoring systems: a meta-analytic review. RER **86**(1), 42–78 (2016)
26. LanSchool Classroom Management Software. https://www.lenovosoftware.com/lanschool
27. Long, Y., Aleven, V.: Supporting students' self-regulated learning with an open learner model in a linear equation tutor. In: Lane, H.C., Yacef, K., Mostow, J., Pavlik, P. (eds.) AIED 2013. LNCS (LNAI), vol. 7926, pp. 219–228. Springer, Heidelberg (2013). https://doi.org/10.1007/978-3-642-39112-5_23
28. Long, Y., Aleven, V.: Gamification of joint student/system control over problem selection in a linear equation tutor. In: Trausan-Matu, S., Boyer, K.E., Crosby, M., Panourgia, K. (eds.) ITS 2014. LNCS, vol. 8474, pp. 378–387. Springer, Cham (2014). https://doi.org/10.1007/978-3-319-07221-0_47
29. LookWhosTalking. bitbucket.org/dadamson/lookwhostalking
30. Martinez-Maldonado, R., Clayphan, A., Yacef, K., Kay, J.: MTFeedback: providing notifications to enhance teacher awareness of small group work in the classroom. IEEE TLT **8**(2), 187–200 (2015)
31. Mavrikis, M., Gutierrez-Santos, S., Poulovassilis, A.: Design and evaluation of teacher assistance tools for exploratory learning environments. In: LAK, pp. 168–172. ACM (2016)
32. Molenaar, I., Knoop-van Campen, C.: Teacher dashboards in practice: usage and impact. In: Lavoué, É., Drachsler, H., Verbert, K., Broisin, J., Pérez-Sanagustín, M. (eds.) EC-TEL 2017. LNCS, vol. 10474, pp. 125–138. Springer, Cham (2017). https://doi.org/10.1007/978-3-319-66610-5_10
33. Nye, B.D.: Barriers to ITS adoption: a systematic mapping study. In: Trausan-Matu, S., Boyer, K.E., Crosby, M., Panourgia, K. (eds.) ITS 2014. LNCS, vol. 8474, pp. 583–590. Springer, Cham (2014). https://doi.org/10.1007/978-3-319-07221-0_74
34. Pelánek, R., Řihák, J.: Experimental analysis of mastery learning criteria. In: UMAP, pp. 156–163. ACM (2017)
35. Prieto, L.P.: Supporting orchestration of blended CSCL scenarios in distributed learning environments. Unpublished doctoral thesis (2012)
36. Prieto, L.P., Sharma, K., Dillenbourg, P., Jesús, M.: Teaching analytics: towards automatic extraction of orchestration graphs using wearable sensors. In: LAK, pp. 148–157. ACM (2016)
37. Ritter, S., Yudelson, M., Fancsali, S.E., Berman, S.R.: How mastery learning works at scale. In: L@S, pp. 71–79. ACM (2016)
38. Ritter, S., Yudelson, M., Fancsali, S., Berman, S.R.: Towards integrating human and automated tutoring systems. In: EDM, pp. 626–627 (2016)
39. Rodríguez-Triana, M.J., Prieto, L.P., Vozniuk, A., Boroujeni, M.S., Schwendimann, B.A., Holzer, A., Gillet, D.: Monitoring, awareness and reflection in blended technology enhanced learning: a systematic review. IJTEL **9**(23), 126–150 (2017)

40. Segal, A., Hindi, S., Prusak, N., Swidan, O., Livni, A., Palatnic, A., Schwarz, B., Gal, Y.: Keeping the teacher in the loop: technologies for monitoring group learning in real-time. In: André, E., Baker, R., Hu, X., Rodrigo, M.M.T., du Boulay, B. (eds.) AIED 2017. LNCS (LNAI), vol. 10331, pp. 64–76. Springer, Cham (2017). https://doi.org/10.1007/978-3-319-61425-0_6
41. Schofield, J.W.: Computers and Classroom Culture. University Press, Cambridge (1995)
42. Stang, J.B., Roll, I.: Interactions between teaching assistants and students boost engagement in physics labs. Phys. Rev. Phys. Educ. Res. **10**(2), 020117 (2014)
43. Tissenbaum, M., Matuk, C.: Real-time visualization of student activities to support classroom orchestration. In: ICLS, pp. 1120–1127 (2016)
44. Xhakaj, F., Aleven, V., McLaren, B.M.: Effects of a teacher dashboard for an intelligent tutoring system on teacher knowledge, lesson planning, lessons and student learning. In: Lavoué, É., Drachsler, H., Verbert, K., Broisin, J., Pérez-Sanagustín, M. (eds.) EC-TEL 2017. LNCS, vol. 10474, pp. 315–329. Springer, Cham (2017). https://doi.org/10.1007/978-3-319-66610-5_23
45. Yacef, K.: Intelligent teaching assistant systems. In: ICCE, pp. 136–140. IEEE (2002)

Opening Up an Intelligent Tutoring System Development Environment for Extensible Student Modeling

Kenneth Holstein[(✉)], Zac Yu, Jonathan Sewall, Octav Popescu,
Bruce M. McLaren, and Vincent Aleven

Carnegie Mellon University, Pittsburgh, PA 15213, USA
{kjholste, zacyl, sewall, bmclaren, aleven}@cs.cmu.edu,
octav@cmu.edu

Abstract. ITS authoring tools make creating intelligent tutoring systems more cost effective, but few authoring tools make it easy to flexibly incorporate an open-ended range of student modeling methods and learning analytics tools. To support a *cumulative* science of student modeling and enhance the impact of real-world tutoring systems, it is critical to extend ITS authoring tools so they easily accommodate novel student modeling methods. We report on extensions to the *CTAT/Tutorshop* architecture to support a plug-in approach to extensible student modeling, which gives an author full control over the content of the student model. The extensions enhance the range of adaptive tutoring behaviors that can be authored and support building external, student- or teacher-facing real-time analytics tools. The contributions of this work are: (1) an open architecture to support the plugging in, sharing, re-mixing, and use of advanced student modeling techniques, ITSs, and dashboards; and (2) case studies illustrating diverse ways authors have used the architecture.

Keywords: Authoring tools · Architectures · Closing the loop
Student modeling · Learning analytics · Intelligent tutoring systems

1 Introduction

Over the last few decades, authoring tools have made the development of intelligent tutoring systems (ITSs) substantially more cost effective [1, 5, 27, 35]. Yet these tools are not always geared towards easily and flexibly accommodating advances in student modeling, which may limit the degree to which they drive innovation in ITS research and the degree to which advances in student modeling spread across ITSs. Student models have long been (and remain) a key element of ITSs. They track many pedagogically-relevant features of student learning and behavior, including the moment-by-moment development of student knowledge (e.g., [8, 11, 23, 43]), metacognitive skills (e.g., [3]), affect (e.g., [10, 14, 25]), and motivation (e.g., [4]). They are a foundation for adaptive tutoring behaviors in ITSs [11], which in turn can lead to more effective instruction [3, 4, 10, 19, 26]. Student models, and learning analytics more broadly, are also increasingly being used in tools such as dashboards, open learner models, and classroom orchestration tools, where they can augment the perceptions of teachers [19, 42] and learners [7, 26].

© Springer International Publishing AG, part of Springer Nature 2018
C. Penstein Rosé et al. (Eds.): AIED 2018, LNAI 10947, pp. 169–183, 2018.
https://doi.org/10.1007/978-3-319-93843-1_13

However, various factors work against novel student modeling methods spreading widely in ITSs. These methods (e.g., [11, 23, 32, 43]) are often developed and tested on historical log data from educational software (i.e., "offline"). They are not commonly implemented or evaluated in real-world educational technologies, as we saw for example with AFM [6], PFA [33], and various innovative extensions to Bayesian Knowledge Tracing (BKT) (e.g., [23, 43]; but see [8]). Even when an advance in student modeling has been demonstrated in a live tutoring system, it often stays confined to that system, without being taken up in other systems (e.g., [3, 4, 10, 16]).

ITS authoring tools, and the ITS architectures with which they are integrated, could help address these challenges if they provided support for easy integration of a wide and open range of student modeling methods and analytics. Given that for many ITS authoring tools, many classroom-proven tutors exist, such authoring tool functionality could facilitate testing the *generality* of new student modeling methods across a range of tutors. Further, easy integration could facilitate further experimentation with new student modeling methods, beyond the initial offline testing, regarding how best to use these methods to enhance an ITS's functionality (e.g., with new adaptive tutoring behaviors or external learning analytics tools). Eventually, researchers may conduct more close-the-loop studies, in which the effects of new student modeling methods and analytics are rigorously tested in "live" tutoring systems (e.g., [3, 4, 7]). Results from such studies could accelerate a cumulative science of student modeling, as well as extend student modeling advances into working ITSs and educational practice.

However, ITS authoring tools rarely support *extensible* student modeling. For example, prior to the work reported in the current paper, *CTAT/Tutorshop*, an authoring environment for cognitive tutors and example-tracing tutors that has been used to build many dozens of ITSs [1], supported only student models comprising a set of BKT mastery probabilities for knowledge components (KCs) within the authored tutors. An author could not add other types of variables to the student model (e.g., to track the student's affective or motivational state, or metacognition) or easily experiment with different methods for updating or using the student model. Similarly, *ASSISTments Builder* [35] and *ASPIRE* [29], other major ITS authoring tools, do not support easy extension of their student models with new types of variables. By contrast, *GIFT* [37] does support an extensible student model based on multiple data sources (e.g., sensor data) with different time scales and granularity. Yet *GIFT* has been designed with a different focus than *CTAT*, and thus has other limitations [15]. For example, unlike *CTAT*, *GIFT* does not support non-programmer authoring of tutors with their own tutor interface and an extended step loop. We see these related, somewhat divergent, efforts as synergistic and a useful point of reference.

To address this challenge, we have extended *CTAT/Tutorshop* so authors can easily plug in an open-ended range of student modeling techniques. The extensions also support the authoring of an open-ended range of adaptive tutoring behaviors and facilitate the development of an open-ended range of student-facing and teacher-facing support tools, including real-time tools for awareness and orchestration [7, 17]. We refer to the new architecture as the *CTAT/TutorShop Analytics (CT+A)* architecture. We aim to lower the barriers to the sharing, re-use, and re-mixing of advanced student modeling methods across researchers and research groups, with the goal of accelerating progress within a *cumulative* science of student modeling (c.f., [11, 32, 37]).

2   The CTAT/Tutorshop Analytics (CT+A) Architecture

2.1   Overview

CTAT is a widely used ITS authoring tool that supports both a non-programmer approach (example-tracing tutors) and an AI-programming approach (Cognitive Tutors, a form of model-tracing tutors) to tutor authoring. *TutorShop* is a learning management system (LMS) built for classroom use of *CTAT* tutors. Use of *CTAT* has been estimated to make ITS development 4–8 times as cost effective, compared to historic estimates of development time [1]. As evidence that *CTAT* and *Tutorshop* are robust and mature, *CTAT* has been used by more than 750 authors. Dozens of tutors built with *CTAT* have been used in real educational settings [1]. As of 2015, *CTAT*-built tutors had been used by 44,000 students, with roughly 48,000,000 student/tutor transactions, for a total of 62,000 h of student work. Since then, there has been substantial additional use.

We first describe key elements of the *CT+A* architecture (shown in Fig. 1) that existed prior to adding the new support for extensible student modeling. At a functional level, each tutor created in this architecture comprises a "step loop" nested within a "task loop" [39, 40]. The step loop supports within-problem tutoring, the task loop supports problem selection. The step loop has two key components, namely, a tutor interface and a tutor engine, both running on the client (i.e., the student's machine). The interface is where the student-tutor interactions happen; it is custom-designed for each problem type. The tutor engine interprets student actions and decides what feedback or hints to give, employing either the model-tracing or example-tracing algorithm, depending on the tutor type. The tutor's task loop is implemented in *TutorShop* and runs on the server. *CT+A* offers various problem selection algorithms that can be used within a tutor, including individualized mastery learning [8]. This method relies on a student model that, as mentioned, contains estimates of the probability that the student has mastered each of a set of KCs targeted in the current tutor unit, computed (by the tutor engine, as part of the step loop) according to a standard BKT model [8]. *TutorShop* takes care of permanent storage of the student model. It also provides learning management functionality for teachers (e.g., managing student accounts and assignments), as well as content management (e.g., it stores tutor curriculum content). This architecture has been used to build many tutors, but it cannot easily accommodate new student modeling methods. To address this limitation, we added the following key extensions:

1. An *extensible student model*. An author can now add new variables to the student model.
2. An API and template for automated plug-in *detectors* for any new student modeling variables (i.e., computational processes – oftentimes machine-learned – that track psychological and behavioral states of learners based on the transaction stream with the ITS). For the time being, we focus on sensor-free detection of student modeling variables. We have started to create a library of compatible detectors [9], so as to facilitate sharing, re-use, and re-mixing of plug-in detectors among authors;

3. Multiple mechanisms by which authors can craft tutor behavior that adapts to student model extensions, in the tutor's step loop and task loop, and
4. A *forwarding* mechanism within *TutorShop* that allows authors to pass student models to web-connected learning analytics displays on a broad range of platforms (from browser-based dashboards to wearable devices).
5. The beginnings of a library of "dashlets," to facilitate building learning analytics tools. Dashlets are re-usable interface components that can be associated with sets of analytics and configured to visualize these analytics.

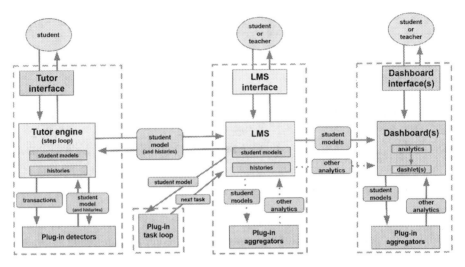

Fig. 1. Overview of the modular *CT+A* architecture, illustrating the flow of information between architectural components, with the top level (ovals) representing users. Components within dotted-line regions run on the same machine. Items in blue represent configurable components. Rounded boxes indicate information being passed between architectural components. Dotted arrows represent pathways that are not presently implemented.

2.2   The Extensible Student Model

Whereas previously the student model of a tutor built in *CTAT/Tutorshop* comprised only a set of KC probabilities, the student model is now extensible, with authors having full control over the set of variables it contains. An author can add any number of variables to the student model that capture student behaviors and inferred psychological states (e.g., knowledge, metacognitive, affective, or motivational states) [11]. The KC probabilities remain as variables in the student model if the author so wishes. With the exception of these KC probabilities, *TutorShop* is oblivious to the semantics of the analytics in the student model (i.e., it does not have any built-in functionality that responds to the student model analytics; all such functionality must be provided by the author). A key advantage of this "semantic ignorance" is flexibility and control on the part of authors defining and using these analytics. Transparent to the author, the *CT+A* architecture maintains, in real time, two up-to-the-second copies of the student model, one within the tutor engine, one within *TutorShop*. Within the tutor engine, the student model can support adaptive tutoring behaviors. Within *TutorShop*, it can support external real-time support tools an author may wish to create or hook in (e.g., a real-time dashboard). The copy of the student model stored by *TutorShop* is kept in between problems and student sessions and is sent back to the tutor engine at the beginning of each problem/session, again transparent to the author.

2.3   Plug-in Detectors

To extend the student model, an author needs to provide automated *detectors* for all new student model variables, that is, code that computes these variables. Tutor authors can write plug-in detectors in Javascript, working from either previously-created detectors or from a generic template, available in a central, open source code repository [9]. The template defines a small number of code modules that each detector should have, namely, student model variable computations, internal feature computations, and trigger conditions for each.

To support a "remix" approach to student modeling, we have started a library of detectors that conform to this template. The library is freely available [9], and we hope it will continue to grow through community authoring. Many of the detectors currently available have been used in running ITSs and dashboards, including: multiple variants of the Help Model [3], BKT [8], various moving average detectors [34], and detectors of unproductive persistence or "wheel-spinning" [21]. Paquette et al. have also recently developed and shared a detector of "gaming the system" behavior in ITSs [4] that generalizes well across a diverse range of systems [32].

Detectors in *CT+A* are plug-in agents that rely on three sources of input. First, they listen to the transaction stream coming from the tutor engine; each transaction describes a student action, such as an attempt at solving a step or a hint request, as well as the tutor's response, such as whether the student action was correct and what KCs were involved. Each detector also listens for updates to the extensible student model (i.e., updates made by other detectors), and has access to all student model variables, in addition to any intermediate variables that the detector itself maintains (see below). Based on these inputs, each detector responds with newly computed values for its targeted student model variables. As a result, both copies of the student model (the one within the tutor engine and the one within *TutorShop*) are updated, transparent to the author. Student model updates are sent to *TutorShop* in a fine-grained, transaction-based message format we have adopted, a subset of *LearnSphere*'s Tutor Message format [15, 36].

Each detector can maintain an internal state in the form of a set of intermediate variables specified to conform to the detector template. Intermediate variables are not considered to be part of the student model and are therefore not accessible to other architectural components such as other detectors or aggregators. They are, however, sent to *TutorShop*, so that *TutorShop* can save a (compact) "history" for each detector. These detector histories are sent back to the tutor engine at the beginning of each problem, so that the previous state of each associated detector can be restored.

Although *CTAT* detectors typically run in live tutoring systems, they can also be used, without modifications, for offline data analyses (e.g., [19, 32]). *LearnSphere* [38], a large online data repository with many analysis tools, provides a workflow component for *CTAT* detectors, in the *Tigris* visual workflow tool, that enables running detectors against historical log data (from the same or other *CTAT* tutors).

2.4   Extended Support for Authoring Adaptive Tutor Behaviors

To enable the authoring of a wide and open range of adaptive tutor behaviors, we added two mechanisms to *CTAT* by which an author can make a tutor's behavior in the *step loop* (i.e., the within-problem tutoring support it offers [2, 40]) contingent on the extensible student model. We also made provisions for plugging in new task selection algorithms in the tutor's *task loop*.

As a first mechanism for creating step-loop tutor behaviors that are responsive to the extensible student model, authors of example-tracing tutors can use Excel-like formulas that reference student model variables. The use of formulas, attached to the tutor's behavior graph, has long been part of CTAT [1]; what's new is that formulas can reference variables in the extensible student model (see Fig. 2). Formulas can affect many aspects of tutor behavior, including how the tutor interprets a student's problem-solving behavior against a behavior graph, the content of feedback and hints, and tutor-performed actions. Using these building blocks, an author can craft a wide and open-ended range of adaptive tutor behaviors, for example, presenting abstract hints to advanced students, presenting empathic hints to frustrated students, presenting unmastered steps as worked-out steps to be explained by the student, and having the tutor perform highly mastered steps for the student to reduce "busy work." Authors of rule-based tutors can also craft rules that support adaptive behaviors, taking of advantage of the extensible student model's availability in working memory.

A second mechanism addresses a limitation of the first, namely, that it cannot be used to craft adaptive tutor behaviors that respond to the very last (i.e., the most recent) student action – it lags by one student action. Sometimes, tutor behaviors are needed that are contingent upon updates of the extensible student model triggered by the very last student action. Our second mechanism lets author craft such tutor behavior, although to do so, the author must write Javascript code. Specifically, all tutors have a dedicated plug-in agent called the "Tutor's Ear", that continuously listens for updates to the student model. The Tutor's Ear has unique access to the tutor engine, meaning that it can directly trigger tutor responses. Authors can customize this detector by specifying (in Javascript code) conditions involving one or more student model variables under which a particular tutor response should be triggered. Authors can then specify desired response actions (e.g., "ShowMessage ('Try explaining to yourself what needs to be done on this step')"), via a simple API. Ideally, *CTAT* would have a single mechanism for step-loop adaptivity based on student model variables, but a substantial re-architecting would be necessary to merge the two mechanisms.

In addition to supporting the authoring of adaptive behaviors in the tutor's step loop, we support the plugging-in of adaptive task selection methods (i.e., plug-in task loops), by making the student model available to external task selection processes.

2.5 Support for Using Learning Analytics in External Support Tools

Finally, authors may use *Tutorshop* to forward student models to web-connected learning analytics displays on a range of platforms, from browser-based dashboards to wearable devices [17]. While detectors in *CT+A* operate client-side, within individual students' tutors, and thus can only compute analytics for individual students, it is often useful for learning analytics applications (e.g., teacher dashboards) to compute analytics at higher units of analysis, such as groups of students or whole classes. For example, in classrooms in which students work with *CTAT* tutors collaboratively (c.f., [31]), information about the relative performance and contributions of the students in a group might be useful to display to teachers. To address this need, the extended architecture provides an "aggregator" API to enable authors to compute custom group- or class-level analytics from student model variables across multiple students.

Authors of learning analytics tools can write custom "aggregators" in JavaScript to calculate new values from detector analytics across specified sets of students. Aggregator calculations can be triggered by incoming student model updates. We created the *Aggregator House* (AggHouse), a JavaScript/Node.js [30] library that can invoke aggregators either on the *Tutorshop* server, or directly on a dashboard client. Results from aggregators can, in turn, be used to update real-time dashboard displays.

To facilitate building analytics tools that can be used in conjunction with *CTAT*-built tutors (e.g., dashboards and orchestration tools), we provide an API called the *CT+A Live Dashboard*, which includes the beginnings of a library of "dashlets," interface components for analytics tools. Authors may use the built-in dashlet components or create new dashlets (using Javascript). In addition to supporting the building and deployment of web browser-based dashboards, *Tutorshop* can also forward analytics to tools running on external hosts, via a real-time event stream in JSON format, to support analytics tools across a range of hardware interfaces.

2.6 Lessons Learned: Guiding Principles for Extensible Student Modeling

In designing *CT+A* so it can support an open range of student modeling applications, with provisions for real-time support tools, a set of guiding architectural principles has emerged. These principles capture the key architectural elements added to *CT+A*.

Maximize Tutor-Side Computations. We have structured detectors to promote incremental (e.g., per transaction) computation of analytics. This supports offloading of student model computations to the tutor clients, rather than the LMS, since incremental computations spread processing load over time.

Keep Data Streams "lean". In designing key data streams (i.e., the transaction stream into the detectors, and the student model update stream from tutor to LMS), we settled on a small subset of the information *CTAT* tutors currently send to *LearnSphere* [24]. We originally attempted to anticipate many possible author needs and build these into the transaction messages [36] that serve as primitive inputs to plug-in detectors, but decided against this approach. Keeping this set small can reduce unnecessary message traffic and redundancy by acknowledging the wide range of analytics authors may wish to compute and enabling them to compute only those needed.

Maintain the Student Model both Locally and Centrally. Prior to these architectural extensions, an up-to-the-second copy of the student model was maintained on the tutor side, but the LMS-side copy was updated only as needed to preserve the student model in-between problems. We have found it valuable to instead maintain both a local (tutor-side) and central (LMS-side) up-to-the-second copy of the student model, with each copy supporting different use cases, namely, tutor adaptivity versus analytics tools; the latter typically require both class-level analytics and real-time updating, which is why central copies of the student models are useful.

Support Easy Re-mixing of Existing Components. In addition to supporting plug-and-play of architectural components, we have found it valuable to make individual components easily-customizable. For example, each detector contains a module that exposes configurable parameters. This feature is intended to facilitate the creation of *variants* of student modeling techniques, including those created and shared by others, to support authors not only in comparing against each other's models, but also in *building upon and contributing to* each other's modeling work (c.f. [22, 37, 38]).

3 Case Studies

In this section, we present case studies of prototype systems that use the *CT+A* architecture to enhance tutoring systems' adaptive capabilities and/or to support teachers.

3.1 A Prototype Tutor that Provides Metacognitive Scaffolding

The experience of some of the participants during our yearly summer school illustrates how a detector library can be helpful in quickly prototyping adaptive tutor behaviors. During this summer school, designers, teachers, and researchers build their own systems using *CT+A*. This past year, participants were able to author detector-enhanced ITSs, by re-using pre-existing detectors available in the detector library. They embedded pre-existing detectors into their tutors and authored custom adaptive tutor behavior based on detectors' outputs.

A team of two students, Dennis Bouvier and Ray Martinez, used the *CT+A* architecture to implement an ITS prototype that provided metacognitive feedback in addition to feedback at the domain level, which is standard in *CTAT* tutors. This tutor, the Binary Search tutor, was intended to help undergraduate Computer Science students learn binary search algorithms. It allows students to practice applying a binary search algorithm to an array of numbers. The *Binary Search Tutor* uses a plug-in implementation of the Help Model, which can identify patterns in student-tutor interactions that indicate *abuse* (e.g., rapidly clicking through hints without reading) or *avoidance* (e.g., not using hints in situations where they are likely to be needed) of the tutoring software's built-in hints [3]. Using custom response actions authored in the Tutor's Ear, the *Binary Search Tutor* responds to both types of student behavior. In the case of hint avoidance, the tutor prompts the student to ask for a hint. In the case of hint abuse, the tutor encourages the student to try attempting more steps without hints.

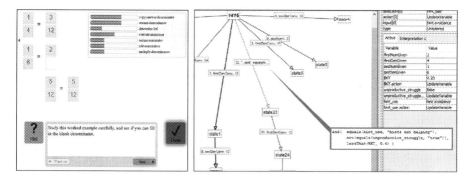

Fig. 2. Left: The *Fraction Addition Tutor* uses multiple plug-in detectors to decide whether to provide more scaffolding. Right: Authoring the *Fraction Addition Tutor* in *CTAT*.

3.2 A Prototype Fraction Addition Tutor with Hybrid Adaptivity

Using *CT+A*, we have also created a tutor prototype that implements a form of "hybrid adaptivity" [2], meaning that it adapts to combinations of student states. This tutor, an example-tracing tutor for 4th and 5th grade fraction addition problems, adjusts the level of scaffolding provided based *jointly* on the values of cognitive variables (skill mastery) and metacognitive variables (hint use, unproductive persistence). For example: if a student is detected as having low knowledge on KCs involved in the current step (by a plug-in of BKT [8]) *and* the student is detected as "using all available hints yet remaining stuck" (by the Help Model [3]) *but* the student is not currently detected as necessarily "unproductively persisting" (by a detector of wheel-spinning [21]), then the *Fraction Addition Tutor* will dynamically convert the student's current problem into a completion problem, by filling out all steps except one, and prompt the student to study the worked-out steps and fill in the remaining step (Fig. 2, left). This capability was authored using a formula (expressed in *CTAT's* formula language) that references student model variables (i.e., the first of the two mechanisms described above for authoring adaptive tutor behavior). This formula was attached to a new path in the behavior graph (the main representation of domain knowledge in an example-tracing tutor), added by the author (Fig. 2, right). The path specified the tutor-performed actions needed to fill in the worked-out steps.

3.3 Teacher Smart Glasses that Support Real-Time Classroom Orchestration

The *CT+A* architecture has been used to implement *Lumilo* [17, 19], a mixed reality smart glasses application, co-designed with K-12 math teachers, and developed for the Microsoft *HoloLens* [28]. *Lumilo* is designed to aid teachers in orchestrating person-alized class sessions, in which students work with ITSs at their own pace. When a teacher puts these glasses on, she/he can see visual indicators floating over students' heads (Fig. 3), based on changes in a student's extensible student model. The teacher can also view more detailed student-level analytics, as well as class-level summaries. *Lumilo* has been used in fifteen K-12 classrooms so far [17, 19].

All student model updates are computed within students' tutor clients (using several plug-in detectors) and forwarded to *TutorShop*, which forwards them to *Lumilo*. Although *Lumilo* is not browser-based (and was thus authored outside of *Live Dashboard*, described above), *TutorShop* provides hooks for *Lumilo* to connect to each classrooms' analytics streams. *Lumilo*'s dashlets are then updated by aggregators on the *Lumilo* client.

Fig. 3. Left: Point-of-view screenshot of teacher using *Lumilo* to monitor a class of students (taken directly after class). Right: Teacher's view through *Lumilo* after selecting a student, to view more detailed information for that student [17].

3.4 A Tablet-Based Real-Time Dashboard for Personalized Class Sessions

In addition to the smart glasses interface of *Lumilo*, a tablet-based companion app is being developed within the *Live Dashboard* and *AggHouse* tools. The tablet companion to *Lumilo* provides the same analytics and allows teachers to toggle between alternative display formats. For example, teachers can use *Live Dashboard*'s Table-View component to display student model updates in a student-by-variable matrix format. Alternatively, teachers can use *Live Dashboard*'s Seating-Chart component to display a "real-time, real-place" visualization [18, 41] of the classroom, using a teacher-provided seating chart, and draggable student components (Fig. 4).

3.5 A Prototype Dashboard that Supports Data-Informed Lesson Planning

The *CT+A* architecture was used to develop *Luna*, a prototype browser-based dashboard front-end for K-12 teachers. Unlike *Lumilo*, which is designed to support real-time monitoring, Luna supports teachers in lesson planning, using analytics generated by an ITS for algebraic equation solving [20, 42]. *Luna* allows teachers to review students' knowledge and amount of practice on each of a number of fine-grained skills and error categories, either at the level of a class summary, or at the individual student level. In addition, teachers can use *Luna* to review individual students' progress through the software, relative to the time they have spent working (Fig. 4). *Luna* was developed using the *Live Dashboard* and *AggHouse* tools. As with *Lumilo*, the primitive level of data upon which *Luna* relies are student model updates, computed by plug-in detectors which are distributed across students' client machines.

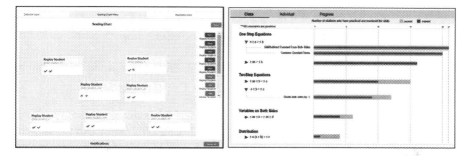

Fig. 4. Left: prototype of the *Lumilo Tablet* real-time dashboard, with students displayed as blocks within a *Live Dashboard* "Seating Chart" component. Right: a prototype of the *Luna* lesson-planning dashboard, showing the class-level view.

3.6 A Fractions Tutor with a Custom Adaptive Task Selection Policy

Finally, the *CT+A* architecture was used to develop an adaptive fractions tutor [12, 13] which can use a variety of custom instructional policies [12] to drive adaptive task selection (e.g., adaptive policies learned via reinforcement learning). The *Fractions Adaptive* tutor makes its student model available to external, custom task selection processes (Python web applications) via the *TutorShop* LMS. *TutorShop*, in turn, selects a next task for each student based on the output of this plug-in task loop.

4   Discussion and Future Work

If advances in student modeling made by the AIED, EDM, and LAK communities are to have a measurable impact on the design and effectiveness of real-world systems, and contribute to a *cumulative* science of student modeling, it is critical to develop authoring tools that can support these goals. Toward this end, we have introduced *CT+A*, an open architecture to support extensible student modeling. This architecture supports the plugging in, sharing, re-mixing, and use of advanced student modeling techniques in ITSs and associated analytics tools. The work is unique in that it supports extensible student models in the context of non-programmer ITS authoring tools that support building tutors with a dedicated problem-solving interface and elaborate step loop. In addition to the architecture itself, we present a set of "lessons learned," in the form of principles summarizing the main architectural elements. We hope they will inform other projects focused on extensible student modeling.

Our case studies illustrate some of the range and flexibility of *CT+A* and demonstrate progress towards four key goals for an analytics-integrated architecture. We have demonstrated that authors can add new variables to the student model by embedding detectors in running tutoring systems. We have presented an API and template for creating these plug-in detectors, requiring only that authors are familiar with basic JavaScript. We demonstrated as well that existing detectors can be reused and that authoring new adaptive tutoring behavior is feasible without programming. Finally, we have shown that the *CT+A* architecture can support the development of a variety of teacher support tools, including both real-time and lesson-planning dashboards, and both web-based and wearable tools.

Limitations of the work are, at least for the time being, that we focus on transaction-based (in other words, sensor-free) student modeling [11]. Although transaction-based student modeling is a practical, proven, and widely useful approach (e.g., [4, 11, 15, 25, 38]), we leave for future work any issues related to how a student model can be updated with multiple data streams of different granularity (transactions and sensor output). As mentioned, such issues are being explored in the *GIFT* architecture [37]. An additional limitation of the current architecture is that, in authoring tutoring behaviors responsive to the extensible student model, immediate tutor responses involve a different mechanism than tutor responses in subsequent tutor cycles. A more flexible and general solution might be give detectors and the tutor engine equal status, with a coordinating agent that has the final word regarding the tutor response [36]. Finally, adding student model extensions requires some programming (namely, to create detectors in Javascript) and thus falls outside *CTAT*'s non-programmer paradigm. The amount of programming required can be reduced, however, by re-using existing detectors, shared among authors in the *CT+A* detector library [9]. In the future, new practices developed and tested within architecture might inform extensions to support their use without programming.

It is our hope that *CT+A* will help lower the barriers to sharing advanced student modeling methods between researchers, which in turn may accelerate progress within a cumulative science of student modeling (c.f., [11, 32, 37]). Support for plugging in and sharing student modeling methods can support authors and researchers not only in comparing against each other's' models (e.g., by evaluating systems that use these models in classroom experiments), but even in *building upon and contributing to* others' student modeling work (c.f., [22, 37, 38]). Also, they might help increase the number of close-the-loop studies that researchers undertake. We also hope that architectures like *CT+A* will result in broader representation of advanced student modeling methods in both research and real-world educational software.

Acknowledgements. This work was supported by NSF Award #1530726, and IES Grant R305B150008 to CMU. Opinions are those of the authors and do not represent views of NSF, IES or the U.S. ED. Special thanks to Ryan Baker, Nupur Chatterji, Mary Beth Kery, Michal Moskal, Luc Paquette, Peter Schaldenbrand, Cindy Tipper, and Franceska Xhakaj.

References

1. Aleven, V., McLaren, B.M., Sewall, J., van Velsen, M., Popescu, O., Demi, S., Ringenberg, M., Koedinger, K.R.: Example-tracing tutors: intelligent tutor development for non-programmers. IJAIED **26**, 224–269 (2016)
2. Aleven, V., Mclaughlin, E.A., Glenn, R.A., Koedinger, K.R.: Instruction based on adaptive learning technologies. In: Mayer, R.E., Alexander, P. (eds.) Handbook of Research on Learning and Instruction. Routledge, London (2017)
3. Aleven, V., Roll, I., McLaren, B.M., Koedinger, K.R.: Help helps, but only so much: research on help seeking with intelligent tutoring systems. IJAIED **26**(1), 205–223 (2016)
4. Baker, R.S.J.D., et al.: Adapting to when students game an intelligent tutoring system. In: Ikeda, M., Ashley, K.D., Chan, T.-W. (eds.) ITS 2006. LNCS, vol. 4053, pp. 392–401. Springer, Heidelberg (2006). https://doi.org/10.1007/11774303_39
5. Blessing, S.B., Aleven, V., Gilbert, S., Heffernan, N.T., Matsuda, N., Mitrovic, A.: Authoring example-based tutors for procedural tasks. In: Design Recommendations for Adaptive Intelligent Tutoring Systems, pp. 71–93. US Army Research Laboratory (2015)
6. Cen, H., Koedinger, K., Junker, B.: Learning factors analysis – a general method for cognitive model evaluation and improvement. In: Ikeda, M., Ashley, K.D., Chan, T.-W. (eds.) ITS 2006. LNCS, vol. 4053, pp. 164–175. Springer, Heidelberg (2006). https://doi.org/10.1007/11774303_17
7. Clow, D.: The learning analytics cycle. In: LAK, pp. 134–138. ACM (2012)
8. Corbett, A.T., Anderson, J.R.: Knowledge tracing: modeling the acquisition of procedural knowledge. UMUAI **4**(4), 253–278 (1995)
9. CT+A - Detector plugins. https://github.com/d19fe8/CTAT-detector-plugins/wiki/
10. D'Mello, S.K., Lehman, B., Graesser, A.: A motivationally supportive affect-sensitive AutoTutor. In: Calvo, R.A., D'Mello, S.K. (eds.) New Perspectives on Affect and Learning Technologies, pp. 113–126. Springer, Heidelberg (2011). https://doi.org/10.1007/978-1-4419-9625-1
11. Desmarais, M.C., Baker, R.S.J.D.: A review of recent advances in learner and skill modeling in intelligent learning environments. UMUAI **22**, 9–38 (2012)
12. Doroudi, S., Aleven, V., Brunskill, E.: Robust evaluation matrix: Towards a more principled offline exploration of instructional policies. In: L@S, pp. 3–12. ACM (2017)
13. Doroudi, S., Holstein, K., Aleven, V., Brunskill, E.: Sequence matters, but how exactly? A method for evaluating activity sequences from data. In: EDM, pp. 70–77 (2016)
14. Fancsali, S.: Causal discovery with models : behavior, affect, and learning in cognitive tutor algebra. In: EDM, pp. 28–35 (2014)
15. Fancsali, S.E., Ritter, S., Stamper, J. and Nixon, T.: Toward "hyper-personalized" cognitive tutors: non-cognitive personalization in the generalized intelligent framework for tutoring. In: AIED, pp. 71–79 (2013)
16. Grawemeyer, B., Holmes, W., Gutiérrez-Santos, S., Hansen, A., Loibl, K., Mavrikis, M.: Light-bulb moment? Towards adaptive presentation of feedback based on students' affective state. In: IUI, pp. 400–404. ACM (2015)
17. Holstein, K., Hong, G., Tegene, M., McLaren, B. M., Aleven, V.: The classroom as a dashboard: co-designing wearable cognitive augmentation for K-12 teachers. In: LAK, pp. 79–88. ACM (2018)
18. Holstein, K., McLaren, B.M., Aleven, V.: SPACLE: investigating learning across virtual and physical spaces using spatial replays. In: LAK, pp. 358–367 (2017)
19. Holstein, K., McLaren, B.M., Aleven, V.: Student learning benefits of a mixed-reality teacher awareness tool in AI-enhanced classrooms. In: AIED (2018, to appear)

20. Holstein, K., Xhakaj, F., Aleven, V., Mclaren, B.M.: Luna: a dashboard for teachers using intelligent tutoring systems. In: IWTA@EC-TEL (2016)

21. Kai, S., Almeda, V.A., Baker, R.S., Shechtman, N., Heffernan, C., Heffernan, N.: Modeling wheel-spinning and productive persistence in Skill Builders. JEDM (2018, to appear)

22. Kery, M.B., Myers, B.A.: Exploring exploratory programming. In: VL/HCC, pp. 25–29 (2018)

23. Khajah, M., Lindsey, R.V., Mozer, M.C.: How deep is knowledge tracing? In: EDM, pp. 94–101 (2015)

24. Koedinger, K.R., Baker, R.S.J.D., Cunningham, K., Skogsholm, A., Leber, B., Stamper, J.: A data repository for the EDM community: the PSLC DataShop. In: Handbook of Educational Data Mining, pp. 43–56. CRC Press, Boca Raton (2010)

25. Liu, Z., Pataranutaporn, V., Ocumpaugh, J., Baker, R.S.J.D.: Sequences of frustration and confusion, and learning. In: EDM, pp. 114–120 (2013)

26. Long, Y., Aleven, V.: Supporting students' self-regulated learning with an open learner model in a linear equation tutor. In: AIED, pp. 219–228 (2013)

27. MacLellan, C.J., Koedinger, K.R., Matsuda, N.: Authoring tutors with SimStudent: an evaluation of efficiency and model quality. In: Trausan-Matu, S., Boyer, K.E., Crosby, M., Panourgia, K. (eds.) ITS 2014. LNCS, vol. 8474, pp. 551–560. Springer, Cham (2014). https://doi.org/10.1007/978-3-319-07221-0_70

28. Microsoft HoloLens. https://www.microsoft.com/en-us/hololens

29. Mitrovic, A., Martin, B., Suraweera, P., Zakharov, K., Milik, N., Holland, J., McGuigan, N.: ASPIRE: an authoring system and deployment environment for constraint-based tutors. IJAIED 19(2), 155–188 (2009)

30. Node.js. https://nodejs.org/en/

31. Olsen, J.K., Belenky, D.M., Aleven, V., Rummel, N., Sewall, J., Ringenberg, M.: Authoring tools for collaborative intelligent tutoring system environments. In: Trausan-Matu, S., Boyer, K.E., Crosby, M., Panourgia, K. (eds.) ITS 2014. LNCS, vol. 8474, pp. 523–528. Springer, Cham (2014). https://doi.org/10.1007/978-3-319-07221-0_66

32. Paquette, L., Baker, R.S., Moskal, M.: A system-general model for the detection of gaming the system behavior in CTAT and LearnSphere. In: AIED (2018, to appear)

33. Pavlik, P.I., Cen, H., Koedinger, K.R.: Performance factors analysis - a new alternative to knowledge tracing, pp. 531–538. IOS Press, Amsterdam (2009)

34. Pelánek, R., Řihák, J.: Experimental analysis of mastery learning criteria. In: UMAP, pp. 156–163 (2017)

35. Razzaq, L., Patvarczki, J., Almeida, S.F., Vartak, M., Feng, M., Heffernan, N.T., Koedinger, K.R.: The assistment builder: supporting the life cycle of tutoring system content creation. IEEE TLT 2(2), 157–166 (2009)

36. Ritter, S., Koedinger, K.: Towards lightweight tutoring agents. In: AIED, pp. 16–19 (1995)

37. Sottilare, R.A., Baker, R.S., Graesser, A.C., Lester, J.C.: Special issue on the Generalized Intelligent Framework for Tutoring (GIFT): creating a stable and flexible platform for innovations in AIED research. In: IJAIED, pp. 1–13 (2017)

38. Stamper, J., Koedinger, K., Pavlik Jr, P.I., Rose, C., Liu, R., Eagle, M., Veeramachaneni, K.: Educational data analysis using LearnSphere. In: EDM 2016 Workshops and Tutorials (2016)

39. VanLehn, K.: The behavior of tutoring systems. IJAIED 16(3), 227–265 (2006)

40. VanLehn, K.: Regulative loops, step loops and task loops. IJAIED 26(1), 107–112 (2016)

41. Vatrapu, R.K., Kocherla, K., Pantazos, K.: iKlassroom: real-time, real-place teaching analytics. In: IWTA@LAK (2013)
42. Xhakaj, F., Aleven, V., McLaren, B.M.: Effects of a teacher dashboard for an intelligent tutoring system on teacher knowledge, lesson planning, lessons and student learning. In: EC-TEL, pp. 315–329 (2017)
43. Yudelson, M.V., Koedinger, K.R., Gordon, G.J.: Individualized Bayesian knowledge tracing models. In: AIED, pp. 171–180 (2013)

Better Late Than Never but Never Late Is Better: Towards Reducing the Answer Response Time to Questions in an Online Learning Community

Oluwabukola Mayowa (Ishola) Idowu[✉] and Gordon McCalla[✉]

ARIES Laboratory, Department of Computer Science, University of Saskatchewan, Saskatoon, Canada
bukola.idowu@usask.ca, mccalla@cs.usask.ca

Abstract. Professionals increasingly turn to online learning communities (OLCs) such as Stack Overflow (SO) to get help with their questions. It is important that the help is appropriate to the learning needs of the professional and is received in a timely fashion. However, we observed in SO a rise in the proportion of questions either answered late or not answered at all, from 5% in 2009 to 23% in 2016. There is clearly a need to be able to quickly find appropriate answerers for the questions asked by users. Our research goal is thus to find techniques that allow us to predict from SO data (using only information available at the time the question was asked) the *actual* answerers who provided the best answers and the most timely answers to users' questions. Such techniques could then be deployed proactively at the time a question is asked to recommend an appropriate answerer. We used a variety of tag-based, response-based, and hybrid approaches in making these predictions. Comparing the approaches, we achieved success rates that varied from a low of .88% to a high of 89.64%, with the hybrid approaches being the best. We also explored the effect of excluding from the pool of possible answerers those users, who had already answered a question "recently", with "recent" varying from 15 min up to 12 h, so as to have well rested helpers. We still achieved reasonable success rates at least for smaller exclusion periods of up to an hour, although naturally not as good as the time exclusion grew longer. We believe our work shows promise for allowing us to predict prospective answerers for questions who are not overworked, hence reducing the number of questions that would otherwise be answered late or not answered at all.

Keywords: Online learning · Learning needs · Help-seeking · Peer-help
Peer recommender systems

1 Introduction

Online learning communities (OLCs) provide interactive learning environments that integrate with the day-to-day tasks of professionals [1, 12]. It is important that the

© Springer International Publishing AG, part of Springer Nature 2018
C. Penstein Rosé et al. (Eds.): AIED 2018, LNAI 10947, pp. 184–197, 2018.
https://doi.org/10.1007/978-3-319-93843-1_14

learning needs[1] of professionals within such communities can be met in a timely fashion [2]. Stack Overflow (SO) is one such online learning community, and it is within SO that we have based our research. In this paper we are interested in the problem of a user[2] who posts questions in SO and either receives an answer that is too late to be of use or, worse, doesn't receive an answer at all, which not only deprives the user himself or herself of useful feedback but also deprives the entire community of such feedback. This is an increasingly serious problem. In this paper we show that there has been a steady rise over the years in the proportion of questions answered late or unanswered within SO. We then devise approaches that allow us to predict the actual answerer to a question. If successful, such approaches could be the basis for a peer recommender system that could proactively find a prospective answerer to a question and thus reduce the time that a user must wait for an answer, and eliminate situations where no answer is given at all. In order to get insight into the issue of "answerer overload" we also explore the impact of eliminating certain potential answerers who have answered a question recently.

Our work builds on an earlier study in which we attempted only to predict the answerers for questions that received their first answer within an hour of being asked [2], answerers that were online at the time the question was asked. We achieved a success rate of about 55%. In our new study we wish to improve upon the success rate achieved in our previous study. Moreover, we wish to extend our analysis to predict the answerers for questions that received late answers to their question. Of course, predicting the prospective answerers for questions that received their first answer much later is a more difficult problem, as the actual question answerer might have been offline when the question was asked. This implies the need to select the prospective answerers from a much larger pool of active question answerers as opposed to choosing only from online available question answerers as we did in our previous study [2].

In predicting the answerers, we employ tag-based, response-based and hybrid approaches. Each of these approaches tracks historical information about the questions and the SO users using its own defined features and generates a ranked list of prospective answerers. The top @N (where N is the number of prospective answerers selected, ranging from 10 to 100 in our study) prospective answerers are selected. The success rate @N of each of the approaches is then evaluated by computing the proportion of questions (compared to the total number of questions considered) where the actual question answerer is in the top @N prospective answerers. The results obtained in this study are an improvement upon the results achieved in our own past study [2] and the results of Tian et al. [3].

---

[1] Learning needs are defined as the gaps in the knowledge of a learner that might be perceived or unperceived by the learner. In this study, we focused on the perceived learning needs of learners which are evident by the questions they asked within the OLC.

[2] We will use the term "user" in this paper rather than "learner" when specifically discussing SO users since they are likely not explicitly learners in their own minds. However, in the future most professionals will be using such forums to meet their lifelong learning needs. Since our research is aimed at helping develop tools for such professional lifelong learners, especially tools that support personalization to each such learner, it is, we believe, deeply and broadly relevant to artificial intelligence in education.

2 Related Work

The value of a help giving system depends on the success of students in receiving help in the past [4]. Results from a study by Aleven and Koedinger [5] show the need for appropriate use of help facilities by students to improve their learning outcomes. Roll et al. [6] in a follow up study using the PACT Geometry Tutor provided appropriate instructions to guide the help-seeking of students, resulting in an increase in the help-seeking behavior of users, although no significance difference was obtained on the learning outcomes of the students. A major take away from the studies by Aleven and co-authors [5, 6] is the need to ensure quality help is provided and used appropriately by students.

Similarly, the I-Help system supported students in helping each other, with the student body being effectively a learning community [7, 8]. The aim was to have students receive help that was just-in-time, even if the help wasn't necessarily of the highest quality. However, feedback provided by students revealed that receiving quality help is even important than receiving timely help [8]. According to Bull et al. [7], it is important to ensure that the help provided is not only just-in-time but also targeted at achieving the learning goals of the help-seeker. This creates the need to identify and recommend the helpers who will provide both quick and quality answers to the questions asked.

In designing a peer recommender system, knowing the learning goals, prior knowledge of the helpers, their learning preferences, groups of helpers with similar learning behavior, historically successful learning paths, and learning strategies are important [9]. This leads to a "cold start" problem where an initial data set is needed for recommendation. MovieLens, a recommender system for movies [10], has addressed this problem by asking new users to rate their preferences for movies before the system can provide recommendations. This solution does not apply to learners who in most cases are not able to rate learning activities in advance because they do not have adequate prior knowledge about the learning activity [9]. Hence, rather than using explicit ratings, recommending learning resources to users is more often based on analyzing posts from discussion forums and online peer-peer interactions to extract information about helpers, to detect learning behaviors and to create awareness about learning activities within the community [11, 12]. In our study we, too, analyzed the past answer posts of each prospective answerer to predict the best and most timely answerers for a question.

Existing studies attempting to support users in the SO community have also attempted to address the issue of late response time to questions. In a companion research project we came up with promising approaches to predicting (at the time the question is asked) whether an SO question will be answered or not, and, if answered, whether the answer will be timely or late [17]. A previous study in SO by Bhat et al. [13] revealed that although most questions get answered within an hour, about 30% of the questions have a response time greater than 1 day. Ishola and McCalla [2] similarly observed a decrease in the proportion of questions that received their first answer within 15 min from 57% in 2009 to 36% in 2015. In an attempt to reduce the response time for the first answer to questions Tian et al. [3] predicted the best answerers to questions using a topic modelling approach. Yang and Manandhar [14] identified the topic modelling approach as a less effective approach because it is too general, while the use of question tags was proposed as a more informative approach. The study by Ishola and McCalla [2] also tried to predict best answerers, and improved upon the success rate achieved by Tian et al. [3] from about 22% to 55%. However, 55% is probably not good enough for real-life application. Hence, one of the goals of the study reported on in this paper is to substantially improve the current success rate in predicting the prospective answerers to a question.

3   Our Study

The first goal of our current study was to examine how serious the problem of late answered and unanswered questions are in Stack Overflow. In 2016 SO data, the median *response time for the first answer* (RTFA) was 38 min while the average RTFA was 12,350 min (about 8 and half days). The wide variation between the median and average RTFA shows that while many questions receive their first answer fairly promptly, some of questions receive their first answer very late. Of course, waiting 8 days to receive the first answer is so late as to be unacceptable. Figure 1, below, shows a steady growth in SO from 5% in 2009 to 23% in 2016 of questions not answered within 1440 min (1 day), which we will call *late answered questions*, and questions that go unanswered.

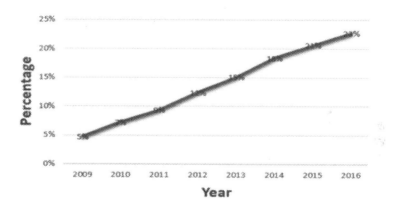

Fig. 1. Proportion of late answered and unanswered questions in SO

Of course, the numbers of questions asked in SO have also increased from 2009 to 2016, so this is even more of a problem than it looks. The actual number of late answered or unanswered questions in SO rose from 16,415 questions in 2009 to 512,060 questions in 2016. Of course even for questions that received their first answer within a day, not all the answers provided would necessarily be helpful to the question askers. The other issue is the quality of the answer: does the answer, late or not, meet the user's learning needs? In SO, question askers can mark as "accepted" one of the answers they received as the most useful in solving their question. This accepted answer can be deemed to have met the user's learning needs. We wanted to gain further insight into the perceived usefulness (user's acceptance) of the answers received by question askers and how this related to how long it took to receive the first answer. To get an overview of how long it took to receive first and best answers to questions we looked at all answered questions asked in 2016 (about 1.87 million questions). Figure 2 shows the time frame for the first answers and the proportion of these first answers that were accepted and not accepted by the user who asked the question.

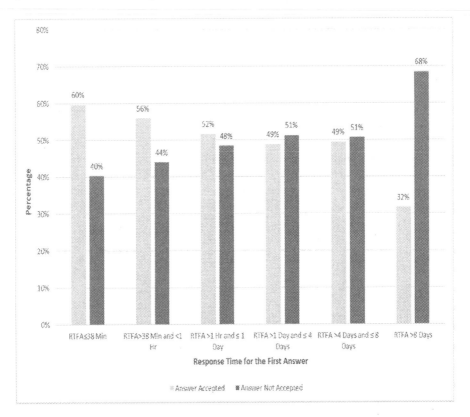

Fig. 2. Proportion of accepted to not accepted answers in SO based on response time for the first answer

The results obtained in Fig. 2 show that as the RTFA increases, the perceived usefulness of the answer reduces (in the eyes of the question asker). This is especially true for question askers who received very late (after 8 days) answers to their question where 69% of the answers received were not useful to the question askers. Of course, some of these answers may prove useful to people other than the question asker. In fact some of the comments provided to the questions which received their first answer after 8 days do indicate that other users are faced with similar issues: *"facing same issue, please help us"*, *"have you resolved the problem? Now I am having the same problem. Help me to resolve it"*, *"What did you do eventually?"* So, if we can find ways of getting an answer earlier to the question asker, there may be others who also benefit. One way would be to proactively recommend prospective answerers who would provide the *best* and *most timely* answer to a question. This sets up the next phase of our study: using SO data to try to find metrics to predict who the actual best and timely answerers were to a question using only information available at the time the question was asked. If successful, these metrics could then be embedded in a recommender system.

4   Approaches to Predicting Question Answerers

In predicting the best and timely answerers for questions, we decided to use questions asked in SO in the period from January to May 2017 inclusive. Then we eliminated questions that received no answers since there is no way to validate that the predicted answerers would eventually be the actual answerers. Since we want to be able to predict good answerers and avoid the cold-start problem [9], we then focused only on questions that were answered by *active question answerers*. These are users who have earned at least one of the tag badges (bronze, silver or gold tag badge) for providing at least 20 quality answers (with at least a score of 100) to questions relating to a specific tag. For this study, we focused only on questions that were answered by active question answerers with at least one *java* or *android* tag. This is still a large sample size since the *java* and *android* tags cover broad areas of software and mobile development and are among the top 5 most used tags in SO. With these foci, we were left with 44,035 questions answered by 14,051 active question answerers over the 5 month time frame. We developed three different general approaches to predicting the answerer to a question: *tag-based*, *response-based* and *hybrid* approaches. We believe the approaches employed in this study would generalize to all the questions asked in SO at large. These approaches are discussed next.

4.1   Tag–Based Approach

The tag-based approach focusses on the past usage of the tags employed in the question by all the active question answerers for a given question [15]. For a given question, we select as *prospective answerers* those active question answerers who have provided at least one answer to questions relating to any of the tags in the question up to a month before the question was asked. We employed a baseline of one month in tracking the historical information about the active question answerers as our previous study [2] shows that tracking past activities of users beyond one month only provides marginal benefits. The selected prospective answerers are thereafter ranked using the combined score calculated by the four metrics described below. More details can be found in [2].

(A) *Regularity:* Regularity is defined by how often the prospective answerer provided an answer to a topic. This feature is a count of the total number of times a prospective answerer has provided answers to questions containing each of the tags employed in the question in the past one month. For instance, if a question contains *java, and android,* tags, we would count the number of questions answered containing either *java or android* o tags for the month before the question was asked.

(B) *Knowledgeability:* Knowledgeability is defined as the know-how of the prospective answerer about a given topic. This is the total score[3] earned by a prospective answerer for providing answers to questions containing each of the tags employed in the question. In our example this would be the total score earned by the prospective answerer for providing answers to *java, android,* or *interface tags* a month before the question was asked.

(C) *Eagerness:* Eagerness is the keenness of the prospective answerer to deal with a topic compared to other topics. This feature represents the likelihood of an answer being given to any of the tags in the question by a prospective answerer. This is computed by dividing the regularity score computed in (A) above with the total number of answers provided by a prospective answerer for the month before the question was asked.

(D) *Willingness:* Willingness is defined by how active the prospective answerer is in providing answers to questions on a topic compared to the total number of answers provided on the topic. This feature is computed using Bayes theorem by multiplying the prior probability of a prospective answerer to provide answers to a question about any of the tags in the question and the likelihood of an answer to any of the tags in the question given by a prospective answerer (as defined in (C) above). The prior probability of a prospective answerer to provide an answer is computed by dividing the total answers provided by a prospective answerer to the total answers provided by all question answerers to questions containing any of the tags used in the question.

As the score computed for each of the features described in (A) to (D) above have different ranges, to prevent a feature from dominating other features when the features are combined, the scores computed above are normalized to range between 0 and 1. The normalized score is computed as described below:

$$Normalized\ Score = \frac{(Actual\ Score - Minimum\ Score)}{(Maximum\ Score - Minimum\ Score)}$$

The actual score is the score computed for a prospective answerer for a question, while the minimum and the maximum score is the minimum score and maximum score for all prospective answerers selected for a given question. In predicting the prospective answerers for a question, the normalized scores computed for a prospective answerer are ranked based on the computed score for each of the features described above.

4.2 Response-Based Approach

With the response-based approach, the overall responsiveness of an active question answerer to provide answers to questions regardless of the tags used in the question is computed. The overall responsiveness of an active question answerer is judged based on all answers they have provided for a month prior to when the question was asked using the three features described below:

---

[3] In SO, the score a question earns is computed by the aggregate of the number of up votes and down votes to the answers provided by other community members in response to the question.

(E) *Probability of First Answer (FirstProb)*: This is the probability that a prospective answerer provides the first answer to a question. It is computed by dividing the number of answers provided by the prospective answerer by the total number of answers provided, in the month prior to the question being asked.

(F) *Probability of Fast Answer (FastProb)*: This is the proportion of answers the prospective answerer provided within 38 min (the median response time, as discussed earlier) of the question being asked to the total number of answers provided within a month from when the question was asked.

(G) *Probability of Best Answer (BestProb)*: This is the probability that a prospective answerer provides the best answer, the one with the highest score. This is the proportion of the number of best answers provided by the prospective answerer to the total number of answers provided within a month from when the question was asked.

Since the scores computed for the three features above range from 0 to 1, there is no need to have the scores normalized. In predicting the actual prospective answerers for a question, the selected prospective answerers are ranked using the computed score from each of the three features described above.

4.3 Hybrid Approach

With the hybrid approach, the goal is to combine the scores from two features taken from the other approaches. Similar to [16], we experimented with 3 different ways of combing the features: the *And-function* (which only selects prospective answerers that have non-zero scores on both features being considered), and the *Or-function* (which selects the top ranked prospective answerers based on the sum of the scores obtained from the two features being considered), and the *Product-function* (which selects the top ranked prospective answerers based on the product of the scores obtained from the two features being considered). Rather than forming hybrids for all combinations of features defined in Sects. 4.1 and 4.2 above (which would be trivial and unlikely to increase the success rate), we formed hybrids combining the best features from the tag-based and response-based approaches. To determine the effectiveness of each feature described in this section, we separately ranked prospective answerers for each feature; we later combined the more successful features in hybrid metrics. The prospective answerers are then ranked according to their scores on the chosen hybrid.

5   Experimental Evaluation and Results

Using the approaches described in the previous section we attempted to predict the *best answerer* (answerer with the highest score), the most *timely answerer* (answerer who will provide an answer within 38 min from when the question was created), and the *best and timely answerer* for a question (answerer who provides the best answer within 38 min response time from when the question was created). Similar to Tian et al. [3] and our earlier work [3], we evaluated the success of our prediction by calculating the success rate (S@N) of our prediction as defined below:

$$S@N = \frac{Total\ Number\ of\ Successes}{Total\ Number\ of\ Questions} * 100\%$$

The total number of successes in predicting the best answerer, for instance, for a particular feature is computed by the total number of instances whereby the answerer who provided the best answer to a question is among the top N of prospective answerers as ranked by that feature. Similar to Tian et al. [3], our N ranges from 10 to 100. Successfully predicting that the actual answerer is in the top 10 or even top 100 is not a trivial task given that there was a pool of about 14,051 active answerers. Moreover, in a real-life recommender application, only a few of the predicted prospective answerers might be available and ready to answer the question. The results obtained are shown below for each of the approaches in Tables 1, 2 and 3.

Table 1. Success rate obtained using tag-based features

Tag-Based	Best Answerer				Timely Answerer				Best and Timely Answerer			
	S@10	S@20	S@50	S@100	S@10	S@20	S@50	S@100	S@10	S@20	S@50	S@100
Regularity	29.98%	42.68%	64.79%	80.33%	35.78%	49.50%	70.27%	83.98%	31.06%	43.95%	65.61%	80.85%
Knowledgeability	24.27%	37.69%	63.37%	83.94%	29.68%	45.37%	70.30%	86.49%	24.90%	38.53%	63.99%	84.05%
Eagerness	19.53%	28.39%	45.25%	58.88%	12.86%	21.60%	40.79%	57.39%	19.39%	28.40%	45.69%	59.49%
Willingness	45.92%	58.17%	75.73%	85.88%	37.25%	50.58%	71.03%	83.11%	37.25%	50.58%	71.03%	83.11%

Table 2. Success rate obtained using response-based features

Response-Based	Best Answerer				Timely Answerer				Best and Timely Answerer			
	S@10	S@20	S@50	S@100	S@10	S@20	S@50	S@100	S@10	S@20	S@50	S@100
FastProb	4.36%	7.84%	27.84%	62.53%	7.07%	12.74%	41.24%	75.37%	4.72%	8.48%	29.21%	63.59%
FirstProb	7.49%	12.81%	31.55%	60.43%	5.12%	9.69%	27.15%	55.01%	7.57%	12.84%	31.54%	60.51%
BestProb	20.60%	23.97%	36.24%	61.77%	11.07%	14.45%	26.04%	52.88%	20.29%	23.72%	35.92%	61.48%

Table 3. Success rate obtained using hybrid-based features

Hybrid-Based	Best Answerer				Timely Answerer				Best and Timely Answerer			
	S@10	S@20	S@50	S@100	S@10	S@20	S@50	S@100	S@10	S@20	S@50	S@100
Intersect{Willingness, Knowledgeability}	17.13%	28.99%	54.22%	75.74%	20.36%	34.10%	58.64%	76.52%	17.74%	29.83%	55.04%	76.13%
Product {Willingness, Knowledgeability}	45.47%	59.18%	78.46%	89.24%	40.00%	54.53%	75.39%	87.73%	45.78%	59.72%	78.90%	89.46%
Sum{Willingness, Knowledgeability}	41.47%	55.66%	76.58%	89.64%	36.70%	52.26%	74.83%	88.71%	41.81%	56.18%	76.97%	89.46%
Intersect{FastProb, BestProb}	0.96%	1.64%	10.04%	43.62%	0.96%	1.64%	10.04%	43.62%	0.76%	1.24%	7.89%	41.50%
Product{FastProb, BestProb}	3.21%	7.74%	30.71%	68.06%	4.89%	12.03%	43.88%	77.81%	3.40%	8.20%	31.68%	68.71%
Sum{FastProb, BestProb}	3.22%	7.79%	30.77%	68.99%	4.92%	12.07%	43.73%	77.36%	3.42%	8.23%	31.73%	69.57%
Intersect{Willingness, FastProb}	0.88%	2.73%	19.15%	53.57%	1.41%	4.30%	28.11%	63.24%	1.30%	4.08%	27.08%	61.99%
Product{Willingness, FastProb}	42.56%	55.00%	71.41%	83.78%	42.95%	57.37%	76.07%	89.08%	41.65%	56.06%	75.08%	88.54%
Sum{Willingness, FastProb}	29.93%	37.01%	55.48%	76.79%	31.94%	40.99%	63.22%	84.32%	30.65%	30.65%	30.65%	83.74%

As shown in Table 1, with the tag-based approach we obtained higher success rates with increasing values of N. Comparing the success rates of the features over all values of N the willingness feature seems to perform best, especially at lower values of N. At higher values of N, both knowledgeability and willingness features performed very well. Similarly, the success rates obtained for the response-based approach (shown in Table 2) with S@10, S@20 and S@50 were poor for all the features, although with S@100 a fairly decent success rate was obtained with FastProb, although not as high as the best tag-based features.

As shown in Table 3, the And-function had the least success rate, and isn't likely to be very useful. However, comparing the results obtained in Table 3 with Tables 1 and 2, a marginally higher success rate was achieved with the best hybrid feature compared to the best tag-based and response-based features. Product-function (Willingness, Knowledgeability) generally outperforms the other hybrid-based features on most measures of success at most values of N. Thus, in our subsequent analysis we will just use the Product-function (Willingness, Knowledgeability) hybrid at S@100.

6   Adopting Work Load Balancing in Predicting Answerers

As Ishola and McCalla [2] and Greer et al. [8] discuss, it is important to avoid over-working a helper by exempting helpers who recently have provided help. Of course, reducing the number of prospective answerers creates a tradeoff between having rested helpers vs. choosing helpers who can provide the best and most timely answers. We wanted to explore this tradeoff. So, our next goal was to determine in the SO data the effect on our predictions of "exempting" potential answerers for a question (removing them from the potential list of prospective helpers) for various *exemption intervals* between the time the question was asked and the time of the previous answer provided by a prospective answerer (to any question). For instance, for an exemption interval of 15 min, we would exempt all prospective answerers who had provided an answer (to any question) within 15 min of when the question was asked. The remaining prospective answerers can then be ranked using whatever metric we are analyzing. The results obtained for exempting "overworked" helpers using Product-function (Willingness, Knowledgeability), our best measure, for various exemption intervals are shown in Fig. 3 below using S@100.

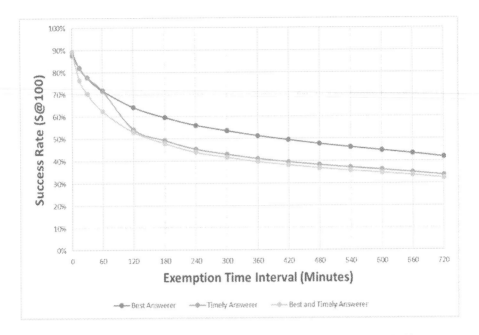

Fig. 3. Success rate obtained with varying exemption intervals for S@100

The data points in Fig. 3 between 0 min and 60 min are at 15 min and 38 min. The exemption interval 0 as shown in Fig. 3 represents the results obtained when no prospective answerers were exempted (as shown in Table 3). As the exemption interval increases, the success rate steadily diminishes, reflecting the increasing likelihood that the actual answerer has been exempted and thus the prediction fails. However, the predictive success rate is still quite good up to a 60 min exemption interval (over 60% for all of our measures). This would provide the opportunity to be able to exempt users for up to an hour after they have answered a question and still be able to recommend good helpers. This would not only rest frequent helpers, but also would encourage a more diverse set of question answerers. Our next goal is to study the performance of our best feature in predicting the answerers for questions answered late, were such a prediction to be made at the point the question is asked.

7   Providing Earlier Answers to Late Answered Questions

In this section we considered only the questions answered late. We want to know how much time can be saved if we were successful at the point the question is asked in predicting the actual answerers to late answered questions. Once again we used the best measure from our earlier analysis: Product-function (Willingness, Knowledgeability) with S@100. For this analysis, we only looked at predicting the best answerer, not the timely answerers nor the best and timely answerers, since by definition there can be no timely answerers for questions that are late. We looked at various categories of late answers, ranging from just a little late (38 min to an hour) all the way up to very late (over 8 days), to determine how the prediction accuracy at S@100 with the 60 min exemption window compares to the prediction accuracy without exempting prospective answerers. The results are shown in Table 4 below.

Table 4. Success rate obtained with varying late RTFA ranges

Product-function (Willing, Knowledgeability)	Best Answerer				
	RTFA>38 Min and <1 Hr	RTFA >1 Hr and ≤ 1 Day	RTFA >1 Hr and ≤ 3 Days	RTFA >3 Days and ≤ 8 Days	RTFA >8 Days
S@100 Without the Exemption Interval	78.67%	93.60%	91.65%	86.83%	86.41%
S@100 With the Exemption Interval	78.67%	87.99%	88.25%	86.12%	79.61%

Overall, the success rates achieved with and without the 60 min exemption interval are both relatively high through all of the late answer categories. However there is a bigger tradeoff between having rested helpers vs. choosing helpers who can provide the best answer for answers that are just a little late (38 min < RTFA ≤ 1 h) as compared to even later answers. Even for questions answered very late (RTFA > 8 days) a success rate of 79.61% was achieved in predicting the best answerers who would also be rested. This implies that if our Product-function (Willingness, Knowledgeabilty) measure were incorporated in a peer recommender system, there is the possibility of saving the question askers many days in waiting for an answer. Moreover, if we can provide quicker answers to a late answered question, especially one that is only answered very late, not only will the question asker benefit but so will other users within the community who can gain insight from the answer.

8   Discussion

Our research is about supporting professional users in meeting their learning needs within an open learning community. In the study reported in this paper we looked at the issue of response time and response quality to questions asked in the Stack Overflow community of programmers. We observed an increasing rise in the proportion of questions answered late and unanswered from 2009 to 2016. Using three different general approaches, tag-based, response-based and hybrid, we developed measures that allowed us to predict the prospective answerers for questions asked in SO over a 5 month period. Such measures could be the basis of a recommender system to proactively find appropriate helpers, thus speeding up response time and quality. In exploring the efficacy of these measures we achieved the best success rates using a hybrid approach that combines information about the user's willingness and knowledgeability to make the prediction. We also took up the issue of "helper overload", and explored the effects on our predictive ability (using our best hybrid approach) if we exempted helpers who had recently given help. Looking at various exemption periods, we discovered a steady decline in predictive ability as the period increased, but still achieved reasonable success for exemption periods of an hour. We showed that these success rates stayed high even for questions that had taken many days to answer, showing the potential of a peer recommender system based on our measures to truly speed up the response time to first answer. Thus, we believe there is promise not only for recommending good helpers in an OLC but also for achieving equitable load balancing among the helpers.

The results achieved in our study are an improvement over previous studies by Tian et al. who achieved a success rate of 18% and 23% using S@50 and S@100 respectively [3]. Likewise, the results obtained are also an improvement over our own previous results when we achieved a success rate of about 55% while predicting the best answerer for questions answered within the first hour [2]. The reason for the higher success rate achieved in this study compared to our past study is likely because we considered all the tags used in the question in computing the score for each of the features defined under the tag-based approach (rather than just the first tag). Also, the hybrid approach where features were combined increased the success rate over the individual features used alone. We could certainly explore more approaches, especially using different machine learning techniques, and perhaps achieve even higher levels of success, but with our best success rates nearing 90% (without the exemption periods) we believe we already have the basis for fairly effective helper recommendation.

Of course, this study was carried out only on questions answered by active question answerers since we need some sort of information about a question answerer to make any reasonable predictions. We thus have no insight into all of those users who might have been good helpers but who were not active answerers. Our hope is that the same measures that allow predictions for active answerers also apply to other answerers, although such users must have some track record for us to be able to compute any of the measures. However, we believe that incorporating these measures into a recommender system that more proactively encourages question answering may stimulate a broader range of helpers. Moreover, generalizing beyond Stack Overflow, in a real world context where developers with an eye to meeting lifelong learning needs had control on what capabilities to include in the software environment supporting an OLC, it would also be possible to gather much more information about the answerers that could be used to form a richer long term learner model to inform the various components of the OLC environment, including a peer recommender system. If we can be as successful as we have been in this study using the fairly minimal information available, such rich models provide promise in achieving much more refined recommendations of appropriate helpers.

Acknowledgements. We would like to thank the Natural Sciences and Engineering Research Council of Canada and the University of Saskatchewan for financially supporting this research.

References

1. Simons, P.R.J., Ruijters, M.C.: Learning professionals: towards an integrated model. In: Boshuizen, H.P.A., Bromme, R., Gruber, H. (eds.) Professional Learning: Gaps and Transitions on the Way from Novice to Expert, pp. 207–229. Kluwer (2004)
2. Ishola (Idowu), O.M., McCalla, G.: Predicting prospective peer helpers to provide just-in-time help to users in question and answer forums. In: 10th International Conference on Educational Data Mining (EDM 2017), Wuhan, China, pp. 238–243, June 2017

3. Tian, Y., Kochhar, P.S., Lim, E.P., Zhu, F., Lo, D.: Predicting best answerers for new questions: an approach leveraging topic modeling and collaborative voting. In: Workshops of the 5th International Conference on Social Informatics (SocInfo 2013), Kyoto, Japan, pp. 55–68, November 2013

4. Howley, I.: Leveraging educational technology to overcome social obstacles to help seeking. Doctoral dissertation, Carnegie Mellon University, Pittsburgh, PA (2015)

5. Aleven, V., Koedinger, K.R.: Investigations into help seeking and learning with a cognitive tutor. In: Papers of the AIED 2001 Workshop on Help Provision and Help Seeking in Interactive Learning Environments, San Antonio, TX, pp. 47–58, May 2001

6. Roll, I., Aleven, V., Koedinger, K.: Promoting effective help-seeking behavior through declarative instruction. In: Lester, J.C., Vicari, R.M., Paraguaçu, F. (eds.) ITS 2004. LNCS, vol. 3220, pp. 857–859. Springer, Heidelberg (2004). https://doi.org/10.1007/978-3-540-30139-4_99

7. Bull, S., Greer, J., McCalla, G., Kettel, L., Bowes, J.: User modelling in I-help: what, why, when and how. In: Bauer, M., Gmytrasiewicz, P.J., Vassileva, J. (eds.) UM 2001. LNCS (LNAI), vol. 2109, pp. 117–126. Springer, Heidelberg (2001). https://doi.org/10.1007/3-540-44566-8_12

8. Greer, J., McCalla, G., Vassileva, J., Deters, R., Bull, S., Kettel, L.: Lessons learned in deploying a multi-agent learning support system: the I-help experience. In: Proceedings 10th International Conference on Artificial Intelligence in Education (AIED 2001), pp. 410–421, San Antonio, TX. IOS, May 2001

9. Drachsler, H., Hummel, H.G., Koper, R.: Personal recommender systems for learners in lifelong learning networks: the requirements, techniques and model. Int. J. Learn. Technol. 3(4), 404–423 (2008)

10. Rashid, A.M., Albert, I., Cosley, D., Lam, S.K., McNee, S.M., Konstan, J.A., Riedl, J.: Getting to know you: learning new user preferences in recommender systems. In: Proceedings of the 7th International Conference on Intelligent User Interfaces (IUI 2002), pp. 127–134, San Francisco, CA. ACM, January 2002

11. Siemens, G.: What are learning analytics? Blog (2010). http://www.elearnspace.org/blog/2010/08/25/what-are-learning-analytics/. Accessed 11 April 2018

12. Fischer, G.: Lifelong learning – more than training. J. Interact. Learn. Res. 11(3), 265–294 (2000)

13. Bhat, V., Gokhale, A., Jadhav, R., Pudipeddi, J., Akoglu, L.: Min (e) d your tags: analysis of question response time in StackOverflow. In: IEEE/ACM International Conference on Advances in Social Networks Analysis and Mining (ASONAM 2014), Beijing, China, pp. 328–335. IEEE, August 2014

14. Yang, B., Manandhar, S.: Tag-based expert recommendation in community question answering. In: IEEE/ACM International Conference on Advances in Social Networks Analysis and Mining (ASONAM 2014), Beijing, China, pp. 960–963. IEEE, August 2014

15. Ishola, O.M., McCalla, G.: Personalized tag-based knowledge diagnosis to predict the quality of answers in a community of learners. In: André, E., Baker, R., Hu, X., Rodrigo, Ma.M.T., du Boulay, B. (eds.) AIED 2017. LNCS (LNAI), vol. 10331, pp. 113–124. Springer, Cham (2017). https://doi.org/10.1007/978-3-319-61425-0_10

16. Guy, I., Zwerdling, N., Ronen, I., Carmel, D., Uziel, E.: Social media recommendation based on people and tags. In: Proceedings of the 33rd International ACM SIGIR Conference on Research and Development in Information Retrieval, Geneva, Switzerland, pp. 194–201. ACM, July 2010

17. Idowu (Ishola), O.M., McCalla, G.: On the value of answerers in early detection of response time to questions for peer recommender systems. In: Penstein Rosé, C., et al. (eds.) AIED 2018, LNCS (LNAI), vol. 10947, pp. 160–165. Springer, Cham (2018)

Expert Feature-Engineering vs. Deep Neural Networks: Which Is Better for Sensor-Free Affect Detection?

Yang Jiang[1]([⊠]), Nigel Bosch[2], Ryan S. Baker[3], Luc Paquette[2],
Jaclyn Ocumpaugh[3], Juliana Ma. Alexandra L. Andres[3],
Allison L. Moore[4], and Gautam Biswas[4]

[1] Teachers College, Columbia University, New York, NY, USA
yj2211@tc.columbia.edu
[2] University of Illinois at Urbana-Champaign, Champaign, IL, USA
{pnb,lpaq}@illinois.edu
[3] University of Pennsylvania, Philadelphia, PA, USA
{rybaker,ojaclyn}@upenn.edu, aandres@gse.upenn.edu
[4] Vanderbilt University, Nashville, TN, USA
{allison.l.moore,gautam.biswas}@vanderbilt.edu

Abstract. The past few years have seen a surge of interest in deep neural networks. The wide application of deep learning in other domains such as image classification has driven considerable recent interest and efforts in applying these methods in educational domains. However, there is still limited research comparing the predictive power of the deep learning approach with the traditional feature engineering approach for common student modeling problems such as sensor-free affect detection. This paper aims to address this gap by presenting a thorough comparison of several deep neural network approaches with a traditional feature engineering approach in the context of affect and behavior modeling. We built detectors of student affective states and behaviors as middle school students learned science in an open-ended learning environment called Betty's Brain, using both approaches. Overall, we observed a tradeoff where the feature engineering models were better when considering a single optimized threshold (for intervention), whereas the deep learning models were better when taking model confidence fully into account (for discovery with models analyses).

Keywords: Student modeling · Feature engineering · Deep learning
Deep neural networks · Affect and behavior detection · Betty's Brain

1 Introduction

Student modeling assumes a crucial role in the field of Artificial Intelligence in Education (AIED). In recent years, there has been a proliferation of models that can infer complex constructs such as scientific reasoning strategies [1, 2], affect [3–5], and disengaged behavior [5–8]. One educational data mining method, commonly used to develop automated models of these types of constructs, is to generate a meaningful set

© Springer International Publishing AG, part of Springer Nature 2018
C. Penstein Rosé et al. (Eds.): AIED 2018, LNAI 10947, pp. 198–211, 2018.
https://doi.org/10.1007/978-3-319-93843-1_15

of features from data (i.e. feature engineering). This feature set is then used within machine learning algorithms to learn the mapping from those features to examples of the construct being modeled, also identified by trained experts [e.g., 2–5, 7].

Automated detectors using feature engineering have achieved reasonably high success in predicting whether a student is engaged, frustrated, confused, or bored, and whether the student will display related affective states and behaviors [3, 5, 9]. In this approach, ground truth (examples of the construct) is typically collected through classroom observations [5, 10], emote-aloud protocols [4], or self-reports [6]. Theoretically-justified features are then created and utilized to build machine-learning predictive models of affective states and behaviors. The resulting detectors make inferences solely using data from student-software interaction, enabling researchers and educators to explore and detect these constructs scalably and in real time. These affect and behavior detectors have been applied to over a dozen learning environments, and have been found to predict long-term learning outcomes [5, 11–13]. They can also be integrated in learning environments to provide timely information on when the system should intervene to respond to the students' affect and behavior in real time and reduce negative affective states [4].

However, with the rapid development of deep learning [14], there is an emerging interest and effort in applying deep learning for various problems within student modeling [15–18]. Deep neural networks have enabled leaps forward in prediction accuracy for models in other domains (e.g., image classification [19]), which has driven recent interest in applying these methods to educational problems. In general, early results have been mixed, with optimism about the potential of deep learning for knowledge modeling and performance prediction [18] giving way to evidence of overstated effectiveness [16], and initial evidence that affect detection could be substantially improved through deep learning [15] transitioning to evidence of the models not working for all populations [20]. As such, the advantages (and disadvantages) of deep neural networks for student modeling are not yet well understood. Therefore, a thorough comparison of deep learning and traditional feature engineering methods is needed in student modeling to determine the strengths and drawbacks of each method.

This paper compares several deep neural network approaches with a traditional feature engineering approach. Specifically, we studied these issues in the context of developing detectors of student affective states and behaviors in an open-ended learning environment for middle school science called Betty's Brain [21]. To our knowledge, this study is the first direct comparison of the two approaches on the same data with a thorough exploration of model types and hyperparameters. The comparison in this paper will lead to a better understanding of the advantages and disadvantages of each approach, including insights into situations where one approach is preferable to the other.

2   Betty's Brain

The Betty's Brain software [21], shown in Fig. 1, is an open-ended computer-based learning environment where students learn science and complete challenging scientific tasks by constructing a causal map describing a scientific phenomenon (e.g., climate change, ecosystems, thermoregulation). It adopts the learning-by-teaching paradigm to help students acquire scientific knowledge and gain cognitive and metacognitive skills. The goal for students in Betty's Brain is to teach a virtual agent, named Betty, about the phenomenon by means of a causal map the students build, where causal relationships (e.g., cold temperature leads to heat loss, as shown in Fig. 1) can be represented by a set of concept entities connected by directed causal links.

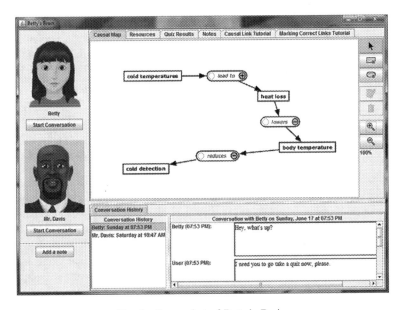

Fig. 1. Screenshot of Betty's Brain.

In this open-ended environment, learners have access to hypermedia resource pages (called the *science book* in Betty's Brain) on relevant scientific concepts to acquire domain-specific knowledge. They can apply what they read about from the resource pages to assist them with the map building. A causal map can be constructed by adding concept entities and creating causal links between specific entities.

Learners can assess their causal map by having Betty, the virtual student, answer questions and explain her answers. Betty's answers to questions are based on the causal map that the student has created, by checking the chain of causal links between the concepts involved in the questions. Students can also request conversations with a pedagogical mentor agent, named Mr. Davis, to evaluate Betty's answer. Additionally, students can have Betty take quizzes (composed of a list of questions to help students improve their causal map) and check the correctness of concepts and causal links and the current state of their causal map, which is compared to the expert model hidden from the system.

Betty's Brain is challenging for students, as it poses high requirements on self-regulated learning. Students need to plan their map construction process, make decisions on when and how to access information pages and which information is important for concept mapping, regularly monitor their causal map by checking Betty's performance, and accordingly modify their causal maps. These processes, together with the complexity of the task and the open-endedness of the environment, all have the potential to influence engagement and elicit affective and behavioral responses. In this paper, we aim to develop automated detectors of student engagement in the system and compare the accuracy of two sets of detectors respectively using feature engineering and deep learning.

3   Method

3.1   Participants

Participants in this study were a total of 93 sixth grade students from four science classes in an urban public middle school in the southeastern region of the United States. They were observed as they used the Betty's Brain system in spring 2017 and their interactions within the system were logged. The interaction log data and the classroom observations of the students' engagement were used to construct affect detectors.

3.2   Procedure

This study was conducted over a seven-day period. Students took a 30–45 min paper-based pretest on Day 1 of the study, and received a 30-min training session on how to use Betty's Brain on the following day. They then spent four class periods working in Betty's Brain to build a causal map about climate change from Days 3–6. They completed a paper-based post-test, which was the same as the pre-test, on Day 7. The pre- and post-tests, composed of multiple-choice items and short response items, were designed to assess students' knowledge of the concepts and the causal relationships underlying the scientific phenomenon in the domain.

3.3   Classroom Observations of Affect and Behavior

While working with Betty's Brain in a classroom setting, students were observed in real-time by two human coders using the Baker Rodrigo Ocumpaugh Monitoring Protocol (BROMP 2.0) [10]. BROMP is a momentary time sampling method where students are observed individually, without interruption, in a pre-determined order. BROMP has been applied to explore student engagement by over 150 coders in four countries, resulting in over 25 publications (see review in [10]). It achieves reliably high inter-rater reliability (each of the 150 coders achieved inter-rater reliability with at least one other coder, achieving Cohen's Kappa over 0.6), obtains data quickly, and BROMP data has been used as the basis for a range of automated detectors of affect and engagement [3, 5, 22].

In this study, two BROMP-certified coders observed and recorded affective states (boredom, confusion, delight, engaged concentration, frustration) and behaviors (on-task, on-task conversation, off-task) using an Android application called the Human Affect Recording Tool (HART) [23]. They observed each student consecutively, for up to 20 s at a time, in a predetermined order and recorded the first affective state and behavior that the student clearly displayed during the interval. Observers cycled through the entire class and moved to the next student once the student's state had been determined or 20 s expired. These observations were time-stamped and synchronized to the data from the students' interactions with Betty's Brain, which included a total of 146,141 actions generated by students. Early in the study, the coders tested whether they agreed on the affect and behavioral codes and achieved inter-rater reliability (Cohen's Kappa $\geq .60$) for affect and behavior.

A total of 5,212 observations of affect and behavior were obtained from the 93 students over the course of this study, with each student being observed 56 times on average across the four class sessions. Engaged concentration was the affective state that was the most commonly identified (4,064 observations; 78.0%), followed by confusion (312 observations; 6%), frustration (241 observations; 4.6%), boredom (220 observations; 4.2%), and delight (149 observations; 2.9%). Student state was marked as *other* if the observer was unsure about the student's affective state or behavior within the 20-s window or the affective state or behavior displayed by the student was not listed in the coding scheme (226 observations; 4.3%).

Behavioral constructs were recorded separately from affect (e.g., a student could be recorded as both bored and off-task). Off-task behavior observations comprised 10.2% (533 observations) of the data, on-task conversation comprised 15.0% (784 observations), and on task behavior comprised 69.0% (3,595 observations).

3.4 Feature Engineering Approach

In the traditional feature engineering approach, we created a set of meaningful features from student interaction log data that could potentially predict specific affective states and behavior. These features were then fed into standard classifiers to train machine-learned predictive models of student affective states and behaviors that were collected via BROMP.

Three broad categories of features were developed for detector construction: (1) basic features, (2) sequence features, and (3) threshold features. The basic features consisted of: (a) time-based features which captured the amount of time spent on specific user activities (e.g., total amount of time spent on viewing the causal map; average duration taken each time the student reads a resource), (b) frequency/count-based features that calculated the number of times the student executed a specific type of action (e.g., total number of causal links created; total number of notes edited; frequency of moving map elements; number of quizzes student has had Betty take so far), (c) ratio/percentage features (e.g., proportion of effective or ineffective actions; concept/link ratio), and d) other descriptive features (e.g., average; standard deviation; minimum and maximum values of map score, which is determined by the difference between the number of correct and incorrect causal links on the map at any point of time). For each feature, we created three variants: a *within 20-s clip*[1] variant, a *thus far* variant, and a *thus far divided by time elapsed* variant. For example,

---

[1] 60-s clip variants were initially tested but were less effective than 20-s clips.

for the feature "total time spent on viewing causal map," we calculated: (1) the total amount of time student has spent on viewing the causal map within the 20-s observation clip (20-s clip feature), (2) the total time the student has spent on viewing the causal map so far – from the beginning of using the system up to the current time (thus far feature), and (3) the total time the student has spent on viewing the causal map thus far divided by the time that has elapsed thus far (thus far divided by time elapsed feature). In total, 123 basic features were designed and extracted in this study (41 features × 3 variants).

The second category of features involved the frequency of sequences of three consecutive actions. Example three-action sequences included *read resource → add concept → add causal link, read resource → read resource → read resource*, etc. Sequence features captured the frequency of common three-action sequences. First, we searched for all possible three-action combinations executed by students, producing a total of 2,228 possible three-action sequences. Next, we selected the frequent three-action sequences that occurred more than 200 times across all students in the logs from Betty's Brain in order to remove infrequent sequences and obtain a reasonable number of three-action sequences. This reduced the number of sequences to 30. Similar to the basic features, we then applied these sequence patterns to log data and calculated the number of times each sequence occurred within the 20-s clip, the number of occurrences thus far, and the occurrences thus far divided by elapsed minutes. This resulted in a total of 90 sequence features.

We also extracted a set of threshold features that involved selecting an optimized threshold. For example, we determined how *long pause* should be defined in the feature "total number of long pauses after creating causal links thus far." For these features, different thresholds were tested in terms of fit; for example, different thresholds were tried at the grain size of 1 s in order to identify the best threshold for the feature "long pause after building causal links." Thresholds were evaluated based on the correlation between the feature with that threshold and the student's post-test performance. A total of 36 threshold features were generated. Thus, in total, there were 249 features (123 basic features + 90 sequence features + 36 threshold features).

In order to refine the detectors and identify the features most predictive of affective states and behaviors, we adopted a stepwise procedure and tested three sets of features in the final models. First, we constructed detectors using the basic features only. Secondly, we then expanded the feature set and added sequence features to explore the change in model performance. Lastly, we fed all features (basic features, sequence features, and threshold features) into machine-learning algorithms to build detectors. In the following sections, we will discuss the process of building machine-learned models.

Feature Selection. Considering the large number of features we distilled (which increases the risk of over-fitting), especially for the second (basic + sequence features) and third feature sets (basic + sequence + threshold features), tolerance analysis was conducted to reduce the number of features inputted to build affect detectors. Tolerance analysis evaluates the multicollinearity of features and eliminates features that are highly collinear (variance inflation factor >5).

Forward selection was implemented for further feature selection for each affect and behavior detector, where the feature that most improved model accuracy was added repeatedly until no more features could be added to improve model performance. Feature selection in this study was conducted within each cross-validation fold and was applied on training data only.

Classification Models. Classification models of affective states and behaviors were constructed in RapidMiner 5.3 [24] in order to determine which features best predict students' affective states and behaviors.

Models were built for each affective and behavioral state using the two-class approach, in which each observation was coded as either the state is present (e.g., bored), or absent (e.g., not bored). For behaviors, we built an off-task detector in order to detect whether the student was off-task or on-task (including on-task conversation). Resampling was implemented (in cross-validated training folds only) using the cloning method in order to make the frequency of each class for each construct balanced.

A small set of classification algorithms that have shown previous success in building affect detectors, including C4.5, RIPPER, Step Regression, Logistic Regression, and Naïve Bayes, were considered and tested for final model.

Detector accuracy was evaluated using two performance metrics: Cohen's kappa and A'. Kappa represents the degree to which the model is better than chance. A detector with a kappa value of 0 performs at chance-level and one with a kappa of 1 performs perfectly. A' is equivalent to the area under the receiver operating characteristic curve and the Wilcoxon U statistic, and represents the probability that the model can distinguish a positive example (e.g., bored) from a negative example (e.g., not bored). An A' value of 0.5 indicates chance-level performance and A' = 1.0 implies perfect performance.

Model performance was evaluated using 10-fold student-level cross-validation. In this process, students were randomly distributed into ten groups. Detectors were trained on nine of the groups and tested on the tenth group. The feature selection was executed on training data only.

3.5 Deep Learning Method

Preprocessing. We converted the event log data to a discrete time series format by coding occurrences of logged actions as 0 or 1 in consecutive three-second intervals. One variable was created for each type of action possible in Betty's Brain. For example, a column was created to denote whether a student was viewing the biology textbook material. If the student quickly browsed the textbook starting 5 s into the learning session and viewed for 4 s, the time series data for that variable would consist of 0, 1, 1, 0, etc. to capture textbook viewing behavior in the 3–6 s and 6–9 s intervals. We removed any variables with standard deviation $\leq .05$, since these variables represented events that rarely occurred and were less likely to be useful indicators of affect or off-task behavior. Nine variables remained: view causal map, view science book, view notes, view graded questions, view graded question explanation, respond to prompt, add causal map link, move causal map link, and other (context-specific action).

Data were then split into sequences of 60 s (20 three-second intervals) leading up to each BROMP observation[2], and two additional variables were added to capture the time since the start of the learning session and the position within the sequences (0 to 60 s). This preprocessing method allowed us to create sequences of equal length for each variable, which allows straightforward application of sequential neural network models such as recurrent neural networks.

Deep Learning Model Types. We considered five different common types of neural network models: fully-connected, recurrent neural network (RNN), long-short term memory (LSTM), gated recurrent unit (GRU), and 1-dimensional temporal convolution (Conv). Fully-connected networks consist of layers of simple neurons that connect to every neuron in the previous layer, with no regard to ordering in the sequence. RNNs connect each step in the sequential data to the previous step, thus reducing the number of parameters in the network and allowing the network to learn patterns over time. LSTM networks are a variety of RNN with more complex neurons that include memory cells that can remember elements of the sequence over a long period of time, to capture longer-term dependencies. GRUs are slightly simplified LSTMs that sacrifice some sequence-learning capabilities but require fewer parameters to be learned and thus may work well for smaller datasets. Finally, Conv networks learn filters that match sequences of a specific length (we used length 5). All of our models had an initial hidden layer with 10 neurons (of one of the five different types considered), followed by a fully-connected hidden layer of size 16, followed by an output fully-connected hidden layer of size 2. Exponential linear unit activation was applied after each fully-connected layer [25].

Hyperparameter Selection. Given the small labeled dataset available, a large, complicated network is unlikely to fit well to the data. However, to explore this possibility we adjusted the size of the first hidden layer in increments of 5 neurons from 5 to 70 neurons and added dropout after each layer [26]. We found no notable improvements, and thus continued experiments with no dropout and 10 neurons in the first hidden layer.

4 Results

4.1 Feature Engineering

Performance of the best-performing detector using the feature engineering approach for each construct are shown in Table 1. Prediction models built using the basic features showed better cross-validated performance (kappa and A' values) for the boredom and delight detectors. This indicated that the count/frequency-based and time-based features were overall better predictors of these affective states than the frequency of action sequences or features that involve threshold fitting. On the other hand, detectors using a combination of feature sets performed better in predicting confusion, engaged concentration, frustration, and off-task behavior.

---

[2] A 20-s clip was also tested for the deep learning models, but it did not work as well as the 60-s clips.

Overall, all the resulting machine-learned models for these constructs performed better than chance (mean kappa = 0.168, $A' = 0.634$), with the detectors for boredom (kappa = 0.278, $A' = 0.682$) and off-task behavior (kappa = 0.369, $A' = 0.725$) yielding better cross-validated performance than detectors for the other constructs. The performance of these detectors was mildly lower than previously published models of affect in other learning environments [3, 5, 27], and moderately lower than past models of off-task behavior [5].

Table 1. Cross-validated performance of affect and behavior detector using feature engineering and deep learning.

Affect/Behavior	Feature engineering				Deep learning		
	Feature set	Classifier	Kappa	A′	Model	Kappa	A′
Boredom	Basic	Logistic regression	0.278	0.682	GRU	0.103	0.672
Confusion	All	Logistic regression	0.091	0.568	GRU	0.091	0.566
Delight	Basic	Step regression	0.070	0.570	GRU	0.035	0.649
Engaged concentration	All	Logistic regression	0.142	0.624	GRU	0.138	0.619
Frustration	All	Logistic regression	0.056	0.634	GRU	0.041	0.572
Off-task behavior	Basic + Sequence	Logistic regression	0.369	0.725	LSTM	0.268	0.761
Average			0.168	0.634		0.112	0.640

Examination of the features selected in each affect and behavior detector indicated that the features that were predictive of each state were similar in nature and could be grouped into the following categories:

- Frequency of causal map construction or causal map annotation actions (e.g., frequency of deleting entity; frequency of deleting causal link; frequency of marking a causal link correct action)
- Status of causal map (e.g., ratio of the number of concepts remaining in map and the number of causal links remaining in map)
- Note-taking behaviors (e.g., frequency of editing note, frequency of viewing notes)
- Evaluation behaviors (e.g., duration of viewing explanation)
- Resource access behaviors (e.g., duration of viewing science book)
- Conversation request (e.g., number of times requesting a conversation with mentor)
- Threshold features (e.g., number of long pauses after taking quiz; number of long pauses after viewing graded explanation from Betty)
- Sequence features (e.g., frequency of sequence *read resource → read resource → read resource*; frequency of sequence *read resource → read resource → add concept*)
- Other (e.g., percent of ineffective actions)

These results indicated that the frequency and duration of relevant actions, especially those that were key to the environment, such as map building, resource accessing, note-taking, requesting conversation, and monitoring and evaluating maps, and the sequence of these actions, are meaningful in predicting affective states and behaviors in Betty's Brain.

4.2 Deep Learning

Several notable patterns of results of the deep learning approach can be seen in Table 1. GRU networks were, on average, the most accurate type across the different detection tasks (mean kappa = 0.110, mean A′ = 0.637). LSTMs were the next most accurate (mean kappa = 0.098, mean A′ = 0.623), demonstrating the efficacy of the simplified structure of GRUs in the current dataset with relatively few instances for deep learning applications — though this pattern was reversed in [15]. The fully-connected network structure was the least accurate (mean kappa = 0.068, mean A′ = 0.577), which is unsurprising given that the fully-connected network does not leverage the sequential nature of the data.

Additionally, there were large differences in the accuracy of neural networks for different detection tasks. Confusion and frustration were particularly difficult to detect (A′ = 0.566 and 0.572 respectively), while boredom was much more effectively detected (A′ = 0.672). Off-task behavior was most accurately detected (A′ = 0.761), indicating that there are clear connections between students' behaviors in Betty's Brain and the BROMP observations of off-task behavior.

Finally, the deep learning models achieved similar or better A′ compared to the feature engineered models for every construct except for frustration, averaging 0.006 higher A′, but achieved worse kappa for every construct except for confusion, averaging 0.056 lower kappa. Examination of ROC curves revealed that the feature engineered models were particularly precise at the pre-selected decision threshold but were less so at other false positive rates, yielding relatively higher kappa values, whereas the deep models were more uniformly effective across decision thresholds.

5 Discussion

The past few years have seen a surge of interest and attention in deep learning [14]. Despite its wide application in other domains such as image classification and natural language processing [14, 19, 28], deep learning is still an emerging area in the field of education with limited studies comparing its predictive power to that of the traditional feature engineering approach. To address this issue, we built predictive models of students' affective states and off-task behavior as they learned science in an open-ended learning environment called Betty's Brain, using both the traditional feature engineering approach and the deep learning approach. Our findings show the advantages and disadvantages of each approach.

5.1   Main Findings

In general, the two approaches yielded similar levels of accuracy, with the detectors using the deep learning approach showing similar or higher A' (for all but the frustration detector), while the detectors using feature engineering approach generally showing higher kappa (for all detectors except for confusion). These results indicated that the detectors using the feature engineering approach were more accurate in differentiating the presence or absence of an affective state or behavior than the deep learning detectors at one specific threshold (therefore higher kappa); whereas the detectors using a deep learning approach were more accurate in distinguishing whether a student was displaying delight/boredom or not across a wide range of other decision thresholds (therefore higher A'). Such a tradeoff should be taken into consideration when selecting final models. For instance, the deep learning model would be preferable if we want to integrate a detector with a tunable threshold or multiple thresholds, but would be less useful for a single threshold making a single distinction at 50% confidence. The difference in the two metrics for the deep models is also consistent with what was found in Botelho et al. [15], where deep learning affect detectors showed a notable increase in A' compared to previously published feature-engineered detectors on the same dataset, whereas kappa was slightly lower for the deep learning models.

Another key result, as illustrated by the confusion models, is that deep neural networks are not a panacea. Features engineered to capture confusion were not effective at much above chance levels, and deep neural networks were not able to capture key details researchers may have missed when engineering features. It is possible that students simply do not interact with Betty's Brain in ways that distinguish confusion from other affective states.

Overall, these affect detectors showed relatively lower performance than those constructed in other learning environments such as Cognitive Tutor [3]. This may be due to the open-ended nature of the environment. In many computerized learning systems, student actions are more restricted and each action can be either correct or incorrect based on the answer. In Betty's Brain, however, there is no single correct path. In order to succeed in the environment, students can execute many possible paths, and they have the freedom to decide their own actions at any time. This might make it difficult to create features that capture attributes of the student's learning, which could help identify affective states and behaviors.

In comparing the two modeling approaches to each other, a key advantage of deep neural networks is their capability to automatically derive meaningful features from raw interaction data. Indeed, this is the core capability that has driven advances in deep learning models, and what distinguishes them from shallow neural networks. However, it is also arguable that time saved by this advantage is lost due to time spent refining the structure of neural networks, which is also an open-ended, time-consuming task for any new domain. As such, further research is needed to quantify this tradeoff.

On the other hand, the traditional feature engineering approach has its own strengths. The resulting models using feature engineering, particularly simple models such as logistic regression, are more interpretable from a psychological and educational perspective because they provide meaningful information on which features are more strongly associated with each affective and behavioral construct of student engagement.

Conversely, deep learning models are typically more complex and the model parameters are difficult to analyze and interpret.

5.2 Limitations and Future Work

In this study, the affect and behavior detectors were built for sixth-grade students in an urban public school as they learned topics from the subject matter of science in Betty's Brain. Sample size was limited due to the difficulties of observing affect and behaviors in class; researchers using expert labels to build detectors of student affect and behavior are unlikely to ever reach the millions of instances frequently employed in other deep learning domains. Thus, results should not be considered a reflection on the potential of deep learning in general but do suggest that it is unlikely to provide breakthroughs for student modeling applications where data is naturally limited.

Future research should explore the generalizability of our findings. For example, recent work indicated that affect detectors might not generalize well to new populations such as rural school students [29], and that deep learning models for affect and behavior detection were less effective in rural settings [20]. As such, it is especially meaningful to implement both approaches for different populations and test whether our comparison results generalize to other student populations, including rural and suburban students. Furthermore, will these results transfer to other contexts (e.g., other types of computer-based learning environments outside the domain of science)? Will the level of accuracy be comparable when we apply the two approaches to predict other constructs beyond affect detection?

Our findings have implications for the implementation of affect/behavior detectors to trigger interventions and observations in the open-ended learning environment. The advantages and disadvantages of each method should be considered in order to make decisions on which approach to pursue to detect affect/behavior with higher confidence in real time and to drive interventions. If the data set size is much larger than seen here, deep neural networks may provide the best results, but for our current data set size the choice of method appears to be based on the eventual application of the model: feature-engineered models for intervention, deep neural networks for discovery with models.

Acknowledgments. We would like to thank the National Science Foundation (NSF) for their support (#DRL-1561567).

References

1. Clarke-Midura, J., Yudelson, M.V.: Towards identifying students' causal reasoning using machine learning. In: Lane, H.C., Yacef, K., Mostow, J., Pavlik, P. (eds.) AIED 2013. LNCS (LNAI), vol. 7926, pp. 704–707. Springer, Heidelberg (2013). https://doi.org/10.1007/978-3-642-39112-5_93

2. Rowe, E., Asbell-Clarke, J., Baker, R.S., Eagle, M., Hicks, A.G., Barnes, T.M., Brown, R.A., Edwards, T.: Assessing implicit science learning in digital games. Comput. Hum. Behav. **76**, 617–630 (2017)

3. Baker, R.S., Gowda, S.M., Wixon, M., Kalka, J., Wagner, A.Z., Salvi, A., Aleven, V., Kusbit, G.W., Ocumpaugh, J., Rossi, L.: Towards sensor-free affect detection in cognitive tutor algebra. In: Proceedings of the 5th International Conference on Educational Data Mining, pp. 126–133 (2012)

4. D'Mello, S., Jackson, T., Craig, S., Morgan, B., Chipman, P., White, H., Person, N., Kort, B., Kaliouby, R.e., Picard, R., Graesser, A.: AutoTutor detects and responds to learners affective and cognitive states. In: Proceedings of the Workshop on Emotional and Cognitive Issues in ITS in Conjunction with the 9th International Conference on ITS, pp. 31–43 (2008)

5. Pardos, Z.A., Baker, R.S., Pedro, M.O.C.Z.S., Gowda, S.M., Gowda, S.M.: Affective states and state tests: investigating how affect throughout the school year predicts end of year learning outcomes. In: Proceedings of the 3rd International Conference on Learning Analytics and Knowledge, pp. 117–124 (2013)

6. Arroyo, I., Cooper, D.G., Burleson, W., Woolf, B.P., Muldner, K., Christopherson, R.: Emotion sensors go to school. In: Proceedings of the 2009 Conference on Artificial Intelligence in Education (AIED 2009), pp. 17–24. IOS Press, Amsterdam (2009)

7. Baker, R.S., Corbett, A.T., Roll, I., Koedinger, K.R.: Developing a generalizable detector of when students game the system. User Model. User-Adapt. Interact. **18**, 287–314 (2008)

8. Cetintas, S., Si, L., Xin, Y.P., Hord, C.: Automatic detection of off-task behaviors in intelligent tutoring systems with machine learning techniques. IEEE Trans. Learn. Technol. **3**, 228–236 (2010)

9. Kai, S., Paquette, L., Baker, R.S., Bosch, N., D'Mello, S., Ocumpaugh, J., Shute, V., Ventura, M.: A comparison of video-based and interaction-based affect detectors in physics playground. In: Proceedings of the 8th International Conference on Educational Data Mining, pp. 77–84 (2015)

10. Ocumpaugh, J., Baker, R.S., Rodrigo, M.M.T.: Baker Rodrigo Ocumpaugh Monitoring Protocol (BROMP) 2.0 technical and training manual. Technical report, Teachers College, Columbia University, Ateneo Laboratory for the Learning Sciences (2015)

11. Fancsali, S.E.: Causal discovery with models: behavior, affect, and learning in cognitive tutor algebra. In: Proceedings of the 7th International Conference on Educational Data Mining (EDM 2014), pp. 28–35 (2014)

12. San Pedro, M.O.Z., Baker, R.S., Bowers, A.J., Heffernan, N.T.: Predicting college enrollment from student interaction with an intelligent tutoring system in middle school. In: Proceedings of the 6th International Conference on Educational Data Mining, pp. 177–184 (2013)

13. San Pedro, M.O.Z., Snow, E.L., Baker, R.S., McNamara, D.S., Heffernan, N.T.: Exploring Dynamic Assessments of Affect, Behavior, and Cognition and Math State Test Achievement. In: Proceedings of the 8th International Conference on Educational Data Mining, pp. 85–92 (2015)

14. LeCun, Y., Bengio, Y., Hinton, G.: Deep learning. Nature **521**, 436–444 (2015)

15. Botelho, A.F., Baker, R.S., Heffernan, N.T.: Improving sensor-free affect detection using deep learning. In: André, E., Baker, R., Hu, X., Rodrigo, M.M.T., du Boulay, B. (eds.) AIED 2017. LNCS (LNAI), vol. 10331, pp. 40–51. Springer, Cham (2017). https://doi.org/10.1007/978-3-319-61425-0_4

16. Khajah, M., Lindsey, R.V., Mozer, M.C.: How deep is knowledge tracing? In: Proceedings of the 9th International Conference on Educational Data Mining (EDM 2016), pp. 94–101 (2016)

17. Lin, C., Chi, M.: A comparisons of BKT, RNN and LSTM for learning gain prediction. In: André, E., Baker, R., Hu, X., Rodrigo, M.M.T., du Boulay, B. (eds.) AIED 2017. LNCS (LNAI), vol. 10331, pp. 536–539. Springer, Cham (2017). https://doi.org/10.1007/978-3-319-61425-0_58

18. Piech, C., Spencer, J., Huang, J., Ganguli, S., Sahami, M., Guibas, L., Sohl-Dickstein, J.: Deep knowledge tracing. In: Advances in Neural Information Processing Systems (NIPS 2015), vol. 28, pp. 505–513. Curran Associates, Inc. (2015)
19. Krizhevsky, A., Sutskever, I., Hinton, G.E.: ImageNet classification with deep convolutional neural networks. In: Proceedings of the 25th International Conference on Neural Information Processing Systems, pp. 1097–1105, Lake Tahoe, Nevada (2012)
20. Botelho, A.F., Baker, R.S., Heffernan, N.T.: Developing and evaluating "deep" sensor-free detectors of student affect. (Manuscript in preparation)
21. Leelawong, K., Biswas, G.: Designing learning by teaching agents: the Betty's brain system. Int J. Artif. Intell. Educ. **18**, 181–208 (2008)
22. Baker, R.S., Ocumpaugh, J., Gowda, S.M., Kamarainen, A.M., Metcalf, S.J.: Extending log-based affect detection to a multi-user virtual environment for science. In: Proceedings of the 22nd Conference on User Modelling, Adaptation, and Personalization, pp. 290–300 (2014)
23. Ocumpaugh, J., Baker, R.S., Rodrigo, M.M., Salvi, A., Velsen, M.V., Aghababyan, A., Martin, T.: HART: the human affect recording tool. In: Proceedings of the 33rd Annual International Conference on the Design of Communication (SIGDOC 2015). ACM, New York (2015)
24. Mierswa, I., Scholz, M., Klinkenberg, R., Wurst, M., Euler, T.: Rapid prototyping for complex data mining tasks. In: Proceedings of KDD 2006, pp. 935–940 (2006)
25. Clevert, D.-A., Unterthiner, T., Hochreiter, S.: Fast and accurate deep network learning by Exponential Linear Units (ELUs). In: ICLR 2016 (2016)
26. Srivastava, N., Hinton, G., Krizhevsky, A., Sutskever, I., Salakhutdinov, R.: Dropout: a simple way to prevent neural networks from overfitting. J. Mach. Learn. Res. **15**, 1929–1958 (2014)
27. Paquette, L., Baker, R.S., Pedro, M.A.S., Gobert, J.D., Rossi, L., Nakama, A., Kauffman-Rogoff, Z.: Sensor-free affect detection for a simulation-based science inquiry learning environment. In: Proceedings of the 12th International Conference on Intelligent Tutoring Systems, pp. 1–10 (2014)
28. Sutskever, I., Vinyals, O., Le, Q.V.: Sequence to sequence learning with neural networks. In: Advances in Neural Information Processing Systems, pp. 3104–3112. Curran Associates, Inc. (2014)
29. Ocumpaugh, J., Baker, R.S., Gowda, S.M., Heffernan, N.T., Heffernan, C.: Population validity for educational data mining: a case study in affect detection. Br. J. Educ. Psychol. **45**, 487–501 (2014)

A Comparison of Tutoring Strategies for Recovering from a Failed Attempt During Faded Support

Pamela Jordan[✉], Patricia Albacete, and Sandra Katz

Learning Research and Development Center, University of Pittsburgh,
Pittsburgh, PA 15260, USA
pjordan@pitt.edu
http://www.pitt.edu/~pjordan

Abstract. The support the tutor provides for a student is expected to fade over time as the student makes progress towards mastery of the learning objectives. One way in which the tutor can fade support is to prompt or elicit a next step that requires the student to fill in some intermediate actions or reasoning on her own. But what should the tutor do if the student is unable to complete such a step? In human-human tutoring interactions, a tutor may remediate by explicitly covering the missing intermediate steps with the student and in some contexts this behavior correlates with learning. But if there are multiple intermediate steps that need to be made explicit, the tutor could focus the student's attention on the last successful step and then move forward through the intermediate steps (forward reasoning) or the tutor could focus the student's attention on the intermediate step just before the failed step and move backward through the intermediate steps (backward reasoning). In this paper we explore when the forward strategy or backward strategy may be beneficial for remediation. We also compare the two faded support+remediation strategies to a control in which support is never faded and found that faded support was not detrimental to student learning outcomes when the two remediation strategies were available and it took significantly less time on task to achieve similar learning gains when starting the tutor-student interaction with faded support.

Keywords: Remediation strategy · Tutorial dialogue
Hinting strategy · Model of teaching

1 Introduction

The support that the tutor provides for a student is expected to fade over time as the student makes progress towards mastery of the learning objectives [12]. One way in which the tutor can fade support is to prompt or elicit a next step in the reasoning or problem solving so that the student needs to fill in some intermediate actions or reasoning on his own without support as in Fig. 1 where the

© Springer International Publishing AG, part of Springer Nature 2018
C. Penstein Rosé et al. (Eds.): AIED 2018, LNAI 10947, pp. 212–224, 2018.
https://doi.org/10.1007/978-3-319-93843-1_16

tutor could elicit just the steps and skip over the microsteps. We will call such a step size coarse-grained, while we call the step size fine-grained if the tutor elicits all the reasoning from the student (i.e. both the steps and microsteps in Fig. 1). But what should the tutor do if the student is unable to complete an elicited coarse-grained step? In human-human tutoring interactions, a tutor may remediate by explicitly covering the missing intermediate microsteps with students and in some contexts this behavior correlates with learning [6]. The tutor may not have a clear idea of which of these microsteps the student needs help with or even if the student applied any reasoning (i.e. maybe the student just guessed an answer to the coarse-grained step). As suggested in [15], the tutor can hint forward or backward depending on the question at hand that the student could not fully answer. Extending this to a context in which reasoning support has been faded, if there are multiple intermediate microsteps that the tutor skipped over, the tutor could focus the student's attention on the last successful step and then move forward through the intermediate microsteps it had left for the student to reason through on his own (forward reasoning remediation) or the tutor could focus the student's attention on the intermediate microstep just before the failed step and move backward through the intermediate microsteps it had left for the student to reason through on his own (backward reasoning remediation). In this paper, we explore the question of when the forward reasoning remediation strategy may be beneficial and when the backward reasoning remediation strategy may be better in a context in which a tutoring system has faded support and always elicits coarse-grained steps except during a remediation. We also compare the two remediation strategies when used in the context of faded support to a control in which the tutor always elicits both steps and microsteps (i.e. reasoning support is never faded). This comparison checks that the faded reasoning support plus remediating when needed vs. never fading support is similar for learning gains while offering a significant savings in time on task.

2   Related Work

Prior research challenged the assumption that microstep-based tutoring (best illustrated by human tutoring) is more effective than step-based tutoring. For example, [13] observed that the learning benefits of microstep-based tutoring relative to less interactive forms of instruction, including step-based tutoring, plateau over time when students in one condition always experience steps, except during remediation, and in the other always experience microsteps. [3] found that augmenting microstep-based tutoring with pedagogical policies that decide who will cover what (the tutor or the student), is significantly more beneficial for learning than tutoring that addresses steps only. However, [3] also noted that microstep-based only discussions between the student and simulated tutor are significantly more time consuming than step-based only discussions.

[7] compared an approach that was all microstep-based tutoring, which involved highly interactive, microstep-based dialogues, to one that alternated between problems that used microstep-based tutoring and non-interactive help

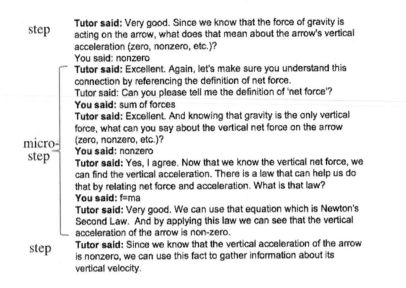

step — Tutor said: Very good. Since we know that the force of gravity is acting on the arrow, what does that mean about the arrow's vertical acceleration (zero, nonzero, etc.)?
You said: nonzero

micro-step —
Tutor said: Excellent. Again, let's make sure you understand this connection by referencing the definition of net force.
Tutor said: Can you please tell me the definition of 'net force'?
You said: sum of forces
Tutor said: Excellent. And knowing that gravity is the only vertical force, what can you say about the vertical net force on the arrow (zero, nonzero, etc.)?
You said: nonzero
Tutor said: Yes, I agree. Now that we know the vertical net force, we can find the vertical acceleration. There is a law that can help us do that by relating net force and acceleration. What is that law?
You said: f=ma
Tutor said: Very good. We can use that equation which is Newton's Second Law. And by applying this law we can see that the vertical acceleration of the arrow is non-zero.

step — Tutor said: Since we know that the vertical acceleration of the arrow is nonzero, we can use this fact to gather information about its vertical velocity.

Fig. 1. An example of steps and microsteps (substeps) in a line of reasoning

that summarized the line of reasoning that leads to a solution. They found that the simple, non-adaptive approach to improving the efficiency of microstep-based tutoring proved to be as beneficial for learning as an all microstep-based tutoring approach. However, the latter was significantly less efficient than the intervention that shifted between interactive and non-interactive problems. [14] showed that the granularity of the reasoning also impacts students' time on task. [5] showed that adapting the granularity of the reasoning throughout an individual's dialogue according to his pretest score reduced time on task without sacrificing learning gains.

Assuming the tutor does decide to elicit a next step instead of a microstep, if the student fails to answer the next step correctly, what should happen next during a remediation? That is the question that we address in this paper. [15] describes the hinting strategies that they found in human tutoring for when a medical student answers incorrectly. One is a strategy for cases in which there are causally related variables and the tutor has left some intermediate links for relating them implicit. The human tutors' strategy is to select a forward or backward direction for the hint depending on which variable was last brought into focus. That suggests that if the coarse-grain reasoning is moving forward the tutoring system should continue forward during a remediation that covers the microsteps and if the course-grain reasoning is moving backward the tutoring system should continue backward during a remediation that covers the microsteps. [9] found that in human-human tutoring students used both forward and backward reasoning when completing geometry proofs but the human tutors tended to hint forward. In experiments with an intelligent tutoring system for geometry proofs, [10] found that students' learning gains were not statistically different when tutored exclusively forward or exclusively backward but that students in the forward condition showed better performance with proof-writing than those in the backward condition.

We explore whether there are time on task differences between the use of forward and backward microstep remediation strategies and whether there could be learning differences in different situations depending on the remediation strategy. We also explore whether students' prior knowledge as measured by pretest impacts the effectiveness and efficiency of different remediation strategies.

3   Experimental Comparison of Remediation Strategies

The two strategies for remediating a missed step that we are exploring further were inspired by a strategy found in human tutoring dialogues for physics that correlated with student learning [6]. In some cases when a student missed a step the human tutor elicited the intermediate microsteps until the student was able to answer one of the microsteps correctly. Afterwards the tutor finished the remaining microsteps for the student before returning to the main line of reasoning (LOR). The human tutor seems to be assuming that once the student can answer correctly that either the remaining microsteps were likely known and just need to be made explicit for the sake of dialogue coherency or that the rest were potentially problematic too and the tutor should make them explicit for the student so as not to overburden the student.

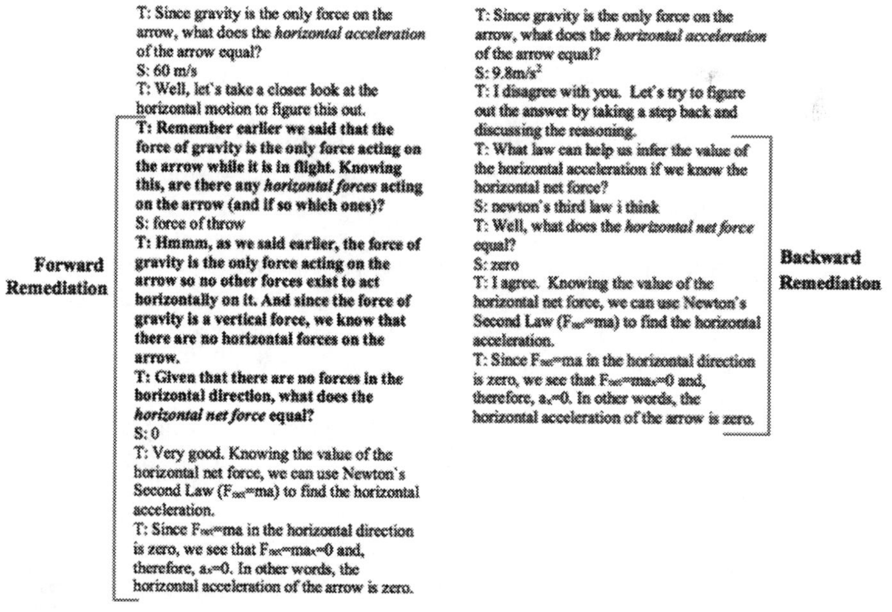

Forward Remediation

T: Since gravity is the only force on the arrow, what does the *horizontal acceleration* of the arrow equal?
S: 60 m/s
T: Well, let's take a closer look at the horizontal motion to figure this out.
T: Remember earlier we said that the force of gravity is the only force acting on the arrow while it is in flight. Knowing this, are there any *horizontal forces* acting on the arrow (and if so which ones)?
S: force of throw
T: Hmmm, as we said earlier, the force of gravity is the only force acting on the arrow so no other forces exist to act horizontally on it. And since the force of gravity is a vertical force, we know that there are no horizontal forces on the arrow.
T: Given that there are no forces in the horizontal direction, what does the *horizontal net force* equal?
S: 0
T: Very good. Knowing the value of the horizontal net force, we can use Newton's Second Law ($F_{ax}=ma$) to find the horizontal acceleration.
T: Since $F_{ax}=ma$ in the horizontal direction is zero, we see that $F_{ax}=ma_x=0$ and, therefore, $a_x=0$. In other words, the horizontal acceleration of the arrow is zero.

Backward Remediation

T: Since gravity is the only force on the arrow, what does the *horizontal acceleration* of the arrow equal?
S: 9.8m/s²
T: I disagree with you. Let's try to figure out the answer by taking a step back and discussing the reasoning.
T: What law can help us infer the value of the horizontal acceleration if we know the horizontal net force?
S: newton's third law i think
T: Well, what does the *horizontal net force* equal?
S: zero
T: I agree. Knowing the value of the horizontal net force, we can use Newton's Second Law ($F_{ax}=ma$) to find the horizontal acceleration.
T: Since $F_{ax}=ma$ in the horizontal direction is zero, we see that $F_{ax}=ma_x=0$ and, therefore, $a_x=0$. In other words, the horizontal acceleration of the arrow is zero.

Fig. 2. An example of forward and backward remediation for the same step

But when implementing such a remediation approach in a tutoring system there are several decisions to make for which we do not yet have guidance from human tutoring corpora. The system could potentially move forward or backward through the microstep level LOR as shown in Fig. 2 in the two dialogues from actual student-system interactions. During the forward remediation on the left, the system elicits the first microstep in the subdialogue and continues forward to the next microstep until the student can answer correctly or reaches the last microstep. When the student answers a microstep correctly, the system acknowledges the correct answer and then completes the remaining microsteps for the student before moving on to the next step in the higher-level LOR just as with the human tutoring scenario described above. During the backward remediation on the right the tutoring system elicits the last microstep in the subdialogue and continues moving backward through the fine-grained LOR until the student can answer correctly or reaches the prior step in the main LOR. When the student answers a microstep correctly, the system acknowledges it and reviews the microsteps that the system attempted to elicit from the student. Note that prior to the student's first correct answer, the system did not provide any corrections for the microsteps the student answered incorrectly. Thus the review of the microsteps at the end serves as corrective feedback. In the forward remediation all of the microsteps are made explicit, but by design in the backward remediation, all of the microsteps may not be explicitly covered with the student. Note in Fig. 2 that the microsteps in bold on the left are not made explicit in the backward remediation on the right.

For the forward remediation the system bridges the remaining reasoning gap towards the missed step which seems necessary to achieve dialogue coherency but at the same time this could help a student who may have trouble completing the remaining reasoning on his own. At the end of the backward remediation the system again moves forward to provide corrective feedback on the microsteps the student could not answer. The forward review to tie into the missed step seems necessary to achieve dialogue coherency but not explicitly completing the full line of reasoning would not be helpful for a student who cannot supply the remaining backward reasoning on his own. This suggests that a forward strategy may be better for a student with lower prior knowledge and a backward strategy may be better for a higher prior knowledge student if the student self explains the remaining backward reasoning that was not made explicit. To explore the impact of these design decisions, we developed a two-condition study to explore this hypothesis; a Forward remediation condition and a Backward remediation condition. Both conditions always cover the LOR at a coarse-grained step size (i.e. the conditions are in faded support mode and cover the steps only in Fig. 1) and remediate either forward or backward through the microsteps only when the student cannot answer the step. We introduced a third control condition in which the fine-grained LOR (i.e. the condition is in full support mode and covers the steps+microsteps in Fig. 1) is pursued so that neither remediation strategy–forward or backward– is needed. Comparing the Forward and Backward remediation conditions to the control condition will confirm that faded reasoning support plus remediation when needed is not detrimental to learning and is more efficient.

3.1   The Rimac Tutoring System

We used the Rimac tutor to test the two microstep remediation strategies. Rimac is a web-based natural-language tutoring system that engages a student one-on-one in conceptual discussions after he solves a quantitative physics problem [1,6]. The dialogues authored for the system can be represented with a finite state machine. Each state contains a single tutor turn. The arcs leaving the state correspond to possible classifications of student turns. When creating a state, the dialogue author enters the text for a tutor's turn and defines classes of student responses (e.g., correct, partially correct, incorrect).

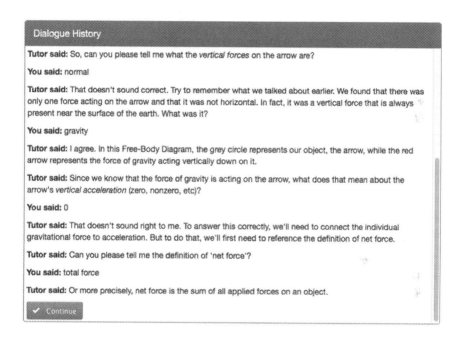

Fig. 3. A sample Rimac dialogue

Rimac's dialogues were developed to model a directed LOR [4] during which the tutor presents a series of carefully ordered questions to the student. In addition, Rimac's dialogues are structured hierarchically as in Fig. 1, so that a step can be expanded into microsteps. Thus the tutor can elicit the LOR at different levels of the hierarchy. For example, the tutor could elicit just the steps in Fig. 1 to elicit a higher level LOR. Regardless of the hierarchy level elicited, if the student answers a question correctly, he advances to the next question in the LOR at the same level. If the student provides an incorrect answer, the system launches a remedial subdialogue which could be at a lower hierarchical level and then returns to the main line of reasoning after the subdialogue has completed. Rimac asks mainly short-answer questions to improve recognition of student responses as shown in Fig. 3, which illustrates the system's follow-up to correct, partially correct and incorrect answers at the lowest level of the hierarchy (i.e. microsteps that cannot be further expanded).

3.2 Experimental Design

The participants in the study were undergraduate students who had not studied physics beyond high school and thus were expected to be physics novices. The students came to our lab for one session which was scheduled to last up to 5 h but on average lasted 4 h. Breaks were encouraged between tasks.

When a student arrived, an experimenter explained the tasks the student would be completing, obtained consent and provided the student with a calculator, access to a short, online physics review text that we had compiled and blank paper to use during the session. First students were given up to 25 min to read the physics review text. Next they were given up to 50 min to complete a 62 item, offline pretest on physics concepts. No test items involved quantitative problem solving and each item received a score from 0 to 1 when graded after the session.

Next the student was introduced to the Rimac tutoring system. The student was asked to alternate working towards solving a quantitative physics problem on paper and then engaging in a discussion of multiple conceptual reflection questions about the problem with the tutoring system.[1] The student was limited to 5 min to work on solving the quantitative problem but had no time limit for completing discussions of the reflection questions with the system. On average, students took 1 to 1.5 h to complete all discussions with the tutoring system as will be discussed in more detail later. The student had access to the online review text throughout his interactions with the tutoring system. The student was assigned 6 problems to complete. For each problem the system asked the student to watch a short video of the problem solution before engaging in a discussion of the concepts involved in solving the problem. The video only showed how to solve the quantitative problem and did not offer any conceptual explanations. Its purpose was to ensure the student knew the correct solution to the problem before the system started discussing the concepts involved in the problem.

After completing all of the problems, the student was given up to 50 min to complete an offline posttest that was isomorphic to the pretest. Finally, at the end of the experiment the student completed a survey to give feedback on his interactions with the system. A total of $N = 129$ students (Females = 82, Males = 47) participated in the study and were paid for their time.

Students were randomly assigned to one of three non-adaptive conditions, Control ($N = 45$: Females = 28, Males = 17), Forward ($N = 42$: Females = 27, Males = 15) or Backward ($N = 42$: Females = 27, Males = 15). Only the version of the reflection dialogue varied between conditions. The Control version

---

[1] There were at least two reflection questions per problem and at most three depending on the problem.

of the dialogue always engaged a student in the discussion at the most fully expanded level (i.e. all steps were expanded into their microsteps). Both the Forward and Backward versions of the dialogue always engaged students in a discussion at the unexpanded level (i.e. at the step level) but behaved differently when the student was unable to correctly answer a question at the step level. All remediations had the potential to cover 3–6 microsteps (depending on the step) to address the missed step but the Forward condition moved through those microsteps in the forward direction while the Backward condition moved in the backward direction.

Table 1. Learning comparisons

Condition	Pretest mean SD (normalized mean SD)	Posttest mean SD (normalized mean SD)	$t(n)$	p
Combined	$M = 39.67\ SD = 11.08$ ($M = .64,\ SD = .18$)	$M = 47.67\ SD = 9.36$ ($M = .77,\ SD = .15$)	$t(128) = 15.698$	<.001
Control	$M = 40.10\ SD = 12.06$ ($M = .65\ SD = .20$)	$M = 49.48\ SD = 9.61$ ($M = .80\ SD = .16$)	$t(44) = 10.106$	<.001
Forward	$M = 37.67\ SD = 9.18$ ($M = .61\ SD = .15$)	$M = 45.95\ SD = 8.89$ ($M = .74\ SD = .14$)	$t(41) = 9.359$	<.001
Backward	$M = 41.21\ SD = 11.69$ ($M = .67\ SD = .19$)	$M = 47.42\ SD = 9.42$ ($M = .77\ SD = .15$)	$t(41) = 8.148$	<.001

3.3   Results

A paired samples t-test comparing pretest and posttest scores on conceptual knowledge showed a statistical significant difference when considering all students together and when separately considering students by condition, as shown in Table 1. These results suggest that the system was successful in promoting learning in all conditions. A one-way ANOVA to test for differences in incoming knowledge (as measured by pretest) among students in each condition showed no statistically significant difference, $p = .33$, suggesting that students in all conditions had comparable prior conceptual knowledge.

There was a statistically significant difference between the average time students in each condition spent in discussions with the tutor as shown in Table 2 where $F(2, 126) = 44.988, p < .001$. A Tukey post hoc pair-wise comparison revealed significant differences between all pairs of conditions at $p < .001$. The differences between Control and the other two conditions are expected since the Control condition always walks students through the most detailed LOR whereas the other two conditions always present the LOR at a coarse-grain step size and only expand into microsteps when a student cannot correctly complete a step. However, finding that the time on task for the Backward condition was significantly less than for the Forward condition was unexpected. We will explore this further in the next section.

Table 2. Time on task comparisons

Condition	Mean time & SD in seconds (Mean time & SD in minutes)
Control	$M = 5011.01$ s, $SD = 897.70$ s ($M = 83.52$ min, $SD = 14.96$ min)
Forward	$M = 4092.85$ s, $SD = 571.92$ s ($M = 68.21$ min, $SD = 9.53$ min)
Backward	$M = 3533.51$ s, $SD = 684.45$ s ($M = 58.89$ min, $SD = 11.41$ min)

When comparing the differences in mean learning gains among conditions, a one-way ANOVA with condition as the independent variable and learning gain[2] as the dependent variable showed a statistically significant difference among conditions $F(2, 126) = 3.475, p = .034$. A Tukey post hoc pair-wise analysis revealed a statistically significant difference between the mean gain of students in the Backward condition ($M = 6.21(10\%), SD = 4.94(8\%)$) and those in the Control condition ($M = 9.38(15\%), SD = 6.23(10\%)$), $p = .028$. An ANCOVA with Condition as the independent factor, Gain as the dependent variable and Time on Task as the covariate showed no effect of Condition on Gain when controlling for time on task $F(2, 125) = .516, p = .60$. This suggests that when controlling for time on task there is no significant difference between the gains of the conditions.

When exploring whether the effectiveness of each treatment varied depending on student aptitude (as measured by pretest), a univariate analysis of variance with Condition, Aptitude, and Condition X Aptitude as independent variables and Gain as the dependent variable showed no interaction between Aptitude and Condition $F(2, 123) = .413, p = .66$. Additionally, when controlling for time on task there was no interaction between Aptitude and Condition $F(2, 122) = .394, p = .68$.

Overall, we expected the Forward/Backward conditions to require less time on task because students only had to go through microsteps when they answered a step incorrectly. And the results suggest that only expanding a step into its microsteps when the student was unable to answer the step correctly was not detrimental to learning. These results where granularity was not adapted during the dialogue are similar to those found in [5] where adapting step granularity increased efficiency with no measurable change to learning. Whereas the study described in [5] expanded a step when it was answered incorrectly or when a lower prior knowledge student answered correctly, this study does not adapt granularity during the dialogue and never expands a correctly answered step. Thus we confirmed that the single trigger we used in our study (i.e. there is an incorrect step response) for expanding a step can also increase efficiency without reducing learning.

---

[2] gain = (PosttestScore-PretestScore)/#TestItems.

4   A Closer Look at Forward and Backward Remediations

While the results described above show that always presenting coarse-grained steps and only expanding them into microsteps when a remediation is needed can increase the efficiency of learning, it does not reveal whether there are differences in how students interact with the two remediation strategies. For this analysis we will examine the results of a number of one-way ANOVAs with condition as the independent variable and a dependent variable of either the number of remediations, the gain or the number of microsteps a student needs to answer to complete a remediation (length per remediation, LPR) for a step. We will look at students' behavior on two problems that were chosen randomly. One problem is midway through a session and the other is near the end of the tutoring session.[3]

A one-way ANOVA with the number of remediations as the dependent variable showed no statistically significant difference $F(1, 77) = 1.5, p = .223$ between the Backward ($M = .186, SD = .119$) and Forward ($M = .223, SD = .143$) conditions. This suggests that the need for remediations were similar across conditions. With LPR as the dependent variable there was a statistically significant difference between the Backward ($M = .30, SD = .13$) and Forward ($M = .40, SD = .16$) conditions $F(1, 77) = 9.20, p < .04$). This suggests that the tutor elicited a smaller number of microsteps from students during a remediation in the Backward condition (i.e. the students in the backward condition answered fewer microsteps incorrectly than students in the forward condition).

Next we compared the behavior of the higher and lower prior knowledge students in the Backward and Forward Conditions as determined by a median split on their pretest scores. With LPR as the dependent variable, there was no significant difference in the number of microsteps that lower prior knowledge students experienced between the Backward ($M = .37, SD = .11$) and Forward ($M = .43, SD = .14$) conditions ($F(1, 37) = 2.08, p = .15$) but higher prior knowledge students experienced significantly fewer microsteps $F(1, 37) = 5.71, p < .03$ in the Backward condition ($M = .25, SD = .11$) than in the Forward condition ($M = .36, SD = .18$). Perhaps the higher prior knowledge students are reasoning backwards to answer the step since they tend to make more microstep errors in their forward reasoning than in their backward reasoning (i.e. they were attempting to reason in the backward direction so the questions may be more familiar to them), while lower prior knowledge students may be guessing or ill-equipped to conduct the reasoning on their own (i.e. they do not know the necessary knowledge well enough to reason with it) since the errors in their reasoning are similar in either direction. This interpretation of the results could mean that lower knowledge students should be told all of the microsteps since they either do not know most of them or how to reason with them and that

---

[3] While it is possible that students may have found these two problems to be more difficult than earlier ones, a one-way ANOVA with the number of problems as the independent variable and the number of remediations needed as the dependent variable showed no statistically significant difference $F(1, 156) = 1.9, p = .166$ between the two problems ($M = .204, SD = .132$) and all of the problems ($M = .178, SD = .106$).

higher knowledge students may do better with the Backward remediation strategy but perhaps the full line of reasoning from the prior step to the missed step should still be made explicit.

Finally, with the gain as the dependent variable there were no significant differences in the gains of lower prior knowledge students in the Backward ($M = .147, SD = .09$) or Forward ($M = .152, SD = .08$) conditions $F(1, 37) = .03, p = .87$ nor in the gains of higher prior knowledge students in the Backward ($M = .06, SD = .05$) or Forward ($M = .10, SD = .10$) conditions $F(1, 38) = 2.35$, $p = .13$. This suggests that there may be room for improvement in both strategies. Perhaps the system should be adaptive during the remediation and look at the student's skill and improvement on the concepts involved in the microsteps to decide what to explicitly cover and who should cover it (tutor or tutor + student) [3] during the remediation.

5   Conclusions and Future Work

We found that the Backward remediation strategy was more efficient than the Forward remediation strategy for all students but more so for higher prior knowledge students who experienced a shorter remediation than for lower prior knowledge students. This might indicate that lower prior knowledge students do not yet know enough to do the reasoning in either direction since they make more errors during a remediation and take longer to exit a remediation than higher prior knowledge students. Furthermore, we found that higher prior knowledge students make more errors in the Forward remediation direction than in the Backward direction. This may reflect that they attempted to reason in the Backward direction on their own and thus the questions in this direction may be more familiar to them. When a higher prior knowledge student makes an error at the step level there is the possibility that he is not yet capable of completing an expert line of reasoning on his own and thus is still relatively closer in behavior to a novice than an expert. We recruited students whom we expected to be physics novices and as observed in [2,8,11], novices tend to reason backwards while experts reason forwards.

When an adaptive tutoring system that tracks the characteristics of an individual student (as in [5]) needs to decide whether to elicit a step or microstep (fade or don't fade reasoning support), our results so far suggest that for a lower knowledge student it should either elicit or tell the microsteps to a lower knowledge student and that for a higher knowledge student it should elicit the step but be prepared to remediate by moving backward through the microsteps instead of forward.

In our future work, we will incorporate the suggestion above into our adaptive version of Rimac. Currently, it remediates missed steps by always moving forward through the microsteps. We will also look at students' proficiency and gains for the knowledge covered during the remediations to gain insight into when it may be better to begin moving forward through a remediation (e.g. the student slipped somewhere in his reasoning and is closer to expert than novice).

Such insights may help us to make the remediations themselves more adaptive to the student's current level of knowledge.

Acknowledgment. We thank Dennis Lusetich, Svetlana Romanova, Catherine Stainton, Sarah Birmingham and Scott Silliman. This research was supported by the Institute of Education Sciences, U.S. Department of Education, through Grant R305A130441 to the University of Pittsburgh. The opinions expressed are those of the authors and do not necessarily represent the views of the Institute or the U.S. Department of Education.

References

1. Albacete, P., Jordan, P., Katz, S.: Is a dialogue-based tutoring system that emulates helpful co-constructed relations during human tutoring effective? In: Conati, C., Heffernan, N., Mitrovic, A., Verdejo, M.F. (eds.) AIED 2015. LNCS (LNAI), vol. 9112, pp. 3–12. Springer, Cham (2015). https://doi.org/10.1007/978-3-319-19773-9_1

2. Chi, M.T.H., Feltovich, P.J., Glaser, R.: Categorization and representation of physics problems by experts and novices. Cogn. Sci. **5**(2), 121–152 (1981)

3. Chi, M., Jordan, P., VanLehn, K.: When is tutorial dialogue more effective than step-based tutoring? In: Trausan-Matu, S., Boyer, K.E., Crosby, M., Panourgia, K. (eds.) ITS 2014. LNCS, vol. 8474, pp. 210–219. Springer, Cham (2014). https://doi.org/10.1007/978-3-319-07221-0_25

4. Evens, M., Michael, J.: One-on-One Tutoring by Humans and Computers. Psychology Press, New York (2006)

5. Jordan, P., Albacete, P., Katz, S.: Adapting step granularity in tutorial dialogue based on pretest scores. In: André, E., Baker, R., Hu, X., Rodrigo, M.M.T., du Boulay, B. (eds.) AIED 2017. LNCS (LNAI), vol. 10331, pp. 137–148. Springer, Cham (2017). https://doi.org/10.1007/978-3-319-61425-0_12

6. Katz, S., Albacete, P.L.: A tutoring system that simulates the highly interactive nature of human tutoring. J. Educ. Psychol. **105**(4), 1126–1141 (2013)

7. Kopp, K.J., Britt, M.A., Millis, K., Graesser, A.C.: Improving the efficiency of dialogue in tutoring. Learn. Instr. **22**(5), 320–330 (2012)

8. Larkin, J., McDermott, J., Simon, D.P., Simon, H.A.: Expert and novice performance in solving physics problems. Science **208**(4450), 1335–1342 (1980)

9. Matsuda, N., VanLehn, K.: Modeling hinting strategies for geometry theorem proving. In: Brusilovsky, P., Corbett, A., de Rosis, F. (eds.) UM 2003. LNCS (LNAI), vol. 2702, pp. 373–377. Springer, Heidelberg (2003). https://doi.org/10.1007/3-540-44963-9_51

10. Matsuda, N., VanLehn, K.: Advanced geometry tutor: an intelligent tutor that teaches proof-writing with construction. AIED **125**, 443–450 (2005)

11. Norman, G.R., Brooks, L.R., Colle, C.L., Hatala, R.M.: The benefit of diagnostic hypotheses in clinical reasoning: experimental study of an instructional intervention for forward and backward reasoning. Cogn. Instr. **17**(4), 433–448 (1999)

12. Van de Pol, J., Volman, M., Beishuizen, J.: Scaffolding in teacher-student interaction: a decade of research. Educ. Psychol. Rev. **22**(3), 271–296 (2010)

13. VanLehn, K.: The relative effectiveness of human tutoring, intelligent tutoring systems, and other tutoring systems. Educ. Psychol. **46**(4), 197–221 (2011)

14. Zhou, G., Price, T.W., Lynch, C., Barnes, T., Chi, M.: The impact of granularity on worked examples and problem solving. In: CogSci, pp. 2817–2822 (2015)
15. Zhou, Y., Freedman, R., Glass, M., Michael, J.A., Rovick, A.A., Evens, M.W.: Delivering hints in a dialogue-based intelligent tutoring system. In: AAAI/IAAI, pp. 128–134 (1999)

Validating Revised Bloom's Taxonomy Using Deep Knowledge Tracing

Amar Lalwani[✉] and Sweety Agrawal

funtoot, Bangalore, India
{amar.lalwani,sweety.agrawal}@funtoot.com

Abstract. Revised Bloom's Taxonomy is used for classifying educational objectives. The said taxonomy describes a hierarchical ordering of cognitive skills from simple to complex. The Revised Taxonomy relaxed the strict cumulative hierarchical assumptions of the Original Taxonomy allowing overlaps. We use a knowledge tracing model, Deep Knowledge Tracing (DKT), to investigate the hierarchical nature of the Revised Taxonomy and also study the overlapping behavior of the Taxonomy. The DKT model is trained on about 42 million problems attempted on funtoot by the students. funtoot is an adaptive learning platform where students learn by answering problems. We propose a novel way to interpret the model's output to measure the effects of each learning objective on every other learning objectives. The results confirm the relaxed hierarchy of the skills from simple to complex. Moreover, the results also suggest overlaps even among the non-adjacent skills.

Keywords: Deep knowledge tracing · Revised Bloom's Taxonomy
Cognitive skills · Hierarchical taxonomy · Deep learning
Student modeling · Domain knowledge · funtoot

1 Introduction

Benjamin S. Bloom, along with a group of educators took up a task of classifying educational goals and objectives. They aimed to classify thinking behaviors that were believed to be important in the process of learning. The output of their research was a taxonomy of three domains:

- The cognitive
- The affective
- The psychomotor

The cognitive domain was further broken down into six cognitive levels of complexity (called, learning objectives): Knowledge, Comprehension, Application, Analysis, Synthesis, and Evaluation.

© Springer International Publishing AG, part of Springer Nature 2018
C. Penstein Rosé et al. (Eds.): AIED 2018, LNAI 10947, pp. 225–238, 2018.
https://doi.org/10.1007/978-3-319-93843-1_17

The levels are often depicted as a stairway, with emphasis on climbing to a higher level of complexity. The taxonomy is hierarchical, each level is subsumed by the higher levels. In other words, a student functioning at the 'Application' level has also mastered the material at the 'Knowledge' and 'Comprehension' levels.

A revision of this framework was developed in a similar manner 45 years later [2]. The Revised Taxonomy is also hierarchical in nature, like the original one. In the Revised Taxonomy, the six major categories - Remember, Understand, Apply, Analyse, Evaluate, and Create, differ in their complexity, with Remember being less complex than Understand, which is less complex than Apply, and so on. However, the complexity of the six categories is allowed to overlap, unlike in the case of Original Bloom's Taxonomy. Great emphasis is placed on the teacher usage rather than on developing a strict hierarchy.

Bloom's Taxonomy has been widely used in curriculum development [7], student assessment [23] and instruction evaluation. In curriculum design it serves as a common vocabulary to structure the curriculum's learning objective within the competency-based curriculum [3]. There are instructors who have applied Bloom's Taxonomy successfully in their classrooms. In circumstances when an instructor desires to move a group of students through a learning process utilizing an organized framework, Bloom's Taxonomy has been proven to be helpful. Research has shown that the implementation of Bloom's taxonomy in the curriculum has shown a positive outcome on students' test score [3,7,18].

Two important points, which various researchers have attempted to validate, have been noted about the original taxonomy, as described in [4,10]:

1. Taxonomy contained the categories ordered from simple to complex and from concrete to abstract.
2. The taxonomy was assumed to have a cumulative hierarchy; that is, mastery of a simple category was a prerequisite to the mastery of the next more complex category.

The authors have mentioned that even though the assumption of strict hierarchy is relaxed in the new taxonomy [2, Appendix A], they do not mean that the Revised Taxonomy is not hierarchical. Although the definition has been changed slightly, the authors believe that the empirical evidence found for the original taxonomy is not invalidated for the Revised Taxonomy. Hence, the empirical evidence found in [2, Appendix A] should apply to the Revised Bloom's Taxonomy as well.

Funoot [1] is a personalized learning tutor which employs Revised Bloom's Taxonomy to organize the domain knowledge. Each problem in funtoot is designed to cater to a specific learning objective as defined in the Revised Taxonomy. We model the students' interactions generated on funtoot using a deep knowledge tracing (DKT) model [19].

---

[1]   http://www.funtoot.com/.

In this study, we use the DKT model to study the interconnections between different skills of the Revised Taxonomy. We then investigate the validity of the above two mentioned assumptions and explore how well those assumptions are realized from the student interaction data. The knowledge tracing model is modeled with *learning objectives* as features, which gives us immense flexibility to simulate a controlled environment. The different behaviors of the student like mastery and learning can be encoded and the effects of learning objectives in the process of learning can be investigated in detail.

The rest of the paper is organized as below: Sect. 2 discusses some of the important prior works. Section 3 describes the dataset used to train the knowledge tracing model. Section 4 describes the knowledge tracing model. Section 5 describes the experiments done. Section 6 reports the results of the experiment. Section 7 concludes the paper with future work.

2   Literature Survey

This section discusses some of the works which also attempt to verify the assumptions and/or claims of Bloom's Taxonomy as discussed in Sect. 1. Multiple attempts have been made in the past using various techniques of analysis to verify the hierarchy of Bloom's Taxonomy as well as Revised Bloom's Taxonomy.

A meta analysis of [5, 6, 9, 11, 17, 22] was conducted by the authors of Revision of Bloom's Taxonomy [2, Chap. 16] to verify the cumulative hierarchical nature in the original Bloom's Taxonomy [4]. These studies were considered for the meta-analysis as they had published their original inter-correlation data, whereas, other similar studies that had not published such data were not included in this study.

The inter-correlation data consisted of the category scores for a sample of students who had taken the same tests. Each test measured a single taxonomic level of the original Bloom's Taxonomy. Each such score was then paired with the score of every other category and correlations of such pairs were computed.

In case if the cumulative hierarchy were present, success in one category would likely be accompanied by success in the category closest to it in the hierarchy. Success in one category is a necessary but not a sufficient condition for success in the more complex adjacent category. The correlations between these categories would be higher than with the still more complex categories. Also, successively more complex categories should show successively lower correlations [2, Chap. 16].

The study concluded that the hierarchical ordering holds for the middle categories - Comprehension, Application and Analysis. Authors had also reversed the last two categories of original taxonomy, Create and Evaluate to the revised taxonomy's, Evaluate and Create to see how the data would look like. The authors concluded that doing so gave somewhat better results.

The conclusion of the meta analysis was similar to the conclusion of most of the six studies individually, namely, that, excluding Knowledge, the support for a cumulative hierarchy was seen in the simpler categories.

Two other studies in [8,15] were done using the data from Kropp and Stoker's [11,20] work. Authors of [15] used step-wise regression, path analysis and factor analysis to reanalyse the data from Kropp and Stoker's [11,20] ninth grade sample of one of their tests - Atomic Structure. They found that all the techniques had rejected a simple hierarchical assumption of the taxonomy. Their results do not align with the analysis of the Kropp and Stoker's study. Authors of [8] applied an alternative method to the Kropp and Stoker's [11,20] data. They concluded that the simplex assumption of the Bloom's Taxonomy is supported when *Knowledge* is removed from the taxonomy.

Study in [12] showed that students are given a task that they can complete, and when memory is tested for the same material, students who operate at higher taxonomic level will produce superior memory scores than the students who operated on the lower taxonomic level. Their results conform and provide a moderately strong support for the hierarchical nature of the taxonomy.

A study done in [16] showed that the activities and assignments for Internet for Business class in the order of cognitive skills of the Revised Bloom's Taxonomy prepare students with higher order thinking skills. They showed that practicing the skills in the order of their difficulties had a positive effect on the higher order skills.

All the above mentioned works except for [15] showed some evidence in support for the hierarchical nature of the taxonomy. The meta-analysis [2, Chap. 16] and [8] both showed the support for the hierarchical nature after removing Knowledge level. Authors of [2] have also discussed the ambiguity of the placement of the Knowledge in the hierarchy based on the meta-analysis.

Madaus et al. have used squared semi-partial correlations and fitted a path model to the levels of the taxonomy in [14]. They found that not only did the magnitude of the paths between the adjacent levels declined as the levels became more complex in the Bloom's Hierarchy, but also that there were significant paths between non-adjacent levels. This results are similar to our findings for the Revised Bloom's Taxonomy presented in this paper.

Authors of [18] attempted to categorize the cognitive skills involved in interpreting medical images. The authors had hypothesized that hierarchical levels of cognitive process would emerge to define different levels of learning medical imaging concepts. The authors have used Revised Bloom's Taxonomy to assign a category to each of the questions of their examination mentioned in the study. The authors concluded that there was an inverse relationship between the depth of cognitive process and mean scores. With the increase in the complexity of the skills, there was a decrease in the score. However, the Revised Taxonomy's original script [2] says that it is not necessary to sequentially achieve each of the levels, that is, students can achieve Create before the Remembering process. This is consistent with the concept of problem-based learning [21], which emphasizes on the early immersion in diagnostic thinking [18].

Athanassiou et al. describes the usage of Bloom's Taxonomy in Management classroom in order to facilitate students with *Scaffolding* in [3]. Usage of Bloom's taxonomy in this fashion allows students to determine the level of her own work. The study concluded that the use of the taxonomy as a scaffolding device helped students improve their skills and become more aware of their learning process and hence, have a pointed way of making improvements. Study in [3,16] shows that the usage of Bloom's Taxonomy helps improve the higher order skills in students.

3 Dataset

In funtoot [13], the curriculum is designed such that a subject is broken down into multiple high level topics. These topics are then divided into smaller units called sub-topics (*sc*). *sc* is further broken down into a smallest teachable unit called sub-sub-topic (*ssc*). This *ssc* can not be broken down further and is the most granular level skill. For instance, subject *Mathematics* has a topic called *Addition*. Topic *Addition* is further broken down into *scs* - *Addition of two digit numbers*, *Addition of three digit numbers* and so on. The *Addition of two digit numbers* contains smallest teachable units - *sscs*, like *Addition of two digit numbers with carry over*, *Addition of two digit numbers without carry over* and so on.

sscs are designed to achieve an expert defined learning objective. Problems are then designed to cater to these learning objectives. A Bloom's Taxonomy learning objective (*btlo*) tag is assigned to each problem based on the learning objective (from the Revised Bloom's Taxonomy) it helps to achieve. We call this a *btlo* tagging. *ssc* may not always have all the six learning objectives as defined in the Revised Bloom's Taxonomy.

Funtoot is a classroom based personalized learning tutor for grades 2 to 9 for subjects - Maths and Science. It is used in over 100 schools following one of the boards of education[2] like: CBSE, KASB, ICSE or IGCSE. There are broadly 74 topics spanning Maths and Science in funtoot. These 74 topics have a total of 682 *sscs*.

In this study, we wish to verify the validity of the claims of the Revised Bloom's Taxonomy and Bloom's Taxonomy. Hence, it is important for us to have at least two *btlos* in an *ssc* to check the effect of one *btlo* on another. For this reason, we have only considered *sscs* with more than two *btlos* which leaves us with 536 *sscs*. Figure 1 shows the distribution of a number of *sscs* for *btlos*.

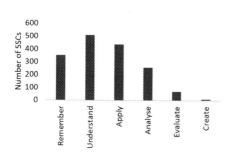

Fig. 1. *ssc* distribution across *btlos*

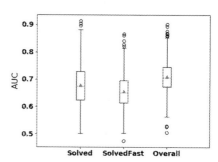

Fig. 2. AUCs

[2] https://en.wikipedia.org/wiki/Boards_of_Education_in_India.

The dataset has a total of 41.7 million problem interaction entries generated by 1,03,593 students while interacting with 10,158 problems. Each interaction represents a problem attempted by the student which is characterized by two attributes: *solved-fast* (got the correct answer in first attempt) and solved (got the correct answer in one or more attempts). While attempting the problem, if the student's response is incorrect, the student is notified about it along with the explanation about why it is incorrect. She then gets another attempt at the problem with a hint (if available). This continues till the predefined number of attempts for that particular problem are exhausted. In the end, a student is also provided with the detailed solution of the problem. Out of 41.7 million data points, 29.7 million are solved (71%) and 22.7 million are solved-fast (54%).

4   Deep Knowledge Tracing (DKT)

Intelligent Tutoring systems like funtoot aim to provide personalized study material to students and help when needed. For this, the knowledge state of the student needs to be monitored frequently and updated as and when students interact with a digital tutor. The models capable of doing this are called Knowledge tracing models. By modeling knowledge acquisition process of the students, predictions can be made on the future interactions and based on these predictions further instructions can be delivered in a personalized manner.

Several knowledge tracing models exist in literature. For this study, we have used a Deep knowledge Tracing (DKT) model proposed in [19]. DKT is a time series model based on Recurrent Neural Network. It takes as input the series of exercises and a bit corresponding to it indicating the outcome from the student interactions with the tutor.

In this study, we want to measure the effect of one *btlo* on its successor in the Revised Bloom's Taxonomy. We need a scope within which the DKT model can capture interlinks between the *btlos*. In funtoot's knowledge hierarchy, the *btlo* is present in the *ssc* scope. Hence, we have trained the models at an *ssc* level for simplicity.

Since we have 536 *sscs*, we have 536 DKT models and *btlos* are used as features. So, the input vector is a series of *btlos* (tagged to the problems attempted by the student) and their corresponding outcomes of the problem attempts: solved and solved-fast in our case. For instance, if an *ssc* consists of three *btlos*, the input consists of three neurons per *btlo*, one representing whether the interaction belonged to that *btlo*, one for solved and one for solved-fast. The model outputs the probability that the problem will be solved and solved-fast for each *btlo*, amounting to two output neurons per *btlo*.

The average AUC of the DKT models is 0.69 ($\sigma = 0.07$) for *solved*, 0.66 ($\sigma = 0.05$) for *solved-fast* and 0.71 ($\sigma = 0.06$) overall. Figure 2 shows the box-plot of the distribution of AUCs across *sscs* for outputs solved, solved-fast, and overall (average of solved and solved-fast).

5   Experiments

The aim of this study is to verify if the skills in the Revised Bloom's Taxonomy are ordered from lower to higher level. We also attempt to see if lower order skills are the prerequisites for higher order skills. In other words, we want to study the effects of mastery of lower order skills on the chances of mastery of higher order skills. We hypothesize that student's *mastery* in the lower order skills should increase her chances of mastery in the higher order skills. The evidence of *mastery* of any skill is shown by solving successively 5 problems from that skill in the first attempt (solved-fast).

We measure the effect of a lower order skill i on the higher order skill j in following ways. Formula 1 measures the change in the solved-fast probability of skill j after having shown the evidence of mastery of skill i compared to the initial state (*).

$$(i \rightarrow j) - (* \rightarrow j) \tag{1}$$

Here, * is the initial state when none of the skills are mastered and none of the problems are solved by the students. This serves as the starting state of the student.

Formula 2 shows the combined effect of skill i and all its lower skills on skill j.

$$(\widehat{i} \rightarrow j) - (* \rightarrow j) \tag{2}$$

Here, $\widehat{i}$ is sequence of skills easier than i, including i, in simple to complex order. In this formula, skill $\widehat{i}$ is mastered and the change of its effect on the probability of skill j is measured compared to the initial state *. The mastery of such a set of skills $(\widehat{i})$ is shown by showing the mastery of each skill in the same order.

Formula 1 represents the effect of skill i on skill j, which might include the effects of the skills easier than i, whereas Formula 2 measures the combined effect of skills $\widehat{i}$ on skill j. Both the above mentioned formulae do not show the individual effect of skill i after the mastery of the lower order skills is achieved. We compute this by Formula 3.

$$(\widehat{i} \rightarrow j) - (\overline{i} \rightarrow j) \tag{3}$$

Here, $\overline{i}$ is the set of the skills lower to skill i in the simple to complex order. Formula 3 shows the isolated effect of skill i on skill j by taking the difference of probability of skill j when skills $\widehat{i}$ and $\overline{i}$ are mastered.

For instance, consider an *ssc* containing four *btlos*: *Remember, Understand, Apply* and *Analyse*. When we say $\widehat{Apply}$, we mean the sequence of skills *Remember, Understand, Apply*. When we say $\overline{Apply}$, we mean the sequence of skills *Remember, Understand*.

If a lower order skill i is a prerequisite of a higher order skill j, then the mastery of the skill j would assure the mastery of skill i. We study this prerequisite nature by measuring the effect of the mastery of the skill j on the mastery of skill i through the following formulas.

In Formula 4, the probability of the skill i after the mastery of skill j is compared against the probability of skill i at the initial state.

$$(j \rightarrow i) - (* \rightarrow i) \qquad (4)$$

If indeed skill i is the prerequisite of skill j, the probabilities of skill i after the mastery of skill j would be the same as the probability of skill i after having mastered the skill i. The difference between these probabilities is captured by Formula 5.

$$(j \rightarrow i) - (i \rightarrow i) \qquad (5)$$

The skills lower than i might also have an effect on the mastery of skill i which is not considered by the Formula 5. Hence, in Formula 6, the probability of skill i after the mastery of skill j is compared against the probability of skill i after the mastery of the skills $\widehat{i}$.

$$(j \rightarrow i) - (\widehat{i} \rightarrow i) \qquad (6)$$

We also compare the probabilities of each pair of skills at the initial state and the final state (when all the skills are mastered in simple to complex order). For this, we have measured the correlations between the probabilities of all pairs of skills and the differences between them are also computed.

The results of the initial and final correlations are shown in Tables 2 and 3 respectively. Tables 4 and 5 show the difference between the probabilities at the initial and final state. The results of all the above formulae 1, 2, 3, 4, 5 and 6 are shown in Tables 6, 7, 8, 9, 10 and 11 respectively.

In Tables 6, 7 and 8, we measure the effect $(i \rightarrow j)$. Here i is the row header and j is the column. That is, the top left most cell $(1,1)$ refers to $(R \rightarrow U)$ in these tables. In Tables 9, 10 and 11, we measure the effect $(j \rightarrow i)$. Here j is the row header and i is the column. That is, the top left most cell $(1,1)$ refers to $(U \rightarrow R)$ in these tables.

To compare a pair of skills, the sscs having both the skills are used and the number of sscs for all the pairs of skills is shown in Table 1. In formula 2, 3 and 6, we consider the sscs where at least one lower skill than i is present. The reduced number of sscs, if any, for all such pairs are shown in the parentheses in Table 1.

Table 1. Counts of SSCs containing BTLO Pairs

	U	Ap	An	E	C
R	339	264	165	39	3
U		411(253)	237(160)	64(39)	7(3)
Ap			222(209)	63(61)	8(7)
An				64(62)	8
E					7

Table 2. Initial correlations

	U	Ap	An	E	C
R	0.39(0.0)	0.14(0.03)	0.1(0.22)	−0.24(0.15)	−0.58(0.61)
U		0.34(0.0)	0.28(0.0)	0.16(0.21)	0.83(0.02)
Ap			0.22(0.0)	−0.07(0.6)	−0.23(0.58)
An				0.36(0.0)	0.07(0.86)
E					0.68(0.09)

6 Results

In Tables 2 and 3, the values in the parentheses are the *p-values*. From Table 2, it can be seen that for the skills *Remember, Understand, Apply* and *Analyse*, their initial correlations with their adjacent more complex skills is the highest and the correlations decrease with the increase in the difficulty of the skills. The correlations at the diagonal cells decreases with the increase in the complexity of the skill. However, there is an increase in the correlation of the pair *Analyse-Evaluate* compared to the previous diagonal pair *Apply-Analyse*. Even though the correlation between the pair *Evaluate-Create* is very high, its *p-value* is 0.09. Ideally, for all the columns, the maximum correlations should be the diagonal entries. This pattern holds for all the *btlos* except for *Analyse* and *Create*. Both *Analyse* and *Create* achieve maximum correlation of 0.28 and 0.83 respectively, with the same *btlo Understand*. The initial differences are negative for the pairs where complex skills are involved in Table 4. The column entries for *Create* are the most negative values.

The pattern where each entry in the matrix is less than the entry to its left and also to the entry below it, is called *simplex* [2, Chap. 16]. The adherence to this simplex behavior in initial correlations is quite prominent. However, this is not the case with final correlations as seen in Table 3. The correlations of skills *Understand* and *Apply* with the complex skills increases with the increase in the complexity of the skills. The first three diagonal correlations see a decrease with the increase in the complexity of the skills. The correlation between the pair *Evaluate* and *Create* is 0.74 but it is marginally significant (*p-value*= 0.06). Like the initial differences, the final differences (Table 5) between the probabilities are negative for the complex skills.

In the rows of the skills *Remember, Understand* and *Apply* in Table 6 of Formula 1, the values decrease with the increase in the complexity of the skills except for the last column *Create*. The effect of the skills *Understand, Apply* and

Table 3. Final correlations

	U	Ap	An	E	C
R	0.2	0.08	0.04	−0.21	−1.0
	(0.0)	(0.19)	(0.64)	(0.2)	(0.02)
U		0.18	0.11	0.27	0.78
		(0.0)	(0.08)	(0.03)	(0.04)
Ap			0.14	0.25	0.77
			(0.04)	(0.05)	(0.03)
An				0.11	0.49
				(0.39)	(0.22)
E					0.74
					(0.06)

Table 4. Initial differences

	U	Ap	An	E	C
R	0.02	0.03	0.01	0.03	−0.02
U		0.01	−0.01	−0.02	−0.11
Ap			−0.03	−0.04	−0.09
An				−0.02	−0.05
E					−0.01

Table 5. Final differences

	U	Ap	An	E	C
R	0.07	0.1	0.04	0.12	0.05
U		0.03	−0.01	−0.04	−0.16
Ap			−0.06	−0.07	−0.07
An				−0.05	−0.03
E					0.01

Table 6. Formula 1

	U	Ap	An	E	C
R	0.1	0.04	0.03	0.01	−0.08
U		0.05	0.03	0.02	0.06
Ap			0.07	0.03	0.08
An				0.05	0.1
E					0.14

Analyse on the skill *Create* is even greater than their effects on their respective adjacent complex skills, *Apply, Analyse* and *Evaluate*. The skill *Evaluate* has the maximum effect of 0.14 on its adjacent complex skill, *Create*.

The effect of *Understand* and *Apply* is maximum on their respective complex adjacent skills, *Apply* and *Analyse* computed using Formula 2 (seen in Table 7). However, the effect of *Apply* and *Analyse* on the skill *Create* is greater than or comparable to their effects on their respective complex adjacent skills - *Analyse* and *Evaluate*. The effect of *Evaluate* on its complex adjacent skill *Create* is the maximum effect in the table.

The isolated effects (computed using Formula 3) of the skills in Table 8 are similar to the effects seen in the Table 7 with a slight reduction in the magnitude. However, there a couple of exceptions where we see a significant change. The isolated effect of *Understand* on the skill *Create* is the maximum (0.1) and the isolated effect of the skill *Analyse* is comparatively lesser on skill *Create*.

Formula 4 captures the effect of each skill on its lower order skills, the results of which can be seen in Table 9. Ideally, the diagonal entries should decrease with the increase in the complexity of the skill. Moreover, the entries in each row should increase as they move further away from the diagonal. Also, the column entries should increase as they move away from the diagonal. This expected behavior is observed very clearly with a few exceptions. The effects of *Create* on *Understand* and *Apply* are lower than expected and the effect of *Create* on *Evaluate* is much higher than expected.

Table 7. Formula 2

	U	Ap	An	E	C
R	-	-	-	-	-
U		0.07	0.07	0.02	0.02
Ap			0.09	0.04	0.08
An				0.07	0.09
E					0.1

Table 8. Formula 3

	U	Ap	An	E	C
R	-	-	-	-	-
U		0.03	0.04	0.01	0.1
Ap			0.04	0.02	0.06
An				0.02	0.02
E					0.07

Table 9. Formula 4

	R	U	Ap	An	E
U	0.12				
Ap	0.13	0.11			
An	0.14	0.11	0.09		
E	0.15	0.12	0.09	0.06	
C	0.18	0.1	0.11	0.14	0.13

Table 10. Formula 5

	R	U	Ap	An	E
U	-0.08				
Ap	-0.06	-0.05			
An	-0.04	-0.03	-0.03		
E	-0.03	-0.05	-0.03	-0.07	
C	0.12	-0.08	0.04	-0.02	0.03

If the effect of a skill j on a simpler skill i computed using Formula 5 happens to be close to zero, that would imply that the skill j completely subsumes skill i. For the cumulative hierarchical assumptions to hold true for the Revised Bloom's Taxonomy, all the values in Table 10 should have been close to zero, which is not the case here.

Table 11. Formula 6

	R	U	Ap	An	E
U	-				
Ap	-	-0.07			
An	-	-0.06	-0.05		
E	-	-0.03	-0.07	-0.1	
C	-	-0.04	0.02	-0.04	0.06

The effects computed using Formula 6, shown in Table 11 are similar to the effect seen in the earlier Table 10 with little reduction in the magnitude. However, the effects of *Evaluate* on *Understand* and the effects of *Create* on *Understand* and *Evaluate* show an unexpected increase. Ideally, all the effects in the Table 11 should have been similar to the effects in the Table 10 if the higher skills were to subsume the lower skills.

7   Discussion and Conclusion

Based on the correlations and the results of Formulae 1, 2 and 3 (Tables 1, 2 and 3), it can be clearly said that skill *Understand* is more complex than skill *Remember* and skill *Apply* is more complex than skill *Understand*. Skill *Apply* has good effect on skill *Analyse* and their probabilities share a moderate correlation indicating the complexity of *Analyse* being more than *Apply*. However, due to the higher complexity of the skill *Analyse*, this effect of *Apply* on *Analyse* is not expected to be very high.

There is a moderate initial correlation of *Analyse* with *Evaluate*. The effect of *Analyse* on *Create* is higher than expected. The effect of *Evaluate* on *Create* is exceptionally good. These points strongly suggest that the difference in complexity between the higher order skills *Analyse*, *Evaluate* and *Create* is not very high.

The correlation of *Understand* with *Analyse* and high effect of *Understand* on *Analyse* indicate some overlap between the two skills. Both *Understand* and *Apply* have significant effects on *Create* which are even higher than their effects on their respective adjacent complex skills, *Apply* and *Analyse*. This hints some overlap between the skills *Understand*, *Apply* and *Create*. The overlap between *Understand* and *Apply* has also been admitted in the script of Revised Bloom's Taxonomy [2].

From the above evidence, *Understand* seems to correlate with almost all the higher order skills. *Understand* might be force fitted and seems out of place. It seems to not have any individual and unique place in the relative ordering of the skills. *Understand* was not included in the Original Taxonomy for the very similar reason that, *Understand* for all the practical purposes actually means anything from *Comprehension* to *Synthesis*. Despite of that, *Understand* was included in the Revised Taxonomy considering its widespread usage as a synonym of *Comprehension*.

Barring few exceptions in the results in Table 9, it can be clearly said that the skills are rightly ordered from simple to complex in the Revised Taxonomy. These results are based on the effects of mastery of skills on their lower order skills $(j \rightarrow i)$ compared to the initial states. Hence, mastery of higher order skills always increased the likelihood of the mastery of simpler skills, with the larger likelihoods for more simpler skills. The exceptions suggested some overlap between the pairs *Create-Understand*, *Create-Apply* and *Create-Evaluate*.

However, when the effects of mastery of skills on its lower order skills $(j \rightarrow i)$ are studied against the effects of already mastered lower order skills on themselves $(i \rightarrow i)$, the results (as seen in Tables 10 and 11) deny the subsumption of the lower order skills by the higher order skills. The chances of the mastery of the lower order skills in the consequence of the mastery of higher order skills do increase, but not to the extent of considering lower order skills as the prerequisites (complete subset) of higher order skills.

In our attempt to generate optimal problem sequences using Revised Bloom's Taxonomy in [1], we found that when the problems are given to the students in the order of the hierarchy, the gains produced were higher when measured using Deep Knowledge Tracing model. These findings indicate that the Revised Bloom's Taxonomy is indeed hierarchical. Similar results were reported in [16] where students practiced the skills in the order of their difficulties (of the Revised Bloom's Taxonomy) and it had a positive effect on the higher order skills.

Our results do not align with the findings of the work [18] which showed that their implementation of Revised Bloom's Taxonomy had a cumulative hierarchy. We conclude that the Revised Bloom's Taxonomy is indeed a hierarchy (clearly observed in the lower learning objectives *Remember*, *Understand* and *Apply*) when the skills are judged on their relative (median) complexity. But, it is not a strict hierarchy in the sense that it allows for overlaps even among the non-adjacent skills, ensuring higher order skills do not subsume lower order skills. Mastery of higher learning objective does not assure mastery of lower learning objectives.

References

1. Agrawal, S., Lalwani, A.: Analysing problem sequencing strategies based on revised Bloom's taxonomy using deep knowledge tracing. In: 14th International Conference on Intelligent Tutoring Systems, June 2018. (to appear)
2. Anderson, L.W., Krathwohl, D.R., Airasian, P., Cruikshank, K., Mayer, R., Pintrich, P., Raths, J., Wittrock, M.: A Taxonomy for Learning, Teaching and Assessing: A Revision of Bloom's Taxonomy. Longman Publishing, New York (2001). Artz, A.F., Armour-Thomas, E. (1992). 9(2), 137–175
3. Athanassiou, N., McNett, J.M., Harvey, C.: Critical thinking in the management classroom: Bloom's taxonomy as a learning tool. J. Manage. Educ. 27(5), 533–555 (2003)
4. Bloom, B.S., Engelhart, M.D., Furst, E.J., Hill, W.H., Krathwohl, D.R.: Taxonomy of Educational Objectives, Handbook I: The Cognitive Domain, vol. 19. David McKay Co. Inc., New York (1956)
5. Davis, F.B.: Research in comprehension in reading. Reading Res. Q. 3(4), 499–545 (1968)
6. Hancock, G.R.: Cognitive complexity and the comparability of multiple-choice and constructed-response test formats. J. Exp. Educ. 62(2), 143–157 (1994)
7. Hawks, K.W.: The effects of implementing Bloom's taxonomy and utilizing the virginia standards of learning curriculum framework to develop mathematics lessons for elementary students (2010)
8. Hill, P., McGaw, B.: Testing the simplex assumption underlying Bloom's taxonomy. Am. Educ. Res. J. 18(1), 93–101 (1981)
9. Klein, M.F.: Use of taxonomy of educational objectives (cognitive domain) in constructing tests for primary school pupils. J. Exp. Educ. 40(3), 38–50 (1972)
10. Krathwohl, D.R.: A revision of Bloom's taxonomy: an overview. Theory Pract. 41(4), 212–218 (2002)
11. Kropp, R.P., Stoker, H.W., Bashaw, W.: The validation of the taxonomy of educational objectives. J. Exp. Educ. 34(3), 69–76 (1966)
12. Kunen, S., Cohen, R., Solman, R.: A levels-of-processing analysis of bloom's taxonomy. J. Educ. Psychol. 73(2), 202 (1981)
13. Lalwani, A., Agrawal, S.: Few hundred parameters outperform few hundred thousand? Educational Data Mining (2017)
14. Madaus, G.F., Woods, E.M., Nuttall, R.L.: A causal model analysis of Bloom's taxonomy. Am. Educ. Res. J. 10(4), 253–262 (1973)
15. Miller, W.G., Snowman, J.: Application of alternative statistical techniques to examine the hierarchical ordering in Bloom's taxonomy. Am. Educ. Res. J. 16(3), 241–248 (1979)
16. Nkhoma, M.Z., Nkhoma, M.Z., Lam, T.K., Lam, T.K., Sriratanaviriyakul, N., Sriratanaviriyakul, N., Richardson, J., Richardson, J., Kam, B., Kam, B., et al.: Unpacking the revised Bloom's taxonomy: developing case-based learning activities. Education + Training 59(3), 250–264 (2017)

17. Pachaury, A.: An empirical validation of taxonomy of educational objectives using McQuitty's hierarchical syndrome analysis. Indian Educ. Rev. **6**(2), 156–164 (1971)
18. Phillips, A.W., Smith, S.G., Straus, C.M.: Driving deeper learning by assessment: an adaptation of the revised Bloom's taxonomy for medical imaging in gross anatomy. Acad. Radiol. **20**(6), 784–789 (2013)
19. Piech, C., Bassen, J., Huang, J., Ganguli, S., Sahami, M., Guibas, L.J., Sohl-Dickstein, J.: Deep knowledge tracing. In: Advances in Neural Information Processing Systems, pp. 505–513 (2015)
20. Stoker, H.W., Kropp, R.P.: Measurement of cognitive processes. J. Educ. Meas. **1**(1), 39–42 (1964)
21. Subramaniam, R.: Problem-based learning: concept, theories, effectiveness and application to radiology teaching. J. Med. Imaging Radiat. Oncol. **50**(4), 339–341 (2006)
22. Thomas, A.M.: Levels of Cognitive Behavior Measured in a Controlled Teaching Situation. Graduate School of Cornell University (1965)
23. Thompson, E., Luxton-Reilly, A., Whalley, J.L., Hu, M., Robbins, P.: Bloom's taxonomy for CS assessment. In: Proceedings of the Tenth Conference on Australasian Computing Education, vol. 78, pp. 155–161. Australian Computer Society, Inc. (2008)

Communication at Scale in a MOOC Using Predictive Engagement Analytics

Christopher V. Le, Zachary A. Pardos[✉], Samuel D. Meyer,
and Rachel Thorp

University of California at Berkeley, Berkeley, CA 94720, USA
{chrisvle,zp,meyer_samuel,rthorp}@berkeley.edu

Abstract. When teaching at scale in the physical classroom or online classroom of a MOOC, the scarce resource of personal instructor communication becomes a differentiating factor between the quality of learning experience available in smaller classrooms. In this paper, through real-time predictive modeling of engagement analytics, we augment a MOOC platform with personalized communication affordances, allowing the instructional staff to direct communication to learners based on individual predictions of three engagement analytics. The three model analytics are the current probability of earning a certificate, of submitting enough materials to pass the class, and of leaving the class and not returning. We engineer an interactive analytics interface in edX which is populated with real-time predictive analytics from a backend API service. The instructor can target messages to, for example, all learners who are predicted to complete all materials but not pass the class. Our approach utilizes the state-of-the-art in recurrent neural network classification, evaluated on a MOOC dataset of 20 courses and deployed in one. We provide evaluation of these courses, comparing a manual feature engineering approach to an automatic feature learning approach using neural networks. Our provided code for the front-end and back-end allows any instructional team to add this personalized communication dashboard to their edX course granted they have access to the historical clickstream data from a previous offering of the course, their course's daily provided log data, and an external machine to run the model service API.

Keywords: Representation learning · MOOCs · Learning analytics
Engagement · Drop-out prediction · Instructor communication
edX · User-interface

1 Introduction

While related work has investigated what features correlate with MOOC drop-out, this work pushes in a different direction of allowing instructional staff to operationalize predictive analytics of engagement in ways that are of pedagogical utility to the learner. We assert that adding the ability for instructors to send messages to groups of learners based on their real-time engagement analytics provides a much-needed intermediary form of communication, in-between the impersonal broadcast announcement and individual discussion forum posts and replies. To realize this utility, we augment edX, our MOOC platform of study, with a D3-powered dashboard which displays real-time

© Springer International Publishing AG, part of Springer Nature 2018
C. Penstein Rosé et al. (Eds.): AIED 2018, LNAI 10947, pp. 239–252, 2018.
https://doi.org/10.1007/978-3-319-93843-1_18

engagement analytics produced from a trained model and served by a node.js backend API. We argue that making predictive models useable in real-world contexts is as valuable an endeavor for the AIED community as is discovery and data mining with those models, and therefore consider this implementation component a primary contribution of the work.

If instructors are to use these analytics to determine which learners receive which communications, it is crucial that the models selected are as accurate as possible. For this reason, our second contribution, which we devote the first half of the paper to, is on conducting a comparison of certification (pass) prediction models on 20 edX courses to establish best practices. This evaluation included (1) various non-neural network models paired with hand engineered features (2) those same models ensembled (3) recurrent neural networks paired with hand engineered features, and (4) recurrent neural networks with features learned automatically from clickstream data. Using the best performing modeling paradigm from this evaluation, we trained two additional models predicting learner course completion and learner course drop-out. These two models, and the certificate model were trained on data from two previous offerings of our chosen live deployment course, BerkeleyX's CS169: Software as a Service. With the three predictive models powering a real-time API backend, we enabled an instructor only viewable interactive dashboard which is used to compose messages and select recipients based on selected ranges of the three models' predictions. For example, an instructor could send a message linking learners to extra review and remediation materials if they were predicted to likely stick with the course (not drop out) but were not predicted to pass.

The outline of the paper begins with related work, followed by the predictive modeling section, which includes a description of our dataset, methods used, and results, followed by the edX dashboard ("Communicator") engineering section, which includes a detailed description of the backend service and the analytics user interface.

2   Related Work

Research on predictive modeling relating to drop-out has been a popular focus of study in MOOCs, given their typically low pass rate (5% in the first year of MIT and Harvard edX MOOCs) [1]. Much of this can be attributed to learners simply curious about the contents of the course or wishing to engage with portions of the course as reference material; however, a considerable portion of learners remain who intend to pass but do not [2]. It has been suggested that a subset of learners, such as those in premium tracks [3], might be a better focus for research seeking to increase achievement, as those learners' intentions to achieve are more explicit. However, others have kept a wholistic approach, attempting to increase engagement among all participants through social interventions [21]. A simple email, soliciting survey responses from students thought to have dropped-out, resulted in a mild retention of those students, who rejoined the class [4]. Very few studies have combined predictive modeling with real-world interventions in a MOOC. In [20], next resource suggestions were made using a predictive model of behavior [19]. On residential campuses, predictive models of drop-out have been operationalized in the form of dispatching counselors for flagged students [18], an approach which can have unintended side effects of signaling to students that they are not likely to pass the course, and thus catalyzing a greater rate of drop-out than without the intervention.

There have been many definitions of how to define *drop-out* in predictive models; [5], for instance, included three unique definitions in their analysis. Research in predicting drop-out using features hand-engineered from the clickstream have used SVMs [6], logistic regression [7], Hidden Markov Models [8], ensembles of other machine learning methods [9], and recurrent neural networks (RNN) applied to hand engineered features [5]. Other work has included information outside the clickstream, such as forum post data analyzed with natural language processing [10, 17]. Frameworks for evaluating various models and their feature sets have also been introduced [15, 22]. While most of these studies focused on only a small set of courses, [11, 22] used a dataset of 20 or more courses to train and predict.

Deep learning, utilizing representation (feature) learning from raw data, has been applied to the knowledge tracing task [11] and to the sequence prediction task in MOOCs [12]. The principle intuitions behind the effectiveness of learning features automatically from raw data has been most saliently established in the task of image classification; once dominated by more manual feature extraction methods now eclipsed by Convolutional Neural Networks powered by representation learning [1].

3   Predictive Modeling

3.1   Dataset and Pre-processing

We began with data from 102 edX MOOCs offered in the 2015–2016 school year[1]. In our analyses we focused only on instructor-paced courses, leaving the prediction of engagement analytics for self-paced courses, which involve a greater variety of learner behavior, for future work. Among the instructor-paced courses, we only considered those where at least 100 learners earned a certified (Fig. 1). In these data, a certified learner included both learners who had earned a paid-for certificate and learners who had earned a passing score in the course but had not paid for an official certificate. To distinguish which courses were instructor-paced, we checked the archived description of the course for indications of being self-paced. As an additional check, a course was considered self-paced if it had only one deadline. This left 21 courses available for use. One outlier course had three times as many students certified as any other instructor-paced course and was excluded from training, leaving 20 courses for analysis (Fig. 1). A total of 13.6 million learner actions were logged in these courses.

Courses came from seven different institutions and varied in length from four weeks to 19 weeks (Table 1). The longest courses had no more than 10 weeks of material released, but some instructors kept the course open for more time after the tenth week. While most courses followed a format of releasing weekly resources and assigning weekly homework, two courses only had two unique deadlines in the course,

---

[1] These data were provided by way of the edX partners' Research Data Exchange (RDX). All data have been anonymized before being received and are restricted in use by MOU.

while lasting more than 7 weeks each. These descriptive statistics of course structure give us an idea of how much variation is to be expected when we later train a single predictive model across many courses.

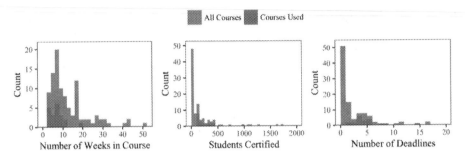

Fig. 1. Histogram of number of weeks (left), number of students certified (center) and number of deadlines in each course (right).

Table 1. Statistical summary of courses used for analysis.

Duration (weeks)			Unique deadlines			Certified students		
Min	Median	Max	Min	Median	Max	Min	Median	Max
4	7.7	19	2	4.5	15	102	189.5	958

In our experiments, we only considered learners who enrolled by the end of the first week of the course, and we attempted to predict which of those learners would eventually obtain certification (as defined by passing the course[2]).

3.2 Methodology

The following subsections describe the process behind building both the feature engineering approach and the automatic feature (representation) learning model based on the raw clickstream. Both models were trained to predict the same binary outcome of the learners eventually passing the course or not. The same set of leaners were used for training all models including the same course level 5-fold cross-validation; training on 16 courses and testing on 4 in each cross-validation phase. During the training portion of each phase, the courses in the training folds were under-sampled to have only twice as many learners who received certification as those who did not. This was done to address the dramatic class imbalance in the dataset. During the testing portion of each phase, the courses in the test fold were predicted in-full, predicting certification of all learners in the course at every week.

---

[2] A student gained certification if the "status" column in the edX provided certificates_generatedcertificate-prod-analytics.sql file was set to "downloadable".

Feature Engineering. We used the standard feature engineering process of taking clickstream data from MOOC event logs and crafting features which are then used as inputs in a variety of machine learning predictors.

Within a set time period of one week, various representative values were calculated to summarize a learner's behavior. We constructed twelve features, most of which were taken from a thoroughly-described set of features of a similar experiment by [13], but with week-by-week comparison features removed — while [13] predicted *when* a learner would drop-out, we are focusing on *if* the learner eventually receives certification. To account for the loss of information about how far a learner has progressed through the course, we included two extra features not included in [13] (see features 6 and 12 in Table 2).

Table 2. Description of all 12 hand-engineered features.

1. Total time[a] spent on learning resources[b]	**7.** Average time difference between submitting a problem and its respective deadline
2. Number of distinct problems attempted	**8.** Duration of the longest-observed learning event
3. Average number of attempts per problem	**9.** Total time spent on video lectures
4. Number of distinct correct problems	**10.** Standard deviation of duration of learning events
5. Ratio of total time spent on learning resources to number of correct problems	**11.** Ratio of number of attempted problems to number of correct problems
6. Total time since last student action	**12.** Percent time through a course

[a]Each non-problem-solving event included a session tag, which identifies continuous periods of time that a student was online for under a single session id; thus, we estimated the total amount of time contained within all of these individual sessions and returned the sum of those session times as a student's total time spent on learning resources.

[b]*Learning resources* and *learning events* include all student events except those related to solving problems on assignments and/or exams.

Table 3 depicts a single learner (single course) example of the feature set used to train the models. In the table, it can be observed that the learner's first week's actions are summarized. In the next row, these increase, as the weekly features are additive from one week to the next. In the row corresponding to the last week of the course (100% through the course), the learner's values have not changed from the second week, indicating the student left the course sometime in week two. All "time spend" based features are estimates, since the log data do not allow us to know how much of the time between events was spent focused on the course vs. off-task.

To improve the generalized performance of our classifiers, we normalized each set of feature values according to: $\text{norm}(f) = \frac{f - \min(F)}{\max(F) - \min(F)}$.

Where f is a single feature value, and F is the corresponding set of all values of that feature; however, in order to avoid peeking at the test set, we computed each feature's respective maximum and minimum on the training set alone for each cross-validation fold, and applied these training set based maximum and minimum normalizations to the test.

Table 3. Example of engineered feature values for one student in a 5-week course before normalization. The complete training dataset included rows from all courses combined. While "Learner" is shown as a column for descriptive purposes, it was not a feature in the model.

Learner	Percent through course	Avg. attempts per problem	...	Total time spent on learning resources (sec)	Certified
Learner_A	20%	1.5	...	3,075	0
Learner_A	40%	3.2	...	20,250	0
...	...	...	...	...	...
Learner_A	100%	3.2	...	20,250	0

Feature Engineering Models. We ran a variety of models on the hand-engineered feature values to replicate methods from the state-of-the-art. In addition to training individual models, we also trained an ensemble [16] which included random forests, logistic regression, and k-nearest neighbors. We also applied a recurrent neural net (RNN) using long short-term memory (LSTM) to the hand-engineered features to compare RNNs learned from raw events (representation learning) to RNNs with hand-engineered features to evaluate the effect of the type of features vs. the algorithm.

Ensemble Learning. Ensemble learning combines predictions from individual classifiers into a more robust prediction output [14]. To perform our baseline ensemble learning prediction, we were guided by [9], and our ensemble classifier combined results from three individual classifiers[3]: logistic regression, random forest, and k-nearest neighbors.

The community default hyperparameters of the respective algorithms were used with two exceptions: (1) the number of estimators in random forest, which we updated from a default value of 10 to 100 and (2) the number of nearest neighbors k from which to take the modal classification of a point, from a default value of 5 to 15.

In [9], four different fusing methods were applied and compared. We chose to implement their most successful method, which was effectively a simple logistic regression, used to weight the various individual classifiers. In particular, for each cross-validation iteration, we trained our three individual classifiers on a sub-training set of 12 courses, and fit ensemble weights on predictions of a 4-course validation subset, using logistic regression to determine respective weights of each classifier. Finally, we took a weighted average of the three classifier prediction results on our test set (4 courses) applying the respective weights determined in the logistic regression fitting process for a final classification prediction.

---

[3] All implemented using Python's scikit-learn machine learning library.

Representing Raw Clickstream Data for Automatic Feature Learning. In representation learning, features are not manually crafted by experts leveraging their domain knowledge but are learned by the model from raw data. This approach underlies all deep learning models and can find abstract relationship between events in a sequence that may not be apparent to a domain expert or researcher working with data in the domain. Obscured, however, is the ability to attempt to interpret the importance of features grounded in domain knowledge. This was a reasonable potential sacrifice for our work, as it focuses on the operationalization of the predictions and not the inspection of the models.

All edX courses have a log file that records an event as a JSON entry each time the user takes an action. Each includes an *event_type* which is either a descriptive verb phrase such as *video_pause* or a URL accessed. The URLs may be a link to a course resource, or can give information about how a student took an action, such as posting a comment in the forums. To allow course-general predictions, all URLs with similar parsed meanings were combined into a single event type. One event, the *problem_check* event type, was broken into *problem_check_correct* and *problem_check_incorrect* based on correctness of the answer. This allowed us to incorporate general assessment performance into the event stream. If an event type occurred less than 1000 times within the 20 courses, or was not used in more than three courses, it was not included. This left 78 event types used for the analysis, 21 of which were types parsed from the URLs. In addition, a week-ending event was added for each of the first 10 weeks to provide some "mile markers" for the model.

A one-hot encoding of these events was presented as the input at each time step in a sequence of ordered events for each learner (Fig. 2). Outliers, with event stream lengths greater than 1.5 IQR above the set of learners within each course who gained certification, were not used for training. This excluded about 5% of learners and significantly reduced model training times.

RNN LSTM Model. A recurrent neural network (RNN) is a sub-class of neural networks that has Markovian properties. Much like a Hidden Markov Model (HMM), an RNN has an input, hidden state, and output per time slice. The hidden state can be represented as one or several multi-node layers. Also like an HMM, the hidden state from one time slice is passed as an input to the hidden layer of the next time slice and the parameters (weights) are shared across time slices.

For a standard RNN, the number of free parameter weights can be calculated by: [input vector size] × [nodes in hidden layer] + [nodes in hidden layer] × [nodes in output layer] + [nodes in hidden layer]^2. In our case, the input vector size was 88 (# of unique event types + 10 week_end markers) and the hidden node size was set to 100. Since our classification is binary, the output was represented with a single node and sigmoid activation. The number of time slices was dynamic with the longest event streams rising to 6,909 events for a single learner[4]. For learners with a shorter event stream, sequences were zero-padded, and a masking index of 0 was used to tell the model to ignore those data points during training. During training, drop-out was applied to 20% of input gates. Training ran for only five epochs due to the computation

---

[4] The longest event streams were in EPFLx "Plasma Physics and Applications".

time required given the size of the data. The output predicts learner certification after each event, making predictions of greater utility earlier in the course.

3.3   Results

In this section we present the prediction results of each model at each week of instruction in our 20 selected edX courses. We evaluated all models by calculating a course-based mean AUC score across the predictions (Fig. 3) and averaging the AUCs of each course. Some courses only lasted four weeks, so averages for later weeks include only as many courses as were available for that week. The representation learning approach performed better than the best feature engineered model up until the last two weeks. In weeks 5 and 6, the difference between the representation learning LSTM and the feature engineered LSTM was statistically significant ($p < 0.05$). The representation learning LSTM was significantly greater than the logistic regression in weeks 3 through 8.

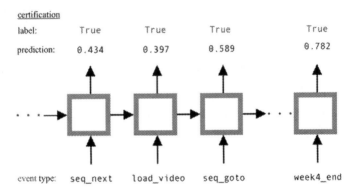

Fig. 2. RNN model showing event types being input for each time slice for a single user. Predictions of certification are made at each time slice by the model but only the predictions at the week_end markers are used in our analysis to serve as the predictions for the respective week.

Among the classifiers used in the ensemble approach, the models from most to leas successful were; logistic regression ($\bar{w}_{lr} = 0.61$), random forests ($\bar{w}_{rf} = 0.32$), and k-nearest neighbors ($\bar{w}_{knn} = 0.07$), where the respective mean weights reported are the normalized weights determined during the logistic regression fitting step of the ensemble fusing process, averaged across each cross-validation fold.

The representation learning model outperformed all other models throughout the majority of course weeks, and the amount by which it underperformed in the last two weeks was not statistically significant.

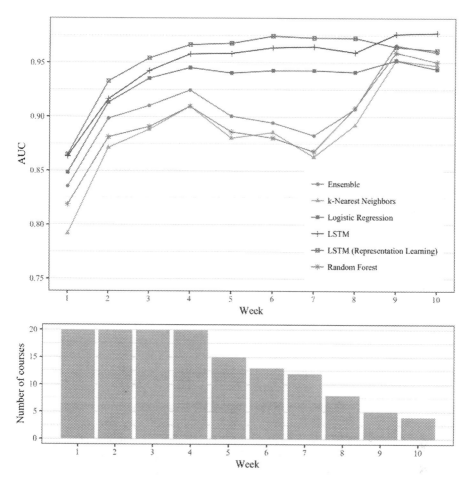

Fig. 3. The Area Under Curve (AUC) score for each model (plot above) cross-validated on 20 edX courses along with the number of courses with activity for each week (plot below).

4 Engineering the edX Communicator Interface

The overall objective of the research effort was to surface analytics to instructors with an interface that allowed for personalized communication based on those analytics. With predictive modeling best practices empirically established in the previous section, we moved on to training a predictive model of passing for two of the previous offerings of our deployment course, BerkeleyX CS169: *Software as a Service*. In addition to predicting passing, we trained a model which predicted if a learner would complete the course, as defined by the student submitting enough materials to possibly pass. We also trained a third model to predict if the learner would leave and never return within the next two days. The same representation learning paradigm which performed best at pass prediction was used for training models of these additional two outcomes. We chose to add to the base functionality of the edX platform, a lightweight, scalable deployment of an intelligent instructor communication dashboard utilizing the models' predictions. The interface presented here can be achieved without modification to Open edX and only requires standard instructional design team/instructor access to edit course material. The dashboard is added as its own separate course page in its own sequential in the edX course structure and an option is turned on for this sequential to be viewable only to instructional staff. A combination of JavaScript and HTML is inserted into this page from edX studio to produce the interactive dashboard seen in Fig. 4.

The labeled dashboard components are described below:

(A) The front end allows for the instructor to send communications to a specific group of learners determined by our D3 tool or to all learners enrolled.

(B) A dropdown list allows the instructor to view or resend past communications.

(C) Pre-sets are included in the pilot that will quickly change the crossfilter to select a specific group of learners (e.g. learners predicted to complete but not earn a certificate or learners predicted to leave and not complete).

(D) The crossfilter is a Javascript library[5] built on top of the D3 visualization library that displays a histogram of all the predictions for each learner and allows a range of probabilities to be selected. Selecting a range thereby selects the learners that pertain to that range. Selecting ranges of multiple analytics selects the learners who are included in both ranges. An instructor, for example, may want to target learners between 70% and 100% predicted to earn a certificate with enrichment material

(E) In the email section, the INSTRUCTOR EMAIL is required and will be the "From: Email" that will appear to learners receiving the email communication.

Within the email section of the front end there is an option to mark the communication for automatic sending. This option is only available when an instructor is sending the communication to a specific group of learners utilizing the Analytics option. With this option enabled, the backend system will check once a day whether there are new learners that fit the profile of the crossfilter criteria selected. Emails will be sent to these new learners without sending another communication to students who have already received it. The Communicator receives anonymous IDs and the three predictive analytics for each ID from the backend API, described in the next section.

4.1 Engineering the Backend Analytics API

The backend framework depends on two sources of data made available by edX to each member institution. One source is the *daily* provided event log for the course being run. The second source is the *weekly* provided roster information for the course, which includes email contact information for all enrolled learners. Every day, the predictions are refreshed given the newly added clickstream data. A typical workflow is as follows (Fig. 5):

---

[5] http://square.github.io/crossfilter/.

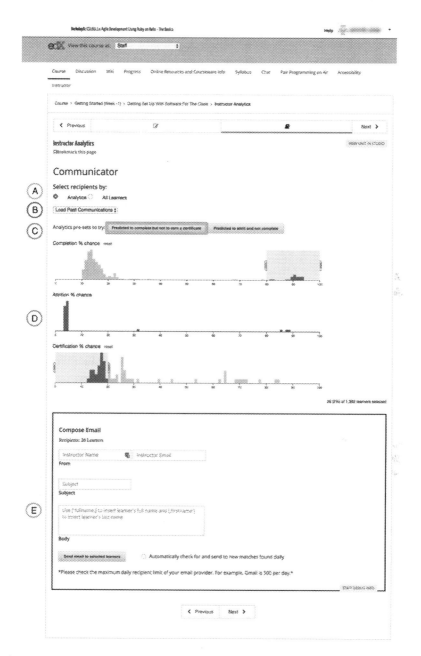

Fig. 4. Interactive "Communicator" dashboard for composing instructor authored directed emails to learners based on their real-time engagement analytics.

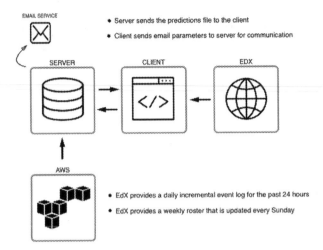

Fig. 5. Backend framework components powering the communicator dashboard

1. The instructor accesses the edX Communicator dashboard and receives the real-time learner analytics from the backend, displayed via three interactive crossfilters.
2. After the instructor selects a specific group of learners using the crossfilter views and fills out the Compose Email form, the backend receives a request to send email to the selected learners.
3. The server receives the data and sends off the emails. A mail provider with bulk messaging capabilities is needed for this step.
4. The communication data (email message and selection criteria) are stored on the server in case the instructor would like to re-send or modify communications from the current course or save communications for use in future offerings of the course.

   The body of the message field has the ability to fill in the learner's first or full name using the following markup: "[:fullname:]" or "[:firstname:]" This information is pulled from the weekly roster provided by edX. All communication is over SSL, with no identifiable data being passed over this communication channel to the front-end.

5   Contributions

We enabled the utilization of predictive models of engagement by instructors for the purpose of personalized communication by engineering a communications interface into the edX platform complete with a backend model API. Using a dataset of 20 edX courses, we compared a variety of modeling approaches, with representation learning using RNNs as the best performing, to ensure that a competent model would be selected for this task. Our prediction findings showed that it is not simply the use of a deep learning model, such as an RNN, that is responsible for improved performance, but rather the combination of this type of modeling technique with the ability to machine learn features from raw clickstream data. Additional hand-engineered features would likely increase prediction accuracy; however, this would require additional domain knowledge and may not be worth the additional effort in a context where it is the predictive analytics that are the end goal, and not knowledge discovery through model interpretation. Our open-source[6] Communicator interface and backend API makes predictive models actionable in the real-world setting of edX MOOCs and opens the door to researchers in the field to explore other types of personalized communication parameters and interventions. Such parameters could include messaging based on common wrong answers given on a question, scores on an assessment or collection of assessments, or other inputs (e.g. surveys) and predictive model outputs.

Acknowledgements. These multi-institution analyses were made possible by anonymized data from the edX partners' Research Data Exchange (RDX) program. This work was supported in part by a grant from the National Science Foundation (Award #1446641).

References

1. Krizhevsky, A., Sutskever, I., Hinton, G.: Imagenet classification with deep convolutional neural networks. In: Advances in Neural Information Processing Systems, pp. 1097–1105 (2012)
2. Ho, A., Reich, J., Nesterko, S., Seaton, D., Mullaney, T., Waldo, J., Chuang, I.: HarvardX and MITx: The first year of open online courses, fall 2012-summer 2013 (2014)
3. Reich, J.: MOOC completion and retention in the context of student intent. EDUCAUSE Review Online (2014)
4. Mass, A., Heather, C., Do, C., Brandman, R., Koller, D., Ng, A.: Offering verified credentials in massive open online courses. In: Ubiquity Symposium (2014)
5. Mi, F., Yeung, D.: Temporal models for predicting student drop-out in massive open online courses. In: 2015 IEEE International Conference Data Mining Workshop (ICDMW) (2015)
6. Kloft, M., Stiehler, F., Zheng, Z., Pinkwart, N.: Predicting MOOC drop-out over weeks using machine learning methods. In: Proceedings of the EMNLP 2014 Workshop on Analysis of Large Scale Social Interaction in MOOCs (2014)
7. Jiang, S., Williams, A., Schenke, K., Warschauer, M., O'dowd, D.: Predicting MOOC performance with week 1 behavior. In: Educational Data Mining 2014 (2014)
8. Balakrishnan, G., Coetzee, D.: Predicting student retention in massive open online courses using hidden markov models (2013)
9. Boyer, S., Veeramachaneni, K.: Robust predictive models on moocs: transferring knowledge across courses. In: Proceedings of the 9th International Conference on Educational Data Mining (2016)
10. Crossley, S., Paquette, L., Dascalu, M., McNamara, D., Baker, R.: Combining click-stream data with NLP tools to better understand MOOC completion. In: Proceedings of the Sixth International Conference on Learning Analytics & Knowledge (2016)
11. Kizilcec, R., Halawa, S.: Attrition and achievement gaps in online learning. In: Proceedings of the Second ACM Conference on Learning@ Scale (2015)
12. Piech, C., Bassen, J., Huang, J., Ganguli, S., Sahami, M., Guibas, L., Sohl-Dickstein, J.: Deep knowledge tracing. In: Advances in Neural Information Processing Systems, pp. 505–513 (2015)

---

[6] https://github.com/CAHLR/Communicator.

13. Tang, S., Peterson, J., Pardos, Z.: Modelling student behavior using granular large scale action data from a MOOC. arXiv:1608.04789 (2016)
14. Whitehill, J., Williams, J., Lopez, C.C., Reich, J.: Beyond prediction: toward automatic intervention to reduce mooc student stopout. In: Educational Data Mining (2015)
15. Boyer, S., Gelman, B., Schreck, B., Veeramachaneni, K.: Data science foundry for MOOCs. In: IEEE International Conference on Data Science and Advanced Analytics (DSAA), 36678 2015 (2015)
16. Pardos, Z.A., Gowda, S., Baker, R., Heffernan, N.: The sum is greater than the parts: ensembling models of student knowledge in educational software. ACM SIGKDD Explor. Newlett. **12**(2), 37–44 (2012)
17. Wise, A., Cui, Y., Vytasek, J.: Bringing order to chaos in MOOC discussion forums with content-related thread identification. In: Proceedings of the Sixth International Conference on Learning Analytics & Knowledge (2016)
18. Jayaprakash, S.M., Moody, E.W., Lauría, E.J., Regan, J.R., Baron, J.D.: Early alert of academically at-risk students: an open source analytics initiative. J. Learn. Analytics **1**(1), 6–47 (2014)
19. Tang, S., Peterson, J., Pardos, Z.: Predictive modelling of student behaviour using granular large-scale action data. In: Lang, C., Siemens, G., Wise, A.F., Gaevic, D. (eds.) The Handbook of Learning Analytics, 1st edn., pp. 223–233. Society for Learning Analytics Research (SoLAR), Alberta (2017)
20. Pardos, Z.A., Tang, S., Davis, D., Le. C.V.: Enabling real-time adaptivity in MOOCs with a personalized next-step recommendation framework. In: Proceedings of the Fourth ACM Conference on Learning @ Scale (L@S). Cambridge, MA. pp. 23–32. ACM (2017)
21. Ferschke, O., Yang, D., Tomar, G., Rosé, C.P.: Positive impact of collaborative chat participation in an edX MOOC. In: Conati, C., Heffernan, N., Mitrovic, A., Verdejo, M. Felisa (eds.) AIED 2015. LNCS (LNAI), vol. 9112, pp. 115–124. Springer, Cham (2015). https://doi.org/10.1007/978-3-319-19773-9_12
22. Andres, J.M.L., Baker, R.S., Siemens, G., Spann, C.A., Gasevic, D., Crossley, S.: Studying MOOC completion at scale using the MOOC replication framework. In: Proceedings of the 10th International Conference on Educational Data Mining, pp. 338–339 (2017)

How to Use Simulation in the Design and Evaluation of Learning Environments with Self-directed Longer-Term Learners

David Edgar Kiprop Lelei[(✉)] and Gordon McCalla[(✉)]

ARIES Laboratory, Department of Computer Science,
University of Saskatchewan, Saskatoon, Canada
davidedgar.lelei@usask.ca, mccalla@cs.usask.ca

Abstract. Designing, developing, and evaluating interactive and adaptive learning environments requires significant investment of financial and human resources. This is especially the case when evaluating the impact of learning environments aimed at supporting self-directed longer-term learners, environments of increasing interest to AIED as the field moves into lifelong learning where mentorship is key. In this paper we propose the use of simulation to help in both the design and evaluation of such environments. As a case study, we have built a simulated university doctoral program (SimDoc) with simulated doctoral students and supervisors (mentors). To make sure SimDoc replicates observed data from a real-world environment as closely as possible, we informed and calibrated the simulation model with data from an actual doctoral program, as well as drawing on various empirical studies of graduate students and supervisors. Next, we used the calibrated simulation model to explore the effect of varying research group sizes of learners and supervisors' mentoring workload on students' completion rates and time-to-completion. Our main goal is to provide insight into how to build simulations of environments that support self-directed longer-term learners through a case study of one such simulation, thus further demonstrating the importance of simulation in AIED.

Keywords: Simulation · Simulated learners
Longer-term learning environments · Self-directed learners · Lifelong learning

1 Introduction

AIED is trending towards lifelong learning as educational technology becomes pervasive and ubiquitous and involves many devices that can collect all sorts of data about learners and their learning in all situations [1, 2]. A big question for AIED, however, is how do we inform and evaluate the designs of learning environments that are meant to be used by learners who are active over the long term? The vast amount of data that such environments will eventually collect will take time to grow to a sufficient size for good analysis. Meanwhile system designers will not be able to easily predict the impact of various design decisions they make about the technology meant to support longer-term learners, thus possibly subjecting learners to badly designed systems. How can system designers explore, test, and accept or reject hypotheses in a cost-effective

© Springer International Publishing AG, part of Springer Nature 2018
C. Penstein Rosé et al. (Eds.): AIED 2018, LNAI 10947, pp. 253–266, 2018.
https://doi.org/10.1007/978-3-319-93843-1_19

manner that doesn't take years? We argue for the use of simulation: the creation of simulated learning environments (SLEs) complete with simulated learners (SLs) and other simulated agents such as mentors. Such SLEs can then be evaluated by the system designer in a reasonable time frame and, importantly, without subjecting learners to unfavorable learning conditions, for example, limited mentoring times when experimenting with mentors' workload. SLEs allow rapid evaluations, comparisons, and modifications of design decisions.

Simulation has been part of AIED for years [3, 4], but mostly in the context of simulated pedagogical agents. There is now a small, but growing, body of AIED literature on simulation exploring the use of simulation for system design and evaluation. The simulations range from high fidelity models such as SimStudent [5] used to develop precise theories of learning, to very low fidelity models such as ones used by Champaign and Cohen [6] and Frost and McCalla [7] to explore issues around learning material sequencing and peer help. But, these systems are focused only on shorter term learning contexts, not longer-term learning environments. With simulation it is possible to examine various system design and development decisions, rejecting undesirable ones and performing more studies on the promising ones. The key is to model and build a simulation that replicates what is happening in the target learning environment (real world) [3] along important attributes and dimensions of the design interests to be explored. Thus, model fidelity is an important factor to consider.

The main intention of this paper is to demonstrate through building and running an actual simulation (i) how to design a simulated learning environment in a long term learning situation (in our case a doctoral program) that is informed with primary data from the target learning environment and evidence derived from the literature, (ii) how to calibrate the resulting model using the primary dataset, and (iii) how to use the resulting model to explore some 'what if' questions. We conclude the paper by discussing the important role of simulation as a necessary tool in an AIED system designer's toolkit especially as AIED moves towards supporting learning in long term learning environments.

2   Related Work

2.1   Simulated Learners Within AIED Research

In their pioneering paper on simulation in AIED VanLehn, Ohlsson, and Nason [4] outlined three applications of simulated learners: (i) formative evaluation of instructional systems, (ii) the use of simulated students to scaffold human student learning by acting in a learning companion capacity, and (iii) the use of simulated learners as a tutoring test-bed for teachers practicing and examining the impact of their tutoring techniques. Subsequent research has, in fact, explored issues closely related to these three foundational uses of simulated learners (SLs). For instance there is a large body of literature exploring the second use of SLs. SLs as learning companions have served a variety of educational purposes such as being adaptable and versatile to human learners' needs [8]; fostering engagement, motivation, and responsibility [9]; and improving learning and performance [10]. Sometimes the simulated learners are used in a reciprocal learning context, where human learners act as teachers, as in SimStudent [5]. Teachable agents have been used in a history class to improve human learners' working memory [11]; in an elementary mathematics class to test transfer of socio-motivation throughout the learning process to testing [12]; and examining which approach leads to better learning between learning by teaching and learning by tutoring [13].

Other researchers have explored applications of SLs that cannot be broadly fitted into any of the three foundational uses of simulation in AIED. For example, Koedinger, Matsuda, Maclellan, and McLaughlin mention four uses of SimStudent [5]. The first two are in line with the VanLehn, Ohlsson, and Nason uses (i) and (ii), and two are new. These four applications of SLs are: first, SLs provide a formative test-bed of alternative instructional techniques; second, when designed as teachable agents (TAs), they offer an opportunity for human learners to learn by teaching; third, SLs enable researchers to develop a precise theory of learning; and fourth SLs help ITS designers to automate authoring of intelligent tutoring systems in at least two ways – authoring by tutoring and authoring by demonstration [14].

Our research into simulating lifelong learning environments broadly fits into VanLehn, Ohlsson, and Nason's category (i), but we go beyond just evaluating instructional systems to also explore design alternatives and hypothetical scenarios.

3   Modeling Simulated Agents

A key element in any simulation in AIED is the agent model underlying the simulated learners. Numerous probabilistic methods have been used in building such agent models that model learner data based on probability distribution functions, as in [15]. The Bayesian Knowledge Tracing technique is one of the most popular approaches for modeling learners' knowledge [16]. A common approach to modeling learner knowledge is combining Bayesian Knowledge Tracing with other methods, for example, Bayesian Knowledge Tracing and Item Response Theory [17]. Still another Bayesian related approach is Bayesian Decision Theory [18].

Another main approach is to use simulation strategies based on cognitive theories in which cognitive problem-solving processes are modelled to produce rich SLs. Faghihi, Fournier-Viger, and Nkambou introduced a technique based on neuroscientific theories that combines several human learning capabilities including emotional, epi-sodic, causal and procedural learning to capture a learner model for a cognitive tutoring agent [19]. Rule-Based Modeling often augments the cognitive approach by repre-senting learners' knowledge using procedural and production rules as in the cognitive tutoring systems [20]. These approaches attempt to create high fidelity agent models based on historical interactions between an ITS and learners.

Alternatively, some researchers have chosen to build low fidelity agent models, that typically don't need to draw on a large amount of human learners' usage data. For instance, Frost and McCalla [7] model very simple abstractions of learning objects and learners. Each SL is modeled to have an attribute called aptitude-of-learner whose value is between (0 and 1). Similarly Champaign and Cohen [6] have used low fidelity models consisting of learners and learning objects. Each learner is modeled to have a level of knowledge, a value between (0 and 1). These low fidelity models are useful for exploring parameter interactions and general pedagogical tendencies in the simulated learning environment. In our research, our agent models could be called "medium fidelity", as we discuss in the next section.

4   The SimDoc Simulation Model

In this section we introduce SimDoc, a simulated learning environment meant to capture aspects of a university doctoral program. A doctoral program is an environment with largely self-directed students who over the long term (usually years) are mentored by supervisors. We show how we modeled a university doctoral program along dimensions of interesting questions we wish to ask. Further, we describe the basic agent models (representing students and supervisors). We also show how the model was informed using a combination of information from a real-world dataset and evidence from the literature, and then how the model was calibrated and validated against the real-world dataset. Finally, we show the results of simulation experiments that shed light on how the overall population mix of the simulated students and supervisors' workload lead to varying learner outcomes in terms of completion time in the program. The main goal of the paper is to be a proof by demonstration of how such a "medium fidelity" simulation can be created.

4.1   SimDoc: Simulated Doctoral Program Conceptual Model

Doctoral programs are complex and dynamic social environments made up of many heterogeneous stakeholders: learners, faculty, administrators, and government. Each play their role interconnecting and interacting in many ways leading to unpredictable nature of the doctoral learning environment (see a more detailed description in [21]). Attrition rates, completion rates, and time-to-completion are important factors influencing the perception and experience of a doctoral program by interested stakeholders [22]. Long time-to-completion and high attrition rates are costly financially to the funding bodies and the learning institutions and costly, timewise, to student(s) and supervisor(s). Literature shows that various factors have influence on doctoral program attrition rates, completion rates, and time-to-completion. These factors include: supervisory style, availability and size of funding, discipline of study, and sense of learning community [23–25]. Heath [24] attributes most of the doctoral students' success or lack thereof to supervisor-student relationships. Regular supervisor-student meetings have been shown to play major roles in the satisfaction of students leading to successful completion of the program [26]. However, the frequency of supervisor-student meetings is a balancing act that is mainly dependent on the availability and style of the supervisor and the readiness of the student to meet. It would be valuable to explore various issues in the supervisor-student relationship affect the completion rates and times-to-completion of doctoral learners. For example, how do various mixes of students and supervisors affect completion rates and students' times-to-degree? How does research group size (a few students vs many students) impact supervisor workload, learners' times-to-degree, and completion rates?

These are issues that can be explored through simulation, in this case capturing important aspects of the supervisor-student relationship that can then be explored through simulation experiments. To this end, we have created a simulation called SimDoc, a medium fidelity simulation model. SimDoc is a modified version of Sim-Grad that we introduced and described in [21]. SimDoc's conceptual model has four key elements (unlike SimGrad which has five): normative model, agents model, dialogic model, and events model based on features for building an electronic institution proposed by Esteva et al. [27]. Each of these is described next.

Agents Model: We devise two types of agents to represent doctoral students (who we will refer to as learners in our simulation) and supervisors. The learner agent model captures the following key attributes: preferred meeting frequency, class workload, class requirements, stage, research group, actual frequency of meeting with supervisor, latent effort (how much they are willing to work), and weekly effort-of-learner (how much they actually work). The supervisor agent model has the following key attributes: research group, workload, meeting frequency, and preferred supervisory style.

Normative Model: We use the notion of a normative model to abstract from the huge complexity of a real doctoral program the requirements and constraints that affect the questions we are exploring. The SimDoc normative model represents programs, research groups, classes, and milestones. According to Erickson et al. [3], to gain better insight about any phenomenon using simulation, it is necessary to model two types of important functions. These functions are *behaviour functions* and *evaluation functions*. Behaviour functions inform how various events and interactions between modeled agents, elements and the simulated learning environment occur. Evaluation functions determine the outcomes of the various interactions between different agents and/or between learner agents and the learning environment. The specific functions we developed will be elaborated in Sect. 4.2, below.

Event Model: An event refers to a happening, a change, or a stimulus within a model environment that triggers (re)action by agents. We model two types of events: *system level* and *agent level*. Agents react to events by initiating appropriate actions. Each event has different enabling conditions associated with it. Further, each event leads to different outcome(s), including other event(s). System level events are handled according to the normative model, including scheduling new events, triggering due ones, and monitoring ongoing ones.

Dialogic Model: The dialogic model refers to interaction strategies and communication mechanisms that the agents use within the simulated learning environment. We use a message passing mechanism [28] to facilitate communication between learner agents and their supervisor agents. We model a learner's desire to have a meeting to be a stochastic event internal to the learner agent based on preferred meeting frequency rate. In the event of a desire for meeting, a learner agent can initiate a meeting event by sending a "request for a meeting" message. This request is handled by the normative model, which inserts the message into the "request for a meeting queue" of the learner's supervisor agent. Before inserting a new request, the normative model checks that a previous request by the same learner agent is not in the queue. A meeting event occurs when a supervisor agent's meeting schedule is triggered (a stochastic event internal to the supervisor agent based on its preferred supervisory style) and the supervisor has a non-empty queue. The supervisor "meets" learners in the queue on a first come first served basis. We have modeled supervisors to have limited time for meetings based on their workload. Therefore, if the queue is long enough, some meetings will have to be postponed. During the actual meeting event, there is no interaction or exchange of messages between the supervisor agent and the learner agent. Instead, the normative model uses an evaluation function (described in the next section) to determine the outcome of the meeting and updates the learner agents' attribute values – which could affect a learner in a positive or a negative way going forward.

4.2   Informing SimDoc's Behaviour and Evaluation Functions

In informing SimDoc's behaviour and evaluation functions, we drew from a real world doctoral program, that of the University of Saskatchewan (U of S). We obtained a dataset (we call it the *UofS dataset*) containing data drawn from UofS doctoral programs over a 10-year period (2005–2014), kept in the University Data Warehouse[1]. In initializing the learner agent models, for those attributes which could not be informed from the UofS dataset directly but were necessary in the model, we got data from other sources. These sources included different departmental web pages about standard times and policies and various studies in the literature about doctoral students and supervisors [23–25, 29, 30]. These sources allowed us to capture a broad spectrum of doctoral students' and supervisors' behaviors along the dimensions we were interested in.

Here are the specific SimDoc behaviour functions which generate a variety of factors in our simulation: *admission numbers*, how many learners join the program each year; *attrition rate*, how many students leave the program on a yearly basis; *graduation and completion times*, the time learners are taking in the program; *learners' class load*, how many classes each learner is allocated and at what stage they complete them; *supervisor style*, the supervisory style of the supervisor; and *frequency* of learner-supervisor meetings.

Of the six behaviour functions, we inform four of them from the UofS dataset. They include: admission numbers, attrition rate, graduation and completion times, and learners' class load. Analysis of the UofS dataset shows that within the 10-year period, there were 2291 doctoral students with 52850 data points about their class registration and other elements of their study e.g. grades and graduation dates. The student population changed constantly starting with a learner population of 721, an average of 184 yearly admission (minimum – 133 and maximum – 223), a yearly mean graduation rate of 108 (minimum – 76 and maximum – 118), and a yearly mean attrition rate of 46 (minimum – 26 and maximum – 87). An analysis of the UofS dataset indicates that 12% of the students did not take classes and of the 88% who took classes, the number of classes range between 1-8 with a majority taking 2.

---

[1] http://www.usask.ca/ict/services/ent-business-intelligence/university-data-warehouse.php, last accessed on February 06, 2018.

The admission behaviour function determines the number of learners to be admitted yearly based on a function derived from the UofS admission pattern, as in Eq. 1:

$$N = at + \frac{\sin(ct)}{d} + e \tag{1}$$

Here N represents the total number of learners who will register in each year, t, and a, c, d, and e are variables necessary to match a sigmoid pattern derived from the UofS admission data. Once learners enroll, the normative model randomly assigns them to different research groups using the research group assignment behaviour function. Each research group is led by a supervisor who also acts as a supervisor to learners assigned to that research group. At admission, the normative model also determines whether a learner receives a class waiver or not. Learners who receive a waiver enter the comprehensive stage straight away while the rest start in the coursework stage.

To provide some fidelity to the determination of supervisor styles, we drew on data from studies carried out by Gatfield [23] and Heath [24]. Gatfield analyzed 60 items found in the literature associated with supervisor-student relationships and PhD completion to identify four supervisory styles along two dimensions: structure and support. These four styles are *laissez-faire, pastoral, directorial*, and *contractual*. Heath provides an analysis of student-supervisor meeting frequency that we used to inform both supervisor population make-up and learner population make-up. Based on percentages found in Gatfield and Heath, the supervisor style behaviour function assigns supervisor styles so that the overall supervisor population breaks down as follows: *laissez-faire* 13%, *pastoral* 19%, *directorial* 30%, and *contractual* 38%. In SimDoc these styles reflect only preferred meeting frequencies: *laissez-faire* – prefers a less frequent meeting schedule of one meeting every one to six months; *pastoral* – favors a monthly meeting schedule; *directorial* – prefers a bi-weekly meeting frequency, and *contractual* – favors a more frequent meeting schedule of at least one meeting a week. Gatfield and Heath also found varying desires for meeting frequency on behalf of students, with slightly different percentages than for supervisors with 38% of students preferring a weekly meeting schedule and another 29% favoring a one meeting every three weeks. Breaking down the remaining 33%: 19% prefer a meeting every three to six weeks, 9% favor a meeting rate of one meeting every six to 12 weeks, and finally, 4% prefer meeting their supervisor once every three to six months. The learner meeting frequency behaviour function generates agents' desired meeting frequency so that these percentages are reflected in the overall SimDoc simulated learner and supervisor population.

To inform SimDoc's evaluation function on learners' performance, we considered modeling completion times rather than learner knowledge states because of the long-term nature of the learning environment. The UofS provides guidance on its web pages[2] on the expected time-to-completion for each student in the doctoral program. According to these guidelines, it is expected that doctoral students spend at least 40 h

---

[2] https://grad.usask.ca/programs/find-a-program.php last accessed on February 06, 2018.

per week on their research work[3]; when it comes to coursework, students are expected to spend 15-20 h per class per week[4]. Overall, in an ideal situation, doctoral students are expected to complete their degree in 4 years. To estimate the total number of hours a simulated learner in SimDoc needs to complete their program, we assume that the total number of hours a learner should invest in their doctoral program, $t_d \approx ymwh_r$ where t_d is the time in hours it takes to finish a doctoral program, $y = 4$ (ideal number of years), $m = 12$ (months in a year), $w \approx 4$ (weeks in a month), and $h_r = 40$ (expected hours allocated to research per week). As such, an estimated value for t_d would be 7680 h. At this point of the model development, we do not consider any other information about learners and milestones except to note that we are modeling four milestones, based on the UofS requirements – coursework, comprehensive, proposal, and dissertation. The smallest time unit in the simulation is a week. Further, it is important to observe that the requirements for each learner in the coursework will vary as learners are allocated different number of classes.

We next describe SimDoc's evaluation function for computing the value of each learner agent's weekly *effort-of-learner* attribute. This evaluation function assumes a linear relationship between a learner's latent effort and a logarithm of time to complete the whole program. This evaluation function is inspired by item response theory (IRT) which has mainly been used to model students' probability of providing correct answers in tests. Other researchers have also used IRT to model students' problem solving times [31]. To determine the probability of a student providing a correct answer in a test item, IRT considers a student's latent ability, the basic difficulty of an item, a discrimination factor, and a random factor. Similarly, SimDoc's evaluation function primarily assumes that a learner's weekly effort can be defined in terms of time-to-completion of a milestone unit, their latent effort θ, the difficulty of the current milestone unit (measured in time) c_{at}, the number of classes taken $e^{\frac{x}{8}}$, the desired supervisor-learner meeting frequency f^{mf}, and a stochastic factor z. Therefore, the SimDoc evaluation function for computing weekly time spent on doctoral program by a learner, c_{tl} is given by Eq. 2 (adapted from a similar IRT equation):

$$c_{tl} = \theta . c_{at} . e^{\frac{x}{8}} . z . f^{mf} \tag{2}$$

where $f^{mf} \approx$ impact factor based on the exponential meeting frequency base f which is a variable and exponential power ^{mf} which is meeting frequency $\frac{number\ of\ meetings\ so\ far}{number\ of\ weeks\ in\ program\ by\ student}$. $e^{\frac{x}{8}} \approx$ exponential of x which is number of classes taken in a semester divided by 8 which is the maximum number of classes a student can take. This evaluation function makes a weekly calculation of effort-of-learner. The weekly effort-of-learner can vary widely as various factors change over time, so the overall time in program can only be determined by simulating the learner's progress through the entire program.

---

[3] http://artsandscience.usask.ca/psychology/department/gradteaching.php last accessed on February 06, 2018.

[4] https://www.grad.ubc.ca/campus-community/life-grad-student-ubc/what-expect last accessed on February 06, 2018.

4.3   Evaluation Function Calibration and Validation

Thus, SimDoc has been equipped with behaviour functions and evaluation functions that have been informed with real world data – some obtained from UofS dataset and other data from literature along relevant attributes to our research questions. However, before using SimDoc to run experiments to explore hypothetical scenarios, it is important to make sure that we start with a version of SimDoc, called the *baseline model*, that has been validated in the target real world environment (UofS in this case) where the simulation outcomes match the outcomes we are concerned with (yearly graduation in this case). This is to give us confidence that we have in fact accurately captured the real world, at least along the dimensions affecting the issues we care about. The process of *calibrating* SimDoc to match UofS consisted of 500 simulation runs where values of three attributes with values not yet specified were varied systematically from run to run. These attributes are stochastic factor z and meeting frequency base f in Eq. 2, and supervisor-learner meeting duration. The values of the three attributes in the validated baseline version of SimDoc can then be determined from their values in the simulation run whose graduation and attrition rates most closely match the UofS data set with the highest confidence level. The 132nd run out of the 500 calibration simulation runs was the best one, with a 93% confidence level as shown Fig. 1 in below.

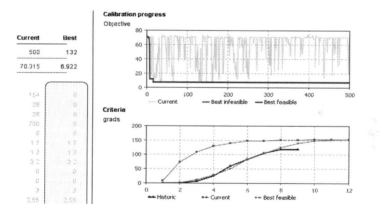

Fig. 1. Calibration process result

In the figure, upper graph shows the objective function numbers that capture the difference between the simulation output and historic data – the lower the value, the better the confidence level. This objective function is only applicable to the calibration process. The light blue line captures the value for each simulation run while the dark blue line captures the value for the current lowest objective function value. The lower graph depicts the graduation numbers each year. The black like represents the data from the real world and that is why it is labeled Historic. The brown line represents the output of the latest simulation run and hence we call it Current. Finally, the light red line represents the closest match so far between the simulation run results and actual real-world data, so we labeled it "Best feasible".

5 Experiment

As a proof-of-concept scenario, we wish to run a simulation experiment to determine the impact of supervisor workload in terms of the number of learners being supervised. The research question we focus on is as follows: how would different sizes of the research groups being supervised by a supervisor affect the learning outcomes of a doctoral program as measured by completion/attrition rates and learners' completion times? To this end, we created an experiment where we ran the simulation under two different conditions on how students are allocated to supervisors: *random* and *structured*. For each of these two conditions, we created five different sub-conditions based on supervisor workload, where each supervisor has one learner, two learners, four learners, six learners, or eight learners. As the name suggests, in the random condition learners are assigned to supervisors randomly without considering the number of learners they already have. With this approach the number of learners supervised by each supervisor will vary. In the structured condition learners are uniformly assigned to supervisors, thus ensuring similar workload for each supervisor. Admission of new learners only takes place when there are vacancies, that is, there are graduations and/or drop outs. Figure 2, below, displays summaries of the simulation runs exploring the various experimental conditions over 10 simulated years.

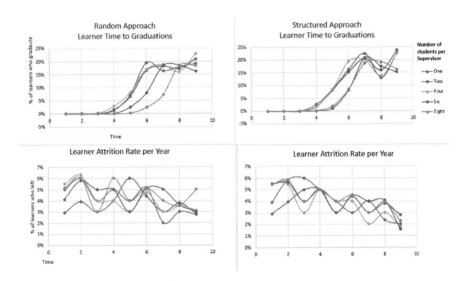

Fig. 2. Results of the simulation runs

The graphs on the right are the random approach; the ones on the left are the structured approach; the coloured lines represent each of the 5 sub-conditions. The upper graphs show the percentage of learners who graduate each year; the lower graphs show the percentage of learners who drop out each year. The results show that bigger supervisor workloads cause learners to slow down and increase their time to degree.

Another interesting phenomenon that we observe is that learners' time-to-degree is slightly better in both random and structured conditions when supervisors are assigned four students. However, an independent-samples t-test shows that there is no significant difference between these two conditions, p = 0.72. The structured approach resulted in graphs lines that are closer together meaning there is less variability, while the random approach resulted in a more spread out graph probably because of statistical variability in the allocation of students to supervisors. Even though not statistically significant, results such as these could indicate trends, at least, and inform various stakeholders at a university, for example trying to target better supervisor group sizes. A key benefit of simulation is that once the underlying simulation model is developed, it is relatively cheap to run simulation experiments to explore many hypotheses that might take an enormous expenditure in time and resources to explore with human subjects. SimDoc could be used, for example, to shed light on the effects of changing the typical milestone sequence to see if learners finish faster or drop out less frequently if they, for example, delay their comprehensive exam until after their proposal. This could affect program design criteria in the doctoral program. Or SimDoc based simulations could investigate the effect of supervisory style on workloads, attrition rates, and time to degree. The results of such an investigation might even inform a system that could be designed to make a personalized recommendation to a student on which supervisor to choose based on a potential supervisor's workload and their supervisory type. Of course, any discoveries made through simulation would eventually have to be confirmed in actual practice with real students and supervisors.

6 Conclusion

The development and importance of simulation is recognized within social science and many other research areas such as physics, engineering, nursing, medicine, and building design. In fact, simulation is regarded as a third way of doing science in addition to the inductive and deductive methods of reasoning [32, 33]. The concept of simulation was introduced to the AIED community more than two decades ago and several systems have used simulated learners in a significant role such as learning companions, animated pedagogical agents, and teachable agents. However, as we discussed earlier the idea of simulating an entire learning environment complete with simulated learners has not been extensively explored within the community, apart from some low fidelity simulations with only one or two variables, aimed at learning over fairly small-time scales of hours, days, or at most the duration of a course. Our primary goal in this research has been to demonstrate how to create a medium fidelity simulation of a complete learning environment and its learners that has medium fidelity along important dimensions with a real learning environment that operates over a time scale of years. Such a simulation would allow a designer to ask hypothetical questions and explore system design decisions that cannot be easily and quickly investigated empirically because of the long-term nature of the learning environment.

We believe SimDoc is a first step towards achieving this goal. Set in the context of a doctoral program in which students spend years, SimDoc is a "proof of concept" example of a long-term simulated learning environment, complete with simulated learners. The architecture of SimDoc and the steps we took to create and validate it are exemplars of how to design any medium fidelity simulation based in a real-world learning environment with longer term learners. We demonstrated how to use data from the target real world learning environment and combine it with data from other relevant studies in the literature to inform the simulation. Further, we showed how to calibrate the simulation model to create a baseline model that matches the real-world data in areas important to the research questions we wished to explore. We then demonstrated how to use the resulting simulation to run an experiment to shed light on one such research question. Although we just showed one simulation experiment, a great advantage of simulation is that many other experiments could be run quickly to explore other research questions. Of course, the results of a simulation are just predictions needing eventual confirmation in the real world.

In the future with so much fine-grained learner data being generated, collected, and stored in many learning environments (e.g. MOOCs) simulations of learning environments will be informed by much better data, and thus have a better chance of making more reliable predictions about a wider variety of pedagogical and design issues. Further, while data mining approaches using such data can allow great insight, simulation provides the extra capability of being able to answer 'what-if' questions, explore hypothetical scenarios, and evaluate the impact of various system design decisions for which there is no real-world data at all. As AIED research moves towards supporting lifelong learning, we strongly feel that system designers and researchers need to incorporate simulation as a key tool in their toolkit. We believe that the research reported in this paper illustrates important aspects of how to build such a simulation for a long-term learning context and shows the way towards building more sophisticated simulations in the future.

Acknowledgements. We would like to thank the University of Saskatchewan University Data Warehouse team for allowing us to access their dataset, and the Natural Sciences and Engineering Research Council of Canada (NSERC) for funding our research.

References

1. Bull, S., Kay, J.: SMILI: a framework for interfaces to learning data in open learner models, learning analytics and related fields. Int. J. Artif. Intell. Educ. **26**(1), 293–331 (2016)
2. Lane, H.C., McCalla, G., Looi, C.-K., Bull, S.: The next 25 years: how advanced interactive learning technologies will change the world. Int. J. Artif. Intell. Educ. **26**(1), 539–543 (2016)
3. Erickson, G., Frost, S., Bateman, S., McCalla, G.: Using the ecological approach to create simulations of learning environments. In: Lane, H.C., Yacef, K., Mostow, J., Pavlik, P. (eds.) AIED 2013. LNCS (LNAI), vol. 7926, pp. 411–420. Springer, Heidelberg (2013). https://doi.org/10.1007/978-3-642-39112-5_42
4. VanLehn, K., Ohlsson, S., Nason, R.: Applications of simulated students: an exploration. Int. J. Artif. Intell. Educ. **5**(2), 1–42 (1994)

5. Koedinger, K.R., Matsuda, N., MacLellan, C.J., McLaughlin, E.A.: Methods for evaluating simulated learners: examples from SimStudent. In: The Proceedings of the 2nd Workshop on Simulated Learners at the 17th International Conference on Artificial Intelligence in Education, vol. 5, pp. 45–54 (2015)
6. Champaign, J., Cohen, R.: A multiagent, ecological approach to content sequencing. In: Proceedings of the 9th International Conference on Autonomous Agents and Multiagent Systems - AAMAS 2010, pp. 10–14 (2010)
7. Frost, S., McCalla, G.: Exploring through simulation an instructional planner for dynamic open-ended learning environments. In: Conati, C., Heffernan, N., Mitrovic, A., Verdejo, M. F. (eds.) AIED 2015. LNCS (LNAI), vol. 9112, pp. 578–581. Springer, Cham (2015). https://doi.org/10.1007/978-3-319-19773-9_66
8. González-Brenes, J.P., Huang, Y.: Using data from real and simulated learners to evaluate adaptive tutoring systems. In: The Proceedings of the 2nd Workshop on Simulated Learners at the 17th International Conference on Artificial Intelligence in Education, vol. 5, pp. 31–34 (2015)
9. Pezzullo, L.G., Wiggins, J.B., Frankosky, M.H., Min, W., Boyer, K.E., Mott, B.W., Wiebe, E.N., Lester, J.C.: "Thanks Alisha, keep in touch": gender effects and engagement with virtual learning companions. In: André, E., Baker, R., Hu, X., Rodrigo, Ma.M.T., du Boulay, B. (eds.) AIED 2017. LNCS (LNAI), vol. 10331, pp. 299–310. Springer, Cham (2017). https://doi.org/10.1007/978-3-319-61425-0_25
10. Pareto, L.: A teachable agent game engaging primary school children to learn arithmetic concepts and reasoning. Int. J. Artif. Intell. Educ. 24(3), 251–283 (2014)
11. Palmqvist, L., Kirkegaard, C., Silvervarg, A., Haake, M., Gulz, A.: The relationship between working memory capacity and students' behaviour in a teachable agent-based software. In: Conati, C., Heffernan, N., Mitrovic, A., Verdejo, M.F. (eds.) AIED 2015. LNCS (LNAI), vol. 9112, pp. 670–673. Springer, Cham (2015). https://doi.org/10.1007/978-3-319-19773-9_88
12. Sjödén, B., Tärning, B., Pareto, L., Gulz, A.: Transferring teaching to testing – an unexplored aspect of teachable agents. In: Biswas, G., Bull, S., Kay, J., Mitrovic, A. (eds.) AIED 2011. LNCS (LNAI), vol. 6738, pp. 337–344. Springer, Heidelberg (2011). https://doi.org/10.1007/978-3-642-21869-9_44
13. Matsuda, N., Yarzebinski, E., Keiser, V., Raizada, R., Stylianides, G.J., Cohen, W.W., Koedinger, K.R.: Learning by teaching SimStudent – an initial classroom baseline study comparing with cognitive tutor. In: Biswas, G., Bull, S., Kay, J., Mitrovic, A. (eds.) AIED 2011. LNCS (LNAI), vol. 6738, pp. 213–221. Springer, Heidelberg (2011). https://doi.org/10.1007/978-3-642-21869-9_29
14. Matsuda, N., Cohen, W.W., Koedinger, K.R.: Teaching the teacher: tutoring Simstudent leads to more effective cognitive tutor authoring. Int. J. Artif. Intell. Educ. 25(1), 1–34 (2015)
15. Pardos, Z.A., Yudelson, M.V.: Towards moment of learning accuracy. In: The Proceedings of the 1st Workshop on Simulated Learners at the 16th International Conference on Artificial Intelligence in Education, vol. 7, pp. 61–70 (2013)
16. Wang, Y., Heffernan, N.: A comparison of two different methods to individualize students and skills. In: Lane, H.C., Yacef, K., Mostow, J., Pavlik, P. (eds.) AIED 2013. LNCS (LNAI), vol. 7926, pp. 836–839. Springer, Heidelberg (2013). https://doi.org/10.1007/978-3-642-39112-5_125
17. Folsom-Kovarik, J.T., Wray, R.E., Hamel, L.: Adaptive assessment in an instructor-mediated system. In: Lane, H.Chad, Yacef, K., Mostow, J., Pavlik, P. (eds.) AIED 2013. LNCS (LNAI), vol. 7926, pp. 571–574. Springer, Heidelberg (2013). https://doi.org/10.1007/978-3-642-39112-5_61

18. Ueno, M.: Adaptive testing based on bayesian decision theory. In: Lane, H.C., Yacef, K., Mostow, J., Pavlik, P. (eds.) AIED 2013. LNCS (LNAI), vol. 7926, pp. 712–716. Springer, Heidelberg (2013). https://doi.org/10.1007/978-3-642-39112-5_95

19. Faghihi, U., Fournier-Viger, P., Nkambou, R.: A cognitive tutoring agent with automatic reasoning capabilities. In: The Proceedings of the 24th International Florida Artificial Intelligence Research Society Conference, pp. 448–449 (2011)

20. Maclellan, C.J., Matsuda, N., Koedinger, K.R.: Toward a reflective SimStudent: using experience to avoid generalization errors. In: The Proceedings of the 1st Workshop on Simulated Learners at the 16th International Conference on Artificial Intelligence in Education, pp. 51–60 (2013)

21. Lelei, D.E.K., McCalla, G.: Exploring the issues in simulating a semi-structured learning environment: the SimGrad doctoral program design. In: The Proceedings of the 2nd Workshop on Simulated Learners at the 17th International Conference on Artificial Intelligence in Education, vol. 5, pp. 11–20 (2015)

22. Groenvynck, H., Vandevelde, K., Van Rossem, R.: The Ph.D. track: who succeeds, who drops out? Res. Eval. 22(4), 199–209 (2013)

23. Gatfield, T.: An investigation into PhD supervisory management styles: development of a dynamic conceptual model and its managerial implications. J. High. Educ. Policy Manag. 27(3), 311–325 (2005)

24. Heath, T.: A quantitative analysis of PhD students' views of supervision. High. Educ. Res. Dev. 21, 37–41 (2002)

25. Torrance, M., Thomas, G.V., Robinson, E.J.: The writing strategies of graduate research students in the social sciences. High. Educ. 27(3), 379–392 (1994)

26. Mainhard, T., van der Rijst, R., van Tartwijk, J., Wubbels, T.: A model for the supervisor-doctoral student relationship. High. Educ. 58(3), 359–373 (2009)

27. Esteva, M., Rodríguez-Aguilar, J.-A., Sierra, C., Garcia, P., Arcos, J.L.: On the formal specification of electronic institutions. In: Dignum, F., Sierra, C. (eds.) Agent Mediated Electronic Commerce. LNCS (LNAI), vol. 1991, pp. 126–147. Springer, Heidelberg (2001). https://doi.org/10.1007/3-540-44682-6_8

28. Berendsen, H.J.C., Van Der Spoel, D., Van Drunen, R.: GROMACS: a message-passing parallel molecular dynamics implementation. Comput. Phys. Commun. 91(1), 43–56 (1995)

29. Lavelle, E., Bushrow, K.: Writing approaches of graduate students. Educ. Psychol. 27(6), 807–822 (2007)

30. Seagram, B.C., Gould, J., Pyke, S.W.: An investigation of gender and other variables on time to completion of doctoral degrees. Res. High. Educ. 39(3), 319–335 (1998)

31. Pelánek, R., Jarušek, P.: Student modeling based on problem solving times. Int. J. Artif. Intell. Educ. 25(4), 493–519 (2015)

32. Axelrod, R.: Advancing the art of simulation in the social sciences. In: Conte, R., Hegselmann, R., Terna, P. (eds.) The Proceedings of the 18th European Meeting on Cybernetics and Systems Research, pp. 1–13. Springer, Heidelberg (2006). https://doi.org/10.1007/978-3-662-03366-1_2

33. Gilbert, N., Terna, P.: How to build and use agent-based models in social science. Mind Soc. 1(1), 57–72 (2000)

Students' Academic Language Use When Constructing Scientific Explanations in an Intelligent Tutoring System

Haiying Li[(✉)], Janice Gobert, Rachel Dickler, and Natali Morad

Rutgers University, New Brunswick, NJ 08901, USA
{haiying.li,janice.gobert,rachel.dickler,
natali.morad}@gse.rutgers.edu

Abstract. In the present study, we examined the use of academic language in students' scientific explanations in the form of written claim, written evidence, and written reasoning (CER) statements during science inquiry within an intelligent tutoring system. Results showed that students tended to use more academic language when constructing their evidence and reasoning statements. Further analyses showed that both the number of words and pronouns used by students were significant predictors for the quality of students' written CER statements. The quality of claim statements was significantly reduced by the lexical density (type-token ratio), but the quality of reasoning significantly increased with lexical density. The quality of evidence statements increased significantly with the inclusion of causal and temporal relationships, verb overlap, and descriptive writing. These findings indicate that students used language differently when constructing their CER statements. Implications are discussed in terms of how to increase students' knowledge of and use of academic language.

Keywords: Academic language · Formality · Scientific explanation

1 Introduction

The Common Core State Standards for English Language Arts (CCSS-ELA) [2] require that students develop academic writing skills. This requirement is expanded upon in the College and Career Readiness Anchor Standards for Reading and Writing in Grades K-12 [22]. The specific abilities outlined in the standards include "write arguments to support claims in an analysis of substantive topics or texts, using valid reasoning and relevant and sufficient evidence" [22, p. 18]. Moreover, the CCSS-ELA demands that students use academic discourse in their writing. As of 2011, however, the National Assessment of Educational Progress [21] reported that secondary students face considerable challenges in meeting these standards. Unfortunately, there is little research on students' academic language use in the context of science inquiry.

Currently, the instruction and evaluation of academic writing in areas such as science has focused on students' understanding of scientific content and processes. With the development of automated scoring tools, researchers have the potential to examine the role of academic language in student writing in science inquiry. Prior studies, however, have primarily used linguistic features to automatically score the quality of student writing [13, 18, 28] rather than examining the use of academic language. Therefore, the relationship between students' writing in the context of science and use of academic language required by the CCSS-ELA have yet to be investigated.

In this study, we examined students' academic language use within scientific explanations in the format of claim, evidence, and reasoning statements using the automated text analysis tool, Coh-Metrix [17]. Coh-Metrix automatically scores 100 linguistic features of written text, which is extremely valuable when examining multiple components of student language use. This study contributes to research on scientific explanations as well as research on students' use of academic writing by addressing the gap in research on the relationship between students' academic language use and writing performance in the context of science inquiry.

1.1   Academic Language

Academic language, also called scientific language, refers to the use of language in scholarly contexts (the classroom, textbooks, etc.) that is often more sophisticated and complex than language used in common day-to-day interactions [25, 26]. Snow and Uccelli [25] developed a comprehensive pragmatic-based framework of academic language that groups linguistic features according to: interpersonal stance (e.g., informational versus conversational), information load (e.g., concise information versus redundant repetition), organization of information (e.g., embedded clauses, connective meta-discourse markers), lexical choices (e.g., academic vocabulary versus colloquial expressions), and representational congruence (e.g., grammatical incongruence, such as nominalization, passive voice). In addition to these linguistic features, they included three core domains of cognitive accomplishment involved in academic-language performance: genre mastery (e.g., narration versus explanation), command of reasoning/argumentative strategies (e.g., ways of argumentation and persuasion), and disciplinary knowledge taxonomies (e.g., facts versus constructed knowledge).

Another multilevel framework developed by Graesser and McNamara [6] has been used primarily to analyze texts on multiple textual levels for reading comprehension and writing. The multilevel components of the framework included the: surface code (e.g., words, syntax), explicit textbase (e.g., overlapping of propositions and idea units), situation model (e.g., causal, intentional, temporal, relationships), the genre (e.g., narrative, expository), rhetorical structure, and pragmatic communication level. While utilizing different labels, there is significant overlap between this framework and Snow and Ucelli's [25] framework. Both frameworks cover multiple textual levels, including words (e.g., pronouns, concrete/abstract words, lexical density/diversity), syntax (e.g., embedded words, phrases, and clauses), referential cohesion (e.g., overlapping of propositions and ideas), deep cohesion (e.g., cohesion represented by connectives), and genre (narrative versus informational). Automated text analysis tools, such as Coh-Metrix [17], have been developed based on the framework proposed by Graesser and McNamara [6].

1.2   Automated Text Analysis Tool: Coh-Metrix

Coh-Metrix (cohmetrix.com) is a computer-based tool that automates language- and text-processing mechanisms for hundreds of measures at multiple textual levels of linguistic analysis, including word characteristics, sentence characteristics, and discourse relationships between ideas [17]. Specifically, Coh-Metrix (3.0) measures include descriptive (e.g., the number of syllables, words, sentences,), word information (e.g., incidence of noun, word frequency, concreteness, imageability), syntactic pattern density (e.g., density of noun phrase), syntactic complexity (e.g., left embedded words before main verbs), connectives (e.g., causal, temporal), lexical density (e.g., type-token ratio, which is the proportion of unique words out of all words), latent semantic analysis (e.g. examining semantics of text [8]), referential cohesion (e.g., noun overlap, argument overlap), and readability (e.g., Flesch-Kincaid grade level). These individual indices have been often used to predict the quality of student writing [12, 13, 18, 28]. For instance, Wiley et al. [28] found that cohesion, causality, and lexical diversity were correlated with the quality of students' explanatory science essays, but only lexical diversity was a significant predictor. Li et al. [13] used Coh-Metrix individual indices to automatically evaluate the quality of summaries after reading scientific texts.

Coh-Metrix also includes five major dimensions identified through a principal component analysis performed on 52 individual indices [17]. These five dimensions include: word concreteness (concrete words can evoke mental images and are thus assumed to be more meaningful to the writer relative to abstract words), syntactic simplicity (sentences are constructed with few words and simple, familiar syntactic structures), narrativity (narrative texts tell stories that are familiar to the reader and are closely associated with everyday oral conversation), referential cohesion (high-cohesion writing contains words and ideas that overlap across sentences and the text as a whole, forming threads that connect the explicit textbase), and deep cohesion (causal, intentional, and other types of connectives are taken as evidence that writing reflects a more coherent and deeper understanding) [17].

The five Coh-Metrix dimensions can be examined together in order to uncover information about the overall language style of a text, also referred to as a measure of formality [9–11]. Text formality provides information on the overall complexity of a piece of writing based on the structure and content of the text. Specifically, formality increases with more abstract words, syntactic complexity, high cohesion, and more informational text. Therefore, formality is helpful for capturing the use of academic language as academic language embodies formal linguistic characteristics [9–11, 14]. Li et al. [9] found that formality as captured by the five Coh-Metrix dimensions was better able to distinguish between text complexity relative to a more traditional index of formality measured at the surface language level. Overall, Coh-Metrix can provide valuable information related to student writing and language use based on the individual indices, individual dimensions, and comprehensive measure of formality.

1.3 Scientific Explanations

Scientific explanations have been used to evaluate students' science inquiry competencies for analyzing and interpreting data and engaging in argument from evidence [23]. Researchers have assessed written scientific explanations in various forms including within the structure of claim, evidence, and reasoning (CER) [5, 19, 20, 24]. The CER format is based on a modified version of Toulmin's [27] framework for argumentation in which students make a claim, provide evidence for their claim, and provide a justification for how their evidence supports their claim. CER has traditionally been scored according to the accuracy of content, as well as the completeness of claim, sufficient and appropriate use of evidence, and justification for how the evidence supports the claim [15, 16, 19, 20, 24]. To date, however, no studies have comprehensively examined students' claims, evidence, and reasoning statements in terms of academic language used within each component. It is necessary to address this gap in the literature, as student performance on each component of CER has been found to vary according to content quality [15, 16]. It would be valuable to understand how or if language use relates to this variation in performance for each component of CER. Also, even though the content may vary across claim, evidence, and reasoning statements, students should still use consistent academic language across each component.

This study examined students' writing of claim, evidence, and reasoning statements constructed within an intelligent tutoring system according to formality and academic language use. Specifically, this study investigated two research questions:

RQ1: To what extent do students use academic (formal) language to write claim, evidence, and reasoning, respectively?
RQ2: What specific language and discourse features are actually used in students' claim, evidence, and reasoning, respectively?

The first question examines whether students used academic language when they wrote their claim, evidence, or reasoning statements. It is important that students use formal language at the appropriate grade level for each of these statements. Students' claim, evidence, and reasoning writing should also meet the academic language requirements for each component of formality (i.e., high levels of deep cohesion, etc.) [2].

The second question investigates which specific Coh-Metrix indices predict claim, evidence, and reasoning in order to determine the features that contribute to the construction of high quality writing for each component of C, E, and R [15, 16]. The measures of academic language and the Coh-Metrix indices that were used in this study are reported in detail in the Methods section.

2 Method

2.1 Participants and Materials

The participants were 293 students in grades 7 through 8 from public middle schools located in Massachusetts, Minnesota, or Oregon. All participants had completed a Density Virtual Lab in Inq-ITS, an inquiry intelligent tutoring system [3, 4]. Inq-ITS virtual labs are for science topics in the domains of Life, Earth, and Physical Science.

Inq-ITS uses machine learned detectors to automatically score students' inquiry practice competencies as they engage in virtual labs [3]. Each virtual lab involves three to six activities in which students conduct an investigation to address a directed question or goal.

The Density Virtual Lab contains three different activities. Only data from the Density, Shape of the Container activity is analyzed in the present study due to space limitations. The goal of the Shape of the Container activity was to "determine how the shape of the container affects the density of the liquid." In the first stage of the virtual lab, students formed a hypothesis as to whether the density of a liquid would change or not when the container shape (wide, narrow, or square) was changed. Students then manipulated a simulation to test their hypothesis. Data from the students' trials were automatically recorded and stored in a data table. In the third stage, students analyzed and interpreted the data from their table. In the final stage of the activity, students responded to each of the following three open response prompts (i.e. CER) in order to explain the findings from their investigation: write a sentence that states what you found out about the scientific question you just investigated (Claim), provide and describe scientific evidence from your data table that supports (or refutes) your claim (Evidence), and explain why your evidence supports your claim (Reasoning).

The present study only uses student data from the final stage of the Shape of the Container Lab. Specifically, the data consisted of students' written claim, evidence, and reasoning statements. Even though 293 students completed the activity, some students wrote gibberish responses for their claim, evidence, or reasoning. These gibberish responses were strings of letters such as "jhhhhhhhhhhhh" or "eciu3ghf." Gibberish responses were removed for analyses resulting in: 288 written claim statements, 288 written evidence statements, and 287 written reasoning statements.

2.2   Measures

Scientific Explanations of CER. Students' written scientific explanations from the final stage of the Density Shape of the Container Activity in the form of a claim, evidence, and reasoning (CER) statement were scored by two human raters according to fine-grained rubrics developed by Li et al. [16].

Students' written claims were scored according to four sub-components, including identifying: the correct independent variable (IV; i.e. shape of the container), the specific shapes of the containers (IVR; i.e. narrow, square, or wide), the correct dependent variable (DV; i.e. density), and whether the density was affected by changing the container shape (DVR; i.e. the density stayed the same). Each subcomponent of claim was worth a maximum of 1 point. Students could receive a maximum total score of 4 points for claim.

Written evidence statements were scored based on three sub-components of: describing at least two relevant trials (Sufficiency), stating numeric data for the mass and volume of a liquid (Appropriate Mass and Volume), and stating numeric data for the density of a liquid (Appropriate Density). Sufficiency was scored out of 2 points. Appropriate Mass and Volume, and Appropriate Density were scored out of 1 point. Students could receive a maximum total score of 4 points for evidence.

Students' written reasoning statements were scored according to five sub-components of: interpreting whether or not the data described in the evidence supports (or refutes) the claim (Connection), describing the IV data and how it was changed (Data IV/IVR), describing the DV (Data DV), describing and interpreting data for the DV (Data DVR), and backing up conclusions with a scientific theory (Theory). The subcomponent of Theory was scored out of 2 points. Sub-components of Connection, Data IV/IVR, Data DV, and Data DVR were scored out of 1 point. Students could receive a maximum total score of 6 points for reasoning.

Cronbach's α was used to calculate inter-rater reliabilities for claim ($\alpha = .99$), evidence ($\alpha = .99$), and reasoning ($\alpha = .94$), respectively [15, 16]. Disagreements between human raters were discussed and the final agreed upon scores were used for analyses.

Academic Language. Academic language of students' written claim statements, written evidence statements, and written reasoning statements was measured by Coh-Metrix formality [7]. Formality increases with word abstractness (i.e. the inverse of word concreteness), syntactic complexity (i.e. the inverse of syntactic simplicity), expository texts (i.e. the inverse of narrativity), and high referential cohesion and deep cohesion. The formula used to calculate formality is listed in Eq. (1):

$$\text{Formality} = (\text{deep cohesion} + \text{referential cohesion} - \text{narrativity} - \text{word concreteness} - \text{syntactic simplicity})/5 \tag{1}$$

Coh-Metrix formality uses the reference corpus TASA (Touchstone Applied Science Associates, now renamed Questar Assessment Inc.), with numbers higher than 0 representing more formal discourse, and numbers below 0 representing more informal discourse [7]. Graesser et al. [7] compared formality in three genres across grades K-12 using 37,650 texts in the TASA corpus and displayed that formality of science reading for middle school students (Grade 6–8) was slightly below 0. This implies that if student formality in writing reaches 0, their use of academic language is equivalent to the academic language used in their informational reading materials.

Individual Coh-Metrix Indices. Students' actual use of language for written claim, written evidence, and written reasoning was measured using individual linguistic features from Coh-Metrix [17]. Coh-Metrix captures and evaluates over 100 individual indices. Not all indices were used to evaluate students' written claim, evidence, and reasoning statements, as there were too few data to apply such a large number of indices. In order to avoid overfitting of our regression model as a result of the small number of data ($N = 285-288$) available in the present study, we followed two regression assumptions. First, if the correlation between each pair of Coh-Metrix indices exceeded the limit of the assumption (less than .70), we removed one variable. We followed the rule that if one index, such as sentence count (the number of sentences in writing) was highly correlated with more than one index, we kept sentence count, but removed other variables. If two indices were highly correlated, we kept the one that was used as a predictor in previous studies. Second, we removed indices whose correlations with the dependent variable were smaller than .30. Table 1 lists the

Coh-Metrix indices used in the present study and their descriptions. The remaining independent indices for written claim scores were LDTTRa, DRPP, WRDPRO, WRDPRP1s, WRDFRQc, WRDPOLc, and RDFKGL. The independent indices for written evidence scores were: DESSC, DESSL, DESSLd, LDTTRa, SMCAUSvp, SMCAUSlsa, SMTEMP, SYNLE, SYNSTRUTa, WRDPRO, WRDIMGc, and RDL2. The indices for written reasoning scores were: DESSC, DESSL, LDTTRa, LDMTLD, SYNNP, and WRDPRO.

Table 1. Descriptions of Coh-Metrix indices

Coh-Metrix Index	Description
LDTTRa	Lexical diversity measured by the type-token ratio, which was calculated by the proportion of unique words out of all words
DRPP	The density of preposition phrases
WRDPRO	The incidence of pronouns
WRDPRP1s	The incidence of first person singular pronouns
WRDFRQc	Word frequency based on the CELEX word data base
WRDPOLc	The mean of polysemy for content words
RDFKGL	The Flesch-Kincaid grade level
DESSC	The number of sentences
DESSL	The average number of words per sentence
DESSLd	The standard deviation of the average number of words per sentence
SMCAUSvp	The incidence of causal verbs and particles
SMCAUSlsa	Verb overlap based on latent semantic analysis
SMTEMP	Temporal cohesion of the text
SYNLE	The syntactic simplicity based on the number of words that occur before the main verb
SYSNTRUTa	Syntactic simplicity based on the average number of adjacent sentences with similar syntactic structures
WRDIMGC	The average number of visually descriptive words
RDL2	The Coh-Metrix readability level
LDMTLD	A measure of textual lexical diversity based on the MTLD word data base
SYNNP	The average number of modifiers per noun phrase

3   Findings and Discussion

3.1   Formality of Claim, Evidence, and Reasoning

To answer the first research question, a one-way ANOVA was performed to compare the formality of language used in students' claim, evidence, and reasoning statements. An analysis of variance showed a significant effect of explanation component on formality, $F(2, 860) = 27.09$, $p < 0.001$, $\eta^2 = 0.06$. Post hoc analyses using the Bonferroni criterion for significance with adjustment for multiple comparisons indicated that claim formality ($M = -.33$, $SD = .50$) was significantly lower than evidence formality ($M = -.03$, $SD = .82$, $p < .001$, Cohen's $d = .43$) and reasoning formality ($M = .08$, $SD = .72$, $p < .001$, Cohen's $d = .67$). No significant difference was found between evidence formality and reasoning formality.

These findings indicate that students used more academic language when they constructed their evidence and reasoning statements relative to their claim statements. The average formality score for evidence and reasoning was about 0 points and the average claim formality score was about $-.33$ points. Graesser et al. [7] indicated that the formality score of science reading texts for middle school students (Grade 6–8) was slightly below 0, whereas a formality score around $-.30$ points was for grades 2–3. Therefore, when the middle school students (grades 7–8) in the present study generated evidence and reasoning, they used academic language to the same extent encountered in their formal science readings (i.e. textbooks). Students were less likely, however to use academic language when constructing their claims relative to evidence and reasoning. Claims only involve stating a conclusion, whereas evidence involves describing at least two pieces of data and reasoning involves using data to support a claim. This difference between explanatory components may lead to different levels of formality between claim and evidence and reasoning.

A simple, stepwise linear regression with 10-fold cross-validation was used to predict the written claim statement scores based on the formality scores. Results showed that formality was not a significant predictor of written claim scores. The same regression analysis was conducted for the written evidence scores and was significant with an R^2 of 0.119. The same regression analysis for the written reasoning scores was also significant with an R^2 of 0.005. The predicted scores of written evidence and written reasoning based on formality are displayed in Eqs. (2) and (3), respectively. These findings further indicated that the more formal language that students used when they generated evidence and reasoning, the higher the scores they received based on content.

$$\text{Written evidence scores} = 1.33 + 0.55 \times \text{Formality} \tag{2}$$

$$\text{Written reasoning scores} = 2.45 + 0.29 \times \text{Formality} \tag{3}$$

Formality scores were computed based on five major Coh-Metrix dimensions (word concreteness, syntactic simplicity, referential cohesion, deep cohesion, and narrativity). To further examine the extent to which student language differed across claim, evidence, and reasoning, three multiple linear regressions with stepwise 10-fold cross-validation were performed. Specifically, each of the five Coh-Metrix dimensions was used to predict scores on written claim, evidence, and reasoning, respectively. A significant regression equation for written claim was found with an R^2 of 0.073. Syntactic Simplicity, Deep Cohesion, and Narrativity were significant predictors, but Referential Cohesion and Word Concreteness were not. Results showed a significant regression equation for evidence with an R^2 of 0.273. Significant predictors for evidence were Syntactic Simplicity, Referential Cohesion, Deep Cohesion, and Narrativity, but not Word Concreteness. Results of the analyses for reasoning showed the same significant predictors as evidence and a significant regression equation with an R^2 of 0.169. The predicted scores of written claim, written evidence, and written reasoning based on the five Coh-Metrix dimensions are displayed in Eqs. 4–6, respectively.

$$\text{Written claim scores} = 2.61 - 0.30 \times \text{Syntactic Simplicity}$$
$$- 0.07 \times \text{Deep Cohesion} - 0.10 \times \text{Narrativity} \quad (4)$$

$$\text{Written evidence scores} = 0.84 - 0.29 \times \text{Syntactic Simplicity} + 0.23 \times \text{Referential}$$
$$\text{Cohesion} + 0.09 \times \text{Deep Cohesion} - 0.15 \times \text{Narrativity} \quad (5)$$

$$\text{Written reasoning scores} = 2.33 - 0.44 \times \text{Syntactic Simplicity} + 0.12 \times \text{Referential}$$
$$\text{Cohesion} + 0.09 \times \text{Deep Cohesion} - 0.11 \times \text{Narrativity} \quad (6)$$

Findings from these fine-grained analyses were consistent with those from analyses for overall formality. Students' quality of written evidence and reasoning increased with more complex sentence structures, cohesion, and expository/informational writing style. Word concreteness was not a significant predictor of evidence or reasoning performance possibly because the density activity did not involve many extremely abstract or concrete words. Written claim showed a different pattern relative to evidence and reasoning. Students' quality of written claim increased with more complex sentence structures and expository style, but less deep cohesion.

The finding that the quality of claim decreases with less deep cohesion was contradictory to the findings for written evidence and written reasoning. Also while referential cohesion was a predictor of evidence and reasoning scores, it was not a predictor of claim scores. It makes sense that deep cohesion could predict quality of claims but not referential cohesion because deep cohesion relates to the use of causal connectives whereas referential cohesion relates to the use of repeated language. Claims are generally causal conclusions that do not contain much repeated information. We examined the written claims where students achieved high scores on claim content, but low scores on the dimension of deep cohesion. We found that claims that received low content scores contained some causal connectives (e.g., so, cause), which dramatically increased the scores of deep cohesion to above 6.00 points (e.g. "Cause I said so and it worked"), even though the content in these claims was inaccurate, irrelevant, or mistakenly spelt. On the other hand, we examined written claims that received high scores and found that students did not specify the causal relationship between the IV and DV (e.g., "i found out that the shape of container going from narrow to wide doesn't change its density"), which led to low deep cohesion scores (less than −4.00 points). While it is possible that the deep cohesion measure from Coh-Metrix may not detect implicit causation as in the prior example, students are still expected to use causal connectives in claims in order to more clearly articulate the relationships between variables. We found that only 11% ($N = 33$) of students' written claims ($N = 288$) showed high Deep Cohesion above the average score of 0 points. These findings reveal that students were able to generally articulate the relationship between the IV and DV in their claims, but did not use causal connectives to state this causal mechanism. Students need to be instructed on how to use appropriate connectives in order to effectively and explicitly express causal relationships when they generate a claim. It is important that claims involve causal language as used in evidence and reasoning, as claims specifically involve drawing a conclusion in regard to the relationship between variables.

3.2   Student Language Use for Claim, Evidence, and Reasoning

In order to investigate the second research question, individual Coh-Metrix indices were used to predict students' writing performance on claim, evidence, and reasoning, respectively. The process used to extract individual indices was based on regression assumptions, as detailed in the Individual Coh-Metrix Indices measures section.

A multiple linear regression with stepwise 10-fold cross-validation was used to predict written claim performance based on seven individual Coh-Metrix indices (LDTTRa, DRPP, WRDPRO, WRDPRP1s, WRDFRQc, WRDPOLc, and RDFKGL). Five indices were significant predictors; DRPP and WRDPOLc were not significant. A significant regression model was found with an R^2 of 0.332. The same analyses for written evidence were conducted based on 12 individual Coh-Metrix indices (DESSC, DESSL, DESSLd, LDTTRa, SMCAUSvp, SMCAUSlsa, SMTEMP, SYNLE, SYN-STRUTa, WRDPRO, WRDIMGc, and RDL2). Eight indices were significant predictors; DESSLd, LDTTRa, SyNSTRUTa, and RDL2 were not significant. A significant regression equation was found with an R^2 of 0.435. The same analyses for written reasoning were performed based on six individual Coh-Metrix indices (DESSC, DESSL, LDTTRa, LDMTLD, SYNNP, and WRDPRO). Five indices were significant predictors; LDTTRa was not significant. A significant regression equation was found with an R^2 of 0.515. The predicted scores of written claim, written evidence, and written reasoning based on Coh-Metrix individual indices are displayed in Eqs. (7), (8), and (9), respectively.

$$\begin{aligned} \text{Written claim scores} = 6.32 - 2.35 \times \text{LDTTRa} - 0.002 \times \text{WRDPRO} - 0.004 \times \text{WRDPRP1s} \\ - 0.89 \times \text{WRDFRQc} + 0.11 \times \text{RDFKGL} \end{aligned} \tag{7}$$

$$\begin{aligned} \text{Written evidence scores} = -0.38 + 0.23 \times \text{DESSC} + 0.04 \times \text{DESSL} \\ - 0.001 \times \text{SMCAUSvp} + 0.90 \times \text{SMCAUSlsa} + 0.26 \times \text{SMTEMP} \\ + 0.03 \times \text{SYNLE} - 0.001 \times \text{WRDPRO} + 0.002 \times \text{WRDIMGc} \end{aligned} \tag{8}$$

$$\begin{aligned} \text{Written reasoning scores} = -0.29 + 0.74 \times \text{DESSC} + 0.08 \times \text{DESSL} + 0.01 \times \text{LDMTLD} \\ + 0.65 \times \text{SYNNP} - 0.003 \times \text{WRDPRO} \end{aligned} \tag{9}$$

These findings indicated that the use of pronouns (WRDPRO) negatively predicted claim, evidence, and reasoning. Therefore, high quality claim, evidence, and reasoning statements contained less pronouns. Pronoun use has been found to be highly correlated with conversational language [1, 9], so the minimal use of pronouns in high quality CER implies that students were using more formal language. The following is an example of a claim that received a full score for quality and did not contain any pronouns: *"when the shape was changed from narrow to wide and eventually square, the density of the liquid stayed the same."* Here is an example of a claim that received 0 points and included the pronoun "it": *"It didn't support my answer."* For this claim, the reader cannot determine what "it" means without additional context.

Other word information was also found to predict claim performance, but not performance on evidence or reasoning. Specifically, when students used less first-person singular pronouns (WRDPRP1s) and less frequently used words (WRDFRQc), their claim scores were higher. This phenomenon was not found in either evidence or reasoning. It is likely that students more often used structures in claims such as "*I found,*" "*my claim/hypothesis,*" and "*I changed*" compared to in their evidence and reasoning. Even though this pattern was not found in evidence, the use of content words that evoked mental images (WRDIMGc) increased the quality of evidence. The following two evidence statements demonstrate the value of including descriptive language: "*When using the oil in both containers (wide and narrow) the mass equaled 425 and the volume equaled 500, it gives you 0.85 for the density, there for the density remains the same*" and "*My experiment proves my evidence.*" The former had an extremely high WRDIMGc score relative to the latter, which received only 0 points. It is hard to obtain any specific data from the latter example, relative to the first example.

Scores of evidence and reasoning increased with both the number of sentences (DESSC) and the number of words (DESSL). However, these two features were not selected as predictors of claim performance because the number of sentences (DESSC) had a low correlation with written claim ($r = 0.003$) and DESSL was highly correlated with the Flesch-Kincaid Grade Level (RDFKGL) ($r = 0.745$), which was partially computed based on the mean number of words per sentence. Thus, RDFKGL was used to present DESSL and RDFKGL was a significant predictor of claim performance. For this reason, we could conclude that number of words was a significant predictor for claim, evidence, and reasoning.

Lexical density significantly predicted claim and reasoning, but not evidence. However, the method used to compute lexical density for claim was different from reasoning. Lexical density for claim was computed by the type-token ration (LDTTRa), namely the number of unique words in writing (i.e., types) divided by the overall number of words (i.e., tokens) in writing. The measure of Textural Lexical Density (LDMTLD) that was used to predict reasoning was computed based on the mean length of sequential word strings in writing that maintained a given type-token ratio. LDTTRa was a Lexical density measure that was entered as a predictor for reasoning but was not a significant predictor based on the step-wise regression procedure. LDTTRa was also used as a predictor for evidence, but it could not significantly predict evidence. One possible explanation is that its function may be counterbalanced by other variables, such as syntactic complexity and the situation model.

Additionally, lexical density largely decreased the scores of claim statements, but increased scores of reasoning statements. High lexical density indicates that there are more unique words, which involves the introduction of more new information. Low lexical density, on the other hand, implies repetition of words and redundancy. In claims with high scores, students tended to elaborate more, which likely led to the repetition of functional words, such as the article "the" in the following example: "*My hypothesis said that if I changed the container from narrow to wide that the density of the liquid would increase*" (LDTTRa = 0.59). On the contrary, in claims with low scores, students articulated general ideas, such as "*My hypothesis was wrong,*" in which each word was unique and resulted in a LDTTRa score of 1.00 point.

Syntactic complexity was related to both evidence and reasoning, but different individual features were selected to predict evidence and reasoning, respectively. Specifically, for evidence, left embedded words before main verbs (SYNLE) was used as a predictor and was found to significantly increase evidence scores. For example, a high-quality evidence statement involved left embeddedness with a large number of words before the main verb, such as "When using…" in the following example, *"When using the oil in both containers (wide and narrow) the mass equaled 425 and ..."* However, the low-quality evidence statements did not contain a large number of words before main verb, such as in the example *"stay the same in both container."*

SYNLE was not used as a predictor for reasoning because its correlation with written reasoning score was below 0.30. The mean number of modifiers per noun phrases (SYNNP) was used as a predictor and it significantly increased reasoning scores. For example, the following reasoning statement had a high score, *"This shows that the container shapes, wide and narrow, will allow the densities of the liquid to stay the same, which supports the claim,"* which contained some modifiers before and after the noun phrases, such as "the container" before "shapes," "wide and narrow" after "shapes," "the liquid" as a modifier of "densities," and the "which" clause was at the end of the statement. Low SYNNP caused reasoning scores to decrease. For example, in this reasoning statement, *"when u changed the container it got bigger,"* no modifiers occurred before or after the noun "container," which meant the reader did not know what about the container was changed (i.e. shape, size, etc.). SYNNP was not used as a predictor for evidence because its correlation with evidence scores was below 0.30.

The indices used only to predict performance on evidence statements included causal verbs and causal particles (SMCAUSvp), LSA verb overlap (SMCAUSlsa), and temporal cohesion based on tense and aspect repetition (SMTEMP). These indices contribute to situation models that represent deep cohesion and clear causality. Here is an example that best illustrates a high-quality evidence statement, *"I used a narrow container of oil getting a mass of 212.5 and volume of 250 getting .85 as my density. Then I used the wide container getting mass 212.5 and volume of 250 and getting .85 again as the density."* In this example, the causality measure (SMCAUSvp) was zero, meaning no casual verbs or causal particles such as "impact" or "as a result" were used in this statement. However, this statement was replete with verbs that have clear links to actions, events, and states (e.g., "used" and "getting"), which is called LSA verb overlap. This example also showed high temporal cohesion (SMTEMP) as represented by the use of temporal particles such as "then," and consistency of tense (e.g., past tense of "used") and aspect (e.g., progressive "getting"). However, these three indices had low correlations (below .30) with written claim and reasoning statement performance. Therefore, they were not included in the claim or reasoning predictive models.

4   Conclusions and Implications

This study examined students' written scientific explanations from two perspectives: academic language and actual language use. Results showed that students used academic language as indicated by high levels of formality when they generated evidence and reasoning statements, but not claim statements. The analyses for the five major Coh-Metrix dimensions showed that students used more complex syntax and informational text when they generated high quality claim, evidence, and reasoning statements. Moreover, high-quality evidence and reasoning statements tended to include more referential cohesion and deep cohesion. The quality of claim, however, decreased with deep cohesion. These findings imply that students may benefit from learning to explicitly use causal connectives in order to generate a high-quality claim statement. Analyses with individual Coh-Metrix indices also showed that students need to be instructed to use causal verbs or causal connectives to explicitly specify relationships in their claims.

Additionally, students need to be instructed to avoid using vague pronouns to refer to a person or a thing in their formal academic writing as this decontextualized language can lead to lack of clarity. Although students demonstrated deep cohesion and used descriptive words in their evidence statements, they require support in order to transfer this language use to their claim and reasoning statements. These various gaps in linguistic formality could be addressed through integrating automated assessments and scaffolding within intelligent tutoring systems. Specifically, scaffolding could gradually direct students to use appropriate forms of language when writing scientific explanations and even provide examples of formal CER statements. While the design of automated assessment and scaffolding of students' CER in terms of content is under way [15, 16], researchers have yet to design automated scoring and feedback specifically to address language use.

The present study unpacks the academic language used when students generate a claim, evidence, and reasoning statement at both the macro-level and micro-level. The findings provide valuable information for teachers and researchers that can be used to enhance students' academic writing. A limitation of this study is that the data came from just one density activity as a result of space limitations. Future studies may include more activities within the same topic or across topics in order to investigate whether domain familiarity is related to academic language use in writing scientific explanations in the form of claim, evidence, and reasoning.

Acknowledgements. This research was supported by the Institute of Education Sciences (R305A120778) and National Science Foundation (1629045) to Janice Gobert, principal investigator at Rutgers University.

References

1. Biber, D.: Variation Across Speech and Writing. Cambridge University Press, New York (1988)
2. Common Core State Standards Initiative: Common Core State Standards for English language arts and literacy in history/social studies, science, and technical subjects (2010). http://www.corestandards.org/ELA-Literacy/
3. Gobert, J.D., Baker, R.S., Sao Pedro, M.A.: Inquiry skills tutoring system. U.S. Patent No. 9,373,082. U.S. Patent and Trademark Office, Washington, DC (2016)
4. Gobert, J., Sao Pedro, M., Betts, C., Baker, R.S.: Inquiry skills tutoring system (alerting system). U.S. Patent No. 9,564,057. U.S. Patent and Trademark Office, Washington, DC (2016)
5. Gotwals, A.W., Songer, N.B.: Reasoning up and down a food chain: using an assessment framework to investigate students' middle knowledge. Sci. Educ. **94**(2), 259–281 (2010). https://doi.org/10.1002/sce.20368

6. Graesser, A.C., McNamara, D.S.: Computational analyses of multilevel discourse comprehension. Topics Cog. Sci. **3**(2), 371–398 (2011). https://doi.org/10.1111/j.1756-8765.2010.01081.x

7. Graesser, A.C., McNamara, D.S., Cai, Z., Conley, M., Li, H., Pennebaker, J.: Coh-Metrix measures text characteristics at multiple levels of language and discourse. Elem. School J. **115**, 210–229 (2014). https://doi.org/10.1086/678293

8. Landauer, T.K., Dumais, S.T.: A solution to Plato's problem: the latent semantic analysis theory of acquisition, induction, and representation of knowledge. Psych. Rev. **104**(2), 211 (1997)

9. Li, H., Cai, Z., Graesser, A.C.: Comparing two measures for formality. In: Boonthum-Denecke, C., Youngblood, G.M. (eds.) Proceedings of the Twenty Sixth International FLAIRS Conference, pp. 220–225 (2013)

10. Li, H., Cheng, C., Graesser, A.C.: A measure of text formality as a human construct. In: Russel, I., Eberle, B. (eds.) Proceedings of the Twenty-Eighth International Florida Artificial Intelligence Research Society Conference, pp. 175–180. AAAI Press, Palo Alto (2015)

11. Li, H., Graesser, A.C., Conley, M., Cai, Z., Pavlik, P., Pennebaker, J.W.: A new measure of text formality: an analysis of discourse of Mao Zedong. Disc. Processes **53**(3), 205–232 (2016). https://doi.org/10.1080/0163853X.2015.1010191

12. Li, H., Cai, Z., Graesser, A.C.: How good is popularity? summary grading in crowdsourcing. In: 9th International Conference on Educational Data Mining, pp. 430–435. EDM Society, Raleigh (2016)

13. Li, H., Cai, Z., Graesser, A.C.: Computerized summary scoring: crowdsourcing-based latent semantic analysis. Behav. Res. Meth. (2017). https://doi.org/10.3758/s13428-017-0982-7

14. Li, H., Graesser, A.: Impact of pedagogical agents' conversational formality on learning and engagement. In: André, E., Baker, R., Hu, X., Rodrigo, M., du Boulay, B. (eds.) AIED 2017. LNCS (LNAI), vol. 10331, pp. 188–200. Springer, Cham (2017). https://doi.org/10.1007/978-3-319-61425-0_16

15. Li, H., Gobert, J., Dicker, R.: Dusting off the messy middle: assessing students' inquiry skills through doing and writing. In: André, E., Baker, R., Hu, X., Rodrigo, Ma.M.T., du Boulay, B. (eds.) AIED 2017. LNCS (LNAI), vol. 10331, pp. 175–187. Springer, Cham (2017). https://doi.org/10.1007/978-3-319-61425-0_15

16. Li, H., Gobert, J., Dickler, R.: Automated assessment for scientific explanations in on-line science inquiry. In: Hu, X., Barnes, T., Hershkovitz, A., Paquette, L. (eds.) Proceedings of the 10th International Conference on Educational Data Mining, pp. 214–219. EDM Society, Wuhan (2017)

17. McNamara, D.S., Graesser, A.C., McCarthy, P.M., Cai, Z.: Automated Evaluation of Text and Discourse with Coh-Metrix. Cambridge University Press, New York (2014)

18. McNamara, D.S., Crossley, S.A., Roscoe, R.D., Allen, L.K., Dai, J.: A hierarchical classification approach to automated essay scoring. Assess. Writ. **23**, 35–59 (2015). https://doi.org/10.1016/j.asw.2014.09.002

19. McNeill, K., Lizotte, D.J., Krajcik, J., Marx, R.W.: Supporting students' construction of scientific explanations by fading scaffolds in instructional materials. J. Learn. Sci. **15**, 153–191 (2006). https://doi.org/10.1207/s15327809jls1502_1

20. McNeill, K.L.: Elementary students' views of explanation, argumentation, and evidence, and their abilities to construct arguments over the school year. J. Res. Sci. Teach. **48**, 793–823 (2011). https://doi.org/10.1002/tea.20430

21. NAEP: 2015 Reading Assessment [Data file] (2015). http://nces.ed.gov/nationsreportcard/subject/publications/stt2015/pdf/2016008AZ4.pdf

22. National Governors Association Center for Best Practices, Council of Chief State School Officers: Common Core State Standards for English Language Arts. Washington D.C. (2010)
23. National Research Council: A framework for K-12 science education: practices, crosscutting concepts, and core ideas. National Academies Press, Washington (2012)
24. Ruiz-Primo, M., Li, M., Shin-Ping, T., Schneider, J.: Testing one premise of scientific inquiry in science classrooms: examining students' scientific explanations and student learning. J. Res. Sci. Teach. **47**, 583–608 (2010). https://doi.org/10.1002/tea.20356
25. Snow, C.E., Uccelli, P.: The challenge of academic language. In: Olson, D.R., Torrance, N. (eds.) The Cambridge Handbook of Literacy, vol. 121, pp. 112–133. Cambridge University Press, Cambridge (2009). https://doi.org/10.1017/cbo9780511609664.008
26. Snow, C.E.: Academic language and the challenge of reading for leaning about science. Science **328** (2010). https://doi.org/10.1126/science.1182597
27. Toulmin, S.: The Uses of Argument. Cambridge University Press, Cambridge (1958)
28. Wiley, J., Hastings, P., Blaum, D., et al.: Different approaches to assessing the quality of explanations following a multiple-document inquiry activity in science. Int. J. Artif. Intell. Educ. **27**, 758 (2017). https://doi.org/10.1007/s40593-017-0138-z

Automated Pitch Convergence Improves Learning in a Social, Teachable Robot for Middle School Mathematics

Nichola Lubold[1(✉)], Erin Walker[1], Heather Pon-Barry[2], and Amy Ogan[3]

[1] Arizona State University, Tempe, AZ 85281, USA
{nlubold,erin.a.walker}@asu.edu
[2] Mount Holyoke College, South Hadley, MA 01075, USA
ponbarry@mtholyoke.edu
[3] Carnegie Mellon University, Pittsburgh, PA 15213, USA
aeo@cs.cmu.edu

Abstract. Pedagogical agents have the potential to provide not only cognitive support to learners but socio-emotional support through social behavior. Socio-emotional support can be a critical element to a learner's success, influencing their self-efficacy and motivation. Several social behaviors have been explored with pedagogical agents including facial expressions, movement, and social dialogue; social dialogue has especially been shown to positively influence interactions. In this work, we explore the role of paraverbal social behavior or social behavior in the form of paraverbal cues such as tone of voice and intensity. To do this, we focus on the phenomenon of entrainment, where individuals adapt their paraverbal features of speech to one another. Paraverbal entrainment in human-human studies has been found to be correlated with rapport and learning. In a study with 72 middle school students, we evaluate the effects of entrainment with a teachable robot, a pedagogical agent that learners teach how to solve ratio problems. We explore how a teachable robot which entrains and introduces social dialogue influences rapport and learning; we compare with two baseline conditions: a social condition, in which the robot speaks socially, and a non-social condition, in which the robot neither entrains nor speaks socially. We find that a robot that does entrain and speaks socially results in significantly more learning.

Keywords: Entrainment · Convergence · Pitch · Teachable robot · Rapport

1 Introduction

Pedagogical agents, including affect-sensitive tutors, emotionally responsive learning companions, and teachable agents, are becoming increasingly sophisticated. They facilitate learning through both cognitive feedback and socio-emotional support, using facial expressions, movement, and social dialogue strategies [1–5]. Social dialogue in particular has been explored in depth and found to influence engagement, motivation, and learning by drawing student attention to salient aspects of the problem domain while building rapport [6, 7]. We are interested in the effects of social behavior with a pedagogical agent in an area which remains largely unexplored—paraverbal behavior.

© Springer International Publishing AG, part of Springer Nature 2018
C. Penstein Rosé et al. (Eds.): AIED 2018, LNAI 10947, pp. 282–296, 2018.
https://doi.org/10.1007/978-3-319-93843-1_21

In human-human interactions, speakers often convey important social information to their listeners through paraverbal cues, by *how* they speak. For example, acoustic-prosodic **entrainment** is a phenomenon of speech where individuals adapt their para-verbal cues (such as their tone of voice or speaking rate) to that of their speaking partner while conversing. Correlated with **rapport** (a feeling of connection, harmony and friendship) as well as conversational flow, entrainment is thought to be a means of achieving social approval [8, 9]. It has been suggested that an individual on the receiving end of a high level of entrainment is likely to feel more rapport for their partner than if they were a receiver of low entrainment. A pedagogical agent which can model a learn-er's paraverbal cues and adapt to them might build a stronger social connection with the learner. In turn, a learner who feels more rapport for their agent may be more engaged and willing to evaluate misconceptions, leading to increased learning.

There are several challenges to implementing acoustic-prosodic entrainment in a pedagogical agent. To begin with, entrainment in human-human dialogue occurs on many features of speech and in many forms; it is unknown what the best method might be for automating entrainment to facilitate learning. Secondly, in exploratory work on implementing entrainment in agents, findings suggest social responses such as engage-ment [10] and likeability [11] may be enhanced by an agent that entrains. However, it is an open question whether automated entrainment will be powerful enough to influence outcomes like learning. In our own prior work, we explored whether a pedagogical agent which adjusted its pitch to match that of the learner could influence learning with college students [12]. While we found effects on social presence, there were no learning effects. There are several possible explanations for the lack of effect on learning. On the one hand, our implementation of entrainment may have been overly simple. On the other, many students were at ceiling on the posttest, and thus the domain content may have been too easy and prevented us from detecting effects.

In this paper, we iterate on our prior implementation of entrainment, deploy it as part of the interaction mechanisms of a teachable robot named Nico, and then explore its effects on learning with middle school students. Nico is a Nao robot that learners can teach how to solve math problems. It interacts with the learner using spoken dialogue and realistic gesture. More specifically, Nico uses social dialogue inspired by strategies successfully implemented in other AIED systems, such as praise [37], enthusiasm [3], and politeness [38]. Because dialogue of this sort has been shown to influence learning, and entrainment is a dialogue-based phenomenon, we investigate whether entrainment as a social behavior can enhance learning above and beyond this social dialogue.

We evaluate the influence of acoustic-prosodic entrainment with Nico using three conditions: a **social-entraining** condition, where Nico entrains and speaks socially, and two baseline conditions: a **social** baseline, where Nico speaks socially but does not entrain, and a **non-social** baseline, where Nico neither speaks socially nor entrains. We hypothesize that when Nico entrains and speaks socially, learners will report feeling more rapport and we will observe greater learning gains when compared to the social and non-social baselines. We also hypothesize that the social baseline will result in higher rapport and learning gains than the control. We further analyze how these three conditions differentially influence students of different genders, as recent research has shown that males and females respond to social behaviors from agents and robots differently, with females sometimes preferring social behavior more than males [21, 24, 42]. We believe it is possible we may observe gender differences with females responding to social behaviors more strongly than males.

In the next section, we review background on teachable agents, acoustic-prosodic entrainment, and gender differences. We then describe Nico and the implementation of acoustic-prosodic entrainment with social dialogue. Section 4 describes our evaluation study at two middle schools with 72 participants. The results of this study are given in Sect. 5; our discussion and conclusions are in the last section.

2   Background

2.1   Teachable Agents

We explore social behavior and effects on learning with a teachable robotic agent. By teaching, learners may attend more to the problem, reflect on their own misconceptions when correcting errors, and elaborate on their knowledge as they construct explanations [13], leading to learning. Teachable agents have demonstrated success in influencing learning [14, 15], and teachable robots have demonstrated similar positive effects [19, 20]. Indeed, due to their physical presence and rich channels of communication, robots have under some circumstances socially engaged users more than agents [22], and this may be the case with teachable agents as well.

It has been hypothesized that there is a social component to the success of teachable agents in influencing learning. Some research has shown that when learners feel rapport for their teachable agent [16] they are more likely to benefit. Others have demonstrated that learners can feel at once more responsible for their agent and believe the onus of failure belongs to the agent, easing the negative repercussions of failure [18]. Heightened feelings of responsibility for the agent can also lead to greater benefits from teaching the agent [17]. These responses may be enhanced by learners' feelings of rapport; within a teachable agent context, greater feelings of rapport may facilitate learning.

While social dialogue has not been extensively explored with teachable agents and acoustic-prosodic signals have received even less attention, there is reason to believe both will enhance learning and rapport. Social dialogue has been shown to build rapport [6, 30, 31] and in pedagogical agents it has been shown to increase learning [6]. In terms of acoustic-prosodic signals, there is some evidence that manipulating the agent's para-verbal behavior can positively influence social factors [23]. However, there is still little known about the potential of automating these signals to influence learning; we seek to provide more insight here.

2.2   Acoustic-Prosodic Entrainment

Entrainment, known also as accommodation, occurs when dialogue partners adapt to each other during an interaction. Acoustic-prosodic entrainment occurs when two people adapt their manner of speaking, including their speaking rate, intensity (i.e. loudness), or pitch (i.e. tone), to one another over a conversation. Explored in-depth in human-human dialogue, individuals can entrain in several ways. The most common forms are known as proximity, convergence, and synchrony. Proximity occurs when individuals match one another. Convergence occurs when speakers gradually grow closer. Synchrony is when speakers adapt in the same direction but do not match one another.

Explorations of automated entrainment are still in the early stages. Three studies have explored entrainment. Levitan and colleagues conducted a small pilot and found people unconsciously trusted an agent entraining proximally on speaking rate and intensity [11]. In our own work, we found college students felt more social presence for a teachable robot entraining proximally on pitch; learning was not affected [12]. Sadoughi and colleagues implemented a model of synchrony on pitch and intensity [10]. Varying whether the robot entrained in the first or second half of the interaction, children had higher engagement with the robot which began with entrainment

In contrast to this previous work, we implement entrainment as pitch convergence. In our own prior work, we implemented entrainment as proximity, matching the robot's pitch to the user's pitch. Both proximity and convergence on pitch have been found to be related to learning [25, 26] and rapport [27]. However, convergence rather than proximity may be more optimal for building rapport. Tickle-Degnen and Rosenthal suggest that the experience of rapport can be observed though behavioral correlates as they change over time [28]; for example, as rapport increases over time, coordination between partners also increases. Proximity does not have a temporal element but convergence does. Convergence is a form of increasing coordination as two speakers become more similar over time. An agent which converges may build more rapport and a partner who feels more rapport may learn more due to the social motivations in 2.1.

2.3 Gender

There is increasing evidence suggesting gender is an indicator of underlying individual differences which influence how individuals respond to social agents. Min and colleagues recently found that females were significantly more engaged with a narrative agent than males [24]. Other work has also suggested social behaviors are more favorable to females [21, 33]. This evidence suggests females respond more strongly to social interventions. There is, however, some work which has found no gender differences [34]. Additional analyses of gender are needed to understand these individual differences which may be indexed by gender. We include gender here, with the expectation that females may respond more strongly to social dialogue with entrainment.

3 Nico: An Entraining, Social Teachable Robot

Nico is an autonomous, social teachable Nao robot for middle school mathematics. Learners, using spoken dialogue and a tablet interface (MS Surface), teach Nico how to solve ratio word problems based on the Common Core Standards [29]. An example problem as displayed on the tablet interface is depicted in Fig. 1. For each problem, Nico and the learner are given partial information; Nico requests the learner's help to solve for missing information. We describe the overall system design for Nico in the next section, followed by the social dialogue design, and the entrainment module.

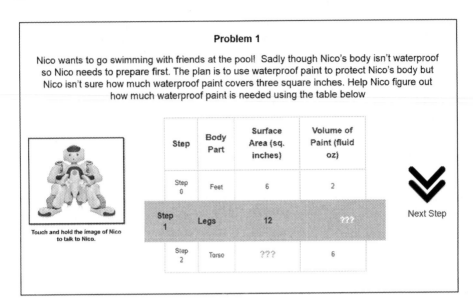

Fig. 1. Example problem in the tablet interface with current problem/step highlighted.

3.1   System

Learners are given a set of problems to teach Nico. The tablet interface displays visual progress to the learner as they move through the problems. Speech recognition is supported through the interface; to speak to Nico, the learner presses a button on the interface. After they are finished speaking, a notice appears on the interface indicating that Nico is 'thinking' while the system processes the input. Average response time is around four seconds. The interface tracks progress as the learner guides Nico through each problem step at their own pace, using buttons to advance forward with the current step highlighted and enlarged on the screen. When Nico 'answers' a step, the corresponding table cell is updated from question marks (see Fig. 1) to the correct answer.

When a learner speaks, the dialogue system depicted in Fig. 2 is engaged. The dialogue system processes the learner's speech, identifies a response, and transforms the response, depending on the condition. The interface captures the user's speech using the tablet's default microphone, and speech recognition is performed using the Google Speech API. The dialogue manager takes as input the recognized speech as well as the current problem and step. Utilizing the Artificial Intelligence Markup Language (AIML) [41], the dialogue manager identifies an appropriate response. Nico's responses are designed to encourage learning by prompting for explanations and providing feedback to encourage learners to feel that they are succeeding in helping Nico. This baseline dialogue is meant to foster learning by encouraging students to attend to the problem and elaborate on their knowledge [13]. An example of this dialogue is given in Table 1. Responses may then be transformed to entrain (see Sect. 3.3).

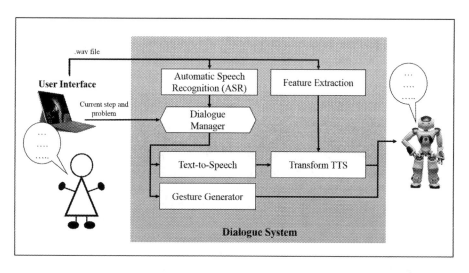

Fig. 2. Dialogue system for Nico

Table 1. Example of non-social and social dialogues

	Non-social dialogue	Social dialogue	Strategy
Nico:	Okay so I setup a ratio with 2.5 over 10. But then what do I do?	*Awesome*! So, *we* setup a ratio with 2.5 over 10. But then what do *we* do?	*Enthusiasm Inclusive*
Learner:	So, then you can reduce it or I guess simplify it to 1 over 4	So, then you can reduce it or I guess simplify it to 1 over 4	
Nico:	Oh, I simplify? How do you know I can do that?	*Sounds great*! So, *we* simplify? How do *we* know *we* can do that?	*Enthusiasm Inclusive*
Learner:	Because we know that 2.5 can go into 10 four times	Because we know that 2.5 can go into 10 four times	
Nico:	Oh, I get it. So, then I have 1 over 4?	Oh, I get it! *Thank you for explaining, [learner name]. You're a great tutor.* So, then *we* have 1 over 4?	*Politeness Praise Name usage*

The dialogue system also introduces gesture. After an appropriate verbal response is identified, the gesture generator determines whether there is a corresponding gesture from a set of eight emblematic or easily recognizable gestures. These include waving 'hello,' nodding head as in 'yes,' shaking head as in 'no,' putting hands on hip to make a point, raising either hand, raising hands in celebration, and shrugging. The system identifies a gesture based on the content of Nico's utterance and times the behavior to the utterance. We also enabled "autonomous life", a default capability in the Nao robot which introduces a slight, swaying movement and listening behavior. Gesture and autonomous life are present in all three conditions and occur at the same rate.

3.2 Social Dialogue

By introducing social dialogue, we hope to replicate the effects of prior work demonstrating that social dialogue can positively influence learning and build rapport. We design Nico's dialogue to be social based on dialogue behaviors from prior work and on theories of rapport. One theory of rapport [30, 43] suggests an individual's use of linguistic politeness is a method for managing rapport. For example, if an individual praises their dialogue partner, this may positively enhance their partner's feelings towards them. If they are rude, this may introduce face-threat, hindering rapport. Following this theory, we utilize verbal behaviors indicative of linguistic politeness such as name usage, inclusive language, praise, and politeness. These verbal behaviors have been found to lead to more rapport in peer tutoring [31]. In addition, enthusiasm and off-task dialogue were found to lead to greater feelings of self-efficacy and learning [3, 6, 7]. We introduce social dialogue as using the learner's name, inclusive language, praise, enthusiasm, and off-task dialogue. Table 1 illustrates Nico's social and non-social dialogue responses to examples of potential student dialogue.

3.3 Acoustic-Prosodic Entrainment: Pitch Convergence

We implement a method for entrainment known as *local convergence* on a single acoustic-prosodic feature, pitch. Convergence occurs when individuals adapt over time to their speaking partner; local convergence refers to this phenomenon happening on a local, turn-by-turn level. Individuals converge towards one another over a series of turns and then 'reset,' moving apart, typically when there is a change in topic or context.

We explore local convergence on pitch by gradually matching Nico's mean pitch to the learner's mean pitch over a series of turns. The mean pitch refers to the average pitch of a speaker's entire turn or utterance. Nico will speak with a mean pitch that is closer and closer to the learner's at each turn. When Nico and the learner move to a new problem, Nico will 'reset' and temporarily stop converging for one turn. Nico has a baseline pitch of approximately 230 Hz. To 'reset,' Nico speaks with a pitch at that baseline. Figure 3 depicts the changing mean pitch values as Nico converges and resets to the learner over a series of turns across two problems.

More specifically, our entrainment algorithm adapts the mean pitch of Nico's utterance utilizing a method which was previously found to produce high ratings of rapport and was perceived to be as natural as regular text-to-speech (TTS) [32]. This method involves generating the non-transformed TTS output and then shifting that output up or down such that the overall mean pitch of Nico's utterance matches a target value. That target value is calculated using the mean pitch of the learner's turn immediately prior. This work differs from previous work in the calculation of the target value. In our previous work, the robot mirrored the learner's pitch exactly, meaning the target value was the mean pitch from the learner's utterance, *target value = learner pitch* [12]. In this work, the calculation mimics local convergence by considering the number of turns

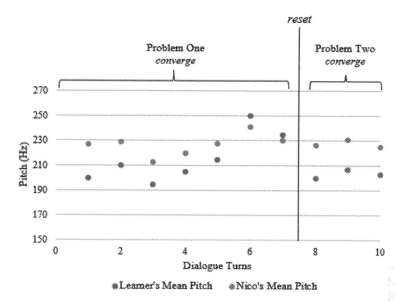

Fig. 3. Mean pitch values for a learner and Nico with entrainment

which have passed, whether this is a new problem, and Nico's current mean pitch. Within a single problem context, the distance between Nico's mean pitch and the learner's mean pitch is gradually reduced. The target value to shift Nico's pitch is determined by the learner's pitch and the number of exchanges that have passed (one exchange = learner speaks, Nico speaks). Depending on the number of exchanges that have passed, Nico's pitch is shifted to be within a certain range of the learner's pitch (e.g., 0–1 exchanges: 50 Hz, 2 exchanges: 40 Hz, …, >8 exchanges: 0 Hz). Thus, after 8 exchanges, Nico's mean pitch will equal the learner's mean pitch.

One additional restriction is placed on the adaptation. Nico will only adapt up to ±75 Hz, to reflect a realistic entrainment distance. Nico speaks with the same voice for both males and females, a version of the default Nao text-to-speech voice, with a baseline pitch of 230 Hz. This means Nico will adapt within the range of 155 Hz–305 Hz. We validated the pitch convergence with four middle school students (2 female/2 male).

4   Study

We conducted a between-subjects experiment in which learners teach Nico how to solve ratio-based problems in one of three conditions: (1) **non-social**: Nico exhibits dialogue meant to foster a learning experience and does not introduce social dialogue or entrainment, (2) **social**: Nico encourages social interaction and rapport through social dialogue, and (3) **social + entrainment**: Nico introduces equivalent social dialogue and additionally entrains via convergence on pitch. Across all three conditions, the experimenter instructions and the content of the activity were held constant.

Participants were 72 middle-school students from two public middle schools in the Southwestern United States. 51% of the students were recruited from one school and 49% from the other, with a mean age of 11.25 (SD = 0.47). The gender breakdown is given in Table 2. Sessions lasted 60 min and took place at the participant's school. As shown in Fig. 4, students sat a desk with a Surface Pro tablet in front of them. Nico stood on the desk next to the Surface Pro, to the right of the participant. Three participants experienced technical issues during the experiment and were excluded from the results. Thus, 22 participants remained in the non-social, 23 participants in the social condition, and 24 participants in the social + entrainment condition.

Table 2. Gender breakdown and dialogue statistics per session

	Females	Males	Total Turns M (SD)	Words per Turn M (SD)
Control	13	11	141.7 (37.0)	8.13 (4.5)
Social dialogue	13	11	124.9 (28.6)	8.56 (3.4)
Social dialogue + Entrainment	13	11	123.8 (26.5)	10.7 (4.9)

Fig. 4. Students interacting with Nico at the two middle schools

Participants began with a 10-min pretest and a short pre-survey to evaluate their initial self-efficacy towards math and tutoring. The participants were then given a few minutes to review the ratio problems and the worked-out solutions. After watching a short video depicting how to interact with Nico, students engaged in a teaching activity with Nico for 30 min. After the activity, they completed a 10-min posttest and a short survey on self-efficacy, rapport, and their goals. Given the scope of this paper and the focus on learning and rapport, we do not explore effects of self-efficacy here.

We measured rapport with 12 questions that we designed and developed based on Tickle-Degnen and Rosenthal's understanding of rapport as being composed of three parts: attention, positivity, and coordination [28]. We developed questions for positivity and attention; we drew upon measures proposed by Sinha and Cassell [26] for coordination. Given our age group, we designed and iterated over the questions in a series of 14 pilot studies, adjusting the questions to target the desired measures and be understandable to middle schoolers. We finalized four questions assessing positivity, four questions measuring attention, and four questions for coordination[1]. We averaged the rapport questions to create a single representative construct with an acceptable internal reliability (Cronbach's $\alpha = 0.83$). To measure learning, we utilized a pretest-posttest design with an A and B form of the test. The two forms were isomorphic and counterbalanced within condition (half of the participants in each condition received test A as the pretest and test B as the posttest, and vice versa). The tests consisted of 10 procedural and conceptual questions around ratios. As with the rapport measures, we piloted and iterated on the design of the questions through 14 pilot studies. We calculated the normalized learning gains according to Hake [36]. If the posttest was lower than the pretest, we used Eq. (2):

$$gain = (posttest - pretest)/(1 - pretest) \qquad (1)$$

$$gain = (posttest - pretest)/(pretest) \qquad (2)$$

5   Results

In this section, we report the results for learning and rapport where individuals interacted with Nico, our teachable robot, in one of three conditions: a **social-entraining** condition where Nico was both social and entrained, a **social** condition where Nico was only social, and a **non-social** where Nico was neither social nor entrained. Studies were conducted across two schools. After analyzing differences between schools, there were no significant differences or interactions with school by condition or gender on learning or rapport. We therefore report the results without the additional factor of school.

5.1   Learning

With learning, we hypothesized that the social-entraining condition would result in greater learning than the social and non-social baselines. We verified this hypothesis by analyzing learning gains in a two-way analysis of variance (ANOVA) with condition and gender as the independent variables and gain as the dependent variable. The means and standard deviations for gain by condition and gender are in Table 3. The gain was significantly different across conditions, $F(2, 63) = 6.06$, $p = 0.004$. Partial eta squared was .16, meaning the effect size was medium. We did not find that gender to be significant, $F(1, 63) = .05$, $p = .82$ and the gender by condition interaction was not significant $F(2, 63) = 2.13$, $p = 0.12$. Tukey post-hoc analyses indicated significant pairwise differences for the social-entraining condition when compared to the non-social. The social-entraining condition was significantly higher than the non-social ($p = .005$). The social condition approached a significantly higher gain than the non-social ($p = .06$). The social-entraining condition was not significantly higher than the social condition ($p = .6$).

---

[1] Survey questions can be found at www.public.asu.edu/~nlubold/surveys/nico_rapport.pdf

Table 3. Means and standard deviations for learning gains and rapport across condition and by gender.

	Non-Social		Social		Social-Entraining	
	Males	Females	Males	Females	Males	Females
Learning Gain	−.11 (.5)	.02 (.34)	.13 (.17)	.17 (.24)	.34 (.2)	.13 (.12)
Rapport	4.0 (.7)	4.3 (.4)	4.2 (.7)	3.8 (.9)	4.1 (.7)	4.2 (.6)

We had hypothesized that the social-entraining condition would result in higher learning gains. Our hypothesis was partially validated; we found that the addition of entrainment results in the highest learning gains and that it was significantly higher than the non-social control. Our hypothesis regarding gender was not verified. We did not find differences in regards learning by gender on the introduction of social behaviors.

5.2 Rapport

We had hypothesized that rapport might increase for the social and the social-entraining conditions. Given prior work, we expected that social dialogue and entrainment might influence rapport and that rapport may be related to learning. The self-reported means and standard deviations for rapport by condition and gender are also in Table 3. We first explored if rapport and gain were correlated but found they were not: Pearson's $r = −.115$, $p = .347$. We then explored if rapport differed by condition by analyzing rapport in an ANOVA with condition and gender as independent variables. We found our hypothesis was rejected. There were no significant differences in rapport across conditions, $F(2, 63) = .751$, $p = .48$, $\eta^2 = 0.02$. There was also no effect of gender, $F(1, 63) = .04$, $p = .84$, $\eta^2 = .001$ or gender by condition, $F(2, 63) = 1.49$, $p = .23$, $\eta^2 = 0.04$.

We found the lack of difference in self-reported rapport across conditions surprising, especially given that there were significant differences in learning. Prior work has suggested that the length of dialogue turns may play a role in learning and potentially rapport [39, 40]. Every learner interacted with Nico for thirty minutes regardless of condition but there may have been differences in number of turns and words per turn issued by each learner. Table 2 gives the means and standard deviations. We explored whether the total number of dialogue turns and average number of words per turn played any role in responses. We did not find any differences across conditions in the number of turns exchanged, $F(2, 63) = 1.22$, $p = .30$, or the number of words used, $F(2,63) = 1.7$, $p = .19$. We did not find a significant influence of turns or words on rapport or learning.

6   Discussion

Paraverbal manipulation is a less-explored modality in learning companions but it has potential for influencing learning. In this work, we explored paraverbal manipulation with our teachable robot, Nico. Nico adapted its pitch to that of the student as the student taught Nico. We were interested in effects of acoustic-prosodic adaptation on learning;

we hypothesized that interactions with the social, entraining version of Nico would result in higher learning gains. Our hypothesis regarding learning was validated; the addition of entrainment with social dialogue significantly improved learning and the learning gains were significantly higher than when Nico did not speak socially and did not entrain. This is the first time that an implementation of acoustic-prosodic entrainment in an agent has shown positive effects on learning, and suggests that entrainment may be useful mechanism for enhancing learning interactions with agents.

We also hypothesized that measures of rapport would increase with the social and the social-entraining conditions as compared to the non-social baseline. Our hypothesis was not validated; self-reported rapport was reported at high and consistent levels across conditions. There are several possible explanations. One is that Nico was very successful in building rapport across all conditions and that our measure was at ceiling. An alternative possibility is that a single post-session survey does not capture the dynamic changes in rapport which occur during interaction and may be more influential to learning. Future work will include assessing behavioral rapport as it changed within interactions, and its relationship to learning across conditions.

Another possibility is that our measure for rapport was accurate, and our conditions simply did not influence social factors but instead influenced cognitive factors. Entrainment has been hypothesized to have social origins but alternative theories have suggested it has a cognitive function as well. The Interactive Alignment Model (IAM) [35] suggests entrainment is an outcome of individuals aligning on their understanding and knowledge of a situation. It is possible our implementation of entrainment facilitated the learners' convergence towards Nico and a deeper understanding of the problem.

For example, the learner might explain to Nico that Nico "*needs to multiply by two.*" Nico will elaborate on this statement, recognizing the need to multiply by two because there are twice as many bags, "*Oh because we have two more bags? We have twice as many and multiply by two?*" Even though learners are given the worked-out solutions, they may not always have full domain knowledge and so Nico's queries lead to deeper understanding of the problem. With local convergence, learners are invited to converge to Nico and Nico's understanding. As Nico and the learner converge, this may facilitate deeper understanding of the domain content. There is evidence that this may occur in human-human peer tutoring. Sinha and Cassell [26] explored relationships of learning, convergence and rapport in dyads of peer tutors with a mean age of 13. They found that the individual who influences entrainment or induces the other speaker to entrain 'to' them, has higher learning gains. They suggest that a virtual peer that both converges to its human partner and invites convergence may be a more effective learning partner. Future work will include exploring the degree to which individuals entrained to Nico and how this may have led to learning considering the cognitive mechanism of IAM.

Finally, we did not observe any differences by gender. We had hypothesized that females might respond to the social behaviors more favorably. That we did not find differences is not unusual, but it may be due to our rapport measure or that we were unsuccessful in influencing the social factors which gave rise to gender differences in other work. In our future work, we intend to explore whether individuals responded differently on other dimensions which may be related to gender differences, including comfort-level in interacting with robots and interactional goals for teaching a robot.

7 Conclusions

In this paper, we explored how acoustic-prosodic entrainment influences learning and rapport in interactions with a social, teachable robot. This is the first evidence of automated entrainment in a pedagogical agent to find a significant effect on learning. In our future work, we plan on exploring how the cognitive mechanism of entrainment may be at work in these interactions and how other measures of rapport might provide insight into how entrainment and social dialogue influence rapport responses.

Acknowledgements. This work is supported by the National Robotics Initiative and the National Science Foundation, grant # CISE-IIS-1637809. We would also like to thank Samantha Baker and Ishrat Ahmed for their help in setting up this study and the data collection process.

References

1. Blanchard, E.G., Volfson, B., Hong, Y.J., Lajoie, S.P.: Affective artificial intelligence in education: from detection to adaptation. In: AIED, pp. 81–88. Springer, Heidelberg (2009)
2. Girard, S., Chavez-Echeagaray, M.E., Gonzalez-Sanchez, J., Hidalgo-Pontet, Y., Zhang, L., Burleson, W., VanLehn, K.: Defining the behavior of an affective learning companion in the affective meta-tutor project. In: Lane, H.C., Yacef, K., Mostow, J., Pavlik, P. (eds.) AIED 2013. LNCS (LNAI), vol. 7926, pp. 21–30. Springer, Heidelberg (2013). https://doi.org/10.1007/978-3-642-39112-5_3
3. Lane, H.C., Cahill, C., Foutz, S., Auerbach, D., Noren, D., Lussenhop, C., Swartout, W.: The effects of a pedagogical agent for informal science education on learner behaviors and self-efficacy. In: Lane, H.C., Yacef, K., Mostow, J., Pavlik, P. (eds.) AIED 2013. LNCS (LNAI), vol. 7926, pp. 309–318. Springer, Heidelberg (2013). https://doi.org/10.1007/978-3-642-39112-5_32
4. Afzal, S., Robinson, P.: A study of affect in intelligent tutoring. In: Workshop on Modeling and Scaffolding Affective Experiences to Impact Learning, vol. 57 (2006)
5. McDaniel, B.T., et al.: Facial features for affective state detection in learning environments. In: Proceedings of the Annual Meeting of the Cognitive Science Society, vol. 29 (2007)
6. Gulz, A., Haake, M., Silvervarg, A.: Extending a teachable agent with a social conversation module – effects on student experiences and learning. In: Biswas, G., Bull, S., Kay, J., Mitrovic, A. (eds.) AIED 2011. LNCS (LNAI), vol. 6738, pp. 106–114. Springer, Heidelberg (2011). https://doi.org/10.1007/978-3-642-21869-9_16
7. Kumar, R., Ai, H., Beuth, J.L., Rosé, C.P.: Socially capable conversational tutors can be effective in collaborative learning situations. In: Aleven, V., Kay, J., Mostow, J. (eds.) ITS 2010. LNCS, vol. 6094, pp. 156–164. Springer, Heidelberg (2010). https://doi.org/10.1007/978-3-642-13388-6_20
8. Gallois, C., Giles, H.: Communication accommodation theory. The International Encyclopedia of Language and Social Interaction (2015)
9. Giles, H.: A new theory of the dynamics of speech. Diogenes **106**, 119–136 (1979)

10. Sadoughi, N., Pereira, A., Jain, R., Leite, I., Lehman, J.F.: Creating prosodic synchrony for a robot co-player in a speech-controlled game for children. In: HRI, pp. 91–99. ACM (2017)
11. Levitan, R., et al.: Implementing acoustic-prosodic entrainment in a conversational avatar. In: INTERSPEECH, vol. 16, pp. 1166–1170 (2016)
12. Lubold, N., Walker, E., Pon-Barry, H.: Effects of voice-adaptation and social dialogue on perceptions of a robotic learning companion. In: HRI, pp. 255–262. IEEE (2016)
13. Roscoe, R.D., Chi, M.T.: Understanding tutor learning: knowledge-building and knowledge-telling in peer tutors' explanations and questions. Rev. Educ. Res. **77**(4), 534–574 (2007)
14. Leelawong, K., Biswas, G.: Designing learning by teaching agents: the betty's brain system. Int. J. Artif. Intell. Educ. **18**(3), 181–208 (2008)
15. Pareto, L., Arvemo, T., Dahl, Y., Haake, M., Gulz, A.: A teachable-agent arithmetic game's effects on mathematics understanding, attitude and self-efficacy. In: Biswas, G., Bull, S., Kay, J., Mitrovic, A. (eds.) AIED 2011. LNCS (LNAI), vol. 6738, pp. 247–255. Springer, Heidelberg (2011). https://doi.org/10.1007/978-3-642-21869-9_33
16. Ogan, A., et al.: Oh dear stacy!: social interaction, elaboration, and learning with teachable agents. In: Proceedings of the SIGCHI Conference on Human Factors in Computing Systems, pp. 39–48. ACM (2012)
17. Biswas, G., Jeong, H., Kinnebrew, J.S., Sulcer, B., Roscoe, R.: Measuring self-regulated learning skills through social interactions in a teachable agent environment. Res. Pract. Technol. Enhanced Learn. **5**(02), 123–152 (2011)
18. Chase, C.C., Chin, D.B., Oppezzo, M.A., Schwartz, D.L.: Teachable agents and the protégé effect: increasing the effort towards learning. J. Sci. Educ. Technol. **18**(4), 334–352 (2009)
19. Hood, D., Lemaignan, S., Dillenbourg, P.: When children teach a robot to write: an autonomous teachable humanoid uses simulated handwriting. In: HRI, pp. 83–90. ACM (2015)
20. Tanaka, F., Matsuzoe, S.: Children teach a care-receiving robot to promote their learning: field experiments in a classroom for vocabulary learning. J. Hum.-Robot Interact. **1**(1) (2012)
21. Arroyo, I., et al.: Affective gendered learning companions. In: AIED, pp. 21–48 (2009)
22. Liu, P., Glas, D.F., Kanda, T., Ishiguro, H., Hagita, N.: It's not polite to point: generating socially appropriate deictic behaviors towards people. In: HRI, pp. 267–274. IEEE (2013)
23. Westlund, K., et al.: Flat vs. expressive storytelling: young children's learning and retention of a social robot's narrative. Front. Hum. Neurosci. **11**, 295 (2017)
24. Pezzullo, L.G., Wiggins, J.B., Frankosky, M.H., Min, W., Boyer, K.E., Mott, B.W., Wiebe, E.N., Lester, J.C.: "Thanks Alisha, keep in touch": gender effects and engagement with virtual learning companions. In: André, E., Baker, R., Hu, X., Rodrigo, M.M.T., du Boulay, B. (eds.) AIED 2017. LNCS (LNAI), vol. 10331, pp. 299–310. Springer, Cham (2017). https://doi.org/10.1007/978-3-319-61425-0_25
25. Thomason, J., Nguyen, H.V., Litman, D.: Prosodic entrainment and tutoring dialogue success. In: Lane, H.C., Yacef, K., Mostow, J., Pavlik, P. (eds.) AIED 2013. LNCS (LNAI), vol. 7926, pp. 750–753. Springer, Heidelberg (2013). https://doi.org/10.1007/978-3-642-39112-5_104
26. Sinha, T., Cassell, J.: We click, we align, we learn: impact of influence and convergence processes on student learning and rapport building. In: Proceedings of the 1st Workshop on Modeling INTERPERsonal SynchrONy And infLuence, pp. 13–20. ACM (2015)
27. Lubold, N., Pon-Barry, H.: Acoustic-prosodic entrainment and rapport in collaborative learning dialogues. In: Proceedings of the 2014 ACM Workshop on Multimodal Learning Analytics Workshop and Grand Challenge, pp. 5–12. ACM (2014)
28. Tickle-Degnen, L., Rosenthal, R.: The nature of rapport and its nonverbal correlates. Psychol. Inq. **1**(4), 285–293 (1990)

29. Common Core State Standards Initiative. Common Core State Standards for Mathematics. National Governors Association Center for Best Practices and the Council of Chief State School Officers, Washington, DC (2010)
30. Spencer-Oatey, H.: (Im) Politeness, face and perceptions of rapport: unpackaging their bases and interrelationships. Politeness Res. 1(1)(Im), 95–119 (2005)
31. Bell, D., Arnold, H., Haddock, R.: Linguistic politeness and peer tutoring. Learn. Assistance Rev. 14(1), pp. 37–54 (2009)
32. Lubold, N., Walker, E., Pon-Barry, H.: Naturalness and rapport in a pitch adaptive learning companion. In: ASRU, pp. 103–110. IEEE (2015)
33. Burleson, W., Picard, R.: Gender-specific approaches to developing emotionally intelligent learning companions. IEEE Intell. Syst. 22(4) (2007)
34. Saerbeck, M., Schut, T., Bartneck, C., Janse, M.D.: Expressive robots in education: varying the degree of social supportive behavior of a robotic tutor. In: Proceedings of the SIGCHI Conference on Human Factors in Computing Systems, pp. 1613–1622. ACM (2010)
35. Pickering, M.J., Garrod, S.: An integrated theory of language production and comprehension. Behav. Brain Sci. 36(4), 329–347 (2013)
36. Hake, R.R.: Relationship of individual student normalized learning gains in mechanics with gender, high-school physics, and pretest scores on mathematics and spatial visualization. In: Physics Education Research Conference, pp. 30–45, (2002)
37. Maldonado, H., et al.: We learn better together: enhancing elearning with emotional characters. In: CSCL, pp. 408–417. International Society of the Learning Sciences (2005)
38. Wang, N., et al.: the politeness effect. Int. J. Hum Comput Stud. 66, 96–112 (2008)
39. Litman, D.J., et al.: Spoken versus typed human and computer dialogue tutoring. Int. J. Artif. Intell. Educ. 16(2), 145–170 (2006)
40. Rosé, C.P., Bhembe, D., Siler, S., Srivastava, R., VanLehn, K.: The role of why questions in effective human tutoring. In: Hoppe, U., Verdejo, F., Kay, J. (eds.) AIED (2003)
41. Wallace, R.: The elements of AIML style. Alice AI Foundation (2003)
42. Kim, Y., Baylor, A., Shen, E.: Pedagogical agents as learning companions: the impact of agent emotion and gender. J. Comput. Assist. Learn. 23(3), 220–234 (2007)
43. Spencer-Oatey, H.: Managing rapport in talk: using rapport sensitive incidents to explore the motivational concerns underlying the management of relations. J. Pragmat. 34(5), 529–545 (2002)

The Influence of Gender, Personality, Cognitive and Affective Student Engagement on Academic Engagement in Educational Virtual Worlds

Anupam Makhija[1], Deborah Richards[1(✉)], Jesse de Haan[1,2],
Frank Dignum[2], and Michael J. Jacobson[3]

[1] Department of Computing, Macquarie University,
Macquarie Park, NSW 2109, Australia
{anupam.makhija,jesse.dehaan}@students.mq.edu.au,
deborah.richards@mq.edu.au
[2] Department of Information and Communication Sciences,
Utrecht University, Utrecht, Netherlands
{j.dehaanl,f.p.m.dignum}@uu.nl
[3] Sydney School of Education and Social Work,
Centre for Research on Learning and Innovation,
The University of Sydney, Camperdown, Australia
michael.jacobson@sydney.edu.au

Abstract. Educational virtual worlds (EVWs) are emerging as immersive learning environments that allow students to engage in experiential learning. However, understanding whether individual student differences influence learning behaviours and adapting the EVW accordingly has not been extensively investigated. This paper reports an experimental study with 115 undergraduate students to explore the link between their gender, personality, cognitive and affective engagement in relation to their academic engagement, measured by a quiz after using the world. We also explore whether providing hints can improve their academic engagement in the EVW. Only personal support (a factor of affective engagement) and intrinsic motivation (a factor of cognitive engagement) were found to be related to the quiz score. Also the personality dimension of Openness indicated student propensity to accept support.

Keywords: Educational virtual world · Personality · Big five factor
Affective engagement · Cognitive engagement · Academic engagement

1 Introduction

Virtual worlds are emerging as a potential platform for a variety of applications especially in the field of education and learning. A virtual world used for education is known as an educational virtual world (EVW). These computer-simulated environments are typically three-dimensional (3D) and have similarities to the real world, usually in the form of physics, movement or topography that enhance the illusion of presence. Though the merits of 2D versus 3D will depend on the learning context [1],

© Springer International Publishing AG, part of Springer Nature 2018
C. Penstein Rosé et al. (Eds.): AIED 2018, LNAI 10947, pp. 297–310, 2018.
https://doi.org/10.1007/978-3-319-93843-1_22

presence in 3D environments can aid experiential learning and can therefore be used to enhance education [2].

Educational virtual worlds have been used successfully in the past, most notably the online virtual world of Second Life that allows users to create avatars to represent themselves and interact with other users in the virtual world [3]. EVWs have capability to offer freedom of navigation for students to learn in their own pace and in their own way, providing features of remote learning [4]. These findings are further supported by Falloon [5] in reference to the features of educational virtual worlds enabling students to exhibit higher order thinking skills along with better communication.

Immersive, graphically rich learning environments seem compelling to increase student engagement, a factor associated with learning. However, as with the use of any educational technology, the technology itself does not guarantee learning. For example, the value of three-dimensional over two-dimensional will be dependent on the concepts to be learnt [1]. As well as different technology affordances, demographic factors such as age and gender and individual factors such as personality and engagement, have been found to significantly predict the way students learn new concepts and achieve the learning outcomes [6, 7]. The understanding of student personality traits and how well they are engaged with the content on different levels can provide additional insight in order to design educational virtual worlds that can deliver enhanced learning outcomes for users. Students with different personality traits and engagement levels may differ in the way they learn and what support they find useful. This study is guided by following research questions:

(1) *Does an individual's gender, personality, level of affective engagement or level of cognitive engagement influence their performance in a quiz after using an educational virtual world?*

(2) *Does the provision of hints assist some individuals more than others?*

This paper is structured as follows. The next section provides background to the study. Methodology appears in Sect. 3, followed by results and discussion in Sects. 4 and 5 respectively. The conclusion, future work and implications appear in the final sections of this paper.

2 Background

Understanding of personality traits in students can help to resolve issues of academic underachievement amongst students. Extensive numerous research studies have been conducted in past to examine the relationship between personality traits and performance [7–9]. For measuring personality, the most commonly used instrument is the Big Five Factor (BFF) model. The personality traits in this model are Openness, Conscientiousness, Extroversion, Agreeableness, Neuroticism sometimes also called OCEAN collectively [10, 11]. Openness trait relates to creativity while Neuroticism relates to emotional stability. Conscientious individuals have traits of being more organised, disciplined and hardworking. Agreeableness represents people with more sympathetic, thoughtful and cooperative nature. People with extravert trait are outgoing and friendly people who tend to form more social connections as compared to their introvert counterparts [12].

A related study done by Chamorro-Premuzic and Furnham [13] for university students emphasised that conscientiousness is a strong determinant of academic results. These ideas were further extended in another study in a school setting where they found that students with conscientious personality trait performed better in science subject [9]. Furnham and Monsen [9] also claimed that people with extravert personality are more interested in studies and perform better if they feel free and have more sense of freedom. Similar results have emerged from another study that points out that people with high level of openness and conscientiousness achieve success at university level [14]. In same direction, Eyong and David [7] revealed that conscientiousness and agreeability traits are associated with the performance of secondary school students in positive manner and focused on promoting the need to encourage students to gain these behavioural traits for better academic achievements.

Student engagement plays a vital role in shaping academic performance in various settings. Disengagement is considered to be a key factor influencing student dropout rates in schools. Understanding of students' engagement in learning context can provide new perspective to narrow the gap of academic achievements.

Student engagement is a multidimensional construct with four primary dimensions namely academic, behavioural, emotional, and cognitive engagement [15]. The first two types of engagement (academic and behaviour) can be objectively measured. Academic engagement can be measured using the variables such as time spent to complete the task or grades received. The level of behavioural engagement of a student can be represented by looking at their attendance, participation in class and extra-curricular activities. The other two types (cognitive and affective), also known as internal forms of engagement are as influential as academic and behavioural engagement but there are not sufficient research evidences to confirm their link with academic performance because of their less observable indicators. The cognitive engagement involves indicators related to self-learning, future goals and intrinsic motivation while affective engagement corresponds to the relationships with peers and teachers [16].

Many studies have explored the relationship between student engagement and student achievement [6, 17, 18]. Fredricks and Blumenfeld [15] demonstrated the positive association between engagement and academic achievement. A few other studies also suggested similar results but the links seemed to be weaker [6, 19].

3 Methodology

To answer the above research questions, we conducted an online study approved by the Macquarie University's Human Research Ethics Committee involving students using an educational virtual world. All participants were invited to participate via the online recruitment program of the Psychology Department and could choose our study to receive half an hour course credit for their participation.

3.1   Experimental Design

To measure whether tailored hints provided by the system improved quiz performance, participants were divided into four groups. Group formation is illustrated in the Fig. 1. Each group used the EVW in two separate rounds. In the first round, Group 1 and Group 2 did scenario 1 while Group 3 and Group 4 did Scenario 2. For second attempt (as shown in part D) Group 1 did scenario 2 receiving hints, referred to as S1/Hint group (S1H). Group 2 did scenario 2 without hints is referred to as S1/Control group (S1C). Group 3 did scenario 1 and received hints is referred to as S2/Hint group (S2H). Group 4 did scenario 1 and did not receive hints referred to as S2/Control group (S2C).

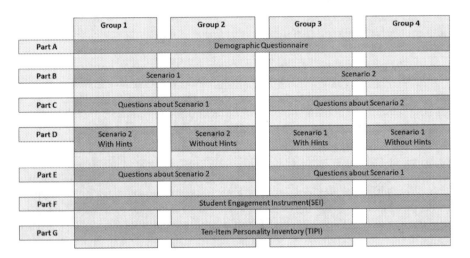

Fig. 1. Experimental groups

3.2   Materials and Methods

The EVW is an island known as Omosa, that is facing a problem with a certain species of animals dying out. The purpose of Omosa is to help students gain knowledge about biology and to learn and practice science inquiry skills. Omosa represents a fictitious island with five main locations: village, research lab, hunting ground, animal counting station and weather station that can be visited by students. There are virtual agents present on main locations that provide information to the students. Students may gather information by talking to these virtual agents and through observation. The animals that inhabit the island are intelligent agents that live in predator-prey relationships and demonstrate emergent behaviours according to the agent-based models that drive them. Omosa has been developed to be used over several class periods and to be used in conjunction with workbooks, use of Netlogo simulation software and classroom activities. For the purpose of this study to test our hints, the value of capturing cognitive and affective engagement and personality, we conducted a shorter study with undergraduate students that involved their navigation around the world, the collection of data and conversation with the Omosan virtual people and observation of the virtual animals. After their visit to Omosa, students were asked to answer a pre-defined set of questions based on the facts about the island covering scientific concepts about biological systems. Participants were allowed to navigate through the island following any path.

3.3   Procedure and Data Collection

Following informed consent, the study procedure took around 30 min and consisted of the following parts:

I.   Demographic questionnaire
II.   Interaction with EVW
III.   First EVW quiz
IV.   Second interaction with EVW
V.   Second EVW quiz
VI.   Personality Traits Questionnaire - Ten Item Personality Measure (TIPI)
VII.   Engagement Questionnaire - Student Engagement Inventory (SEI)

The study started with demographic questionnaire with participants. The demographic questionnaire included questions to extract participants' information related to gender, cultural group, age, and how many hours they play computer games per week.

The next step in this study involved use of virtual world by participants. There were two interactions with the EVW depending on which group participants belonged to, as illustrated in experimental design section. The educational virtual world described above in methodology section was used for this purpose.

Parts III and IV involved assessing the participants performance by asking ten relevant questions based on the information that was collected during navigation of virtual world either by conversing with the characters or by observing the environment. After both scenario, a set of ten questions were asked from each participant from all four groups (S1C, S1H, S2C, S2H) as illustrated in Table 1. One of the example of a question was, "What do the villagers usually eat?" The answer to this question can be obtained from one of the villager in the virtual world. We used the number of correct answers to categorise participants into groups to represent their performance in educational virtual world based (Low = 1 to 4 correct; Medium = 5 to 6 correct; High = 7 or more correct).

The online nature of study allowed more people to participate in their own time and place. The questionnaire was made using Qualtrics, a web site where surveys can be created. The virtual world was embedded within the survey to let participants complete it without the need to leave the survey website.

After each scenario, we asked participants how much on a scale of 1 to 5 they found the experience enjoyable, with 1 being not enjoyable, and 5 enjoyable. Participants were also asked to elaborate why they thought the experience was enjoyable or not. The participants were also asked for usefulness of the hints, if they belonged to a group where hints were given for second scenario. These strategies provide us with the possibility for better comprehension of the behaviour of participants and more sophisticated interpretation of data during analysis.

Participants also answered the Ten Item Personality Instrument (TIPI) that consisted of 10 questions. TIPI allows for a quick measurement of the Big-Five personality dimensions, extraversion, agreeableness, conscientiousness, emotional stability, and openness to experiences [11]. The instrument was included to gather data to determine the influence of participant's personality on the performance and the likelihood of being engaged with the virtual world. To measure cognitive and affective engagement we used the Student Engagement Instrument (SEI) [16]. SEI was designed for use on students in middle school, so we modified it for university students. For example, we replaced the word "school" with university. SEI includes 32 items, nineteen items to measure affective engagement and fourteen to measure cognitive engagement. Participants responded to statements by rating their level on likert scale of 1–4 with 1 indicating that they never felt or acted that way, and 4 indicating that they certainly acted that way.

The student's behavioural engagement was captured via their interactions within the world consisting of how many characters they spoke to, where they had visited, how long they were in the world, the number of navigation steps and navigational patterns. Academic engagement was captured via the number of correct answers (min = 0, max = 10) to the 10 questions in the quizzes given after using the EVW. The virtual world was deliberately laid out in such a way that participants may not always know what to do, or where to go next. Omosa is a fictitious world and thus the answers to the questions could not be based on prior knowledge. We did not ask students to self-report about behavioural or academic engagement.

To facilitate analysis, the data were transformed and prepared. Preparation included checking response values were valid and complete. First, data regarding participants' demographics were tabulated. This information was used to report the demographic characteristics of the participants. The demographic characteristics of age, gender, cultural group were also relevant to the current study. We calculated a score from 0–10 for each quiz. The quizzes included multiple choice questions, with one correct answer that received a score of 1. To answer the research questions and to identify potential significant relationships between the categorical variables such as gender, cultural groups, personality, different types of engagement levels and quiz scores, we calculated chi-square test on results.

4   Results

A sample of 115 undergraduate Psychology students participated in our study. Of the total number of respondents, 37 were male and 78 were female. Ages ranged from 17–33 with the mean age of these participants was 19.80 and standard deviation of 2.84. Only 43.48% of participants played computer games, for an average of 7.35 h per week, ranging from 1 h to 50 h. Groups 1, 2, 3, and 4 had 37 (S1H), 29 (S1C), 25 (S2H) and 24 (S2C), participants, respectively. Thus, a total of 62 were assigned to hints and 53 to control. While the Qualtrics randomiser equally distributed participants into each group, some participants chose to stop participation (possibly due to having to download and install the Unity3D EVW). The results regarding cultural background are shown in Table 1. We can see that there are two largest cultural groups "Oceania" (which includes Australia) and "South East Asia".

Table 1. Cultural background

Cultural group	%	N
Oceania	20	23
Northern-Western European	13.91%	16
Southern-Eastern European	10.43%	12
North African and Middle Eastern	9.57%	11
South-East Asian	20	23
North-East Asian	3.48%	4
Southern and Central Asian	6.09%	7
People of the Americas	0.87%	1
Sub-Saharan African	0.00%	0
I don't identify with any cultural group	15.65%	18
Total	100	115

4.1   Personality Data

Means were calculated for each of the five personality dimensions for each individual. We categorized each dimension into low, medium and high for better identification of patterns and profiles. Table 2 shows the data, further categorized by gender. Chi-square tests revealed no significant differences for gender and personality except for gender and agreeability $X2$ $(N = 115) = 10.31$, $p = 0.04$. A relationship between game playing characteristic and personality was also observed. Out of 65 people who play games, 39 (69.64%) are highly agreeable suggesting an association between agreeableness trait and playing games.

Table 2. Categorised personality results (L = low, M = medium, H = High)

	Openness				Conscientious				Extraversion				Agreeableness				Neuroticism			
	L	M	H	Total	L	M	H	Total	L	M	H	Total	L	M	H	Total	L	M	H	Total
Female	9	27	42	78	8	38	32	78	20	32	26	78	3	29	46	78	24	28	26	78
Male	3	11	23	37	3	19	15	37	10	14	13	37	3	24	10	37	7	9	21	37
Total	12	38	65	115	11	57	47	115	30	46	39	115	6	53	56	115	31	37	47	115

4.2   Engagement Data

Affective engagement (AE) is comprised of: Teacher-Student Relationships (TSR) (mean = 1.66, s.d = 0.62), Peer Support at School (PSS) (mean = 1.73, s.d = 0.64), Family Support for Learning (FSL) (mean = 1.72, s.d = 0.63), Cognitive engagement (CE) is comprised of Control and Relevance of School Work (CRSW) (mean = 1.21, s.d = 0.45), Future Aspirations and Goals (FG) (mean = 1.78, s.d = 0.62), Intrinsic Motivation (IM) (mean = 1.97, s.d = 0.73). For comparison we categorized the mean results into low, high and medium as shown in Table 3. After averaging the results for the three components in each type of engagement, 58 (50.43%) participants had high AE and 57 (49.57%) had low AE; 77 (66.96%) participants had high CE and 38 (33.04%) had low CE.

Table 3. Number of participants in engagement categories. **TSR** = Teacher-Student Relationships, **PSS** = Peer Support at School, **FSL** = Family Support for Learning, **CRSW** = Control and Relevance of School Work, **FG** = Future Aspirations and Goals, **IM** = Intrinsic Motivation

Category	TSR		PSS		FSL		CRSW		FG		IM	
Low < 3	48	41.74%	43	37.39%	43	37.39%	93	80.87%	37	32.17%	33	28.70%
Mid >=3	58	50.43%	60	52.17%	61	53.04%	20	17.39%	66	57.39%	53	46.09%
High >=3.5	9	7.83%	12	10.43%	12	9.57%	2	1.74%	12	10.43%	29	25.22%

Cross tabulations showed that out of 38 participants with high cognitive engagement, 84.21% have high affective engagement and out of 77 participants with low cognitive engagement, 67.53% also have low affective engagement. Participants with high affective engagements, 56.14% of the 57 are also highly engaged cognitively. Similar results are observed for all groups, including those receiving hints or not. Chi-square tests revealed significant relationship between cognitive and affective engagement $X2$ (N = 115) = 27.25, p = 0.00.

Chi-square tests reveal significant associations between some personality dimensions and engagement levels: affective engagement and disorganised $X2$ (N = 115) = 20.64, p = 0.00; cognitive engagement and disorganised $X2$ (N = 115) = 40.15, p = 0.00; cognitive engagement and conscientiousness $X2$ (N = 115) = 9.24, p = 0.01.

Cross tabulations showed that participants with low affective engagement most commonly (44.83%) chose the Likert scale option "agree a little to being disorganised and careless. Whereas, participants with high affective engagement most commonly (33.33%) chose "disagree moderately" to being disorganized and careless. This suggests that organised people are more affectively engaged. Regarding being disorganised, 37.66% of participants with low CE "agreed a little" along with 10.39% who "agreed moderately", whereas 47.37% participants of participants with high CE chose 'disagree moderately' and 5.26% chose 'disagree a little'. Highly cognitively engaged participants, were also more likely (60.53%) to score high for the conscientiousness personality dimensions. These results show a link between being organised and conscientious and is related positively to being cognitive engaged.

Chi-square tests revealed a significant relationship between game playing behaviour and cognitive engagement $X2$ (N = 115) = 4.88, p = 0.03. People who do not play games were more cognitively engaged. There were 38 people with high cognitive engagement. 71.05% of them do not play games. From 77 (66.96%) participants who are low on cognitive engagement category, 50.65% play games.

4.3   Performance Scores

For each treatment group we calculated the average number of correct answers in Table 4. The categorized quiz scores are compared with levels of affective and cognitive engagement in Table 5.

Chi-square tests comparing gender with quiz scores and engagement variables for any scenario did not reveal any significant

Table 4. Correct answers for each Group

Group	N participants	Avg.	Quiz 1 correct answers	Quiz 2 answers
S1Control	29	5.43	4.5	6.4
S1Hints	37	5.6	4.6	6.6
S2Control	24	4.46	3.8	5.2
S2Hints	25	5.74	5.0	6.5

differences. Cultural group shows statistical significant difference in results with quiz 2 score $X2$ (N = 115) = 29.93, p = 0.04. Oceania (27.27%) and Northern Western European (21.82%) groups are the highest scoring groups for quiz score 2 as compared to other cultural groups while for first scenario there were far less people in high scoring group and most participants belonged to Oceania group (35.71%). There was also a link between quiz scores and playing games in both scenarios. People who played games tended to perform less 46/65 (70.77%). This is further confirmed from second scenario where 61.76% students scored mid and 29.23% students scored low. The results do not show any statistical differences for CE and quiz scores for any of the attempt but looking at the data we can see that 65.79% of high CE people scored low in first scenario but this number reduced to 23.68% for second scenario.

Table 5. Quiz 1 (top) and Quiz 2 (bottom) scores by category (L = low, M = medium, H = high, T = Total) compared with engagement categories;

	Affective engagement (n %)						Cognitive engagement (n %)							
	Low		Medium		High		Low		Medium		High		Total	
Q L	32	48.48	32	48.48	2	3.03	41	62.12	23	34.85	2	3.03	66	57.39
1M	14	66.67	5	23.81	2	9.52	15	71.43	4	19.05	2	9.52	21	18.26
H	12	42.86	16	57.14	0	0	21	75	6	21.43	1	3.57	28	24.35
Q L	14	53.85	10	38.46	2	7.69	17	65.38	8	30.77	1	3.85	26	22.61
2M	14	41.18	18	52.94	2	5.88	21	61.76	10	29.41	3	8.82	34	29.57
H	30	54.55	25	45.45	0	0	39	70.91	15	27.27	1	1.82	55	47.83
T	58	50.43	53	46.09	4	3.48	77	66.96	33	28.7	5	4.35	115	100

We also tested the relationship between individual engagement factors and performance score for different groups. For hint groups (Group 1 and 3), the chi-square test showed the significant difference between Peer Support at School (PSS) variable and quiz score 1 X2 (N = 62) = 12.84, p = 0.01 for hint groups. There are 26 students with low PSS category. 53.85% of them scored low quiz score for attempt 1. While for second attempt, there is improvement in scores for this category with 65.38% in high quiz score category.

For all groups, the chi-square test showed statistically significant different results for Peer Support at School (PSS) variable with the quiz score 1 X2 (N = 115) = 10.43, p = 0.03, demonstrating statistical differences between these two variables. For all groups that is mix of students with hints and no hints, there are 43 people with low PSS category and 58.14% scored low but for second scenario 53.49% scored high. As some of the students with low PSS score received hints, explains the reason of improvement for people with low PSS score as described for above relation.

On average participants answered 6.23 questions correct in second scenario as compared to 4.47 questions correct in the first scenario. All personality types showed an improvement after the first scenario. Most participants (67.82%) in all groups performed better for second scenario however the improvement for hint groups is more than the control groups.

Table 6 presents the summary data for participants who scored high in the quizzes and personality dimensions. We calculated chi-square test on personality and performance results. For all groups, chi-square tests reveal significant differences in performance (measured by the quiz) between participants with different levels of openness (X2 (N = 115) = 8.86, p = 0.06). The majority (56.52%) of participants scored high on the Openness personality dimension; just over half (50.7%) of these achieved a score of 4/10 or less in the quiz test, while 29.23% achieved a score of 7/10 or over. These high achievers represent 67.86% of the participants achieving a high score. No significant differences were found between Openness and the second quiz score. We note that the participants in the bottom 10% did not improve their score. So the hints or practice did not help. This is in contrast to the medium and high achieving categories, where for example, the percentage of low achievers with high Openness reduced to 20% (from 50.7%) after the second round.

Table 6. Participants in high personality categories with high quiz scores

Categories		Openness		Conscientious		Extroversion		Agreeableness		Neurotic	
Score 1	28	19	67.86%	12	42.86%	8	28.57%	10	35.71%	11	39.29%
Score 2	55	35	63.64%	22	40%	21	38.18%	23	41.82%	21	38.18%

5   Discussion

The goal of this study is to investigate the influence of personality and engagement (Cognitive and Affective) on the students' performance in an EVW. We also investigated whether gender, gaming hours, and providing hints influenced performance. In this paper, measurement of performance was restricted to the quiz scores achieved.

We did not include in our analyses any of the behavioural engagement data. In a previous study we captured navigation data, identified navigation path patterns and analysed navigation paths to identify their relationship to quiz score in order to derive suitable tips [20]. We used those patterns to provide tips that were used in the study presented in this paper. A forthcoming paper focuses on the relationship between scores, hints and navigation paths, but does not consider any other factors [21]. We have yet to combine the navigation data with the data presented in this paper. We also intend to look at performance as measured by time spent in the world. The goal of this body of work is to increase our understanding of the learner and their performance in EVWs, to gain insights for effective EVW learning design and how the EVW should adapt according to specific student features and needs.

The literature suggests a strong positive correlation between student engagement and student achievement [6, 15, 17, 18]. The results of this study (Table 5) show that some students with low engagement were able to achieve high scores, and overall 57.39% of students (61.12% with low cognitive engagement compared to 48.48% with low affective engagement) achieved a low score in the first quiz, and more than half of these students were able to improve their score after using the EVW a second time. This is probably because students were unfamiliar with the EVW and what was expected of them, but in the second round they applied the knowledge and experience gained from the first round. This was true regardless of whether they were in the hints or control group. In answer to the first research question, we cannot, in general, confirm a relationship between levels of engagement and performance, although our results show some evidence of relationships of individual engagement categories (i.e. peer support at school (PSS) and intrinsic motivation (IM)) with performance.

Consistent with the literature, the results do confirm a positive relationship between affective engagement with cognitive engagement. The students who are highly engaged in affective manner are also engaged cognitively as well and vice versa. This result is supported by same pattern for control groups and hint groups as well with statistical significant results. While the differences are not significant, our results show evidence that students with high cognitive engagement improved more as compared to low cognitively engaged students in their second scenario.

Regarding the influence of personality, our cohort had a majority of people with high Openness personality dimension and most of this category attained high score for scenario 1. Low achievers with high Openness performed better in their second attempt. This supports the argument that people with open personalities are more creative and curious. They tend to perform better in subsequent tasks with their creative ideas. Our results indicated positive relationship between openness to experience and performance, consistent with other relevant study [14]. It appears that they learnt from their experience from using the EVW for the first time. This improvement was true whether participants received hints or not.

Participants who are more organized have higher level of affective and cognitive engagement as compared to disorganized individuals (with low conscientiousness personality trait). This suggests that organized people are more engaged. Given that, being organised is one of the attribute of conscientiousness and it is often used to describe hard working and high achieving students, it is not surprising that there is a connection between the conscientious personality trait and engagement levels. From the results it is apparent that the personal trait of being organised and conscientiousness is related positively to the cognitive engagement.

Related to our second research questions concerning the usefulness of hints for different individuals, the performance of participants in the low peer support at school (PSS) category improved for hint groups in the second round. These findings may indicate that providing hints to the people with low PSS was useful. This supports the argument that peer support encourages social and emotional learning, positive psychology among students and helps in learning [22]. Except for this finding, our analysis of the five personality dimensions with the second quiz score did not reveal any significant differences, regardless of group and whether they received hints or not. Thus, we don't have any clear evidence to suggest that different personality types benefit more from hints or help than others. The participants that were in the hint group in general did not do significantly better than those in the control group. Larger sample size and different populations might show different results. Also, since our results suggest that scenario 1 was harder than scenario 2 and receiving scenario 1 first provided a greater learning opportunity than scenario 2, a future study should balance the difficulty of two scenarios better (we had intended them to be equally difficult). In line with productive failure [23] and impasse learning [24], the implication of our results is that we should provide a challenge to students at the start, rather than a highly structured or guided task. Our study suggests that all participants might benefit from providing all the hints after using the EVW once. Further studies are needed to confirm the importance of tailoring hints, though intuitively and also supported by impasse learning concepts, offering help before it is needed is usually unwanted and unhelpful.

Besides answers to our research questions, there are some interested findings in this study that are worth mentioning. More specifically, this research found that students who play games achieved lower quiz scores. These findings suggest that previous gaming experience does not help students to perform well in virtual environments rather it affects their performance negatively. It is not suggested that participants have a better performance when they have more experience with games compared to others. Another study is necessary to confirm the link between gaming hours and performance. The results suggested that there is no direct relation between gaming hours and performance in terms of number of correct answers. Another finding from this study was that people who do not play games are more cognitively engaged. This suggests that participants who do not play games can be more attentive and emotionally aware hence more cognitively engaged.

No gender specific differences were observed in this study from performance perspective as quiz scores did not show any significant differences. However the results revealed that females are (or perceive themselves to be) more agreeable than males, or conversely that males are more likely than females to sometimes describe themselves as disagreeable. This may reflect cultural norms where it may be more acceptable for males to argue and analysis of gender differences showing that females tend to be more cooperative and agreeable [25].

6 Conclusion and Future Work

Towards creation of more intelligent EVWs, we sought to understand the possible influences of individual differences of the learner (such as personality, cognitive and affective engagement) on their performance and behaviours. Deeper and accurate understanding of learner features and behaviours in EVWs can facilitate better artificially intelligent technologies to improve the learning effectiveness of EVWs. Our study found some differences in performance depending on personality, engagement level, gender and a few other factors. These factors were captured outside the EVW. In the future we intend to capture this information and pass it to the EVW so that it might adapt appropriately using the rules uncovered from our current experimental datasets.

Further research with larger cohorts and other non-psychology students would strengthen the generality of the results. The findings of this study stress the significance of understanding the learner better in order to design more efficient virtual learning platforms. As future work, school student population can be included for further examination of links studied in this study. New research could be based on these findings as to specify more clearly what helps to improve performance via EVW and in what way help can be provided to students depending on their personality traits to improve their performance.

Acknowledgement. We would like to thank the participants in our study. Also, we thank Meredith Taylor for her assistance with Omosa. This work has in part been supported by Australian Research Council Discovery Project DP150102144.

References

1. Richards, D., Taylor, M.: A comparison of learning gains when using a 2D simulation tool versus a 3D virtual world: an experiment to find the right representation involving the marginal value theorem. Comput. Educ. **86**, 157–171 (2015)
2. Rickel, J.: Intelligent virtual agents for education and training: opportunities and challenges. In: de Antonio, A., Aylett, R., Ballin, D. (eds.) IVA 2001. LNCS (LNAI), vol. 2190, pp. 15–22. Springer, Heidelberg (2001). https://doi.org/10.1007/3-540-44812-8_2
3. Baker, S.C., Wentz, R.K., Woods, M.M.: Using virtual worlds in education: Second Life® as an educational tool. Teach. Psychol. **36**(1), 59–64 (2009)
4. Eschenbrenner, B., Nah, F.F.-H., Siau, K.: 3-D virtual worlds in education: applications, benefits, issues, and opportunities. J. Database Manag. (JDM) **19**(4), 91–110 (2008)
5. Falloon, G.: Using avatars and virtual environments in learning: What do they have to offer? Br. J. Educ. Technol. **41**(1), 108–122 (2010)
6. Carini, R.M., Kuh, G.D., Klein, S.P.: Student engagement and student learning: testing the linkages. Res. High. Educ. **47**(1), 1–32 (2006)
7. Eyong, E.I., David, B.E., Umoh, A.J.: The influence of personality trait on the academic performance of secondary school students in Cross River State. Nigeria. IOSR J. Humanit. Soc. Sci. **19**(3), 12–19 (2014)
8. Fosse, T.H., et al.: The impact of personality and self-efficacy on academic and military performance: the mediating role of self-efficacy. J. Mil. Stud. **6**(1), 47–65 (2015)

9. Furnham, A., Monsen, J.: Personality traits and intelligence predict academic school grades. Learn. Individ. Differ. **19**(1), 28–33 (2009)

10. Goldberg, L.R.: An alternative "description of personality": the big-five factor structure. J. Pers. Soc. Psychol. **59**(6), 1216 (1990)

11. Gosling, S.D., Rentfrow, P.J., Swann, W.B.: A very brief measure of the Big-Five personality domains. J. Res. Pers. **37**(6), 504–528 (2003)

12. McCrae, R.R., Costa Jr., P.T.: A five-factor theory of personality. In: Handbook of Personality: Theory and Research, vol. 2, pp. 139–153 (1999)

13. Chamorro-Premuzic, T., Furnham, A.: Personality, intelligence and approaches to learning as predictors of academic performance. Pers. Individ. Differ. **44**(7), 1596–1603 (2008)

14. Hazrati-Viari, A., Rad, A.T., Torabi, S.S.: The effect of personality traits on academic performance: The mediating role of academic motivation. Procedia Soc. Behav. Sci. **32**, 367–371 (2012)

15. Fredricks, J.A., Blumenfeld, P.C., Paris, A.H.: School engagement: potential of the concept, state of the evidence. Rev. Educ. Res. **74**(1), 59–109 (2004)

16. Appleton, J.J., et al.: Measuring cognitive and psychological engagement: validation of the Student Engagement Instrument. J. Sch. Psychol. **44**(5), 427–445 (2006)

17. Hassaskhah, J., Khanzadeh, A.A., Mohamad Zade, S.: The relationship between internal forms of engagement (cognitive-affective) and academic success across years of study. Issues Lang. Teach. **1**(2), 251–272 (2013)

18. Hoff, J., Lopus, J.S.: Does student engagement affect student achievement in high school economics classes. In: The Annual Meetings of the Allied Social Science Association, Philadelphia, PA (2014)

19. Ewell, P., An analysis of relationships between NSSE and selected student learning outcomes measures for seniors attending public institutions in South Dakota. National Center for Higher Education Management Systems, Boulder, CO (2002)

20. de Haan, J., Richards, D.: Navigation Paths and Performance in Educational Virtual Worlds. Navigation (2017)

21. de Haan, J., Richards, D., Dignum, F.: Aiding learning efficiency in virtual worlds. In: Virtual Systems and Multimedia, 26–30 October 2018, Dublin, Ireland (2017, forthcoming)

22. Carter, E.W., Cushing, L.S., Kennedy, C.H.: Peer support strategies for improving all students' social lives and learning. Educ. Rev. Reseñas Educativas (2009)

23. Kapur, M.: Productive failure. Cognit. Instr. **26**(3), 379–424 (2008)

24. VanLehn, K., et al.: Why do only some events cause learning during human tutoring? Cognit. Instr. **21**(3), 209–249 (2003)

25. Weisberg, Y.J., DeYoung, C.G., Hirsh, J.B.: Gender differences in personality across the ten aspects of the Big Five. Front. Psychol. **2**, 178 (2011)

Metacognitive Scaffolding Amplifies the Effect of Learning by Teaching a Teachable Agent

Noboru Matsuda[✉], Vishnu Priya Chandra Sekar, and Natalie Wall

Texas A&M University, College Station, TX 77843, USA
{Noboru.Matsuda,Vchandsekar,Natalie.Wall}@tamu.edu

Abstract. Learning by teaching has been compared with learning by being tutored, aka cognitive tutoring, to learn algebra linear equations for 7th to 8th grade algebra. Two randomized-controlled trials with 46 and 141 6th through 8th grade students were conducted in 3 public schools in two different years. Students in the learning by teaching (LBT) condition used an online learning environment (APLUS), where they interactively taught a teachable agent (SimStudent) how to solve equations with a goal to have the teachable agent pass the quiz. Students in the learning by being tutored condition used a version of cognitive tutor that uses the same user interface as APLUS, but no teachable agent. Instead, a teacher agent tutored students how to solve equations. The goal for students in this condition was to pass the quiz by themselves. Students selected and entered problems to be tutored by themselves. This condition is hence called Goal-Oriented Practice (GOP). For both conditions, students received metacognitive scaffolding on how to teach the teachable agent (LBT) and how to regulate their learning (GOP). The results from the classroom studies show that (1) students in both conditions learned equally well, measured as pre- and post-test scores, (2) prior competency does not influence the effect of LBT nor GOP (i.e., no aptitude-treatment inter-action observed), and (3) GOP students primarily focused on submitting the quiz rather than practicing on problems. These results suggest that with the metacognitive scaffolding, learning by teaching is equally effective as cognitive tutoring regardless of the prior competency.

Keywords: Learning by teaching · Goal-Oriented Practice · Teachable agent
Cognitive tutor · Algebra

1 Introduction

The goal of the current paper is to investigate the relative effectiveness of learning by teaching and learning by being tutored, aka cognitive tutoring. In particular, we investigate how the presence of metacognitive scaffolding to help students appropriately teach their peers affects the effect of learning by teaching.

Learning by teaching is a promising style of learning with strong empirical evidence of its positive effect [1, 2]. In recent years, along with the advancement of artificial intelligence technology, researchers have investigated the effect of online environments for learning by teaching where students learn by interactively teaching a synthetic peer, often called a teachable agent [3]. A seminal study on Betty's Brain, for learning causal

© Springer International Publishing AG, part of Springer Nature 2018
C. Penstein Rosé et al. (Eds.): AIED 2018, LNAI 10947, pp. 311–323, 2018.
https://doi.org/10.1007/978-3-319-93843-1_23

relationships such as the river ecological system, has probably the longest history in the discipline with a numerous number of field trials [4]. There are other systems that have been field tested both in the lab and actual classroom settings such as TAAG [5] and DynaLearn [6] (among other systems).

Learning by being tutored, on the other hand, is driven by a cognitive tutor, a well-known effective learning technology that provides students with mastery learning on problem-solving skill acquisition [7]. Cognitive tutors implement macro- and micro-level adaptive instructions. The macro-level adaptation is to determine a sequence of problems to practice, whereas the micro-level adaptation is to provide scaffolding in the form of immediate corrective feedback and a just-in-time hint while a student is solving a problem.

Using a teachable agent, researchers conduct tightly controlled studies to test specific hypotheses. So far, to evaluate the effect of learning by teaching, it has been mostly compared against itself while controlling particular features of interest. For example, the students' belief of the mind of the teachable agent [8], the roll of semantic-based feedback [9], and the presence of a meta-tutor agent [10]. As a consequence, despite intensive research on the efficacy of these two types of learning (i.e., learning by teaching and learning by being tutored), little is known about the comparison between them. To advance the theory of effective learning technology and how people learn, it is important to understand the relative advantages and disadvantages of different learning strategies and corresponding assistive learning technologies.

Betty's Brain is probably the first learning by teaching system that was compared with direct instruction [11]. While learning the concept of a river ecosystem by building a concept map, students in the learning by teaching condition gave the concept map (that they created) to Betty and let her solve the quiz. Students in the direct instruction condition made a concept map in the same way, but they solved the quiz by themselves while receiving assistance from the mentor agent. The results show that students in the learning by teaching condition outperformed students in the direct instruction condition on the delayed-test in identifying more core concepts and causal relations in concept maps. A question is whether the same result applies to learning procedural skills such as algebra equation solving.

We have developed an online learning by teaching environment, called APLUS (Artificial Peer Learning environment Using SimStudent) on which students learn to solve algebra equations by teaching a teachable agent, called SimStudent [12]. SimStudent is a machine learning agent that interactively learns procedural skills. The underlying assumption of SimStudent's learning is similar to cognitive tutoring—it assumes that students (and SimStudent) learn skills through induction from examples. When teaching SimStudent, students act like a cognitive tutor for SimStudent (Sect. 3.1). Therefore, comparing learning by teaching SimStudent with cognitive tutoring provides us a tight control to understand how students learn to solve equations with different learning strategies.

We conducted a study comparing an early version of APLUS with Carnegie Learning Algebra I™, a commercially available cognitive tutor [12] —we shall call this study the 2011 Study hereafter. In the 2011 Study, *we found an aptitude-treatment interaction that suggests students with low prior competency (measured as pre-test score) benefited more from learning by being tutored than learning by teaching.* We then hypothesized that to make learning by teaching effective, students should be provided scaffolding while they are teaching their teachable agents. We further hypothesized students needed either cognitive scaffolding that helps students solve equations, or metacognitive scaffolding that helps students teach their teachable agent appropriately. A later classroom evaluation study revealed that *the metacognitive scaffolding facilitated the effect of learning by teaching, but not the cognitive scaffolding* [13].

In the current study, we are particularly interested in comparing the effect of learning by teaching with metacognitive scaffolding against learning by being tutored. We are particularly interested in how the presence of the metacognitive scaffolding influences the effect of learning by teaching across various prior competency levels. The next section further elaborates our research question and hypothesis. The rest of the paper then provides the details of our interventions, evaluation studies and their results, followed by the discussion.

2   Research Questions and Hypotheses

Given our past research experience and background mentioned above, the current paper aims to answer the following central research question: How does the presence of metacognitive scaffolding affect the effect of learning by teaching relative to learning by being tutored?

In the current study, we extend APLUS with metacognitive scaffolding. We also develop a version of cognitive tutor that provides the same metacognitive scaffolding (in addition to immediate feedback and a just-in-time hint that an ordinal cognitive tutor provides). By controlling the presence of scaffolding, we will be able to better compare the two learning strategies.

We will answer this research question by testing the following specific hypothesis. *Metacognitive Scaffolding Hypothesis*: The presence of metacognitive scaffolding will help students teach appropriately even when they have low prior competency hence will increase the effect of learning by teaching regardless of their prior competency. As a consequence, there will be no aptitude-treatment interaction between learning by teaching and learning by being tutored when adaptive scaffolding is provided for both.

3   Interventions

3.1   APLUS: **A**rtificial Peer **L**earning Environment **U**sing **S**imStudent

APLUS is an online learning environment where students learn to solve equations by teaching a synthetic peer. Figure 1 shows an example screenshot of APLUS. While details about APLUS have been published elsewhere [14], we provide a brief overview of the intervention below.

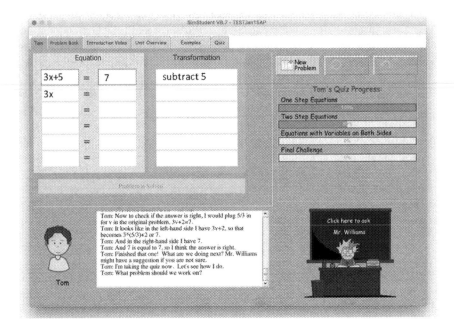

Fig. 1. Example screenshot of APLUS

The synthetic peer, SimStudent, is visualized as an avatar in the lower left corner. SimStudent is a machine learning agent that interactively learns skills to solve problems through guided-problem solving—i.e., a student using APLUS acts as a tutor for SimStudent through guided-problem solving—i.e., a student using APLUS acts as a tutor for SimStudent [15]. SimStudent applies inductive logic programming to induce skills in the form of production rules by generalizing given examples.

The goal for students using APLUS is to have their SimStudent pass the quiz. SimStudent applies productions learned thus far to solve quiz problems. Solutions made by SimStudent are graded by the system and results are displayed for students to review. The quiz has four sections—One Step Equation (1 problem), Two Step Equations (2 problems), Equations with Variables on Both Sides (4 problems), and Final Challenge (8 problems that are all equations with variables on both sides).

Students must tutor their SimStudent with problems that help SimStudent learn the appropriate skills to pass the quiz. Students either make up problems or choose from the Problem Bank. While tutoring, SimStudent asks for feedback on the correctness of each step performed. When the student answers "no" to SimStudent's suggestion, SimStudent tries to make another attempt. If SimStudent has no alternate skills to apply, SimStudent asks the student for help. The student then must suggest the next step by entering it in the Tutoring Interface.

SimStudent occasionally asks the student *why-questions* about steps that the student has suggested or his/her negative feedback (i.e., "no") to a step performed by SimStudent. The student replies to SimStudent's question with free text in a pop-up dialogue box.

There are learning resources available for students to review: (1) Unit Overview, that provides a brief overview of how to solve algebra equations, (2) Examples, that provides worked-out examples for the target equations, (3) Intro Video, that is a brief video explaining how to use APLUS, and (4) Problem Bank that provides a list of suggested equation problems to be used for teaching.

APLUS also features a meta-tutor, known as Mr. Williams, depicted in the lower right-hand corner of Fig. 1 Mr. Williams provides students metacognitive scaffolding on how to teach their SimStudent appropriately. A student can either request help at any time or receive it proactively. For both requested and proactive help, a message from Mr. Williams is shown in a separate dialogue box to give students a perception that it is a private message. There are five types of skills for teaching that the metacognitive scaffolding is designed for: (1) Selecting an appropriate next problem to teach—either a problem from the quiz or a similar one. (2) Administering the quiz at an appropriate time. (3) Reviewing a resource (e.g., Unit Overview) when SimStudent has not made any progress on the quiz. (4) Providing feedback to SimStudent. (5) Demonstrating a step when SimStudent is stuck.

3.2 AplusTutor

AplusTutor is a version of cognitive tutor that provides cognitive tutoring implemented with the Cognitive Tutor Algebra I™ back-end. Figure 2 shows an example screenshot of AplusTutor. AplusTutor does not employ the knowledge tracing technique for problem selection. Instead, students enter problems of their own choice, either from the Problem Bank or one they make-up. The lack of knowledge tracing implies that Aplus-Tutor does not compute a student's mastery level. Instead, the goal for students using AplusTutor is to pass the quiz by themselves. The quiz is organized in the same way as APLUS. Students using AplusTutor must therefore choose problems to practice so that they can pass all the quiz sections. We shall call this style of learning Goal-Oriented Practice.

When the student enters a problem in the Tutoring Interface, the cognitive-tutor backend provides adaptive assistance (i.e., immediate feedback and a just-in-time hint) while he/she is solving the problem. The student can click on the [Quiz] tab at any time to take a quiz. The student is asked to submit a solution for one quiz item at a time, and the system provides feedback on the correctness of the solution. The student can modify an incorrect solution and resubmit (even without practicing on a problem with the cognitive tutor).

The interface of AplusTutor is almost identical to APLUS, except there is no synthetic peer present. Instead, Mr. Williams provides cognitive and metacognitive scaffolding either proactively or by request. Mr. Williams provides metacognitive scaffolding for the following: (1) Selecting an appropriate next problem, (2) Taking the quiz at an appropriate time, and (3) Reviewing Resources. These three types of metacognitive scaffolding are equivalent to the ones provided by APLUS. Like in APLUS, the same resources are available for students to review at any time.

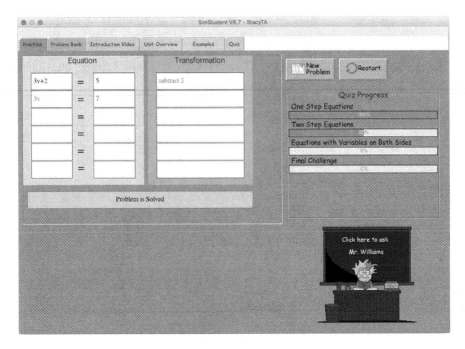

Fig. 2. Example screenshot of APLUSTUTOR

4   Evaluation Study

To test the specific hypothesis discussed in Sect. 2, we conducted two evaluation studies at our partner schools. The first study was conducted in 2016 in the greater Pittsburgh, PA area, whereas the second study was conducted in 2017 in the Houston, TX area. The study sessions were held in algebra classroom settings as part of their business-as-usual classroom instruction.

4.1   Method and Participants

The evaluation studies were randomized controlled trials with two study conditions: (1) *Learning by Teaching* (LBT) where students used APLUS with the goal to have their synthetic peer pass the quiz. (2) *Goal-Oriented Practice* (GOP) where students used APLUSTUTOR with the goal to pass the quiz by themselves.

For the 2016 Study, two public schools were involved with a total of 184 students (7th and 8th grades) in 12 algebra classrooms. For the 2017 Study, one public school was involved with 276 students (6th and 7th grades) in 12 algebra classrooms. For both studies, the condition assignment was done by within-class randomization, i.e., in each classroom, students were randomly assigned to one of two conditions.

The study ran for six days, one classroom period (45 to 50 min) per day. On the first day, all participants took the pre-test (as described below). On the 2nd through 5th day, participants used a corresponding version of software. On the last day, participants took the post-test (as described below).

4.2 Measures

We measured learning outcome and learning activity. Students' learning outcome was measured with an online test that contains 10 equation problems—2 one-step equations, 2 two-step equations, and 6 equations with variables on both sides.

Students' learning activity was measured using learning process data that showed detailed interactions between a student and the system. The interactions are automatically collected by the system including problems used for tutoring or practice, solutions entered by the student and the synthetic peer, quiz progress, hint requested, etc.

5 Results

For the analysis below, only students who took both pre- and post-tests and attended class while using the intervention for at least 3 (out of 4) days were included. For the 2016 Study, there were 60 students out of 184, whereas for the 2017 Study, there were 144 students out of 276 who met these criteria. Among these students, we excluded 14 students from 2016 Study and 3 students from the 2017 who were at the "ceiling," i.e., who scored 100% correct on the pre-test. As a consequence, there are 46 students for the 2016 Study (24 in Learning by Teaching (LBT) and 22 in Goal-Oriented Practice (GOP)) and 141 students for the 2017 Study (71 in LBT and 70 in GOP) in the following analysis.

5.1 Learning Outcomes

Figure 3 shows the average test score. To see if there is a condition difference in students' learning, repeated-measures ANOVAs were run for each study (2016 and 2017) separately with test score as the dependent variable, and test-time (pre vs. post) and condition (GOP vs. LBT) as independent variables.

For both studies, students in both conditions showed an equal pattern of increase from pre- to post-test—i.e., the test-time was a main effect for test score: for 2016, $F(1, 44) = 5.91, p < 0.05$; for 2017, $F(1, 139) = 45.91, p < 0.001$. However, at the same time, for the 2017 Study, there was a (relatively weak) condition difference on the post-test score when pre-test score was controlled. An ANCOVA revealed condition as a main effect for post-test score when pre-test is entered as a covariate; $F(1, 138) = 3.84, p = 0.05$. The condition difference on the post-test was not detected for the 2016 Study.

To understand if and how the students' prior competency affected the effect of two learning strategies, students were split into three groups based on their pre-test score. Table 1 shows a comparison of the test scores among these three groups of students. We conducted a two-way ANCOVA with pre-test as a covariate and prior (High, Mid, Low) and condition (GOP vs LBT) as independent variables. For both studies, there was no

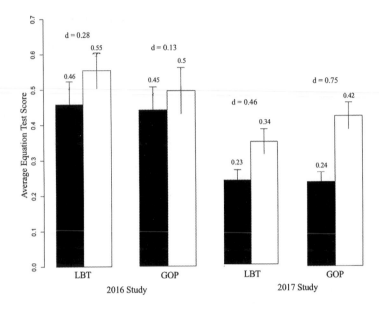

Fig. 3. Test scores. The y-axis shows an average test score (10 equation problems). LBT: Learning by Teaching. GOP: Goal-Oriented Practice

interaction between prior and condition; for 2016, F (4, 39) = 0.81, p = 0.52; for 2017, F (4, 134) = 1.25, p = 0.29.

Table 1. Comparison of test scores among students with different prior competency.

		High			Mid			Low		
		Pre	Post	d	Pre	Post	d	Pre	Post	d
2016 Study	LBT	0.84(0.07)	0.76(0.16)	−1.14	0.48(0.12)	0.53(0.19)	0.42	0.06(0.08)	0.32(0.21)	3.25
	GOP	0.81(0.09)	0.81(0.20)	0	0.19(0.10)	0.33(0.18)	1.4	0.13(0.07)	0.23(0.19)	1.42
2017 Study	LBT	0.54(0.20)	0.62(0.25)	0.40	0.20(0.05)	0.26(0.24)	1.2	0.02(0.04)	0.19(0.22)	4.25
	GOP	0.46(0.21)	0.63(0.31)	0.81	0.17(0.06)	0.33(0.21)	2.66	0.01(0.03)	0.26(0.26)	8.33

These findings imply that Learning by Teaching is as effective as Goal-Oriented Practice to learn to solve algebra equations when the metacognitive scaffolding is provided. Our current data do not reveal an aptitude-treatment interaction for the effect of learning strategies—i.e., both strategies are equally effective regardless of student's prior competency.

5.2 Learning Process

To understand the process of learning and how students interacted with the intervention —Learning by Teaching (LBT) and Goal-Oriented Practice (GOP)—we analyzed learning process data.

We first analyzed how students' "competency" in solving equations improved over time. The competency was operationalized as follows. For LBT, the accuracy of students' responses (i.e., feedback and hint) to their teachable agents was computed. For GOP, the accuracy of steps performed by students while they were getting tutored on the problems they entered was computed. We then computed a linear regression with competency as the dependent variable, and condition (LBT vs. GOP) and participation day (1 through 4) as the independent variables. Notice a subtle difference between study day and participation day—study day is defined by the calendar day hence everybody has the same count of study days whereas participation day shows a sequential number of days a particular student was present in the class. For example, the 2nd participation day might be the 3rd study day if a student was absent from the class on the 3rd day of the intervention. Figure 4 shows the average competency for each condition per participation day aggregated across all students in two studies (2016 and 2017). Numbers at a data point indicates the number of observations—there were students who were present in the class but did not tutor SimStudent or did not do any practice on solving equations. The data showed that participation day was a significant predictor of competency, $F(1, 464) = 9.76, p < 0.01$, but there was no condition difference, $F(1, 464) = 0.39, p = 0.53$. This result indicates that students in both conditions equally improve their "competency" in solving equations over time during the intervention.

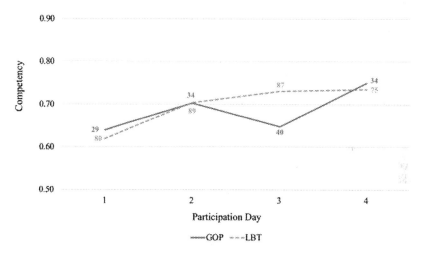

Fig. 4. The average competency of teaching (LBT) and practice (GOP) per participation day. The number at a data point shows the number of students who actually taught or practiced.

Next, we analyzed the number of problems students practiced. For LBT, this means the number of problems that students entered to teach their synthetic peer. For GOP, this means the number of problems that students entered to receive cognitive tutoring. Figure 5 shows the box plot showing the number of problems students practiced. To our surprise, GOP students practiced on noticeably fewer problems than LBT. Since these two learning strategies are quite different in their natures, comparing the number of "practiced" problems requires some caution. Yet, the number of practice problems for GOP shown in the figure motivated us to further explore how GOP students interacted with the system.

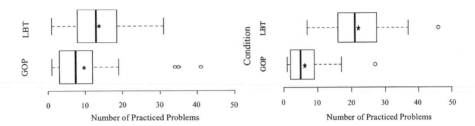

Fig. 5. The number of problems a student practiced.

A further analysis revealed that GOP students spent a considerable amount of time on the quiz. Figure 6 shows the number of times that the quiz was submitted as well as the number of problems practiced per GOP student (aggregated across all students). As the graph shows, on average students submitted quiz 7.8 (2016 Study) and 6.3 (2017 Study) times while practicing on one problem. This implies that *GOP students learned to solve equations through the quiz, which involved reviewing the quiz results (corrective feedback on the correctness of solution steps) and editing and re-submitting their solutions.*

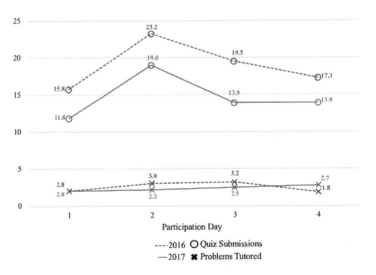

Fig. 6. The number of quiz submission and problems practices on APLUSTUTOR.

6 Discussion

The Metacognitive Scaffolding hypothesis was supported. The current data show that adaptive metacognitive scaffolding facilitated the effect of learning by teaching equally well as learning by being tutored regardless of the students' prior competency. The aptitude-treatment interaction observed in the 2011 Study [12] that students with low-prior received more benefit from cognitive tutoring than learning by teaching does not appear when the metacognitive scaffolding was provided.

It is worthwhile remembering that the behavior of the cognitive tutor used in the current study is different from the one in the previous study—passing the quiz in place of the mastery learning criteria, the mechanism of problem selection, and the availability of the metacognitive scaffolding. It is therefore desired to conduct a follow-up study to compare learning by teaching with the metacognitive scaffolding against a genuine cognitive tutor (i.e., the one used in the 2011 Study).

We designed APLUSTUTOR to provide cognitive tutoring on the problems that students enter by themselves, and we anticipated that students would practice on the problems that appear on the quiz. However, one of the notable findings from the current study is that students in the Goal-Oriented Practice condition learned to solve equations primarily by submitting and re-submitting the quiz multiple times with corrective feedback from the system.

It is interesting to see that two different learning goals, i.e., (1) students passing the quiz by themselves (Goal-Oriented Practice with APLUSTUTOR) and (2) having the synthetic peer pass the quiz (Learning by Teaching with APLUS) have equal impact on *student's* learning outcome. This result somewhat contradicts a previous finding on the ego protective buffer [8] —students' learning is facilitated when they perceive a third party agent (e.g., a synthetic peer) as the target for blame of a failure. Further investigations are necessary to understand why we do not observe this phenomenon.

The submission/re-submission behavior on the quiz might be considered as "gaming" the system [16]. In other words, by simply re-submitting the quiz, students committed to "shallow" learning that only allows them to solve particular problems that are on the quiz and the test. However, there are three types of equation problems (one-step equation, two-step equation, and equations with variables on both sides), and three measures all have different equations (pre-test with 10 equations, post-test with 10 equations, and quiz with 15 equations). It is therefore arguably fair not to assume that the increase on the test score from pre- to post-test is merely due to shallow learning. Yet, it is intriguing that students improved their proficiency in solving equations primarily by repeatedly modifying and re-submitting quiz solutions with occasional practice on a relatively small number of problems.

The current two studies show relatively small effect sizes. Although a meta-analysis reported that learning by teaching in face-to-face settings tended to show a small effect size [1], we anticipate that the effect of learning by teaching will be amplified with the adaptive technology support. Further investigation is necessary to achieve this goal.

7   Conclusion

We found that by adding the metacognitive scaffolding that helps students appropriately teach their synthetic peer, learning by teaching becomes as effective as cognitive tutoring regardless of students' prior competency. In the current study, a version of cognitive tutor, AplusTutor, was used for which the student's goal was to pass the quiz by themselves. When using AplusTutor, students also entered problems to practice by themselves. On the other hand, for learning by teaching, an online learning environment, APLUS, on which students can interactively teach a teachable agent was used. For both APLUS and AplusTutor, metacognitive scaffolding on how to teach and how to regulate learning was provided.

To provide effective instruction for a diverse student population with various backgrounds, preferable learning styles, and needs, it is crucial to understand the strengths and weaknesses of different learning strategies and learning technologies. Two particular learning technologies used in the current study do not show an overall difference in a particular setting. Yet, there are students who do not benefit as well as others. No one size fits all. Further investigation is necessary to understand how best we can combine various learning strategies including learning by teaching and cognitive tutoring to meet individual students' needs.

Acknowledgement. This study was supported by National Science Foundation grant No. 1643185.

References

1. Roscoe, R.D., Chi, M.T.H.: Understanding tutor learning: Knowledge-building and knowledge-telling in peer tutors' explanations and questions. Rev. Educ. Res. **77**(4), 534–574 (2007)
2. Cohen, E.G.: Restructuring the classroom: Conditions for productive small groups. Rev. Educ. Res. **64**(1), 1–35 (1994)
3. Schwartz, D., et al.: Animations of thought: interactivity in the teachable agent paradigm, in learning with animation: research and implications for design. In: Lowe, R., Schnotz, W. (eds.), pp. 114–140. Cambrige University Press, UK (2007)
4. Biswas, G., Segedy, J.R., Bunchongchit, K.: From design to implementation to practice a learning by teaching system: Betty's brain. Int. J. Artif. Intell. Educ. **26**(1), 350–364 (2016)
5. Pareto, L.: A teachable agent game engaging primary school children to learn arithmetic concepts and reasoning. Int. J. Artif. Intell. Educ. **24**(3), 251–283 (2014)
6. Bredeweg, B., et al.: DynaLearn – an intelligent learning environment for learning conceptual knowledge. AI Mag. **34**(4), 46–65 (2013)
7. Koedinger, K.R., Corbett, A.T.: Cognitive tutors: technology bringing learning sciences to the classroom. In: Sawyer, R.K. (ed.) The Cambridge Handbook of the Learning Sciences, pp. 61–78. Cambridge University Press, New York (2006)
8. Chase, C., et al.: Teachable agents and the protégé effect: increasing the effort towards learning. J. Sci. Educ. Technol. **18**(4), 334–352 (2009)
9. Lozano, E., et al.: Problem-based learning supported by semantic techniques. Interact. Learn. Environ. **20**(4), 351–357 (2012)
10. Matsuda, N., Stylianides, G.J., Koedinger, K.R.: Studying the effect of guided learning by teaching in learning algebra equations. In: Paper Presented at the Annual Meeting of the American Educational Research Association, Chicago, IL (2015)
11. Viswanath, K., et al.: A multi-agent architecture implementation of learning by teaching systems. In: Proceedings of the IEEE International Conference on Advanced Learning Technologies, Joensuu, Finland, pp. 61–65 (2004)

12. Matsuda, N., Yarzebinski, E., Keiser, V., Raizada, R., Stylianides, G.J., Cohen, W.W., Koedinger, K.R.: Learning by teaching simstudent – an initial classroom baseline study comparing with cognitive tutor. In: Biswas, G., Bull, S., Kay, J., Mitrovic, A. (eds.) AIED 2011. LNCS (LNAI), vol. 6738, pp. 213–221. Springer, Heidelberg (2011). https://doi.org/10.1007/978-3-642-21869-9_29

13. Matsuda, N., Barbalios, N., Zhao, Z., Ramamurthy, A., Stylianides, G.J., Koedinger, K.R.: Tell me how to teach, I'll learn how to solve problems. In: Micarelli, A., Stamper, J., Panourgia, K. (eds.) ITS 2016. LNCS, vol. 9684, pp. 111–121. Springer, Cham (2016). https://doi.org/10.1007/978-3-319-39583-8_11

14. Matsuda, N., et al.: Cognitive anatomy of tutor learning: lessons learned with simstudent. J. Educ. Psychol. **105**(4), 1152–1163 (2013)

15. Matsuda, N., Cohen, W.W., Koedinger, K.R.: Teaching the teacher: tutoring simstudent leads to more effective cognitive tutor authoring. Int. J. Artif. Intell. Educ. **25**, 1–34 (2015)

16. Baker, R., et al.: Developing a generalizable detector of when students game the system. User Model. User-Adapt. Interact. **18**(3), 287–314 (2008)

A Data-Driven Method for Helping Teachers Improve Feedback in Computer Programming Automated Tutors

Jessica McBroom[1]([✉]), Kalina Yacef[1], Irena Koprinska[1],
and James R. Curran[2]

[1] The University of Sydney,
School of Information Technologies, Sydney, Australia
jmcb6755@uni.sydney.edu.au,
{kalina.yacef, irena.koprinska}@sydney.edu.au
[2] Grok Learning, Sydney, Australia
james@groklearning.com

Abstract. The increasing prevalence and sophistication of automated tutoring systems necessitates the development of new methods for their evaluation and improvement. In particular, data-driven methods offer the opportunity to provide teachers with insight about student interactions with online systems, facilitating their improvement to maximise their educational value. In this paper, we present a new technique for analysing feedback in an automated programming tutor. Our method involves first clustering submitted programs with the same functionality together, then applying sequential pattern mining and graphically visualising student progress through an exercise. Using data from a beginner Python course, we demonstrate how this method can be applied to programming exercises to analyse student approaches, responses to feedback, areas of greatest difficulty and repetition of mistakes. This process could be used by teachers to more effectively understand student behaviour, allowing them to adapt both traditional and online teaching materials and feedback to optimise student experiences and outcomes.

Keywords: Data-driven teacher support · Automated tutoring systems
Feedback improvement · Tutoring system evaluation

1 Introduction

In recent years, steady progress has been made towards developing new data-driven methods for feedback generation in automated tutoring systems. These are online systems which provide automated marking of submissions and feedback to students. This work has led to an increase in the sophistication of tutoring systems, with great potential to improve educational outcomes. However, it has also increased the difficulty of analysing and assessing the automated feedback given by these systems. As the systems become more complex, teachers become more distanced from the direct feedback and instruction given to individuals, and this is exacerbated by the increasing number of students. It is therefore very challenging for teachers to identify and

© Springer International Publishing AG, part of Springer Nature 2018
C. Penstein Rosé et al. (Eds.): AIED 2018, LNAI 10947, pp. 324–337, 2018.
https://doi.org/10.1007/978-3-319-93843-1_24

diagnose issues with the system and monitor whether the instructional material they have created is appropriate or could be improved.

Thus, to ensure that automated tutoring systems meet their potential to enhance student experiences, it is essential to close the loop between teachers, systems and students, by ensuring that information about student interactions with these systems is passed back to teachers. In particular, it is important to develop data-driven methods for assessing automated tutoring systems alongside methods of extending them. These methods can allow teachers to use the wealth of data collected by the tutoring systems to modify and improve these systems. They can also provide useful insights into student learning, which can be applied in other contexts, such as inside the classroom, to improve learning.

In this paper, we present a new data-driven method for assessing automated tutoring systems in the context of a computer programming course. This method helps teachers to understand the kinds of programs students write and how they change over time in response to feedback. This allows them to: (i) gain insight into student learning, e.g. by finding exercise parts where students have trouble, or identifying common mistakes and difficult concepts, and (ii) improve the tutoring system, e.g. by revising the pre-set feedback and testing cases in the system based on student behaviour. We demonstrate an application of this method to real data from a beginner programming course in Python, and also discuss possible extensions and broader applications of the method to other areas.

2   Related Work

A variety of automated marking and tutoring systems have been reported in computer science courses [1–7] and other areas [8–11] in recent years, and there has been much work focused on improving the sophistication of feedback provided by these systems [1, 5, 6, 8–11] Evaluations of these systems have often focused on functionality of the system, including its usability [2] and the availability of hints [5, 6, 8, 10], student opinions and engagement [4, 11, 12], before and after studies [11, 12] or comparisons with expert opinions. These evaluation methods provide valuable feedback to teachers, but some (e.g. comparative studies) do not scale well to large numbers of students due to the significant manual work and time required, and the information provided about how students interact with the system is often more general. Our work aims to address this by providing teachers with a way to understand and visualise how large numbers of students interact with an automated tutoring system, including how they respond to feedback, which can lead to clear and actionable ways to improve the system.

An important part of our work involves clustering similar programs. Previous work related to this includes clustering programs based on features or on their structure by using metrics such as the tree edit distance [13]. Gross et al. [14] investigated the usefulness of different similarity metrics in the context of programming and Paassen et al. [15] discussed a scheme for learning parameters of structure metrics, which could be used to determine program similarity. Another method is to focus on functionality or semantics of programs. In [16], similar programs were grouped by renaming all similar variables across programs (determined by running the programs), then combining programs with the same sets of lines of code. Our clustering involves applying functionality-preserving transformations to programs, followed by further processing to account for differences that are irrelevant in the context of the exercise. Functionality-preserving transformations have been applied in other work for different purposes and languages [1, 5].

Our work falls into the broader area of mining log data from automated tutoring systems to provide teachers with information to improve educational outcomes. Other related work includes predicting students at risk of failing early in the semester [17], characterizing and predicting the performance of different groups of students [18] and analysing student behaviour and its evolution throughout the semester [19, 20].

3 Data

Our data come from Grok Learning [19], an online platform offering various programming courses of different difficulty levels to students, each consisting of a series of interactive lessons and exercises for students to complete. The exercises are marked automatically using a series of test cases written in advance by teachers, and students are provided with feedback based on the tests passed and failed. The students can then use this feedback to improve their programs, re-submit and re-test them, until all tests are passed.

The dataset used in this paper is extracted from a beginner Python programming challenge run through Grok Learning in 2017. It comprises of programming attempts, failed or successful, from two programming exercises ('What Rhymes with Grok' and 'Letter from the Queen'). Each exercise was attempted by over 5000 students, and the data includes all student programs that were run through the system or submitted for marking, any tests passed or failed by the programs, the feedback automatically generated by the tests, submission times and information on any errors from running the programs.

4 Method

The method we propose aims to give teachers an overview of student interactions with an automated tutor for computer programming for a given exercise. This includes: the types of programs students submit, how students respond to the given feedback, the student progression through the exercise and the exercise parts where students experience difficulty. This knowledge can assist teachers in identifying system strengths and areas for improvement, and also in gaining insights into student learning.

Importantly, as our method is data-driven, using real student programs and their subsequent revisions after receiving feedback, it can reveal underlying problems experienced by students that were not necessarily anticipated by the teacher when devising the test feedback. For example, in Table 1, a sample student submission for an exercise discussed in the next section is shown, along with the feedback received. The issue with the program is that it prints a hardcoded answer, instead of the user's input, and the feedback given addresses the issue by reminding the student to use a variable instead. However, our data-driven approach reveals that 100/172 students in this situation simply changed their hardcoded message after receiving the feedback. This is not what a teacher would expect, and so highlights the value of data-driven analysis techniques. Our approach can also reveal bugs in test cases, opportunities to make these tests more targeted and whether students make similar mistakes in later exercises.

Table 1. Sample student program and feedback received. The feedback seems useful, but many students do not respond as expected to it.

Student Program	Feedback
```input('What rhymes with Grok? ')``` ```print('rock')```	Testing the second example in the question (when the user enters sock). Your submission did not produce the correct output. Your program output: What rhymes with Grok? **sock** rock when it was meant to output: What rhymes with Grok? **sock** sock Remember to store the user input in a variable, and to use the variable name with print

Our approach consists of two main steps, summarised in Fig. 1. The first is to cluster student programs based on their functionality, and the second is to extract useful information from the clusters by building an interaction graph and using sequential pattern mining. We describe these steps in more detail below.

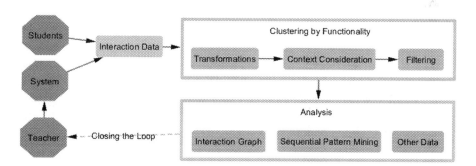

Fig. 1. Summary of our approach to closing the loop between teachers, systems and students

4.1 Clustering

To allow teachers to interpret a large number of student program submissions, we begin by clustering programs based on their functionality. Two programs are considered to have the same functionality if an observer with access to any input/output examples cannot distinguish between the two programs. This definition is consistent with how the testing is done using the pre-specified test cases. The advantage of using this clustering approach is that a group of programs functioning similarly is easily exemplified by a single example, so the clusters are easy to interpret. Though differences in syntax and efficiency can reveal further interesting information about student understanding, we do not focus on these here.

The clustering in the form we describe is applicable to 'calculation-based' programs. That is, programs employing any of the following: literals, mathematical operators, variables, simple functions and console-based input and output. However, this could be extended to broader classes of programs in future.

The method consists of three steps: the application of functionality-preserving transformations, considering context and filtering, which we outline in turn.

Functionality-Preserving Transformations. We describe a number of transformations with Python in mind, but these could be generalised to other languages. Some examples are shown in Table 2.

Table 2. Examples of Python programs and their standardised forms

Original Program	Standardised	Explanation

`print(input('Quo`
`kka '))`
	`print('Quokka ', end='')`
	`i1 = input()`
	`print(i1)`
		separate input into printing and input, new variable for changing value, standardised variable naming

`a = input()`
`b = '…'`
`c = a + b`
`print(c)`
	`i1 = input()`
	`print(i1 + '…\n',`
	`end='')`
		substitute variables, standardise printing, standardised naming

`'''comment'''`
`a = 2`
`print(7*12)`
	`print('84', end = '')`	remove comments and unused variables, evaluate expressions, standardise printing

Variables. In general, transformations are applied so that variables are used only and always for values that can vary on different runs of the program. Such values include the output from random or input functions. If variables are not being used for these values, they are introduced. Variables used for all other values (such as literals) are removed and any occurrences of them are replaced by their value. The names of variables are then standardised.

Expressions. Expressions are simplified where possible. This includes the evaluation of consecutive literals or literals in commutative expressions and the elimination of trivial operations, such as empty string addition. If the value of an expression can be determined without complete knowledge of all operands, it is also evaluated (e.g. an expression with multiplication by 0).

Expressions are also expanded to standardise their form. This includes application of distributive laws and replacement of some operations involving literals. For example, `a**2` would be replaced by `a*a`. For consistency, commutative expressions are ordered by operand types, e.g. integers are placed first.

Function-Specific Transformations. Transformations specific to allowed functions are applied to standardise programs further. For example, an `input` call can be separated into a `print` call followed by an `input` call with no arguments. Consecutive print statements are collapsed into a single statement with no varying keywords. Type casts are removed where possible.

Other. If two variable declarations can be swapped without altering the function of the program, a standardised ordering is applied, for example, based on the variable used first. Whitespace, comments and any lines that do not affect the program's functionality are removed.

Considering Context. After transformations are applied and functionally equivalent programs are clustered together, the number of clusters is then reduced by ignoring differences that do not matter. An example of such a difference is whether a program prints 'hi' or 'hello' in an exercise where the goal is to print 'How are you?': in both cases, the programs are incorrect for the same reason.

This reduction is achieved by combining programs with a similar standardised form together, so long as they fail the same test cases. For simple programs, this can just be differences in strings or numerical values. For more complex programs, some mathematical expressions could be treated as equivalent, or some statements with the same general purpose. In our case study, we combined programs with exactly the same abstract syntax tree structure and node types so, for example, differences in strings would be ignored, so long as the same tests were passed and failed.

Filtering. Finally, to ensure teachers are left with a manageable number of clusters to consider, clusters containing less than a specified number of programs are filtered out. In the case study we describe next, this threshold was 10.

4.2 Analysis

After clustering, student interactions with the system are analysed using a combination of different methods: building an interaction graph and finding frequent patterns.

In the interaction graph, nodes and edges represent student program clusters and their transitions between these clusters respectively. By providing a general overview of how students progress through the exercise, this graph can reveal places where students struggle and therefore can be used to improve feedback. For example, cycles in the graph could be indicative of student confusion or misleading feedback. Student starting positions in the graph could also indicate how prepared students were for the exercise, and ending positions in the graph could highlight areas of difficulty.

Next, sequential pattern mining is used to find common consecutive transitions between clusters. This is done by iterating through the transitions of each student and adding all unique paths of a given length to a tally. For example, a tally of 370 for the path *abc* would indicate that 370 unique students submitted three consecutive programs in clusters a, b then c at some point when completing the exercise. Paths can then be assessed for their efficiency and how reflective they are of the teacher's expectations.

Any potentially interesting areas can be analysed in conjunction with other data from the tutoring system, including submission times, how often students run their code before marking it, which tests are passed and failed and samples of feedback for different program clusters. This can allow teachers to assess whether feedback was appropriate and students responded to it as expected, and how it could be improved in future. It can also highlight opportunities to make testing more targeted if different types of programs are failing the same test, and reveal issues with testing procedures if some programs are passing tests they shouldn't pass.

Finally, the performance of students across exercises can be observed to assess their learning progress. For example, teachers can see if students continue to make similar mistakes or continue to require similar feedback to earlier exercises.

5   Case Study

We demonstrate the application of this method using two beginner programming questions from the Grok Learning programming challenge. These questions are particularly interesting because their completion rate is very high (over 97%), so a traditional analysis could risk skipping over them. However, the small percentage of students who do not complete the tasks still represent a large enough group to be interested in helping, and any improvements could help all students to interact more usefully with the system.

In the first example, we will show how the method can be used to assess whether student responses in different contexts reflect what an instructor might expect, and how this can be used to improve the system test cases and the feedback provided to students. In the second example, we focus on how the method can be used to understand student learning and help to develop more targeted testing and feedback.

5.1   Example 1 – What Rhymes with Grok?

In this exercise, students write a program to print user input. Details of the exercise from a student's perspective are shown in Fig. 2, with instructions on the left, sample code in the top right and details of tests run on the code in the bottom right.

Figure 3 shows the interaction graph produced by clustering programs of 5874 students who attempted this question. Circular nodes represent student program clusters, and edges show the number of times a submission in the source node cluster was followed by a submission in the target node cluster. Node and edge size correspond to the number of submissions, so larger nodes and edges are more important. Edges from the start and end nodes show the number of students who started and ended in each cluster. Table 3 shows the most common cluster paths of length 3 and 4 among students from the sequential pattern mining, ordered by the number of students taking the paths.

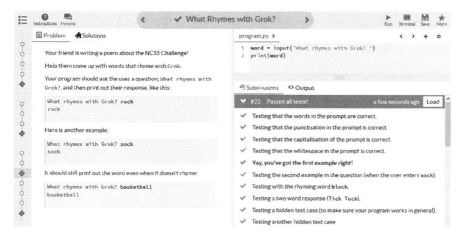

Fig. 2. A screenshot from a student's perspective of the exercise "What Rhymes with Grok?"

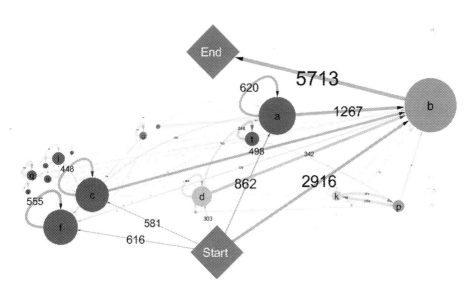

Fig. 3. Interaction graph for the exercise "What Rhymes with Grok"

Identifying Areas of Interest. From the graph and common paths, we can make some general observations about student interactions with the system. Firstly, cluster b is the most common starting point, followed by a, f, c and d. In the graph, there are self-loops on a, f, c and d and a cycle between p and k, and repetitions of these also appear in many common paths. The paths cab and dab, with three different nodes, could also be interesting. Table 4 shows a summary of the potentially interesting clusters just identified, including a sample program from each cluster.

Table 3. Path patterns for the exercise 'What Rhymes with Grok?"

Path Length	Cluster Path and Number of Students										
3	*aab* 306	*ccb* 170	*aaa* 134	*fff* 129	*ccc* 102	*cab* 94	*dab* 85	*ddb* 82	*ffb* 59	*pkp* 53	*ttt* 52
4	*aaab* 119		*cccb* 72		*aaaa* 64		*ffff* 47		*cccc* 47		*tttt* 34

Table 4. Cluster summaries

Cluster	Size	Failed test	Sample Program
b	5713	None	`x = input("What rhymes with Grok? ")` `print(x)`
a	2044	prompt ws	`x = input("What rhymes with Grok?")` `print(x)`
f	1455	prompt words	`print('Hello!')`
c	1281	prompt words	`name = input('what is your name ')` `print(name)`
d	691	prompt case	`name = input('what rhymes with Grok? ')` `print(name)`
p	397	eg2	`input('What rhymes with Grok? ')` `print('rock')`
k	338	eg1	`name = input('What rhymes with Grok? ')` `print('clock')`

Investigating Areas of Interest. From where students began, it is clear many were generally well prepared for the exercise: cluster *b* indicates a correct solution, and clusters *a*, *c* and *d* are close to a correct solution, with just some issues with the prompt string. The students who began at *f*, however, were missing some key concepts as they were only using the print function.

In relation to the cycle between *p* and *k*, both clusters are similar in that students used the input function, but printed out a hardcoded message instead of the user's response. When this hardcoded message was not 'rock', the first example test was failed. Otherwise, the second test was failed. A cycle between these clusters suggests students were changing the hardcoded string instead of correcting the issue. The feedback given to these students, shown in Table 5, consisted of a notification that their output was incorrect and, in the case of *p*, a suggestion on how to correct this was given. However, according to the data, 50% of submissions (200/397) in cluster *p* were followed by a submission in cluster *k*, and this involved 58% of unique students (100/172) who had a program in cluster *p*. For *k*, the figures were similar: 171/338 submissions (51%) and 84/139 students (60%). Though a teacher might expect students to change the hardcoded string based on the feedback at *k*, the fact that the same is true

Table 5. Sample feedback for programs in clusters k and p

k Sample Feedback	p Sample Feedback
Testing the first example in the question. Your submission did not produce the correct output. Your program output: What rhymes with Grok? **rock** clock when it was meant to output: What rhymes with Grok? **rock** rock	Testing the second example in the question (when the user enters sock). Your submission did not produce the correct output. Your program output: What rhymes with Grok? **sock** rock when it was meant to output: What rhymes with Grok? **sock** sock Remember to store the user input in a variable, and to use the variable name with print

of p is surprising. One possibility is that students try to modify their code as soon as they see the output is wrong, without reading all of the feedback. This could perhaps be addressed by including the suggestion at the beginning of the feedback.

The common paths, *dab* and *cab*, are examples of students responding to feedback as expected, being guided efficiently to the solution. At d, c and a, the feedback directs students to correct the words, capitalisation and whitespace respectively in their input prompts. The median time taken for each of the transitions (*ca*, *da* and *ab*) was 54, 32 and 44 s respectively, and the median number of times students ran their code after correcting their code was one, the required number. This suggests students on these paths quickly understood and responded to the given feedback.

Of the clusters with self-loops, students in f seemed to experience the most difficulty: it has the largest proportion of repeated submissions (38%) by the largest proportion of unique students (42%), and the largest median time between repeats (42 s). In fact, 24% of the 161 students who did not complete the exercise stopped at f. Though this number was still small relative to the total number of students, it could still be an opportunity to improve feedback. The feedback given for the sample program in cluster f focused on the input prompt not containing the correct words, but perhaps it could be changed to target the presence of certain features in a student program instead, such as an input function.

Unexpected Clusters. This exercise provides an example of how unexpected clusters of programs can reveal potential issues with test cases. One small cluster of programs (21 instances) that failed the first example test had an interesting structure: the programs asked for input from the user and printed it correctly, but the input prompt was incorrect. This was interesting, because they passed the four tests checking the input prompt. By analysing the programs in this cluster, teachers could correct the tests, which could improve not only this exercise, but any others using similar tests.

5.2   Example 2 - Letter from the Queen

We briefly discuss a later exercise to show how this method can be used to measure student improvement over time. This exercise requires students to prompt the user for their age, convert the input to an integer, subtract it from 100 and print out the result. The interaction graph for this exercise is shown in Fig. 4.

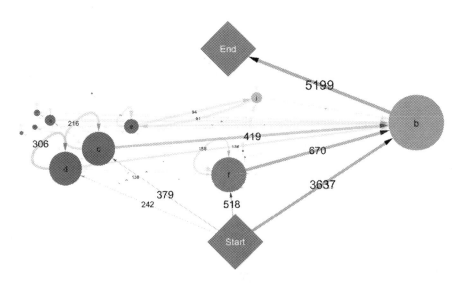

Fig. 4. Interaction graph for the exercise "Letter from the Queen"

Measuring Improvement. Despite the exercise being more difficult, a greater proportion of students (69% compared to 50%) submitted a correct program on their first try, and 99% completed the exercise, indicating students improved in this later problem. A similar hardcoded cycle as in the last problem can be seen (between e and j), suggesting some students were repeating the same mistakes, but this occurred for a smaller number of students. Similarly, the cycles on f and c are similar to the cycles on d, c and a in the earlier exercise in that they involve mostly correct student programs with incorrect prompt strings. These too involve fewer students than previously, suggesting improvement. Cluster d represents programs attempting to read too much input, which was much less frequent in the previous exercise. This new issue could be a result of students needing to print more output, which they mistakenly did by overusing the input function. This overall suggests students were generally improving, with less making the same mistakes as before and more making new mistakes as the question increased in difficulty.

Targeting Tests. In this exercise, 9 tests were run on student programs, but almost all failing programs were caught by the first three tests. This suggests there is an opportunity to make the tests more targeted to student code. From the clustering, teachers can see different kinds of programs failing the same test, such as is shown in Table 6. This can then be used to create tests targeted at the different approaches. For example, one could be targeted towards hardcoded answers (*t*), another could check the subtraction is done correctly (*g*) and another could check for correct strings (*f*).

Table 6. Sample programs from clusters that fail the second test, which checks grammar

Cluster	Cluster Size	Sample Program

f	847	`print("Years until your letter...")`
		`time = 100 - age`
		`print(time)`

t	46	`input('How old are you?')`
		`print('Years until your letter...')`
		`print('85')`

g	41	`age=input ('How old are you?')`
		`print ('Years until your letter...')`
		`print ( int(age) - int( 100))`

6 Discussion and Conclusions

In this paper we have explored a new data-driven method for the assessment of online automated tutors in the context of computer programming. This method involves clustering student programs based on their functionality, building an interaction graph and applying sequential pattern mining, while also using other data from the system, to analyse student interactions and progress.

Our method can be used to gain insights into student learning, including how students begin and end an exercise (e.g. indicating if they had the required prior knowledge), common paths taken and cycles that may be indicative of difficulty. By investigating these areas, teachers can identify difficult concepts and common mistakes. The differences in student behaviour across exercises can allow teachers to measure student learning by observing similarities and differences in the types of progressions and mistakes made by students in each exercise.

This information can also facilitate the improvement of tutoring systems. For example, the identification of areas where the feedback provided to students works well, and areas where it can be improved, including in places where student responses may be unexpected, can help teachers to revise automated feedback. In addition, it can assist in the improvement of test cases: unexpected student program clusters can be used to find problems with the sequence of tests, and different program clusters that fail the same test can be used to create more targeted tests. This information can also be used to provide feedback to students within the classroom, e.g. by explaining common issues and how to address them before attempting an exercise.

In future, this method could be improved by evaluating it with other teachers and extending it to a broader class of computer programs and languages. It could also be combined with other methods for clustering and analysis to provide further information to teachers on the quality of the student programs, such as style, time and space complexity, and could possibly be applied to all exercises in the course at once rather than individual exercises.

Another direction for future work is extending the method to generate automated feedback for students. For example, students could be encouraged to try new styles of coding: by identifying parts of their code that functioned similarly to parts of other students' code, a tutoring system could suggest they try the other style, which might be shorter or more efficient. Our method could also potentially be used in the generation of feedback by identifying functionally similar past examples and adapting the given feedback to new problems.

Ultimately, in a society where automated tutoring systems are becoming increasingly complex and serving larger and larger cohorts of students, data-driven methods such as the proposed method are essential to support teachers in their assessment with empirical evidence. In this way, we can close the loop between teachers, students and tutoring systems, ensuring teachers can diagnose and correct unexpected issues and, in doing so, allow these systems to meet their full potential as effective learning tools. Thus we believe the method we have presented is useful, not only to aid teachers now, but as a stepping stone to the continued improvement of tutoring systems in the future.

References

1. Gerdes, A., Heeren, B., Jeuring, J., van Binsbergen, L.T.: Ask-Elle: an adaptable programming tutor for haskell giving automated feedback. Int. J. Artif. Intell. Educ. **27**(1), 65–100 (2017). https://doi.org/10.1007/s40593-015-0080-x
2. Venables, A., Haywood, L.: Programming students NEED instant feedback! In: Proceedings of the Fifth Australasian Conference on Computing (ACE), pp. 267–272. ACM, Adelaide (2003)
3. Edwards, S.H., Perez-Quinones, M.A.: Web-CAT: automatically grading programming assignments. In: Proceedings of the 13th Annual Conference on Innovation and Technology in Computer Science Education (ITiCSE), p. 328. ACM, Madrid (2008). https://doi.org/10.1145/1597849.1384371
4. Enstrom, E., Kreitz, G., Niemela, F., Soderman, P., Kann, V.: Five years with Kattis using an automated assessment system in teaching. In: Proceedings - Frontiers in Education Conference (FIE), pp. T3 J-1–T3 J-6, IEEE, Rapid City (2011). https://doi.org/10.1109/fie.2011.6142931
5. Rivers, K., Koedinger, K.: Data-driven hint generation in vast solution spaces: a self-improving python programming tutor. Int. J. Artif. Intell. Educ. **27**(1), 37–64 (2017). https://doi.org/10.1007/s40593-015-0070-z
6. Chow, S., Yacef, K., Koprinska, I., Curran, J.: Automated data-driven hints for computer programming students. In: Adjunct Proceedings of the 25th Conference on User Modeling, Adaptation and Personalization (UMAP), pp. 5–10, ACM, Bratislava, Slovakia (2017). https://doi.org/10.1145/3099023.3099065
7. Gramoli, V., Charleston, M., Jeffries, B., Koprinksa, I., McGrane, M., Radu, A., Viglas, A., Yacef, K.: Mining autograding data in computer science education. In: Proceedings of the Australasian Computer Science Week Multiconference. ACM, Canberra (2016). https://doi.org/10.1145/2843043.2843070
8. Stamper, J., Barnes, T., Lehmann, L., Croy, M.: The hint factory: automatic generation of contextualized help for existing computer aided instruction. In: Proceedings of the 9th International Conference on Intelligent Tutoring Systems (ITS), pp. 71–78. Springer, Montreal, Canada (2008)

9. Johnson, S., Zaiane, O.: Deciding on feedback polarity and timing. In: Proceedings of the International Conference on Educational Data Mining (EDM), IEDMS, Chania, Greece, pp. 220−222 (2012)
10. Barnes, T., Stampler, J.: Automatic hint generation for logic proof tutoring using historical data. J. Educ. Technol. Soc. **13**(1), 3–12 (2010). https://doi.org/10.1007/978-3-540-69132-7_41
11. Perikos, I., Grivokostopoulou, F., Hatzilygeroudis, I.: Assistance and feedback mechanism in an intelligent tutoring system for teaching conversion of natural language into logic. Int. J. Artif. Intell. Educ. **27**(3), 475–514 (2017). https://doi.org/10.1007/s40593-017-0139-y
12. Dominguez, A., Yacef, K., Curran, J.: Data mining for individualized hints in eLearning. In: Proceedings of the International Conference on Educational Data Mining (EDM), IEDMS, Pittsburgh, PA, United States, pp. 91−100 (2010)
13. Yin, H., Moghadam, J., Fox, A.: Clustering student programming assignments to multiply instructor leverage. In: Proceedings of the Learning at Scale Conference (L@S), pp. 367−372. ACM, Vancouver (2015). https://doi.org/10.1145/2724660.2728695
14. Gross, S., Mokbel, B., Paassen, B., Hammer, B., Pinkwart, N.: Example-based feedback provision using structured solution spaces. Int. J. Learn. Technol. **9**(3), 248–280 (2014). https://doi.org/10.1504/ijlt.2014.065752
15. Paassen, B., Mokbel, B., Hammer, B.: Adaptive structure metrics for automated feedback provision in intelligent tutoring systems. Neurocomputing **192**, 3–13 (2016). https://doi.org/10.1016/j.neucom.2015.12.108
16. Glassman, E., Scott, J., Singh, R., Guo, P.J., Miller, R.C.: Overcode: visualizing variation in student solutions to programming problems at scale. ACM Trans. Comput. Hum. Interact. **22**(2), 1–35 (2015). https://doi.org/10.1145/2699751
17. Koprinska, I., Stretton, J., Yacef, K.: Students at risk: detection and remediation. In: Proceedings of the International Conference on Educational Data Mining (EDM), IEDMS, Madrid, Spain, pp. 512−515 (2015)
18. Koprinska, I., Stretton, J., Yacef, K.: Predicting student performance from multiple data sources. In: Conati, C., Heffernan, N., Mitrovic, A., Verdejo, M.F. (eds.) AIED 2015. LNCS (LNAI), vol. 9112, pp. 678–681. Springer, Cham (2015). https://doi.org/10.1007/978-3-319-19773-9_90
19. McBroom, J., Jeffries, B., Koprinska, I., Yacef, K.: Mining behaviours of students in autograding submission. In: Proceedings of the International Conference on Educational Data Mining (EDM), IEDMS, Raleigh, NC, United States, pp. 159−166 (2016)
20. McBroom, J., Jeffries, B., Koprinska, I., Yacef, K.: Exploring and following students' strategies when completing their weekly tasks. In: Proceedings of the International Conference on Educational Data Mining (EDM), IEDMS, Raleigh, NC, United States, pp. 609−610 (2016)
21. Grok Learning. https://groklearning.com. Accessed 8 Feb 2018
22. Figures 1, 3 and 4 produced using Cytoscape graphing software Cytoscape. www.cytoscape.org. Accessed 8 Feb 2018

Student Agency and Game-Based Learning: A Study Comparing Low and High Agency

Huy Nguyen[1(✉)], Erik Harpstead[2], Yeyu Wang[2], and Bruce M. McLaren[2]

[1] Lafayette College, Easton, PA, USA
nguyenha@lafayette.edu
[2] Carnegie Mellon University, Pittsburgh, PA, USA

Abstract. A key feature of most computer-based games is agency: the capability for students to make their own decisions in how they play. Agency is assumed to lead to engagement and fun, but may or may not be helpful to learning. While the best learners are often good self-regulated learners, many students are not, only benefiting from instructional choices made for them. In the study presented in this paper, involving a total of 158 fifth and sixth grade students, children played a mathematics learning game called *Decimal Point*, which helps middle-school students learn decimals. One group of students (79) played and learned with a *low-agency* version of the game, in which they were guided to play all "mini-games" in a prescribed sequence. The other group of students (79) played and learned with a *high-agency* version of the game, in which they could choose how many and in what order they would play the mini-games. The results show there were no significant differences in learning or enjoyment across the low and high-agency conditions. A key reason for this may be that students across conditions did not substantially vary in the way they played, perhaps due to the indirect control features present in the game. It may also be the case that the young students who participated in this study did not exercise their agency or self-regulated learning. This work is relevant to the AIED community, as it explores how game-based learning can be adapted. In general, once we know which game and learning features lead to the best learning outcomes, as well as the circumstances that maximize those outcomes, we can better design AI-powered, adaptive games for learning.

Keywords: Student agency · Educational game · Mathematics

1 Introduction

There is palpable interest in the potential of educational games to engage students and enhance learning. Teachers are particularly excited about the use of educational games in their classrooms, with a high percentage having their students use games for learning at least once a week (55% of 513, according to [9]).

© Springer International Publishing AG, part of Springer Nature 2018
C. Penstein Rosé et al. (Eds.): AIED 2018, LNAI 10947, pp. 338–351, 2018.
https://doi.org/10.1007/978-3-319-93843-1_25

At the same time, young people are playing computer games at an ever increasing rate. For instance, [15] reported a playing frequency of 4.9 to 5.8 h per week for children age 7 to 12. The enthusiasm for educational games, combined with the increasing interest of young people in playing computer games, is leading to a revolution in education, with educational games in the forefront.

At the same time, scientific research has started to provide evidence that games can be effective for learning [2,4,14,19,31]. For instance, research has shown the benefits of learning decimal mathematics with an educational game called *Decimal Point*, which was designed based on theory and evidence about common student misconceptions [8]. In a study involving more than 150 middle school students, *Decimal Point* led to significantly more learning and was self-reported by students as significantly more enjoyable than a more conventional computer-based tutoring approach [20]. Other studies, in the areas of mathematics [11,22], science [1,12], and language learning [29,32], have shown similar learning and/or engagement benefits for educational games.

The search is now on for the specific features of games that lead to engagement and learning benefits, as well as how we can best leverage those features to maximize the potential of educational games [2]. Potential game features to explore include game challenge, fantasy, in-game actions, in-game objects, animation, game environment, and feedback [6,18]. For instance, Lomas and colleagues have explored the benefits of increasing challenge in an educational game, finding that increasing challenge doesn't necessarily increase motivation and learning; instead students were generally more motivated by "easy" versions of games [16,17]. Another key feature of educational games is *agency*, the capability for students to decide how to play games - what aspects of a game they will explore, how long they will play, and when they will try out various game features. Agency is often seen as a component of engagement [23], which in turn leads to fun. Yet, agency, which is closely related to self-regulated learning [34], may or may not be helpful for learning. While the best learners, those who demonstrate achievement on tests, are often good self-regulated learners [26,34], many students are not good at regulating their learning, benefiting from instructional choices being made for them through direct instruction [33].

Several past studies have explored the effects of agency by giving students control over the way they play an educational game. For example, [30] showed that letting students decide the amount of time to work on different lessons can lead to higher learning outcomes. On the other hand, allowing students to make choices on instructionally irrelevant components of a learning environment has also been shown to make a difference to learning. For instance, [3] let students customize game icons and names in their arithmetic tutor, while [27] provided in-game currency, which could be spent on personalizing the system interface or extra game play. In these studies, the idea was to provide students with a sense of control without the risk of making poor pedagogical decisions. The general results across these studies showed that students who exercised their agency became more involved and learned more.

A notable example of studying student agency, in which students were given instructionally relevant choices, comes from Sawyer et al. [24] who explored variations in agency within the game *Crystal Island*. In *Crystal Island*, students are tasked with exploring an island and interacting with people and objects to gather knowledge about a spreading disease, learning about microbiology along the way. Three agency conditions were present in this study: high-agency, which allowed students to navigate to locations in the environment in any order; low-agency, which restricted students to a prescribed order, and no-agency, where students simply watched a video of an expert playing the game. In their study Sawyer et al. found that students in the low-agency condition attempted more incorrect submissions but also attained significantly higher learning gains, which might be attributed to their extensively engaging with instructional materials. Their results suggest that limiting agency improves learning performance but can also lead to undesirable student behaviors, such as a propensity for guessing.

In our study we explore variations of agency within *Decimal Point*, the educational game briefly described above. Our study compares a low-agency version of the game, in which students are guided to play in a prescribed sequence, playing all possible "mini-games," to a high-agency version of the game, in which students can choose how many and in what order they will play the mini-games. The study is comparable to Sawyer et al. [24] in its exploration of agency; students are compelled either to play the game in a lock-step order or to exercise autonomy by making their own choices about game play. In addition, the choices students are presented with in both *Decimal Point* and *Crystal Island* are pedagogically relevant. In the high-agency version of *Decimal Point*, a student can choose to play mini-games that focus on specific aspects of the content domain (e.g., adding decimals, comparing decimals, completing decimal sequences), as well as choosing to get more or less practice with decimals (and game playing). Our research questions and hypotheses for the study are as follows.

Research Question 1. *Is there a difference in learning between students who play the low-agency version of the game versus the students who play the high-agency version of the game?* Given the results of the Sawyer et al. study [24], as well as the similarities between our implementation of agency and theirs, we hypothesized that the low-agency version of the game would lead to better learning outcomes than the high-agency version of the game.

Research Question 2. *Is there a difference in enjoyment between students who play the low-agency version of the game versus the students who play the high-agency version of the game?* Given past research on agency showing that students prefer to make their own choices, regardless of whether those choices are pedagogically beneficial [3,24], we hypothesized that the high-agency version of the game would lead to higher levels of enjoyment than the low-agency version.

2   The Educational Game: *Decimal Point*

Decimal Point is a single-player game designed to help middle-school students learn decimals. The game is based on an amusement park metaphor (Fig. 1), with the student traveling to different theme areas (e.g., "Haunted House," "Wild West"), playing a variety of mini-games within each area (e.g., "Western Shooter," and "OK Corral," within the Wild West theme area). The mini-games are targeted at helping students overcome common decimal misconceptions [10, 13, 28]. Students do not score points or compete with their fellow students. Instead, they simply play the mini-games in the amusement park and are commended upon completing the journey. There are no other activities within *Decimal Point* beyond playing of the mini-games.

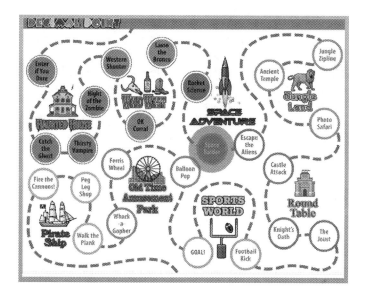

Fig. 1. The *Decimal Point* game (low-agency version).

An example mini-game, "Space Raider," is shown in Fig. 2. This game challenges the student to use laser guns (lower left and right of Fig. 2) to shoot decimal-labeled spaceships (e.g., 0.3234, 0.5, 0.82, 0.634) in the order from smallest to largest decimal. The "Space Raider" mini-game is targeted at "whole number thinking," a common misconception in which students think longer decimals are larger than shorter decimals [28]. The student tries to shoot the spaceships in the requested order and, if they make mistakes, are prompted to correct their solution by dragging and dropping the numbers into the correct sequence. Feedback in this mini-game is provided at the end of the game, once all spaceships have been shot. In Fig. 2, the student has exhibited the misconception by shooting the spaceships in length order: 0.5, 0.82, 0.634.

In the original version of *Decimal Point*, students are prompted to play each mini-game in a pre-specified sequence, according to the dashed path shown in Fig. 1, starting from the upper left. In the study discussed in this paper, this setting is referred to as the *low-agency* version of the game, since student choice

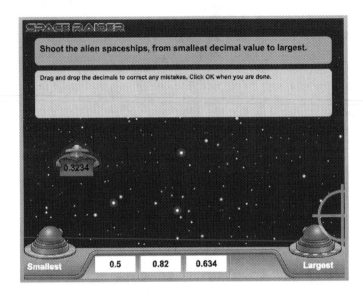

Fig. 2. A student playing the "Space Raider" mini-game.

is limited. In order to explore agency, we extended the game to a *high-agency* version that allows students more control over their experience and learning. As depicted in Fig. 3, students are given several choices. First, they can play the mini-games in any order they choose. Students are also presented with a dashboard that displays the five different categories of mini-games (i.e., (1) "Addition - Add decimals", (2) "Bucket - Compare decimals", (3) "Sequence - Complete a decimal sequence", (4) "Number Line - Place point on number line", (5) "Sorting - Ordering decimals"), as well as the specific mini-games within each category. In Fig. 3 four mini-games have been played, indicated by their icons being colored in the map and their names shown in red font in the dashboard. By mousing over the various game icons, the student can learn about each game and thus access information and gain knowledge to make informed choices.

Second, students can stop playing *Decimal Point* once they have finished playing at least one-half of the mini-games, as shown in Fig. 4. When they reach the halfway point, they are presented with a dialogue that says "You have finished playing half of the mini-games. You can keep playing until all games have been played or stop at any time by clicking on the Stop Playing button," and a new "Stop Playing" button appears in the upper left, as in Fig. 4. At any time from this point until they finish playing all of the games, students can click on "Stop Playing" to quit playing and proceed to the next item in the materials.

Finally, once students have completed every mini-game once (2 problems per mini-game), they can play more mini-games, any of the original 24 games, for one additional problem each. They are also presented with a dialogue telling them they can keep playing (i.e., "You have played all of the mini-games. You can now either quit (by clicking on Stop Playing) or replay some of the

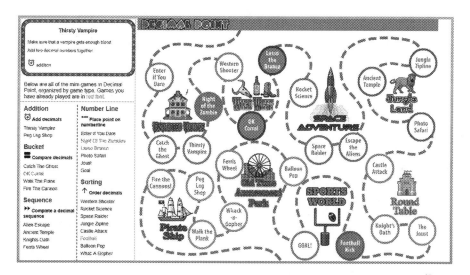

Fig. 3. High-agency version of the *Decimal Point* game. The mouse cursor is currently over the "Thirsty Vampire" icon, displaying that mini-game's info in the dashboard.

mini-games") and a "Stop Playing" button that allows them to stop playing at any time (Fig. 4). Taken together, these changes mean that students playing the high-agency version of *Decimal Point* can play from 24 up to 72 mini-games (compared to the standard 48 in the low-agency condition), in any order of their choosing.

As mentioned, the original (low-agency) version of the game has been empirically demonstrated to be effective for engagement and learning. In our previous study [20], students were assigned to one of two conditions that were compared: the game condition or the non-game condition. Students in the game condition were presented with two problems to solve for each of the mini-games shown in Fig. 1. The non-game condition presented a more conventional user interface to the students, prompting students to solve precisely the same decimal problems, in the same order. [20] compared 75 game-playing students to 83 non-game-playing students and found that the game-playing students enjoyed their experience more and learned more. In subsequent data analyses, we also found that female students benefited more from *Decimal Point* than male students, and the game made difficult problems more tractable for all students, as students in the game condition made significantly fewer errors on the difficult problems [21]. In this paper, we describe a study to explore how extending the agency feature of the game might alter student learning.

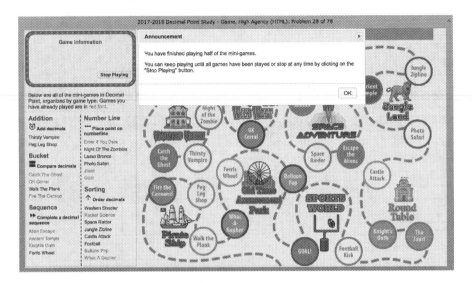

Fig. 4. High-agency version of the *Decimal Point* game after the student has played one-half of the mini-games and is given the option to stop. A "Stop Playing" button appears on the dashboard in the upper left.

3   Method

3.1   Participants and Design

The original participants were 197 students from two schools in a large U.S. city (45 fifth and 152 sixth graders). Students were randomly assigned to either the high-agency (HA) or the low-agency (LA) condition. Thirty-two (32) participants (19 HA, 13 LA) were excluded from the analyses because they did not fully complete all materials and measures in the study. An additional seven (7) participants were removed due to having gain scores 2.5 standard deviations above or below the mean between the pretest and the immediate posttest or between the pretest and the delayed posttest. The remaining 158 students (79 HA; 79 LA; 81 male, 77 female) had a mean age of 11.15 (SD = 0.60).

3.2   Materials

A web-based learning environment was used to deploy the experiment, and the instructional materials were assigned to each group as outlined in Table 1. Materials included three tests (pretest, posttest, delayed posttest), the two game versions, and two questionnaires (demographic, evaluation). Details about the materials are provided in the remainder of this section.

Pretest, Immediate Posttest, and Delayed Posttest. The pretest, immediate posttest, and delayed posttest (one week after the posttest), were administered online. Each test consisted of 24 items, some of which had multiple parts, comprising 61 possible points. Participants received points for each correct part. There was an A, B, and C form of the base test, which were isomorphic to one another and which were positionally counter-balanced within condition (i.e., approximately 1/3 of the students in each condition received Test A as the pretest, 1/3 received Test B as the pretest, and 1/3 received Test C as the pretest; likewise for the posttest and delayed posttest). According to the result of an ANOVA, there was no difference, in terms of the difficulty level, among the three versions of the test: A, B and C ($F(2, 155) = 1.14$, $p = 0.322$).

Table 1. Conditions and Materials used in the study. *Italicized* items vary across conditions.

High-agency game	Low-agency game
Pretest (A, B or C)	Pretest (A, B or C)
Demographic questionnaire	Demographic questionnaire
Game play *(between 24 and 72 mini-game items played, in order of student choice.)*	Game play *(exactly 48 mini-game items played, in prescribed order.)*
Evaluation questionnaire	Evaluation questionnaire
Immediate posttest (A, B or C)	Immediate posttest (A, B or C)
Delayed posttest (A, B or C)	Delayed posttest (A, B or C)

Test items were designed to probe for specific decimal misconceptions and took a variety of forms, for instance: adding, multiplying, and dividing decimal numbers (e.g., `0.387 + 0.05 = ____`), choosing the largest of a given set of decimals (e.g., "Choose the largest of the following three numbers: `5.413`, `5.75`, `5.6`"), and placing a given decimal number on a number line.

Questionnaire. After the lesson, an online evaluation questionnaire was presented to the students, prompting them to rate their experience of interacting with the instructional materials. Students could respond on a 5-point Likert scale, ranging from 1 = "strongly disagree" to 5 = "strongly agree". For the purpose of our analysis, the eight items in the evaluation questionnaire were combined into the following three different categories:

1. *Lesson Enjoyment* indicates how much students like the lesson, such as "I liked doing this lesson" and "I would like to do more lessons like this."
2. *Ease of Interface Use* indicates how easy it was to interact with the intervention items and interface for the lesson, such as "I liked the way the material was presented on the screen," "I liked the way the computer responded to my input," "I think the interface of the system was confusing," and "It was easy to enter my answer into the system."
3. *Attitude towards Math* indicates how students felt about math after completing the intervention, such as "The lesson made me feel more like I am good at math" and "The lesson made me feel that math is fun. "

4   Results

First, a repeated measures ANOVA showed that students in both conditions learned from the pretest to the immediate posttest (LA: ($F(1,78) = 70.803$, $p < 0.0005$); HA: ($F(1,78) = 49.043$, $p < 0.0005$)) and from the pretest to the delayed posttest (LA: ($F(1,78) = 67.931$, $p < 0.0005$); HA: ($F(1,78) = 109.64$, $p < 0.0005$)). Next, we conducted analyses related to our two research questions, as well as conducting other post-hoc analyses.

Research Question 1. *Is there a difference in learning performance between students who play the low-agency version of the game versus the students who play the high-agency version of the game?* With pretest scores used as a covariate, we ran an ANCOVA for both pretest-immediate posttest and pretest-delayed posttest. Results are shown in Table 2. The LA group performed slightly better than the HA group on the immediate posttest ($F(1,155) = 1.8$, $p = 0.182$, $d = 0.13$) but worse on the delayed posttest ($F(1,155) = 2.465$, $p = 0.118$, $d = -0.14$). Neither result is significant.

Interestingly, when broken down by separate schools - one in which we experimented with sixth graders (School 1) and a second in which we experimented with fifth graders (School 2) - we see a significant result. Again, applying ANCOVA with pretest scores as covariates, in School 1 (6th graders) the low-agency group ($n = 61$) performed significantly better than the high-agency group ($n = 61$) on the immediate posttest ($F(1,119) = 4.534$, $p = 0.035$, $d = 0.18$). However, the low-agency group performed slightly worse, but not significantly so, on the delayed posttest ($F(1,119) = 1.286$, $p = 0.259$, $d = -0.15$).

Table 2. Learning results across conditions.

	Low agency (n = 79)	High agency (n = 79)	Effect size (d)
Pretest (max = 61)	35.9 (12.4)	35.9 (12.2)	–
Immediate posttest (max = 61)	42.0 (9.5)	40.8 (10.5)	0.13
Delayed posttest (max = 61)	41.7 (10.5)	43.1 (11.0)	−0.14

For School 2 (5th graders) the low-agency group ($n = 18$) performed slightly better, but not significantly, than the high-agency group ($n = 18$) on the immediate posttest ($F(1,33) = 0.621$, $p = 0.436$, $d = -0.08$). The low-agency group performed slightly worse, but not significantly so, on the delayed posttest ($F(1,33) = 1.68$, $p = 0.204$, $d = -0.12$).

In summary, our hypothesis that the LA group would learn more than the HA group was not confirmed, except with respect to one of the schools, and only on the immediate posttest at that school.

Research Question 2. *Is there a difference in enjoyment between students who play the low-agency version of the game versus the students who play the* *high-agency version of the game?* Three categories that roughly summarize how students enjoyed and felt about the game (i.e.. Enjoyment in the Lesson, Ease of Interface Using, Attitude towards Math) were assessed by one-way ANOVA (Table 3). For lesson enjoyment, the high-agency and low-agency groups did not differ significantly ($F(1, 156) = 0.007$, $p = 0.935$, $d = -0.01$). For Ease of Interface, again, the two groups did not differ significantly ($F(1, 156) = 0.285$, $p = 0.594$, $d = -0.085$). Also, for Attitude towards Math the groups did not differ significantly ($F(1, 156) = 0.584$, $p = 0.446$, $d = 0.122$).

In summary, our hypothesis was not confirmed that the HA group would experience a higher level of enjoyment with the game than the LA group.

Table 3. Engagement results across conditions.

	Low agency (n = 79)	High agency (n = 79)	Effect size (d)
Lesson Enjoyment (1–5)	4.0 (1.0)	4.0 (0.9)	−0.01
Ease of Interface (1–5)	3.5 (0.5)	3.6 (0.5)	−0.09
Attitude towards Math (1–5)	4.0 (1.0)	3.9 (1.0)	0.12

Posthoc Analyses. Given the results and answers to our research questions, we performed post-hoc analyses to better understand why we did not see the differences we expected between the high-agency and low-agency game conditions. In particular, we were interested in exploring what the high-agency students did with the additional control they were given in game play. Did they take advantage of it, to explore the game and have more fun? Did they leverage their autonomy to make self-regulated learning choices?

To explore these questions, we looked at the specific mini-games and mini-game sequences that were chosen by players in the HA condition. The number of high-agency students who did less than, exactly the same, and more than the canonical number of problems was 15, 54, and 10, respectively. Thus, a significant majority of the HA students (68%) played the same mini-games as the LA students. Furthermore, we found that 22% of students in the HA condition precisely followed the canonical sequence (i.e., the sequence prescribed in the LA condition, as shown in Fig. 1). To get a sense of how different the sequences of students in the HA condition were from the canonical sequence, we calculated Damerau-Levenshtein distance between each students' sequence and the canonical one. Damerau-Levenshtein distance counts the number of insertions, deletions, substitutions, and transpositions needed to turn one string into another [5]. In addition to raw Damerau-Levenshtein distance we also calculated a length matched distance, which measured either the edit distance between a student's sequence and a subsequence of the canonical sequence in the event the student played less than 24 mini-games or a subset of the student's sequence of equal length to the canonical sequence in the event they played more mini-games. This modified edit distance avoids inflating the distance for those students who chose to play more or less while still giving a qualitative sense of how similar their path was to the standard path.

In general, the distributions of edit distances were lopsided, due to so many players following the prescribed order. On average, players' sequences differed by about 13.07 edits (SD = 9.73) from the canonical sequence, meaning roughly half of the mini-games they played followed the expected sequence. When controlling for sequence length (i.e., when students chose to play more or less mini-games) this effect is further tempered to 10.77 edits (SD 8.83) from the standard order.

In addition to the distributional information we also checked to see whether a student's edit distance from the canonical sequence had any effect on their pretest - posttest or pretest - delayed posttest learning gains. Repeated-measures ANCOVA showed no significant effects for pretest - posttest ($F(1, 78) = 0.18$, $p = 0.67$) or pretest - delayed posttest ($F(1, 78) = 0.00$, $p = 1.00$). This means that the amount of difference between a student's chosen ordering and the prescribed ordering had little effect on their learning gains.

5   Discussion

We hypothesized that our findings would (roughly) replicate those of Sawyer et al. [24], given the similarities in implementation of agency between the two games. However, other than the finding at School 1, in which the low-agency students did exhibit a better learning outcome than the high-agency students, we did not replicate their findings. Instead, we found no overall differences in learning between the low- and high-agency students who played *Decimal Point*. Given that our results only partially replicate those of Sawyer et al., we are left with the question of explaining why this happened.

As stated earlier, our implementation of agency has key aspects in common with [24]. For instance, students are compelled either to play the game in a specific order (low-agency condition) or to have autonomy to make choices about the order of game play (high-agency condition). In addition, the choices students are presented with in both games are pedagogically relevant, unlike other studies of agency, such as [3, 27], in which the choices were unrelated to learning elements in the games. However, one key difference between *Decimal Point* and *Crystal Island* is that the *Decimal Point* high-agency game displays student progress (through the dashboard - Figs. 3 and 4), allowing students to make informed choices about their next step. Perhaps more importantly, in *Decimal Point* the high-agency students are given the choice to stop or continue playing, a game feature that is not part of the high-agency version of *Crystal Island*. In particular, the *Decimal Point* high-agency students were in control of how much practice on the relevant domain problems they wanted, by choosing to play anywhere from 12 less to 24 more mini-games than the standard number.

Interestingly, however, it appears that the high-agency *Decimal Point* students did not exercise their given agency very much. As mentioned above, 68% of the high-agency students tackled precisely the same problems as the low-agency students. Additionally, the sequences of mini-games chosen by the students did not substantially vary from that of the low-agency condition. One potential reason for this lies in the visual design of the amusement park map (Fig. 2). In particular, the dotted line connecting all the mini-games could have implicitly, yet unintentionally, communicated the sequence of mini-games to follow. This could be a case of "indirect control" [25], where subtle pieces of visual design can draw students' attention and guide behavior without explicit direction.

Another interpretation points to the nuanced nature of agency versus autonomy. In our study, while the students were given the choice of which mini-games to play (autonomy), they may not have felt their choices were consequential (agency). When the students finished a mini-game, the only change visible to them was a game icon "blocked" on the map. In other words, playing *Space Raider* before *Thirsty Vampire* or vice versa would lead to the exact same state, where both games are blocked, so which game being picked first would not matter. A recent study by Flowerday and Shell [7] also shows that providing instructional choices alone does not increase motivation and learning outcome; instead, the key motivator is situational interest. Based on this finding, we could redesign the high-agency condition so that student choices have a more significant impact on their subsequent game experience. On the other hand, the freedom to stop early or play additional games *is* an instructionally relevant instance of agency. Yet, students did not take advantage of this, possibly because they are often not good self-regulated learners [34]; younger students are likely to be even weaker in this aspect.

Finally, we note that our study was conducted in a classroom setting, where students' performance on the tests were used for class grades. Thus, there may have been some felt pressure, causing students to be hesitant about finishing early and skipping some materials. As noted in [23], when one feels controlled in pursuing an activity, one's sense of autonomy and motivation becomes diminished. Conducting the same study in a pressure-free environment could potentially yield more pronounced differences between the two agency conditions.

6   Conclusion

This study of student agency was intended to explore the earlier results of [24], investigating whether providing students agency in a game context would increase or decrease their learning. In this study, we did not find that students in a low-agency condition learned more than the students in a high-agency condition (except for one school). As is often the case, shifting the context of instruction can change the results. In our study, the effects of indirect control or teachers' pressure might play an important role. It could also be the case that students did not experience much agency or were not good self-regulated learners. Nevertheless, educational game studies such as this are important in helping us better understand and make decisions about how to implement adaptivity in games, which ultimately artificial intelligence will control. Once we have a better understanding of the specific context in which, for instance, agency leads to better learning, we can develop AIED-infused games that adapt to those contexts.

References

1. Barab, S.A., Scott, B., Siyahhan, S., Goldstone, R., Ingram-Goble, A., Zuiker, S.J., Warren, S.: Transformational play as a curricular scaffold: using videogames to support science education. J. Sci. Educ. Technol. **18**(4), 305 (2009)
2. Clark, D.B., Tanner-Smith, E.E., Killingsworth, S.S.: Digital games, design, and learning: a systematic review and meta-analysis. Rev. Educ. Res. **86**(1), 79–122 (2016)
3. Cordova, D.I., Lepper, M.R.: Intrinsic motivation and the process of learning: beneficial effects of contextualization, personalization, and choice. J. Educ. Psychol. **88**(4), 715 (1996)
4. Crocco, F., Offenholley, K., Hernandez, C.: A proof-of-concept study of game-based learning in higher education. Simul. Gam. **47**(4), 403–422 (2016)
5. Damerau, F.J.: A technique for computer detection and correction of spelling errors. Commun. ACM **7**(3), 171–176 (1964)
6. Deterding, S., Dixon, D., Khaled, R., Nacke, L.: From game design elements to gamefulness: defining gamification. In: Proceedings of the 15th International Academic MindTrek Conference: Envisioning Future Media Environments, pp. 9–15. ACM (2011)
7. Flowerday, T., Shell, D.F.: Disentangling the effects of interest and choice on learning, engagement, and attitude. Learn. Ind. Differ. **40**, 134–140 (2015)
8. Forlizzi, J., McLaren, B.M., Ganoe, C., McLaren, P.B., Kihumba, G., Lister, K.: Decimal point: designing and developing an educational game to teach decimals to middle school students. In: 8th European Conference on Games-Based Learning: ECGBL 2014, pp. 128–135 (2014)
9. Gamesandlearning.org: teachers surveyed on using digital games in class. Technical report (2015). http://www.gamesandlearning.org/2014/06/09/teachers-on-using-games-in-class/
10. Glasgow, R., Ragan, G., Fields, W.M., Reysi, R., Wasman, D.: The decimal dilemma. Teach. Child. Math. **7**(2), 89 (2000)
11. Habgood, M.J., Ainsworth, S.E.: Motivating children to learn effectively: exploring the value of intrinsic integration in educational games. J. Learn. Sci. **20**(2), 169–206 (2011)
12. Hwang, G.J., Wu, P.H., Chen, C.C.: An online game approach for improving students learning performance in web-based problem-solving activities. Comput. Educ. **59**(4), 1246–1256 (2012)
13. Isotani, S., McLaren, B.M., Altman, M.: Towards Intelligent tutoring with erroneous examples: a taxonomy of decimal misconceptions. In: Aleven, V., Kay, J., Mostow, J. (eds.) ITS 2010. LNCS, vol. 6095, pp. 346–348. Springer, Heidelberg (2010). https://doi.org/10.1007/978-3-642-13437-1_66
14. Ke, F.: Designing and integrating purposeful learning in game play: a systematic review. Educ. Technol. Res. Dev. **64**(2), 219–244 (2016)
15. Lobel, A., Engels, R.C., Stone, L.L., Burk, W.J., Granic, I.: Video gaming and childrens psychosocial wellbeing: a longitudinal study. J. Youth Adolesc. **46**(4), 884–897 (2017)
16. Lomas, D., Patel, K., Forlizzi, J.L., Koedinger, K.R.: Optimizing challenge in an educational game using large-scale design experiments. In: Proceedings of the SIGCHI Conference on Human Factors in Computing Systems, pp. 89–98. ACM (2013)

17. Lomas, J.D., Koedinger, K., Patel, N., Shodhan, S., Poonwala, N., Forlizzi, J.L.: Is difficulty overrated?: the effects of choice, novelty and suspense on intrinsic motivation in educational games. In: Proceedings of the 2017 CHI Conference on Human Factors in Computing Systems, pp. 1028–1039. ACM (2017)
18. Malone, T.W.: Toward a theory of intrinsically motivating instruction. Cogn. Sci. 5(4), 333–369 (1981)
19. Mayer, R.E.: Computer Games for Learning: An Evidence-Based Approach. MIT Press, Cambridge (2014)
20. McLaren, B.M., Adams, D.M., Mayer, R.E., Forlizzi, J.: A computer-based game that promotes mathematics learning more than a conventional approach. Int. J. Game Based Learn. 7(1), 36–56 (2017)
21. McLaren, B., Farzan, R., Adams, D., Mayer, R., Forlizzi, J.: Uncovering gender and problem difficulty effects in learning with an educational game. In: André, E., Baker, R., Hu, X., Rodrigo, M.M.T., du Boulay, B. (eds.) AIED 2017. LNCS (LNAI), vol. 10331, pp. 540–543. Springer, Cham (2017). https://doi.org/10.1007/978-3-319-61425-0_59
22. Riconscente, M.M.: Results from a controlled study of the ipad fractions game motion math. Games Cult. 8(4), 186–214 (2013)
23. Ryan, R.M., Rigby, C.S., Przybylski, A.: The motivational pull of video games: a self-determination theory approach. Motiv. Emot. 30(4), 344–360 (2006)
24. Sawyer, R., Smith, A., Rowe, J., Azevedo, R., Lester, J.: Is more agency better? The impact of student agency on game-based learning. In: André, E., Baker, R., Hu, X., Rodrigo, M.M.T., du Boulay, B. (eds.) AIED 2017. LNCS, vol. 10331, pp. 335–346. Springer, Cham (2017). https://doi.org/10.1007/978-3-319-61425-0_28
25. Schell, J.: The Art of Game Design: A Book of Lenses. CRC Press, New York (2014)
26. Schunk, D.H., Zimmerman, B.J.: Influencing children's self-efficacy and self-regulation of reading and writing through modeling. Read. Writ. Q. 23(1), 7–25 (2007)
27. Snow, E.L., Allen, L.K., Jacovina, M.E., McNamara, D.S.: Does agency matter?: exploring the impact of controlled behaviors within a game-based environment. Comput. Educ. 82, 378–392 (2015)
28. Stacey, K., Helme, S., Steinle, V.: Confusions between decimals, fractions and negative numbers: a consequence of the mirror as a conceptual metaphor in three different ways. In: PME Conference, vol. 4, pp. 4–217 (2001)
29. Suh, S., Kim, S.W., Kim, N.J.: Effectiveness of MMORPG-based instruction in elementary english education in Korea. J. Comput. Assist. Learn. 26(5), 370–378 (2010)
30. Tabbers, H.K., de Koeijer, B.: Learner control in animated multimedia instructions. Instruc. Sci. 38(5), 441–453 (2010)
31. Wouters, P., Van Oostendorp, H.: Instructional Techniques to Facilitate Learning and Motivation of Serious Games. Springer, Cham (2016). https://doi.org/10.1007/978-3-319-39298-1
32. Yip, F.W., Kwan, A.C.: Online vocabulary games as a tool for teaching and learning english vocabulary. Educ. Media Int. 43(3), 233–249 (2006)
33. Zimmerman, B.J.: Self-efficacy: an essential motive to learn. Contemp. Educ. Psychol. 25(1), 82–91 (2000)
34. Zimmerman, B.J.: Investigating self-regulation and motivation: historical background, methodological developments, and future prospects. Am. Educ. Res. J. 45(1), 166–183 (2008)

Engaging with the Scenario: Affect and Facial Patterns from a Scenario-Based Intelligent Tutoring System

Benjamin D. Nye[1]([✉]), Shamya Karumbaiah[2], S. Tugba Tokel[3], Mark G. Core[1], Giota Stratou[4], Daniel Auerbach[1], and Kallirroi Georgila[1]

[1] Institute for Creative Technologies, University of Southern California, Los Angeles, USA
`{nye,core,auerbach,kgeorgila}@ict.usc.edu`
[2] Penn Center for Learning Analytics, University of Pennsylvania, Philadelphia, USA
`shamya16@gmail.com`
[3] Department of Computer Education and Instructional Technology, METU, Ankara, Turkey
`stugba@metu.edu.tr`
[4] Keysight Technologies, Atlanta, USA
`giotastr@gmail.com`

Abstract. Facial expression trackers output measures for facial action units (AUs), and are increasingly being used in learning technologies. In this paper, we compile patterns of AUs seen in related work as well as use factor analysis to search for categories implicit in our corpus. Although there was some overlap between the factors in our data and previous work, we also identified factors seen in the broader literature but not previously reported in the context of learning environments. In a correlational analysis, we found evidence for relationships between factors and self-reported traits such as academic effort, study habits, and interest in the subject. In addition, we saw differences in average levels of factors between a video watching activity, and a decision making activity. However, in this analysis, we were not able to isolate any facial expressions having a significant positive or negative relationship with either learning gain, or performance once question difficulty and related factors were also considered. Given the overall low levels of facial affect in the corpus, further research will explore different populations and learning tasks to test the possible hypothesis that learners may have been in a pattern of "Over-Flow" in which they were engaged with the system, but not deeply thinking about the content or their errors.

1 Introduction

Engagement, confusion, frustration, boredom, and related states have been demonstrated to impact learning gains on many traditional learning tasks, such as

© Springer International Publishing AG, part of Springer Nature 2018
C. Penstein Rosé et al. (Eds.): AIED 2018, LNAI 10947, pp. 352–366, 2018.
https://doi.org/10.1007/978-3-319-93843-1_26

math problems, reading text, and generating short-answers to questions [2, 6, 7]. There are many hardware/software systems available to detect learner emotions through physical signs. Facial expression trackers such as the Computer Expression Recognition Toolbox (CERT) [19] output measures for facial action units (AUs [10]), and based on the AU values, also output measures for general emotion categories (e.g., neutral, confusion, frustration). AUs are numeric codes representing the muscular movements that produce facial appearance changes. In this paper, we explore the utility of bottom-up information such as facial AUs which are fine-grained but not tied directly to cognitive-affective states (e.g., boredom). We use factor analysis to search for categories implicit in patterns of facial AUs. We also explore the use of top-down information such as the CERT emotion categories which are more coarse-grained and not designed for learning environments, where many affective states (e.g., fear, joy, disgust) are less relevant [6].

To explore the insights provided by learner facial cues during computer-based learning scenarios, we instrumented an intelligent tutoring system (ITS) for leadership training called the Emergent Leader Immersive Training Environment (ELITE)-Lite [16] to unobtrusively collect facial expressions from users and align this data to behavioral log files of system context and user behavior. This data allowed us to analyze the relationship of facial cues to other components of the experience (e.g., type of learning activity, correctness of responses) and to look for opportunities where it may be effective to leverage such cues to improve learning. The bottom-up factors enable a different perspective on the facial data, which is hypothesized to help identify patterns that might not be discovered by a top-down approach. In the following sections, we describe the theoretical background, data sample, and analysis of results, and discuss the findings.

2   Theoretical Background

A growing body of literature has studied emotions during computer-based learning and interaction, with affect measured using techniques such as self-report, human observation, text analysis, facial expression cues, speech audio analysis, physical sensors (e.g., pressure, conductance), and inferences from patterns of learner task behavior [2, 9, 15]. More recently, there has also been a shift toward multimodal affect detection such as through systematic analysis of combinations of tutor-student dialogue, facial affect, and task behavior [14]. A significant number of adaptive and non-adaptive learning tasks have been studied, which range from passive tasks (e.g., reading text and watching videos) to active tasks such as procedural problems (e.g., solving equations) or generative responses (e.g., deep reasoning questions, programming).

Within the space of learning environments that have been studied, some consensus has emerged about the utility of four key cognitive-affective states: engagement/flow, confusion/disequillibrium, frustration, and disengagement/boredom [6]. By comparison, traditional emotion categories such as disgust, fear and sadness have not been relevant to most learning tasks studied.

Among the four key emotions that occur during learning, engagement/flow has generally been shown to be positive and indicating greater attention and processing, and more recently evidence has also been found for confusion as a predictor of learning [7]. In the area of scenario-based learning, researchers studying the Crystal Island ITS found engagement to be associated with better learning outcomes [23]. In contrast, disengagement and boredom are generally understood to hinder learning [2]. The impact of frustration is not as well established - possibly because some students like extreme challenges while others prefer steady difficulty, as seen in video game players [17].

Overall, the majority of studies on cognitive and affective cues have relied on a combination of self-report and human raters. This introduces two limitations. First, human annotation may not provide results that are actionable in a real-time system. Second, since affect taxonomies are determined prior to observing the data, common facial cues or patterns that predict user outcomes might be missed because they did not fit into an expected category. This is particularly relevant because certain cognitive-affective cues are not necessarily social in nature and do not fit directly into traditional taxonomies of affect (e.g., looking "lost in thought"). Thus, human emotion annotation may not be able to be automated and might also miss important signals. A subset of literature has specifically studied how facial action units (AUs [10]) interact with behavior and learning with computers [14]. However, although AUs are fine-grained enough to avoid missing information, they need to be aggregated into metrics that can be interpreted.

To look for patterns in prior literature, we reviewed studies of AUs of learning technology users. Eleven such studies were identified based on data sets from users in seven different systems [1,3,8,12,26–28], which are summarized in Table 1. Each row indicates the AUs that were reported as associated with learning behaviors or outcomes in that study. AUs that were not reported in any of these studies are excluded from the table. In most cases, AUs were studied individually for effects on learning, though studies on AutoTutor and Brain-Skills aligned AUs to engagement, confusion, frustration, boredom, and delight [5,8,21,27]. These alignments are noted with subscripts. Across these studies, AUs relevant to learning in at least three studies were associated with the eyebrows (e.g., raised eyebrows AU1 + AU2, wrinkled/furrowed brow A4), lip corners, dimples, and tightening (AU12, AU14, AU23), and eye lids (tightened lids AU7). Some of these cues also tended to co-occur across studies. For example, raised inner eyebrows (AU1) were reported with raised outer eyebrows (AU2) in five out of seven studies in which either AU1 or AU2 was highlighted.

As such, there is some evidence that certain combinations of AUs indicate events or cognitive states that influence learning. For example, Grafsgaard et al. [14] reported that their best model of learning gains includes facial AUs in addition to data from textual dialogue and behavioral logs. While systematic exploration of these factors will require study of many systems and scenarios over time, this framing underpins certain decisions made for the data collection and analysis presented next.

Table 1. Relevant Action Units (AUs) in different learning systems

Study	Platform	N	1	2	4	5	6	7	10	12	14	15	17	18	20	23	24	25	26	28	43	45
[13]	JavaTutor	65	X	X	X	-	-	-	-	-	X	-	-	-	-	-	-	-	-	-	-	-
[14]	JavaTutor	63	-	X	X	-	-	-	-	-	X	-	-	-	-	-	-	-	-	-	-	-
[12]	JavaTutor	65	-	-	X	-	-	-	-	-	X	-	-	-	-	-	-	-	-	-	-	-
[26]	JavaTutor	67	-	-	X	X	-	-	-	-	-	-	-	-	-	X	-	-	-	-	-	-
[28]	Crystal Island	65	-	-	-	X	-	-	-	-	-	X	-	X	-	X	-	-	-	-	-	-
[3]	Physics Playground	137	X	X	-	-	X	-	X	X	X	X	X	X	X	X	-	-	X	X	-	-
[8]	AutoTutor	30	X_f	X_f	X_c	-	-	X_c	-	X_c	X_f	-	-	-	-	-	-	-	-	-	X_b	-
[21]	AutoTutor	28	-	-	X_c	-	-	$X_{c,d}$	-	$X_{f,d}$	-	-	-	-	-	-	X_d	X_d	-	-	-	-
[5]	AutoTutor	5	X_f	X_f	X_c	-	-	X_c	-	X_c	X_f	-	-	-	-	-	-	-	-	-	X_b	-
[27]	BrainSkills	34	X_e	-	-	-	-	-	X_e	-	-	-	-	-	-	-	-	-	-	-	-	X_e
[1]	TeachTown Basics	7	X	X	X	-	X	X	-	X	-	-	-	-	-	-	-	-	-	-	-	X
	Count		6	6	8	2	2	4	2	5	6	2	1	2	1	3	1	1	1	2	2	2

f = frustration, c = confusion, e = engagement, d = delight, b = boredom

3 Data Collection and Methodology

We summarize the data collection below; for more details see [4]. Data was collected on learners using the ELITE-Lite system, which was instrumented to collect a corpus of video logs via laptop web cameras. ELITE-Lite is a scenario-based ITS which uses multiple-choice-based role-playing interactions to allow learners to practice basic counseling skills, while a virtual coach proactively provides hints and feedback [16]. Each video log is a 30–60 min clip of participants interacting with ELITE-Lite.

The experiment was conducted at a competitive private university in California in Fall 2015. Data was collected across two randomly-assigned conditions that varied by the prevalence of guidance for partially-correct (mixed) answers, with one condition always giving hints/feedback for mixed answers and the other never giving hints/feedback for mixed answers. Correct answers never resulted in textual coach guidance (only graphical flag feedback), while incorrect answers always resulted in textual guidance. Users in the two conditions had only very subtle differences in their experiences, making both conditions relatively equivalent from the standpoint of this analysis.

A total of 80 students participated in the study, but only 39 had complete and usable data for affect analysis. Recordings were collected in an open lab with potential distractions, which in some cases added noise to the audio/video log. All students wore headphones for sound, and some minor confounds are that some wore glasses or had facial hair. As noted in prior log file analysis [4], 6 participants were omitted because their game logs were incomplete. A large number of videos were omitted from this analysis because the video/audio recording was corrupted, the participant's face was consistently obscured or cropped, or automated analysis identified problems (e.g., poor results due to issues with lighting or missing frames). Of the 39 participants with complete data (29 male and 10 female), 33 participants identified themselves as Asian/Pacific Islander, 3 as White, 2 as Black/African American and 1 preferred not to respond. Most of the participants came from technical majors such as computer science and thus expressed high comfort with computers. No significant differences were observed in learning gains between participants omitted versus those included.

The experimental procedure consisted of (1) one pre-survey, (2) one pre-test, (3) one ELITE-Lite Introductory Video, (4) two sessions of the same scenario (Being Heard) with a virtual coach providing hints and feedback, (5) one session with a second scenario (Bearing Down) without coach support, (6) one post-survey, and (7) one post-test. Excluding surveys and tests, participants spent close to an hour in ELITE-Lite. In each scenario, learners play the role of a military supervisor helping a subordinate with a problem. Each scenario is relevant to a broad audience: Being Heard addresses a request to transfer due to sexual harassment and Bearing Down addresses a fight between two subordinates. The first scenario was repeated to allow the participants to identify and correct their mistakes.

Learning gain was measured using two types of tests - a shallow knowledge test (e.g., definitions of skills like *active listening*) and a deeper Situational Judgment Test (SJT) which required rating possible actions. Both tests may be considered transfer tasks, in that they test skills under substantially different conditions than the training scenarios. The pre-survey collected self-reported traits: help seeking, growth mindset, interest, lack of anxiety, organization, confidence, and experience. In addition to the web camera recordings, game logs recorded participant responses and interactions with the system. Based on the game logs, each response event was coded by Question Difficulty, whether the question had been seen before (Repeat), Correctness, Time Taken to Answer, if Hint and/or Feedback was presented, the Phase (e.g., session), and a Unique Question ID. Game logs were also aligned to video annotation, so that the system phase was known for each video frame.

Video analysis was conducted using a commercial version of the Computer Expression Recognition Toolbox (CERT) [19], which performs real-time facial expression recognition. CERT reports emotion estimates as well as the activation of 20 action units (AUs), following the well-validated Facial Action Coding System (FACS). CERT estimates are trained primarily on posed facial expressions aligned to Ekman's taxonomy (Baseline, Joy, Anger, Surprise, Fear, Contempt, Sadness, Disgust) [11,19,20]. The commercial version extends this to estimate Confusion and Frustration. This tool processed the video logs outputting evidence levels for each AU and emotion measure for each frame.

Human annotators labeled a sample of the data to assist in interpretation of the data. CERT output was compared with the annotations from two humans for a sample of 6 videos, examining block sizes of 3 s. This interval length has been used by other research [26], and was appropriate for this system as events (e.g., decision points, feedback) did not typically occur longer than this rate. A sweep examining other block sizes (1 s to 5 s) was briefly explored, but 3 s remained the most interpretable and consistent between raters. One concern was whether participants looked off-screen, a sign of boredom, but this turned out to be rare, and so this was not analyzed further.

The human annotators found large amounts of Baseline facial expressions that appeared to range from deliberate engagement to mild boredom, and a true lack of pronounced facial expression. Some Confusion was seen, but the other emotion categories including Frustration were so infrequent that we created an Other category from the maximum of the CERT evidence levels across all other remaining emotions. These "top-down" emotion categories were analyzed based on their evidence levels for the overall experiment (Overall), for specific learning tasks (Phases), and for the 3 s windows before and after each participant decision since decision points are highly likely to be relevant to learning.

In addition, for these 3 s windows, we also considered the AU evidence levels for each learner. In general, evidence levels in CERT can be positive, suggesting the feature is present, negative, suggesting the feature is absent, or zero, indicating uncertainty. AU levels below zero were treated as zero, so that we only account for variation during activation (similar to [25]). A factor analysis was applied to identify linear combinations of AUs that co-occurred in patterns in our data sample. These bottom-up factors were then calculated and analyzed similarly to the top-down emotion categories, to identify new insights with respect to learning events.

4   Results and Analysis

For overall learning gains, the impact of hints, and student traits as well as a preliminary exploration of coarse-grained affect, see [4,22]. The current analysis concerns these questions: (1) What were the distributions of top-down affect detected overall and during different phases of using the system?, (2) What bottom-up patterns of facial cues occur and how do these relate to phases of system use?, (3) How does student affect relate to responses (e.g., correctness, before/after submitting an answer) and to learning gains?, and (4) What self-reported student traits were associated with differences in affect detected?

4.1   Affect Results (Top-Down Categories)

Table 2 summarizes the descriptive statistics of the three top-down emotion categories reported by CERT for the whole session (Overall), for system phases, and for an average over each user's windows of ± 3 s around submitting a decision (N = 39 users). The system phases reported are the introduction video (Intro), then one scenario twice in a row (Being Heard: Scen 1 and Scen 2) before continuing to a second scenario (Bearing Down: Scen 3). For each affective state, the table shows the average evidence level across all recorded frames. Across subjects, there was substantial variability, as seen in the standard deviations. As would be expected, Pearson's correlations showed significant pairwise correlations between each emotion overall (p < .01 for all). Baseline was negatively

Table 2. CERT evidence level means and standard deviations for overall, system phases, and around decisions

Condition	Baseline	Confusion	Other
Overall	0.92 ± 0.52	−0.72 ± 0.68	0.25 ± 0.44
Intro	0.83 ± 0.70	−0.81 ± 0.87	0.36 ± 0.40
Scen 1	0.84 ± 0.65	−0.50 ± 0.87	0.27 ± 0.49
Scen 2	0.58 ± 0.64	−0.47 ± 0.93	0.46 ± 0.40
Scen 3	0.73 ± 0.57	−0.50 ± 0.99	0.48 ± 0.52
Decisions	0.64 ± 0.57	−0.41 ± 0.70	0.20 ± 0.44

correlated with Confusion ($r = -.35$) and Other ($r = -.88$), with Confusion positively correlated with Other ($r = .36$).

Since each measure varies over time, different expressions dominate at different times. If it were assumed that only one affective state could be active at a time (e.g., discretized to the one with maximum evidence), then the prevalence of each would be 69% Baseline, 5% Confusion, and 26% Other. Overall, there are relatively low evidence levels of Confusion and Other emotions. Among emotions included in Other, the average values were all less than zero ($-.38$ to -2.51; $-.96$ for Frustration). The highest estimated emotion in Other was Contempt ($-.42 \pm .43$), which was still quite uncommon. However, Contempt did show a positive but non-significant increase between Intro and Scen 3 ($-.43$ to $-.34$; $p = .08$), which might indicate it could be a useful indicator of decreasing engagement or study fatigue over the course of about an hour. Human annotation indicated similar patterns over a set of 2316 tags for 3 s intervals, with a relatively neutral but engaged expression (Baseline) dominating the experience (92.9%), while clear signs of Confusion (3.5%) or strong evidence of Other affect (6.8%) were rare.

Different system phases of learning activities (Phase) influenced these emotion estimates. Analyses showed a significant main effect for Phase, $F(9,324) = 2.78$, $p < .00$. Baseline and Other emotions were not statistically significant for different Phases overall ($p > .06$ and $p > .41$, respectively). However, a statistically significant effect was found for Confusion $F(3,108) = 3.37$, $p < .02$, partial eta-squared $= .09$. Furthermore, within-subjects analysis showed that there was a significant linear trend for Confusion over Phases, $F(1,36) = 5.67$, $p < .02$, partial eta-squared $= .14$. Overall, confusion was very low during the introductory video and rose for the first two sessions to a steady-state for the final session.

Compared to Overall affect, affect around decisions showed lower levels of Baseline and higher Confusion, with Other remaining similar, as shown in Table 2. Discretizing to only consider the maximal state, the average prevalence over 3 s before a decision to 3 s after was 69% Baseline, 7% Confusion, and 24% Other. As such, Baseline was still dominant.

4.2   AU Factor Results (Bottom-Up)

A factor analysis was applied to the non-negative AUs for all 3 s periods before and after user decisions, for each frame recorded. These periods were chosen because they were anticipated to have the highest volatility of affective reactions, since they covered both the decision-making process, the delivery of hints/feedback after a decision, and the beginning of the virtual agent's response to the learner. Direct Oblimin (Oblique) rotation and structure matrix coefficients were used, since it is reasonable that the same AU could appear in multiple factors. A loading cutoff of .5 was chosen based on reviewing the scree plot, which resulted in seven distinct factors that explained 69.5% of the variance. This cutoff resulted in the factors presented in Table 3. To facilitate interpretation, these factors are mapped to related reference citations that presented similar combinations of factors and a summary label is given to each factor next to it.

A few factors showed significant and non-trivial correlations (N = 1954 decision events). Factor 1 correlated moderately with Factor 5 ($r = .45$, $p < .05$) and weakly with Factor 4 ($r = .16$, $p < .05$). Factor 3 correlated with Factors 5, 6, and 7 ($r = .16$, $r = .14$, and $r = .14$; $p < .05$ for all). Factor 4 correlated negatively with Factor 6 ($r = -.11$; $p < .05$).

Table 3. Factor AU Loadings and related work

Factor: Summary Label	AUs (loadings)	Related Refs: AUs
Factor 1: Mouth Tightened	14, 17, 23, 24, 28 (0.86, 0.62, 0.89, 0.90, 0.62)	[25]: 14, 17, 23
Factor 2: Surprise/Mouth Covered	5, 25, 26 (0.77, 0.92, 0.95)	[11]: 1, 2, 5, 25, 26 [25]: 20, 25, 26
Factor 3: Eyebrows Raised	1, 2 (0.93, 0.92)	[25]: 1, 2
Factor 4: Happy/Smile	6, 12 (0.78, 0.78)	[11]: 6, 7 [1]: 12
Factor 5: Frown/Pursed lips	9, 10, 15, 17 (0.58, 0.77, 0.54, 0.50)	[25]: 10, 15, 17
Factor 6: Thinking/Uncertain	4, 18, 43 (0.74, 0.81, 0.56)	[8], [21], [5]: 4, 7, 12
Factor 7: Lips Stretched	20 (0.54)	[18]

It is important to note that these factors represent relatively subtle differences in facial expression. Figure 1 shows examples of Factor 1, 3, 5, and 6. Three images are of a single user to demonstrate that while differences within a participant can be identified through careful inspection, they are not immediately obvious. The final image for Factor 1 is included because it indicates a second issue: users tend to move their hands as they think and use computers in a natural manner. In general, this appeared to be either consistent (e.g., their face was so consistently covered that their data was excluded from processing) or random (e.g., unrelated to detected cues). However, there is some possibility that Factor 2 represents both mouth opening or a hand placed near the mouth area, since frames with high levels of this factor appeared more likely to have a hand near the chin or mouth. All other factors appear to be related exclusively to facial AUs.

These factors map reasonably to prior literature on facial affect patterns, though not all factors map to traditional emotion labels. For example, Factor 2 and Factor 4 share action units with Eckman's Surprise and Happy/Smile categories, respectively [10]. Factor 6 has some similarity with D'Mello and Graesser's confusion [6], in that the shared AU4 represents a furrowed brow. However, Factor 1 (Mouth Tightening), Factor 3 (Eyebrows Raised), and Factor 5 (Frown) appear to be facial cues related to cognition that do not necessarily map neatly to a traditional emotion category. These factors are instead similar to bottom-up factor patterns that have been found when studying users in other cognitively-demanding tasks such as negotiating with a computer agent [25]. Finally, AU20 has been associated with embarrassment [18] but Factor 7 might not represent a significant pattern. It contains only a single action unit and the scree plot indicates that Factor 7 is the first point of the relatively flat tail. As a group, the factors found in the data may offer indicators related to engagement, which could not be measured directly in the earlier analyses using the top-down emotion categories (i.e., Baseline was used as a noisy proxy instead).

Fig. 1. Example factors (from left to right) - Factor 3, Factor 6, Factor 5 and Factor 1

To explore individual differences in the prevalence of factors, an analysis was conducted that counted the number of decision points where each learner was at least one standard deviation above the mean value for that factor across all participants. This approach found that strong presentations of factors were reasonably spread across participants, as shown in Fig. 2. Factor 4 was a notable exception, with nearly 50% of strong presentations by one subject. The most pronounced pattern however was that the facial affect detection showed much higher evidence of emotions for some subjects versus others. This pattern was also observed for the top-down emotions. This may indicate that certain learners were more reactive, or that the affect detection software shows systematic biases toward certain kinds of faces.

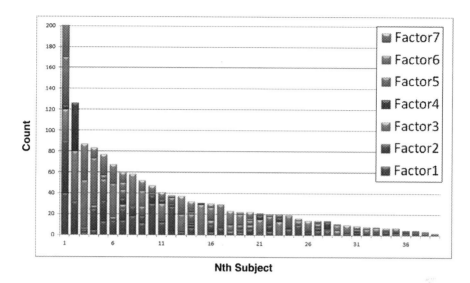

Fig. 2. Counts of factors 1σ above mean, by participant

To consider if the factors differed qualitatively from the top-down categories, we reviewed the most-correlated top-down emotion for each bottom-up factor. No factors are direct analogs to CERT categories, but some are at least moderately correlated while others appear to capture different dimensions of cognitive-affective states. Correlations were calculated based on the set of 3 s-window averages before decisions (N = 1655 complete cases; p < .001 for all reported). Factors which might be considered fairly similar are Factor 6 with Confusion (r = .46) and Factor 4 with Joy (r = .42). Factor 1 correlates fairly evenly with a number of emotions (Frustration r = .35; Contempt r = .30; negatively with Baseline r = −.32). Factor 3 has small correlations with a mixed group of more passive emotions (Sadness r = .41; Surprise r = .29; Fear r = .28). Factor 5 has only small correlations with top-down categories, but may relate to an active negative reaction such as a response to negative feedback (Disgust r = .29; Sadness r = .26). Factor 7 shows no correlations above .2 magnitude with any top-down emotion. As such, the bottom-up factors offer a different interpretation on the AUs than the top-down categories.

Table 4 shows the means for these factors overall and for each experimental phase. Each factor was normalized to fall in a range of [0, 1] by dividing by its maximum possible weight. Two values for Factor 2 were so small (< .001) that they were rounded to zero for presentation. Due to space constraints, standard deviations are not shown but they were roughly on the same order of magnitude as each factor mean.

Among factors that showed changes between phases, within-subjects paired two-tailed t-tests were applied to test significance of differences between each successive phase. Supporting some of the intuitions from the correlation data,

Factor 1 was highest around active decision-making and lowest during passive videos, while Factor 3 showed the reverse relationship. Between the Intro and Scen 1, Factor 1 increased (p < .05), Factor 2 decreased to nearly zero (p < .01) and Factor 4 also decreased (p < .01). Between Scen 1 and Scen 2, Factor 4 increased (p < .001). Between Scen 2 and Scen 3 Factor 3 increased (p < .01). When comparing Decision points against the Overall average, Factor 1 was higher around decisions (p < .001) as was Factor 5 (p < .02), and Factor 7 was lower (p < .05).

Table 4. Factor overall and phase means of subjects (N = 39)

Phase	F1	F2	F3	F4	F5	F6	F7
Overall	0.11	0.003	0.15	0.03	0.12	0.27	0.01
Intro	0.08	0.004	0.18	0.04	0.09	0.34	0.01
Scen 1	0.11	~0	0.14	0.01	0.08	0.37	0.004
Scen 2	0.12	0.01	0.14	0.03	0.08	0.34	0.002
Scen 3	0.10	~0	0.18	0.02	0.08	0.35	0.01
Decisions	0.14	0.003	0.13	0.03	0.13	0.27	0.003

4.3   Relationship of Learner Outcomes to Facial Cues

To look at the relationship between detected affect prior to a response and its correctness (i.e., correct, rather than mixed or incorrect), two mixed models were evaluated using the *afex* R package [24]. These models were selected by including the affective cues studied in this work, then adding a limited set of factors known to affect correctness from prior exploratory analysis [4]. First, a mixed model was built that examined the predictive value of top-down emotions, in the form: *IsCorrect ~ Confusion + Other + Repeat + TimeTaken + QuestionDifficulty + Hint + (1 + Confusion + Other − Subject.Id)* where Repeat refers to whether the question had been seen before, and Hint refers to whether a hint was given. Second, a similarly-structured mixed model was evaluated for factors (i.e., each factor having a fixed effect and a random effect conditional on the subject, to address potential systematic differences in the prevalence of factors between subjects). In both cases, statistically significant models were produced (emotions marginal R^2 = .16 and conditional R^2 = .18; factors marginal R^2 = .16 and conditional R^2 = .23). However, for both models, only QuestionDifficulty, Repeat, and TimeTaken were significant at p < .05 with QuestionDifficulty explaining the majority of the variance.

The next analysis attempted to estimate learning gains between the pre- and post-tests. This analysis was complicated by the fact that overall learning gains were relatively modest. Across the sample of all participants with log files (N = 74), the learning gain for participants was 0.08 (from 0.57 to 0.65). While this represents a fairly small variance, there was higher gain for SJT items (0.11 out of 1) than for Knowledge (0.04 out of 1) [4]. The subset of 39 with full data for this analysis was not significantly different in terms of gains (0.10 for SJT, 0.05 for Knowledge). A model was fit for each type of facial measure (e.g., the set of top-down or bottom-up measures) averaged across all decision events. For both sets of metrics these models did not reach significance.

4.4 Relationship of Self-reported Traits to Facial Indicators

As noted earlier, students were pre-surveyed for traits related to experience/interest in the domain, learning strategies, growth mindset, and a limited subset of academic emotions. Under Pearson's correlations with Bonferroni adjustment for repeated tests, few self-reported traits showed statistically significant results for this sample size, with only Experience and Anxiety (e.g., test anxiety) notable. Experience was positively correlated with Baseline prior to decisions ($r = .40$, $p < .01$) and negatively with Other ($r = -.40$, $p < .01$), which captured strong affect other than Confusion. Lack of anxiety was negatively correlated with Confusion ($r = -.34$, $p < .05$), with students who reported more academic anxiety also showing more confusion evidence. Post-surveys, which focused primarily on impressions of the system, showed no significant correlations with affect for this sample size.

Bottom-up factors correlated with indicators of interest and effort, unlike the correlations for the top-down emotion categories which correlated with confidence and anxiety. However, the majority of these correlations were still small to moderate (.2–.4). Factor 2 showed moderate negative correlations with self-reported academic effort ($r = -.39$; $p < .05$) and with organized study habits ($r = -.40$; $p < .05$). Two factors were near significance for positive correlations with effort as well, Factor 3 ($r = .29$; $p = .08$) and Factor 5 ($r = .28$; $p = .08$). Factor 4 correlated negatively with interest in the subject ($r = -.43$; $p < .05$). Factors 2 and 4 may indicate taking the learning experience less seriously, while Factors 3 and 5 might be related to greater engagement or deliberate practice.

5   Conclusions and Future Directions

Facial expression trackers such as the Computer Expression Recognition Toolbox (CERT) [19] output measures for facial action units (AUs [10]) as well as emotion categories from traditional taxonomies. Using factor analysis to search for categories implicit in AU patterns, we explored the utility of this bottom-up information which is fine-grained but not tied directly to cognitive-affective states (e.g., boredom).

Bottom-up factors show the potential to add value beyond the traditional emotion taxonomies. In our review of related work (Sect. 2), we compiled a unified map of AU patterns studied by learning science researchers. Comparing this map to the factors we found in our data (Table 3), we see that only one (Factor 6) has been previously seen in a learning context while the other factors have been observed in other cognitive software tasks [25] and mentioned in Ekman and Friesen's book on facial expressions [11]. These tables provide a template for building an ongoing record as new studies report results, and meta-analyses compile them.

Results suggest that the factors we identified may be relevant to engagement. Correlations with self-reported traits show negative relationships between Factor 2 and academic effort and organized study habits as well as a negative relationship between Factor 4 and interest in the subject. It could be the case that these traits correspond with a flow state in which Factor 2 and Factor 4 are less active. We also compared average evidence for each factor across the four phases of the experiment as well as the 3 s before and after decisions (Table 4). Factor 1 was highest in these decision making windows and lowest during the video watching phase while Factor 3 was the reverse. Learners might have been more likely to be in the flow state during the video, but humor and graphics in the video may have also triggered emotional reactions. However, these factors must be interpreted with care, since they are based on a limited set of tasks and a particular subject population: factor analysis from other systems is necessary to find common patterns.

Engagement/flow has generally been shown to be positive (e.g., [23]) and indicating greater attention and processing. However, this research did not isolate any facial expressions having a significant positive or negative relationship with either learning gain, or performance once question difficulty was also considered. These results indicate that the detected facial cues give insight into the learner's mental state, but as potential cues to predict learning did not offer a consistent signal.

It is important to note that learners on average showed limited signs of facial affect, either for top-down emotion categories (e.g., Confusion) or the bottom-up factors. For example, the high level of baseline and lack of confusion (69% and 5% when discretized) differs substantially from some previous research such as D'Mello and Graesser [6], which reported only 42% in Flow + Neutral and 19% in Confusion. The scenario-based learning context may have damped academic emotions such as confusion due to sense of flow in the scenario. Considering the low levels of confusion, frustration, and no signs of overt disengagement, all supporting evidence indicates that learners were in an engaged/equilibrium state as per D'Mello and Graesser's model [6]. This state might indicate a pattern of "Over-Flow" where learners are engaged in the experience and content, but float past their failures and potential impasses (e.g., insufficient confusion). Alternatively, this sample of learners (who were primarily computer science students) might have relatively low presentation of affect. A broader sample might include more variance in facial affect and offer more insight into performance.

To explore these issues, research is underway to examine these contributing factors. First, we have changed recruiting methods to attract a more diverse pool of learners. Second, a new activity (an interactive after-action review) has been added to promote impasses by prompting learners to diagnose or retry decisions where they made a mistake. By studying the same system with a new task and different subject population, it may be possible to disentangle if lower facial affect was due to insufficient impasses during scenario flow (i.e., over-flow).

This should contribute to the broader discussion on how to balance scenario flow against creating impasses that promote learning.

Acknowledgments. The effort described here is sponsored by the U.S. Army Research Laboratory (ARL) under contract number W911NF-14-D-0005. Any opinion, content or information presented does not necessarily reflect the position or the policy of the United States Government, and no official endorsement should be inferred.

References

1. Ahmed, A.A., Goodwin, M.S.: Automated detection of facial expressions during computer-assisted instruction in individuals on the autism spectrum. In: CHI Conference on Human Factors in Computing Systems (2017)
2. Baker, R.S., D'Mello, S.K., Rodrigo, M.M.T., Graesser, A.C.: Better to be frustrated than bored: the incidence, persistence, and impact of learners' cognitive-affective states during interactions with three different computer-based learning environments. Int. J. Hum. Comput. Stud. **68**(4), 223–241 (2010)
3. Bosch, N., D'Mello, S.K., Ocumpaugh, J., Baker, R.S., Shute, V.: Using video to automatically detect learner affect in computer-enabled classrooms. ACM Trans. Interac. Intell. Syst. (TiiS) **6**, 17 (2016)
4. Core, M.G., Georgila, K., Nye, B.D., Auerbach, D., Liu, Z.F., DiNinni, R.: Learning, adaptive support, student traits, and engagement in scenario-based learning. In: Interservice/Industry Training, Simulation, and Education Conference (I/ITSEC) (2016)
5. Craig, S.D., D'Mello, S., Witherspoon, A., Graesser, A.: Emote aloud during learning with AutoTutor: applying the facial action coding system to cognitive-affective states during learning. Cogn. Emot. **22**(5), 777–788 (2008)
6. D'Mello, S., Graesser, A.: Dynamics of affective states during complex learning. Learn. Instr. **22**(2), 145–157 (2012)
7. D'Mello, S., Lehman, B., Pekrun, R., Graesser, A.: Confusion can be beneficial for learning. Learn. Instr. **29**, 153–170 (2014)
8. D'Mello, S.K., Craig, S.D., Gholson, B., Franklin, S., Picard, R., Graesser, A.C.: Integrating affect sensors in an intelligent tutoring system. In: Affective Interactions: The Computer in the Affective Loop Workshop, pp. 7–13 (2005)
9. D'Mello, S.K., Craig, S.D., Sullins, J., Graesser, A.C.: Predicting affective states expressed through an emote-aloud procedure from AutoTutor's mixed-initiative dialogue. Int. J. Artif. Intell. Educ. **16**(1), 3–28 (2006)
10. Ekman, P., Friesen, W.V.: Facial Action Coding System. Consulting Psychologists Press, Stanford University, Palo Alto (1977)
11. Ekman, P., Friesen, W.V.: Unmasking the Face: A Guide to Recognizing Emotions From Facial Clues. Malor Books, Cambridge (2003)
12. Grafsgaard, J., Wiggins, J., Boyer, K.E., Wiebe, E., Lester, J.: Predicting learning and affect from multimodal data streams in task-oriented tutorial dialogue. In: Educational Data Mining (2014)
13. Grafsgaard, J., Wiggins, J.B., Boyer, K.E., Wiebe, E.N., Lester, J.: Automatically recognizing facial expression: predicting engagement and frustration. In: Educational Data Mining (2013)

14. Grafsgaard, J.F., Wiggins, J.B., Vail, A.K., Boyer, K.E., Wiebe, E.N., Lester, J.C.: The additive value of multimodal features for predicting engagement, frustration, and learning during tutoring. In: International Conference on Multimodal Interaction (ICMI), pp. 42–49. ACM (2014)

15. Guo, P.J., Kim, J., Rubin, R.: How video production affects student engagement: an empirical study of MOOC videos. In: Learning at Scale Conference, pp. 41–50. ACM (2014)

16. Hays, M.J., Campbell, J.C., Trimmer, M.A., Poore, J.C., Webb, A.K., King, T.K.: Can role-play with virtual humans teach interpersonal skills? In: Interservice/Industry Training, Simulation, and Education Conference (I/ITSEC) (2012)

17. Juul, J.: Fear of failing? The many meanings of difficulty in video games. Video Game Theor. Read. **2**, 237–252 (2009)

18. Keltner, D.: Signs of appeasement: evidence for the distinct displays of embarrassment, amusement, and shame. J. Pers. Soc. Psychol. **68**(3), 441–454 (1995)

19. Littlewort, G., Whitehill, J., Wu, T., Fasel, I., Frank, M., Movellan, J., Bartlett, M.: The computer expression recognition toolbox (CERT). In: IEEE International Conference on Automatic Face and Gesture Recognition, pp. 298–305 (2011)

20. Lucey, P., Cohn, J.F., Kanade, T., Saragih, J., Ambadar, Z., Matthews, I.: The extended Cohn-Kanade dataset (CK+): a complete dataset for action unit and emotion-specified expression. In: IEEE Computer Vision and Pattern Recognition Workshops (CVPRW), pp. 94–101 (2010)

21. McDaniel, B., D'Mello, S., King, B., Chipman, P., Tapp, K., Graesser, A.: Facial features for affective state detection in learning environments. In: Annual Meeting of the Cognitive Science Society, pp. 467–472 (2007)

22. Nye, B., Karumbaiah, S., Tokel, S.T., Core, M.G., Stratou, G., Auerbach, D., Georgila, K.: Analyzing learner affect in a scenario-based intelligent tutoring system. In: André, E., Baker, R., Hu, X., Rodrigo, M.M.T., du Boulay, B. (eds.) AIED 2017. LNCS, vol. 10331, pp. 544–547. Springer, Cham (2017). https://doi.org/10.1007/978-3-319-61425-0_60

23. Rowe, J.P., Shores, L.R., Mott, B.W., Lester, J.C.: Integrating learning, problem solving, and engagement in narrative-centered learning environments. Int. J. Artif. Intell. Educ. **21**(1–2), 115–133 (2011)

24. Singmann, H., Bolker, B., Westfall, J., Aust, F.: afex: Analysis of Factorial Experiments (2018). https://CRAN.R-project.org/package=afex. r package version 0.19-1

25. Stratou, G., Morency, L.P.: Multisense - context-aware nonverbal behavior analysis framework: a psychological distress use case. IEEE Trans. Affect. Comput. **8**(2), 190–203 (2017)

26. Vail, A.K., Grafsgaard, J.F., Boyer, K.E., Wiebe, E.N., Lester, J.C.: Predicting learning from student affective response to tutor questions. In: International Conference on Intelligent Tutoring Systems, pp. 154–164 (2016)

27. Whitehill, J., Serpell, Z., Lin, Y.C., Foster, A., Movellan, J.R.: The faces of engagement: automatic recognition of student engagement from facial expressions. IEEE Trans. Affec. Comput. **5**(1), 86–98 (2014)

28. Xu, Z., Woodruff, E.: Person-centered approach to explore learner's emotionality in learning within a 3D narrative game. In: Learning Analytics & Knowledge Conference, pp. 439–443 (2017)

Role of Socio-cultural Differences in Labeling Students' Affective States

Eda Okur[1(✉)], Sinem Aslan[1], Nese Alyuz[1], Asli Arslan Esme[1], and Ryan S. Baker[2]

[1] Intel Labs, Intel Corporation, Hillsboro, OR, USA
{eda.okur,sinem.aslan,nese.alyuz.civitci,
asli.arslan.esme}@intel.com
[2] University of Pennsylvania, Philadelphia, PA, USA
rybaker@upenn.edu

Abstract. The development of real-time affect detection models often depends upon obtaining annotated data for supervised learning by employing human experts to label the student data. One open question in labeling affective data for affect detection is whether the labelers (i.e., human experts) need to be socio-culturally similar to the students being labeled, as this impacts the cost and feasibility of obtaining the labels. In this study, we investigate the following research questions: For affective state labeling, how does the socio-cultural background of human expert labelers, compared to the subjects (i.e., students), impact the degree of consensus and distribution of affective states obtained? Secondly, how do differences in labeler background impact the performance of affect detection models that are trained using these labels? To address these questions, we employed experts from Turkey and the United States to label the same data collected through authentic classroom pilots with students in Turkey. We analyzed within-country and cross-country inter-rater agreements, finding that experts from Turkey obtained moderately better inter-rater agreement than the experts from the U.S., and the two groups did not agree with each other. In addition, we observed differences between the distributions of affective states provided by experts in the U.S. versus Turkey, and between the performances of the resulting affect detectors. These results suggest that there are indeed implications to using human experts who do not belong to the same population as the research subjects.

Keywords: Affective state labeling · Student affect detection · Cross-cultural Inter-rater agreement · Intelligent Tutoring Systems (ITS)

1 Introduction

Automated detection of learner affect has matured as an area of Artificial Intelligence in Education (AIED) research, with models of learner affect now published for a range of learning environments [1–3]. These models have formed the basis of a range of scientific analyses, including the relationship between affect and student outcomes [3], and the differences in learning outcomes between brief and extended affect [4]. They have also been used as the basis for automated interventions which improve students'

© Springer International Publishing AG, part of Springer Nature 2018
C. Penstein Rosé et al. (Eds.): AIED 2018, LNAI 10947, pp. 367–380, 2018.
https://doi.org/10.1007/978-3-319-93843-1_27

affect and engagement, and in turn their learning, by responding to negative affect in real time [5, 6].

These automated detectors of affect are typically created through a supervised learning approach, where the first step is to collect some kind of external, ground-truth measure of a student's affect at specific points in time, whether those labels are from self-report, video coding, or field observation. These ground-truth labels are often useful scientific interests in their own right, and are used for analyses such as understanding the dynamics of student affect over time [7], and the affect that students experience within MOOCs [8].

Early work on the expert coding of affect and emotion, such as the Facial Action Coding System (FACS) focused on deriving rationally understandable and widely-agreed, culturally universal indicators of affect [9]. However, the inter-rater reliability for this approach was poor [10]. More recent approaches to the expert coding of affect have relied on more subjective judgments. Two such approaches, the Baker Rodrigo Ocumpaugh Monitoring Protocol (BROMP) [11] and the Human Expert Labeling Process (HELP) [12], have each achieved inter-rater agreement measures over 0.6, indicating considerably higher levels of agreement than FACS. Neither BROMP nor HELP makes claims to cultural universality; in fact BROMP has been re-normed in four different countries and its coding manual explicitly warns against using raters from a different national origin than the students whose affect is being coded [11]. However, the empirical basis for this caution remains insufficient, and many affective computing research groups continue to use raters from a different national origin than the subjects they are studying, both for AIED research and within other application areas. Even with BROMP, there are anecdotal reports of individuals successfully achieving acceptably high inter-rater reliability outside their original home country, after living in a different country for several years [11].

If it was possible to use the same affect labeling protocol internationally without re-norming, wide use of affect labeling would become considerably more feasible. In addition, if it were feasible to use raters of any national origin, it would become more feasible to conduct affective computing research and development even in countries where protocols have already been normed.

As such, this paper investigates the degree to which human expert labelers from the same country as the students being labeled actually achieve higher inter-rater reliability than experts from a different country, when labeling the affective states of learners using an online platform for mathematics. In doing so, we analyze both the within-country and cross-country agreements in affect labeling, as it is possible that experts from a different country than students may agree with each other but disagree with experts from the students' country, a pattern that would suggest systematic error and bias in affect labeling.

2   Methodology Overview

2.1   Research Questions

In this research, we investigate whether human experts who are from the same country as the subjects (i.e., students) would provide different affective state labels than the ones who are from another country. We hypothesize that such difference could be attributed to the fact that same-culture experts will be familiar with the learners' context (going through the same schooling experience, being familiar with the learning context) and culture (sharing the similar values and conceptions about affect in learning, as well as similar modes of expressing affect). Hence, they could provide more reliable affect labels. Towards this end, this study investigates the following research questions: How is the socio-cultural background of human expert labelers, compared to the students, associated with the degree of consensus and distribution of affective states labeled, for the task of affective state labeling? Secondly, how would the differences in labelers' background impact the performance of affect detection models that are trained using these labels?

2.2   Data Collection and Labeling

Research Context and Data Collection. We collected data from 9th-grade students (ages 14–15) through authentic classroom pilots in an urban high-school in Turkey. The pilots took place in an optional Math course offered during school hours throughout a school semester. 13 pilot sessions of 40 min each were provided to 17 volunteering students; around 113 hours of student data is collected in total. During the pilots, the students used an online learning platform where they watched instructional videos (i.e., *Instructional* sections) and solved objective assessments to test their mastery (i.e., *Assessment* sections). A Math teacher participated in the course as a facilitator of the learning process – i.e., whenever the students needed her input, she got involved. The curriculum of the course was designed in collaboration with the course teacher. The data for each student was collected individually, using a laptop equipped with a camera. While the students were involved in learning activities on the online platform, we collected two streams of videos: (1) videos of the student from the camera, to enable monitoring of observable cues available in the individual's face or upper body; and (2) student desktop videos, to observe contextual information from the learning activity. We also recorded system interaction logs and whether students were participating in instructional or assessment activities.

Data Labeling. Using the Human Expert Labeling Process (HELP) [12], detailed below, we had five human experts from Turkey and five human experts from the United States with at least a B.S. degree in Psychology/Educational Psychology label the same portion of the student data collected from the pilots. Each group of human experts labeled around 14 hours of data collected from ten students in two sessions. The experts defined segments based on observed state changes (i.e., an expert defined segments based on identifying a change in affect rather than using pre-defined segments of pre-defined length) and provided labels with regards to affective states during learning. These experts labeled student data after receiving face-to-face, instructor-led training provided by the research team. The training involved a presentation explaining operational definitions of labels and providing examples, as well as a practice session with the labeling tool. Note that the training was not prescriptive in that we did not give directive instructors such as telling the experts that the student's fist on their cheek indicates boredom. This is because annotating affective states is a highly subjective task and we expected the human experts to infer emotional states just as teachers would do in classrooms. This more subjective coding approach is similar to what is seen in BROMP [11], and distinct from FACS [13], which is more prescriptive. The research team provided the same training materials for operational definitions of these labels within both countries (translated), and attempted to use similar training procedures, though there remained some slight differences in the actual training process due to differences between the experts and the settings where they were being trained. The definitions of emotional states provided to the human experts are given in Table 1.

Table 1. Operational definitions of emotional states.

Satisfied	If a student is not having any emotional challenges during a learning task. This can include all positive emotional states of the student from being neutral to being excited during the learning task
Bored	If the student is feeling bored during the learning task
Confused	If the student is getting confused during the learning task – in some cases this state might include some other negative states such as frustration (which can be viewed as an increased level of confusion)

In addition to these emotional states, the experts also had two other labels: *Can't Decide* (i.e., if the expert cannot decide on the final emotional state) and *N/A* (i.e., if the data cannot be labeled - e.g., there is no one in front of the camera). Using the HELP Labeling Tool (see Fig. 1 for a sample view), the experts annotated the data using all available cues, such as video and audio capture of the student, desktop recording with mouse cursor locations emphasized, and contextual logs from the device and content platform. Both of the human expert groups completed labeling on the same student data using the same labeling tool; the labeling itself took place at different times and locations.

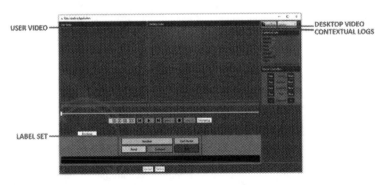

Fig. 1. HELP labeling tool (sample view).

Human Experts' Demographics. The demographics for the human experts in Turkey were rather different than the ones in the United States. The age-range was 20 s–30 s in the former group, whereas in the latter it ranged from 30 s–60 s. All the experts in Turkey were female whereas we had one male expert in the United States. All experts had a

Psychology/Educational Psychology degree in both groups and some of them had experience as a classroom teacher.

2.3   Data Analysis

Data Pre-processing. In order to obtain the inter-rater agreement measures, the labeled data was pre-processed as follows: First of all, we applied data aggregation (i.e., creating instances by sliding-windows) on the labeling outputs of all the experts. The labeling data provided by each expert were pre-processed and divided into instances, where for each 8-seconds sliding-window (with an overlap of 4-seconds), an emotional label was assigned by each expert. The section type information is taken into account while creating these windowed data, so that none of the instances contained both instructional and assessment activities. These instance labels were employed to calculate the inter-rater agreement measures.

To compute each affective state's proportion labeled, we distilled a single label (per population of experts) for each time window, which served as a final ground truth label for each group of human experts. In order to do this, we applied majority voting across all five experts within each group. For each data instance, a majority label (i.e., label with at least three-out-of-five votes) was obtained. We also applied majority voting across the best three experts (i.e., three-out-of-five labelers with the highest consensus) within each group, to eliminate the possible influence of an outlier on final ground truth labels for each group. These final majority labels were utilized to train our supervised models for affect detection.

Metrics for Analysis. We calculated the inter-rater agreement among multiple experts to investigate the effect of the socio-cultural background of human experts on the degree of agreement achieved for the affective state labeling. For inter-rater agreement, we used consensus measures which are designed to estimate the degree of agreement among multiple raters [14, 15]. In this study, we used Krippendorff's alpha [16], because it is both suitable for multiple raters and robust for missing rates: It provides a corrected consensus estimate by comparing the observed agreement to the expected agreement (i.e., the agreement that would be obtained by chance alone) [16]. As summarized in [17], there is no gold standard on the interpretation of Krippendorff's alpha values, and different thresholds are utilized throughout the literature. However, [17] states that values above 0.4 are often considered to represent moderate agreement.

Methods for Analysis. To investigate differences between the human experts from Turkey and the U.S., inter-rater agreement measures were calculated separately in several ways.

First, we calculated within-country agreements. When doing so, we considered both all five experts, and the best three experts of each group, to mitigate against poor results due to outlier experts. Note that "best" refers to the three experts having the highest consensus among all possible three-out-of-five combinations of experts within each group. For the pairwise agreement cases, agreement is computed for each pair of experts, and then averaged across all possible pairs within the corresponding set of experts. We calculated:

- Inter-rater agreement of all five U.S. experts ("US-all-5").
- Pairwise agreement of all five U.S. experts ("US-all-5-pairwise").
- Inter-rater agreement of all five Turkey experts ("TR-all-5").
- Pairwise agreement of all five Turkey experts ("TR-all-5-pairwise").
- Inter-rater agreement of the best three U.S. experts, where "best" is calculated as the highest agreement between three raters (among all combinations of five raters) in the same country ("US-best-3").
- Pairwise agreement of the best three U.S. experts ("US-best-3-pairwise").
- Inter-rater agreement of the best three Turkey experts, where "best" is calculated as the highest agreement between three raters (among all combinations of five raters) in the same country ("TR-best-3").
- Pairwise agreement of the best three Turkey experts ("TR-best-3-pairwise").

Next, we analyzed agreement involving two groups of experts, mixed between both countries, to see how well they agreed with each other, on the whole. Calculating mixed-country group agreements gives us an idea of what the result might be if a research group hired a set of human experts with various backgrounds. We calculated:

- Inter-rater agreement of all ten experts ("Both-all-10").
- Pairwise agreement of all ten experts ("Both-all-10-pairwise").
- Inter-rater agreement of the best three experts from the U.S. and the best three experts from Turkey ("Both-best-6").
- Pairwise agreement of the best three experts from the U.S. and the best three experts from Turkey ("Both-best-6-pairwise").

Finally, we compared between experts in different countries to see how well they agreed with each other, solely in cross-country comparisons. Here, each U.S. expert is compared to each Turkey expert, and the results are averaged across all such pairs. We calculated:

- Pairwise agreement of all ten experts, between cross-country pairs ("Intercountry-all-10-pairwise").
- Pairwise agreement of the best three experts from the U.S. and the best three experts from Turkey, between cross-country pairs ("Intercountry-best-6-pairwise").

By conducting these comparisons, we aimed to understand how much agreement can be achieved within a culture, and how agreement would change when comparing experts from different cultures. Note that *N/A* labels are simply treated as missing values in all of our inter-rater agreement calculations, to avoid misleading higher agreements due to this relatively objective label for which most experts agree on. As a result, we computed inter-rater agreements for the other four labels (i.e., *Satisfied*, *Bored*, *Confused*, *Can't Decide*).

In addition to examining the degree of agreement between experts, we also computed summary statistics on the overall prevalence of affective states labeled by each group, in order to see whether one group of experts generally identified specific affective states more than others (potentially indicating some degree of bias in observation among the U.S. experts, who were labeling students from a different country). We calculated these proportions for all the content taken together (i.e., *Overall*), as well as for each of the system's two types of content (i.e., *Instructional* and *Assessment*), taken individually. These proportions were calculated on the final ground truths computed by majority voting of best three experts of each group separately, again to avoid the influence of an outlier within each group. Note that after this point, we are solely interested in the affective states (i.e., *Satisfied, Bored, Confused*) so we no longer consider *Can't Decide* final labels for either proportions or models of affective states.

As a last step, we explored whether there were differences in the performance of affect detection models trained using final majority labels obtained by each group of expert labelers. In this study, we considered two modalities for affect detection as follows: (1) *Appearance*: upper-body information of students from the camera, (2) *Context & Performance* (C&P): interaction and performance logs of students from the online learning platform. For feature extraction, in order to obtain instance features for each modality, we utilized the same 8-seconds sliding window (with an overlap of 4-seconds) approach that we used to derive the instance labels. For *Appearance*, the raw video data are segmented into instances and time series analysis methods were utilized to extract appearance features, consisting of motion and energy measures (e.g., trend of pose energy), robust statistical estimators (e.g., trimean) of head velocity, and frequency domain features related to head position, pose, and facial expressions. More details of the *Appearance* modality can be found in our previous study [18] where we used the same appearance features in this study. For C&P, we extracted features for inferring affect from the raw user interaction logs collected from the content platform together with the user profile (e.g., gender), consisting of features related to time (e.g., video duration, time from beginning, time spent on attempts/questions, etc.), student performance (e.g., success/failure of attempts, percentage of attempts correct, etc.), attempts made (trial number, number of attempts taken until success, etc.), hints (number of hints used on attempts/questions, etc.), and others (question number, etc.). Some of these extracted C&P features are adapted from the study [3] selecting the subset which are applicable to the content platform we used. More details of the C&P features employed in this study can be found in our previous study [19]. In total, we extracted 188 appearance and 24 C&P features per each instance, which are fed into separate classifiers as feature vectors along with the ground truth labels. For both modalities, we trained Random Forest classifiers with 100 trees. For model training and testing, the labeled datasets (14 hours of data collected from ten students) are partitioned into training (80%) and test (20%) sets, stratifying to keep the distribution of each state and student similar within each group. We applied leave-one-subject-out cross-validation to prevent overfitting, where for each test student, the training samples of all other students were used to construct subject-specific training sets. Due to the class imbalance problem, we employed 10-fold random sample selection to obtain balanced training sets. We compared the performance results of affect detection models trained on the same feature sets but different label sets (i.e., ground truths). In each case, we trained and tested on the final majority labels obtained from the best three experts from the U.S. versus the best three experts from Turkey.

3   Experimental Results

3.1   Results: Inter-rater Agreement

Inter-rater agreement values among the human experts for the several comparison sets given in Sect. 2.3 are outlined in Table 2. The results of within-country agreements with all five experts given in Table 2 show that when comparing between the experts from the U.S. and Turkey as two separate groups, the experts from Turkey perform moderately better in terms of inter-rater reliability. The results for within-country agreements with the best three experts (discarding the worst, potentially outlier, experts), given in Table 2, is similar although the difference between the two groups decreases. Note that when eliminating the outliers, the improvement we achieve is higher for the U.S. experts than the experts from Turkey, which suggests that the outliers had a more negative impact on the agreement for the U.S. experts.

Table 2. Inter-rater agreement (Krippendorff's alpha) measures among human experts from the United States (US) and Turkey (TR).

Human expert comparison sets	Krippendorff's alpha	Human expert comparison sets	Krippendorff's alpha
Within-country (all-5)		Mixed-country	
US-all-5	0.469	Both-all-10	0.452
US-all-5-pairwise	0.472	Both-all-10-pairwise	0.446
TR-all-5	0.578	Both-best-6	0.483
TR-all-5-pairwise	0.585	Both-best-6-pairwise	0.478
Within-country (best-3)		Cross-country	
US-best-3	0.560	Intercountry-all-10-pairwise	0.379
US-best-3-pairwise	0.564	Intercountry-best-6-pairwise	0.400
TR-best-3	0.617		
TR-best-3-pairwise	0.626		

At first, the within-country results with the best three experts given in Table 2 might look promising, suggesting that the better raters among the U.S. experts perform almost as well as the Turkey experts. However, the mixed-country results given in Table 2 show that when we combine these two groups and obtain a mixed-cultural set, the agreement scores go down, even for the best experts within each group.

Finally, we can look at how closely the two groups agree directly with each other, by comparing pairs of experts (one from the U.S. and one from Turkey), shown as the cross-country results in Table 2. These results indicate that pair-wise cross-cultural comparison has the lowest degree of agreement of any of the comparisons conducted here, reaching a value of 0.4 or lower. Such results might signify that although the experts from the same country could agree with each reasonably well, their agreement drops when comparing their labels with another group from a different country. In a way, this could be the worst possible result for using experts from a different country than participants – it suggests that experts may be systematically biased in their evaluations of student affect, agreeing on a label that may not actually reflect the student's affect. We investigate this possibility in greater depth in the following sections.

3.2 Results: Overall Proportions of Affect

There are also differences in the proportions of labels provided by human experts in the U.S. versus Turkey, as shown in Fig. 2. As Fig. 2 demonstrates, although both of the groups labeled *Confused* at a similar frequency (18.0% vs. 18.7%), the experts in the U.S. thought that students were *Satisfied* almost twice more frequently as the experts in Turkey (55.5% vs. 29.2%). For *Instructional* content, the difference in the *Satisfied* state distribution is even greater (49.1% vs. 18.1%). Similarly, for the *Assessment* content, although the Turkey experts thought that students were *Bored* fairly frequently (27.7%), the U.S. experts considered those students to be *Bored* substantially less frequently (7.7%). The U.S. experts instead annotated the majority of these students as *Satisfied* (60.5%) while solving questions. Note that neither group of experts identified students as *Confused* during the *Instructional* activities.

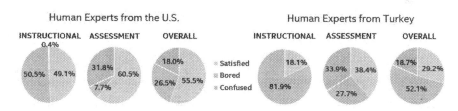

Fig. 2. Students' emotional-state distributions for different section types (i.e., *Instructional*, *Assessment*, and *Overall*) as labeled by the human experts from the U.S. and Turkey.

3.3 Results: Performance of Affect Detection Models

Finally, we compared whether using ground truth labels from same-culture expert labelers (from Turkey) produced better affect detectors than ground truth labels from cross-culture expert labelers (from U.S.). For each modality (i.e., Appr: *Appearance* and C&P: *Context & Performance*), we trained separate models for different activities (i.e., *Instructional* and *Assessment*), and trained separate models for each group of experts: U.S. and Turkey. The generic (i.e., subject-independent) results for each of these two modalities (Appr and C&P) and activity types (*Instructional* and *Assessment*) are reported in Table 3, broken out by each affective state and by labeler background. We also report the average training set sizes (i.e., average of ten students, where balanced training sets differ for each student due to the leave-one-subject-out methodology) and total test set sizes (i.e., total of ten students' unbalanced test sets).

Table 3. Affect detection classifier results (F1-scores) for separate modalities (Appr: *Appearance*, C&P: *Context & Performance*) and different section types (Instr: *Instructional*, Assess: *Assessment*) trained using labels by experts from the United States and Turkey.

Section type	Class	Labels: Experts from the U.S.				Labels: Experts from Turkey			
		Avg. train count	*Total test count*	Appr F1	C&P F1	*Avg. train count*	*Total test count*	Appr F1	C&P F1
Instr.	Satisfied	*888*	*265*	0.62	0.58	*336*	*94*	0.41	0.42
	Bored	*888*	*271*	0.67	0.59	*336*	*425*	0.86	0.88
	OVERALL	*1776*	*536*	0.65	0.58	*672*	*519*	0.77	0.80
Assess.	Satisfied	*787*	*416*	0.59	0.80	*769*	*243*	0.43	0.73
	Confused	*787*	*219*	0.45	0.63	*769*	*215*	0.57	0.66
	OVERALL	*1574*	*635*	0.53	0.74	*1538*	*458*	0.51	0.70

Note that no students were labeled as *Confused* during *Instructional* activities, so our analysis of the *Instructional* models consists solely of examples of *Satisfied* and *Bored*. For *Assessment* models, although we have relatively balanced classes among the Turkey experts, the U.S. experts seldom labeled students as *Bored* (7.7%), too small a sample to develop detectors on. As our goal here is to compare models between same-culture and cross-culture labels, we trained our *Assessment* models to detect *Satisfied* and *Confused* states only, for both groups of experts.

In Table 3, we report mean F1-scores which are computed by weighted averaging over all folds (10-fold for random selection; times ten for all students), where weights are the test counts of each model. These mean F1-scores are computed for each class (i.e., affective state) and for overall classification performance. In addition to F1, mean AUC (i.e., the area under the ROC curve) values are reported in Table 4, which are again computed by weighted averaging over all folds. We report single AUC value for each model, which reflects the overall performance of binary classifiers.

Table 4. Affect detection classifier results (AUC values) for separate modalities (Appr: *Appearance*, C&P: *Context & Performance*) and different section types (Instr: *Instructional*, Assess: *Assessment*) trained using labels by experts from the United States and Turkey

Section type	Labels: Experts from the U.S.				Labels: Experts from Turkey			
	Avg. train count	*Total test count*	Appr AUC	C&P AUC	*Avg. train count*	*Total test count*	Appr AUC	C&P AUC
Instr.	*1776*	*536*	0.62	0.57	*672*	*519*	0.66	0.76
Assess.	*1574*	*635*	0.54	0.81	*1538*	*458*	0.53	0.78

As shown in Table 3, there are notable differences in the affect detection performances when models are trained using labels provided by experts in the U.S. versus Turkey. For *Instructional* models, both modalities had higher F1-scores for the overall performance when labels provided by Turkey experts are utilized instead of the U.S. experts (US vs. TR: 0.65 vs. 0.77 for Appr, 0.58 vs. 0.80 for C&P). This difference is particularly strong for the case of detecting *Bored* states (US vs. TR: 0.67 vs. 0.86 for

Appr, 0.59 vs. 0.88 for C&P). Note that we achieved better F1-scores even with the lower number of training samples provided by Turkey experts (672) compared to the U.S. experts (1776). For *Assessment* models, where we have comparable training set sizes (1574 vs. 1538), although both modalities performed slightly better overall when trained on expert labels from the U.S. compared to Turkey (US vs. TR: 0.53 vs. 0.51 for Appr, 0.74 vs. 0.70 for C&P), we observed that *Confused* state had higher F1-scores when expert labels were obtained from Turkey rather than U.S. (US vs. TR: 0.45 vs. 0.57 for Appr, 0.63 vs. 0.66 for C&P). In Table 4, we observed very similar trends with AUC values as we had with F1-scores for the overall performance results of models trained on expert labels from Turkey versus the U.S.

4   Discussion and Conclusions

In this study, we explored whether having expert labelers from the same country as the students would lead to more reliable affective state labels than having experts from a different country. Our findings show that experts from Turkey obtained moderately better inter-rater agreement than the experts from the U.S. These results are perhaps unsurprising, given that the original data collected was on learners from Turkey, and experts from Turkey have shared culture (common values and perceptions; modes of expressing affect) and context (similar school experience, shared environment). More importantly, even though the U.S. experts agree with each other, they agree fairly poorly with the Turkey experts, even when only the best U.S. experts are taken into account. Again, this finding may not be surprising. However, these findings have not been previously demonstrated in a quantitative comparison, and cross-cultural affect coding is common in the field of AIED. These results argue that the cross-cultural affect coding should be done with extreme caution.

On the other hand, it should be noted that these two expert groups had slightly different training due to being trained in a different setting and language; the two groups were also somewhat demographically different in terms of their age. This is the type of limitation that is difficult to surmount when comparing experts from different populations, but it suggests that replication with larger samples is probably warranted.

This difference between what the Turkey experts and U.S. experts saw, within the same student data, can also be seen in the differences between the distributions of affective states obtained from the two groups. In particular, these two distinct expert groups interpreted and assigned *Bored* and *Satisfied* states rather differently, with U.S. experts assigning a label of *Satisfied* much more frequently and *Bored* much less frequently. This may be due in part to the type of affect commonly experienced during online learning. Students' emotions may be less intense in a 1:1 learning using an online content platform (i.e., watching instructional videos or solving assessment questions) than in other contexts [20]. Qualitatively, several experts in both Turkey and the U.S. commented that the students were often very close to the neutral state. To differentiate between student emotional states, the human expert might need to understand subtle signals of shifts in emotion. This issue might explain the differences in the state distributions: There could be a cultural impact in interpreting such ambiguities in close-to-neutral states of students. Alternatively, U.S. experts may simply have been unable to recognize some of the key signs of boredom among the students from Turkey. This possible difference or limitation of U.S. experts in understanding subtle differences between emotions might also explain the higher F1-scores obtained for *Bored* and *Confused* states of students from Turkey when experts also from Turkey are utilized to provide somewhat more reliable ground truth labels for training affect detection models. Although we have limited data in these experiments, considering the challenges of affect detection both for human experts and machines, the differences in model results suggest that it is important to obtain labels as reliable as possible to achieve high-performing detection of student affect. These results might also suggest that although the best three experts from the same country could agree with each other reasonably well, we should be careful when using human experts from a different country than participants as this can impact the final model results.

These findings argue in general, then, that inter-country labeling of student affect is non-ideal. This finding raises some questions for going forward, however. First and foremost is, how different can labelers be from students and still produce acceptable labels? Living in the same country is an easy shorthand for belonging to the same culture, but culture and country do not perfectly coincide. Could a Canadian reliably label American data? Could a New Yorker reliably label a Texan's affect? And how long must someone have lived in the same country as the subject contributing data, to be reliable? What if they are married to a member of the target population? These questions are difficult to answer, but essential if we are to fully leverage this type of finding for data collection for affective computing research. One suggested take-away message from this research is that cross-national or cross-cultural expert labelers should be vetted for inter-rater agreement very carefully (a practice recommended in [11]), but having said that, similar precautions should be taken with any set of experts.

It has been a matter of debate within the field for decades whether it is wise to conduct affect labeling cross-culturally (for example, [9] argues in favor and [11] against). Our conclusion indicates that if a researcher's goal is to obtain high-quality labels of student affect, whether for use in affect detection or analysis on their own, it is probably not ideal to simply take a convenience sample of expert labelers who do not belong to the same population as the research subjects. Ultimately, AIED models and interventions based on those models have the highest chance of being effective if they are based on more reliable data.

References

1. Sabourin, J., Mott, B., Lester, J.C.: Modeling learner affect with theoretically grounded dynamic Bayesian networks. In: D'Mello, S., Graesser, A., Schuller, B., Martin, J.-C. (eds.) ACII 2011. LNCS, vol. 6974, pp. 286–295. Springer, Heidelberg (2011). https://doi.org/10.1007/978-3-642-24600-5_32

2. Jaques, N., Conati, C., Harley, Jason M., Azevedo, R.: Predicting affect from gaze data during interaction with an intelligent tutoring system. In: Trausan-Matu, S., Boyer, K.E., Crosby, M., Panourgia, K. (eds.) ITS 2014. LNCS, vol. 8474, pp. 29–38. Springer, Cham (2014). https://doi.org/10.1007/978-3-319-07221-0_4

3. Pardos, Z.A., Baker, R.S., San Pedro, M.O.C.Z., Gowda, S.M., Gowda, S.M.: Affective states and state tests: investigating how affect and engagement during the school year predict end of year learning outcomes. J. Learn. Anal. **1**(1), 107–128 (2014)

4. Liu, Z., Pataranutaporn, V., Ocumpaugh, J., Baker, R.S.J.d.: Sequences of frustration and confusion, and learning. In: Proceedings of the 6th International Conference on Educational Data Mining, pp. 114–120. International Educational Data Mining Society (2013)

5. D'Mello, S., Lehman, B., Sullins, J., Daigle, R., Combs, R., Vogt, K., Perkins, L., Graesser, A.: A time for emoting: when affect-sensitivity is and isn't effective at promoting deep learning. In: Aleven, V., Kay, J., Mostow, J. (eds.) ITS 2010. LNCS, vol. 6094, pp. 245–254. Springer, Heidelberg (2010). https://doi.org/10.1007/978-3-642-13388-6_29

6. Arroyo, I., Woolf, B.P., Burleson, W., Muldner, K., Rai, D., Tai, M.: A multimedia adaptive tutoring system for mathematics that addresses cognition, metacognition and affect. Int. J. Artif. Intell. Educ. **24**(4), 387–426 (2014)

7. D'Mello, S.K., Graesser, A.C.: Dynamics of affective states during complex learning. J. Learn. Instr. **22**(2), 145–157 (2012)

8. Dillon, J., Ambrose, G.A., Wanigasekara, N., Chetlur, M., Dey, P., Sengupta, B., D'Mello, S.K.: Student affect during learning with a MOOC. In: Proceedings of the Sixth International Conference on Learning Analytics & Knowledge, pp. 528–529. ACM (2016)

9. Ekman, P., Friesen, W.: Facial action coding system: a technique for the measurement of facial movement. Consulting Psychologists, Palo Alto (1978)

10. Sayette, M.A., Cohn, J.F., Wertz, J.M., Perrott, M.A., Parrott, D.J.: A psychometric evaluation of the facial action coding system for assessing spontaneous expression. J. Nonverbal Behav. **25**(3), 167–185 (2001)

11. Ocumpaugh, J., Baker, R., Rodrigo, M.M.T.: Baker Rodrigo Ocumpaugh monitoring protocol (BROMP) 2.0 technical and training manual. Teachers College, Columbia University and Ateneo Laboratory for the Learning Sciences, New York, NY and Manila, Philippines (2015)

12. Aslan, S., Mete, S.E., Okur, E., Oktay, E., Alyuz, N., Genc, U., Stanhill, D., Arslan Esme, A.: Human expert labeling process (HELP): towards a reliable higher-order user state labeling process and tool to assess student engagement. J. Educ. Technol. **57**(1), 53–59 (2017)

13. Cohn, J.F., Ambadar, Z., Ekman, P.: Observer-based measurement of facial expression with the facial action coding system. In: The Handbook of Emotion Elicitation and Assessment, pp. 203–221. Oxford University Press, New York (2007)

14. Stemler, S.E.: A comparison of consensus, consistency, and measurement approaches to estimating interrater reliability. Pract. Assess. Res. Eval. **9**(4), 1–19 (2004)

15. Gwet, K.L.: Handbook of Inter-Rater Reliability. Advanced Analytics. LLC, New York (2010)

16. Krippendorff, K.: Computing Krippendorff's alpha-reliability. Departmental Papers (ASC), 43. (2011) Retrieved from. http://repository.upenn.edu/asc_papers/43

17. Siegert, L., Böck, R., Wendemuth, A.: Inter-rater reliability for emotion annotation in human–computer interaction: comparison and methodological improvements. J. Multimodal User Interfaces **8**(1), 17–28 (2014)

18. Okur, E., Alyuz, N., Aslan, S., Genc, U., Tanriover, C., Arslan Esme, A.: Behavioral engagement detection of students in the wild. In: André, E., Baker, R., Hu, X., Rodrigo, Ma.M.T., du Boulay, B. (eds.) AIED 2017. LNCS (LNAI), vol. 10331, pp. 250–261. Springer, Cham (2017). https://doi.org/10.1007/978-3-319-61425-0_21

19. Alyuz, N., Okur, E., Genc, U., Aslan, S., Tanriover, C., Arslan Esme, A.: An unobtrusive and multimodal approach for behavioral engagement detection of students. In: Proceedings of the 1st International Workshop on Multimodal Interaction for Education, pp. 26–32. ACM (2017)
20. Lehman, B., Matthews, M., D'Mello, S., Person, N.: What are you feeling? investigating student affective states during expert human tutoring sessions. In: Woolf, Beverley P., Aïmeur, E., Nkambou, R., Lajoie, S. (eds.) ITS 2008. LNCS, vol. 5091, pp. 50–59. Springer, Heidelberg (2008). https://doi.org/10.1007/978-3-540-69132-7_10

Testing the Validity and Reliability of Intrinsic Motivation Inventory Subscales Within ASSISTments

Korinn S. Ostrow[(⊠)] and Neil T. Heffernan

Worcester Polytechnic Institute, Worcester, MA 01609, USA
{ksostrow,nth}@wpi.edu

Abstract. Online learning environments allow for the implementation of psychometric scales on diverse samples of students participating in authentic learning tasks. One such scale, the Intrinsic Motivation Inventory (IMI) can be used to inform stakeholders of students' subjective motivational and regulatory styles. The IMI is a multidimensional scale developed in support of Self-Determination Theory [1–3], a strongly validated theory stating that motivation and regulation are moderated by three innate needs: autonomy, belonging, and competence. As applied to education, the theory posits that students who perceive volition in a task, those who report stronger connections with peers and teachers, and those who perceive themselves as competent in a task are more likely to internalize the task and excel. ASSISTments, an online mathematics platform, is hosting a series of randomized controlled trials targeting these needs to promote integrated learning. The present work supports these studies by attempting to validate four subscales of the IMI within ASSISTments. Iterative factor analysis and item reduction techniques are used to optimize the reliability of these subscales and limit the obtrusive nature of future data collection efforts. Such scale validation efforts are valuable because student perceptions can serve as powerful covariates in differentiating effective learning interventions.

Keywords: Intrinsic Motivation Inventory · Self-Determination Theory
ASSISTments · Factor analysis · Validity · Reliability

1 Introduction

1.1 Psychometric Research in Online Learning: Value for AIED

Online learning environments allow for the implementation of psychometric scales on diverse samples of students participating in authentic learning tasks. Scales measuring personality traits, values, beliefs, motivation, and other self-reported psychological characteristics, have supported educational research for many years. However, it seems that recent opportunities for data collection at scale, made possible by omnipresent technology, have led many researchers to overlook the procedures necessary to ensure valid measurement.

© Springer International Publishing AG, part of Springer Nature 2018
C. Penstein Rosé et al. (Eds.): AIED 2018, LNAI 10947, pp. 381–394, 2018.
https://doi.org/10.1007/978-3-319-93843-1_28

Although this may not seem like an issue of particular interest to the AIED community, it should be of critical concern. Validating a measure in a learning environment before its formal use strengthens the validity and reliability of resulting claims. AIED researchers commonly focus on advancing models of student learning or affect [4, 5]. Models featuring data collected from a clickstream or sensors can be supplemented by student self-reports from psychometric scales to explain additional variance or reduce error. A recent article in the *Journal of Learning Analytics* highlighted psychometric variables relevant to academic performance including measures of cognitive ability, temperament, personality, motivation, and learning strategies [6]. Although researchers tend to cite published reliability statistics before implementing popular psychometric scales, few employ the exploratory or confirmatory factor analyses (or similar methods) necessary to validate use of the scale in their specific domain, population, and/or learning environment. This is not to say that these techniques are completely foreign to researchers in the field; one positive example observed during a review of related literature established and validated a measure of learners' perceptions of pedagogical agents prior to its use in further research [7]. In contrast, it is common practice in psychology to cite an initial publication as proof of a scale's validation prior to its formal use. As such, the AIED community may benefit from stronger approaches to psychometric application.

A concrete example of the importance of scale validation stems from recent focus in the AIED community toward personalization [8]. Researchers tackle this problem by using learner analytics, data mining techniques, and randomized controlled trials to isolate the most effective learning interventions for each student based on a set of predefined characteristics. In such contexts, self-report measures from psychometric scales can provide an opportunity to explain additional variance between students. Scale scores can be used as dependent measures for the purpose of prediction (i.e., "students with *high prior knowledge* are more likely to report feeling *competent*") or as independent variables for exploring interactions or mechanism (i.e., "students with *high perceptions of autonomy* outperformed those with *low perceptions of autonomy* differentially by treatment condition"). Thus, it is critical to strengthen these metrics by taking steps to validate psychometric scales within specific domains, populations, and/or learning environments.

1.2   Self-Determination Theory and the Intrinsic Motivation Inventory

The Intrinsic Motivation Inventory (IMI) [9] is a multidimensional scale developed in support of Self-Determination Theory (SDT) [1–3], a strongly validated theory claiming that motivation and regulation are guided by three innate needs: autonomy, belonging, and competence. As applied to education, this theory posits that students who perceive volition in a task, those who report stronger connections with peers and teachers, and those who perceive themselves as competent in the task at hand are more likely to internalize the task and excel. It has been shown that promotion of these needs in educational environments can lead to higher quality learning, as well as greater conceptual understanding, personal growth, and positive adjustment [10]. If validated in an online learning environment, the IMI could potentially be used to inform stakeholders of students' motivational and regulatory styles, alerting them to pertinent implications for learning outcomes and appropriate interventions.

In their landmark review outlining the growth of SDT, Ryan and Deci [2] cite applications of the theory across research domains including education, health care, religion, health and exercise, political activity, environmental activism, and intimate relationships. The IMI has also been applied broadly, with past work validating versions of its subscales in contexts including sports and competition [11, 12], reading [13], mathematics [14], language learning [14], psychiatry [15], medicine [16], puzzle completion [17], computer tasks [18], and teacher training [19]. Past work has also shown IMI subscales to have strong temporal reliability [20]. While examples of IMI application have clearly varied by domain, task, and sample population, it is important to note that they have also varied by scale and item inclusion, scale and item order, and data collection environment. As such, the developers of the IMI encourage researchers to validate the scale within their specific domains, populations, and/or environments of interest [9].

1.3 The Present Work

The present work provides an example of scale validation in an online learning environment using iterative exploratory factor analysis and item reduction techniques. ASSISTments (www.assistments.org), an online learning environment known for its embrace of educational research at scale [21, 22], is currently hosting a series of randomized controlled trials examining learning interventions that target the innate needs defined by SDT with the goal of promoting integrated learning and thereby improving student performance. In support of this research, the present work attempts to validate four subscales of the IMI measuring students' perceptions of autonomy, belonging (or relatedness), competence, and interest/enjoyment within ASSISTments. Validation of IMI subscales within ASSISTments is valuable because students' perceptions can serve as powerful independent or dependent measures when isolating effective learning interventions. Goals of the present work are to achieve convergent, discriminant, and face validity for each subscale, to achieve high reliability for each subscale, and to reduce the number of items within each subscale for future implementation. The latter goal will make future data collection less obtrusive (by requiring fewer items), thereby allowing survey efforts to more easily scale to the broader ASSISTments user population (approximately 50,000 users).

2 Methods

2.1 Sample

Five teachers who regularly work with ASSISTments were contacted with the request that their students participate in a 28-item Likert scale survey. Teachers were notified that the survey would immediately follow a brief assignment (of their choice) used for classwork or homework, and that it would add five to ten minutes to the assignment based on students' reading levels. Four teachers chose to participate and provided assignments that were modified by the primary author to include two additional items, one introducing the survey as a data collection tool to strengthen students' experiences within ASSISTments and one providing access to the IMI subscales.

Participating teachers and their students were representative of different subpopulations and sampling styles. A total of 226 students participated in at least one of the four subscales. Students of Teacher 1 (n = 73) and Teacher 2 (n = 54) were enrolled in 7th grade math classes at two schools in two different suburban/rural locations in Massachusetts. Teacher 1 chose to embed the IMI subscales after an 8-question homework assignment. Teacher 2 split delivery of the subscales, enrolling her students in a randomized controlled trial including two scales (Interest/Enjoyment and Competence) for homework, and choosing to embed the remaining two scales (Autonomy and Belonging) following an 8-question classwork assignment. These two assignments were strongly conceptually linked and split scale delivery was embraced to examine the potential consequences for reliability and score interpretation within teachers. Students of Teacher 3 (n = 46) were enrolled in high school level math courses in an urban location in Massachusetts and were highly representative of ESL and low SES populations. Teacher 3 chose to embed the subscales after a "class opener" with two multiple choice questions. Students of Teacher 4 (n = 53) were enrolled in high school level engineering courses in an urban location in Massachusetts and represented accelerated learners. Teacher 4 chose to embed the survey following a 20-question assignment on velocity.

All students were familiar with ASSISTments and used the system regularly for classwork and homework in the courses in which they were surveyed. In general, students were not allowed to opt out of survey participation up front but were allowed to skip scale responses and progress to the end of their assignments at any time during their participation. For the RCT-bound scales delivered by Teacher 2, students were prompted to opt-in to survey participation causing unbalanced scale responses between subscales within Teacher 2. This caused average overall missingness (%) to vary by scale across teachers: Interest/Enjoyment (M = 13.60, SD = 0.33), Autonomy (M = 2.16, SD = 0.46), Belonging (M = 3.70, SD = 0.35), and Competence (M = 14.38, SD = 0.37). The analytic sample was reduced based on missing data using listwise deletion. This approach is appropriate for factor analysis because unbalanced items can sway factor loadings [23]. As such, results are based on samples with complete response patterns for modeled scale items.

2.2   Intrinsic Motivation Inventory (IMI)

The IMI is a multidimensional scale intended to measure the subjective experiences of participants following task participation [1, 9]. Various iterations of the IMI have been in use for more than 30 years, with well-established validity and subscale reliability across tasks, conditions, and settings [9]. The scale has six primary subscales that can be mixed and matched to suit research needs: interest/enjoyment, perceived competence, effort, value/usefulness, felt pressure and tension, and perceived choice. A seventh subscale intended to measure perceived relatedness or belonging was added in recent years and has not yet been established as valid or reliable.

Subscales. All scale items were modified slightly to reflect an academic task or setting; such modifications are thought to be inconsequential to outcomes [9]. Students were asked to indicate how true each statement was for them using a Likert scale (1 = *Not at All True*, 7 = *Very True*). Past work has suggested that order effects of scale and item delivery are negligible and that subscales can be included or excluded as necessary [9, 24]. The four subscales considered in the present work align with the basic psychological needs defined by Self-Determination Theory, as detailed in the subsections below.

Interest/Enjoyment. This subscale is the primary measure of intrinsic motivation. It includes seven items regarding intrinsic motivation (i.e., "I enjoyed doing this assignment very much"), with two items reverse scored (i.e., "This assignment did not hold my attention at all").

Autonomy. This subscale is the primary measure of perceived autonomy, also known as choice, volition, or task-based locus of control. Scores on this scale have previously been shown to predict Interest/Enjoyment scores [9]. This subscale includes seven items regarding perceived autonomy (i.e., "I did this assignment because I wanted to"), with five items reverse scored (i.e., "I did this assignment because I had to").

Belonging. This subscale is the primary measure of perceived relatedness or belonging. This scale was added to the IMI in recent years and does not have well established validity or reliability. In addition, modifications to items in this subscale to capture how well students felt they related to their classmates may have been more significant than modifications to other scales because the effect was extrapolated to a collective group (i.e., changing "task" or "activity" to "assignment" does not extrapolate to *many tasks*). This subscale includes eight items (i.e., "I'd like a chance to interact with my classmates more often") with four items reverse scored (i.e., "I don't feel like I could really trust my classmates").

Competence. This subscale is the primary measure of perceived competence or feeling capable and confident. Scores on this scale have previously been shown to predict Interest/Enjoyment scores [9]. This subscale includes six items (i.e., "I am satisfied with my performance on this assignment") with one item reverse scored (i.e., "This was an assignment that I couldn't do very well").

2.3   Procedure

Data was retrieved by integrating Qualtrics, a readily accessible survey infrastructure, with ASSISTments using the ASSISTments Survey System available through the ASSISTments TestBed [25]. This system uses an iframe to establish a connection between the two platforms, resulting in the ability to link survey data to ASSISTments performance through anonymized student and assignment identification numbers. Two items were added to the end of each participating teacher's assignment: a verification item introducing the survey as a data collection tool to strengthen students' experiences within ASSISTments, and an item with an embedded iframe that connected students to the survey content in Qualtrics while they worked in ASSISTments.

IMI items were delivered through Qualtrics using subscale alignment. Except for those of Teacher 2, all students were asked to respond to all items pertaining to Interest/Enjoyment in a single page view. When finished, or if opting not to answer, they could select "Next" to move on to the next page and subscale. Students cycled through the Autonomy, Belonging, and Competence subscales in this fashion until ultimately completing the survey. Due to Teacher 2's split delivery, her students opted-in to the Interest/Enjoyment and Competence subscales after a homework assignment and received the Autonomy and Belonging subscales after a subsequent class assignment using the same protocol and infrastructure noted above.

The data collection period lasted one week. Data was retrieved from Qualtrics and ASSISTments, compiled, and preprocessed for IBM SPSS Statistics. Variables were cleaned, and missing data was labelled for proper exclusion from analysis. Redundancies were removed while merging data (24 students accessed the survey multiple times; in these cases, only first responses were retained). The resulting data file contained responses from 226 students. Items were reverse scored as necessary - a step not required for factor analysis, but critical for calculating reliability using Cronbach's α [23]. Higher score values indicated higher levels of scale sentiment across all scales (i.e., greater enjoyment). De-identified survey data is available at [26] for additional reference.

Following the guidelines set forth by Field [23] iterative scale reduction was conducted using principal axis factor analyses. Given the likelihood of correlations between subscales, oblique rotation (i.e., direct oblimin) offered a more appropriate approach than orthogonal rotation (i.e., varimax). Factors were established using traditional methods: factors with eigenvalues greater than 1.0 were considered valid for inclusion using Kaiser's criterion, and scree plots were developed to confirm factor count by estimating the point of inflexion. Items were removed as part of the iterative process to establish stronger validity and reliability. Inter-item correlations and subscale reliability measures were consulted for scale reduction. Where items were removed, factor analysis was repeated to assess potential changes to factors and loadings and to optimize the model.

3 Results

3.1 Iterative Scale Reduction

28-Item Factor Analysis. A principal axis factor analysis was conducted on all 28 items from the IMI subscales using direct oblimin oblique rotation. After listwise deletion of missing responses the analytic sample consisted of 180 students. The Kaiser-Meyer-Olkin measure verified the sample was large enough for analysis, KMO = .81, and Bartlett's Test of Sphericity was significant, χ^2 (378) = 2,818.75, p < .001 (as desired). In addition, the diagonals of the anti-image correlation matrix were above .5 (as desired). Thus, 180 students provided an adequate sample size for analysis.

This analysis was conducted to assess initial model structure and examine the potential for item reduction. The model had poor structure, as suggested by a determinant of 5.61E−008 (denoting issues of multicollinearity), numerous after extraction communalities below 0.70, and an average communality of 0.58 denoting that Kaiser's criterion was not necessarily an appropriate threshold for factor inclusion. The model resolved to six factors using Kaiser's criterion and four or six factors based on interpretation of the scree plot's point of inflexion. Four factors, as desired based on the initial subscales, accounted for 56% of the variance in the model, with the remaining two factors accounting for an additional 11%.

The correlation matrix attained from this analysis (Table 1) was helpful in reducing scale items to establish a stronger model. Field [23] suggests beginning the reduction process by assessing the correlation matrix for multiple inter-item correlations over .90 or under .30. As none of the correlations exceeded .90, items were slated for removal from the model if 50% or more of the within-scale inter-item correlations were .30 or less (i.e., item E4 had 3/6 correlations of .30 or smaller; suppressed correlations are all less than .30). Using this approach, eight items were removed from the model: Interest/Enjoyment Item 4 (50%), Autonomy Item 6 (50%), Belonging Items 2 (57%), 3 (57%), 4 (86%), 5 (57%), and 7 (57%), and Competence Item 6 (100%).

20-Item Factor Analysis. Following removal of these eight items, a second principal axis factor analysis was conducted on the remaining 20 items, again using direct oblimin oblique rotation. The analytic sample again consisted of an adequate sample size of 180 students: the Kaiser-Meyer-Olkin measure verified the sample was large enough for the analysis, KMO = .84, and Bartlett's Test of Sphericity was significant, χ^2 (190) = 2,066.79, p < .001.

Model structure was still not ideal. The expected structure was resolved, with four factors retained (using Kaiser's criterion), explaining 66% of the variance and with all items loading on their expected subscales. However, although the determinant increased to 5.84E−006, it remained lower than the desired minimum of 1.00E−005, suggesting that a multicollinearity issue remained and that additional items should be considered for removal.

Having addressed the issue through the correlation matrix, no additional reductions were suggested using this approach. Thus, reliability analyses were conducted on each subscale to determine candidates for removal. Cronbach's α was used with listwise deletion of missing values by scale. Analysis suggested that reliability of the six remaining items in the Interest/Enjoyment subscale was high, α = .91 (n = 191), but could be increased by removing Item 3. Reliability for other subscales was mixed, as shown in Table 2, but no other items met qualifications for removal using this approach. Therefore, Interest/Enjoyment Item 3 was removed from the model, leaving 19 items.

19-Item Factor Analysis. Following item removal, a final principal axis factor analysis was conducted on the remaining 19 items, again using direct oblimin oblique rotation. Listwise deletion of missing data left an analytic sample of 181 students. The Kaiser-Meyer-Olkin measure verified the sample was large enough for the analysis, KMO = .83, and Bartlett's Test of Sphericity was significant, χ^2 (171) = 1,988.72, p < .001.

Table 1. Inter-item correlations in the 28-item model (n = 180).

Scale/Item	Interest/Enjoyment							Autonomy							Belonging								Competence					
	1	2	3	4	5	6	7	1	2	3	4	5	6	7	1	2	3	4	5	6	7	8	1	2	3	4	5	6
Enjoyment																												
E1	—																											
E2	.83	—																										
E3	.52	.53	—																									
E4	.32	.33	.62	—																								
E5	.69	.67	.43	.19	—																							
E6	.75	.77	.47	.30	.74	—																						
E7	.62	.64	.34		.70	.65	—																					
Autonomy																												
A1	.42	.37	.36	.21	.41	.35	.36	—																				
A2	.15		.24	.25	.18		.14	.39	—																			
A3	.17	.17	.32	.24		.17		.43	.53	—																		
A4	.13	.15	.20	.17	.24	.15	.18	.31	.39	.53	—																	
A5	.24	.20	.30	.25	.30	.31	.23	.51	.42	.57	.48	—																
A6	.47	.52	.37	.21	.56	.43	.44	.45	.24	.31	.21	.45	—															
A7	.18		.23	.17	.26	.22	.22	.39	.36	.40	.58	.59	.24	—														
Belonging																												
B1	-.13				-.14	-.14								.15	—													
B2													-.13	.14	.67	—												
B3							.15								.23	.18	—											
B4																	.25	—										
B5					-.23	-.14	-.16	-.23					-.23		.45	.39	.26		—									
B6															.43	.35	.38		.47	—								
B7															.16		.40	.44	.26	.31	—							
B8					.13		.19							-.18	.35	.24	.64	.18	.27	.31	.47	—						
Competence																												
C1									-.24	-.18	-.19	-.14			.24	.13	.19		.18			.16	—					
C2									-.21	-.16	-.23	-.25		-.21	.18	.13	.27				.14	.19	.61	—				
C3	.13	.17			.13				-.18	-.13	-.15		.16	-.15	.17		.33		.17		.21	.26	.62	.56	—			
C4									-.16	-.13	-.15				.34	.22	.21		.17		.20	.17	.77	.61	.66	—		
C5		-.14	-.14					-.12	-.29	-.25	-.18	-.22			.28	.15	.29		.18		.23	.25	.78	.70	.68	.83	—	
C6	-.25	-.15	-.21		-.26	-.15	-.18	-.33	-.27	-.16	-.23	-.27			.22	.31	.15		.29	.24		.25	.15	.14	.17	.19	.29	—

Note. Bold correlations, $p < .01$; all others, $p < .05$. Suppressed correlations were not significant at $p < .05$.

Table 2. Reliability of subscales in the 20-item model and candidate items for removal.

Scale	*n*	*Scale Items*	α	α *if item removed*
Interest/Enjoyment	191	6	91	.92 (Item 3)
Autonomy	220	6	.83	--
Belonging	217	3	.56*	--
Competence	192	5	.92	--

*The Belonging subscale does not have well-established validity or reliability; low reliability of this scale was not of immediate concern.

This final iteration established adequate model structure. Four factors were retained using Kaiser's criterion, explaining 68% of the variance, with all items loading on their expected subscales. Four factors were also suggested via scree plot interpretation, as shown in Fig. 1. The determinant increased to 1.01E−005, just surpassing the threshold of 1.00E−005 and suggesting that multicollinearity had been sufficiently resolved. Average communality increased to 0.595, bordering the 0.60 threshold for adequacy of the Kaiser criterion. Additionally, only 12% of the residuals in the reproduced matrix had absolute values greater than 0.05. Reliability results were unchanged from those presented in Table 2, with the noted increase in reliability for the Interest/Enjoyment subscale following item removal. Further, all corrected item-total correlations were above 0.30, suggesting that each item correlated well with its respective overall scale score. Values were lowest for items in the Belonging subscale, suggesting issues with

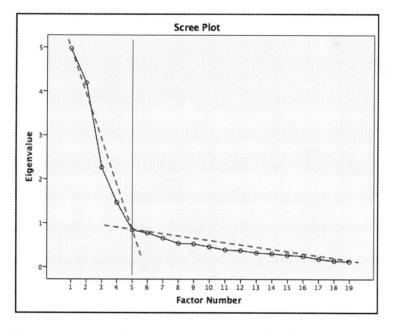

Fig. 1. Scree plot with point of inflexion mapped. The red vertical line at factor 5 designates the non-inclusive cutoff factor, or the 'elbow' of the graph. (Color figure online)

Table 3. Summary of exploratory factor analysis results in the 19-item model (n = 181).

Scale/Item	Interest/Enjoyment	Competence	Autonomy	Belonging
Interest/Enjoyment				
IE2 – This assignment was fun to do.	.879			
IE1 – I enjoyed doing this assignment very much.	.858			
IE6 – I thought this assignment was quite enjoyable.	.857			
IE5 – I would describe this assignment as very interesting.	.810			
IE7 – While I was doing this assignment, I was thinking about how much I enjoyed it.	.767			
Competence				
C4 – I am satisfied with my performance on this assignment.		.935		
C5 – I was pretty skilled at this assignment.		.915		
C1 – I think I am pretty good at this assignment.		.868		
C3 – After working at this assignment for a while, I felt pretty competent.		.709		
C2 – I think I did pretty well at this assignment, compared to other students.		.664		
Autonomy				
A5 – I did this assignment because I had no choice. (R)			.780	
A3 – I didn't really have a choice about doing this assignment. (R)			.720	
A7 – I did this assignment because I had to. (R)			.704	
A4 – I felt like I had to do this assignment. (R)			.663	
A2 – I felt like it was not my own choice to do this assignment. (R)			.581	
A1 – I believe I had some choice about doing this assignment.			.518	
Belonging				
B6 – I'd really prefer not to interact with my classmates in the future. (R)				.665
B1 – I feel really distant to my classmates. (R)				.643
B8 – It is likely that my classmates and I could become friends if we interacted a lot.				.492
Eigenvalues	4.97	4.19	2.27	1.47
% of variance	26.16	22.07	11.92	7.74
α	.92	.92	.83	.56

the validity of using this subscale alongside others in the IMI. Overall reliability of all 19 items in the model was moderate, $\alpha = .78$.

3.2   Resulting Subscales in the 19-Item Model

The four resulting factors aligned with expected subscales. Table 3 provides each scale item with factor loadings from the pattern matrix after rotation. The pattern matrix was used for interpretation because it ignores shared variance and shows the unique contribution of items to factors [23]. Factor 1 aligned with the Interest/Enjoyment subscale, explaining 26.14% of model variance. Similarly, Factor 2 aligned with the Competence subscale (22.07%), Factor 3 aligned with the Autonomy subscale (11.92%), and Factor 4 aligned with the Belonging subscale (7.74%). The Interest/Enjoyment, Autonomy, and Competence subscales showed substantial convergent validity and high reliability, and all scales displayed high discriminant and face validity.

3.3   Class Variations

A brief investigation was conducted to examine how scale scores using the 19-item model varied across participating teachers. Split-file analysis was used to assess the reliability of each subscale using Teacher as the grouping variable. Results are shown in Table 4. Subscales showed similar patterns of reliability regardless of teacher, with some variation in magnitude across teachers. Of note, Teacher 2 and Teacher 3 exhibited the lowest reliability on the Belonging subscale, while Teacher 2 and Teacher 4 exhibited lower than anticipated reliability on the Competence subscale.

Table 4. Subscale reliability by teacher.

Scale	Teacher 1		Teacher 2		Teacher 3		Teacher 4	
	n	α	n	α	n	α	n	α
Interest/Enjoyment	73	.93	27	.88	38	.92	53	.93
Autonomy	71	.81	54	.77	41	.78	53	.88
Belonging	71	.71	54	.29	39	.23	53	.75
Competence	70	.93	29	.82	40	.90	53	.82

Scale scores were defined for each student by averaging factor items and then aggregated by teacher for final comparison (see Fig. 2). Such aggregates offer an example of how this psychometric scale could be used to establish useful variables or covariates for future research. ANOVAs revealed significant differences between teachers on all subscales: Interest/Enjoyment, $F (3, 190) = 3.71$, $p < .05$; Autonomy, $F (3, 218) = 6.98$, $p < .001$; Belonging, $F (3, 216) = 6.76$, $p < .001$; and Competence, $F (3, 191) = 21.08$, $p < .001$. Given numerous confounds in present survey collection (e.g., teacher, assignment, skill level, age range) further assessment was not considered. However, future work could control for potential sources of variance to better define the mechanisms underlying these significant differences.

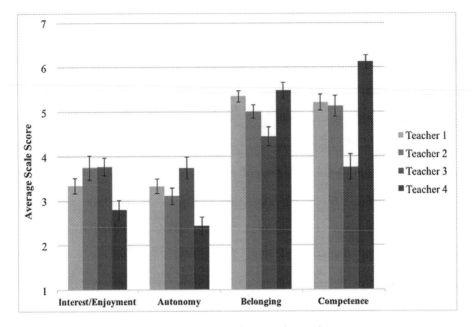

Fig. 2. Resulting scale scores by teacher.

4   Contributions and Limitations

The goal of the present work was to validate subscales of the IMI within ASSISTments to support a series of randomized controlled trials assessing the efficacy of learning interventions that target students' perceptions of autonomy, belonging, and competence. Employing an iterative factor analysis and item reduction approach with an analytic sample of 181 students established substantial convergent validity and high reliability for three reduced IMI subscales (Interest/Enjoyment, Autonomy, and Competence). Issues were observed with the reliability of the Belonging subscale, due in part to the high proportion of items removed to optimize the model. This subscale is not well-established as valid or reliable [9] and it did not perform well within ASSISTments. As such, the Belonging subscale will not be used in future data collection efforts and students' aggregate scores on this subscale will not be used in future analyses. Results also suggested that all four subscales exhibited high discriminant and face validity.

Limitations of this work include potential bias introduced by varied delivery protocol of subscales (i.e., Teacher 2's split delivery), delivery of items aligned within subscales (although previously addressed as inconsequential for psychometric scales [9, 24]), and the potential for reduced external validity due to item reduction. The randomized controlled trials supported by this work will use the subscales established by the 19-item model when compiling aggregate scores for use in future analyses. The reduction of 9 items from these subscales will also make future data collection using the IMI within ASSISTments less obtrusive, thereby allowing survey efforts to scale.

With hope, these results also serve as a valuable reminder for the AIED community that contextually validating a psychometric scale prior to its formal use strengthens the validity and reliability of resulting claims.

Acknowledgments. We acknowledge funding from NSF grants (ACI-1440753, DRL-1252297, DRL-1109483, DRL-1316736, DGE-1535428, OAC-1724889, OAC-1636782 & DRL-1031398), the U.S. Department of Education (IES R305A120125 & R305C100024 and GAANN), the ONR, and the Gates Foundation. Thanks to S.O. & L.P.B.O.

References

1. Ryan, R.: Control and information in the intrapersonal sphere an extension of cognitive evaluation theory. J. Pers. Soc. Psychol. **43**, 450–461 (1982)
2. Ryan, R.M., Deci, E.L.: Self-determination theory and the facilitation of intrinsic motivation, social development, and well-being. Am. Psychol. **55**, 68–78 (2000)
3. Ryan, R.M., Deci, E.L.: An overview of self-determination theory. In: Deci, E.L., Ryan, R. M. (eds.) Handbook of Self-Determination Research. University of Rochester Press, Rochester (2002)
4. Brusilovsky, P., Millán, E.: User models for adaptive hypermedia and adaptive educational systems. In: Brusilovsky, P., Kobsa, A., Nejdl, W. (eds.) The Adaptive Web. LNCS, vol. 4321, pp. 3–53. Springer, Heidelberg (2007). https://doi.org/10.1007/978-3-540-72079-9_1
5. Calvo, R.A., D'Mello, S.: Affect detection: an interdisciplinary review of models, methods, and their applications. IEEE Trans. Affect. Comput. **1**(1), 18–37 (2010)
6. Gray, G., McGuinness, C., Owende, P., Carthy, A.: A review of psychometric data analysis and application in modelling of academic achievement in tertiary education. J. Learn. Anal. **1** (1), 75–106 (2014)
7. Ryu, J., Baylor, A.L.: The psychometric structure of pedagogical agent persona. Tech. Inst. Cogn. Learn. **22**, 291–314 (2005)
8. Santos, O.C., Kravcik, M., Boticario, J.G.: Preface to special issue on user modelling to support personalization in enhanced educational settings. Int. J. Artif. Intell. Educ. **26**(3), 809–820 (2016)
9. Intrinsic Motivation Inventory. http://selfdeterminationtheory.org/questionnaires/. Accessed 07 Feb 2018
10. Deci, E., Vallerand, R., Pelletier, L., Ryan, R.: Motivation and education: the self-determination perspective. Educ. Psychol. **26**, 325–346 (1991)
11. McAuley, E., Duncan, T., Tammen, V.V.: Psychometric properties of the Intrinsic Motivation Inventory in a competitive sport setting: a confirmatory factor analysis. Res. Q. Exerc. Sport **60**, 48–58 (1987)
12. McAuley, E., Tammen, V.V.: The effects of subjective and objective competitive outcomes on intrinsic motivation. J. Sport Exerc. Psychol. **11**, 84–93 (1989)
13. Grolnick, W., Ryan, R.: Autonomy in children's learning: an experimental and individual difference investigation. J. Pers. Soc. Psychol. **52**, 890–898 (1987)
14. Monteiro, V., Mata, L., Peixoto, F.: Intrinsic Motivation Inventory: psychometric properties in the context of first language and mathematics learning. Psicologia Reflexao e Critica **28** (3), 434–443 (2015)
15. Choi, J., Mogami, T., Medalia, A.: Intrinsic Motivation Inventory: an adapted measure for schizophrenia research. Schizophr. Bull. **36**(5), 966–976 (2010)

16. Williams, G.C., Deci, E.L.: Supporting autonomy to motivate glucose control in patients with diabetes. Diab. Care **21**, 1644–1651 (1998)

17. Ryan, R., Mims, V., Koestner, R.: Relation of reward and interpersonal context to intrinsic motivation: a review and test using Cognitive Evaluation Theory. J. Pers. Soc. Psychol. **45**, 736–750 (1983)

18. Deci, E., Eghrari, H., Patrick, B., Leone, D.: Facilitating internalization: the self-determination theory perspective. J. Pers. **62**, 119–142 (1994)

19. Filak, V., Sheldon, K.: Student psychological need satisfaction and college teacher-course evaluation. Educ. Psychol. **23**, 235–247 (2003)

20. Tsigilis, N., Theodosiou, A.: Temporal stability of the Intrinsic Motivation Inventory. Percept. Mot. Skills **97**(1), 271–280 (2003)

21. Heffernan, N., Heffernan, C.: The ASSISTments ecosystem: building a platform that brings scientists and teachers together for minimally invasive research on human learning and teaching. Int. J. Artif. Intell. Educ. **24**(4), 470–497 (2014)

22. Ostrow, K.S., Heffernan, N.T., Williams, J.J.: Tomorrow's edtech today: establishing a learning platform as a collaborative research tool for sound science. Teachers Coll. Rec. **119** (3), 1–36 (2017)

23. Field, A.: Discovering statistics using IBM SPSS Statistics, 4th edn. SAGE Publications, London (2013)

24. Schell, K.L., Oswald, F.L.: Item grouping and item randomization in personality measurement. Pers. Individ. Differ. **55**, 317–321 (2013)

25. ASSISTments TestBed Resource Guide. https://www.assistmentstestbed.org. Accessed 06 Feb 2018

26. Submission Data. https://osf.io/4gwuc/. Accessed 07 Feb 2018

Correctness- and Confidence-Based Adaptive Feedback of Kit-Build Concept Map with Confidence Tagging

Jaruwat Pailai[✉], Warunya Wunnasri, Yusuke Hayashi, and Tsukasa Hirashima

Graduate School of Engineering, Hiroshima University, Higashihiroshima, Japan
{jaruwat,warunya,hayashi,tsukasa}@lel.hiroshima-u.ac.jp

Abstract. In this paper, we present an adaptive feedback of Kit-Build concept map with confidence tagging (KB map-CT) for improving the understanding of learners in a reading situation. KB map-CT is a digital tool that supports the concept maps strategy where learners can construct concept maps for representing their understanding as learner maps and can identify their confidence in each proposition of the learner maps as a degree of their understanding. Kit-Build concept map (KB map) has been already realized the propositional level automatic diagnosis of the learner maps. Therefore, KB map-CT can utilize both correctness and confidence information for each proposition to design and distinguish feedback, that is, (1) correct and confident, (2) correct and unconfident, (3) incorrect and confident, and (4) incorrect and unconfident. An experiment was conducted to investigate the effectiveness of the adaptive feedback. The results suggest that learners can revise their maps after receiving feedback appropriately. In "correct and unconfident" case, adaptive feedback is useful to improve the confidence. In the case of "incorrect and confident," improvement of the propositions was the same ratio with the case of "incorrect and unconfident." The results of the delay test demonstrate that learners can retain their understanding and confidence one week later.

Keywords: Adaptive feedback · Kit-Build concept map · Confidence tagging

1 Introduction

Feedback has a powerful influence in helping the learners to improve their learning achievements, thus it should be individually aligned with the characteristics of each learner as much as possible [1]. The correctness of learner's answer is generally used to estimate the characteristic of the learner, which the correct answer was interpreted as a representing the knowledge, while the incorrect answer was interpreted as a representing the misunderstanding. Especially the incorrect answers indicate that the learners require help to correct their misunderstandings. Moreover, the certainty of knowledge is an essential component to represent the belief of the learner as the quality of the knowledge [2–6]. For instance, confidence can encourage a deeper understanding of the material [7] and can increase reflection and justification of the answers [8]. Consequently, the answers of learners represent their understanding, and the confidence in their answer indicates the degree of their understanding, such as the different degrees of the understanding between a learner who is sure in the correct answer and a learner who is unsure in the correct answer.

Although the correctness and confidence information can describe the degree of learner's understanding, this two information is not utilized to provide individual feedback for improving the understanding of learners generally. Because of the different degrees of learner's understanding, learners should be given different feedback in the same way as the different correctness which is given the feedback differently. Furthermore, the adaptive feedback regarding confidence information aims to ensure the confidence of learners who have an accurate understanding but lack confidence for encouraging the retaining of their understanding. The adaptive feedback also aims to reduce the confidence of learners who are confident in their misunderstanding, then correct the misunderstanding.

In this paper, we propose a mechanism to provide individual feedback based on the correctness and confidence information as an adaptive feedback of the Kit-Build concept map with confidence tagging (KB map-CT). The Kit-Build concept map (KB map) is a digital tool for supporting the concept maps strategy [9]. The instructor-built map is called a goal map, illustrating a learning goal, and the goal map will also be used as criteria for identifying the correctness. The goal map is decomposed into a list of concepts and linking words (called the "kit"), while the learner-built map, which is called a learner map, is used to represent the understanding of learner. The structuring task of the KB map-CT is to gather learning evidence that consists of the learner map and the confidence of the learner. Learners can construct learner maps as the learning evidence by connecting the kit to form the propositions [10]. A completed proposition, which can be tagged with the confidence of the learner, comprises one connected linking word between two concepts. The confidence of the learning evidence is simplified in the form of confidence- or unconfidence-value, which the learner can assign to every complete proposition. Hence, the KB map-CT can elicit learning evidence that includes the understanding of learners and the degree of the understanding in the gathering process. The adaptive feedback based on the correctness and confidence information is provided for learners in a reflection task for improving their understanding individually. The mechanism of the adaptive feedback is to provide different interactions as different feedback for encouraging the learners to reconsider their current understanding according to the correctness and confidence information of each proposition. For instance, the evidence identification task requests the learners to identify the evidence of all their confident propositions for ensuring the confidence of correct propositions by themselves and for reducing the confidence of incorrect propositions before correcting the misunderstanding. The related content of the material and the correct proposition of the goal map will be visualized along with the proposition of learners to promote the learners to reconsider their incorrect propositions. Therefore, we present an experiment of the adaptive feedback of the KB map-CT in a reading situation for illustrating the effectiveness of the feedback.

This paper is structured as follows: Sect. 2 mentions to related works of the concept mapping tools and its feedback. An introduction of the KB map and the KB map-CT are also described in this section. Section 3 presents the adaptive feedback of the KB map-CT based on the correctness and confidence information and the description of the experiment. The results section, outlined in Sect. 4 presents the learning achievements and the proposition revising after the learners received feedback with a discussion about the effectiveness of the adaptive feedback. The discussion of the feedback implementation with confidence information is mentioned in Sects. 5, and 6 is the conclusion of this study.

2   Background

2.1   Concept Mapping Tools and Its Individual Feedback

Concept maps are graphical tools that are used to represent and organize knowledge [11]. A proposition is constructed by connecting two concepts via a relation with a linking word to represent a unit of meaning. The propositions are a core component of measuring a map score. The concept maps strategy is utilized to represent and assess the knowledge of learners in classes as the learning evidence. An instructor can gain information to utilize in various situations, such as using individual or group discussions to contribute a self-awareness of learners [12]. The concept maps strategy is simple to use, effective, satisfactory for problem-solving, and compared to lectures, significantly improves the learning achievements of learners. It is also more effective than traditional lectures in encouraging meaningful learning [13–16].

The correctness information of the concept map is primarily used as feedback. Several concept mapping tools provide the correctness for each component to learners based on the criteria map, such as COMPASS [17–19], ICMLS [20], KAS [21, 22], and CMfl [23]. Some special assessment methodologies were used for scoring the map, such as the weight of the important components of ICMLS and KAS, and the modified pathfinder of CMfl. Although different mapping tools have different details of their systems, the common methodology is a criterion-referenced assessment with the benefit of automatic assessment. The systems can identify the correctness of each component of the learner's map compared to the criteria map. The results of the comparison are provided for the learners as the system feedback for informing their performance, and the display of the related material content is general feedback for correcting the misunderstandings of learners regarding their incorrect propositions.

2.2   KB Map-CT and Its Experiment in Classes

The KB map framework is a digital tool for supporting the concept maps strategy, which is realized as an automatic diagnosis of the concept maps in propositional level exact matching for identifying the correctness information automatically in the form of the diagnosis results [9]. An instructor constructs the traditional concept map to indicate a learning goal of the class as a goal map, while the learning evidence is constructed by the learners by connecting the provided components. The provided components are a list of concepts and linking words that are decomposed components of the goal map as a kit. Additionally, the figure of the KB map framework is shown in [9], due to the page limitation. The diagnosis results of the KB map were utilized by the instructor for recognizing the current learning situation. The instructors used the diagnosis results to design and provide feedback to improve the learning achievements in the lecture classes effectively [24–26]. In addition, the propositional level exact matching of the KB map can attain almost the same validity as the well-known manual method [27, 28].

To gather learning evidence and identify the degree of the learner's understanding, the KB map-CT was developed to elicit learning evidence and associate the correctness and confidence information. Then, the KB map-CT has been experimentally used in classrooms conducted by teachers in elementary schools, and the results have been reported in [10]. The system allows learners to indicate their confidence as "sure" or "not sure" on all complete propositions. Accordingly, the system can generate diagnosis results based on the correctness and confidence information automatically. An example of a learner map on the structuring task with the confidence tagging is displayed in Fig. 1. The correctness and confidence information can be used to classify the propositions into the four following types: (1) A correct proposition with confidence (COR-CON), (2) A correct proposition with unconfidence (COR-UNC), (3) An incorrect proposition with confidence (INC-CON), and (4) An incorrect proposition with unconfidence (INC-UNC).

Fig. 1. An example of a learner map on the structuring task and a group-goal difference map

The diagnosis results of the KB map-CT consist of four different visualized maps following an individual overlay map, an individual-goal difference map, a group map, and a group-goal difference map. For instance, Fig. 1 shows an example of a group-goal difference map where the correctness and confidence information is reported to the instructor. The other figures of the diagnosis results are illustrated in [10]. The group-goal difference map is a visualization of the mistake of learners in the form of three types of error link, and the linking word of correct propositions are dis-appeared in this map. The three types of error link consist of excessive links, leaving links, and lacking links. The excessive link (solid line) indicates the incorrect answer, and the lacking link (dashed line) represents the correct information. The leaving link is the link that is not connected to any concept. A badge is added to the linking word to indicate the confidence of the learners on the link. The colon is a punctuation mark for separating the number of learners. The number of learners who indicated "sure" is displayed on the left-hand side of the mark, while the right-hand side number displays the number of learners who indicated "not sure." In the experiment, the correctness and confidence information of learners were utilized to design and provide the instructor's feedback in the lecture classes. The results suggest that the instructors accepted the confidence information of learners as valuable information for recognizing the learning situation [10].

Table 1 illustrates the revision rate of each proposition type from 2,067 complete propositions in the uses of the KB map-CT in classrooms. The instructors provided feedback to improve the understanding of learners based on the diagnosis results of the KB map-CT. The results of the experiment demonstrate that the propositions without confidence are easier to be changed than the confident propositions. Although the instructor's feedback can improve the understanding of the learners, the correction rate of the incorrect propositions is different, depending on the learner's confidence. The results suggest that adequate feedback should be different, depending on the confidence of learners.

Table 1. The revision rate of each proposition type in the experiment of KB map-CT

Proposition type	INC-CON	INC-UNC	COR-CON	COR-UNC
Revision rate	66.66%	84.72%	5.93%	71.27%

In this paper, we propose the correctness- and confidence-based adaptive feedback that promotes improving the understanding and ensuring the confidence of an individual learner. A goal map structuring task for an instructor and a reflection task for learners were developed to support the automatic adaptive feedback. The goal map structuring task facilitates building a goal map for the instructor and linking each component of the goal map with the content of the material. The reflection task facilitates accessing personalized feedback and revising their learner maps for the learners. Accordingly, the system has adequate information for providing individual feedback according to each learner's characteristics. The adaptive feedback was designed for emphasizing the correctness and confidence information for each proposition type, which the instructor's feedback cannot deal with a large number of learners.

3   Methodology

3.1   Goal Map Structuring Task

The traditional concept map is constructed by an instructor to represent the learning goal. The instructor must type keywords to create labels of concepts or linking words. In this study, the goal map construction tool of the KB map-CT facilitates displaying the learning material in the form of a sentence by sentence for the instructor. The instructor can easily select keywords from the learning material instead of typing, can choose between concepts and linking words to create the components of the goal map. Then the instructor can connect them to each other. The goal map structuring task encourages a clear learning goal because all of the words that appear in the goal map also appear in the learning material. Moreover, the system can track the relationship between the content of the material and each component of the goal map as a related sentence. That means the system can link between each component of the goal map and the content of the material. The related sentences are utilized in the adaptive feedback that is described in the next section.

3.2 Reflection Task

The reflection task is provided for learners after they completed learner maps, where the adaptive feedback is available. The learners will receive the information for recognizing their performance that includes a learner map score and an overlay map between their map and the goal map. The four different proposition types are distinguished using the different displayed line, while the confidence tagging also appears to determine the confidence in each proposition. The adaptive feedback is promptly provided for the learners according to each proposition type. The system allows learners to revise their map and change their confidence freely. Figure 2 demonstrates the system architecture of the KB map-CT and its adaptive feedback.

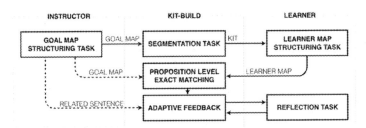

Fig. 2. The system architecture of the KB map-CT and its adaptive feedback

3.3 Adaptive Feedback

The adaptive feedback of the KB map-CT was designed to deal with both the correctness and confidence information of learners. The objective was defined based on four types of the propositions to encourage a positive change of the learning achievements. The primary objective is to correct the misunderstandings of learners in both INC-CON and INC-UNC, while increasing the confidence in COR-UNC. For the remaining proposition type, COR-CON, the aim is to encourage the learners to retain both the correctness and confidence. In other words, the adaptive feedback should correct the misunderstandings of learners and give more confidence to learners regarding the understanding appropriately. Accordingly, the adaptive feedback of the KB map-CT consists of four layers following:

Error Identification Layer
The error identifying layer visualizes the correctness and confidence information of the learner map in three different lines. Solid lines present COR-CON and dashed lines represent INC-CON. COR-UNC and INC-UNC are displayed as a dotted line. An example of the error identification layer is displayed in Fig. 3.

Fig. 3. An example of a learner map and the error identification layer

Evidence Identification Layer

The evidence identification layer emphasizes learners who have the confidence in their propositions by promoting them to identify the evidence for each confident proposition. Its procedure contains a sentence selection and a sentence suggestion. The sentence selection requests learners who have the confidence to select a sentence of the material as a selected sentence for tracking the source of their understanding. The objective is to ensure the confidence of learners who can construct COR-CON and can select the sentence accurately. On the other hand, the sentence selection aims to reduce the confidence of learners who constructed INC-CON. The sentence suggestion provides the related sentence regarding the linking word of the unconfident proposition to the learners who do not have confidence. The objective is to increase the confidence on COR-UNC and to correct the misunderstandings on INC-UNC.

Explanation Layer

The explanation layer emphasizes the proposition revision. Its procedure contains a proposition suggestion and a proposition selection. The proposition suggestion provides the proposition of the goal map to learners as the affirmation of learner's understanding on COR-UNC. The proposition selection aims to change the misunderstanding of learners who constructed INC-CON and INC-UNC. The feedback requests the learners to select an appropriate proposition of the selected sentence (INC-CON) or the provided related sentence (INC-UNC) between their incorrect proposition and the proposition of the goal map.

Guidance Layer

The guidance layer is an instruction suggestion of the next actions regarding the previous activities of learners. For instance, the confirmation message is displayed when the learners selected the appropriate sentence in the same way as the related sentence of the goal map for ensuring the confidence of COR-CON.

Figure 4 represents scenarios of the adaptive feedback based on the correctness and confidence information that demonstrates the provided different feedback for each proposition type. The different scenarios create different feedback, which aspires to provide adequate feedback based on each combination of correctness and confidence information. The confidence information is utilized in the evidence identification layer to separate the learners into two cases. The learners who have confidence in their understanding have to indicate the source of the confidence in the sentence selection task. This task leads learners to reconsider their proposition and the material content thoroughly. For the learners who have no confidence, they are necessary to receive the accurate source of the material in the sentence suggestion task.

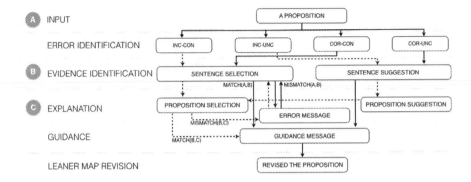

Fig. 4. The scenarios of the adaptive feedback for each proposition type

The correctness information is utilized in the explanation layer for correcting the misunderstanding of learners. Despite only visualizing the correct proposition, it may directly guide how to revise their incorrect proposition. The adaptive feedback requests learners to determine the proper proposition according to the related sentence in case of the incorrect proposition. The proposition suggestion is to affirm the understanding of learners by presenting the related sentence of the material according to the correct proposition for ensuring the confidence.

Figure 5 illustrates an example of the adaptive feedback on INC-CON, in which the proposition is incorrect with confidence of the learner. The system will provide the sentence selection to request learners to identify their evidence as a selected sentence and then will provide the proposition selection for adjusting the misunderstanding according to the selected sentence. Even if the learner can select the correct proposition in the proposition selection task, they have to revise their learner map by themselves after this process.

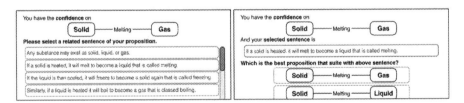

Fig. 5. An example of the adaptive feedback on the incorrect proposition with confidence

3.4   Experiment Procedure

The experiment was conducted to investigate whether the adaptive feedback encourages the learners to correct the misunderstanding and increase their confidence. The goal map was constructed via the goal map structuring task to create a learning goal, generate a kit, and pair the related sentence of each proposition. The goal map consists of eight propositions from eight linking words and seven concepts. The participants are 24 university students who read a 104-word article in five minutes and constructed a learner map in five minutes to represent their understanding as a formative map. The reflection task is provided for learners who uploaded the formative map. The learners have ten minutes to receive feedback and revise their map as a reflective map. Lastly, the learners have to construct the learner map again one week later as a delay map to evaluate the retention of the understanding. Hence, there are three learner maps for each learner: the formative map, the reflective map, and the delay map.

In this paper, the investigation emphasizes on the proposition changing from the formative map to the reflective map to observe the direct effect of the adaptive feedback on the learning achievements. Moreover, the correctness and confidence of each proposition type were analyzed to demonstrate the effectiveness of the adaptive feedback. Using the adaptive feedback, we expected that (1) INC-CON and INC-UNC would be changed to correct propositions, (2) COR-UNC would be changed to COR-CON, and (3) COR-CON would be retained as the same proposition type.

4   Results

4.1   Learner Map Score

The learner map is used to estimate the understanding of learner, and the average learner map score represents an overview of the learning achievements. Table 2 presents the average score of each map in the experiment. The formative map score shows the first understanding of learners after they read the material. The reflective map score presents the understanding of learners after they received feedback. The delay map score represents the understanding of learners one week later.

Table 2. The average scores and p-value of the formative-, the reflective-, and the delay-map

Variables	Formative Map	Reflective Map	Delay Map
Average score: full mark is 1.00	0.69 ($SD = 0.21$)	0.90 ($SD = 0.14$)	0.84 ($SD = 0.16$)
p-value from t-test with Bonferroni correction (Cohen's d)	$p = 0.00$ ($d = 1.15$)		$p = 0.70$ ($d = 0.35$)
	$p = 0.02$ ($d = 0.83$)		

Accordingly, the average score demonstrates that the adaptive feedback can encourage the learners to improve their map score, which the average score of the reflective map is higher than the formative map. There were also significant differences between the formative map scores and the reflective map scores, and between the formative map scores and the delay map scores according to the t-test with Bonferroni correction. Their effective sizes were large by Cohen's d criteria. These results suggest that the adaptive feedback can effectively encourage learners to improve their map score.

4.2   Proposition Transitions

The different feedback was provided for learners according to the correctness and confidence information of each proposition. The changing of the proposition type from the incorrect propositions to the correct propositions after the learners received the adaptive feedback produced the significant improvement in the learner map score. Figure 6 demonstrates the forward transition of the propositions from the formative map to the delay map. Although a few INC-CONs are unchanged to the other proposition types, the learners revised all of those propositions after receiving feedback. The revised propositions mean the learners changed at least one component of the two concepts and one linking word. The results suggest that the adaptive feedback promotes the revising INC-CON and feedback is possible to reduce the confidence of learners and encourage them to correct their misunderstanding.

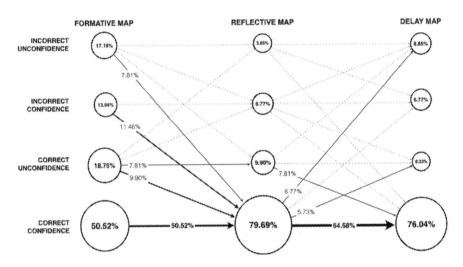

Fig. 6. The forward transition (The dashed line represents the proportions transitions that less than or equal to five percent.) of the propositions from the formative map to the delay map

Moreover, the previous study of the KB map-CT [10] demonstrated that the propositions without confidence tend to change more easily than the propositions with confidence when the learners received the instructor's feedback. The results suggest that the INC-CON should be the most difficult to overcome in the classroom situation. However, the adaptive feedback is possible to reduce the number of INC-CON similar to that of the INC-UNC on the reflective map. The forward proposition transition suggests that the adaptive feedback is adequate for correcting the misunderstanding of learners, even those learners who have the confidence in that misunderstanding. The learners can change the INC-CON to the correct proposition, similar to INC-UNC.

The retaining of COR-CON is one of the objectives of the adaptive feedback. The forward proposition transition illustrates that the learners can keep all COR-CON from the formative map to the reflective map. The transition suggests that the adaptive feedback did not disturb the learners from maintaining confidence in their accurate understanding. On the other hand, ensuring confidence is another objective of the adaptive feedback for COR-UNC. The most revised COR-UNC were changed to COR-CON following the objective. There are some COR-UNC that retained the same type, and a few propositions were changed to INC-UNC and INC-CON. Moreover, the results of the experiment demonstrate that the learners can keep COR-CON of the formative map 46.88% from 50.52% through the delay map. The average score of the delay test is 84.28% correct propositions with and without confidence, which comprise 53.10% of the first understanding, 19.63% from the improvement between the formative map and the reflective map, and 11.55% are undescriptive.

Discrimination and Certainty of the Understanding

The discrimination value (d_r) represents the recognition of the difference between what they know and what they do not know [2]. The value is measured based on COR-CON and INC-UNC against all of the complete propositions in the learner map. A perfect score indicates that the learners are able to discriminate their understanding according to the appropriate confidence. Table 3 shows the improvement of the discrimination value after the learners received feedback. The results suggest that the adaptive feedback encourages the learners to discriminate progressively between the different understandings based on correctness and confidence. Moreover, the hit rate (HR) represents the consistency with the interpretation that, if a correct response is covertly selected, then its execution helps the learner to confirm its correctness [2]. The value is measured based on COR-CON against the number of correct propositions in the learner map. The hit rate of the experiment is displayed in Table 3. The results suggest that the adaptive feedback encourages the learners to present consistency with the interpretation of the correct proposition more accurately.

Table 3. The discrimination value (d_r) and hit rate (HR)

Variables	Formative map	Reflective map	Delay map
Discrimination of the understanding (d_r)	0.68	0.83	0.85
Certainty of the understanding (HR)	0.73	0.89	0.90

5   Discussion

The general feedback aims to correct the misunderstanding of learners based on the correctness of learning evidence. The automatic assessment of the concept maps creates an opportunity to provide individual feedback, such as visualization of the discrepancies of learner map against the goal map. The related content of the material can be part of individual feedback with some preparation. Only incorrect answers of learners are regularly treated with one kind of feedback, while the correct answer is interpreted as accurate understanding without treatment, which indicates that even if the learners have a different degree of the misunderstanding, they will receive the same feedback. Moreover, it is necessary to ensure the accurate understanding of the learners who are unsure in their understanding. However, it is impossible to identify the degree of the learner's understanding with only the correctness information.

The confidence information of learning evidence demonstrates the difference in the same correctness of the evidence, which is used to represent the degree of learner's understanding. Correspondingly, the association of correctness and confidence information can describe the learning situation. The different correctness information is treated with different approaches, the different confidence also requires different approaches. Thus, the combination of correctness and confidence information should be treated appropriately. The adaptive feedback of the KB map-CT represents the utilization of correctness and confidence information to reduce or ensure the confidence, correct the misunderstanding, and confirm the accurate understanding of learners, which is the effect of confidence information on automatic individual feedback implementation. The results of the experiment present the improvement of learning achievements and retention of the understanding of learners. The forward transition of the propositions demonstrates that the learners can change INC-CON in the same way as INC-UNC, which is different from the previous experiment in the classrooms in which all learners received the same feedback from the instructor. Moreover, the learners who received the adaptive feedback are also able to associate the appropriate confidence in their understanding more accurately.

6   Conclusion and Future Work

The correctness and confidence information is valuable for recognizing the understanding of learners and identifying the degree of learner's understanding. Thus, the adaptive feedback of KB map-CT utilized both correctness and confidence information to correct the misunderstandings of learners and ensure the confidence of learners. The goal map structuring task and the reflection task were developed to support the automatic adaptive feedback. The experiment in the reading situation was conducted to demonstrate the effectiveness of the adaptive feedback. The results suggest that the adaptive feedback based on the correctness and confidence information can significantly improve the learning achievements. Moreover, the adaptive feedback encourages the ability of learners to discriminate the different understandings based on the correctness and confidence, and encourages the learners to promote their confidence in the correct propositions accurately. For future work, increasing the number of participants and comparing with the other feedback should be considered to contextualize the effectiveness of the adaptive feedback.

Acknowledgement. This work was supported by JSPS KAKENHI Grant Number 17H0183901.

References

1. Jonassen, D.H., Grabowski, B.L.: Handbook of Individual Differences, Learning, and Instruction. Routledge, Hillsdale (1993)
2. Hunt, D.P.: The concept of knowledge and how to measure it. J. Intellect. Capital **4**(1), 100–113 (2003)
3. Bruine de Bruin, W., Parker, A.M., Fischhoff, B.: Individual differences in adult decision-making competence. J. Pers. Soc. Psychol. **92**(5), 938–956 (2007)
4. Kleitman, S., Moscrop, T.: Self-confidence and academic achievements in primary-school children: their relationships and links to parental bonds, intelligence, age, and gender. In: Efklides, A., Misailidi, P. (eds.) Trends and Prospects in Metacognition Research, pp. 293–326. Springer, Boston (2010). https://doi.org/10.1007/978-1-4419-6546-2_14

5. Kleitman, S., Stankov, L., Allwood, C.M., Young, S., Mak, K.K.L.: Metacognitive self-confidence in school-aged children. In: Self-directed Learning Oriented Assessments in the Asia-Pacific, pp. 139–153 (2012)
6. Stankov, L., Lee, J., Paek, I.: Realism of confidence judgments. Eur. J. Psychol. Assess. **25**(2), 123–130 (2009)
7. Heron, G., Lerpiniere, J.: Re-engineering the multiple choice question exam for social work. Eur. J. Soc. Work **16**(4), 521–535 (2013)
8. Cisar, S.M., Cisar, P., Pinter, R.: True/false questions analysis using computerized certainty-based marking tests. In: Proceedings of the 7th International Symposium on Intelligent Systems and Informatics SISY, Subotica, Serbia, pp. 171–174 (2009)
9. Hirashima, T., Yamasaki, K., Fukuda, H., Funaoi, H.: Framework of Kit-Build concept map for automatic diagnosis and its preliminary use. Res. Pract. Technol. Enhanced Learn. **10**(1), 1–21 (2015)
10. Pailai, J., Wunnasri, W., Yoshida, K., Hayashi, Y., Hirashima, T.: Kit-build concept map with confidence tagging in practical uses for assessing the understanding of learners. Int. J. Adv. Comput. Sci. Appl. **9**(1), 79–91 (2018)
11. Novak, J.D., Cañas, A.J.: The theory underlying concept maps and how to construct and use them. Technical Report IHMC CmapTools (2008)
12. Buldu, M., Buldu, N.: Concept mapping as a formative assessment in college classrooms: measuring usefulness and student satisfaction. Proc. Soc. Behav. Sci. **2**(2), 2099–2104 (2010)
13. Schacter, J., Herl, H.E., Chung, G.K.W.K., Dennis, R.A., O'Neil Jr., H.F.: Computer-based performance assessments: a solution to the narrow measurement and reporting of problem-solving☆. Comput. Hum. Behav. **15**(3–4), 403–418 (1999)
14. Hsieh, I.L.G., O'Neil Jr., H.F.: Types of feedback in a computer-based collaborative problem-solving group task. Comput. Hum. Behav. **18**(6), 699–715 (2002)
15. Chiou, C.C.: The effect of concept mapping on students' learning achievements and interests. Innov. Educ. Teach. Int. **45**(4), 375–387 (2008)
16. Chularut, P., DeBacker, T.K.: The influence of concept mapping on achievement, self-regulation, and self-efficacy in students of English as a second language. Contemp. Educ. Psychol. **29**(3), 248–263 (2004)
17. Gouli, E., Gogoulou, A., Papanikolaou, K., Grigoriadou, M.: COMPASS: an adaptive web-based concept map assessment tool. In: Concept Maps: Theory, Methodology, Technology. Proceedings of the First International Conference on Concept Mapping, Pamplona, Spain, pp. 295–302 (2004)
18. Gouli, E., Gogoulou, A., Papanikolaou, K., Grigoriadou, M.: Evaluating learner's knowledge level on concept mapping tasks. In: Fifth IEEE International Conference on Advanced Learning Technologies, pp. 424–428 (2005)
19. Gouli, E., Gogoulou, A., Papanikolaou, K.A., Grigoriadou, M.: An adaptive feedback framework to support reflection, guiding and tutoring. In: Advances in Web-Based Education: Personalized Learning Environments, pp. 178–202 (2006)
20. Wu, P.H., Hwang, G.J., Milrad, M., Ke, H.R., Huang, Y.M.: An innovative concept map approach for improving students' learning performance with an instant feedback mechanism. Brit. J. Educ. Technol. **43**(2), 217–232 (2012)
21. Grundspenkis, J., Anohina, A.: Evolution of the concept map based adaptive knowledge assessment system: implementation and evaluation results. Sci. J. Riga Tech. Univ. Comput. Sci. **38**(38), 13–24 (2009)
22. Lukasenko, R., Anohina-Naumeca, A., Vilkelis, M., Grundspenkis, J.: Feedback in the concept map based intelligent knowledge assessment system. Sci. J. Riga Tech. Univ. Comput. Sci. **41**(1), 17–26 (2010)

23. Filiz, M., Trumpower, D.L., Ghani, S., Atas, S., Vanapalli, A.: The potential contributions of concept maps for learning website to assessment for learning practices. Knowl. Manag. E-Learn. **7**(1), 134–148 (2015)
24. Yoshida, K., Sugihara, K., Nino, Y., Shida, M., Hirashima, T.: Practical use of kit-build concept map system for formative assessment of learners' comprehension in a lecture. In: Proceedings of ICCE 2013, pp. 892–901 (2013)
25. Yoshida, K., Osada, T., Sugihara, K., Nino, Y., Shida, M., Hirashima, T.: Instantaneous assessment of learners' comprehension for lecture by using kit-build concept map system. In: Yamamoto, S. (ed.) HIMI 2013. LNCS, vol. 8018, pp. 175–181. Springer, Heidelberg (2013). https://doi.org/10.1007/978-3-642-39226-9_20
26. Pailai, J., Wunnasri, W., Yoshida, K., Hayashi, Y., Hirashima, T.: The practical use of Kit-Build concept map on formative assessment. Res. Pract. Technol. Enhanced Learn. **20**(12), 1–23 (2017)
27. Wunnasri, W., Pailai, J., Hayashi, Y., Hirashima, T.: Reliability investigation of automatic assessment of learner-build concept map with Kit-Build method by comparing with manual methods. In: Proceeding of 18th International Conference on Artificial Intelligence in Education, Hubei, China, pp. 418–429 (2017)
28. Wunnasri, W., Pailai, J., Hayashi, Y., Hirashima, T.: Validity of kit-build method for assessment of learner-build map by comparing with manual methods. IEICE E-D **101**(4), 1141–1150 (2018)

Bring It on! Challenges Encountered While Building a Comprehensive Tutoring System Using *ReaderBench*

Marilena Panaite[1], Mihai Dascalu[1,2(✉)], Amy Johnson[3],
Renu Balyan[3], Jianmin Dai[3], Danielle S. McNamara[3],
and Stefan Trausan-Matu[1,2]

[1] Faculty of Automatic Control and Computers,
University "Politehnica" of Bucharest,
313 Splaiul Independenței, 60042 Bucharest, Romania
marilena.panaite@cti.pub.ro,
{mihai.dascalu,stefan.trausan}@cs.pub.ro
[2] Academy of Romanian Scientists,
Splaiul Independenței 54, 050094 Bucharest, Romania
[3] Institute for the Science of Teaching and Learning, Arizona State University,
PO Box 872111, Tempe, AZ 85287, USA
{amjohn43,renu.balyan,jianmin.dai,dsmcnama}@asu.edu

Abstract. Intelligent Tutoring Systems (ITSs) are aimed at promoting acquisition of knowledge and skills by providing relevant and appropriate feedback during students' practice activities. ITSs for literacy instruction commonly assess typed responses using Natural Language Processing (NLP) algorithms. One step in this direction often requires building a scoring mechanism that matches human judgments. This paper describes the challenges encountered while implementing an automated evaluation workflow and adopting solutions for increasing performance of the tutoring system. The algorithm described here comprises multiple stages, including initial pre-processing, a rule-based system for pre-classifying self-explanations, followed by classification using a Support Virtual Machine (SVM) learning algorithm. The SVM model hyper-parameters were optimized using grid search approach with 4,109 different self-explanations scored 0 to 3 (i.e., poor to great). The accuracy achieved for the model was 59% (adjacent accuracy = 97%; Kappa = .43).

Keywords: Natural language processing · Intelligent tutoring systems
Self-explanations · Support vector machines · *ReaderBench*

1 Introduction

This study presents the challenges faced while implementing a comprehensive processing pipeline for automatically scoring self-explanations in the context of Interactive Strategy Training for Active Reading and Thinking (iSTART), a tutoring system that helps students learn and practice using comprehension strategies in the context of self-explanation. The workflow described in this paper integrates advanced Natural Language Processing

© Springer International Publishing AG, part of Springer Nature 2018
C. Penstein Rosé et al. (Eds.): AIED 2018, LNAI 10947, pp. 409–419, 2018.
https://doi.org/10.1007/978-3-319-93843-1_30

(NLP) techniques [1], a wide range of textual complexity indices available in the *ReaderBench* framework [2, 3], fine-tuned heuristics, and Support Vector Machine (SVM) classification [4] applied on primary data consisting of student self-explanations.

In the next section, we discuss the instructions in iSTART along with its practical applications for learning processes. In Sect. 3, the end-to-end development of the feedback system is explained, providing insights into the training dataset, the rule-based system, and the limitations encountered during the process. Section 4 presents the experimental results and analyses use of grid search optimization over the SVM training process. The last section concludes the paper and presents future improvements for the machine-learning model.

2   iSTART

iSTART [5] was designed to improve the quality of self-explanations and the effective use of comprehension strategies while reading a challenging text. iSTART is an intelligent tutoring system that provides extended practice applying high-order comprehension strategies during self-explanation [5, 6]. Because students are provided with automated feedback using natural language processing (NLP), the system affords the ability to provide individualized reading strategy instruction to multiple classrooms of students, each of them interacting in parallel with iSTART [5, 7]. Initial training modules in iSTART provide instruction on five comprehension strategies: comprehension monitoring, paraphrasing, prediction, bridging, and elaboration. These strategies promote and scaffold the generation of inferences, which helps students to construct more complete and accurate mental representations of text [8].

Instruction in iSTART proceeds from training modules to an initial practice phase, and then to extended practice. During the initial training videos, animated agents explain and present examples of the reading strategies that improve comprehension of difficult science texts [5]. Within both initial and extended practice, the student practices generating self-explanation using the repertoire of comprehension strategies. In one of iSTART's generative practice modules, coached practice (see Fig. 1), the animated agent provides feedback that is driven by NLP to evaluate the self-explanations. During these interactions, iSTART's feedback encourages students to use strategies that enhance comprehension.

This paper describes recent advances to improve the accuracy of the NLP algorithm driving assessment and delivery of just-in-time feedback [9, 10]. The major computational challenge faced in the practice modules is providing relevant and appropriate feedback based on the quality of the self-explanation. Assessment of self-explanation quality proceeds through three stages: (a) pre-processing, which includes spell checking, lemmatization, and noise filtering, (b) rule-based pre-checks for particular student response types, and (c) classification of self-explanation quality. The initial pre-check (stage 2) rules identify submission types including copy/pasting, irrelevant responses, and simple paraphrases. Targeted feedback is provided when these response types are recognized, and follow-up automated classifications are not applied. For example, if the system detects close paraphrases, the student receives feedback indicating that the response is too similar to the text content, and suggests the student use their own words to self-explain (e.g., "That looks very similar to the text. It will help you to understand the text better if you put it in your own words"). When the self-explanation does not trigger any of the pre-checks, it proceeds to the classification algorithm (stage 3). At this stage, the quality of the student's self-explanation is scored from 1 (fair) to 3 (great), and the pedagogical agent delivers formative feedback to improve future self-explanations.

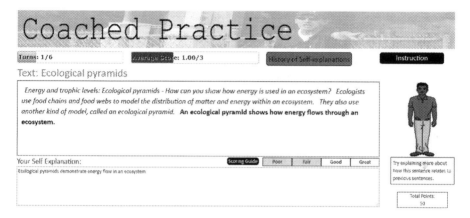

Fig. 1. iSTART's coached practice provides generative self-explanation practice with formative feedback.

3   Method

3.1   Corpus

We collected 4,109 self-explanations using responses from 277 high school participants. Participants completed the self-explanation task for two texts, "Heart Disease" (~ 300 words) and "Red Blood Cells" (~ 280 words). They were shown the texts in segments, delimited by target sentences. Each segment of text ended with a target sentence, which the participants were instructed to self-explain: "Please read the text and provide a self-explanation for the **bolded** sentence below." Both texts included 9 target sentences.

Two trained researchers applied the self-explanation coding scheme, which classifies self-explanations from 0 to 3. Self-explanations that were scored 0 (poor) included unrelated, vague, or non-informative information, were too short, or too similar to the target sentence. Scores of 1 (fair) were focused on the target sentence, primarily paraphrasing content from the target. Scores of 2 (good) included 1–2 ideas that were outside of the target sentence. Scores of 3 (great) incorporated information at a global level, tying in information from prior knowledge, or multiple connections across ideas in the text. Before applying the coding scheme to the entire self-explanation corpus, the researchers completed two training rounds on a subset dataset to achieve acceptable interrater reliability. Both raters scored 60% of the full dataset to obtain 20% overlap for the final interrater reliability (*kappa* = .81). Table 1 shows the distribution of human scores.

Table 1. Distribution of human scores.

Scores	0 (poor)	1 (fair)	2 (good)	3 (great)
# of SEs	124	1,514	1,740	731

3.2   Algorithm Workflow

The main purpose of our comprehensive assessment pipeline is to provide learners with automated scores for their self-explanations ranging from 0 to 3, along with formative feedback as described in the previous section. The algorithm receives as input the self-explanation text from the learner, the target sentence and the previous text and computes an automated score along with relevant feedback for the participant. The algorithm also receives the previous self-explanation as an input in order to check the relevance between successive responses. One consideration in iSTART is that an instructor may enter new texts into the system, and thus the algorithm cannot apply a domain specific model for each new text. This constraint increases the challenge of developing an accurate algorithm. However, this occurs seldom, and most experiments are performed using the existing collection of 24 documents covering general knowledge.

As presented in Fig. 2, the first step of the workflow pre-processes the input text, checking the spelling of words and applying the default NLP processing pipeline from *ReaderBench*. The next step in the process checks a list of rules for detecting different scenarios of poor self-explanations and provides appropriate feedback. The first rule verifies presence of frozen expressions in the student's self-explanation based on predefined lists of regular expressions that match certain conditions (e.g., misunderstanding patterns, prediction, boredom, etc.). If more than 75% of the self-explanation contains frozen expression, then the learner is assigned a 0 score, and an appropriate feedback message is generated (e.g., "Please focus more on the task at hand.").

The second rule checks the semantic cohesion between the participant's explanation and the targeted text; if the cohesion value is below a specific threshold, a poor score is assigned, and relevant feedback provided (e.g., "You should relate more to the given text."). The next criterion considers the length of self-explanation. If the self-explanation is too short when compared with the target text; the student is instructed to add more to the self-explanation (e.g., "Can you please provide more details?"). The threshold for short length was determined using *grid-search* optimization over the SVM hyper-parameters in order to find the optimal parameters in the formula that detects short sentences, as presented later in the Results section. The last rule identifies self-explanations that are copied directly from the target sentence (the text that the student self-explains) or the text prior to the target sentence. This rule uses n-grams from the target text, prior text and self-explanation to perform this copy-related check.

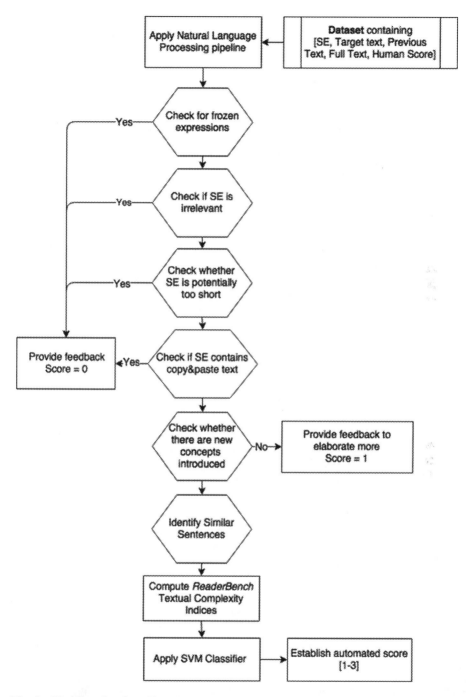

Fig. 2. Workflow for the self-explanation scoring comprehensive tutoring system (including pre-processing, rule-based system and automatic assessment).

Apart from the checks performed to identify low-scoring self-explanations, an additional rule identifies any new concepts that the learner may have introduced while self-explaining the text. In this step, we extract words that are neither identical lemmas nor synonyms of target content words (i.e., non stopwords that have as corresponding part-of-speech one of the following tags: noun, verb, adjective or adverb). In this case, the proposed score for the student is 1 (fair) with paraphrase related feedback to include new concepts - e.g., "Good. Now can you try to explain the text using your own words and ideas".

The last part of the algorithm automatically predicts the self-explanation score as 1 (fair), 2 (good) or 3 (great) using the pre-trained SVM model. The features computed for each self-explanation include: a) the semantic similarities between the self-explanation and target text (including LSA, LDA and word2vec), and b) the textual complexity indices from *ReaderBench*. A nu-SVM [11] algorithm from libsvm Java library [12] was implemented for the prediction model. In this specific implementation of the SVM algorithm, a multi-class "one vs one" strategy is used meaning that a separate classifier is trained for each pair of labels. In addition, ten-fold cross-validation was used for model evaluation, and grid search [11] optimization was performed to tune the parameters for determining the short sentence threshold using parameter variance [0.00; 0.05; 0.10; 0.15; 0.20]. Other hyper-parameters used for training the SVM models are: kernel-RBF (radial basis function), gamma-0.0017 (free parameter of the Gaussian function) and 3 prediction classes. Performance details of the grid search optimization are presented in the results section.

3.3   Encountered Challenges and Envisioned Solutions

Several iterations over the modules were performed before finalizing the format of the algorithm. The iterations included tuning the parameters used in the rule-based system for selecting the most suitable parameters for the SVM model. The first step accounted for evaluation of prediction of score 0 (poor) after passing through the rule-based module. We discovered that some self-explanations were assigned score 0 by the rule-base with "too-short self-explanation" feedback, even though human experts had scored them as 1 (fair). In order to address this issue, the *grid-search* optimization was performed on the full processing pipeline including the SVM, and parameters with the best average prediction were selected. The alternative was using a singular learning model exclusively for the two parameters corresponding to the short length formula, which would not have been globally efficient.

Another challenge encountered in the process was identifying the most relevant parameters from *ReaderBench* textual complexity indices for training the SVM model. The textual complexity parameters from the ReaderBench framework resulted in 1,322 parameters. These textual complexity features were obtained for a dataset consisting of approximately 4,000 SEs presented in the corpus sub-section. Some of these parameters were not relevant for predicting self-explanation scores and could led to overfitting for the model; as a result these parameters were eliminated using a variance threshold [13] feature selection algorithm on the whole dataset. Elimination of features using variance threshold resulted in 250 features, which were used to train the model.

While designing workflow for an interactive system, it is important that users receive instant feedback. Initial iteration implementing the complete workflow that included pre-processing, the rule-based system, and automatic evaluation using the SVM model, resulted in an average response time of 7 s for a single SE (measured when running the system on a single machine with 16 GB of memory). We observed that the default NLP processing pipeline in *ReaderBench* accounted for most of this delay. The stages in *ReaderBench* that resulted in this delay included computation of parameters for discourse analysis, dialogism, Cohesion Network Analysis [14] and sentiment analysis.

The best solution to avoid these delays was to eliminate the unnecessary steps from the pipeline and include only the relevant indices for the SVM model to predict the scores. As a result, we computed only those indices that were relevant to the trained dataset – surface, syntax, cohesion, word-complexity, word-list and connectives. In addition, the cohesion graph [14] from the discourse analysis was also retained in the workflow. The average response time for a self-explanation was reduced to 5 s once all these optimizations were performed. In addition, caching for the targeted sentence model was also implemented, but this did not improve the overall response time because students' responses vary greatly and require full processing for each input.

4   Results

This section presents the results obtained after training the SVM model over the 4019 self-explanations from "Heart Disease" and "Red Blood Cells" datasets. In the early stages of training, the short-sentence rule was generating false 0 scores, so we tuned the parameters for calculating a suitable short threshold value (see Eq. 1 inspired from the algorithm implemented in iSTART. for which the threshold values were experimentally set; *noWords* refers to the number of words from the SE).

$$short\ threshold = \begin{cases} [\min(no\ Words, 20) * (0.4 + \Delta x)], \text{if } noWords \text{ from target text} \geq 15 \\ [noWords * (0.5 + \Delta y)], otherwise \end{cases}$$

$$(1)$$

In order to perform *grid-search* over SVM training, the $\Delta x/\Delta y$ hyper-parameters were varied from 0 to 0.2. During each model-training step, the dataset was divided into train and test using a ten-fold split. For each combination of the *grid-search* parameters, average accuracy was calculated over the test prediction accuracies obtained for all the 10 folds. The results are shown in Table 2. The best accuracy for test dataset is 59% and the corresponding hyper-parameters for short threshold are 45% and 50%. A Kappa of .43 between the algorithm-produced scores and the human rating denotes a moderate agreement.

Table 2. Accuracy for 10-fold SVM with grid search optimization.

$\Delta x/\Delta y$ parameters	0.00	0.05	0.10	0.15	0.20
0.00	.57	**.59**	.56	.56	.56
0.05	.57	.57	.57	.57	.56
0.10	.57	.57	.57	.57	.57
0.15	.56	.56	.56	.56	.57
0.20	.56	.56	.56	.56	.57

We also computed adjacent accuracy, which accounts for the percentage of predicted scores which differ from the human score by less than or equal to 1. The results for adjacent accuracy are given in Table 3 for each stage of the grid search optimization. The adjacent accuracy for the system is very high (97%), demonstrating that the system-predicted scores are close enough to the human experts' scores, though these could be further tuned with additional features to improve exact accuracy.

Table 3. Adjacent accuracy for the 10-fold SVM.

$\Delta x/\Delta y$ parameters	0.00	0.05	0.10	0.15	0.20
0.00	.96	**.97**	.97	.96	.96
0.05	.96	.96	.95	.96	.96
0.10	.94	.94	.96	.96	.96
0.15	.95	.95	.96	.96	.96
0.20	.95	.95	.96	.95	.96

The adjacent accuracy of 97% is also reflected in the confusion matrix obtained over the ten-fold SVM, as well as the evaluation with the best results for the hyperparameters (see Table 4). In contrast to the human scores (see Table 1), the classes with scores of 2 and 3 are more distributed over all the automated score categories (see Table 5).

Table 4. Confusion matrix for the best parameters ($\Delta x = 0.05$ and $\Delta y = 0.00$) of the grid search optimization over the SEs.

SVM score/Human score	1	2	3
1	994	409	108
2	450	915	325
3	115	265	351

Table 5. Distribution of automated scores.

Scores	0 (poor)	1 (fair)	2 (good)	3 (great)
# of SEs	70	1559	1589	784

5   Conclusions

This paper reported the development of an automated self-explanation evaluation workflow, and the challenges encountered when implementing the workflow in the tutoring system. The proposed workflow integrating the textual complexity indices from the *ReaderBench* framework is specifically designed to provide automated comprehensive feedback in iSTART's self-explanation practice. The formative feedback is designed to improve students' comprehension strategy use while the self-explain texts.

iSTART's rule-based evaluation first identifies clear deficiencies, including irrelevant, too short, or copied responses. Using this first level of self-explanation assessment, iSTART's instructional model intervenes to provide targeted feedback to address such deficiencies. We leveraged machine learning algorithms to predict the self-explanation scores and evaluated the resulting model against the human experts scores.

In the final workflow, the rule-based system is used to detect poor self-explanations based on noise, relevancy, length, and similarity that are scored 0, and the SVM trained model for scoring self-explanations from 1 (fair) to 3 (great). Scores resulting from the SVM model also inform iSTART's instructional model, resulting in feedback aimed at improving the overall quality of the student's self-explanation. Despite the fact that the overall accuracy is 59% for the testing set, the adjacency measure of 97% demonstrates that the model classifies majority of the SEs near the targeted class.

During the development of the algorithm workflow, we encountered several problems. One was finding the most relevant and suitable set of features for the SVM model. We opted to select indices that exhibited sufficient linguistic coverage (experimentally set at a minimum 20%) and complement one another by expressing different traits (Pearson correlation lower than .9).

The second major issue faced during implementation of the workflow was response time due to evaluation of the rule-based system and NLP processing pipeline computation from *ReaderBench*. The solution proposed for improving the response time was to compute only the features and textual complexity indices that were necessary for the SVM classification model. We found that the *ReaderBench* framework utilizes a large number of NLP processes such as part-of-speech (PoS) tagging, parsing, dependency parsing, co-reference resolution and named entity recognition (NER) for generating the vast set of linguistic indices. However, the only set of features that were relevant for the task in this study were related to PoS tagging and textual complexity indices. As a result, we eliminated the unnecessary phases (dependency parsing, co-reference resolution, and NER) from the NLP pipeline, thus reducing the processing time to some extent.

However, our sense is that even with all these optimizations, the processing time due to the NLP pipeline remains excessive; waiting 5 s for feedback every time one generates a self-explanation would be excessively annoying. This processing cost currently renders it unfeasible to integrate this algorithm within learning scenarios that require near real-time responses. Nevertheless, this scoring system is highly accurate, nearing the accuracy obtained between two highly trained human scorers; in addition, it is more efficient for students to obtain immediate feedback for their answers. Hence, we do intend to use the algorithm to provide scores in contexts where system response time is not a critical factor. Moreover, we expect the processing power of computers to continue to increase, rendering the processing time shorter for these types of implementations.

Taken together, this study can provide valuable lessons for the larger NLP and educational research community. First, having a too wide range of textual features without a proper systematic preprocessing of data and appropriate classification rules established by human experts can be cumbersome and exhibit lower accuracies, despite using more advanced automated classification methods. Additionally, NLP researchers must consider the constraints of the particular environment into which the evaluation approach is being implemented. In our case, the response time of the initial workflow was not practical, due to iSTART learners' interaction behaviors and their expectations of the system.

Our next steps will focus on further tuning the model hyper-parameters in order to better differentiate between scores, including *grid-search* optimization over other SVM parameters. Moreover, we can apply more advanced feature selection algorithms, such as L1-based [15] or Tree-Based [16], for improving the prediction of each class. All these improvements can lead to the integration of the pipeline in a near real-time tutoring system that performs comprehensive automated evaluations of student response.

Acknowledgments. This research was partially supported by the 644187 EC H2020 *Realising an Applied Gaming Eco-system* (RAGE) project, the FP7 2008-212578 LTfLL project, the Department of Education, Institute of Education Sciences - Grant R305A130124, as well as by the Department of Defense, Office of Naval Research - Grants N00014140343 and N000141712300. We would also like to thank Tricia Guerrero and Matthew Jacovina for their support in scoring the self-explanations.

References

1. Jurafsky, D., Martin, J.H.: An Introduction to Natural Language Processing Computational Linguistics, and Speech Recognition. Pearson Prentice Hall, London (2009)
2. Dascalu, M., Dessus, P., Bianco, M., Trausan-Matu, S., Nardy, A.: Mining texts, learner productions and strategies with *ReaderBench*. In: Peña-Ayala, A. (ed.) Educational Data Mining. SCI, vol. 524, pp. 345–377. Springer, Cham (2014). https://doi.org/10.1007/978-3-319-02738-8_13
3. Dascalu, M., Dessus, P., Trausan-Matu, Ş., Bianco, M., Nardy, A.: *ReaderBench*, an environment for analyzing text complexity and reading strategies. In: Lane, H.C., Yacef, K., Mostow, J., Pavlik, P. (eds.) AIED 2013. LNCS (LNAI), vol. 7926, pp. 379–388. Springer, Heidelberg (2013). https://doi.org/10.1007/978-3-642-39112-5_39
4. Drucker, H., Burges, C.J., Kaufman, L., Smola, A.J., Vapnik, V.: Support vector regression machines. In: Advances in Neural Information Processing Systems, pp. 155–161 (1997)
5. McNamara, D.S., Levinstein, I., Boonthum, C.: iSTART: interactive strategy training for active reading and thinking. Behav. Res. Methods Instrum. Comput. **36**(2), 222–233 (2004)

6. O'Reilly, T., Sinclair, G., McNamara, D.S.: iStart: A Web-Based Reading Strategy Intervention That Improves Students's Science Comprehension. In: CELDA, pp. 173–180 (2004)
7. McNamara, D.S.: SERT: self-explanation reading training. Discourse Process. **38**(1), 1–30 (2004)
8. McNamara, D.S., Magliano, J.P.: Self-explanation and metacognition. In: Handbook of Metacognition in Education, pp. 60–81 (2009)
9. McNamara, D.S., O'Reilly, T.P., Rowe, M., Boonthum, C., Levinstein, I.B.: iSTART: A web-based tutor that teaches self-explanation and metacognitive reading strategies. In: McNamara, D.S. (ed.) Reading comprehension strategies: Theories, interventions, and technologies, pp. 397–420. Erlbaum, Mahwah (2007)
10. Boonthum, C., Levinstein, I., McNamara, D.S.: Evaluating self-explanations in iSTART: word matching, latent semantic analysis, and topic models. In: Kao, A., Poteet, S. (eds.) Natural Language Processing and Text Mining, pp. 91–106. Springer, London (2007). https://doi.org/10.1007/978-1-84628-754-1_6
11. Liu, R., Liu, E., Yang, J., Li, M., Wang, F.: Optimizing the hyper-parameters for SVM by combining evolution strategies with a grid search. In: Huang, D.S., Li, K., Irwin, G.W. (eds.) Intelligent Control and Automation, pp. 712–721. Springer, Heidelberg (2006). https://doi.org/10.1007/978-3-540-37256-1_87
12. Chang, C.-C., Lin, C.-J.: LIBSVM: a library for support vector machines. ACM Trans. Intell. Syst. Technol. **2**(3), 27:21–27:27 (2011)
13. Cherkassky, V., Ma, Y.: Practical selection of SVM parameters and noise estimation for SVM regression. Neural Netw. **17**(1), 113–126 (2004)
14. Dascalu, M., McNamara, D.S., Trausan-Matu, S., Allen, L.K.: Cohesion network analysis of CSCL participation. Behav. Res. Methods **50**, 1–16 (2017)
15. Gilad-Bachrach, R., Navot, A., Tishby, N.: Margin based feature selection-theory and algorithms. In: Proceedings of the Twenty-First International Conference on Machine Learning, p. 43. ACM (2004)
16. Sugumaran, V., Muralidharan, V., Ramachandran, K.: Feature selection using decision tree and classification through proximal support vector machine for fault diagnostics of roller bearing. Mech. Syst. Signal Process. **21**(2), 930–942 (2007)

Predicting the Temporal and Social Dynamics of Curiosity in Small Group Learning

Bhargavi Paranjape$^{(\boxtimes)}$, Zhen Bai, and Justine Cassell

Carnegie Mellon University, Pittsburgh, PA, USA
{bvp,zhenb,justine}@cs.cmu.edu

Abstract. Curiosity is an intrinsic motivation for learning, but is highly dynamic and changes moment to moment in response to environmental stimuli. In spite of the prevalence of small group learning in and outside of modern classrooms, little is known about the social nature of curiosity. In this paper, we present a model that predicts the temporal and social dynamics of curiosity based on sequences of behaviors exhibited by individuals engaged in group learning. This model reveals distinct sequential behavior patterns that predict increase and decrease of curiosity in individuals, and convergence to high and low curiosity among group members. In particular, convergence of the entire group to a state of high curiosity is highly correlated with sequences of behaviors that involve the most social of group behaviors - such as questions and answers, arguments and sharing findings, as well as scientific reasoning behaviors such as hypothesis generation and justification. The implications of these findings are discussed for educational systems that intend to evoke and scaffold curiosity in group learning contexts.

1 Introduction and Motivation

Profound transformations in employment may require increased socio-emotional learning (SEL) skills that improve the ability to learn new things throughout the lifespan. Curiosity, the strong desire to learn or know more about something or someone [19], is recognized as a vital SEL skill that leads to learning through constructing one's own understanding, rather than "being told" or "instructed" [1]. Curiosity is traditionally considered as a psychological state in individuals evoked by novelty, surprise, conceptual conflict and uncertainty [5]. Existing educational technologies that support curiosity through social means mainly focus on dyadic scenarios and are equipped with a limited set of curiosity elicitation strategies. We propose to investigate how curiosity is promoted or suppressed in groups and present here a social account of curiosity, adding to constructivist accounts of how knowledge may be actively constructed through social interactions in small groups [10]. The larger context of our research is to develop a virtual peer [6] that can evoke curiosity among human peers in group learning.

© Springer International Publishing AG, part of Springer Nature 2018
C. Penstein Rosé et al. (Eds.): AIED 2018, LNAI 10947, pp. 420–435, 2018.
https://doi.org/10.1007/978-3-319-93843-1_31

Curiosity changes moment to moment in response to environmental stimuli [31] and underlying psychological states such as anticipation and satisfaction of knowledge seeking [25,28]. Although there has not been much study of how individuals' curiosity influences others, research shows that cognitive, behavioral and affective states in group members are not independent of one another. For example, convergence and alignment among individuals' dialogue, gestures, emotions and even learning are commonly seen during conversation and group work [26,35,36]. Previous work [33] developed a fine-grained theoretical framework to quantify and investigate curiosity at ten-second intervals. Still, there is a lack of studies that extract the underlying temporal and social *dynamics* of curiosity.

In this paper, we present a prediction model that describes social scaffoldings that evoke curiosity at both the individual and group level. To build the model, we extracted *instantaneous changes in individual curiosity* and *convergence of curiosity across group members*. We then used temporal association rule mining to identify sequences of multi-modal behaviors that predict these dynamics and condensed them into a small set of interpretable rule clusters. Behavioral sequences extracted from the model reveal distinct patterns of social interaction that predict curiosity increase and decrease in individuals, and group convergence to high and low curiosity. We observe that an increase in individual curiosity, and convergence at high levels of group curiosity, are predicted by behavioral sequences involving verbalizing and justifying ideas, followed by argument, question asking and uncertainty. In particular, behavioral sequences involving the most social of group behaviors (question asking, argument and sharing findings) and underlying science reasoning (hypothesis generation and justification) best predict the convergence of all group members to high curiosity.

The main contributions of the paper are threefold. First, the prediction model initiates the study of the temporal and social dynamics of curiosity at both, individual and group level, from sequences of verbal and non-verbal behaviors occurring in small-group learning tasks. Second, the behavior patterns extracted from the model serve as fine-grained heuristics of social scaffoldings that guide the design of educational technologies and pedagogical curriculum to support curiosity-driven learning. Third, our approach informs the combination of temporal and social dynamics analysis of underlying learning states that are subject to change in response to complex interpersonal activities.

2   Related Work

Curiosity motivates information-seeking and reasoning, even when external rewards for learning are absent. It is therefore a strong predictor of academic performance [34], and yet is often found to decrease with age and schooling [20]. For this reason, a number of studies examine how to trigger and sustain curiosity. Most research investigates the cognitive factors that trigger curiosity in an individual, such as uncertainty, incongruity, novelty and surprise ([19] for a review). These theories have led to the development of computational models for educational technologies such as curious virtual learners [38] and robots [14].

However, these studies are limited to modeling individual curiosity, while we know that knowledge is also acquired through social interaction [8]. What of a social account of curiosity during peer-peer interaction? Two recent studies shed light on how the interpersonal effects curiosity. One showed that a curious robot with a limited repertoire of social interactions (e.g. asking questions, making suggestions) can elicit curiosity in a child [16]. The other provided an elaboration of the interpersonal drivers of curiosity, based on fine-grained analysis of verbal and non-verbal behaviors occurring during small group learning, and it showed a strong influence of social interaction on curiosity [33]. In spite of these promising discoveries about curiosity in social contexts, learning in groups does not guarantee to lead to curiosity. For instance, curiosity rarely occurs while interacting with intelligent tutors [24], and is more frequent when the learning tasks are harder [18]. Sinha et al. [32] developed a preliminary approach to elicit multimodal behaviors for maintaining individual curiosity in response to real-time social interactions. This approach, however, does not model the instant change of curiosity over time and among different members of the group, which is an essential first step towards evoking curiosity during social interactions.

The larger scope of our work is to build a virtual child to engage in small group learning and elicit curiosity. So far, intelligent tutoring and scaffolding systems focus on promoting learning by adapting towards student's activities within a computer-based learning environment [3,23]. When students learn in a group, social interaction through verbal and non-verbal communication becomes a prominent learning resource [8]. The spontaneity and complexity of social interactions influence dynamic learning states such as curiosity. Previous work on socio-emotional states such as rapport [39] and attitude [9] reveals the advantages of using data mining technologies to capture the predictive relationship between real-time social interactions and underlying states. Furthermore, learning is a collective experience, and group performance is more complex than the simple aggregation of individual's performance [7,27,37]. Previous work has studied collective phenomena such as physical interactivity [12] and learning efficiency [21] in collaborative learning tasks. However, the collective aspect of socio-emotional learning states, curiosity in particular, has not been adequately studied in small-group learning.

In this paper, we initiate a study of the moment-by-moment change and collective aspects of curiosity by presenting a prediction model that uncovers the association between complex social interactions and curiosity dynamics at individual and group level.

3   Method

We collected audio and video for 12 groups of children (aged 10–12, 16 males and 28 females, 3–4 children per group, 44 in total)[1]. Each group collaboratively built a Rube Goldberg machine(RGM) for about 35–40 min. The RGM task included building creative chain reactions using a variety of simple objects such as rubber

---

[1] Experimental setup at https://tinyurl.com/experimental-setup.

bands, pipe cleaners, toy cars, clothespins, etc. We choose the RGM task since it enables collaborative hands-on learning and creative problem solving [29], and supports scientific inquiry for key science knowledge such as force, motion and energy transfer for students in 5th and 6th grades [2]. In our analysis, we used the first 30 min of the RGM task from the first 6 groups, that we annotated for curiosity and curiosity-related behavior.

3.1   Annotating Individual Curiosity

We used Amazon Mechanical Turk to quantify curiosity for every group member via the thin-slice approach [4]. We chose 10-s thin-slices, which showed the highest inter-rater reliability compared to 20 and 30-s in a pilot annotation. This corroborates with previous studies on detecting learning effects [18]. AMT workers were given the definition "curiosity is a strong desire to learn or know more about something or someone", and asked four naive annotators to rate every 10 s thin-slice of the video of every child on a scale of 0 (not curious), 1 (curious) and 2 (extremely curious). Slices were presented in random order. A single measure of inter-class correlation coefficient (ICC) was computed for each possible subset of raters for a particular HIT, and the subset that had the best reliability was retained[2]. The average ICC was 0.46 (Krippendorff's alpha)[3] and aligns with reliability of curiosity ratings in previous work [11].

3.2   Annotating Curiosity-Related Behaviors

We used semi-automatic (machine learning + human judgment) and manual (human judgment)[4] procedures to annotate every clause in our corpus for 11 verbal behaviors chosen from a combination of prior research and empirical observation. Verbal behaviors included: *Uncertainty* (Lack of certainty about ones choices or beliefs), *Argument* (A coherent series of reasons or facts to support or establish a point of view), *Justification* (showing something to be right or reasonable by making it clear), *Suggestion* (idea or plan put forward for consideration), *Question asking* (related to the task or unrelated), *Idea Verbalization* (explicitly saying an idea in response to own or others' actions), *Sharing Findings* (explicit communication of results, findings and discoveries to the group), *Hypothesis Generation* (Expressing one or more different possibilities or theories to explain a phenomenon by relating two variables), *Agreement* (Harmony or accordance in opinion or feeling), *Sentiment towards task* (positive, negative) and *Evaluation of other's actions* (positive, negative)[5]. Inter rater reliability (Krippendorf's alpha) for each of these was above 0.7. In addition, we used

---

[2] We remove raters who take less than 1.5 std. deviation time to rate and used inverse-based bias correlation to counter label over- & under-use.

[3] 0.72 Cronbach's alpha intra-class correlation.

[4] Outlined in [32].

[5] Coding scheme for verbal and non-verbal behaviors at http://tinyurl.com/codingschemecuriosity.

automated detection of facial-landmark features using *OpenFace* and a rule-based classifier to indicate the presence of the following expressions of affective states: *Joy, Delight, Surprise, Confusion* and *Flow (intense concentration)*[6].

3.3   Prediction Model

Our prediction model was developed in three steps. (a) We mined instances of temporal and social dynamics of curiosity, treated as discrete *events* occurring during the group activity. (b) We then mined temporal association rules [22] that employ sequences of multi-modal behaviors to predict the occurrence of these events. (c) finally, we use agglomerative clustering technique to group these association rules into distinct clusters that can serve as strategies for curiosity scaffolding in group learning tasks.

3.3.1   Detecting Moment-by-Moment Dynamics of Curiosity

We study curiosity dynamics along two orthogonal dimensions: (a) Temporal dynamics of one group member's curiosity as represented by the increase and decrease of its value in short intervals of time (b) Social dynamic of curiosity - instances of *convergence* of the curiosity values of all the group members. We chose convergence as it is a common measure of group reciprocal influence [35,36].

Temporal Dynamic of Individual Curiosity: We detect moment-by-moment increases or decreases in individual curiosity by modeling thin-slice curiosity data of each group member as a time series and using a sliding window-based outlier detection technique to extract discrete events. We use a moving window average to smooth the curiosity time series and reduce short-term noise. We track anomalous changes by segmenting the series into short overlapping intervals using a fixed-length sliding window and extracting intervals that end in an anomalous peak. Standard score (z-score), which is the signed number of standard deviations a data point is above the mean of the data series, is used to decide thresholds for outliers. For every segmented interval, we calculate absolute deviation of the last thin-slice from the interval average and select intervals where z-score of the deviation exceeds 2. Events can be further divided as (a) curiosity increase and (b) curiosity decrease.

Social Dynamic of Curiosity in the Group: To study curiosity convergence in the group, we focus on instances during the interaction when more than 3 members of the group simultaneously display high or low curiosity. We calculate the standard deviation of the smoothed curiosity signals of concerning group members and, as before, select segmented intervals of time where this deviation is consistently less than one Z-score to extract events of convergence. Convergence events are distinguished as either high or low based on the group average of

---

[6] Facial-landmark feature coding and classification heuristics at https://tinyurl.com/curiositynonverbal.

curiosity in the selected interval. Figure 1 shows the temporal and social dynamic events mined for individuals and the group, respectively[7].

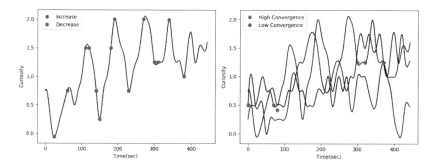

Fig. 1. (Left) curiosity increase and decrease events in Individuals. (Right) curiosity high and low convergence events in 3-member group

3.3.2 Extracting Rules Associating Sequences of Behaviors with Curiosity Dynamics

Multi-party interaction is dynamic, in that behaviors exhibited by some group members influence future behaviors exhibited by others. To capture this complex interaction of behaviors over time, we mine sequential multi-modal behaviors, which then serve as input features to predict the curiosity dynamic events we previously extracted. To this end, we use the Temporal Interval Tree Association Rule Learning (TITARL) algorithm [17] to mine frequently occurring association rules such as the one in Fig. 2. TITARL incorporates a degree of uncertainty in the interval between two behaviors in the sequential rule using a discrete prob-abilistic distribution over time. It then constructs a Random Forest Classifier that uses these sequences as input features for multi-class classification. We use TITARL to predict the occurrence of temporal change in individual curiosity (increase, decrease, no change) or social convergence (high, low and no convergence) events in a 20 s interval. We only mine TITA rules that have a minimum occurrence of 5% and prediction confidence of 50%. For curiosity change in one individual, we make the distinction between behaviors expressed by that individual (*target T*) and *other (O)* members of the group. For group curiosity convergence, we consider all members of the group as *targets*. To verify our hypothesis about the predictive power of sequential behaviors, we consider a baseline that treats every behavior as an independent feature to a Support Vector Machine classifier with an RBF Kernel ($\gamma = 2$, C = 1). To compare with other sequential models of prediction, we also implement a recurrent neural network baseline that

---

[7] Event mining is robust as we use z-score-based thresholds to select individual and group specific intervals.

models sequential inputs in a 20 s interval using 128 hidden dimensions to classify events. Figure 3 depicts the extraction of behavioral sequences and dynamic events of curiosity along the temporal and social dimension. We report the average performance on 5-fold cross validation for 100 runs, where association rule mining and fusion was done separately for each training fold.

Fig. 2. A TITA rule. Between any two input behaviors, the temporal constraint is a discrete probability distribution over time (shown as a Histogram).

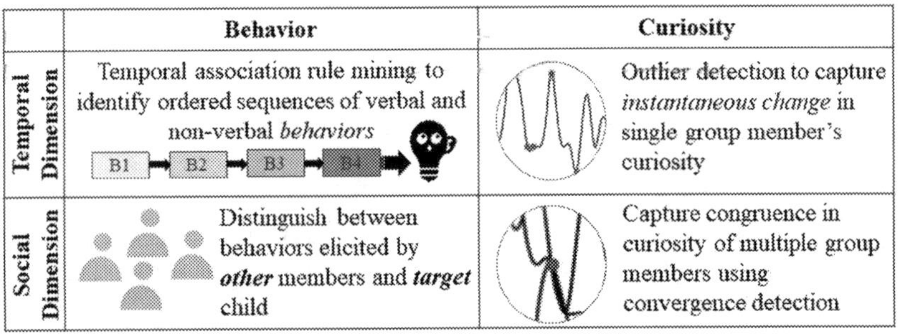

		Behavior	Curiosity
Temporal Dimension		Temporal association rule mining to identify ordered sequences of verbal and non-verbal *behaviors*	Outlier detection to capture *instantaneous change* in single group member's curiosity
Social Dimension		Distinguish between behaviors elicited by *other* members and *target* child	Capture congruence in curiosity of multiple group members using convergence detection

Fig. 3. Computational framework for prediction of curiosity dynamics

3.3.3   Extracting Predominant Clusters of Association Rules

TITARL results in a large set of rules that suffer from inter-rule temporal redundancies, making them hard to analyze and interpret. To counter this, authors employ supervised fusion that uses a training dataset of input behaviors and output events to learn correlation between TITA rules and fuse them. To further reduce the set of mined TITA rules into a feasible set that can be operationalized, we employ an edit-distance based hierarchical clustering technique to cluster rules with similar behavioral patterns. In the next section, we present TITA rules with the highest confidence categorized into their respective clusters.

4   Results and Discussion

4.1   Predicting Individual Curiosity Change

Table 1 shows the prediction performance of TITARL for anomalous change in individual curiosity and comparisons with baselines. TITARL outperforms the SVC baseline, increasing prediction recall. This indicates that it can model fine-grained behavioral associations that index social interactions and can consequently predict changes in curiosity more accurately. TITARL outperforms RNN on F1 measure. RNNs require a lot of training data and are hard to interpret and operationalize. This performance evaluation is promising given the relatively few occurrences of temporal dynamic events in the dataset (Class imbalance of 33%).

Table 1. Cross-validation evaluation of TITARL and RNN, SVC Baselines for Prediction of *temporal* and *social* dynamics in curiosity, averaged over 100 runs

Dynamic	Method	Performance			
		Accuracy	Precision	Recall	F1
Temporal dynamic	**TITARL**	0.69	0.66	0.69	**0.67**
	RNN	0.74	0.60	0.75	0.64
	SVC	0.57	0.49	0.57	0.52
Social dynamic	**TITARL**	**0.81**	**0.78**	**0.82**	**0.79**
	RNN	0.79	0.74	0.81	0.77
	SVC	0.75	0.69	0.76	0.72

Table 2 lists examples of extracted temporal association rules that predict increase and decrease in curiosity. Rules have been grouped according to the clusters to which they belong, along with a few sequence of behaviors that make up the cluster. In Clusters 1, 2, 3 and 4 for curiosity increase, a recurring sequence of *Idea Verbalization(O)* followed by *Justification(O)* indicates that other group members (apart from target T) express an idea and justify its validity. Following this, a *Negative Evaluation* (Cluster 1) by another member indicates disagreement with the stated idea, exposing to the target child a conflict about the proposed solution and perhaps triggering a need to resolve this conflict (leading to increased curiosity). Clusters 2 and 3 show that the *Idea verbalization* -followed by *Justification* behavior of others may also trigger uncertainty or conceptual conflict about the stated idea in the target child (Cluster 3) or another group member (Cluster 2), which manifests as a *confused facial expression*. Confusion displayed by others (Cluster 2) may provide stimulus to the target child to think critically about the proposed idea. A knowledge-gap or conceptual conflict about the proposed idea may stimulate another group member to ask a question (Cluster 4), which in turn may trigger awareness in the target member of his/her own knowledge gap or conflict. In cluster 5, if evidence and validation is put forth by the target group member about a previously mentioned idea, and then another group member *argues* for a different view-point, the target is exposed to diverse aspects of the problem and that may stimulate critical thinking.

Sequences that predict decrease in curiosity include more behaviors carried out by the target group members themselves than others in the group. Prominent among these is *Agreement* and *Positive Sentiment evaluation* by the target of

Table 2. Rule examples for change in individual's curiosity

Rule Clusters that Predict Curiosity Increase
Cluster 1: Other's Idea Verbalization(IV), and Justification(J) followed by Negative Sentiment Evaluation(NSE)
1. $J(O) \rightarrow \{ IV(O), J(O), NSE(O)\} \rightarrow NSE(O) \Rightarrow$ Increase
2. $\{J(O), IV(O)\} \rightarrow \{J(O), IV(O)\} \rightarrow NSE(O) \Rightarrow Increase$
Cluster 2 : Other's Justification(J), Negative Sentiment Evaluation(NSE) and Idea Verbalization(IV) followed by Other's Confusion(CONF)
1. $J(O) \rightarrow \{NSE(O), J(O)\} \rightarrow IV(O) \rightarrow CONF(O) \Rightarrow Increase$
2. $NSE(O) \rightarrow \{NSE(O), J(O)\} \rightarrow \{IV(O), J(O)\} \rightarrow CONF(O) \Rightarrow Increase$
Cluster 3: Other's Agreement(AG) followed by Idea Verbalization(IV)and Justification (J) followed by Target's Confusion(CONF)
1. $AG(O) \rightarrow AG(O) \rightarrow \{IV(O), J(O)\} \rightarrow CONF(T) \Rightarrow Increase$
2. $\{J(O), AG(O)\} \rightarrow \{IV(O), J(O)\} \rightarrow CONF(T) \Rightarrow Increase$
Cluster 4: Other's Idea Verbalization (IV), Justification followed by Other's Negative Sentiment Evaluation and Question Asking (QA)
1. $IV(O) \rightarrow \{IV(O), J(O)\} \rightarrow NSE(O) \rightarrow QA(O) \Rightarrow Increase$
2. $IV(O) \rightarrow J(O) \rightarrow NSE(O) \rightarrow QA(O) \Rightarrow Increase$
Cluster 5: Target's Justification(J) followed by Argument and/or Justification by Others
1. $J(O) \rightarrow \{J(O), J(O)\} \rightarrow J(T) \rightarrow Argument(O) \Rightarrow Increase$
2. $\{IV(O), Argument(O)\} \rightarrow \{J(T), Argument(O)\} \rightarrow J(O) \Rightarrow Increase$
Rule Clusters that Predict Curiosity Decrease
Cluster 1: Other's Idea Verbalization(IV) and Justification(J) followed by Target's Positive Sentiment Evaluation(PSE) and Agreement (AG)
1. $\{IV(O), J(O)\} \rightarrow \{PSE(T), IV(O)\} \rightarrow AG(T) \Rightarrow Decrease$
2. $IV(O) \rightarrow \{PSE(T), IV(O), IV(O)\} \rightarrow AG(T) \Rightarrow Decrease$
Cluster 2: Target's Justification(J), Idea verbalization(IV) or Positive Sentiment Evaluation (PSE) followed by Target's Agreement
1. $J(O) \rightarrow J(T) \rightarrow \{PSE(T), PSE(T)\} \rightarrow AG(T) \Rightarrow Decrease$
2. $\{J(T)\} \rightarrow \{PSE(T), PSE(T), IV(O)\} \rightarrow AG(T) \Rightarrow Decrease$
Cluster 3: Target's Idea Verbalization and Positive Sentiment Evaluation(PSE) followed by other's Agreement (AG)
1. $IV(O) \rightarrow \{PSE(T), IV(T), IV(T)\} \rightarrow AG(O) \Rightarrow Decrease$
2. $J(T) \rightarrow \{PSE(T), IV(T), IV(T)\} \rightarrow AG(O) \Rightarrow Decrease$

an idea or solution proposed by other group members (in Table 2, Clusters 1,2). Both behaviors are indicators that the target child approves of the solution. This may be an indication of closing an information-gap, which may lead to curiosity decrease. In general, we observe that sequences predicting curiosity increase have more behaviors elicited by other group members than the target member (35% more), which corroborate with findings in [32] that interpersonal interactions have a larger influence on positive curiosity than intra-personal behaviors.

4.2   Predicting Group Curiosity Convergence

Table 1 also summarizes the performance of TITARL for convergence of group members' curiosity to high and low values. Again, the model outperforms baselines and performs comparatively better predicting individual curiosity change ($F1_{TITARL} = 0.69$), despite group convergence events occurring half as frequently during the group activity as individual change events.

Table 3 lists examples of extracted temporal association rules that predict convergence of curiosity to high and low values, respectively. Rules that cause several group members' curiosity to simultaneously converge to high values tend

Table 3. Rule clusters for convergence in group members

Rule Clusters for Convergence to High Curiosity
Cluster 1: Sharing Findings(SF) followed by Idea Verbalization(IV) and Justification(J) or Negative Sentiment Evaluation(NSE)
1. $IV \rightarrow \{SF, NSE\} \rightarrow IV \Rightarrow High$
2. $\{NSE, IV\} \rightarrow \{SF, J\} \rightarrow IV \Rightarrow High$
Cluster 2: Suggestions(SUGG), Arguments(ARG) and Idea verbalization (IV) in that order
1. $SUGG \rightarrow ARG \rightarrow IV \rightarrow J \Rightarrow High$
2. $SUGG \rightarrow \{IV, ARG\} \rightarrow \{IV, J\} \Rightarrow High$
Cluster 3: Uncertainty(UNC) followed by Idea Verbalization(IV) and Hypothesis Generation(HG)
1. $\{J, UNC, UNC\} \rightarrow IV \rightarrow HG \Rightarrow High$
2. $UNC \rightarrow \{UNC, IV\} \rightarrow HG \Rightarrow High$
Cluster 4: Question Asking(QA) followed by Uncertainty(UNC) and Idea verbalization(IV)
1. $\{QA, J\} \rightarrow UNC \rightarrow IV \Rightarrow High$
2. $Confusion \rightarrow QA \rightarrow UNC \rightarrow IV \Rightarrow High$
Cluster 5: Arguments(ARG) followed by Idea Verbalization(IV), Justification(J) and/or Negative Sentiment Evaluation(NSE)
1. $\{IV, ARG\} \rightarrow \{IV, J\} \Rightarrow High$
2. $ARG \rightarrow \{IV, IV, J\} \Rightarrow High$
Rule Clusters for Convergence to Low Curiosity
Cluster 1: Question Asking(QA) followed by both Negative and Positive Sentiment Task (PST, NST) and Confusion
1. $\{QA, Confusion\} \rightarrow \{PST, NST\} \rightarrow Confusion \Rightarrow Low$
2. $\{QA, NST\} \rightarrow \{PST, NST\} \rightarrow Confusion \Rightarrow Low$
Cluster 2: Justification(J) and Agreement(AGREE) followed by both Positive and Negative sentiment task(PST, NST) followed by Confusion
1. $\{J, AGREE\} \rightarrow \{PST, NST\}Confusion \Rightarrow Low$
Cluster 3: Confusion and Idea Verbalization(IV) followed by more confusion
1. $\{IV, Confusion\} \rightarrow \{IV, Confusion\} \rightarrow \{IV, Confusion\} \Rightarrow Low$
Cluster 4: Uncertainty(UNC) and Idea Verbalization(IV) followed by more uncertainty
1. $UNC \rightarrow \{IV, Confusion\} \rightarrow UNC \Rightarrow Low$
2. $UNC \rightarrow \{IV, IV\} \rightarrow UNC \Rightarrow Low$

to contain a sequence of behaviors uttered with the purpose of (a) evaluation of the proposed approach/solution by the group (Table 3, Clusters 1, 2) or (b) resolution of conflicts, knowledge gaps or opposing beliefs amongst different group members (Cluster 3, 4, 5). In particular, *Sharing Findings* (Cluster 1) or *Suggestions* (Cluster 2) made by one group member followed by *Negative Sentiment Evaluations* or *Argumentative* evaluations by other group members appears to lead to engagement and constructive debate in the group that stimulates critical thinking of alternative solutions and conflicting beliefs. Similarly, in Clusters 3, 4 and 5, when one group member reveals a knowledge-gap through the expression of *Uncertainty* (Cluster 3) or *Question Asking* (Cluster 4), or *Argues* (Cluster 5) for an alternative point of view, this knowledge-gap or conflict may be perceived by the group and jointly resolved through the use of ideas and supporting evidence (*Idea Verbalization, Justification*) or by building different possibilities and theories using a creative thought process (*hypothesis generation*).

A general explanation for these results is that the importance of a member's lack of knowledge is intensified through (i) explicit demand for response via sharing findings and question asking; (ii) high engagement with other's ideation through argument; and (iii) science reasoning involved in hypothesis generation [30]. These behaviors may lead to increased joint attention towards the information-gap, and thereby a high level of curiosity among group members [15]. This indicates that both cognitive and social engagement in conversation and group work plays an important role in joint curiosity at the group level and has previously been shown to produce a positive impact in edX MOOCs [13]. Rules where members' curiosity converges to low values contain the common theme of unresolved *Uncertainty* and *Confusion* in several members, revealing an unsolved knowledge-gap or conflict. This confusion is further exacerbated with the combination of both, *Positive* and *Negative* evaluations of the task (in Table 3, Clusters 1 and 2). Specifically, when curiosity converges at a low value across members, we observe more non-verbal behaviors (e.g. facial expressions of confusion, surprise) than verbal behaviors. The prominence of more non-verbal than verbal behaviors is indicative of low interactivity among group members (Table 4).

In summary, we observe that rules that predict a positive dynamic of curiosity (Increase and High Convergence) contain behavioral sequences where a possible solution to a problem is expressed with supporting evidence and is either critically evaluated through negative sentiments and arguments or triggers awareness of a knowledge gap leading to uncertainty and question asking. This is indicative of the desire to resolve conflicts arising from the critical evaluation or to bridge the perceived knowledge gap and is perceived as a positive scaffold for curiosity. Another interesting finding that contrasts curiosity as a group phenomenon with an individual state is that, compared to sequences that predict individual curiosity increase, sequences for high convergence contain a)more behaviors such as sharing findings and on-task question asking that elicit others' response and b)verbal behaviors with higher-order of reasoning such as justification and hypothesis generation. This is in spite of the rare occurrence of hypothesis generation, which emerges later compared to other scientific reasoning skills such as

Table 4. Examples of group conversations where association rules for curiosity increase and convergence are triggered

---

Conversation 1: Others Show Idea Verbalization(IV), Justification(J) followed by Negative Sentiment Evaluation(NSE) ⇒ Curiosity Increase

P1: If we bring the ball down in here... **(J)**

P1: Alright, it would need more space. **(IV)**

P4: Oh! use this, use this.

P1: Oh ain't it better.. **(NSE)**

P1: No, no, no! i just- look, i just got it

P1: Just need to aim it a little bit better, see?

P2: what are you trying to do ? **(Person 2's curiosity increases)**

Conversation 2: Uncertainty(UNC) followed by Justification(J) or Idea Verbalization(IV) and Hypothesis Generation(HG) ⇒ High Convergence

P3: We could have made- we didn't actually need this. **(UNC)**

P2: P3 how's that?

P3: We could have put this here **(J) (IV)**

P1: Uh we really need to make it really like on it's edge **(IV)**

P4: And then the ball could have landed in the boot, kicking this, kicking another ball.**(J)(HG) (Everyone is now curious)**

---

evidence evaluation among primary school students [30]. This initial observation opens up a new direction for differential social scaffolding of curiosity at different social granularities, individual and group.

We present conversation examples from a group building the RGM where association rules for curiosity increase (Conversation 1) and convergence at high levels (Conversation 2) are triggered. These association rule clusters can serve as the base of the reasoning model that determines real-time social scaffoldings to evoke curiosity in response to sequences of interactions in small group learning.

5   Implications and Future Work

Curiosity is an important motivation for learning, and our work demonstrates the ways in which curiosity is heavily influenced by social interactions in small groups. Findings of this work lead us to conceive of curiosity as socially as well as cognitively driven, and to ensure that in small group learning, we look not just at individual members' curiosity, but also the curiosity of the group. Our prediction model lays the foundation for determining what kinds of social scaffolding can evoke an increase in curiosity at both the individual and group level. Technically, this can be realized by monitoring the social interaction stream, and estimating the likelihood of future behaviors that may lead to curiosity increase or convergence to a high level, and to them choose the most appropriate social scaffolding based on the real-time learning contexts. We aim to integrate this solution into a curiosity reasoner for an intelligent virtual peer, that can evoke curiosity in small group scientific inquiry. It can also, however, be employed by teachers as they monitor small groups in learning activities, and by those who develop curricula and serious games for group learning activities.

The computational model presented here identifies temporal and social dynamics as two essential aspects of the association between complex social interactions and dynamic learning states like curiosity. The temporal dynamics we investigated were sequential behavior patterns and anomalous curiosity changes. The social dynamics were sequential behaviors across group members and curiosity convergence among group members. Although the study only explores basic temporal and social dynamics, it reveals promising directions for the AIED community to develop future theories and adaptive technologies for learning in social contexts. The approach of combining temporal association rule mining and curiosity dynamics is a technique that can be applied to investigate the temporal and social dynamics of other socio-emotional learning states in group work. Our study is limited by sample size since multi-party data collection and human-annotation of behavior and curiosity is a resource-intensive process. However, the promising results obtained in this work will encourage the community towards the creation of larger datasets, fine-grained analysis of the dynamics of learning states and development of adaptive SEL technology for collaborative group learning. In the future, we plan to enhance the model with multi-modal information at the turn-level to add a higher resolution to the social dimension of behaviors. We will also, of course, take the next step and assess whether implementing these sequences raises, not just curiosity, but also learning gains.

6   Conclusion

To our knowledge, this work is the first attempt to understand and build a prediction model of the dynamic interpersonal nature of curiosity in small group learning contexts. The computational model associates temporal sequences of verbal and non-verbal behaviors displayed by children in small learning groups with curiosity change in individuals as well as curiosity convergence of the group. Our model reliably predicts these events and extracts rules with distinct sequential patterns for each dynamic, thus uncovering different social interaction influences that lead to different curiosity dynamics. We observe that an increase in curiosity is associated with behavioral sequences where a solution to a problem is expressed together with supporting evidence and is either critically evaluated or triggers awareness of a knowledge gap. Convergence of high curiosity in a group tends to be associated with both scientific discourse (such as hypothesis generation) and interpersonal discourse (such as sharing findings). The extracted association rules provide heuristics for educators and designers to develop curricula and educational technologies that support curiosity in peer-peer learning environments. Furthermore, our approach provides a way for future adaptive learning technologies to incorporate social and temporal dynamics of positive learning states in supporting peer learning in small group.

Acknowledgement. We would like to thank the Heinz Endowment, all student interns, teachers and instructors of local school and summer camps, as well our collaborators Dr. Jessica Hammer, Dr. Louis-Phillppe Morency, Dr. Geoff Kaufman and Alexandra To for supporting the SCIPR project.

References

1. World economic forum (2016) new vision for education: Fostering social and emotional learning through technology (2016). http://www3.weforum.org/docs/WEF_New_Vision_for_Education.pdf
2. Standards aligned system (2018). https://www.pdesas.org/
3. Aleven, V., Connolly, H., Popescu, O., Marks, J., Lamnina, M., Chase, C.: An adaptive coach for invention activities. In: André, E., Baker, R., Hu, X., Rodrigo, M.M.T., du Boulay, B. (eds.) AIED 2017. LNCS (LNAI), vol. 10331, pp. 3–14. Springer, Cham (2017). https://doi.org/10.1007/978-3-319-61425-0_1
4. Ambady, N., Rosenthal, R.: Thin slices of expressive behavior as predictors of interpersonal consequences: a meta-analysis. Psychol. Bull. **111**(2), 256 (1992)
5. Berlyne, D.E.: Conflict, arousal, and curiosity (1960)
6. Cassell, J., Ananny, M., Basu, A., Bickmore, T., Chong, P., Mellis, D., Ryokai, K., Smith, J., Vilhjálmsson, H., Yan, H.: Shared reality: physical collaboration with a virtual peer. In: CHI 2000 Extended Abstracts on Human Factors in Computing Systems, pp. 259–260. ACM (2000)
7. Cen, L., Ruta, D., Powell, L., Hirsch, B., Ng, J.: Quantitative approach to collaborative learning: performance prediction, individual assessment, and group composition. Int. J. Comput. Support. Collaborative Learn. **11**(2), 187–225 (2016)
8. Chi, M.T., Wylie, R.: The icap framework: linking cognitive engagement to active learning outcomes. Educ. Psychol. **49**(4), 219–243 (2014)
9. Chollet, M., Ochs, M., Pelachaud, C.: From non-verbal signals sequence mining to bayesian networks for interpersonal attitudes expression. In: Bickmore, T., Marsella, S., Sidner, C. (eds.) IVA 2014. LNCS (LNAI), vol. 8637, pp. 120–133. Springer, Cham (2014). https://doi.org/10.1007/978-3-319-09767-1_15
10. Cohen, E.G., Lotan, R.A.: Designing Groupwork: Strategies for the Heterogeneous Classroom, 3rd edn. Teachers College Press (2014)
11. Craig, S.D., D'Mello, S., Witherspoon, A., Graesser, A.: Emote aloud during learning with autotutor: applying the facial action coding system to cognitive-affective states during learning. Cogn. Emot. **22**(5), 777–788 (2008)
12. Cukurova, M., Luckin, R., Millán, E., Mavrikis, M., Spikol, D.: Diagnosing collaboration in practice-based learning: equality and intra-individual variability of physical interactivity. In: Lavoué, É., Drachsler, H., Verbert, K., Broisin, J., Pérez-Sanagustín, M. (eds.) EC-TEL 2017. LNCS, vol. 10474, pp. 30–42. Springer, Cham (2017). https://doi.org/10.1007/978-3-319-66610-5_3
13. Ferschke, O., Yang, D., Tomar, G., Rosé, C.P.: Positive impact of collaborative chat participation in an edX MOOC. In: Conati, C., Heffernan, N., Mitrovic, A., Verdejo, M.F. (eds.) AIED 2015. LNCS (LNAI), vol. 9112, pp. 115–124. Springer, Cham (2015). https://doi.org/10.1007/978-3-319-19773-9_12
14. Forestier, S., Oudeyer, P.Y.: Curiosity-driven development of tool use precursors: a computational model. In: 38th Annual Conference of the Cognitive Science Society (COGSCI 2016), pp. 1859–1864 (2016)
15. Golman, R., Loewenstein, G.: An information-gap theory of feelings about uncertainty (2016)

16. Gordon, G., Breazeal, C., Engel, S.: Can children catch curiosity from a social robot? In: Proceedings of the Tenth Annual ACM/IEEE International Conference on Human-Robot Interaction, pp. 91–98. ACM (2015)
17. Guillame-Bert, M., Crowley, J.L.: Learning temporal association rules on symbolic time sequences. In: Asian Conference on Machine Learning, pp. 159–174 (2012)
18. Hussain, M.S., AlZoubi, O., Calvo, R.A., D'Mello, S.K.: Affect detection from multichannel physiology during learning sessions with autotutor. In: Biswas, G., Bull, S., Kay, J., Mitrovic, A. (eds.) AIED 2011. LNCS (LNAI), vol. 6738, pp. 131–138. Springer, Heidelberg (2011). https://doi.org/10.1007/978-3-642-21869-9_19
19. Kidd, C., Hayden, B.Y.: The psychology and neuroscience of curiosity. Neuron 88(3), 449–460 (2015)
20. Kim, K.H.: The creativity crisis: the decrease in creative thinking scores on the torrance tests of creative thinking. Creativity Res. J. 23(4), 285–295 (2011)
21. Kirschner, F., Paas, F., Kirschner, P.A.: Task complexity as a driver for collaborative learning efficiency: the collective working-memory effect. Appl. Cognit. Psychol. 25(4), 615–624 (2011)
22. Kotsiantis, S., Kanellopoulos, D.: Association rules mining: a recent overview. GESTS Int. Trans. Comput. Sci. Eng. 32(1), 71–82 (2006)
23. Lehman, B., D'Mello, S., Graesser, A.: Who benefits from confusion induction during learning? An individual differences cluster analysis. In: Lane, H.C., Yacef, K., Mostow, J., Pavlik, P. (eds.) AIED 2013. LNCS (LNAI), vol. 7926, pp. 51–60. Springer, Heidelberg (2013). https://doi.org/10.1007/978-3-642-39112-5_6
24. Lehman, B., Matthews, M., D'Mello, S., Person, N.: What are you feeling? investigating student affective states during expert human tutoring sessions. In: Woolf, B.P., Aïmeur, E., Nkambou, R., Lajoie, S. (eds.) ITS 2008. LNCS, vol. 5091, pp. 50–59. Springer, Heidelberg (2008). https://doi.org/10.1007/978-3-540-69132-7_10
25. Loewenstein, G.: The psychology of curiosity: a review and reinterpretation. Psychol. Bull. 116(1), 75 (1994)
26. Louwerse, M.M., Dale, R., Bard, E.G., Jeuniaux, P.: Behavior matching in multimodal communication is synchronized. Cognit. Sci. 36(8), 1404–1426 (2012)
27. Ludvigsen, S.: CSCL: connecting the social, emotional and cognitive dimensions. Int. J. Comput. Support. Collaborative Learn. 11(2), 115–121 (2016)
28. Noordewier, M.K., van Dijk, E.: Curiosity and time: from not knowing to almost knowing. Cogn. Emot. 31(3), 411–421 (2017)
29. O'Connor, D.: Application sharing in K-12 education: teaching and learning with Rube Goldberg. TechTrends 47(5), 6–13 (2003)
30. Piekny, J., Maehler, C.: Scientific reasoning in early and middle childhood: the development of domain-general evidence evaluation, experimentation, and hypothesis generation skills. Br. J. Dev. Psychol. 31(2), 153–179 (2013)
31. Silvia, P.J., Kashdan, T.B.: Interesting things and curious people: exploration and engagement as transient states and enduring strengths. Soc. Pers. Psychol. Compass 3(5), 785–797 (2009)
32. Sinha, T., Bai, Z., Cassell, J.: Curious minds wonder alike: studying multimodal behavioral dynamics to design social scaffolding of curiosity. In: Lavoué, É., Drachsler, H., Verbert, K., Broisin, J., Pérez-Sanagustín, M. (eds.) EC-TEL 2017. LNCS, vol. 10474, pp. 270–285. Springer, Cham (2017). https://doi.org/10.1007/978-3-319-66610-5_20

33. Sinha, T., Bai, Z., Cassell, J.: A new theoretical framework for curiosity for learning in social contexts. In: Lavoué, É., Drachsler, H., Verbert, K., Broisin, J., Pérez-Sanagustín, M. (eds.) EC-TEL 2017. LNCS, vol. 10474, pp. 254–269. Springer, Cham (2017). https://doi.org/10.1007/978-3-319-66610-5_19

34. Von Stumm, S., Hell, B., Chamorro-Premuzic, T.: The hungry mind: intellectual curiosity is the third pillar of academic performance. Perspect. Psychol. Sci. **6**(6), 574–588 (2011)

35. Walter, F., Bruch, H.: The positive group affect spiral: a dynamic model of the emergence of positive affective similarity in work groups. J. Organ. Behav. **29**(2), 239–261 (2008)

36. Weinberger, A., Stegmann, K., Fischer, F.: Knowledge convergence in collaborative learning: concepts and assessment. Learn. Instr. **17**(4), 416–426 (2007)

37. Wen, M., Yang, D., Rosé, C.P.: Virtual teams in massive open online courses. In: Conati, C., Heffernan, N., Mitrovic, A., Verdejo, M.F. (eds.) AIED 2015. LNCS (LNAI), vol. 9112, pp. 820–824. Springer, Cham (2015). https://doi.org/10.1007/978-3-319-19773-9_124

38. Wu, Q., Miao, C.: Modeling curiosity-related emotions for virtual peer learners. IEEE Comput. Intell. Mag. **8**(2), 50–62 (2013)

39. Zhao, R., Sinha, T., Black, A.W., Cassell, J.: Socially-aware virtual agents: automatically assessing dyadic rapport from temporal patterns of behavior. In: Traum, D., Swartout, W., Khooshabeh, P., Kopp, S., Scherer, S., Leuski, A. (eds.) IVA 2016. LNCS (LNAI), vol. 10011, pp. 218–233. Springer, Cham (2016). https://doi.org/10.1007/978-3-319-47665-0_20

Learning Curve Analysis in a Large-Scale, Drill-and-Practice Serious Math Game: Where Is Learning Support Needed?

Zhongxiu Peddycord-Liu$^{(\boxtimes)}$, Rachel Harred, Sarah Karamarkovich,
Tiffany Barnes, Collin Lynch, and Teomara Rutherford

North Carolina State University, Raleigh, NC, USA
{zliu24,rlharred,skessle,tmbarnes,cflynch,taruther}@ncsu.edu

Abstract. This paper applies data-driven methods to understand learning and derives game design insights in a large-scale, drill-and-practice game: Spatial Temporal (ST) Math. In order for serious games to thrive we must develop efficient, scalable methods to evaluate games against their educational goals. Learning models have matured in recent years and have been applied across e-learning platforms but they have not been used widely in serious games. We applied empirical learning curve analyses to ST Math under different assumptions of how knowledge components are defined in the game and map to game contents. We derived actionable game design feedback and educational insights regarding fraction learning. Our results revealed cases where students failed to transfer knowledge between math skills, content, and problem representations. This work stresses the importance of designing games that support students' comprehension of math concepts, rather than the learning of content- and situation-specific skills to pass games.

Keywords: Learning analytics · Serious games
Educational data mining · Fraction learning

1 Introduction

Serious games are in high demand with a fast-growing market [1]. As such, they are poised to significantly impact future generations of learners. As more games emerge, we face unprecedented challenges in evaluating the games against their educational goals. Traditional methods fall short. Games are growing in size and complexity, making it increasingly costly to evaluate games through controlled-trial experiments. Games evolve quickly during production and maintenance cycles, making it necessary to pinpoint design flaws and to derive actionable feedback efficiently. We need new methods to penetrate the black box between pre- and post-tests and to inform game design in an efficient, scalable fashion.

Serious game analytics [14] is an emerging field that uses data to connect gameplay with learning. In contrast to traditional game analytics [7] that primarily focuses on player enjoyment, serious game analytics grounds game design

© Springer International Publishing AG, part of Springer Nature 2018
C. Penstein Rosé et al. (Eds.): AIED 2018, LNAI 10947, pp. 436–449, 2018.
https://doi.org/10.1007/978-3-319-93843-1_32

in students' learning and performance on targeted skills. Serious game analytics is extremely valuable for large-scale, curriculum-integrated games. This approach not only helps pinpoint game design issues efficiently, but can also be used to investigate the learning process and derive educational insights across domains [13,14,19]. Serious game analytics shares similar and potentially transferable methods with Learning Analytics [27] and Educational Data Mining [23]. However, serious game analytics is concerned with more specific domains, where learning is interleaved with game mechanisms as well as other factors. We need more research to verify the applicability of these methods across domains, and to adapt these methods to solve contemporary challenges in serious games.

In this paper, we applied empirical learning curve analyses. We fit and combined learning curves under different assumptions of how knowledge components are defined in the game and mapped to game contents. Our analyses aim to: (1) Understand and model learning in ST Math–a large-scale, drill-and-practice game that introduces and reinforces math skills through various problem-solving scenarios. (2) Derive actionable feedback to help game designers better design game content to support learning. (3) Provide data-driven insights on fraction learning and the knowledge transfer between problem-solving scenarios. (4) Suggest future research that analyzes and models learning in serious games.

1.1 Spatial Temporal Math (ST Math)

ST Math is designed to act as a supplemental program to a school's existing mathematics curriculum [13,19,24]. In ST Math, mathematical concepts are taught through spatial puzzles within various game-like arenas. These games are structured at the top level by *objective*, which cover broad learning concepts. Within each objective, individual *games* teach more targeted concepts through presentation of *puzzles*, which are grouped into *levels* for students to play. Students begin by completing a series of training games on the use of the ST Math platform and features. They are then guided to complete the first available objective in their grade-level curriculum, such as "Multiplication Concepts." Within an objective, games represent scenarios for problem-solving using a particular mathematical concept, such as finding the right number of boots for X animals with Y legs. Each game contains between one and ten levels, which follow the same general structure of the game, but with increasing difficulty. Students must unlock the games and levels in their designed order.

As with many games, students are given a set number of 'lives' per level. Every time they answer a puzzle incorrectly they lose one life. Each answer attempt is followed by animated feedback. For example, in a game asking students to select a number of boots for two dogs, a wrong answer of six will show that one dog has two feet without boots. After the feedback, students must attempt the same puzzle again until they answer it correctly or they exhaust all lives. If all lives for a given level are exhausted, students must re-attempt the level. When students re-attempt a level there is a probability that they may encounter a previously attempted puzzle, as puzzles are either randomly generated following a template, or randomly selected from a pre-designed puzzle pool.

Once students pass a level, they can play the next level or any previously-passed level. A general description and additional figures of ST Math can be found in [13,19,24].

2   Literature Review

Learning Curves are derived from the cognitive theory of Newell and Rosebloom [17]. This theory assumes that with more practice, a students' speed and accuracy at answering a question increase logarithmically. In other words, a good learning curve shows that students' accuracy increases, but the increase gets smaller over time. After enough practice, the increase will be negligible, and students can be considered to have reached their best performance.

Several learning models have been applied to fit learning curves. The Additive Factors Model (AFM) [4] is a logistic regression that assumes the probability of correctly answering a question depends on individual students' parameters, the skill difficulties, and the number of previous practices. For questions containing multiple skills, the difficulty and practices of these skills are summed together. This assumes that a student can correctly answer a question without knowing all of the skills involved, provided the summation of known skills passes a certain threshold. The Conjunctive Factor Model (CFM) [5] is similar to AFM, but assumes that the difficulties and practices of skills are multiplied together for questions with multiple skills. This means that a student can never answer a question correctly unless they know all the required skills. Another method is Performance Factor Analysis (PFA) [18], which is similar to AFM with an additional assumption that success and failure have different impacts on learning. Because we don't currently have evidence that this additional assumption holds in ST Math, we focused on applying AFM and CFM in this paper.

Despite the wide application of empirical Learning Curves on intelligent tutors and other e-learning platforms, there has been little application in serious games. As one exception, Harpstead and Aleven [8] applied the AFM model in a physics game. Through examining learning curves, they identified an unforeseen shortcut strategy with which students could pass the game without sufficiently mastering its underlying math concepts. Similarly, Baker et al. [3] fit learning curves in a action-based math game to model gains in speed and accuracy over time. They found that modeling accuracy helped to identify skills that needed extra support and scaffolding. However, modeling speed was difficult, because it was hard to separate gains in math fluency from familiarity with the gameplay. Lomas et al. [15] applied learning curves to a game locating numbers on a number line. They found when students were allowed to pass the game with less accurate estimations, the learning rate was lower. In these cases, estimating learning curves revealed areas for modification and improvement within serious games. However, in all previous work, the games studied represented a single problem-solving scenario. In contrast, games such as ST Math practice math skills through various problem-solving scenarios. Applying learning curves to ST Math can yield not only game design insights, but help understand how students transfer knowledge across different problem solving scenarios.

3   Data

MIND Research Institute, the developer of ST Math, collected and provided the researchers with sample data from 3rd grade students who played ST Math from August 2016 to February 2017. We focused on the "Comparing Fractions" objective. Performance on fractions has been found to predict future mathematical achievement [2,26,28]. Thus, investigating this objective will allow us to contribute suggestions for game design of instruction around a crucial math concept. This objective contains 26 levels across seven games; 1,007 students completed the first game, and 860 students completed the last game. ST Math recorded students' IDs, answers, and response times for each puzzle attempt. The data also included the correct answer for each puzzle, and the level, game, and objective to which it belonged. We filtered out students' replay of previously passed levels [13] to focus solely on their attempts to pass an unlearned case. The final data contains 146,498 unique puzzle attempts.

4   Analyses

Our goal was to understand and model learning in ST Math, and to suggest better game design that would foster greater learning. ST Math is structured at the top level by objectives, where games representing different problem-solving scenarios and levels are puzzle sets of increasing difficulty. Puzzles are either randomly generated following a template, or randomly selected from a pre-designed puzzle pool. We first fit learning curves to the puzzles to identify the learning patterns at each level. We then combined the levels hierarchically within each game. We sought to find similarities between the levels–modeling levels as continuations within a single learning curve. Lastly, we sought to find associations between games. We used an expert-designed Q-matrix with knowledge components describing the shared math skills and problem representations across games. We fit learning curves using different assumptions to identify how these knowledge components interacted and affected students' learning across games.

4.1   Fitting Learning Curves

We used the AFM [4] and CFM [5] models to fit learning curves. We decided to model the probability that a student answered a puzzle correctly on the first attempt only. This is because students receive animated feedback after each answer, with some feedback enabling them to quickly correct a wrong answer without having to redo the entire problem. Thus, subsequent attempts may not truly reflect each student's knowledge of the mathematics content. Next, we decided to fit a learning curve on the first N puzzles in each level, where N is the number of puzzles that must be answered correctly in order to pass the level. We chose N because students who passed the level without exhausting all of their lives (which is the majority in most levels) will not need another attempt. Attempts following N will only contain data from low-performing students who had to attempt the level multiple times to pass. Thus, we only consider students' first N puzzles (practice opportunities) in order to fit our learning curve on the same population. Lastly, for student variables in AFM and CFM, we used students' average performance in the prior two objectives: "Fraction Concepts" and "Fractions on a Number Line." These two reflect students' knowledge of fractions prior to attempting this objective.

4.2 Analyzing Puzzles in Levels

In ST Math, each level stresses skills of increasing difficulty under a problem-solving scenario defined by the game. The increased difficulty can be introduced by changes in math content (e.g., using larger numbers), changes in problem representation (e.g., use of math symbols instead of an visual object), or other factors. However, in each case the problem-solving scenario (e.g., finding shoes for animals) remains the same. Thus, we started by assuming one-to-one mappings between levels and knowledge components, and fit learning curves with AFM.

Figure 1 shows the learning curve fit, with content of representative games described in the later text. We applied 10-fold cross-validation and reported the model's accuracy as the percentage of instances correctly predicted by the logistic regression models. The majority of puzzles were answered correctly by over 50% of students, therefore we include the AUROC to describe how well models can differentiate between true positive and false positive.

We looked for four specific patterns to derive game-design feedback. A *good learning curve* displays a logarithmic pattern indicating that students increased their accuracy with practice and thus that learning appears to be well-supported. An *incomplete learning curve* is similar to a good learning curve except it does not include a flat tail. This indicates that students can still improve with more practice. Next, a *flat learning curve*, which we defined here as having a smooth curve with $e <= 0.05$, means that students' performance did not improve substantially with practice. It could be that the level is too difficult or that the game content is not well-designed thus students did not learn with practice. It could also be that the level is too easy: students started with near perfect performance. Lastly, a *non-learning curve* does not follow a logarithmic or flat pattern. Performance in this type of learning curve increased or decreased suddenly at specific attempts. When this happens, it means that there was a change in the puzzle's template that introduced what the students perceived to be a new knowledge component. For example, a level can have half of the puzzles randomly generated with odd denominators, and the other half randomly generated with even denominators. If students failed to transfer the knowledge when denominators changed, we will see two *disjointed learning curves*.

The majority of levels (16 of 26) showed the logarithmic pattern of a learning curve, which means that the game design helped students learn (or improve their performance). A few learning curves are incomplete (e.g., Game 7 L3), suggesting that game designers should increase the number of puzzles required to pass the levels (L) as students still have room for improvement.

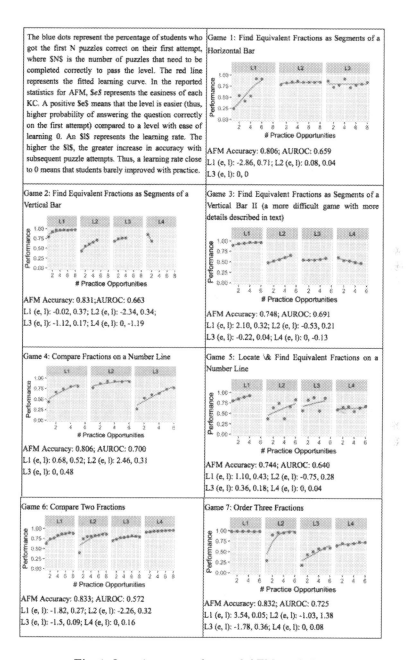

The blue dots represent the percentage of students who got the first N puzzles correct on their first attempt, where N is the number of puzzles that need to be completed correctly to pass the level. The red line represents the fitted learning curve. In the reported statistics for AFM, e represents the easiness of each KC. A positive e means that the level is easier (thus, higher probability of answering the question correctly on the first attempt) compared to a level with ease of learning 0. An l represents the learning rate. The higher the l, the greater increase in accuracy with subsequent puzzle attempts. Thus, a learning rate close to 0 means that students barely improved with practice.

Game 1: Find Equivalent Fractions as Segments of a Horizontal Bar

AFM Accuracy: 0.806; AUROC: 0.659
L1 (e, l): -2.86, 0.71; L2 (e, l): 0.08, 0.04
L3 (e, l): 0, 0

Game 2: Find Equivalent Fractions as Segments of a Vertical Bar

AFM Accuracy: 0.831; AUROC: 0.663
L1 (e, l): -0.02, 0.37; L2 (e, l): -2.34, 0.34;
L3 (e, l): -1.12, 0.17; L4 (e, l): 0, -1.19

Game 3: Find Equivalent Fractions as Segments of a Vertical Bar II (a more difficult game with more details described in text)

AFM Accuracy: 0.748; AUROC: 0.691
L1 (e, l): 2.10, 0.32; L2 (e, l): -0.53, 0.21
L3 (e, l): -0.22, 0.04; L4 (e, l): 0, -0.13

Game 4: Compare Fractions on a Number Line

AFM Accuracy: 0.806; AUROC: 0.700
L1 (e, l): 0.68, 0.52; L2 (e, l): 2.46, 0.31
L3 (e, l): 0, 0.48

Game 5: Locate \& Find Equivalent Fractions on a Number Line

AFM Accuracy: 0.744; AUROC: 0.640
L1 (e, l): 1.10, 0.43; L2 (e, l): -0.75, 0.28
L3 (e, l): 0.36, 0.18; L4 (e, l): 0, 0.04

Game 6: Compare Two Fractions

AFM Accuracy: 0.833; AUROC: 0.572
L1 (e, l): -1.82, 0.27; L2 (e, l): -2.26, 0.32
L3 (e, l): -1.5, 0.09; L4 (e, l): 0, 0.16

Game 7: Order Three Fractions

AFM Accuracy: 0.832; AUROC: 0.725
L1 (e, l): 3.54, 0.05; L2 (e, l): -1.03, 1.38
L3 (e, l): -1.78, 0.36; L4 (e, l): 0, 0.08

Fig. 1. Learning curve plots and AFM statistics.

Four of the 26 levels had flat learning curves. Among these, Game 3 L3&4 appear too difficult and need to be re-designed to support learning. L3 presents a fraction and requires students to find two different ways of dividing a vertical bar by selecting the number of segments that equals the given fraction, as shown in Fig. 2. However, the denominator of the given fraction is not allowed as a choice. For example, if the fraction is 3/4, the option to divide the bar into fourths is grayed out, forcing students to divide the bar into eighths and choose 6/8, and then 9/12. L4 concerns a similar skill with more difficult content. A longitudinal study by Hansen et al. also found questions where the denominator of the fraction did not correspond directly to the pieces in the presented model posed the most difficulties for low-achieving students [9]. Thus, designers may wish to offer extra scaffolding on these two levels. On the contrary, Game 1 L2 and Game 7 L1 appeared to be too easy because performance is consistently near perfect. For example, in Game 7 L1 students order fractions with the same denominator and different numerators, with visualizations showing the size of these fractions as the widths of bars. This level is too easy because students can, without understanding fractions, visually compare the bar widths. However, this level serves to teach the game mechanics for the subsequent levels in this game. Thus, we suggest designers either reduce the number of puzzles, or use one puzzle in this level as a tutorial for L2, instead of as an independent level.

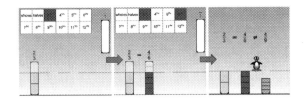

Fig. 2. An example of a too difficult level with flat learning curve.

Six levels follow a non-learning curve pattern. Two levels (Game 1 L1, Game 2 L4) present the same puzzles at the same attempt for all students to make a specific point, such as understanding fractions equal to 1. These non-randomized puzzles are easier, causing a jump in performance. However, we do not suggest changing them due to their educational value. Four levels showed disjointed learning curves. These learning curves revealed cases where students failed to transfer between specific number content. For example, the first three puzzles of Game 5 L2 require students to locate a fraction X/8 on a number line divided into one fourths, and the last three require locating X/4 on a number line marked with one eighths. Game 5 L3 has a similar setup, with X/6 and X/3. Although these puzzles cover the same concept, the four disjointed learning curves show that students failed to transfer between puzzle sets of different fixed denominators (the four puzzles types shown in Fig. 3). It could be that some students do not understand the underlying concepts, but learned pattern matching based on specific number content. Another possible explanation is that the number of partitions prevented transfer between the two puzzle sets. Mitchell and Horne found that some students may incorrectly count the number of lines to determine where a fraction falls on the number line instead of considering the spaces between the lines [10]. Thus, game designers may consider providing practice with randomized numbers instead of presenting fixed numbers separately to reduce the ease of content-specific pattern matching or counting.

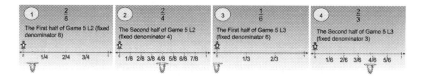

Fig. 3. An example where students failed to transfer. The below four types of puzzles showed four disjointed learning curves.

To summarize, fitting learning curves to each game's level derived specific game design insights, and helped us better understand how learning is structured in the ST Math environment. However, a general trend was that a number of the learning curves were disjointed. In many games, each level seemed to form its own learning curve instead of forming a single learning curve with the other levels. The lack of connection and the cases of disjointed learning curves implied that 3rd graders may rely on content- and problem-specific procedural knowledge or pattern matching strategies to solve puzzles, instead of transferring the understanding of underlying math concepts [12,22]. When new content or problem representations were introduced to practice the same math concept, students treated them as new knowledge components.

4.3   Analyzing Levels in Games

In this section, we sought to find similarities between levels by looking for level combinations that would form a continuous learning curve. Based on the previous analyses, we started by considering each level as a separate Knowledge Component (KC), and applied a bottom-up approach to hierarchically combine levels within a game based on learning curve fitting. We then searched for KC pairs that, once combined as the same KC, yielded AFM models with the lowest Bayesian information criterion (BIC) values as compared to other combination choices. A lower BIC means that the model fit was comparatively better considering both the fit (maximum likelihood) and complexity (number of parameters). This approach is similar to Cen and Koedinger's work [4], except that they used a top-down approach that searches to split one KC into multiple KCs to improve the model. We applied this method to levels within a game instead of across games. We did so because the conjunction of learning curves only makes sense if the different levels involve practicing the same skill (KC). We excluded levels with disjointed or flat learning curves. This is because disjointed learning curves, if split into multiple learning curves, have too few puzzles to study a pattern. Flat learning curves, especially those with high performance, may be appended to the tail of any previous learning curves that reached high performance in the last attempts. Such conjunctions may not have empirical meanings.

Figure 4 shows the hierarchical combinations of levels in Game 6. The algorithm first combined L1&4, which resulted in a lower BIC than the original model in which each level is a different KC. Both L1&4 ask students to compare two fractions with the same denominator and different numerators, with one requiring students to answer with a ladder and the other with math symbols. Similarly, L2&3 require comparing fractions of the same numerator with ladders or math symbols, and were suggested to be combined next. This hierarchy showed that students can transfer easily between ladder and math symbols, but not as easily from comparing fractions with the same denominator to comparing fractions with the same numerator and different denominators. This is likely due to the simplicity of comparing fractions with the same numerator (or denominator)–students only have to compare one number rather than considering the relationship between the numerator and denominator [6]. In other words, comparing fractions was still a difficult skill and it wasn't the symbolic representation of greater than/less than that tripped students up. Thus, we suggest re-positioning L4 to come after L1 or even removing ladders and using math symbols only. However, when introducing comparing fractions with the same numerator and different denominators in the next level, designers should provide other scaffolding to make connections between the two skills.

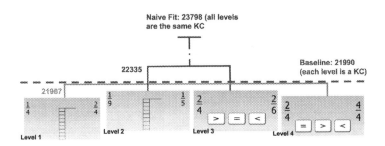

Fig. 4. Hierarchical combinations of game 6 levels that led to models with different BICs. BIC similar to baseline indicates that the combined levels share a similar KC.

In the rest of the games, the algorithm suggested combining the following levels without much increase in BIC: L2&3 of Game 2 (BIC 14138 compared to baseline 14127), L1&2 of Game 4 (BIC 14731 compared to baseline 14702), and L3&4 of Game 7 (BIC 14425 compared to baseline 14352). The combination in Game 4 shows that by locating fractions one by one on a number line, students can easily transfer from comparing fractions with the same denominator and different numerators to comparing fractions with the same numerator and different denominators. This implies that locating fractions on a number line is a strategy that facilitates such a transfer (see the integrated theory of numerical development in [21,25]). However, for comparing fractions with the same denominator, the transfer between fractions smaller than 1 to larger than 1 is much more difficult. It could be that students rely on the numbers in the fractions rather than their magnitude [9,11], so when the fraction is greater than 1, they do not have a conceptual understanding of where the fraction is located on a number line in order to use the number line to help with comparisons. Thus, designers may consider more scaffolding to help students make this transfer.

The other suggested combinations are pairs of levels concerning the same skill with the same problem representation. To summarize, hierarchically combining learning curves helped us identify where students may need extra support to transfer between math skills and problem representations.

4.4   Analyze Games in Objective

From previous analyses, we learned that the performance in ST Math is influenced by both targeted math skills and problem representations. Thus, in this subsection, we sought to further investigate how math skills and problem representations interact with each other and influence students' learning across games. We started with designing an expert Q-matrix (mapping from puzzles to knowledge components) with two types of knowledge component: math skill (KC-S) and problem representation (KC-R). Each level was mapped to at least one KC-S and one KC-R, but not all KCs were mutually exclusive, which means a level could contain multiple KC-Ss and/or KC-Rs. We constructed a total of four KC-Rs, including: number line, vertical bar, horizontal bar, and representation containing visual cues that help students solve the puzzle through pattern-matching. We constructed 6 KC-S, including: presenting fractions (e.g., as segments of a bar); finding equivalent fractions; comparing three types of fractions: same numerators, same denominators, and different in both numerators and denominators; and comparing fractions greater than 1.

Next, we fit learning curves on the expert-designed Q-matrix with three assumptions. The **first** assumption was that each KC contributed to performance *additively*, as assumed by the AFM model. The **second** was that each KC contributed to performance *conjunctively*(modeling the conjunctivity as a multiplication of skill parameters), as assumed by the CFM model. We used R's optim package with BFGS optimization method to estimate the parameters of CFM through maximizing the likelihood function. The **third** assumption was that the KCs interacted neither additively nor conjunctively. This means the same math skill presented in two separate levels would be viewed as two distinct skills that students learned under different representations. Thus, a *combination* of KCs forms a new KC. In other words, each level would be mapped to only one KC, and levels with the same KC-R and KC-S combinations shared the same KC. When each level had one KC, AFM and CFM were equivalent. This assumption yielded 15 KCs (15 different combinations of KC-R and KC-S) across 26 levels.

Table 1. Learning models under different assumptions of KC interactions.

KC assumptions	Model	Accuracy	AUROC	BIC
High Baseline: Each level is a KC (26 KC, each level has 1 KC)	AFM/CFM	0.782	0.622	134831 (+0.0%)
Combined (15 KC, each level has 1 KC)	AFM/CFM	0.775	0.602	137425 (+1.9%)
Additive (9 KC, each level has >1 KC)	AFM	0.768	0.58	141607 (+5.0%)
Conjunctive(9 KC, each level has >1 KC)	CFM	0.761	0.54	149002 (+10.5%)
Low Baseline: Each game is a KC (7 KC, each level has 1 KC)	AFM/CFM	0.756	0.54	150787 (+11.8%)

As shown in Table 1, our models have low discrimination ability based on AUROC from 10-fold cross-validation. Thus, there are limitations when applying traditional learning models to serious games, where it is easier for children to guess or pattern match with visual cues in specific game environments. The model based on the third assumption had the best fit, with only 1.9% increase in BIC as compared to the most ideal model assuming each level is a KC. Our result implies that ST Math's targeted skills and problem representations do not contribute to performance simply through additive or conjunctive relationships. Instead, the same skill would be treated as different skills when combined with other skills and problem representations. It could be that when students play ST Math, they do not use math skills alone. Rather, students develop new skills that are content- and situation-specific, based on the combinations of targeted math skills and problem representations.

5   Discussion and Conclusion

In this paper, we demonstrated using learning curves as a simple, efficient way to evaluate how well an educational game supports learning. Our results pinpointed problematic levels and cases where students needed extra support to transfer between math skills, content, and problem representations. We derived actionable feedback for ST Math and general insights on fraction learning.

This work has several limitations. First, ST Math is designed as a curriculum-integrated game, but our data does not capture factors in classrooms. Future research will include teacher interviews and classroom observations to better assess the impact of classroom factors. Second, we limited the data to only the number of puzzles required to pass a level which excluded some attempts by low-performing students. Future research may explore methods to separate learning curves for student sub-populations [16] in order to increase external validity.

Our results suggest that students developed new 'skills' based on the combination of targeted math skills and problem representations, rather than simply combining them as assumed in the additive or conjunctive factor models. The variety in ST Math's problem-solving scenarios may improve students' understanding of math concepts. However, this variety could distract learning if students focus more on content- and situation-specific practice than the underlying math concepts. The literature review by Lehtinen and Hannula-Sormune [12] argues that in cases of transfer failures, the (new) situations are not necessarily interpreted as mathematical by children. For example, students may see Game 1–3 as 'selecting divided bars and the number of segments to match a given bar's height/width,' instead of 'understanding fractions as proportions and finding equivalent fractions by multiplying or dividing the numerator and denominator by the same number.' Thus, when bars are replaced with a number line to practice the same math skill, it becomes a different task. Similarly, work by Rau et al. [20] found that providing multiple representations can promote better learning than a single graphical representation, but only when students are prompted to self-explain how the graphics relate to the symbolic fraction representations. With the increasing popularity of mini-games collections, it is important to design scaffolding that facilitates transfer by focusing students on the underlying math concepts instead of reinforcing simple strategies like pattern matching. Such scaffolding should also be considered in other e-learning platforms that offer multiple problem-solving scenarios for young children.

We learned several lessons from applying learning curves to this serious game environment. Learning in game environments is inseparable from the games' mechanisms, structures, and designs. Researchers should consider starting analyses at a low granularity, such as the individual level we used here. Understanding students' learning at a low granularity would help illuminate factors that contribute to learning, and help structure analyses at higher granularities where these factors may combine or evolve. Moreover, game performance does not solely comprise learning. This means traditional learning modeling methods may have limited power in serious games. Thus, researchers should be flexible with different models and assumptions to work within specific game environments. Regardless, researchers should triangulate results with human interpretations and the literature to make sure the results do not derive from unforeseen game scenarios or the large amount of data. For example, Harpstead and Aleven [8] used both data and human judgment to examine the fit of learning curves in a physics game and identified an unforeseen pattern matching strategy. Liu et al. [19] mined predictive relationships between ST Math objectives, and used both human interpretation and literature to suggest game design feedback. Thus, when analyzing serious game data, it is extremely important to not solely focus on the performance of models, but also consider the models' interpretation and practical value.

Acknowledgments. This work was supported by NSF grant IUSE #1544273 "Evaluation for Actionable Change: A Data-Driven Approach" Teomara Rutherford, Tiffany Barnes & Collin Lynch Co-PIs.

References

1. Adkins, S.: The 2016–2021 Global Game-based Learning Market. In: Serious Play Conference (2016)
2. Bailey, D.H., Hoard, M.K., Nugent, L., Geary, D.C.: Competence with fractions predicts gains in Mathematics achievement. J. Exp. Child Psychol. **113**(3), 447–455 (2012)
3. Baker, R.S.J.D., Jacob Habgood, M.P., Ainsworth, S.E., Corbett, A.T.: Modeling the acquisition of fluent skill in educational action games. In: Conati, C., McCoy, K., Paliouras, G. (eds.) UM 2007. LNCS (LNAI), vol. 4511, pp. 17–26. Springer, Heidelberg (2007). https://doi.org/10.1007/978-3-540-73078-1_5
4. Cen, H., Koedinger, K., Junker, B.: Learning factors analysis – a general method for cognitive model evaluation and improvement. In: Ikeda, M., Ashley, K.D., Chan, T.-W. (eds.) ITS 2006. LNCS, vol. 4053, pp. 164–175. Springer, Heidelberg (2006). https://doi.org/10.1007/11774303_17
5. Cen, H., Koedinger, K., Junker, B.: Comparing two IRT models for conjunctive skills. In: Woolf, B.P., Aïmeur, E., Nkambou, R., Lajoie, S. (eds.) ITS 2008. LNCS, vol. 5091, pp. 796–798. Springer, Heidelberg (2008). https://doi.org/10.1007/978-3-540-69132-7_111
6. Rittle-Johnson, B., Siegler, R., Alibali, M.: Students' fraction comparison strategies as a window into robust understanding and possible pointers for instruction. Educ. Stud. Math. **72**(1), 127–138 (2009)
7. El-Nasr, M.S., Drachen, A., Canossa, A.: Game Analytics. Springer, London (2016). https://doi.org/10.1007/978-1-4471-4769-5
8. Harpstead, E., Aleven, V.: Using empirical learning curve analysis to inform design in an educational game. In: Proceedings of the 2015 Annual Symposium on Computer-Human Interaction in Play, pp. 197–207. ACM, October 2015
9. Hansen, N., Jordan, N.C., Rodrigues, J.: Identifying learning difficulties with fractions: a longitudinal study of student growth from third through sixth grade. Contemp. Educ. Psychol. **50**, 45–59 (2017)
10. Mitchell, A., Horne, M.: Fraction number line tasks and the additivity concept of length measurement. In: Proceedings of the 31st Annual Conference of the Mathematics Education Research Group of Australasia, pp. 353–360 (2008)
11. Jordan, N.C., Resnick, I., Rodrigues, J., Hansen, N., Dyson, N.: Delaware longitudinal study of fraction learning: implications for helping children with mathematics difficulties. J. Learn. Disabil. **50**(6), 621–630 (2017)
12. Lehtinen, E., Hannula, M.M.: Attentional processes, abstraction and transfer in early mathematical development. Instructional psychology: past, present and future trends. Fifteen Essays Honour Erik De Corte **49**, 39–55 (2006)
13. Liu, Z., Cody, C., Barnes, T., Lynch, C., Rutherford, T.: The antecedents of and associations with elective replay in an educational game: is replay worth it. In: Proceedings of the 10th International Conference on Educational Data Mining (EDM) (2017)
14. Loh, C.S., Sheng, Y., Ifenthaler, D. (eds.): Serious Games Analytics. AGL. Springer, Cham (2015). https://doi.org/10.1007/978-3-319-05834-4
15. Lomas, D., Patel, K., Forlizzi, J.L., Koedinger, K.R.: Optimizing challenge in an educational game using large-scale design experiments. In: Proceedings of the SIGCHI Conference on Human Factors in Computing Systems, pp. 89–98. ACM, April 2013

16. Murray, R.C., Ritter, S., Nixon, T., Schwiebert, R., Hausmann, R.G.M., Towle, B., Fancsali, S.E., Vuong, A.: Revealing the learning in learning curves. In: Lane, H.C., Yacef, K., Mostow, J., Pavlik, P. (eds.) AIED 2013. LNCS (LNAI), vol. 7926, pp. 473–482. Springer, Heidelberg (2013). https://doi.org/10.1007/978-3-642-39112-5_48

17. Newell, A., Rosenbloom, P.S.: Mechanisms of skill acquisition and the law of practice. Cognit. Skills Acquis. **1**(1981), 1–55 (1981)

18. Pavlik, P.I., Yudelson, M., Koedinger, K.R.: A measurement model of microgenetic transfer for improving instructional outcomes. Int. J. Artif. Intell. Educ. **25**(3), 346–379 (2015)

19. Peddycord-Liu, Z., Cody, C., Kessler, S., Barnes, T., Lynch, C.F., Rutherford, T.: Using serious game analytics to inform digital curricular sequencing: what math objective should students play next? In: Proceedings of the Annual Symposium on Computer-Human Interaction in Play, pp. 195–204. ACM, October 2017

20. Rau, M.A., Aleven, V., Rummel, N.: Intelligent tutoring systems with multiple representations and self-explanation prompts support learning of fractions. In: AIED, pp. 441–448, July 2009

21. Rinne, L., Ye, A., Jordan, N.C.: Development of fraction comparison strategies: a latent transition analysis. Dev. Psychol. **53**(4), 713–730 (2017)

22. Rittle-Johnson, B., Siegler, R., Alibali, M.: Developing conceptual understanding and procedural skill in mathematics: an iterative process. J. Educ. Psychol. **93**(2), 346–362 (2001)

23. Romero, C., Ventura, S.: Educational data mining: a review of the state of the art. IEEE Trans. Syst. Man Cybern. Part C (Appl. Rev.) **40**(6), 601–618 (2010)

24. Rutherford, T., Farkas, G., Duncan, G., Burchinal, M., Kibrick, M., Graham, J., Richland, L., Tran, N., Schneider, S., Duran, L., Martinez, M.E.: A randomized trial of an elementary school Mathematics software intervention: spatial-temporal math. J. Res. Educ. Effectiveness **7**(4), 358–383 (2014)

25. Siegler, R., Thompson, C., Schneider, M.: An integrated theory of whole number and fractions development. Cogn. Psychol. **62**(4), 273–296 (2011)

26. Siegler, R.S., Duncan, G.J., Davis-Kean, P.E., Duckworth, K., Claessens, A., Engel, M., Ines Susperreguy, M., Chen, M.: Early predictors of high school Mathematics achievement. Psychol. Sci. **23**(7), 691–697 (2012)

27. Siemens, G., Baker, R.S.D.: Learning analytics and educational data mining: towards communication and collaboration. In: Proceedings of the 2nd International Conference on Learning Analytics And Knowledge, pp. 252–254. ACM, April 2012

28. Torbeyns, J., Schneider, M., Xin, Z., Siegler, R.S.: Bridging the gap: fraction understanding is central to mathematics achievement in students from three different continents. Learn. Instr. **37**, 5–13 (2015)

Conceptual Issues in Mastery Criteria: Differentiating Uncertainty and Degrees of Knowledge

Radek Pelánek[(✉)]

Masaryk University, Brno, Czech Republic
pelanek@fi.muni.cz

Abstract. Mastery learning is a common personalization strategy in adaptive educational systems. A mastery criterion decides whether a learner should continue practice of a current topic or move to a more advanced topic. This decision is typically done based on comparison with a mastery threshold. We argue that the commonly used mastery criteria combine two different aspects of knowledge estimate in the comparison to this threshold: the degree of achieved knowledge and the uncertainty of the estimate. We propose a novel learner model that provides conceptually clear treatment of these two aspects. The model is a generalization of the commonly used Bayesian knowledge tracing and logistic models and thus also provides insight into the relationship of these two types of learner models. We compare the proposed mastery criterion to commonly used criteria and discuss consequences for practical development of educational systems.

Keywords: Learner modeling · Mastery learning · Uncertainty

1 Introduction

A common approach to personalization in educational systems is mastery learning, which is an instructional strategy that requires learners to master a topic before moving to more advanced topics [15]. A key aspect of mastery learning is a mastery criterion – a rule that determines whether a learner has achieved mastery [13]. A typical application of mastery criterion within a modern educational system is the following. A learner solves problems or answers questions in the system. Data about learner performance are summarized by a model of learner knowledge or by some summary statistic. This number is compared to a threshold that specifies the strictness of the criterion. A simple example of such a criterion is "N consecutive correct" – performance is summarized as the number of correctly answered question in a row and the threshold is a natural number N. The choice of the threshold involves a trade-off between unnecessary over-practice and the risk of premature declaration of mastery.

But what exactly is the meaning of the threshold? Does it specify how large portion of the practiced topic the learner has mastered? Or does it specify how

ⓒ Springer International Publishing AG, part of Springer Nature 2018
C. Penstein Rosé et al. (Eds.): AIED 2018, LNAI 10947, pp. 450–461, 2018.
https://doi.org/10.1007/978-3-319-93843-1_33

certain can we be that the learner has sufficiently mastered the topic? The main point of this work is that it is useful to explicitly differentiate these two aspects of mastery: degrees of knowledge and certainty of knowledge estimation.

The current state-of-the-art makes the issues of threshold choice and interpretation obfuscated. There are two influential families of learner models: models based on Bayesian knowledge tracing (BKT) and family of logistic models [12]. These approaches estimate knowledge using different assumptions, which leads to significantly different interpretations of mastery thresholds.

The BKT model [3] makes a key simplifying assumption that knowledge can be modeled as a binary state (known/unknown). The model provides a probability estimate quantifying the certainty that the learner is in the known state. This estimate is commonly compared to a threshold 0.95, which leads to a clear interpretation that there is 95% chance that the learner has already mastered the topic. This interpretation, however, holds only under the idealistic assumption of binary knowledge. The assumption may be reasonable for very fine-grained knowledge components with homogeneous items (e.g., "addition of fractions with the same denominator"). In many practical cases, however, learner models are applied to more coarse-grained knowledge components, where the assumption of binary knowledge is far from satisfied. This degrades the performance of the model, and – for our discussion more importantly – it obfuscates the interpretation of the model estimate and the threshold. In these cases the BKT incorporates the degrees of knowledge aspect into the skill estimate, which thus loses the clear probabilistic interpretation.

Another common learner modeling approach is the family of models based on the logistic function, e.g., Rasch model, Performance factor analysis [10], or the Elo rating system [11]. These models utilize assumption of a continuous latent skill θ and for the relation between the skill and the probability of correct answer use the logistic function $\sigma(\theta) = \frac{1}{1+e^{-\theta}}$. The skill is estimated based on the learner's performance, for example in the Performance factor analysis model the skill is given by a weighted combination of correct and incorrect responses. These models thus utilize continuous knowledge scale, but do not explicitly quantify the uncertainty of estimates – they typically provide only a point estimate of the skill, which combines uncertainty and knowledge estimate into one number.

To address these issues, we propose a relatively simple model that generalizes both BKT and logistic model and provides clear differentiation of the degrees of knowledge and the uncertainty of estimates. The model is a special case of the hidden Markov model that uses a logistic function for specifying emission probabilities. The model leads to a conceptually clear mastery criterion with two thresholds. The first threshold specifies what degree of knowledge we consider to be sufficient for mastery. The second threshold specifies the degree of uncertainty we are willing to tolerate in the mastery decision. We then compare this criterion to other mastery criteria and discuss relation to previous work.

2   Modeling Uncertainty and Degrees of Knowledge

The BKT model provides a conceptual treatment of uncertainty, but does not address the degrees of knowledge, whereas logistic models model different degrees of knowledge, but do not address uncertainty in systematic way. We can address both these aspects by using a more general hidden Markov model than BKT.

2.1   LogisticHMM Model

A general Hidden markov model (HMM) models a process with a discrete latent state and noisy observations. A state at time t is denoted q_t, observation is denoted O_t. An HMM has the following elements:

- discrete set of latent states $\{s_0, s_1, \ldots, s_{n-1}\}$ of size n,
- discrete set of of observation $\{o_0, o_1, \ldots, o_{m-1}\}$ of size m,
- transition probabilities $T_{ij} = P(q_{t+1} = s_j | q_t = s_i)$ (a matrix $n \times n$ with rows summing to 1),
- emission probabilities $E_{ij} = P(O_t = o_j | q_t = s_i)$ (a matrix $n \times m$ with rows summing to 1),
- initial state probabilities: $\pi_i = P(q_1 = s_i)$.

For discussion of mastery criteria we propose "LogisticHMM" – a special version of the HMM that is general enough to generalize both the BKT and logistic models, and yet specific enough to be practically applicable (e.g., it has a small number of parameters). When modeling knowledge, the n latent states correspond to skill modeled with n degrees of knowledge. The observations correspond to learners answers to questions. We consider only the basic case with two observations: correct and incorrect.

Transition probabilities model learning. The basic version is to consider a single parameter l (speed of learning) and define the transition function as:

- $T_{ii} = 1 - l$ (learning did not occur and learner states in the same state),
- $T_{i(i+1)} = l$ (a learner learned and moves to the next knowledge states),
- T_{ij} is zero in all other cases (i.e., we model neither forgetting, nor sudden large increases in knowledge).

The emission probabilities are specified using the logistic function:

$$P(correct|s_i) = \sigma(a(i/(n-1) - b)) \tag{1}$$

where $\sigma(x) = 1/(1 + e^{-x})$ is the logistic function and a, b are parameters that specify the difficulty b and discrimination a of the modeled knowledge component. Figure 1 provides an illustration of the emission probabilities.

The model can be easily generalized. For example, we can model forgetting or more important increases in knowledge in transition probabilities. For observations we can consider more general distribution functions over more fine-grained observations, e.g., using partial credit scoring, utilizing response times, or taking into account difficulty of individual items. Distribution of the initial skill estimate can be used to incorporate information from other KCs (prerequisite skills). However, for our discussion of relations of modeling and mastery learning the presented version is sufficient.

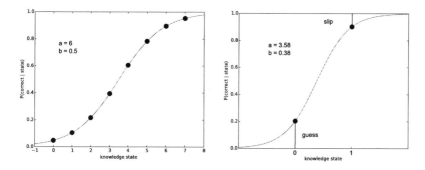

Fig. 1. Examples of emission probabilities in the LogisticHMM model. Left: A running example used throughout the paper. Right: An example illustrating that BKT is a special case of the LogisticHMM model.

2.2 BKT and Logistic Models as Special Versions

BKT and logistic models can be seen as special versions of the model or closely approximated by special versions of the model. The standard Bayesian knowledge tracing [3] is a hidden Markov model where skill is a binary latent variable (either learned or unlearned). The model has 4 parameters: P_i is the probability that the skill is initially learned, P_l is the probability of learning a skill in one step, P_s is the probability of an incorrect answer when the skill is learned (slip), and P_g is the probability of a correct answer when the skill is unlearned (guess). This can be expressed a special case of our LogisticHMM for $n = 2$. The probability that the skill is initially learned and the probability of learning a skill in one step remain the same. The slip and guess parameters can be transformed into a, b parameters without loss of generality. Figure 1 (right) provides illustration of the basic relation. By substituting $n = 2$ and $i = 0, i = 1$ into Eq. 1 we get: $P_g = \sigma(-ab); (1 - P_s) = \sigma(a(1 - b))$. From this we can solve for a, b:

$$a = logit(1 - P_s) - logit(P_g)$$
$$b = -logit(P_g)/a$$

where *logit* is the inverse of logistic function, i.e., $logit(p) = \log((1 - p)/p)$.

Logistic models utilize continuous skill, but from practical perspective the difference between continuous skill and discrete skill with large n is negligible. Even $n = 10$ should be in most practical cases sufficient, since the model clearly involves other, more important simplification with respect to the reality, and thus the difference between continuous skill and its discretized approximation is not a fundamental one.

2.3 Using the Model in Mastery Criterion

Given a sequence of observations, the skill estimates can be computed using the standard forward algorithm for HMMs, i.e., using the Bayes theorem for computing the posterior distribution after the observation and updating it with the transition probability. Specifically, for our case the computation can be performed as follows. The skill estimate after observing t answers is $\boldsymbol{p}_t$ – a vector of length n summing to one; p_{ti} is the probability of student being in the state i at time t. Initial estimate is given by the initial state probabilities: $\boldsymbol{p}_0 = \pi$. The estimate for $\boldsymbol{p}_{t+1}$ is computed from the estimate $\boldsymbol{p}_t$ by:

1. Taking into account the observation o_t at $t + 1$ we compute an auxiliary estimate $\boldsymbol{p}'_{t+1}$:

$$p'_{(t+1)i} \propto p_{ti} L(o_t | s_i)$$

   where $L(o_t | s_i)$ is the likelihood of observing a given answer, i.e., $\sigma(a(i/(n-1)) - b)$ for a correct answer and $1 - \sigma(a(i/(n-1) - b))$ for an incorrect answer.
2. Updating $\boldsymbol{p}'_{t+1}$ by transition probabilities we obtain the new estimate $\boldsymbol{p}_{t+1}$:

$$p_{(t+1)i} \propto \sum_j p'_{(t+1)j} T_{ji}$$

Both vectors $\boldsymbol{p}'_{t+1}$ and $\boldsymbol{p}_{t+1}$ need to be normalized to sum to one. Note that the procedure is just a slightly more general version of the commonly used procedure for computing skill estimate under the Bayesian knowledge tracing model [12].

   Figure 2 shows a specific illustration using our running example from Fig. 1 with the learning speed $l = 0.3$. The initial distribution is depicted in the first graph; the other three graphs show the estimated skill distribution after 5th, 10th, and 19th answer.

   With this model we can do mastery detection with systematic treatment of uncertainty and degrees of knowledge. The mastery criterion has two parameters:

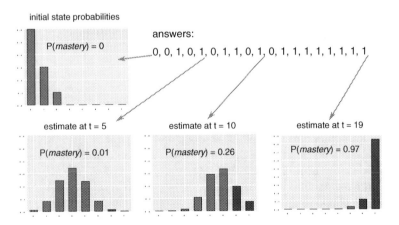

Fig. 2. Example of model estimates for a sample sequence of answers. The diagrams show estimated skill before the first attempt (i.e., the initial distribution π) and after the 5th, 10th, and 19th attempts. The probability of mastery is computed for the mastery state 6 ($T_m = 6$).

- threshold T_m specifying which state is sufficient for mastery,
- threshold T_u specifying how certain we want to be.

We declare mastery when the probability that the skill is larger than T_m is larger than T_u, i.e., $P(\theta \geq T_m) \geq T_u$. For the example in Fig. 2 with $T_m = 6$ and $T_u = 0.95$ mastery is declared after the 19th answer.

3 Comparison with Other Mastery Criteria

The presented model provides a conceptually clear approach to thresholds in mastery criteria. Is this just a conceptual tool for thinking about mastery, or does the usage of the model also lead to practically important differences in mastery decisions?

Evaluation of mastery criteria is very complex. For data from real systems we do not have "ground truth", so it is difficult to perform fair comparison of different criteria [13]. Moreover, the performance of criteria interacts with issues like parameter fitting of used models. Therefore, to explore our question we perform experiments with simulated data – comparing the behavior of criteria based on the LogisticHMM model with other commonly used criteria. We use the following approach. Using the LogisticHMM model we generate simulated learner data. For the generated data we perform mastery decision using both the LogisticHMM model and other mastery criteria. We compare the decision to the ground truth and analyze their agreement.

This is, of course, a simplified setting. It is also optimistic for the LogisticHMM model, since we avoid the issue of parameter fitting and use the same model parameters for generating the data and making the mastery decisions. Our purpose, however, is not to evaluate whether the LogisticHMM *is* better than other criteria, but whether it *could* be better and under what circumstances.

3.1 Comparison with N Consecutive Correct Criterion

If the noise in observations is low (parameter a in the LogisticHMM model is high), then even the the basic N consecutive correct (NCC) criterion leads to good estimates. By a suitable choice of N in the NCC criterion we can achieve nearly the same decisions as by the LogisticHMM model. In these cases the advantage of the LogisticHMM model is only the better interpretability of threshold parameters.

The NCC criterion has worse performance when observations are noisy (parameter a in the LogisticHMM model is low). Intuitively, this is because the NCC criterion has very limited "memory" – once incorrect answer is observed, the counting of correct answers starts from zero and all information about previous attempts is forbidden. When observations are noisy, incorrect answers are relatively common even for skilled learners and thus it is advantageous to remember a summary of previous performance, which the LogisticHMM model does using the estimated skill distribution.

3.2 Comparison with Exponential Moving Average

Simple, yet flexible and pragmatically advantageous approach to mastery decision is the exponential moving average (EMA) approach [13]. With this approach we compute the exponentially weighted average of past answers and compare this statistics to a threshold. The moving average can be, of course, consider also with other weights; the exponential weighting has the advantage that it can be computed without the need to store and access the whole history of learners attempts. It can be computed using the update rule $\theta_k = \alpha \cdot \theta_{k-1} + (1-\alpha) \cdot c_k$, where θ_k is the skill estimate after k-th answer, c_k is the correctness of the k-th answer, and α is a discounting parameter, which controls the relative weight of recent attempts. The mastery criterion is the basic comparison to a threshold: $\theta_k \geq T$.

This approach overcomes the NCC limitation of "limited memory" – the skill estimate θ_k now summarizes the whole history of answers, just giving the more recent attempts more weight. The approach has two parameters: α and T. Results of experiments with simulated data suggest that by tuning these parameters the EMA approach can quite well imitate the LogisticHMM – the correlation of their decisions is often over 0.9. However, the exact setting and interpretation of these parameters is not straightforward. For example, the optimal value of α depends not just on both the requested degree of mastery and level of uncertainty, but also on the the expected speed of learning (if learning is fast, α should be low, so that the estimate is not influenced much by old data).

Table 1. Best EMA parameters for different setting of threshold parameters for the running example from Fig. 1 (with $l = 0.1$ and the initial state distribution same as in Fig. 2).

Best fitting parameter α						
$T_m \backslash T_u$	0.6	0.7	0.8	0.9	0.95	0.98
5	0.85	0.85	0.9	0.85	0.9	0.9
6	0.85	0.85	0.9	0.9	0.85	0.9
7	0.9	0.85	0.9	0.9	0.95	0.9
Best fitting parameter T						
$T_m \backslash T_u$	0.6	0.7	0.8	0.9	0.95	0.98
5	0.65	0.7	0.65	0.8	0.75	0.8
6	0.8	0.85	0.8	0.85	0.95	0.92
7	0.85	0.92	0.9	0.92	0.85	0.97

Table 1 provides a specific illustration. For the LogisticHMM illustrated in Fig. 1 (with $l = 0.1$), we have fitted the optimal values of α and T of the EMA approach. The values were fitted using a grid search while trying to optimize the agreement of mastery decision between the LogisticHMM model and the EMA approach (for 1000 simulated learners). As we can see, both these parameters change depending on both T_m and T_u, i.e., they are not easily linked to the interpretable parameters of the LogisticHMM approach.

3.3 Comparison with Bayesian Knowledge Tracing

The BKT model is typically used for detecting mastery using the basic threshold policy. The model estimates the probability of being in the learned states and declares mastery when this probability is over a given threshold T (with the commonly used value 0.95). Under the assumption of binary knowledge state, this method has a clear interpretation – it uses a threshold on the uncertainty of the skill estimate. However, when the learner performance is based on multiple degrees of knowledge, the BKT model estimate starts to combine both uncertainty and degrees of knowledge and becomes hard to interpret.

As a specific example, consider our running example from Fig. 1 (with $l = 0.3$) and let us use the BKT model to do mastery decisions for this case. At first, we need to estimate the BKT parameters. Note that the fitted parameters of BKT depend on the number of attempts per learner that we use for fitting (this aspect has been previously noted [14], but mostly it is not taken into account in literature):

	init	learn	guess	slip
15 attempts per learner	0.01	0.10	0.12	0.31
50 attempts per learner	0.00	0.11	0.18	0.07

In both cases we can notice the relatively high guess and slip parameters. These do not correspond to the behaviour of learners – according to the model that generated the data, learners who really know the topic have very high probability of answering correctly. The high guess and slip parameters are due to the simplifying binary assumption of BKT. BKT parameters reported in research paper often have high guess and slip parameters. As this example illustrates, the reason for this may be inappropriateness of the model assumptions rather than high propensity of students to slip or guess.

If we use the common 0.95 threshold under these circumstances, BKT model leads to premature declaration of mastery for all learners. Figure 3 provides illustration that shows the results for our running example. Each dot corresponds to one simulated learner. The x axis shows the ground truth mastery (when did the learner reach the mastery state). The y axis shows when the mastery was declared according to the BKT model and according to the LogisticHMM (which uses the same parameters as the ground truth model, but estimates mastery from the generated noisy observations). Both the LogisticHMM and BKT model use the threshold 0.95 on uncertainty. As we can see, the LogisticHMM mastery estimates lag behind the ground truth moments of mastery. This is necessary – if we want to detect mastery with reasonable certainty from noisy observations, there is a necessary lag. The BKT model, on the other hand, nearly always declares mastery too early, which is an unwelcomed behaviour that is caused by the unsatisfied assumptions of the model.

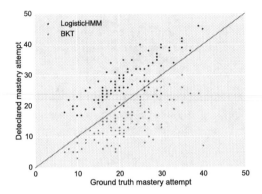

Fig. 3. Comparison of mastery decisions made by the LogisticHMM model and th BKT model with the threshold on uncertainty 0.95.

4   Discussion and Related Work

We presented a proposal for conceptual approach to mastery learning based on a specific version of the hidden Markov model and compared the mastery criterion based on this model to several common mastery criteria. We now discuss consequences of this work to practical applications and relations to previous research.

4.1   Consequences for Practice

Although we present a new learner model, the point is not that this model should be used in implementations of educational systems. The use of the model would require additional steps, for example the choice of the number of states and parameter estimation, which we have not discussed. Based on our analysis of simulated data and on the general experience in the field of educational data mining, we do not expect that the model would bring a significant improvement in predictive accuracy or significantly different mastery decisions in real applications.

The main point of the model is that it provides conceptually clear way to think about mastery criteria and thresholds. Our experiments with mastery criteria suggest that simple criteria (specifically exponential moving average) may be expressive enough for practical purposes. However, such pragmatic approaches have parameters, which do not have clear interpretation and which are hard to set. We propose the LogisticHMM model primarily as tool for clarification and better usage of such more pragmatic approaches.

One specific clarification that our analysis brings concerns the interpretation of BKT in mastery learning. Based on the current research literature, one may be tempted to use the BKT model, fit it to the available data and use it for mastery decisions with a threshold 0.95 with an interpretation "mastery is declared when there is 95% certainty that the learner mastered the skill". This interpretation is, however, misleading. Unless the data correspond very closely to the strong assumptions of the BKT model, the interpretation is incorrect (possibly quite seriously).

The pragmatic conclusion for developers of educational systems can be formulated as follows: Instead of using a complex model that presents summary of knowledge as a single number, it may be preferable to utilize a simple approach that explicitly separates the estimated degree of knowledge the uncertainty of the estimate. Even using statistics like "average performance" and "number of attempts" may be in some cases sufficient. Such approach may lack statistical sophistication, but it can possibly provide similar decisions as complex models, clearer interpretability, and easier setting of thresholds.

4.2   Learner Modeling

Another purpose of the proposed LogisticHMM model is that it connects and clarifies previous research on learner modeling using BKT and logistic models. Our discussion highlights the simplifying assumption of binary knowledge state in the BKT model. On one hand, this assumption is quite clear and explicit in the model and was appropriate for the original use of the model in cognitive tutors [3]. However, the model is now widely used, often in situations where the assumption of binary knowledge is not appropriate. Previous work has proposed BKT extension with multiple states ("spectral BKT") [4], but such work is currently marginal in the field.

Recently, several works have tried to combine BKT and models based on logistic function. This has been done specifically in two closely related approaches: one based on incorporation of features to knowledge tracing [5], another using integration of latent-factors and knowledge tracing [8]. Although these approaches enable inclusion of "learners ability" into BKT and utilize the logistic function for predictions, they still keep the basic BKT assumption of binary knowledge state. Moreover, these works focused on predicting learner performance and not on mastery criteria.

A fully conceptual approach to treatment of uncertainty and skill estimation is to use dynamic Bayesian networks [2,6], which can be used to capture relations between skill. Bayesian networks provide clean conceptual approach, but are difficult to apply in a practical implementation (e.g., it is difficult to specify or fit model parameters). Existing realization thus typically revert to simplifying assumptions, specifically to the assumption of binary knowledge state for each skill.

Bayesian methods in connection with mastery criteria have been used in computerized adaptive testing [9,18]. But the context of testing has several differences from the context of online educational systems, the main difference is learning – in the context of testing the models typically assume that knowledge is not changing during the test; in educational systems the main goal is to increase knowledge during practice and thus the change of knowledge is a fundamental aspect of models.

4.3   More General Stopping Criteria

In this work we have studied the problem of stopping practice in the case of mastery. The stopping problem can be formulated more generally – we may want to stop the practice once asking more questions does not have any merit. Specifically, in addition to mastery we may want to detect "wheel-spinning learners" who are unable to master a topic [1]. Previous research have proposed criteria that can deal with this more general problem: instructional policies called predictive similarity [16] and predictive stability [7]. These works, however, pay little attention to the choice of thresholds. Specifically, they add a parameter ϵ, which specifies the size of the difference in model predictions that is considered large enough to warrant further practice. It is not clear how to set and interpret this parameter.

A more conceptual approach to the general stopping problem could be mixture modeling, which has been previously proposed for modeling individual learning curves [17]. We can use a mixture model, with one component specifying learners who are improving and are able to eventually reach mastery and a second component specifying wheel-spinning learners. Using such model we can estimate the probability that a learner belongs to each class. This leads to a stopping criterion where thresholds are probabilities with clear interpretation.

References

1. Beck, J.E., Gong, Y.: Wheel-spinning: students who fail to master a skill. In: Lane, H.C., Yacef, K., Mostow, J., Pavlik, P. (eds.) AIED 2013. LNCS (LNAI), vol. 7926, pp. 431–440. Springer, Heidelberg (2013). https://doi.org/10.1007/978-3-642-39112-5_44
2. Conati, C., Gertner, A., Vanlehn, K.: Using Bayesian networks to manage uncertainty in student modeling. User Model. User Adap. Inter. **12**(4), 371–417 (2002)
3. Corbett, A.T., Anderson, J.R.: Knowledge tracing: modeling the acquisition of procedural knowledge. User Model. User Adap. Inter. **4**(4), 253–278 (1994)
4. Falakmasir, M., Yudelson, M., Ritter, S., Koedinger, K.: Spectral Bayesian knowledge tracing. In: Proceedings of Educational Data Mining, pp. 360–363 (2015)
5. González-Brenes, J., Huang, Y., Brusilovsky, P.: General features in knowledge tracing: applications to multiple subskills, temporal item response theory, and expert knowledge. In: Proceedings of Educational Data Mining, pp. 84–91 (2014)
6. Kaeser, T., Klingler, S., Schwing, A.G., Gross, M.: Dynamic Bayesian networks for student modeling. IEEE Trans. Learn. Technol. (2017)
7. Käser, T., Klingler, S., Gross, M.: When to stop?: Towards universal instructional policies. In: Proceedings of Learning Analytics & Knowledge, pp. 289–298. ACM (2016)
8. Khajah, M., Wing, R.M., Lindsey, R.V., Mozer, M.C.: Integrating latent-factor and knowledge-tracing models to predict individual differences in learning. In: Proceedings of Educational Data Mining (2014)
9. Lewis, C., Sheehan, K.: Using Bayesian decision theory to design a computerized mastery test. Appl. Psychol. Meas. **14**(4), 367–386 (1990)
10. Pavlik, P.I., Cen, H., Koedinger, K.R.: Performance factors analysis-a new alternative to knowledge tracing. In: Proceedings of Artificial Intelligence in Education, pp. 531–538. IOS Press (2009)

11. Pelánek, R.: Applications of the ELO rating system in adaptive educational systems. Comput. Educ. **98**, 169–179 (2016)
12. Pelánek, R.: Bayesian knowledge tracing, logistic models, and beyond: an overview of learner modeling techniques. User Model. User Adap. Inter. **27**(3), 313–350 (2017)
13. Pelánek, R., Řihák, J.: Experimental analysis of mastery learning criteria. In: Proceedings of User Modelling, Adaptation and Personalization, pp. 156–163. ACM (2017)
14. Pelánek, R., Řihák, J., Papoušek, J.: Impact of data collection on interpretation and evaluation of student model. In: Proceedings of Learning Analytics & Knowledge, pp. 40–47. ACM (2016)
15. Ritter, S., Yudelson, M., Fancsali, S.E., Berman, S.R.: How mastery learning works at scale. In: Proceedings of ACM Conference on Learning@Scale, pp. 71–79. ACM (2016)
16. Rollinson, J., Brunskill, E.: From predictive models to instructional policies. In: Proceedings of Educational Data Mining, pp. 179–186 (2015)
17. Streeter, M.: Mixture modeling of individual learning curves. In: Proceedings of Educational Data Mining. pp. 45–52 (2015)
18. Vos, H.J.: A bayesian procedure in the context of sequential mastery testing. Psicológica **21**(1), 191–211 (2000)

Reciprocal Content Recommendation for Peer Learning Study Sessions

Boyd A. Potts[✉], Hassan Khosravi, and Carl Reidsema

The University of Queensland, Brisbane, Australia
b.potts@uqconnect.edu.au

Abstract. Recognition of peer learning as a valuable supplement to formal education has lead to a rich literature formalising peer learning as an institutional resource. Facilitating peer learning support sessions alone however, without providing guidance or context, risks being ineffective in terms of any targeted, measurable effects on learning. Building on an existing open-source, student-facing platform called RiPPLE, which recommends peer study sessions based on the availability, competencies and compatibility of learners, this paper aims to supplement these study sessions by providing content from a repository of multiple-choice questions to facilitate topical discussion and aid productiveness. We exploit a knowledge tracing algorithm alongside a simple Gaussian scoring model to select questions that promote relevant learning and that reciprocally meet the expectations of both learners. Primary results using synthetic data indicate that the model works well at scale in terms of the number of sessions and number of items recommended, and capably recommends from a large repository the content that best approximates a proposed difficulty gradient.

Keywords: Reciprocal recommender · Peer learning · Peer support RecSysTEL

1 Introduction

The use of peers in teaching, mentoring or other learning support roles has long been recognised as a valuable addition to the learning environment and has developed from early beginnings in understaffed village schools [8] to the development of formalised, systematic guidelines [24]. The proposed academic and social benefit to students' engagement in formal or informal peer support forms the basis of a rich body of literature in education and psychology, grounded in a fundamental acknowledgement of the importance of peers in successful learning and positive university experience. Learners who engage in peer learning and peer support not only contribute to the existing community, but can create entirely new communities of practice [3].

These communities can be supplemented with fit-for-purpose technology to increase the frequency of interaction and communication between students and

C. Penstein Rosé et al. (Eds.): AIED 2018, LNAI 10947, pp. 462–475, 2018.
https://doi.org/10.1007/978-3-319-93843-1_34

create an awareness of a community for them to "belong" to and draw upon as a resource over the course of their studies [6].

However, peer interactions are often topically disconnected from academic objectives and even with the intent to provide academic support [17], simply encouraging connectedness in learning environments risks being ineffective in terms of any targeted, measurable effects on learning. As part a comprehensive evaluation of students' experiences with Peer Assisted Study Sessions (PASS), [16] surveyed participating students over their satisfaction and the program's effectiveness. In an open-ended question of students' suggestions for improving the PASS program, 36% of usable responses related to the focus of the sessions. More specifically, approximately half of this group wanted questions and examples reflecting those in exams and assignments. The other half were concerned specifically with a standard of preparation in PASS sessions, such as an organised outline for each session, commenting that some facilitators were poorly organised. Among the quoted examples of feedback in [16] was "More structure, follow some kind of plan would be helpful" p11. Other feedback included a desire for notes/handouts for the session and even some feedback that tutors were not able to answer specific questions about the content. These results demonstrate that it is not enough to simply arrange study sessions with peers without any guidance or support.

RiPPLE (Recommendation in Personalised Peer Learning Environments) [12] is an open-source, adaptive, crowdsourced, web-based, student-facing learning platform that provides personalised content and peer learning support tailored to the needs of each individual at scale. RiPPLE has two main features: (1) recommendation of formative exercises based on the knowledge state of each learner, as described in [13]; and recommendation of peer learning study sessions based on the availability, learning preferences and needs of each learner, as described in [23].

In this paper, we extend the functionality of RiPPLE to use the knowledge state of users to recommend content from the RiPPLE repository for the scheduled study sessions, addressing the peer learning problems outlined by [17] and [16]. We propose that supplementing these sessions will facilitate communication between peers and productivity. The selection of items is based on the students' abilities able to answer a given item correctly given their competencies (modelled using BKT), and the students' roles in the session (providing or receiving support). In preparation for trialling RiPPLE in four large face-to-face courses, an initial set of experiments were conducted. The evaluation concentrates on the feasibility of the recommender by evaluating the impacts of the size of the question repository and model parameter settings. Synthetic data sets were created for this purpose. Primary results indicate that the system can recommend content for study sessions that reciprocally meets the expectations of both learners.

2 Background

The area of reciprocal content recommendation is closely related to two research areas: (1) knowledge tracing, which is briefly covered in Sect. 2.1; and two subfields tied to recommender systems, namely, recommender systems in technology enhanced learning (RecSysTEL) and reciprocal recommender systems, which are briefly covered in Sect. 2.2.

2.1 Knowledge Tracing

Heavily studied within the intelligent tutoring community [4], knowledge tracing is the task of modeling the knowledge state of students so that their future performance on learning activities can accurately be predicted [5]. The Bayesian Knowledge tracing (BKT) algorithm [5] is one of the most prominent methods used for knowledge tracing, using Hidden Markov Models to capture the student knowledge states as a set of binary variables representing whether or not a concept has been mastered.

BKT has received significant attention and improvement since it was first proposed. [1] introduced parameters for slipping (where a student has the required skill but mistakenly provides the wrong answer) and guessing (where a student provides the right answer despite not having the required skill for solving the problem). Later, [18] effectively extended BKT to capture item difficulty which led to improved prediction accuracy. More recently, [29] introducing a new set of parameters capturing prior knowledge of individual learners further improved BKT. Other algorithms with comparable or superior predictive power to BKT have also been proposed for predicting student performance, such as the Learning Factors Analysis Framework [2] and the Performance Factor Analysis framework [19]. [11] incorporated Item Response theory (IRT) into knowledge tracing, and more recently, [20,25] used recurrent neural networks for deep knowledge tracing.

Knowledge tracing algorithms are often used as a part of a intelligent tutoring systems [4] or in adaptive learning environments [5] to provide content for an individual learner. In the work presented in this paper, we use the algorithms developed by [13] to provide reciprocal content to satisfy the roles of two learners attending the study session.

2.2 RecSysTEL and Reciprocal Recommender Systems

Recommender systems for technology enhanced learning is an active and rapidly evolving research field. In the educational setting, much of the primary research on recommender systems is directed at the recommendation of relevant content and resources for learning, such as context-aware recommendations on learning objects [14], resources within e-learning environments to expand or reinforce knowledge [15], and appropriate exercises based on students' performance predictions [26]. More broadly, researchers with a focus on intelligent tutoring systems and adaptive learning environments have been using knowledge tracing algorithms for recommendation of content to learners.

Reciprocal recommender systems have widely applied to online dating [21], job matching [10], and social networking [9]. They comprise the popular approach to any problem involving a match between two or more entities, tailored by the best consideration of the specific needs and constraints of the immediate environment. Fundamentally they seek solutions such as a list of recommendations that fulfill users' preferences and expectations to a higher degree than competing items. In reciprocal recommendation, the preferences of two or more users must be satisfied concurrently. That is, a recommendation is made on the extent to which the preferences of one user are compatible with those of another, inducing a higher level of complexity than other recommender systems [22].

Previous work by [23] developed a reciprocal recommender in RiPPLE that allows students to find peers and establish study sessions for the purposes of providing or receiving topical peer support and find study partners. Peers were matched on the basis of coursework competencies and compatibility of preferences, such as weekly availability, and received a short list of recommendations with invitations to connect with recommended peers through the platform (Fig. 1).

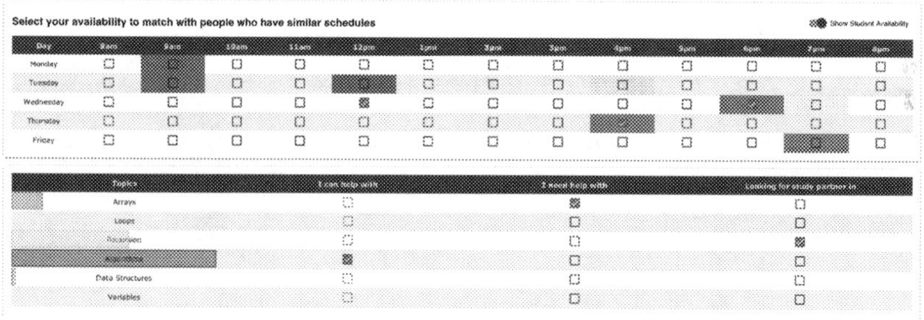

Fig. 1. User preferences in RiPPLE.

3   Formal Notation and Problem Formulation

Let $U_N = \{u_1 \ldots u_N\}$ denote the set of users that are enrolled in a course in RiPPLE, where u_n and $u_{n'}$ refer to arbitrary users.

Let $Q_M = \{q_1 \ldots q_M\}$ denote the repository of the questions that are available to users in a course in RiPPLE, where q_m and $q_{m'}$ refer to arbitrary questions. A two-dimensional array $A_{N \times M}$ keeps track of question answers, where $a_{nm} = 1$ indicates that user u_n has answered question q_m correctly, and $a_{nm} = 0$ indicates that user u_n has answered question q_m incorrectly.

Each course consists of a set of knowledge units $\Delta_L = \{\delta_1 \ldots \delta_L\}$ referred to as a knowledge space, where δ_l refers to an arbitrary knowledge unit. Questions can be tagged with one or more knowledge units; $\Omega_{M \times L}$ is a two-dimensional array, where ω_{ml} is 1 if question q_m is tagged with δ_l and 0 otherwise. A two-dimensional array $\Lambda_{N \times L}$ is used for representing students' knowledge states approximated by the system, where λ_{nl} represents the knowledge state of u_n on δ_l. This information is used to produce a two-dimensional array $\Phi_{N \times M}$, where ϕ_{nm} shows the probability of user u_n answering question q_m correctly. Values in Φ are computed using algorithms introduced by Khosravi et al. in [13].

Students can hold different roles for participation in peer learning sessions, where e_1 is used to present providing peer learning support, e_2 for seeking peer learning support.

Using algorithms introduced by Potts et al. in [23], a list of study sessions is generated. Each study session is in the form $[u_n, u_{n'}, \delta]$ indicating that user u_n has received recommendation to connect with user $u_{n'}$ on topics δ. The notion of a study session is extended with information from $\Phi_{N \times M}$ to be of the form $[u_n, u_{n'}, \delta, Q'_k]$ indicating that a list of k questions $Q'_k \in Q_M$ are to be covered during the session.

4   Reciprocal Content Recommendation

This section focuses on the problem of how best to algorithmically select a suitable set of multiple choice questions for a study session between two peers, that match their role preferences (providing support or receiving support) and provide learning opportunities in terms of subjective difficulty, from a large repository of items. We proceeded within the framework of the following propositions:

1. A user receiving support, u_n, should work through a set of items of increasing difficulty so as to initially orient the session and increasingly provide opportunities for new learning; and
2. The user providing support, $u_{n'}$, should be able to answer these same questions with a high probability of being correct. This should be true of all items such that $u_{n'}$ can adequately assist in learning that u_n would be less likely to accomplish without assistance.

With respect to proposition 1, a difficulty gradient d was computed based on the nominated maximum probability that a user answers an item correctly (p_{max}), the nominated minimum probability that a user answers an item correctly (p_{min}) and the number of items to be recommended for a session (k), as input parameters for the characteristic linear slope function

$$d(p_{min}, p_{max}, k) = \frac{p_{min} - p_{max}}{k - 1} \qquad (1)$$

where d represents the increase in subjective item difficulty (with respect to ϕ_{nm}; the probability of user u_n answering question q_m correctly) for each sequential item in the recommended set of k items.

Figure 2 illustrates the concept of the difficulty gradient in terms of the zone of proximal development (ZPD) [28], a popular concept in learning and education that refers to the range of tasks that a learner is capable of completing if provided with guidance. The ZPD exists between those tasks that can be done autonomously and those that are beyond the person's current capability. Proposition 1 aims to traverse outward with respect to the ZPD of the user receiving support as shown in Fig. 2a.

It is important to note that the parameter values of p_{min} and p_{max} can be system-set, applying to all users in seeking-support role. Recall that values in Φ

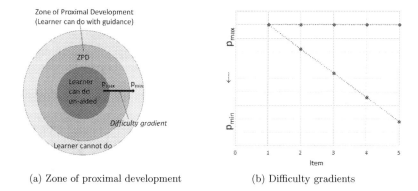

(a) Zone of proximal development   (b) Difficulty gradients

Fig. 2. Difficulty gradients and relationship to the zone of proximal development

are inherently personalised to each user, reflecting the probability that a given user answers the item correctly as computed by the algorithm from [13]. As such, personalised item recommendations will result from system-set values of p_{min} and p_{max} for all users without the need for users to specify these variably as explicit preferences.

The slope function in Eq. 1 was used to create a one-dimensional array, $D_k = \{d_1, d_2, ..., d_k\}$, where elements d_i represent the difficulty of item $i \in \{1, 2, ..., k\}$ across the set of k recommendations. Setting $p_{min} < p_{max}$ ensures items increase in subjective difficulty.

Under proposition 2, users in a providing support role should have $p_{min} = p_{max}$ and should be a high value. That is, for an item to be a suitable inclusion for a study session in which a user is providing support, that user should be able to answer the item correctly with a high probability. This should be true of all k items. This feature aims to address the feedback in [27] that peer facilitators were unable to answer some questions relating to the session content. Study material for each session should take into account the known or inferred competencies of each participant as a basis for selecting the study items to be included in the session plan.

Then for a given difficulty gradient, a scoring function for multiple choice items in the repository that preferences those that most closely align with the gradient is required. That is, a function with maxima at each point d_k in the difficulty gradient with the fitness of any given item assessed by the function height.

Tagged items in the repository were assessed for fitness for each point in D, using a Gaussian function g,

$$g(\phi_{nm}, d_i, \sigma, \delta_l) = \begin{cases} 0 & \delta_l = 0 \\ \\ e^{\frac{-(\phi_{nm}-d_i)^2}{2\sigma^2}} & \delta_l = 1 \end{cases} \tag{2}$$

such that items with subjective difficulties (ϕ_{nm}; the probability of the user answering the item correctly) that more closely approximated the desired values in D received higher scores than those that did not. Items that are not tagged as belonging to the relevant topic ($\delta_l = 0$) receive a score of zero.

The probability of an item being allocated to a less-than-optimal position (i.e. relatively too hard or easy compared to d_i) in D is controlled by the value of σ. Using known properties of the standard normal distribution (z-scores) we calculated the value of σ using the function $\sigma(d, z) = \frac{(d - \frac{d}{2})}{z}$.

For example, to ensure that the probability of an item being sub-optimally allocated to a position along D was less than .001, a value of $z = 3.1$ would be required.[1] For users providing support, setting $p_{min} = p_{max}$ results in a difficulty gradient of zero. Consequently $\sigma = 0$ incurs an undefined result of g. The function g in Eq. 2 therefore uses the same σ derived for the user receiving support. The effects of σ on recommendations are detailed in the evaluation section.

Figure 2b illustrates the values in the array D for two users, where the user providing support has $p_{min} = p_{max} = 1$, and the user receiving support has $p_{max} = 1$ and $p_{min} = .1$, resulting in $d = -.225$, giving $D = \{1, .775, .55, .325, .1\}$ and the set of Gaussian functions, centered on d_i, against which potential items were scored for their suitability for recommendation as the ith item in the set.

The first panel in Fig. 3 shows the function g for five items ($k = 5$) increasing in difficulty from $p_{max} = 1$ to $p_{min} = .1$ Topically-tagged items in the MCQ repository are evaluated for their suitability by the height of the relevant function centered on the desired difficulty d_i. For the user providing support, $p_{min} = p_{max} = 1$ resulting in all items being evaluated under the same g function with center $p_{min} = p_{max}$.

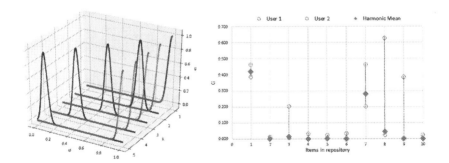

Fig. 3. Panel 1: Gaussian scoring functions along difficulty gradients with $k = 5$, $p_{min} = .1$, $p_{max} = 1$, $z = 3.1$ for the user receiving support (blue), and $p_{min} = p_{max} = 1$ for the user providing support (red). Items with difficulties more closely approximating the desired gradient receive higher scores than those that do not. Panel 2: Example scoring of ten candidate items for $k = 1$. Item 1 is recommended, having the highest harmonic mean of both users' function scores (cf. Table 1). (Color figure online)

---

[1] Evaluated as the probability that a random score under a standard normal distribution is greater than the midpoint between two sequential items, ($\frac{d}{2}$).

A three-dimensional array $G_{U \times Q \times k}$ is created in which g_{nmi} shows the height of the Gaussian function centered on d_i and evaluated at ϕ_{nm} for user u_n and question m, given by Eq. 2. The degree of fit for each item can be computed by the harmonic mean of the corresponding scores in G for u_n and $u_{n'}$ for each item. Those items with the highest fit were selected for recommendation. This is shown in the second panel of Fig. 3. Note that the harmonic mean gives preference to the score of the user receiving support. This was a design decision that recommendations should be made with the user receiving learning support as the priority.

A simple example is shown in Table 1 for $k = 3$, $p_{min} = .1$, $p_{max} = 1$, $z = 3.1$ and $N = 6$. The function has selected the set of items [1, 5, 2] as suitable for the study session (shown in bold). The user providing support has $p_{min} = p_{max} = 1$ for all items, and the user receiving support has items increasing in difficulty along gradient $D = [1, .55, .1]$. It is important to note again that the g scores reflect the extent to which the item's subjective difficulty (ϕ) for the individual user matches the values along the gradient. With respect to making recommendations, g scores (and their harmonic means) have ordinal, rather than cardinal, value. The actual ability of a user is reflected only in ϕ.

Table 1. Item scoring example

| Item | u_n Providing support | | | | $u_{n'}$ Receiving support | | | | Harmonic mean | | |
| | g_{nm} | | | | $g_{n'm}$ | | | | harmonic mean | | |
	ϕ	$d_1 = 1$	$d_2 = 1$	$d_3 = 1$	ϕ	$d_1 = 1$	$d_2 = .55$	$d_3 = .1$	fit_1	fit_2	fit_3
1	0.91	0.464	0.464	0.464	0.90	0.387	$< 10^{-3}$	$< 10^{-3}$	**0.422**	$< 10^{-3}$	$< 10^{-3}$
2	0.78	0.010	0.010	0.010	0.35	$< 10^{-3}$	0.022	0.003	$< 10^{-3}$	0.014	**0.004**
3	0.87	0.201	0.201	0.201	0.77	0.007	0.010	$< 10^{-3}$	0.013	0.019	$< 10^{-3}$
4	0.93	0.628	0.628	0.628	0.80	0.022	0.003	$< 10^{-3}$	0.043	0.005	$< 10^{-3}$
5	0.9	0.387	0.387	0.387	0.62	$< 10^{-3}$	0.628	$< 10^{-3}$	$< 10^{-3}$	**0.479**	$< 10^{-3}$
6	0.8	0.022	0.022	0.022	0.43	$< 10^{-3}$	0.255	$< 10^{-3}$	$< 10^{-3}$	0.041	$< 10^{-3}$

5   Algorithm

Pseudocode for the recommender is shown in Algorithm 1. It takes inputs of the session (S; an agreed study partnership for two users) and for the parameters described in Eqs. 1 and 2 generates a list (Q') of k items from the repository (Q) which are appended to the overall session recommendation (S) in RiPPLE. For brevity, we have referred to mentors and mentees in the pseudocode to represent providing and receiving support, respectively, but acknowledge these titles have different implications in the wider literature.

The function to find the highest reciprocal (harmonic mean) scores in line 16 searches the array for the maximum value and assigns that item to its corresponding gradient position in the set. Both the selected item (array row) and the position along the gradient (array column) are then assigned as empty sets, and the array is searched for the next maximum, and so on in a loop until all positions in the set have been assigned an item. For example, in Table 1 item 5, having the highest score in the array, was recommended first and allocated to its position (second) in the set. Both row 5 and column 2 were then emptied, and the new array consisting of only the remaining items and positions was searched, with item 1 being recommended to its position (first) in the set. This ensures that the recommendations are always the best available, without repeating items.

Algorithm 1. Recommending items

    Input : $S, \Phi_{N \times M}, k, p_{min}, p_{max}, \sigma$

1 $G_{U \times M \times k} = \{\}$;

2 $dMentor = \text{findOptimalDifLevels}(p_{max}, p_{max}, k)$;

3 $dMentee = \text{findOptimalDifLevels}(p_{min}, p_{max}, k)$;

4 **foreach** $studySession \in S$ **do**

5     $u_n = retrieveMentor(studySession)$;

6     $u'_n = retrieveMentee(studySession)$;

7     $\delta = retrieveTopics(studySession)$;

8     $reciprocalScore_{M \times k} = \{\}$;

9   **for** $m \leftarrow 0$ **to** M **do**

10   **for** $i \leftarrow 0$ **to** k **do**

11         $G_{nmi} = g(\phi_{nm}, dMentor_i, \sigma, \delta)$;

12         $G_{n'mi} = g(\phi_{n'm}, dMentee_i, \sigma, \delta)$;

13         $reciprocalScore_{mi} = harmonicMean(G_{nmi}, G_{n'mi})$;

14   **end**

15   **end**

16     $Q' \leftarrow findBestquestions(reciprocalScore)$;

17     $S'.append([u_n, u_{n'}, \delta, Q'])$;

18 **end**

19 **return** S';

---

6 Evaluation

6.1 Simulated Data

User data were simulated for 20,000 users, with competencies (α) drawn from a random normal distribution with mean $\mu = .65$ and standard deviation $sd = .25$. Users with competency greater or equal to .9 ($\mu + 1sd$) were assigned to providing support roles ($N = 1,565$), and users with competency less than or equal to .65 (μ) assigned to seeking support roles ($N = 10,017$). Item data were then simulated for 5000 questions (Q), with difficulties (β) between 0 and 1 drawn from a random uniform distribution.

Simulated user data for Φ were generated using the three parameter logistic model from classical Item Response Theory outlined in [7] as $\phi_{nm} = c + \frac{1-c}{1+e^{\beta-\alpha}}$, where β represents the difficulty level of question m, α represents the competency level of user u_n and c representing the probability of randomly guessing correctly (e.g. $c = .25$ for a four-choice question). We used a low value for random guess probability $c = .05$ to better reflect the current context, which is to encourage discussion and knowledge-building rather than simply selecting the correct response, and to better simulate the users' states of knowledge about the question were they to be given no opportunity to guess from a list of answers known to contain the correct response.

Simulated values of Φ typically ranged between $\approx .50$–$.75$ and $\approx .24$–$.67$ for providing support and seeking support users, respectively. Recommender parameters for all simulations were set to $p_{min} = .1$ and $p_{max} = 1$. Despite these values being outside the range of simulated values in Φ, the recommender functions were designed to capture the best fit from the available data, and setting $p_{max} = 1$ ensures that where required (such as in item 1), the item most likely to be correctly answered (highest ϕ value) is selected.

6.2   Scalability and Quality

Firstly, to test the recommender's ability to return the optimal items under a range of settings for σ, we used the simulated Φ data but planted ideal values for the relevant difficulty gradient at known items. If the recommender worked correctly, these items would be returned in the list of recommendations without interference from other items. Using a random sample of 300 study sessions (pairs of users) from the simulated data, and a high value of $k = 50$, it was found that all planted values were reliably selected by the recommender without error. This process was used to justify the theoretical correctness of the algorithm.

The quality of recommendations was conceptualised as the extent to which the subjective difficulties (ϕ_{nm}) of recommended items reflects the optimal difficulties calculated by the difficulty gradient D. This was approached using recommendations for $k = 5, 10, 20$ and 50 using independent random samples (with replacement) of 300 sessions from the simulated data set.

The **Root-Mean-Square Error** (RMSE) represents the standard deviation of the differences between model data and observed data and is widely used as a measure of accuracy. In each sampled partnership, the RMSE was calculated between the values in D (model) and the actual ϕ values of the items that were recommended (observed).

Spearman's rank correlation coefficient (Spearman's rho) is a measure of the dependence between item rankings in two sets. It is the nonparametric equivalent of Pearson's correlation (r), ranging from 0 to 1 and is appropriate for discrete ordinal variables. It was used in conjunction with the RMSE to assess the extent to which the difficulty of recommended items aligned with the model values in D. Specifically, for users receiving support Spearman's rho was used to check that recommended items were in ranked order of difficulty, given the difficulty gradient D.

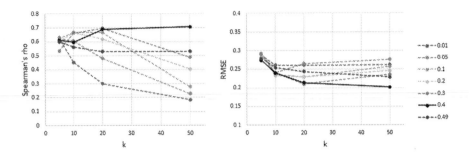

Fig. 4. Mean Spearman's correlation and Root-Mean-Square Error for n = 300 samples with varying k and overlap between Gaussian functions.

The average correlation was moderate-to-high and varied with the setting for z (controlling the overlap between sequential Gaussian functions). Recommendations using large values of z (incurring less overlap) degraded with higher values for k. Figure 4 shows the dependency between the amount of overlap and the quality measures. Interestingly this was independent of the number of items (Q) in the simulated data. The RMSE was both independent of the size of Q and k, consistently $\approx .27$. Simulations demonstrated that allowing an overlap value of $\approx .4$ (shown in bold lines) yielded the best recommendations, especially for higher values of k where restricting the overlap severely degraded the ability of recommendations to fit the difficulty gradient.

Running time was examined over a range of 5 to 50 items recommended (k) and a range of 100 to 500 study partnerships, for 3000 repository items. The algorithm runs in linear time for both dimensions as shown in Fig. 5. It is also linear in the number of repository items. In practice the number of recommended items k should be small, approximately five per hour of study, to encourage discussion and communication rather than having students complete as many multiple choice items as quickly as possible.

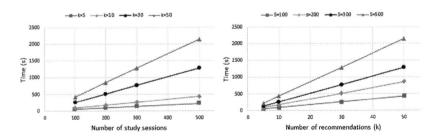

Fig. 5. Run time for variable k and number of study sessions with repository of 3000 items

7   Conclusion and Future Work

The aim of this paper was to recommend study content in the form of MCQs from a large repository to support peer learning study sessions. Items were recommended on the basis of their subjective difficulty for each user, derived through existing BKT algorithms, such that a set of recommended items conformed concurrently to two propositions - that items should increase in difficulty for the user who is receiving peer support, and that all items should be easily answered by the user providing support. A Gaussian scoring model was applied and using synthetic data containing known ideal values it was demonstrated that the recommender reliably finds the optimal items at scale for large numbers of users, recommendations and repositories of items. For simulated data (without ideal values), the root-mean-square error and Spearman's rank correlation of the recommended item difficulties and the proposed ideal difficulties were calculated to evaluate the extent to which recommendations reflected the desired difficulty gradient and correct ordering, respectively.

These statistics depend on the availability of data values that closely approximate the model gradient, and it is a reasonable limitation to expect in future testing with real students. Nonetheless, the moderate-to-high positive values of Spearman's coefficient demonstrates that the recommended ordering of items in increasing difficulty is achievable, and that the Gaussian model ensures the best items are chosen from those available. The recommender performs more consistently for smaller values of k, with the quality dependent on the overlap settings for higher values of k. The quality is otherwise unaffected by the size of the item repository or cohort of students.

A role for two users simply seeking study partners is available in [23] and not addressed by this paper. A preference model for two learners of approximately equal competency was deceptively more complicated than that of the providing/receiving support roles. For example, should recommended items attempt complementarity, such that items that are difficult for one user be answerable by the other and alternate in this fashion? If items are recommended on the basis of being similarly difficult (or easy) to both users, will effective learning occur? Users whose competencies fall between the range of the provider/supporter dichotomy used in this paper will need to be addressed in future work.

These simulations pave the way for online deployment and the incorporation of feedback mechanisms from real students who engage in peer learning through RiPPLE's recommendations. Simply collecting MCQ responses session data on students' progress would be a poor measurement of primary aim of stimulating discussion, interaction and learning. Indeed this measurement problem is a common limitation of many learning analytic tools, which often collect proxy indicators at best. Session feedback via well-designed but brief survey components will be valuable both in the refinement of the recommenders and in understanding users' engagement with, and effectiveness of, the content towards the contribution to theories of technology-enhanced learning. Properly designed, recommender systems such as those used by RiPPLE can be deployed as both learning resources and measurement tools for further research.

References

1. Baker, R.S.J., Corbett, A.T., Aleven, V.: More accurate student modeling through contextual estimation of slip and guess probabilities in bayesian knowledge tracing. In: Woolf, B.P., Aïmeur, E., Nkambou, R., Lajoie, S. (eds.) ITS 2008. LNCS, vol. 5091, pp. 406–415. Springer, Heidelberg (2008). https://doi.org/10.1007/978-3-540-69132-7_44

2. Cen, H., Koedinger, K., Junker, B.: Learning factors analysis – a general method for cognitive model evaluation and improvement. In: Ikeda, M., Ashley, K.D., Chan, T.-W. (eds.) ITS 2006. LNCS, vol. 4053, pp. 164–175. Springer, Heidelberg (2006). https://doi.org/10.1007/11774303_17

3. Conole, G.: Review of Pedagogical Models and Their Use in e-Learning. Open University, Milton Keynes (2010)

4. Corbett, A.: Cognitive computer tutors: solving the two-sigma problem. In: Bauer, M., Gmytrasiewicz, P.J., Vassileva, J. (eds.) UM 2001. LNCS (LNAI), vol. 2109, pp. 137–147. Springer, Heidelberg (2001). https://doi.org/10.1007/3-540-44566-8_14

5. Corbett, A.T., Anderson, J.R.: Knowledge tracing: modeling the acquisition of procedural knowledge. User Model. User-Adap. Inter. 4(4), 253–278 (1994)

6. Dawson, S.: A study of the relationship between student communication interaction and sense of community. Internet High. Educ. 9(3), 153–162 (2006)

7. Drasgow, F., Hulin, C.L.: Item response theory (1990)

8. Goldschmid, B., Goldschmid, M.L.: Peer teaching in higher education: a review. High. Educ. 5(1), 9–33 (1976)

9. Guy, I.: Social recommender systems. In: Ricci, F., Rokach, L., Shapira, B. (eds.) Recommender Systems Handbook, pp. 511–543. Springer, Boston, MA (2015). https://doi.org/10.1007/978-1-4899-7637-6_15

10. Hong, W., Zheng, S., Wang, H., Shi, J.: A job recommender system based on user clustering. J. Comput. 8(8), 1960–1967 (2013)

11. Khajah, M.M., Huang, Y., González-Brenes, J.P., Mozer, M.C., Brusilovsky, P.: Integrating knowledge tracing and item response theory: A tale of two frameworks. In: Proceedings of Workshop on Personalization Approaches in Learning Environments (PALE 2014) at the 22th International Conference on User Modeling, Adaptation, and Personalization, pp. 7–12. University of Pittsburgh (2014)

12. Khosravi, H.: Recommendation in personalised peer-learning environments. arXiv preprint arXiv:1712.03077 (2017)

13. Khosravi, H., Cooper, K., Kitto, K.: Riple: recommendation in peer-learning environments based on knowledge gaps and interests. JEDM-J. Educ. Data Min. 9(1), 42–67 (2017)

14. Lemire, D., Boley, H., McGrath, S., Ball, M.: Collaborative filtering and inference rules for context-aware learning object recommendation. Interact. Technol. Smart Educ. 2(3), 179–188 (2005)

15. Mangina, E., Kilbride, J.: Evaluation of keyphrase extraction algorithm and tiling process for a document/resource recommender within e-learning environments. Comput. Educ. 50(3), 807–820 (2008)

16. van der Meer, J., Scott, C.: Students experiences and perceptions of peer assisted study sessions: towards ongoing improvement. J. Peer Learn. 2(1), 3–22 (2009)

17. Newcomb, T.: A conversation with theodore newcomb. Psychol. Today, 73–80 (1974)

18. Pardos, Z., Heffernan, N.: Kt-idem: introducing item difficulty to the knowledge tracing model. In: User Modeling, Adaption and Personalization, pp. 243–254 (2011)

19. Pavlik Jr., P.I., Cen, H., Koedinger, K.R.: Performance factors analysis-a new alternative to knowledge tracing. Online Submission (2009)

20. Piech, C., Bassen, J., Huang, J., Ganguli, S., Sahami, M., Guibas, L.J., Sohl-Dickstein, J.: Deep knowledge tracing. In: Advances in Neural Information Processing Systems, pp. 505–513 (2015)

21. Pizzato, L., Rej, T., Akehurst, J., Koprinska, I., Yacef, K., Kay, J.: Recommending people to people: the nature of reciprocal recommenders with a case study in online dating. User Model. User-Adap. Inter. **23**(5), 447–488 (2013)

22. Pizzato, L., Rej, T., Chung, T., Yacef, K., Koprinska, I., Kay, J.: Reciprocal recommenders. In: 8th Workshop on Intelligent Techniques for Web Personalization and Recommender Systems, UMAP (2010)

23. Potts, B., Khosravi, H., Reidsema, C., Bakharia, A., Belonogoff, M., Fleming, M.: Reciprocal peer recommendation for learning purposes. In: Proceedings of the 8th International Conference on Learning Analytics and Knowledge (2018)

24. Ross, M.T., Cameron, H.S.: Peer assisted learning: a planning and implementation framework: amee guide no. 30. Med. Teach. **29**(6), 527–545 (2007)

25. Sha, L., Hong, P.: Neural knowledge tracing. Brain Function Assessment in Learning. LNCS (LNAI), vol. 10512, pp. 108–117. Springer, Cham (2017). https://doi.org/10.1007/978-3-319-67615-9_10

26. Thai-Nghe, N., Drumond, L., Horváth, T., Krohn-Grimberghe, A., Nanopoulos, A., Schmidt-Thieme, L.: Factorization techniques for predicting student performance. In: Educational Recommender Systems and Technologies: Practices and Challenges, pp. 129–153 (2011)

27. Van Der Heijden, B., Boon, J., Van der Klink, M., Meijs, E.: Employability enhancement through formal and informal learning: an empirical study among dutch non-academic university staff members. Int. J. Training Dev. **13**(1), 19–37 (2009)

28. Vygotsky, L.S.: Mind in Society: The Development of Higher Psychological Processes. Harvard University Press, Cambridge (1980)

29. Yudelson, M.V., Koedinger, K.R., Gordon, G.J.: Individualized bayesian knowledge tracing models. In: Lane, H.C., Yacef, K., Mostow, J., Pavlik, P. (eds.) AIED 2013. LNCS (LNAI), vol. 7926, pp. 171–180. Springer, Heidelberg (2013). https://doi.org/10.1007/978-3-642-39112-5_18

The Impact of Data Quantity and Source on the Quality of Data-Driven Hints for Programming

Thomas W. Price$^{(\boxtimes)}$ ⓘ, Rui Zhi, Yihuan Dong, Nicholas Lytle, and Tiffany Barnes

North Carolina State University, Raleigh, NC 27606, USA
{twprice,rzhi,ydong2,nalytle,tmbarnes}@ncsu.edu

Abstract. In the domain of programming, intelligent tutoring systems increasingly employ data-driven methods to automate hint generation. Evaluations of these systems have largely focused on whether they can reliably provide hints for most students, and how much data is needed to do so, rather than how useful the resulting hints are to students. We present a method for evaluating the quality of data-driven hints and how their quality is impacted by the data used to generate them. Using two datasets, we investigate how the quantity of data and the source of data (whether it comes from students or experts) impact one hint generation algorithm. We find that with student training data, hint quality stops improving after 15–20 training solutions and can decrease with additional data. We also find that student data outperforms a single expert solution but that a comprehensive set of expert solutions generally performs best.

Keywords: Data-driven hints · Programming · Hint quality
Cold start

1 Introduction

Intelligent tutoring systems (ITSs) increasingly use student data to drive their decision making. Rather than relying on extensive knowledge engineering, authors can employ data-driven methods to automate the development of both "outer loop" [27] components of an ITS (e.g. constructing [30] and improving [10] student models) and "inner loop" components (e.g. automatically generating hints [1] and worked examples [14]). Authors of data-driven systems argue that these approaches avoid the need for experts to spend time constructing complex domain models [1,23] and can lead to additional insights that experts alone would not achieve [10].

However, empirical evaluations of the costs and benefits of data-driven approaches are still rare. This is especially true in the case of data-driven hint generation, where student data is used to automatically generate hints, rather than relying on expert models (e.g. model tracing [3] or constraint-based modeling [13]). Many evaluations of data-driven hints have focused on whether a

© Springer International Publishing AG, part of Springer Nature 2018
C. Penstein Rosé et al. (Eds.): AIED 2018, LNAI 10947, pp. 476–490, 2018.
https://doi.org/10.1007/978-3-319-93843-1_35

system can reliably provide hints to students [16, 28], as well as how much data is necessary to do so [1, 15, 23], a challenge called the "cold start problem" [1]. However, a cold start analysis can only measure the availability of hints; it makes no claims about how useful the hints will be for students. This is particularly concerning in the domain of programming, where a recent evaluation of data-driven hints suggests that their quality varies considerably and that lower quality hints can deter students from seeking help when they need it [21].

In this paper, we present a reframing of the cold start problem in which we evaluate the *quality*, rather than the *availability*, of data-driven hints for programming. We use this analysis to investigate the following research questions:

RQ1: How does the quantity of available training data affect the quality of data-driven programming hints?

RQ2: How does data from students data compare to expert-authored data for generating high-quality programming hints?

We address these questions using datasets from two different programming environments that offer data-driven hints. We find that with student training data, hint quality stops improving after adding 15–20 training solutions and that additional data may harm hint quality. We also find that student data can outperform a single expert solution, but that a comprehensive set of expert solutions generally performs best. Our results suggest that some data-driven hint algorithms can be oversensitive to individual training solutions. We show that this can be reduced by weighting hints using multiple training solutions, which also significantly improves hint quality. The primary contributions of this work are a new procedure for assessing the quality of data-driven hints and results from the first investigation of the impact of data quantity and source on data-driven hint quality.

2   Related Work

The Hint Factory [1] was the first data-driven hint generation algorithm, originally used for logic proof problems. It constructs an Interaction Network [4] that models how students progress through discrete states during problem solving. When a student requests a hint, the Hint Factory looks up their current state in the network and, if it finds a match, suggests a successive state based on how other students successfully solved the problem. More recent approaches to data-driven hint generation have focused on the domain of computer programming. Because programming problems have a large space of possible states [19, 23], it is often infeasible to match hint-requesting students exactly to other students in the database, as the Hint Factory does. Researchers have addressed this by finding the closest match, rather than an exact one [18, 23, 31], matching only some parts of the program [11, 19, 28], matching the student to a cluster of solutions [6], or matching using program output instead of source code [15].

2.1   The Cold Start Problem

Barnes and Stamper [1] recognized that one challenge with the Hint Factory is that when it does not have enough data, it will be unable to provide hints to students who have no match in the network – the "cold start problem." They devised a procedure to investigate how much data would be needed to reliably provide hints to students. They added student attempts to the network, one at a time, and after each addition calculated the likelihood that the next student would have a hint available, averaged over many trails. This produced a "cold start curve," which plots the amount of training data used to generate hints against the percent of students with a hint available. Their results showed that 75% hint coverage can be achieved with as few as 49 training attempts, improving to 91% coverage with over 500 attempts. A later evaluation [25] showed that with a few expert-authored "seed" solutions in the training dataset, hint coverage starts at over 55% and then quickly reverts to the original data-only curve.

Others have performed similar cold start experiments to show that data-driven hint generation for programming requires relatively little student data to achieve high hint coverage [2,5]. Peddycord et al. [15] used cold start curves to show how a different representation of student state improved hint availability. Rivers and Koedinger's ITAP tutor [23] can generate hints for over 98% of student attempts, since ITAP matches students with the closest partial solution in its dataset. Rather than measuring *hint availability* in their cold start analysis, they measured path length, or the number of edits needed to fully correct a student's code, which generally decreased as training data increased.

2.2   Other Evaluations of Data-Driven Hints

Other methods for evaluating data-driven hints include the following categories:

Availability Evaluations estimate how often a system will be able to provide a hint to a requesting student using all training data. Perelman et al. [16] found that their test-driven synthesis algorithm could generate hints for 65% of incorrect attempts in the CodeHunt programming game, while the iGrader system [28] could generate hints for 54% of incorrect attempts in a C# course.

Correction Evaluations estimate how often a system can *correct* an incorrect problem attempt. For the attempts where iGrader [28] was able to generate hints, it could fully correct 72% of these attempts with at most three "fixes." Lazar and Bratko's hint system [11] was able to correct 35–70% of incorrect attempts at a set of Prolog problems. The DeepFix system [7] could correct 27% of incorrect C programs fully and an additional 19% partially.

Student Choice Evaluations generate hints for students seen in historical data and then determine whether the students' later edits align with the hints' suggestions. Lazar et al. [12] found that 97% and 56% of their "buggy" and "intent" hints, respectively, were later enacted by students. Price et al. [19] found that 32–35% of their CTD algorithm's hints would have brought students closer to their own submitted solution, while 61% of students' actions did so.

Student Outcome Evaluations investigate the impact of hints on student outcomes in classroom and laboratory studies. Fossati et al. [5] found that their iList tutor, which provides data-driven hints, led to learning gains comparable to working with a human tutor. Stamper et al. [26] compared a version of their DeepThought logic tutor with and without data-driven hints across semesters and found that students with hints performed better in the tutor and the course.

Expert Evaluations directly measure the quality of data-driven hints using experts. Stamper and Barnes [24] compared two hint generation methods by having an expert select which method generated the better hint. Others have asked experts to rate hints directly on a validity scale [8,21,29]. Piech et al. [17] asked a group of experts to generate single, "gold standard" hints for student programs, and they evaluated hint systems based on their accuracy in matching these gold standard hints. Price et al. [18] extended this approach by having experts identify a *set* of valid hints, rather than a single best hint. Gross et al. [6] found that experts often disagreed with their cluster-based hint generation system about which exemplar solution should be used to generate feedback.

We argue that the first three evaluation categories are insufficient to demonstrate that data-driven hints are useful to students, since even hints that lead to a correct solution may not be easily understood [20]. While student outcome evaluations are ideal for evaluating whole systems, in this paper we focus on expert evaluation to understand how data impacts hint quality.

3 Method

We used the SourceCheck data-driven hint generation algorithm [18] to investigate our research questions. Like many hint generation algorithms in the domain of programming (e.g. [23,28,31]), SourceCheck generates hints for a hint-requesting student in two phases. First, it searches a training dataset of correct solutions for the one that best matches the hint-requesting student's code, using a code-specific distance metric. It then constructs a set of edits to transform the student's code into the matching solution and suggests these edits as hints.

3.1 Data

We analyzed datasets from two programming environments that offer on-demand, data-driven hints: iSnap [20], a block-based programming environment and ITAP [23], an intelligent tutoring system (ITS) for Python programming. Both datasets consist of log data collected from students working on multiple programming problems, including complete traces of their code and records of hints they requested. The iSnap dataset was collected from an introductory programming course for non-majors during the Fall 2016 and Spring 2017 semesters, with 120 total students completing 6 programming problems. The ITAP dataset was collected from two introductory programming courses in Spring 2016, with 89 total students completing up to 40 Python problems (see [22] for details). Both datasets are available from the PSLC Datashop (pslcdatashop.org) [9].

Our evaluation of data-driven hint quality required two sets of data: a set of *hint requests* for which to generate hints, and a set of *training data* used to generate those hints. From the iSnap dataset, we randomly sampled one hint request per problem from each student who used hints. This ensured that no student was overrepresented in the set of hint requests. From the ITAP dataset, we randomly sampled up to two unique hint requests per problem from each student who used hints, since there were fewer students who requested hints than in the iSnap dataset. We only sampled hint requests where the student's Python code could be parsed, since this is required by SourceCheck. We also extracted a set of training data from each dataset consisting of the traces of each student who submitted a correct solution and did not request hints.

We selected a subset of problems from each dataset to analyze, since our method for evaluating hint quality (explained in Sect. 3.2) involves time-intensive hint generation by expert tutors. From the iSnap dataset, we selected two representative problems, GuessingGame and Squiral, which have been used in previous evaluation of SourceCheck [18]. The two problems had 23 and 24 hint requests respectively (47 total). Common solutions to these problems are approximately 13 and 10 lines of code, respectively, and require loops, conditionals, variables and procedure definitions. From the ITAP dataset, we selected all 5 problems that had at least 7 associated hint requests, for a total of 51 hint requests (7–14 per problem). These simpler problems had common solutions with 2–5 lines of code, which included variables, API calls, arithmetic operators and, for one problem, loops. An important difference between the datasets is that the iSnap problems are considerably longer and more open-ended, while the ITAP problems often involve single-line functions, evaluated with test cases.

3.2   Assessing Hint Quality

To address our RQs, we developed a method to measure data-driven hint quality. As in previous work [17,18], we used a group of experts to generate a set of "gold standard" hints for each hint request, and we labeled data-driven hints as high-quality if they matched the gold standard hints. First, three tutors independently reviewed each hint request, including the history of the student's code before the hint request. Each tutor then generated a set of all hints they considered to be valid, useful, and not confusing. Each hint was represented as one or more edits to the student's code, making these hints comparable to the edit-based hints offered by many data-driven algorithms. Tutors were instructed to limit their hints to one edit (e.g. one insertion) unless multiple edits were needed to avoid confusion. Hints were designed to be independently useful, with the understanding that the student would receive any *one* hint, not the whole set.

Next, each tutor independently reviewed the hints generated by the other two tutors and marked each hint as valid or invalid by the same criteria used to generate hints. We included in our gold standard set any hint which at least two out of three tutors considered to be valid. Our goal was not to determine a definitive, objective set of correct hints but rather to identify a large number of hints that a reasonable human tutor might generate. Requiring that two tutors agreed on each hint provided a higher quality standard than is used in most classrooms, while allowing for differences of opinion among tutors. This produced between 1 and 11 gold standard hints per hint request for the iSnap dataset (Med = 5) and between 1 and 5 for the ITAP dataset (Med = 2)[1].

We use this set of gold standard hints to automatically assign a QUALITYSCORE to a hint generation algorithm for a set of hint requests. For each hint request, we first generate a set of candidate hints, H, using the algorithm. Since some algorithms (including SourceCheck) generate multiple hints for a given request, the algorithm must also assign a confidence weight to each hint, with the weights summing to 1. We then mark each candidate hint $h \in H$ as valid if it matches one of the gold standard hints, after standardizing the names of any newly created variables, methods and string literals. We also detect *partial* matches where a candidate hint consists of a subset of the edits suggested by the tutor. The final QUALITYSCORE is the sum of the weights of all valid hints in H. The QUALITYSCORE ranges from 0 (no valid hints) to 1 (all valid hints) and can be calculated to include partial matches or only full matches. We average this score over all hint requests to produce a final QUALITYSCORE for the algorithm.

In our analysis, we compared two different approaches for assigning weights to the set of hints generated by SourceCheck, H, for a given hint request. The first, uniform weighting, simply assigns a weight of $1/|H|$ to each hint. The second, voting-based weighting, uses multiple solutions in the training dataset to assign weights. Recall that SourceCheck uses a single, closest matching target solution in the training dataset to generate hints (a 1-nearest-neighbor approach). With voting-based weighting, hints are also generated using the top-k closest solutions in the training dataset. The weight of each hint $h \in H$ is the percentage of these top-k solutions which, if used for hint generation, would also have generated h. The weights are then normalized to sum to 1. In our analysis we chose $k = 10$, though other values of $k = 5 \ldots 15$ produced similar outcomes. Note that the weighting approach does not change which hints are generated, only each hint's weight in determining the QUALITYSCORE.

3.3 Cold Start Procedure

To investigate RQ1, we developed a cold start procedure that measures the relationship between the quantity of available data and the resulting hint QUALITYSCORE. Unlike other cold start procedures (e.g. [1,5,23]), our evaluation considers only *actual* student hint requests, rather than all states observed in historical data. For each dataset, we start with the full set of training traces, T, the set of hint requests, R, and a sample set of training traces, $S = \emptyset$. We repeatedly select a random trace in T, remove it and add it to S. After each addition, we use the SourceCheck algorithm to generate a set of hints for each hint request in R and calculate a QUALITYSCORE for these hints. We repeat this until T is empty. The end result is a QUALITYSCORE for each $i \in 1..|T|$,

---

[1] Full datasets and hint ratings are available at go.ncsu.edu/hint-quality-data.

where i is the number of traces used to generate hints. We repeated this whole procedure for the iSnap and ITAP datasets 200 times and averaged the results[2].

3.4   Comparing with Expert-Authored Data

In order to investigate RQ2, comparing data from students and expert-authored data, we created two expert-authored training datasets to use as baselines. The first baseline dataset, ONEEXPERT, consists of a single solution, authored by an expert to reflect a straightforward approach to solving each problem. This is a minimal baseline, since almost any problem will already have at least one teacher-authored solution available. The second baseline dataset, ALLEXPERT, consists of *all* solutions considered by an expert to be useful for hint generation. To assign a QUALITYSCORE to these baselines, we still generate hints with the SourceCheck algorithm, but we provide it the expert training dataset.

To allow an expert author to generate a comprehensive set of correct solutions, we developed a simple solution templating language. Using this language, an author can write solution code that includes "branches," indicating where there are multiple ways of writing an acceptable solution. These branches may represent different high-level programming strategies, or different ways of expressing the same idea programmatically. Branches can be nested to produce a wide variety of solutions. Additionally, authors can mark parts of the solution code as order-invariant and add wildcards that can match any code element. One researcher, familiar with the problems, authored the expert solutions for both baselines, using the set of students solutions as a reference. For the larger iSnap problems, ALLEXPERT solution sets took 60–90 min each to author and test, producing 960 and 1,152 unique solutions for GuessingGame and Squiral, respectively. The smaller ITAP problems took 15–60 min each, producing only 2 solutions for most problems, though one problem (KthDigit) had 16.

4   Results

Figure 1 shows cold start curves for the iSnap dataset, plotting how SourceCheck's QUALITYSCORE (averaged over all trials) changes for both weighting approaches as the number of solutions in the training dataset increases. In many ways, the curves resemble a traditional cold start curve, with the QUALITYSCORE increasing rapidly as the first 10–15 solutions are added to the training data and then leveling off. Comparing the uniform and voting-based weighting approaches, we can see that the voting-based approach consistently performs better, achieving a 19.1% and 15.4% higher final QUALITYSCORE on the GuessingGame and Squiral problems, respectively. A Wilcoxon signed-rank test showed that this difference in the final QUALITYSCORE was significant for the sample of 47 iSnap hint requests ($V = 331$; $p = 0.015$; Cohen's $d = 0.143$).

---

[2] Over 200 trials, the standard error of the averaged QUALITYSCORES was always less than 0.01, and averaged less than 0.0025 across values of i.

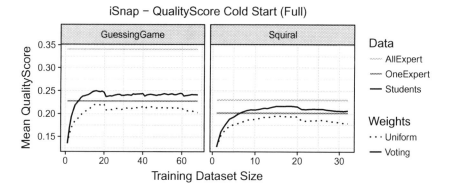

Fig. 1. Cold start curves for the iSnap dataset (black) with uniform (solid) and voting-based weighting (dotted) with ALLEXPERT (green) and ONEEXPERT (blue) baselines. (Color figure online)

Traditional cold start curves measure hint *coverage* and are guaranteed to increase monotonically with more data. However, our QUALITYSCORE curves show clear fluctuations as more training solutions are added, sometimes decreasing in QUALITYSCORE. Here too we see a difference between weighting approaches. The uniform weighting curves have a final QUALITYSCORE 8.4% and 8.3% lower than their peak score on GuessingGame and Squiral, respectively, while the voting-based weighting curves lose only 3.4% and 4.8% of their peak QUALITYSCORE, respectively. Recall that Fig. 1 shows QUALITYSCORE averaged over all hint requests for a given problem. To further investigate why additional data may decrease hint QUALITYSCORE in the iSnap dataset, we calculated cold start curves for each of the 47 iSnap hint requests individually, and we found a wide variety of curve shapes. For voting-based weighting, 39.1% and 33.3% of hint requests on GuessingGame and Squiral showed a negative correlation between quantity of data and hint QUALITYSCORE, while 47.8% and 45.8% showed a positive correlation. This trend was similar for uniform weighting. This suggests the fluctuations at the end of the cold start curves are due to competing positive and negative effects of data quantity on different hint requests.

Figure 1 shows lines indicating the ONEEXPERT and ALLEXPERT baseline QUALITYSCORES[3]. They have a constant value, since they are calculated using a set of expert solutions, not student data. Student data with uniform weighting fails to surpass the ONEEXPERT baseline. However, with voting-based weighting, student data outperforms ONEEXPERT with only 7 training solutions for both problems, achieving a peak QUALITYSCORE 9.8% and 7.5% higher than ONEEXPERT on GuessingGame and Squiral. Even with voting-based weighting, student data falls short of the ALLEXPERT baseline, with the peak student

---

[3] Because the ONEEXPERT baseline uses only one training solution, both weighting approaches produce the same results. For simplicity, Fig. 1 shows only voting-based weighting for the ALLEXPERT baseline.

QUALITYSCORE 73.3% and 94.3% as high as the ALLEXPERT baseline. However, a Wilcoxon signed-rank test shows that this difference between the final student data QUALITYSCORE and the ALLEXPERT baseline was not significant for the sample of 47 iSnap hint requests ($V = 181$; $p = 0.077$; Cohen's $d = 0.221$).

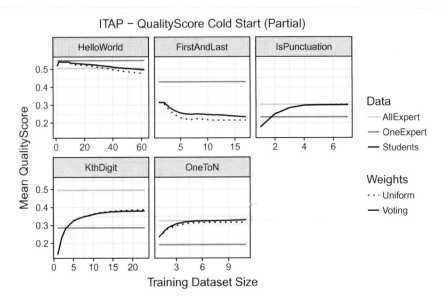

Fig. 2. Cold start curves and baselines for the ITAP dataset.

Figure 2 shows cold start curves for the ITAP dataset. Note that unlike in the iSnap dataset, QUALITYSCORES for ITAP curves were calculated including *partial* matches (see Sect. 3.2), since Python ASTs are more complex, and many of SourceCheck's hints matched only part of the gold standard hints. The IsPunctuation, KthDigit, and OneToN problems have a similar curve shape to the iSnap problems; however, rather than fluctuating, they increase monotonically in QUALITYSCORE with additional data. They also show almost no difference between uniform and voting-based weighting. Student data easily outperforms the ONEEXPERT baseline and, in the IsPunctuation and OneToN problems, matches the ALLEXPERT baseline. These problems have much smaller training datasets, so it is unclear how the curves would continue with additional training data.

The other two curves, for HelloWorld and FirstAndLast, have unique shapes. For both problems, additional data has a clear negative impact on hint quality. Additionally, the ONEEXPERT baseline has equal or better performance compared to the ALLEXPERT baseline. HelloWorld and FirstAndLast are the simplest problems we investigated, each with a common, one-line solution that comprised 47.1% and 93.5% of the training dataset, respectively. This solution was also used in the ONEEXPERT baseline. The curves suggest that the presence of other solutions in the training dataset lowered hint QUALITYSCORE. For FirstAndLast, the second most common solution comprised 35.3% of the training dataset. It used a more advanced Python feature (using `s[-1]` to get the last character in a string), which the human tutors never suggested to struggling students, preferring a more straightforward approach (`s[len(s) - 1]`). SourceCheck often selected the more advanced approach as the target solution, since it is shorter, which accounts for the lower QUALITYSCORE for student data on this problem. It is also important to note that QUALITYSCORES for these two problems were based on the fewest number of hint requests (7 each), which may not be fully representative of all likely hint requests.

5   Discussion

RQ1: *How does the quantity of available training data affect the quality of data-driven programming hints?* Our results suggest increased training data has a positive impact on hint quality up to a point. For our datasets, hint quality stops increasing after 15–20 training solutions. However, for the more complex problems in the iSnap dataset, additional data had either no positive effect, or even a slight negative effect, on hint quality. While this does validate the claim of many data-driven algorithms that little student data is needed to generate hints [1,5], it is concerning that additional data fails to improve SourceCheck's effectiveness. A similar problem was noted by Rivers et al. [23] on some problems, where ITAP's hint generation performance decreased with additional data. We could interpret the analysis presented here as a method to measure a data-driven algorithm's ability to effectively make use of all of its data. Ideally, a data-driven algorithm should have monotonically increasing hint quality as it is given additional training data, selecting useful solutions and ignoring unhelpful ones. By this interpretation, the SourceCheck algorithm has mixed success, especially on the iSnap dataset.

In considering why additional data may be harmful, recall that this evaluation relied on the SourceCheck algorithm to generate all the hints we evaluated. Like many data-driven hint generation algorithms (e.g. [23,28,31]), SourceCheck generates hints using the single best-matching target solution from the training dataset (a "1-nearest neighbor" approach). This makes it sensitive to additional training data. Our training data consists of *all correct* student solutions, and some of these will contain unnecessary code, unique design choices, or advanced features (e.g. `s[-1]` in FirstAndLast) that make them problematic for hint generation. This is especially true for the more open-ended problems found in the iSnap dataset [20]. As more of these problematic solutions are added to the training dataset, it becomes increasingly likely that one of them will be the closest match for the hint-requesting student (e.g. if the student added similar unnecessary code). Since only the closest match in the training dataset is used for hint generation, a single problematic solution can eclipse others that are more useful.

Our comparison of uniform and voting-based hint weighting lends some support to the hypothesis that this "1-nearest-neighbor" approach to hint generation is overly sensitive to additional data. When SourceCheck uses the top 10 best matches in the training dataset to weight hints, its final QUALITYSCORE improves significantly and less quality is lost from additional training data. However, this weighting does not change the hints themselves, which may still suffer from a bad match. Another way to reduce this sensitivity to additional data is the approach of Gross et al. [6], which selects a matching *cluster* of solutions, rather than a single target, and uses an exemplar solution from that cluster for hint generation. Rivers and Koedinger [23] address this in part by discovering new target solutions through path construction, which better match the hint requesting student's code. We could also attempt to filter training solutions (manually or automatically) to retain only those useful for hint generation. Importantly, both the decrease in QUALITYSCORE with additional training data and the difference in QUALITYSCORE between weighting approaches appeared only in the iSnap dataset. This may be because the iSnap dataset featured larger and more complex problems than the ITAP dataset, but it is also possible that these trends result from more specific features of the iSnap dataset itself.

RQ2: *How does data from students compare to expert-authored data for generating high-quality programming hints?* The use of student data for hint generation makes the implicit assumption that it will yield better hints than using a single expert solution, and our results suggest that this is not always the case. In the iSnap dataset, student data failed to outperform the ONEEXPERT baseline when using uniform hint weighting. However, we also showed that this can be addressed with voting-based weighting. On the simpler ITAP dataset, student data seems to perform better, outperforming ONEEXPERT with only 1–3 training solutions on 3 problems, regardless of the hint weighting. However, our results also show that for the simplest problems (HelloWorld and FirstAndLast), a single expert solution may be all the data that is required.

The ALLEXPERT baseline is more robust, and it outperformed student data on the three problems where more than 2 expert solutions were generated as training data (GuessingGame, Squiral, KthDigit), as well as on FirstAndLast. While this difference was not significant on the iSnap dataset, this may be due to our relatively small sample size (47 hint requests). On the remaining problems, student data has similar performance to the ALLEXPERT baseline. These results suggest that for all but the simplest problems, a comprehensive set of expert solutions is likely to be more useful for hint generation than student data. This is not surprising, since our expert solutions were authored by a researcher familiar with the problems (as most instructors would be), using student solutions as a reference, so in many ways they represent an ideal training dataset. It would also be possible to author expert solutions without the benefit of referencing student solutions, but this may yield lower-quality hints.

The template-based data generation technique used in the ALLEXPERT baseline is not the focus of this paper, but we do note some advantages to this approach. In addition to outperforming student data in terms of QUALITYSCORE, this approach solves the cold start problem entirely. Also, if a problem changes from one semester to the next (e.g. adding an additional objective), it is easy to modify the corresponding template, while any student solutions would be rendered useless. Previous work suggests that even a few low-quality hints may deter students from using a help system [21], so the consistency of expert-authored data is desirable. However, like expert models, the templates are time intensive to produce, taking 15–90 min per problem and likely longer for more complex problems. This process may therefore not scale well to larger problem sets.

5.1 Considerations and Limitations

Automatically assessing the quality of hints is a difficult and inherently subjective task. Our method for generating gold standard tutor hints strikes a balance between including many hints (generated by three separate tutors) and ensuring hint quality (all hints were "seconded" by another tutor). However, our results may have been different if we had used more than 3 tutors or a higher standard of agreement (consensus among all tutors). The process of matching an automatically-generated hint to a gold standard hint is also imperfect, and it is likely that some hints were marked invalid despite being similar to a gold standard hint. For all of these reasons, the QUALITYSCORES reported here may seem low. However, raw QUALITYSCORES are difficult to interpret, so we use them primarily for *comparing* hint generation approaches.

One important limitation of this work is that the QUALITYSCORE metric was calculated based on a moderate number of hint requests for each problem (23–24 for iSnap; 7–14 for ITAP). The QUALITYSCORE metric is therefore only as accurate as these hint requests are representative of all hint requests. The tutors generating hints for these requests noted that students' code often contained a range of strange misconceptions and creative mistakes and often did not resemble other students' solutions. However, we see this as an important feature of our data and analysis. The set of code states where students request hints is *not* representative of students' code generally, since it reflects students' need to request outside help. Hint requests are full of strange design choices and incorrect code, and this is exactly what a hint generation algorithm should be designed to address. One limitation of this work is that these hint-requesting students were not included in the training datasets, diminishing their diversity. Lastly, most problems in the ITAP dataset had fewer training solutions (7 to 22), and it is unclear how the cold start curves would have continued with additional data.

6 Conclusion

In this paper we presented a detailed method for evaluating the quality of data-driven hints, and we applied that method to investigate how the quantity and source of data impacts data-driven hint quality for one algorithm. We showed that a relatively small number of student solutions can outperform a single expert-authored solution, but they fall short of a comprehensive set of expert-authored solutions. We also introduced a voting-based hint weighting approach that significantly improves hint quality. We compared our results across 2 datasets that used different programming languages – to our knowledge, the first evaluation of data-driven hints to do so. While our quality evaluation procedure comes with limitations, we argue that research on data-driven hint generation should hold itself to the more rigorous standard of evaluation presented here, rather than relying on availability evaluations. We have suggested that part of that standard should be an algorithm's ability to effectively leverage training data, as assessed with the cold start curves presented here. In future work, we hope to use our method to benchmark and compare hint generation algorithms on common datasets to better understand their strengths and weaknesses.

Acknowledgements. The authors thank Veronica Cateté for her contributions to this research. This work was supported by the National Science Foundation under grant 1623470.

References

1. Barnes, T., Stamper, J.: Automatic hint generation for logic proof tutoring using historical data. J. Educ. Technol. Soc. **13**(1), 3 (2010)
2. Chow, S., Yacef, K., Koprinska, I., Curran, J.: Automated data-driven hints for computer programming students. In: Adjunct Publication of the 25th Conference on User Modeling, Adaptation and Personalization, pp. 5–10 (2017)
3. Corbett, A.T., Anderson, J.R.: Locus of feedback control in computer-based tutoring: impact on learning rate, achievement and attitudes. In: Proceedings of the SIGCHI Conference on Human Factors in Computing Systems, pp. 245–252 (2001)
4. Eagle, M., Johnson, M., Barnes, T.: Interaction networks: generating high level hints based on network community clustering. In: International Educational Data Mining Society (2012)
5. Fossati, D., Di Eugenio, B., Ohlsson, S., Brown, C., Chen, L.: Data driven automatic feedback generation in the ilist intelligent tutoring system. Technol. Inst. Cogn. Learn. **10**(1), 5–26 (2015)
6. Gross, S., Mokbel, B., Paaßen, B., Hammer, B., Pinkwart, N.: Example-based feedback provision using structured solution spaces. Int. J. Learn. Technol. 10 **9**(3), 248–280 (2014)
7. Gupta, R., Pal, S., Kanade, A., Shevade, S.: Deepfix: fixing common C language errors by deep learning. In: AAAI, pp. 1345–1351 (2017)
8. Hartmann, B., MacDougall, D., Brandt, J., Klemmer, S.R.: What would other programmers do: suggesting solutions to error messages. In: Proceedings of the SIGCHI Conference on Human Factors in Computing Systems, pp. 1019–1028 (2010)
9. Koedinger, K.R., Baker, R.S., Cunningham, K., Skogsholm, A., Leber, B., Stamper, J.: A data repository for the EDM community: the PSLC DataShop. In: Handbook of Educational Data Mining, p. 43 (2010)

10. Koedinger, K.R., Stamper, J.C., McLaughlin, E.A., Nixon, T.: Using data-driven discovery of better student models to improve student learning. In: Lane, H.C., Yacef, K., Mostow, J., Pavlik, P. (eds.) AIED 2013. LNCS (LNAI), vol. 7926, pp. 421–430. Springer, Heidelberg (2013). https://doi.org/10.1007/978-3-642-39112-5_43

11. Lazar, T., Bratko, I.: Data-driven program synthesis for hint generation in programming tutors. In: Trausan-Matu, S., Boyer, K.E., Crosby, M., Panourgia, K. (eds.) ITS 2014. LNCS, vol. 8474, pp. 306–311. Springer, Cham (2014). https://doi.org/10.1007/978-3-319-07221-0_38

12. Lazar, T., Možina, M., Bratko, I.: Automatic extraction of AST patterns for debugging student programs. In: André, E., Baker, R., Hu, X., Rodrigo, M.M.T., du Boulay, B. (eds.) AIED 2017. LNCS (LNAI), vol. 10331, pp. 162–174. Springer, Cham (2017). https://doi.org/10.1007/978-3-319-61425-0_14

13. Mitrovic, A.: A knowledge-based teaching system for SQL. In: Proceedings of ED-MEDIA, vol. 98, 1027–1032 (1998)

14. Mostafavi, B., Zhou, G., Lynch, C., Chi, M., Barnes, T.: Data-driven worked examples improve retention and completion in a logic tutor. In: Conati, C., Heffernan, N., Mitrovic, A., Verdejo, M.F. (eds.) AIED 2015. LNCS (LNAI), vol. 9112, pp. 726–729. Springer, Cham (2015). https://doi.org/10.1007/978-3-319-19773-9_102

15. Peddycord III, B., Hicks, A., Barnes, T.: Generating hints for programming problems using intermediate output. In: Proceedings of Educational Data Mining (2014)

16. Perelman, D., Gulwani, S., Grossman, D.: Test-driven synthesis for automated feedback for introductory computer science assignments. In: Proceedings of Data Mining for Educational Assessment and Feedback (ASSESS 2014) (2014)

17. Piech, C., Sahami, M., Huang, J., Guibas, L.: Autonomously generating hints by inferring problem solving policies. In: Proceedings of the Second ACM Conference on Learning@ Scale, pp. 195–204 (2015)

18. Price, T., Zhi, R., Barnes, T.: Evaluation of a data-driven feedback algorithm for open-ended programming. In: Proceedings of Educational Data Mining (2017)

19. Price, T.W., Dong, Y., Barnes, T.: Generating data-driven hints for open-ended programming. In: Proceedings of Educational Data Mining, pp. 191–198 (2016)

20. Price, T.W., Dong, Y., Lipovac, D.: iSnap: towards intelligent tutoring in novice programming environments. In: Proceedings of the 2017 ACM SIGCSE Technical Symposium on Computer Science Education, pp. 483–488 (2017)

21. Price, T.W., Zhi, R., Barnes, T.: Hint generation under uncertainty: the effect of hint quality on help-seeking behavior. In: André, E., Baker, R., Hu, X., Rodrigo, M.M.T., du Boulay, B. (eds.) AIED 2017. LNCS (LNAI), vol. 10331, pp. 311–322. Springer, Cham (2017). https://doi.org/10.1007/978-3-319-61425-0_26

22. Rivers, K., Harpstead, E., Koedinger, K.R.: Learning curve analysis for programming: which concepts do students struggle with? In: Proceedings of the 12th Annual International ACM Conference on International Computing Education Research, pp. 143–151 (2016)

23. Rivers, K., Koedinger, K.R.: Data-driven hint generation in vast solution spaces: a self-improving python programming tutor. Int. J. Artif. Intell. Educ. **27**(1), 37–64 (2017)

24. Stamper, J., Barnes, T.: An unsupervised, frequency-based metric for selecting hints in an MDP-based tutor. In: Proceedings of Educational Data Mining (2009)

25. Stamper, J., Barnes, T., Croy, M.: Enhancing the automatic generation of hints with expert seeding. Int. J. Artif. Intell. Educ. **21**(1–2), 153–167 (2011)

26. Stamper, J., Eagle, M., Barnes, T., Croy, M.: Experimental evaluation of automatic hint generation for a logic tutor. Int. J. Artif. Intell. Educ. **22**(1–2), 3–17 (2013)

27. VanLehn, K.: The behavior of tutoring systems. Int. J. Artif. Intell. Educ. **16**(3), 227–265 (2006)
28. Wang, K., Lin, B., Rettig, B., Pardi, P., Singh, R.: Data-driven feedback generator for online programing courses. In: Proceedings of the Fourth ACM Conference on Learning@ Scale, pp. 257–260 (2017)
29. Watson, C., Li, F.W.B., Godwin, J.L.: BlueFix: using crowd-sourced feedback to support programming students in error diagnosis and repair. In: Popescu, E., Li, Q., Klamma, R., Leung, H., Specht, M. (eds.) ICWL 2012. LNCS, vol. 7558, pp. 228–239. Springer, Heidelberg (2012). https://doi.org/10.1007/978-3-642-33642-3_25
30. Yudelson, M., Hosseini, R., Vihavainen, A., Brusilovsky, P.: Investigating automated student modeling in a Java MOOC. In: Proceedings of Educational Data Mining, pp. 261–264 (2014)
31. Zimmerman, K., Rupakheti, C.R.: An automated framework for recommending program elements to novices (n). In: Proceedings of the 30th IEEE/ACM International Conference on Automated Software Engineering (ASE), pp. 283–288 (2015)

Predicting Question Quality Using Recurrent Neural Networks

Stefan Ruseti[1], Mihai Dascalu[1,2(✉)], Amy M. Johnson[3], Renu Balyan[3],
Kristopher J. Kopp[3], Danielle S. McNamara[3], Scott A. Crossley[4],
and Stefan Trausan-Matu[1,2]

[1] Faculty of Automatic Control and Computers, University "Politehnica" of Bucharest,
313 Splaiul Independenței, 60042 Bucharest, Romania
{stefan.ruseti,mihai.dascalu,stefan.trausan}@cs.pub.ro
[2] Academy of Romanian Scientists, Splaiul Independenței 54, 050094 Bucharest, Romania
[3] Institute for the Science of Teaching and Learning, Arizona State University, PO Box 872111,
Tempe, AZ 85287, USA
{amjohn43,renu.balyan,kristopher.kopp,dsmcnama}@asu.edu
[4] Department of Applied Linguistics/ESL, Georgia State University, Atlanta, GA 30303, USA
scrossley@gsu.edu

Abstract. This study assesses the extent to which machine learning techniques can be used to predict question quality. An algorithm based on textual complexity indices was previously developed to assess question quality to provide feedback on questions generated by students within iSTART (an intelligent tutoring system that teaches reading strategies). In this study, 4,575 questions were coded by human raters based on their corresponding depth, classifying questions into four categories: 1-very shallow to 4-very deep. Here we propose a novel approach to assessing question quality within this dataset based on Recurrent Neural Networks (RNNs) and word embeddings. The experiments evaluated multiple RNN architectures using GRU, BiGRU and LSTM cell types of different sizes, and different word embeddings (i.e., FastText and Glove). The most precise model achieved a classification accuracy of 81.22%, which surpasses the previous prediction results using lexical sophistication complexity indices (accuracy = 41.6%). These results are promising and have implications for the future development of automated assessment tools within computer-based learning environments.

Keywords: Question asking · Recurrent neural network · Word embeddings

1 Introduction

Many students experience difficulty understanding text content, principally due to individual differences related to prior domain knowledge, skills, and motivation [1]. Nonetheless, extended practice using active comprehension strategies, such as question asking, summarization, and elaboration, can support the development of reading comprehension [2–4]. However, a common difficulty facing educators is lack of classroom time to provide feedback to students about their success on using such reading strategies. To address this concern, intelligent tutoring systems can be used to

© Springer International Publishing AG, part of Springer Nature 2018
C. Penstein Rosé et al. (Eds.): AIED 2018, LNAI 10947, pp. 491–502, 2018.
https://doi.org/10.1007/978-3-319-93843-1_36

supplement classroom instruction, offering individual students automated feedback on the use of comprehension strategies. In these situations, ITSs commonly use Natural Language Processing (NLP) algorithms to automatically evaluate various linguistic and semantic features of students' typed input and subsequently provide summative scores and formative feedback. Students can use this feedback to improve their application of comprehension strategies, and in turn their ability to comprehend challenging text.

The goal of the current project is to develop algorithms that provide automated classifications to the instructional model, which in turn selects and delivers student feedback within a new question-asking practice module in the Interactive Strategy Training for Active Reading and Thinking (iSTART) system [5]. There is evidence demonstrating the efficacy of interventions that provide students with instruction on how to ask questions while reading [4], indicating that the development of an ITS which provides instruction and practice would benefit from methods to automatically assess the quality of the questions posed by the student with relation to the text being read. Although systems exist that automatically *generate* questions and *select* appropriate questions [6], we are unaware of any system that automatically assesses the quality of questions produced by readers. In the envisioned practice activity, students will read a text and, at pre-selected points in the text, construct questions about the content of the text. iSTART will automatically assess the quality of each question and provide the student scores and formative feedback to improve the students' questions. Thus, more accurate algorithms need to be developed. This study reports on one such attempt using deep learning techniques, specifically recurrent neural networks, to assess the quality of student-generated questions during reading.

2   Related Work

Classifying a question to assess its quality is useful in multiple scenarios such as classroom learning, reading exploration, and tutoring [7, 8]. We discuss the related work relevant to our approach using four threads. We first review question generation and its role in learning. We then describe existing question taxonomies along with existing work on question classification. Finally, we discuss recent work related to deep-learning models used for question classification and other related natural language processing (NLP) tasks.

2.1   Question Generation and Learning

Motivating students to generate questions is foundational in learning sciences [9]. Question generation supports comprehension, and promotes active learning, knowledge construction, problem solving, reasoning, and the development of sophisticated meta-cognitive skills [10]. Instruction on question asking generally focuses on generating deep-level reasoning questions, or questions that focus on reasoning about causal, logical, or goal-oriented systems [11]. Asking *good* questions is associated with improved comprehension, learning, and memory for targeted content [12]. In turn, comprehension and learning increase when students are trained to ask good questions

[4, 13], However, school children and adult learners tend to generate shallow level questions, and show substantial difficulties while generating questions that require deep level understanding [8].

2.2 Question Taxonomies

Questions can be categorized using a variety of taxonomies [14]. Several question taxonomies have been proposed by researchers developing models of question asking and answering in artificial intelligence, computational linguistics, discourse processing, education, and cognitive science [9, 11].

Several taxonomies originated from the Text REtrieval Conference-Question Answering (TREC-QA) track. For instance, the Ittycheriah et al. [15] taxonomy consists of 31 question types, whereas Hovy et al. [16] defined 141 question types. Harabagiu et al. [17] and Gerber [18] defined large question taxonomies spanning over 180 categories. Li and Roth [19] created a taxonomy with 6 coarse-grained and 50 fine-grained categories. Most of these taxonomies are hierarchical in nature and developed for question-answering and information retrieval systems. The focus for most of these taxonomies is on classifying entities such as person, location, organization, quantity, abbreviations and so on.

In this study, we have based our question classification categories on the Graesser–Person taxonomy [11] because their taxonomy is contextually related to learning. The Graesser–Person taxonomy [11] classifies questions into 16 categories covering different categories based on knowledge and cognitive proficiencies. These question categories are closely tied to Bloom's [20] taxonomy of cognitive activities. They further classify these categories into shallow ("who", "when", "what", "where") and deep ("why", "how", "what if") levels. Along similar lines, Mosenthal [21] developed a coding system to scale questions on five levels of abstractness, namely most concrete, highly concrete, intermediate, highly abstract and most abstract. Wisher and Graesser [8] defined categories based on knowledge such as agents and entities, class inclusion, spatial layout, compositional structures, procedures and plans, and causal chains and networks.

2.3 Question Classification

The methods used for automated question classification have varied greatly, from rule-based systems to advanced NLP techniques. Most approaches in the past relied on handcrafted rules that, though effective, are tedious to create and not scalable for matching questions. Olney et al. [22] manually built custom rules utilizing only surface features, ignoring the semantic and pragmatic context of the questions, for classifying the questions. The classifier performed quite well in distinguishing "questions" from "contributions" (F-measure = 0.99). However, classification of question type, within those identified as questions, achieved more modest accuracy (F-measure = 0.48).

More recently machine-learning techniques have been successfully applied to question classification. IBM's TREC-9 system [15] utilized maximum entropy models [23] for classifying questions labeled according to Message Understanding Conference (MUC) categories [24]. Another question classification system used the Sparse Network of Winnows (SNoW) architecture [19]. Several question classification systems have made use of support vector machines (SVMs) [25, 26] and log-linear models [27] for classification of question types. Kopp et al. [28] used discriminant function analysis (DFA) using leave-one-out cross validation (LOOCV) for classifying question levels. A DFA on the entire set achieved an accuracy of 41.6%, while a LOOCV analysis obtained 40.1% accuracy when questions were classified for 4 levels (1 through 4). Notably, the accuracy improved when only 2 levels (shallow vs deep) were considered, up 61.1% in the LOOCV analysis.

Many more systems utilized NLP techniques including headwords and their hypernyms [14], conditional random field (CRF) [29], hierarchical directed acyclic graph (HDAG) Kernel, which is well suited to handle structured natural language data [30], parsing for classification [31], and automatic construction of grammars to match against question types [32]. Most of these systems have achieved high accuracy (nearing 90% or above) for general and coarse-grained question types.

2.4   Deep Learning Models for Question Classification

This study uses deep learning models, in particular recurrent neural networks (RNNs) [33], for classification of questions. Researchers have used deep learning for NLP tasks such as semantic parsing [34], sentence modeling [35], question answering [36], and other traditional NLP tasks [37]. Neural networks have also been used in question classification tasks. For instance, CNN has been used for semantic modeling of a sentence and later applied for six-way question classification using the TREC dataset [19, 35]. Fei et al. [38] investigated the effectiveness of neural network learning techniques for automatic classification of 233 objective questions into three difficulty levels (i.e., hard, medium, and easy), achieving an accuracy ranging between 76% and 78%. In their study, they opted to use a five-dimensional feature vector and a classic neural network architecture to characterize each question comprising of the following: (a) query-text relevance expressed as cosine similarity between the text, and question and answer pair (Q&A) vectors; (b) mean term frequency, (c) length of Q&A sequences, (d) term frequency distribution (variance) and (e) distribution of Q&A in original text.

While there has been a substantial amount of work for text classification using deep learning models [39, 40], there is little work available that has implemented deep learning models for classification of questions besides the previous studies that mostly rely on classic neural network architectures. To address this gap, this study evaluates the use of RNNs to predict the quality of questions.

3   Method

3.1   Corpus Description

We used the same data described in Kopp et al. [28]. For that study, participants read short texts and generated questions for each text read. These questions were coded by human raters using a four-level taxonomy that classified questions as shallow to deep. NLP indices were then calculated for each generated question and machine learning techniques were used to predict the human ratings. This is the first study performed on this corpus that makes use of neural-network based methods.

To collect the questions corpus, Kopp et al. enlisted responses from 233 participants from Amazon Mechanical Turk (MTurk) [41]. With approval from the California Distance Learning Project (CDLP)[1], they collected 30 texts, which were life-relevant for adult readers. All texts were four to seven paragraphs long and had between 128 and 452 words. For each text, participants constructed questions for three to seven target sentences. Trained researchers identified these target sentences because they included information for which prior knowledge or prior information within the text could be used to elaborate on or make inferences using the sentence. Using an online survey software (www.qualtrics.com), each participant was shown three randomly-selected texts, segmented into chunks by the target sentences (i.e., a target sentence ended each chunk of text). At each target sentence, participants were instructed to type a question about the sentence content and given up to 6 min to submit. Participants' average response time was 85.2 s ($SD = 33.9$). Of the 4,629 collected responses, 4,575 were included in the final dataset. Those items that were excluded were statements, rather than questions.

From the original 16 question categories in the Graesser and Person [11] taxonomy, a modified question coding scheme was developed by Kopp et al. [28]. Table 1 contains the original 16 question categories as well as examples of the modified coding scheme. For the initial coding process, questions were classified into the original 16 categories. Within the modified scheme, two of the original question categories (instrumental/ procedural and enablement) were collapsed into one category because researchers' initial training revealed they were not able to differentiate the categories reliably. The coding process also classified the questions according to the depth of the question (from 1-very shallow to 4-very deep). These differences in depth were annotated as (1) required answers are typically one word (e.g., yes or no), (2) required answers are still very short but may involve two or more elements (e.g., definitions), (3) required answers are longer, but do not relate to causal mechanisms (e.g., comparisons of two entities), and (4) required answers are lengthy and address systems' causal functions (e.g., which antecedent led to a consequence).

Table 1. The modified Graesser Person question taxonomy from Kopp et al. [28].

Level	Question categories from Graesser and Person Taxonomy [11]	Examples
Very shallow (1)	Verification, Disjunctive, Concept Completion, Quantification	Is 911 the emergency number everywhere?
Shallow (2)	Feature Specification, Definition, Example	What Constitutes and Emergency?
Deep (3)	Comparison Instrumental/ procedural, enablement, Judgmental	Why are the majority from cell phones?
Very deep (4)	Interpretational, Antecedent, Consequence, Goal Orientation, Expectational	What happens if you call 911 in a non-emergency?

[1] www.cdlponline.org.

Before coding the complete dataset, two researchers went through a training process, twice coding approximately a randomly selected group of 20% of the corpus. After each training round, interrater reliability was established using Cohen's kappa, bivariate correlation (r), percent exact, and percent adjacent agreement for the depth of questions. Reliability between the researchers increased from the first training round (kappa = .74; r = .78; 76% exact agreement; 92% adjacent agreement) to the second (kappa = .80; r = .86; 79% exact agreement; 95% adjacent agreement). Once the interrater reliability for each training round was assessed, the researchers met to discuss discrepancies on that subset of the data. After the two training rounds, the entire dataset was coded. Questions were randomly selected and each researcher coded 60% of the question corpus. Interrater reliability on the final overlapping subset of the corpus was: kappa = .84, r = .67, exact agreement = 82%, adjacent agreement = 92%. Within this subset, discussions were conducted to resolve any discrepancies between the two researchers' assigned codes. Each question was assigned a final score, from 1 (very shallow) to 4 (very deep).

3.2   Network Architecture

Each entry from the corpus contains a text that provides previous contextual information, the target sentence and a question related to the given sentence. For predicting the question quality score, a neural network could use either the question and the sentence, the question and the text, or all three. We performed several experiments with different architectures, varying the input of the network and the model representation.

In all our experiments, the text was represented using a Recurrent Neural Network with variable input size for the word embeddings. We opted to use pre-trained Glove [42] and FastText [43] word and/or n-gram vectors. *Glove* is an unsupervised log-bilinear regression model that computes word embeddings using the global word co-occurrence matrix. In our experiments, we chose vectors of size 100 and 300 that were pre-trained on Wikipedia. *FastText* enriches the skip-gram model from Word2Vec [44] with vector representations for n-grams; for FastText, the embedding size is 300. This way, the embedding of a word can be influenced by the way it is written, which has been shown to correlate with the meaning of the word [45]. Moreover, unknown word embedding can be constructed from their corresponding n-gram embeddings.

The next step in building our architecture consisted of choosing a text representation model, usually called an encoder. We selected two of the most frequently used recurrent neural models, namely Long Short-Term Memory networks (LSTM) [46] and the Gated Recurrent Units (GRU) [47]. GRUs are considerably simpler and do not have the same representation power, but can be useful on smaller datasets because there are fewer parameters for the network to learn. Both models are usually used as bi-directional networks [48] in which two different networks are used for the forward and backward direction in the text; thus, all words are equally important in the final encoded representation.

Each encoder outputs a matrix of variable size because of the different number of words from the text. In order to be compared, the size has to be reduced to a fixed dimension. Common ways include concatenation of the last outputs from the forward and backward networks, max-pooling over all outputs, or an attention mechanism that provides different weights to each word in the text, depending on the representation of the other text. Similar to the work of Santos et al. [49], we implemented a two-way attention pooling mechanism depicted in Fig. 1 that takes into account only the last sentence from the text and the question.

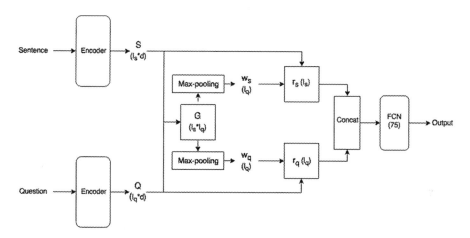

Fig. 1. Attentive pooling network architecture.

In Fig. 1, G is a matrix of size $l_s * l_q$, obtained from the outputs produced by the encoders (S and Q), as shown in Eq. 1, where U is a matrix of size $d * d$, l_s and l_q are the lengths of the sentence and question, and d is the output size of the encoder (in the case of the bidirectional encoders, the output is the double cell size). The matrix G can be perceived as a similarity function between each word in the question and each word from the sentence, which also takes into account the context in which they occur, since the similarity is computed on the encoders' outputs.

$$G = \tanh(S^t U Q) \tag{1}$$

Afterwards, the attention vectors (w_s and w_q) are constructed, which reflect the importance of each word in the sentence/question by applying max-pooling row-wise for the question, and column-wise for the sentence, followed by a softmax normalization. The question and sentence representations (r_q and r_s) are obtained by computing the dot product between the attention vectors and the encoders' outputs, as shown in Eq. 2.

$$r_q = w_q^t Q; \quad r_s = w_s^t S \tag{2}$$

The resulting representations are concatenated and passed through a dropout layer in order to minimize overfitting, followed by a hidden layer with the *tanh* activation function. Last, a softmax layer is applied to compute the probabilities for the four possible output classes. Training is performed using the Adam optimizer [50] and the cross-entropy loss function.

4   Results

The corpus was randomly split into training, validation, and test partitions each containing approximately 60%, 20% and 20% from the whole dataset. No texts were in two different partitions. Several experiments were performed with different network architectures and embedding models. Not all the results are included in this paper. Only the best configurations, with performance measured as accuracy on the validation set, were further fine-tuned with grid search, varying the cell size (50–300), hidden size (50–100), dropout probability (0–0.5) and training epochs (1–30). The reported results (see Table 2) were obtained on the test set, with the best hyper-parameters detected by the grid search. Experiments using linear regressions instead of a 4-way classification were also performed, but the results were less predictive and were not included in Table 2. LSTM results were also dropped because lower accuracy.

Table 2.   Accuracy on 4-way classification on test set.

Model	Embeddings	Cell size	Hidden size	Accuracy (%)
BiGRU text, GRU question	Glove-100	75	50	75.22
GRU sentence, GRU question	Glove-100	175	50	77.11
BiGRU sentence, BiGRU question	Glove-100	100	100	78.11
BiGRU sentence, GRU question	Glove-300	100	75	77.11
BiGRU sentence, GRU question	Glove-100	200	75	80.11
BiGRU sentence, GRU question with attention	Glove-100	100	50	79.33
BiGRU sentence, GRU question	**FastText-300**	**100**	**75**	**81.22**

5   Discussion

This study introduced a new approach to classifying student-generated questions during reading, based on human ratings of depth. Using RNN architectures informed by GRU, BiGRU and LSTM cell types of different sizes, and different word embeddings (i.e., FastText and Glove), results revealed that the strongest model achieved a classification accuracy of 81.22%, which surpasses previous prediction results on the same dataset, that reported an accuracy of 41.6%. However, the results are lower than accuracies reported on other specific tasks of question classification using NLP techniques.

One observation that can be extracted from the results is that sentence encoding performed slightly better than encoding the text, probably since the text contains a lot of information not necessary to evaluate the question quality. In addition, the results may indicate that the network was not able to learn how to ignore potential noise from the text encoding. Arguably, adding more training examples would improve the results for the text encoder version.

Regarding the type of encoders used, the experiments showed that GRU models perform better than LSTM for this dataset likely because fewer parameters are required. The same reasoning can explain the results of the bidirectional networks. Although

BiGRUs have better expressing power (i.e., capability to encode the text based on word embeddings) than normal GRU models, they did not improve the results when used for questions. This indicates that the questions were short enough to be well represented by a simple GRU and the extra parameters were not useful.

Albeit successful in recent studies [51, 52], adding an attention layer did not improve the results, probably because of the additional matrix which needed to be learned by the neural network. In all other experiments, max-pooling was used to reduce the dimensionality of the encoders' output. Experiments using the concatenation between the last outputs of the forward and backward direction were also performed, but were not as accurate on the validation set, compared to the other solutions. As a result, they were not included in Table 2.

The best result was obtained using FastText word embeddings, which performed better than the equivalent network architecture relying on Glove word vectors of the same size (300). Smaller Glove vectors (100) achieved a higher accuracy compared to the larger ones (300) most likely because the network required fewer training parameters.

6   Conclusions

Many students, especially those with low prior knowledge, have difficulty making inferences necessary for text comprehension. iSTART is an ITS that provides reading strategy instruction to promote self-explanation and inference generation, in order to promote comprehension. Question asking can also improve readers' comprehension, especially when the questions generated are deep.

This study contributes to the development of question asking practice within iSTART. As such, practice modules for question asking require the application of NLP techniques to automatically assess the quality of students' questions. Thus, an overarching objective of this project is to create algorithms that are sensitive to the types of questions students ask during reading. Identification of particular question types would then trigger appropriate formative feedback with the hopes that the feedback would promote generation of deeper questions and improve comprehension. For example, when the algorithm detects shallow question asking, the feedback mechanism in iSTART would trigger a message prompting the reader to ask deep questions that would, for example, require learners to identify a causal mechanism.

This study describes a series of experiments that used recurrent neural networks to assess the quality of questions. The obtained results are very promising, with the best model exceeding 81% accuracy classifying questions into 4 classes of question depth. The results reported here indicate that successful classification models for question depth can be integrated into iSTART. These models could provide students with accurate formative feedback that may lead to increased reading strategy skills and overall reading comprehension.

Our next steps consist of implementing and testing these models in iSTART. Moreover, experiments should be conducted to further development of question depth classification. For instance, an experiment testing all three encoders at once (text, sentence, question) could assess how a network making more informant decision, at the cost of increasing the needed parameters, could improve accuracy. Another experiment could test the use of only one encoder for text and extract the sentence representation from the hidden states corresponding to the words in that sentence. In addition, simpler solutions could also be tested on this corpus and compared with the deep learning methods. One example that proved successful on smaller datasets uses neural networks on top of string kernels [53] for answer selection. Although the tasks are not identical, simple similarity measures could be effective for evaluating questions, either stand-alone or as additional features in a more complex network.

Acknowledgments. This research was partially supported by the 644187 EC H2020 *Realising an Applied Gaming Eco-system* (RAGE) project, the FP7 2008-212578 LTfLL project, the Department of Education, Institute of Education Sciences - Grant R305A130124, as well as the Department of Defense, Office of Naval Research - Grants N00014140343 and N000141712300.

References

1. Snow, C.: Reading for Understanding Toward an R&D Program in Reading Comprehension. Rand Corporation, Santa Monica (2002)
2. Palincsar, A.S., Brown, A.L.: Interactive promote learning teaching independent from text to. Read. Teach. **39**, 771–777 (1986)
3. Rosenshine, B., Meister, C.: Reciprocal teaching: a review of the research. Rev. Educ. Res. **64**, 479–530 (1994)
4. Rosenshine, B., Meister, C., Chapman, S.: Teaching students to generate questions: a review of the intervention studies. Rev. Educ. Res. **66**, 181–221 (1996)
5. McNamara, D.S., O'Reilly, T., Rowe, M., Boonthum, C., Levinstein, I.: iSTART: a web-based tutor that teaches self-explanation and metacognitive reading strategies. In: Reading Comprehension Strategies: Theories, Interventions, and Technologies, pp. 397–420 (2007)
6. VanLehn, K., Graesser, A.C., Jackson, G.T., Jordan, P., Olney, A., Rosé, C.P.: When are tutorial dialogues more effective than reading? Cogn. Sci. **31**, 3–62 (2007)
7. Graesser, A.C., McMahen, C.L.: Anomalous information triggers questions when adults solve quantitative problems and comprehend stories. J. Educ. Psychol. **85**, 136–151 (1993)
8. Wisher, R.A., Graesser, A.C.: Question-asking in advanced distributed learning environments. In: Toward a Science of Distributed Learning and Training, pp. 209–234. American Psychological Association, Washington, D.C. (2007)
9. Beck, I., McKeown, M.G., Hamilton, R.L., Kucan, L.: Questioning the Author: An Approach for Enhancing Student Engagement (1997). https://eric.ed.gov/?id=ED408562
10. Kintsch, W.: Comprehension: A Paradigm for Cognition. Cambridge University Press, New York (1998)
11. Graesser, A.C., Person, N.K.: Question asking during tutoring. Am. Educ. Res. J. **31**, 104–137 (1994)
12. Davey, B., McBride, S.: Effects of question-generation training on reading comprehension. J. Educ. Psychol. **78**, 256–262 (1986)
13. Craig, S.D., Gholson, B., Ventura, M., Graesser, A.C.: Overhearing dialogues and monologues in virtual tutoring sessions: effects on questioning and vicarious learning. Int. J. Artif. Intell. Educ. **11**, 242–253 (2000)

14. Silva, J., Coheur, L., Mendes, A.C., Wichert, A.: From symbolic to sub-symbolic information in question classification. Artif. Intell. Rev. **35**, 137–154 (2011)
15. Ittycheriah, A., Franz, M., Zhu, W., Ratnaparkhi, A., Mammone, R.J.: IBM's statistical question answering system. In: Proceedings of TREC-9 Conference, pp. 229–234 (2000)
16. Hovy, E., Gerber, L., Hermjakob, U., Lin, C.-Y., Ravichandran, D.: Toward semantics-based answer pinpointing. In: Proceedings of the First International Conference on Human Language Technology Research, pp. 1–7 (2001)
17. Harabagiu, S., Moldovan, D., Pasca, M., Mihalcea, R., Surdeanu, M., Bunescu, R., Girju, R., Rus, V., Morarescu, P.: FALCON: boosting knowledge for answer engines. In: Proceedings of Ninth Text Retrieval Conference (TREC 2000), pp. 479–488 (2000)
18. Gerber, L.: A QA Typology for Webclopedia (2001)
19. Li, X., Roth, D.: Learning question classifiers. In: Proceedings of the 19th International Conference on Computational Linguistics, vol. 1, pp. 1–7 (2002)
20. Bloom, B.S.: Taxonomy of Educational Objectives, Cognitive Domain, pp. 20–24. McKay, New York (1956)
21. Mosenthal, P.B.: Understanding the strategies of document literacy and their conditions of use. J. Educ. Psychol. **88**, 314–332 (1996)
22. Olney, A., Louwerse, M., Matthews, E., Marineau, J., Hite-Mitchell, H., Graesser, A.: Utterance classification in AutoTutor. In: Proceedings of HLT-NAACL 2003 Workshop on Building Educational Applications Using Natural Language Processing, vol. 2, pp. 1–8. ACL, Morristown (2003)
23. Pietra, S.D., Pietra, V.D., Lafferty, J.: Inducing features of random fields. IEEE Trans. Pattern Anal. Mach. Intell. **19**, 380–393 (1997)
24. Chinchor, N., Robinson, P.: MUC-7 named entity task definition. In: Proceedings of the 7th Conference on Message Understanding, MUC6, p. 21 (1997)
25. Hacioglu, K., Ward, W.: Question classification with support vector machines and error correcting codes. In: Proceedings of HLT-NAACL 2003, pp. 28–30. Association for Computational Linguistics, Morristown (2003)
26. Zhang, D., Lee, W.S.: Question classification using support vector machines. In: Proceedings of the 26th Annual International ACM SIGIR Conference on Research and Development in Information Retrieval, SIGIR 2003, p. 26. ACM Press, New York (2003)
27. Blunsom, P., Kocik, K., Curran, J.R.: Question classification with log-linear models. In: Proceedings of the 29th Annual International ACM SIGIR Conference on Research and Development in Information Retrieval, SIGIR 2006, p. 615 (2006)
28. Kopp, K.J., Johnson, A.M., Crossley, S.A., McNamara, D.S.: Assessing question quality using NLP. In: André, E., Baker, R., Hu, X., Rodrigo, Ma.M.T., du Boulay, B. (eds.) AIED 2017. LNCS, vol. 10331, pp. 523–527. Springer, Cham (2017). https://doi.org/10.1007/978-3-319-61425-0_55
29. Krishnan, V., Das, S., Chakrabarti, S.: Enhanced answer type inference from questions using sequential models. In: Proceedings of Human Language Technology Conference and Conference on Empirical Methods in Natural Language Processing, HLT 2005, pp. 315–322 (2005)
30. Suzuki, J., Taira, H., Sasaki, Y., Maeda, E.: Question classification using HDAG kernel. In: Proceedings of the ACL 2003 Workshop on Multilingual Summarization and Question Answering, vol. 12, pp. 61–68 (2003)
31. Hermjakob, U.: Parsing and question classification for question answering. In: Proceedings of Working Open-domain Question Answering, vol. 12, pp. 1–6 (2001)
32. Mishra, M., Mishra, V.K., Sharma, H.R.: Question classification using semantic, syntactic and lexical features. Int. J. Web Semant. Technol. **4**, 39–47 (2013)

33. Elman, J.L.: Finding structure in time. Cogn. Sci. **14**, 179–211 (1990)
34. Yih, W., He, X., Meek, C.: Semantic parsing for single-relation question answering. In: Association for Computational Linguistics, pp. 643–648 (2014)
35. Kalchbrenner, N., Grefenstette, E., Blunsom, P.: A convolutional neural network for modelling sentences. In: Proceedings of 52nd Annual Meeting of the Association for Computational Linguistics, pp. 655–665 (2014)
36. Iyyer, M., Boyd-graber, J., Claudino, L., Socher, R., Daum, H.: A neural network for factoid question answering over paragraphs. In: Proceedings of the 2014 Conference on Empirical Methods in Natural Language Processing (EMNLP) (2014)
37. Collobert, R., Weston, J., Bottou, L., Karlen, M., Kavukcuoglu, K., Kuksa, P.: Natural language processing (Almost) from scratch. J. Mach. Learn. Res. **12**, 2493–2537 (2011)
38. Fei, T., Heng, W.J., Toh, K.C., Qi, T.: Question classification for e-learning by artificial neural network. In: ICICS-PCM 2003, pp. 1757–1761. IEEE (2003)
39. Kim, Y.: Convolutional neural networks for sentence classification. In: Proceedings of 2014 Conference on Empirical Methods Natural Language Processing (EMNLP 2014), pp. 1746–1751 (2014)
40. Lai, S., Xu, L., Liu, K., Zhao, J.: Recurrent convolutional neural networks for text classification. In: Twenty-Ninth AAAI Conference on Artificial Intelligence, pp. 2267–2273 (2015)
41. Crump, M.J.C., McDonnell, J.V., Gureckis, T.M.: Evaluating Amazon's mechanical turk as a tool for experimental behavioral research. PLoS One **8**, e57410 (2013)
42. Pennington, J., Socher, R., Manning, C.D.: GloVe: global vectors for word representation. In: Proceedings of the 2014 Conference on Empirical Methods in Natural Language Processing (EMNLP), pp. 1532–1543 (2014)
43. Bojanowski, P., Grave, E., Joulin, A., Mikolov, T.: Enriching Word Vectors with Subword Information (2016)
44. Mikolov, T., Corrado, G., Chen, K., Dean, J.: Efficient estimation of word representations in vector space. In: Proceedings of ICLR 2013, pp. 1–12 (2013)
45. Darío Gutiérrez, E., Levy, R., Bergen, B.K.: Finding non-arbitrary form-meaning systematicity using string-metric learning for Kernel regression. In: ACL, pp. 2379–2388 (2016)
46. Hochreiter, S., Urgen Schmidhuber, J.: Long short-term memory. Neural Comput. **9**, 1735–1780 (1997)
47. Cho, K., van Merrienboer, B., Gulcehre, C., Bahdanau, D., Bougares, F., Schwenk, H., Bengio, Y.: Learning phrase representations using RNN encoder-decoder for statistical machine translation. In: EMNLP 2014, pp. 1724–1734 (2014)
48. Graves, A., Schmidhuber, J.: Framewise phoneme classification with bidirectional LSTM and other neural network architectures. Neural Netw. **18**, 602–610 (2005)
49. dos Santos, C., Tan, M., Xiang, B., Zhou, B.: Attentive Pooling Networks. CoRR, abs/1602.03609. 2, 4 (2016)
50. Kingma, D., Ba, J.: Adam: a method for stochastic optimization. In: 3rd International Conference on Learning Representations (2015)
51. Xiong, C., Zhong, V., Socher, R.: Dynamic coattention networks for question answering. In: ICLR Submission, pp. 1–13 (2017)
52. Seo, M., Kembhavi, A., Farhadi, A., Hajishirzi, H.: Bidirectional attention flow for machine comprehension. In: ICLR 2017 (2017)
53. Masala, M., Ruseti, S., Rebedea, T.: Sentence selection with neural networks using string kernels. Proc. Comput. Sci. **112**, 1774–1782 (2017)

Sentence Level or Token Level Features for Automatic Short Answer Grading?: Use Both

Swarnadeep Saha[⊠], Tejas I. Dhamecha, Smit Marvaniya,
Renuka Sindhgatta, and Bikram Sengupta

IBM Research, Bangalore, India
{swarnads,tidhamecha,smarvani,renuka.sr,bsengupt}@in.ibm.com

Abstract. Automatic short answer grading for Intelligent Tutoring Systems has attracted much attention of the researchers over the years. While the traditional techniques for short answer grading are rooted in statistical learning and hand-crafted features, recent research has explored sentence embedding based techniques. We observe that sentence embedding techniques, while being effective for grading in-domain student answers, may not be best suited for out-of-domain answers. Further, sentence embeddings can be affected by non-sentential answers (answers given in the context of the question). On the other hand, token level hand-crafted features can be fairly domain independent and are less affected by non-sentential forms. We propose a novel feature encoding based on partial similarities of tokens (Histogram of Partial Similarities or HoPS), its extension to part-of-speech tags (HoPSTags) and question type information. On combining the proposed features with sentence embedding based features, we are able to further improve the grading performance. Our final model achieves better or competitive results in experimental evaluation on multiple benchmarking datasets and a large scale industry dataset.

Keywords: Short answer grading · Sentence embeddings
Histogram of Partial Similarity · Supervised learning · Feature fusion

1 Introduction

Short answer grading, an integral part of Intelligent Tutoring Systems, is positioned as a research problem at the intersection of natural language understanding and its application to educational technologies. Formally, the problem is to grade a student answer in the context of a question and its reference answer(s). The grades are either discrete or bounded real numbers. Thus, traditionally, the short answer grading problem is often modeled as a classification or regression task.

While early works on automatic short answer grading [17,21,25] used manually generated patterns from reference answers, recently Ramachandran et al. [23] proposed a method to automate the generation of patterns. However, patterns do not scale well across domains. They are not a good fit for grading

© Springer International Publishing AG, part of Springer Nature 2018
C. Penstein Rosé et al. (Eds.): AIED 2018, LNAI 10947, pp. 503–517, 2018.
https://doi.org/10.1007/978-3-319-93843-1_37

non-sentential student answers as they violate the structural patterns of the corresponding reference answers. The *non-sentential* answers, also called fragments [19], lack a complete sentential form but whose meaning can be inferred from the question context.

While some research efforts have proposed dedicated techniques for short answer grading, others view this problem as a specific application of generic natural language understanding tasks of textual entailment or semantic textual similarity. Traditionally, all machine learning based techniques have revolved around hand-crafted features. It is only recently that techniques have been proposed to utilize deep learning based approaches for short answer grading.

Table 1. An illustrative example showing non-sentential and well-formed student answers.

Question	Reference answer	Student answer 1 (Non-sentential)	Student answer 2 (Well-formed)
What is meant by monotonically increasing functions?	Monotonically increasing functions are the ones that are entirely not decreasing	Entirely not decreasing	Monotonically increasing functions are the ones that are either entirely increasing or remain constant

Hand-crafted Features

Mohler et al. [18] proposed a method involving graph alignment and lexical semantic similarity features. Heilman and Madnani [9] proposed a short answer scoring method that uses stacking and domain adaptation techniques. Jimenez et al. [10] proposed a 42 dimensional soft cardinality based feature representation for student answer analysis. The abstraction of the feature representation makes it more suitable for *unseen domain* scenarios. In an ensemble approach, Ott et al. [22] learn a meta-classifier by combining three different grade prediction systems. In one of the recent works, Sultan et al. [26] proposed a method for short answer grading in a feature ensemble approach involving text alignment, semantic similarity, question demoting, term weighting, and length ratios.

Overall, the hand-crafted features often rely on dependency or constituency parsers to encode the structural as well as semantic information of the student answers and the reference answers. However, it becomes restrictive in dialog-based tutoring systems, as the student answers can be non-sentential. Additionally, dependency parsers are slow and are not suitable for deployment in real-world systems.

Apart from these task-specific approaches, there have been numerous research efforts to model short answer grading as problems of textual entailment [5,12,21] or textual similarity [1–3,13].

Deep Learning Approaches

Deep learning techniques, mostly using Recurrent Neural Networks (RNN) and their variants, particularly Long Short-Term Memory (LSTM) have achieved state-of-the-art results in various natural language understanding tasks including textual similarity and textual entailment. A few of such efforts include an LSTM based approach [4], a Siamese LSTM model [20] and a Siamese bi-LSTM model using earth mover's distance [11]. Recently, LSTMs have also been used in the education community for detecting misconceptions from students' responses [14]. Conneau et al. [7] proposed a method, termed as InferSent, for learning universal sentence representations using a bi-LSTM network with max pooling. They trained the network on the Stanford Natural Language Inference corpus [6] to generate sentence embeddings, which are shown to work well across various natural language understanding tasks.

These techniques either train an end-to-end deep neural network or learn an embedding network followed by training a classifier. The former requires a large labeled data to learn, which is often a limitation for short answer grading. The later (embedding learning techniques) can be problematic for non-sentential answers, which is a common occurrence in dialog-based tutoring systems. However, Conneau et al. [7] showed that their pre-trained sentence embeddings can be transferred to other NLP tasks without having to learn them. Thus, we use these embeddings to obtain sentence level features for short answer grading.

Limitations and Research Contributions

We observe that in dialog-based tutoring systems, the student answers are either (1) well-formed, or (2) non-sentential responses. Table 1 presents such an example. The second category of answers can derail techniques that depend on accurate parsing, non-contextual completeness, and grammatical structure of answers. Further, there is significant scope for fine-tuning hand-crafted features to make them suitable for *partial* answers in dialog-based tutors. We have also observed that hand-crafted features generalize better across domains, as compared to sentence embedding based approaches. To this end, we believe that using hand-crafted features in conjunction with sentence embedding features is necessary for improved short answer grading. In keeping with this goal, we make the following salient contributions.

- We develop novel token level features that are specifically tuned for understanding partially correct student answers. We call them Histogram of Partial Similarities (HoPS).
- Certain Part-of-Speech tags are more important than others for certain question types. Thus, we use question type information and combine HoPS per POS Tag of the expected answer tokens to further refine our features. To the best of our knowledge, using question types and POS tags as features for short answer grading is another novel contribution of our work.
- Our features are fast, easy to compute, and domain-independent.

– We combine token level features with sentence level features obtained using InferSent. The effectiveness of this expanded feature set is verified empirically across a variety of short answer grading tasks and datasets.

We also present comparable or better results than previously reported state-of-the-art results on SemEval-2013 task, Mohler et al. dataset, and a large-scale industry dataset. Further, we showcase that our features work equally well on both in-domain and out-of-domain data across various classification and regression tasks in short answer grading. The following section provides a detailed description of the proposed features.

2   Proposed Features

We devise and combine two broad categories of features: (1) sentence level features and (2) token level features. The following two subsections discuss both the categories as well as the individual components of our token level features - Word Overlap (WO), Question Types (QT) and Histogram of Partial Similarity on POS tags (HoPSTag). Our proposed architecture combining sentence and token level features is shown in Fig. 1.

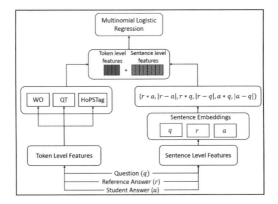

Fig. 1. Our proposed architecture that combines sentence and token level features. WO, QT and HoPSTag refer to word overlap, question type, and histogram of partial similarity on POS tags, respectively.

2.1   Sentence Level Features

For a triple *(question, reference answer, student answer)*, we first obtain sentence embeddings for the question (q), reference answer (r) and student answer (a) using InferSent [7][1]. Once the sentence embeddings are generated, we compute the sentence level features as:

$$S_{feat}(q, r, a) = (r * a, |r - a|, r * q, |r - q|, a * q, |a - q|) \tag{1}$$

---

[1] https://github.com/facebookresearch/InferSent.

where $r * a$ represents the element-wise multiplication of vectors r and a, while $|r - a|$ represents their absolute element-wise difference. Overall, this representation captures (1) the information gap between student and reference answer ($r*a$ and $|r - a|$), (2) the novel information expected in answer ($r * q$ and $|r - q|$), and (3) the novel information expressed in the student answer ($a * q$ and $|a - q|$). We find that incorporating the question embedding in the sentence level features is novel to our feature representation and is particularly useful in scenarios where the question at test time is already seen at train time. The following subsection describes the token level feature extraction process in detail.

2.2   Token Level Features

The idea of token level features largely stems from the fact that in a dialog-based tutoring scenario, students often only mention the important tokens. Such responses, although correct, are non-sentential and may not necessarily entail the reference answer. The preprocessing step for calculating token level features first involves stop words removal from the reference answer and the student answer. Subsequently, question demoting [18,26] is performed that removes words from reference answer and student answer that are also present in the question. This leads to the generation of two bags of words, one for the reference answer and another for the student answer. The token level features are based on the following three key insights.

Word Overlap: We extract token based similarity features using the reference answer bag (RA) and the student answer bag (SA). The similarity features are calculated based on the number of word overlaps between the bags. A word w_i in reference answer bag is considered overlapping if (1) its score with student answer bag, as calculated in Eq. 2, is greater than a certain threshold δ, or (2) it is part of the Wordnet [16] synsets of any word from the student answer bag. $Cos(w_i, w_j)$ represents the cosine similarity between the word vectors of words w_i and w_j. Based on the number of word overlaps between the bags, we calculate three features - (1) Precision - word overlap count upon the number of words in the student answer bag, (2) Recall - word overlap count upon the number of words in the reference answer bag, and (3) Precision×Recall.

$$Score(w_i, SA) = \max_{w_j \in SA} Cos(w_i, w_j), \text{ where } w_i \in RA \qquad (2)$$

Histogram of Partial Similarity (HoPS): The objective of computing the partial similarity histogram is to capture the similarity pattern between the student answer and the reference answer. For each word w_i in reference answer bag, we compute the similarity score $Score(w_i, SA)$ with respect to student answer bag (SA) using Eq. 2. The similarity between two words is computed as the cosine similarity between their word embeddings. The similarity score for a word w_i with respect to the student answer SA is the maximum of the its similarities with all the tokens in SA. These similarity scores are partitioned into N bins. The bin index I for word w_i is computed as:

$$I(w_i) = min\left(\left\lfloor\frac{Score(w_i, SA) + 1}{h}\right\rfloor, N - 1\right) \text{ where } h = \frac{2}{N} \qquad (3)$$

where indices are zero-indexed, and h is the width of the bin, and N is the number of bins. A histogram is created after binning each word in the reference answer bag. Our HoPS features are calculated by dividing each bin value by the size of the reference answer bag. This ensures that the HoPS features are invariant of the size of the reference answer bag. Unlike word overlap features, HoPS incorporates all words in the reference answer bag without thresholding on a similarity score, and thus helps model the class of partially correct student answers.

Table 2. Question type distributions of SemEval-2013 dataset and the large scale industry dataset.

	How	What	Why	Who	Which	When	Where	Whom	Other	Total
SemEval-2013 dataset										
Train	38	58	44	4	19	34	2	0	10	135
Unseen answer	38	58	44	4	19	34	2	0	10	135
Unseen question	4	8	4	1	1	4	0	0	1	15
Unseen domain	10	23	12	0	6	15	3	0	0	46
Large-scale industry dataset										
Train and test	172	278	13	13	6	19	2	2	0	483

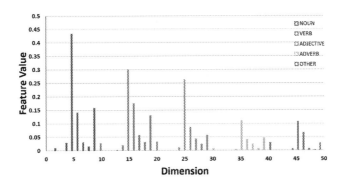

Fig. 2. A 50-dimensional average HoPSTag feature representation over all partially correct student answers from SemEval-2013 5-way classification subtask.

Histogram of Partial Similarity with POS Tags (HoPSTags) and Question Types: As an extension to HoPS, we segregate the histogram counts on the basis of various part of speech tags of the reference answer tokens. Specifically, for each of the 5 POS tags - Verb, Noun, Adjective, Adverb and Other, we create a histogram as before. The bin values of each histogram are divided by the number of tokens in the reference answer bag having the corresponding POS tag. We term this extended set of features as HoPSTag.

The utility of these features is understood best in the context of specific types of questions. Depending on the question type, reference answer tokens of certain POS tags become more important than others. For example, a factoid question like *'Who is the prime minister of India'* expects a noun (*Modi*) in the student answer. We find that short answer grading questions almost always belong to a fixed taxonomy of questions types, given by the set {*How, What, Why, Who, Which, When, Where, Whom*}. Thus, we generate 8 binary features, one for each question type depicting the presence of that question type. Table 2 shows the question type distributions of the SemEval-2013 dataset and the large scale dataset.

In Fig. 2, we show a HoPSTag feature representation averaged over all the partially correct student answers from SemEval-2013 5-way classification dataset. A significant number of reference answer tokens in the middle to high similarity bins indicates partially correct student answers. In a strict word overlap based setting, a large portion of these similarity values may not get incorporated; which we are able to preserve in HoPSTag features.

2.3 Combined Features

Our final feature representation is a combination of the sentence and token level features. Each sentence embedding is a S dimensional vector, making our sentence level feature size as $6S$ dimensional. Token level feature representation is a concatenation of 3 word overlap features, 8 binary question type features, and $5N$ HoPSTag features, where N is the number of bins. Thus, the final combined feature representation is $6S + 5N + 11$ dimensional.

3 Experiments

To evaluate the effectiveness of our proposed approach, we perform experiments on three datasets.

1. **Large Scale Industry Dataset:** The dataset consists of student answers collected for Psychology domain. The task is a 3-way classification task which requires predicting a student answer as `correct`, `partial`, or `incorrect`.
2. **SemEval-2013 [8] Dataset:** We use the SciEntsBank corpus of the SemEval-2013 dataset consisting of 197 questions in Science domain. The task involves three classification subtasks on unseen-answers (UA), unseen-question (UQ), and unseen-domain (UD) scenarios.

3. **Mohler et al.** [18] **Dataset:** This dataset is from Computer Science domain and consists of 80 undergraduate data structures questions. The task is a regression task and requires computing a real valued score for a student answer on a scale of 0 to 5.

Table 3 provides details pertaining to dataset sizes and experimental protocols. Further, we provide an ablation study to analyze the importance of individual components of the proposed feature representation. For the large scale industry dataset and the SemEval-2013 dataset, the results are reported in terms of accuracy (Acc), macro-average F1 (M-F1), and weighted-F1 (W-F1). Since Mohler's task is a regression one, the performance is measured in terms of root mean square error (RMSE) and Pearson's correlation.

Table 3. Characteristics of the large scale industry dataset, SemEval-2013 dataset, and Mohler's dataset.

Dataset	Responses	Protocol		
		Train	Test	
Large scale industry dataset	16,458	12,317	4,141	
SemEval-2013 dataset [8]	10,804	4,969	UA	UQ	UD
			540	733	4,562
Mohler et al. dataset [18]	2,273 (12 assignments)	Leave-one-assignment-out		

In all our experiments, we use NLTK[2] for stop words removal and Scikit-learn[3] for the classifiers. We have used $N = 10$ as the number of bins, overlap threshold $\delta = 0.7$, and sentence embedding size $S = 4,096$. For the large scale industry dataset, we specifically use word vectors trained on a Psychology domain corpus from which the questions have been curated. For others, we use pre-trained word vectors [15]. Our 61 dimensional token level features are trained using a Random Forest classifier with 100 estimators. All reported results using Random Forests are averaged across 100 runs of the system. The sentence level features as well as its combination with token level features are trained using a Multinomial Logistic Regression classifier. The best parameters are chosen using 5-fold cross-validation over the training data. The regression task on Mohler et al. dataset is trained using a ridge regression model.

While reporting comparative results for these datasets, we also show experiments with five variants of the proposed features, including (1) only token level features (TF), (2) only sentence level features without question embedding (SF(-Q)), (3) only sentence level features with question embedding (SF(+Q)), (4) combination of token level and sentence level features without question embedding (TF+SF(-Q)), and (5) combination of token level and sentence level features with question embedding (TF+SF(+Q)).

---

[2] http://www.nltk.org/.
[3] http://scikit-learn.org/stable/.

3.1 Large Scale Industry Dataset

Our first experiment is on a first of its kind large scale industry dataset on Psychology domain. The test data has the same set of questions and reference answers as the training set. We compare our models against SEMILAR [24] and Sultan et al. [26][4]. SEMILAR[5] is a semantic similarity toolkit, widely used in various core NLP tasks including paraphrase identification, question answering, and short answer grading. We choose to compare against Sultan et al. [26] as their model outperformed all existing models in short answer grading. Their system was trained using a Random Forest classifier with 500 estimators, as mentioned in their paper. Table 4 shows the comparative results of all the models. We list the salient observations below.

Table 4. Results of the proposed approach on large scale industry dataset.

	Acc	M-F1	W-F1
SEMILAR	0.3485	0.3367	0.3470
Sultan et al. [26]	0.5274	0.4722	0.5111
TF	0.5881	0.5419	0.5749
SF(−Q)	0.6184	0.5773	0.6066
SF(+Q)	0.6508	0.6177	0.6426
TF+SF(−Q)	0.6341	0.5958	0.6229
TF+SF(+Q)	**0.6636**	**0.6309**	**0.6558**

- Our token level features (TF) alone significantly outperforms SEMILAR and Sultan et al. [26]'s system in all the three metrics.
- The sentence level features (SF) outperform our token level features. Further, our results are significantly better when the question embedding is used for feature encoding (SF(+Q)). This, however, is unsurprising because the questions at test time were already seen at training time, thus enabling the classifier to capture the semantics of the question as well.
- Results improve further when we combine our token level features and sentence level features (TF+SF(+Q)), leading to an overall gain of 14 points in Weighted-F1 over the existing best system of Sultan et al. [26].

3.2 SemEval-2013 [8] Dataset

SemEval-2013 task on student answer analysis consists of three classification subtasks - (1) 2-way classification into `correct` and `incorrect` classes, (2) 3-way

---

[4] All experiments on Sultan et al. 's system were performed using their publicly available code at https://github.com/ma-sultan/short-answer-grader.

[5] http://www.semanticsimilarity.org/.

classification into correct, incorrect and contradictory classes, (3) 5-way classification into correct, partially correct, contradictory, irrelevant and contradictory classes. Each subtask comprises of three kinds of test data - Unseen Answers (UA), Unseen Questions (UQ) and Unseen Domains (UD). As shown in Table 3, the split sizes as well as the samples are exactly same in all the three subtasks. However, the labels change as the subtasks become more fine grained. For this dataset, we show comparative results with four systems

Table 5. Results for all the classification subtasks of SemEval-2013 task.

(a) 2-way

	UA			UQ			UD		
	Acc	M-F1	W-F1	Acc	M-F1	W-F1	Acc	M-F1	W-F1
CoMeT	0.7740	**0.7680**	**0.7730**	0.6030	0.5790	0.5970	0.6760	0.6700	0.6770
ETS	**0.7760**	0.7620	0.7700	0.6330	0.6020	0.6220	0.6270	0.5430	0.5740
SOFTCAR	0.7240	0.7150	0.7220	**0.7450**	**0.7370**	**0.7450**	0.7110	0.7050	0.7120
Sultan et al. [26]	0.7087	0.6768	0.6907	0.7050	0.6786	0.6951	**0.7129**	**0.7038**	**0.7121**
TF	0.7451	0.7339	0.7414	0.6878	0.6517	0.6717	0.7097	0.7009	0.7091
SF(-Q)	0.7315	0.7250	0.7308	0.6753	0.6617	0.6738	0.6357	0.5909	0.6125
SF(+Q)	0.7481	0.7422	0.7476	0.6303	0.6204	0.6314	0.6324	0.6109	0.6253
TF+SF(-Q)	0.7796	0.7710	0.7771	**0.7490**	**0.7385**	**0.7478**	0.7087	0.6903	0.7023
TF+SF(+Q)	**0.7926**	**0.7858**	**0.7910**	0.7026	0.6850	0.6983	**0.7196**	**0.7089**	**0.7178**

(b) 3-way

	UA			UQ			UD		
	Acc	M-F1	W-F1	Acc	M-F1	W-F1	Acc	M-F1	W-F1
CoMeT	0.7130	0.6400	0.7070	0.5460	0.3800	0.5220	0.5790	0.4040	0.5500
ETS	**0.7200**	**0.6470**	**0.7080**	0.5830	0.3930	0.5370	0.5430	0.3330	0.4610
SOFTCAR	0.6590	0.5550	0.6470	**0.6520**	**0.4690**	**0.6340**	**0.6370**	**0.4860**	**0.6200**
Sultan et al. [26]	0.6042	0.4439	0.5696	0.6426	0.4550	0.6154	0.6269	0.4516	0.6033
TF	0.6489	0.5537	0.6385	0.6152	0.4239	0.5844	0.6325	0.4491	0.6084
SF(-Q)	0.6963	0.6408	0.6908	0.5484	0.4508	0.5594	0.5601	0.4217	0.5322
SF(+Q)	0.6907	0.6373	0.6860	0.5948	0.4541	0.5818	0.5686	0.4176	0.5468
TF+SF(-Q)	**0.7185**	**0.6662**	**0.7143**	0.6139	**0.4912**	0.6281	0.6324	**0.4794**	**0.6115**
TF+SF(+Q)	0.7185	0.6574	0.7112	**0.6535**	0.4890	**0.6362**	**0.6403**	0.4524	0.6107

(c) 5-way

	UA			UQ			UD		
	Acc	M-F1	W-F1	Acc	M-F1	W-F1	Acc	M-F1	W-F1
CoMeT	0.6000	0.4410	0.5980	0.4370	0.1610	0.2990	0.4210	0.1210	0.2520
ETS	**0.6430**	**0.4780**	**0.6400**	0.4320	0.2630	0.4110	0.4410	**0.3800**	0.4140
SOFTCAR	0.5440	0.3800	0.5370	**0.5250**	**0.3070**	**0.4920**	**0.5120**	0.3000	**0.4710**
Sultan et al. [26]	0.4898	0.3298	0.4875	0.4808	0.3020	0.4676	0.5065	0.3440	0.4847
TF	0.5523	0.3920	0.5510	0.4966	0.3628	0.4748	0.5194	0.2986	0.4822
SF(-Q)	0.6111	0.4603	0.6098	0.3943	0.3395	0.3973	0.4014	0.3229	0.4004
SF(+Q)	0.6074	0.4645	0.6089	0.4325	0.3127	0.3964	0.4213	0.3114	0.4064
TF+SF(-Q)	**0.6444**	**0.4808**	**0.6420**	0.5007	0.3168	**0.4881**	0.5088	**0.3574**	**0.4923**
TF+SF(+Q)	0.6296	0.4724	0.6303	**0.5061**	**0.3763**	0.4719	**0.5107**	0.3420	0.4862

including the top performing ones from the task leader board[6]. Particularly, we present comparisons with CoMeT [22], ETS [9], SOFTCAR [10], and Sultan et al. [26]. The results are shown in Table 5. We summarize our key observations below.

- State-of-the-art techniques do not perform well across all kinds of test data. However, our domain-independent token level features have balanced performance throughout, as shown by competitive results in 2-way, 3-way, and 5-way across UA, UQ and UD (See *TF* rows in the tables).
- The sentence level features, on the other hand, suffer from lack of domain adaptability, as shown by significantly poor results on UD (See *SF* rows).
- We see substantial improvement in all the metrics when we combine our token level and sentence level features (See *TF+SF* rows). Specifically, in UA, we achieve 5, 2, and 4 points improvement in 2-way, 3-way, and 5-way respectively. This again testifies the need for both kinds of features and also verifies our hypothesis.
- Our final model combining sentence and token level features (TF+SF) outperforms or produces competitive results as compared to all existing models. We find it even more creditable, since there is no single state-of-the-art model that has best performances across all the test sets.

3.3   Mohler et al. [18] Dataset

The dataset includes responses from 12 Computer Science assignments. The experimental protocol uses one assignment each for test and development set, and the remaining ten assignments as the train set. This procedure is repeated 12 times, once per assignment. Finally, the RMSE and Pearson's correlation are computed between the predicted scores and the ground truths across all the assignments. For this dataset, we compare results against four approaches, including Mohler et al. [18] and Sultan et al. [26]. The results are reported in Table 6. The key observations are listed below.

- While sentence level features benefit from encoding the question information, the overall performance is still poorer compared to the token level features. This is largely down to the presence of a sizable number of factoid questions in the dataset.
- Compared to Mohler et al. [18], we report significant improvement. However, we report competitive results compared to Sultan et al. [26]. Note that Sultan et al. [26] relies on dependency parsing, which is computationally expensive and slow compared to the proposed features.
- Similar to experiments on the previous two datasets, the combination of token and sentence level features again shows significant improvement as compared to when used individually.

---

[6] https://docs.google.com/spreadsheets/d/1Xe3lCi9jnZQiZW97hBfkg0x4cI3oDfztZP hK3TGO_gw/pub?output=html.

Table 6. Results on Mohler et al. [18] dataset.

	Pearson's r	RMSE
tf-idf[†]	0.327	1.022
Lesk[†]	0.45	1.05
Mohler et al. [18]	**0.518**	**0.978**
Sultan et al. [26]	**0.592**	**0.887**
TF	0.531	0.929
SF(-Q)	0.376	1.015
SF(+Q)	0.448	0.98
TF+SF(-Q)	0.542	0.921
TF+SF(+Q)	**0.570**	**0.902**

[†] Results are as reported in Mohler et al. [18]

3.4 Ablation Study of Token Level Features

In order to gain a detailed understanding of our proposed features, we perform an ablation study on the large scale industry dataset. We start with the simple 3 dimensional word overlap (WO) features, and cumulatively add HoPS, POS tag, HOPSTag, and question type (QT) features to finally obtain the 61 dimensional representation (WO+HoPSTag+QT). Table 7 shows the results of the ablation study on large scale industry dataset. We list the key observations.

Table 7. Ablation study of our token level features on large scale industry dataset.

	Dim	Acc	M-F1	W-F1
WO	3	0.4868	0.376	0.4398
WO+HoPS	13	0.5077	0.4728	0.5069
WO+POS tag	8	0.4957	0.4116	0.4658
WO+POS tag+QT	16	0.5147	0.4855	0.5183
WO+HoPSTag	53	0.5646	0.5153	0.5509
WO+HoPSTag+QT	61	**0.5881**	**0.5419**	**0.5749**

- The WO features do not capture the partial similarity between the student and the reference answers, as shown by very low macro-average F1.
- Encoding partial similarities using HoPS features significantly improves the performance, particularly in terms of macro-average F1.
- Further, computing HoPSTag features yield additional 4 points improvement in macro-average F1.
- Enriching the HoPSTag features with question type information yields another 3 points improvement. This validates the intuition that tokens of certain POS tags are important for certain question types.

4   Conclusion

In this work, we propose an approach combining token and sentence level features for short answer grading. By using the proposed features, we show that we can overcome the limited accuracy of token level features and also the domain dependence of sentence level features. Our feature representation is based on three key insights – (1) the partial similarities of tokens between the reference and the student answer, termed as HoPS, (2) its extension to POS tags, termed as HoPSTags, and (3) question type information. Empirical evaluation of the proposed approach across benchmarking datasets show better or competitive results as compared to state-of-the-art. This demonstrates the effectiveness and generalizability of our method. Overall, the results suggest that sentence and token level features encode some non-overlapping aspects of information. We believe that this observation will be helpful in devising better features in the broader domain of semantic textual similarity. This remains one of the key future directions of our work.

References

1. Agirre, E., Banea, C., Cardie, C., Cer, D., Diab, M., Gonzalez-Agirre, A., Guo, W., Lopez-Gazpio, I., Maritxalar, M., Mihalcea, R., et al.: Semeval-2015 task 2: semantic textual similarity, English, Spanish and pilot on interpretability. In: Proceedings of the International Workshop on Semantic Evaluation, pp. 252–263 (2015)
2. Agirre, E., Cer, D., Diab, M., Gonzalez-Agirre, A., Guo, W.: * SEM 2013 shared task: semantic textual similarity. In: Proceedings of the Joint Conference on Lexical and Computational Semantics, vol. 1, pp. 32–43 (2013)
3. Agirre, E., Diab, M., Cer, D., Gonzalez-Agirre, A.: Semeval-2012 task 6: a pilot on semantic textual similarity. In: Proceedings of the Joint Conference on Lexical and Computational Semantics, pp. 385–393 (2012)
4. Alikaniotis, D., Yannakoudakis, H., Rei, M.: Automatic text scoring using neural networks. In: Proceedings of the Annual Meeting of the Association for Computational Linguistics, vol. 1, pp. 715–725 (2016)
5. Bjerva, J., Bos, J., Van der Goot, R., Nissim, M.: The meaning factory: formal semantics for recognizing textual entailment and determining semantic similarity. In: Proceedings of the International Workshop on Semantic Evaluation. pp. 642–646 (2014)
6. Bowman, S.R., Angeli, G., Potts, C., Manning, C.D.: A large annotated corpus for learning natural language inference. In: Proceedings of the Conference on Empirical Methods in Natural Language Processing (2015)
7. Conneau, A., Kiela, D., Schwenk, H., Barrault, L., Bordes, A.: Supervised learning of universal sentence representations from natural language inference data. In: Proceedings of the Conference on Empirical Methods in Natural Language Processing, pp. 670–680 (2017)

8. Dzikovska, M.O., Nielsen, R.D., Brew, C., Leacock, C., Giampiccolo, D., Bentivogli, L., Clark, P., Dagan, I., Dang, H.T.: SemEval-2013 Task 7: the joint student response analysis and 8th recognizing textual entailment challenge. In: Proceedings of the NAACL-HLT International Workshop on Semantic Evaluation, pp. 263–274 (2013)

9. Heilman, M., Madnani, N.: ETS: domain adaptation and stacking for short answer scoring. In: Proceedings of the Joint Conference on Lexical and Computational Semantics, vol. 2, pp. 275–279 (2013)

10. Jimenez, S., Becerra, C., Gelbukh, A.: SOFTCARDINALITY: hierarchical text overlap for student response analysis. In: Proceedings of the Joint Conference on Lexical and Computational Semantics, vol. 2, pp. 280–284 (2013)

11. Kumar, S., Chakrabarti, S., Roy, S.: Earth movers distance pooling over siamese LSTMS for automatic short answer grading. In: Proceedings of the International Joint Conference on Artificial Intelligence, pp. 2046–2052 (2017)

12. Levy, O., Zesch, T., Dagan, I., Gurevych, I.: Recognizing partial textual entailment. In: Proceedings of the Annual Meeting of the Association for Computational Linguistics, vol. 2, pp. 451–455 (2013)

13. Lopez-Gazpio, I., Maritxalar, M., Gonzalez-Agirre, A., Rigau, G., Uria, L., Agirre, E.: Interpretable semantic textual similarity: finding and explaining differences between sentences. Knowl. Based Syst. **119**, 186–199 (2017)

14. Michalenko, J.J., Lan, A.S., Baraniuk, R.G.: D.TRUMP: data-mining textual responses to uncover misconception patterns. In: Proceedings of the Fourth ACM Conference on Learning @ Scale L@S., pp. 245–248 (2017)

15. Mikolov, T., Sutskever, I., Chen, K., Corrado, G.S., Dean, J.: Distributed representations of words and phrases and their compositionality. In: Proceedings of the Advances in Neural Information Processing Systems, pp. 3111–3119 (2013)

16. Miller, G.A.: WordNet: a lexical database for English. Commun. ACM **38**(11), 39–41 (1995)

17. Mitchell, T., Russell, T., Broomhead, P., Aldridge, N.: Towards robust computerised marking of free-text responses. In: Proceedings of the International Computer Assisted Assessment Conference (2002)

18. Mohler, M., Bunescu, R.C., Mihalcea, R.: Learning to grade short answer questions using semantic similarity measures and dependency graph alignments. In: Proceedings of the Annual Meeting of the Association for Computational Linguistics: Human Language Technologies, pp. 752–762 (2011)

19. Morgan, J.: Sentence fragments and the notion sentence. Issues Linguistics: Paper in Honor of Henry Renée Kahane, pp. 719–751 (1973)

20. Mueller, J., Thyagarajan, A.: Siamese recurrent architectures for learning sentence similarity. In: Proceedings of the Association for the Advancement of Artificial Intelligence, pp. 2786–2792 (2016)

21. Nielsen, R.D., Ward, W., Martin, J.H.: Recognizing entailment in intelligent tutoring systems. Nat. Lang. Eng. **15**(4), 479–501 (2009)

22. Ott, N., Ziai, R., Hahn, M., Meurers, D.: CoMeT: integrating different levels of linguistic modeling for meaning assessment. In: Proceedings of the Joint Conference on Lexical and Computational Semantics, vol. 2, pp. 608–616 (2013)

23. Ramachandran, L., Cheng, J., Foltz, P.: Identifying patterns for short answer scoring using graph-based lexico-semantic text matching. In: Proceedings of the Workshop on Innovative Use of NLP for Building Educational Applications, pp. 97–106 (2015)

24. Rus, V., Lintean, M., Banjade, R., Niraula, N., Stefanescu, D.: Semilar: the semantic similarity toolkit. In: Proceedings of the Annual Meeting of the Association for Computational Linguistics: System Demonstrationsm, pp. 163–168 (2013)
25. Sukkarieh, J.Z., Pulman, S.G., Raikes, N.: Auto-marking 2: an update on the UCLES-Oxford University research into using computational linguistics to score short, free text responses. Int. Assoc. Educ. Assess. (2004)
26. Sultan, M.A., Salazar, C., Sumner, T.: Fast and easy short answer grading with high accuracy. In: Proceedings of the Conference of the North American Chapter of the Association for Computational Linguistics: Human Language Technologies, pp. 1070–1075 (2016)

When Optimal Team Formation Is a Choice - Self-selection Versus Intelligent Team Formation Strategies in a Large Online Project-Based Course

Sreecharan Sankaranarayanan[(✉)], Cameron Dashti, Chris Bogart, Xu Wang, Majd Sakr, and Carolyn Penstein Rosé

Carnegie Mellon University, Pittsburgh, PA 15213, USA
{sreechas,cdashti1,cbogart,xuwang,msakr,cprose}@andrew.cmu.edu

Abstract. Prior research in Team-Based Massive Open Online Project courses (TB-MOOPs) has demonstrated both the importance of effective group composition and the potential for using automated methods for forming effective teams. Past work on automated team assignment has produced both spectacular failures and spectacular successes. In either case, different contexts pose particular challenges that may interfere with the applicability of approaches that have succeeded in other contexts. This paper reports on a case study investigating the applicability of an automated team assignment approach that has succeeded spectacularly in TB-MOOP contexts to a large online project-based course. The analysis offers both evidence of partial success of the paradigm as well as insights into areas for growth.

Keywords: Automated team formation · Transactivity
Team-Based Massive Open Online Project Course · TB-MOOP
Peer learning

1 Introduction

Effective collaborative learning experiences are known to provide many cognitive, meta-cognitive and social benefits to learners [14,26]. Several MOOC studies have tried to replicate the successes that peer learning has had in offline contexts but have been met with mixed results. Attempts to encourage unstructured discussions using real-time chat did not find improvements in students' retention rate or academic achievement [5] whereas chat facilitated by an intelligent agent led of an approximately 50% reduction in dropout [7].

Early work on Massive Open Online Courses (MOOCs) revealed that although online students call for more social interaction, peer learning opportunities fail without support [15]. Students may fail to provide feedback on the work of their peers; they may not show up for a discussion session they signed up for; or they may quit working with their team altogether as they drop out of the

© Springer International Publishing AG, part of Springer Nature 2018
C. Penstein Rosé et al. (Eds.): AIED 2018, LNAI 10947, pp. 518–531, 2018.
https://doi.org/10.1007/978-3-319-93843-1_38

course [15]. Learners have reported facing more frustration with groups formed online than in face-to-face learning environments [21]. Simply providing communication technology has also proven insufficient. For example, an early MOOC that offered optional learning groups found that only 300 out of a total of 7350 participants in the course signed up for one of the 12 learning groups [16]. One explanation is that students don't fully recognize the role that social interaction is meant to play in their learning. It has thus become clear that offering effective social interaction in MOOCs is a research problem in its own right [22]. In this paper, we investigate a particularly challenging aspect of this broader agenda, namely supporting team-based project learning at scale in online learning environments.

While the bulk of the research on introducing social interaction opportunities are either as informal discussion forums or short-term chat activities, some recent work, including our own past work, takes on the more ambitious challenge of importing team-based projects into MOOCs [24,27,28]. Team projects are common in face-to-face courses, however, from the beginning of the MOOC movement, there has been skepticism about whether such forms of learning would work in MOOCs. One of the many challenges cited has been the difficulty of forming well-functioning teams [8,17,30]. In the MOOC context, prior work has addressed the problems of forming effective teams and supporting coordination and interaction within teams once they are formed. Work on team formation has investigated what evidence can be identified in the behavior traces of students that can be used to do the team formation, ideally in an automated fashion [9,19,20,29,30].

In our work, we begin with a fully automated approach that has been successful in a large controlled lab study [28] as well as a 4 week MOOC [27]. While this empirically grounded paradigm has worked well in short term studies where stakes are low, it remains an open question whether the paradigm will hold up in a much longer course where stakes are higher. Specifically, it is essential to investigate how the idiosyncrasies of the context might affect the paradigms and further create more generalizable and scalable approaches that can be applied in a variety of contexts. This paper therefore provides a case study applying this successful paradigm [27] to a 16 week large online project course on Cloud Computing offered as a part of degree-granting programs by Carnegie Mellon University's (CMU) Open Learning Initiative (OLI) on 3 CMU campuses. Our analysis provides evidence of partial success and several insights into how the paradigm might need to be adapted for this new context.

In the remainder of the paper we first describe past work on team formation in at-scale learning environments. Next, we describe the context of the course in which the current study was conducted. The following section then describes the method and experimental setup. We then describe our experiments and the results we obtained. We conclude with a discussion of our findings and future work.

2   Past Work on Automated Team Formation

Algorithmic team formation approaches that have emerged have seen both successes and failures. Attempts at providing support for team formation have sparked research on criteria that leads to better teams and algorithms that can then optimize over those criteria. Many automated approaches to team formation base their team assignments on characteristics of individual learners such as learning style, personality or demographic information [6]. This information however needs to first be assessed or discovered before it can be provided to the algorithm for optimization. Therefore, these approaches are often not feasible in typical online course environments. Further, forming teams based on typical demographic features such as gender and time zone has not been shown to significantly improve team engagement or success in MOOCs [30].

Approaches to automated team formation that have succeeded have focused on inducing buy-in among the participants. Opportunistic group formation for instance [12], triggers a negotiation process between learners to form groups once it detects that the learners can move from the individual learning phase to the group learning phase. The negotiation process allows learners to be assigned to roles based on their learning goals and the goals for the whole group thus creating buy-in. The approach showed that learners using the framework performed as well as students in face-to-face situations. Another such successful strategy has made use of a collaborative process measure called transactivity, which can be defined as the reasoning of one utterance building off or operating on the reasoning of another utterance [4]. The construct of transactivity stems from a Piagetian learning paradigm where it is believed to flourish in social settings that have a balance of respect and a desire to build common ground. Groups that exhibited high transactivity were shown in previous studies to be associated with higher learning [23], higher knowledge transfer [10] and better problem solving [3].

In the case of team formation, it is the social underpinnings, the signal of mutual interest and respect that a transactive exchange entails that renders this construct an estimate of collaboration potential between students. The automated strategy makes use of evidence of transactive exchanges in a whole course online discussion process that happens prior to the team activity. The resultant teams were shown to perform better than random teams first in a synthetic environment on Amazon Mechanical Turk [28] and then externally validated in a Team-Based Massive Open Online Project-Based (TB-MOOP) course offered on edX [27].

3   Course Context and Intervention

The Open Learning Initiative[1] (OLI) Cloud Computing Course is a semester-long completely online course offered to Carnegie Mellon University (CMU) students on its various campuses[2]. The fall 2017 semester offering of the course

---

[1] http://oli.cmu.edu/.

[2] http://www.cs.cmu.edu/~msakr/15619-f17/.

saw participation from three CMU campuses - Pittsburgh, Silicon Valley and Rwanda. In past offerings of the course, students were required to complete 10 individual projects and then self-select into teams for a 7 week team project. Students complete conceptual topics and assessments on the OLI platform and use a homegrown platform, TheProject.Zone[3] to complete individual and team programming projects. There is no lecture to attend, so students do not have the opportunity to meet face-to-face as part of the course. However, students at the same campus may have encountered each other face-to-face outside of class, and all students in the course do interact with the teaching staff and with other students on Piazza[4], a question and answer forum. The course has been offered 9 times before, so students came in with the expectation that they need to form a team for the group project. Many students started forming teams on their own from the beginning of the semester.

In order to introduce Transactivity-Based matching for team formation in the course, we needed to make two adjustments to the course practices. First, during the initial part of the semester when students were working through their ten individual project assignments, they were required to post a reflection to the discussion forum after each project and offer feedback to three other students. This feedback exchange provided both the opportunity for students to experience more social interaction in the course as well as provide the data for estimating collaborative potential for pairs of students based on their exchange of transactive feedback contributions. We refer to this repeated reflective exchange henceforth as the Reflection-Feedback Setup. An automated measure of transactivity exchange between students in this context is then used to estimate pairwise collaboration potential, and then a constraint satisfaction algorithm is used to assign teams in such a way that students are more likely to be part of teams with the other students they have interacted with transactively than those they have not interacted transactively with. The second adjustment was that rather than asking students to find their own teams, which is what had been done in the past, in this offering we provided automated recommendations for team assignment based on the Transactivity-Based matching algorithm. However, we did not force students to take the recommendations. Instead, we provided these as suggestions with the idea of observing the extent to which receiving recommendations would be viewed as attractive to students.

3.1 The Reflection-Feedback Setup

As mentioned, after each individual project, students reflected on their projects by answering questions similar to those shown below:

- Pick a task you found most challenging. Why was it challenging and how did you end up solving it?
- Pick a task and choose among different solutions paths for this task. What were the trade-offs you ended up making?

---

[3] https://theproject.zone/.
[4] https://piazza.com/.

– Describe how you tested one of the tasks. How did you design your test? Was your initial test sufficient? If not, how did you improve it?

Their answers were then shared to a discussion forum that the entire class could access and the students were encouraged to provide constructive feedback on these reflection posts. An example reflection, prompt and feedback post can be seen in Fig. 1.   Substantive discussions resulted from this reflection-feedback

Fig. 1. Examples of a reflection post, a prompt soliciting constructive feedback and a feedback post. Feedback post highlights instances of common ground, synthesis and encouragement.

setup as shown in the example feedback post. These posts showed evidence of students synthesizing knowledge from several posts, achieving common ground and providing encouragement to each other. An example of a transactive and non-transactive exchange between students from this reflection-feedback setup is shown below:

– **Transactive Exchange**
    Student 1: *"... I used 'f.readlines()' to read the wiki log file. It worked well on my own computer, but it caused a 'MemoryError' when I tested it on AWS ..."*
    Student 2: *"The file object itself is a iterator. So if you 'for x in file', you get lines as x. This is a more pythonic way than using 'readline()'."*

– **Non-Transactive Exchange**
Student 1: *"...I approached the problem by breaking it out into different modules and functions which made it possible to test different cases really fast. ..."*
Student 2: *"Well done!"*

In the first case, the second student is referring explicitly to the reasoning of the first student and building on that reasoning further with their own reasoning. The interaction is therefore transactive. In the second case, the second student is referring to the reasoning of the first student but is not contributing original reasoning of their own and the interaction is therefore non-transactive. Evidence of transactive exchanges can thus be mined from these interactions to automatically inform our team formation algorithm.

3.2 Transactivity-Based Team Formation

Data from the feedback exchange in the discussion forums was used as input to the Transactivity-Based matching algorithm.

Automatic Transactivity Analysis and Team Assignment. Before an estimate of pairwise transactivity exchange can be computed, posts from the discussion forum must first be annotated as transactive or not. In our work, this was accomplished using a text classification approach developed in prior work on automated collaborative learning process analysis [2,13,28]. This approach requires training data including a validated and reliable coding of transactivity [11]. For our work, we used a previously validated coding manual [11] and coded 200 feedback exchanges by hand. Using this training data, we trained a model to perform the transactivity analysis over the whole set automatically.

Team assignment was based on behavior traces for the first five weeks of the course. By that point, students had completed 3 individual assignments and had written a total of 1007 discussion forum posts. For each pair of students, we computed the total number of threads where either they both contributed a transactive post to the discussion or one of them started the thread and the other contributed a transactive post. We refer to this quantity henceforth as the Pairwise Transactivity Score for this pair of students. Once the Pairwise Transactivity Score is computed for each pair of students, a team score can be computed by averaging the Pairwise Transactivity Score for each pair within the group. A score for the resulting teams across the whole class can be computed by averaging across the team scores. The goal of the automated team-matching algorithm is to assign students to teams in such a way that the score over the whole class is maximized. An exhaustive search would take inordinately long. Thus, a constraint satisfaction algorithm is used to find an approximate solution that comes close to the optimal assignment that maximizes the score across the class without having to do an exhaustive search. The specific constraint satisfaction algorithm we used is called the minimal cost max network flow constraint satisfaction algorithm [1]. The algorithm generally tackles the resource allocation problem with constraints and in prior work, role assignments such as the roles of a Jigsaw condition were used as constraints [28]. In this paper, location was used as the constraint in addition to maximizing average transactivity across teams i.e., all members of the team are to be located on the same CMU campus. This was because, based on past runs of the course, it was observed by the course staff that co-located teams worked better together and co-location was an expressed desire of students who had taken the course in the past also. The algorithm finds an optimal grouping within $O(N^3)$ time complexity where N is the number of students. A brute force approach would have $O(N!)$ time complexity and would be infeasible in practice.

The algorithm is capable of forming teams of arbitrary size and approximates the solution in admissible time by maximizing the transactivity post count between two adjacent pairs of users instead of the total accumulated transactivity post count. A discussion network which is a directed weighted graph of the student's discussion in the reflection-feedback phase weighted by the transactivity score is built and the successive shortest paths algorithm shown in Algorithm 1 greedily finds the minimum cost flow until there is no remaining flow in the network.

Algorithm 1. Successive Shortest Paths for Minimum Cost Max Flow

---

1: $f(v_1, v_2) \leftarrow 0 \ \forall \ (v_1, v_2) \in E$
2: $E' \leftarrow a(v_1, v_2) \ \forall \ (v_1, v_2) \in E$
3: **while** $\exists \Pi \in G' = (V, E')$ s.t. Π, a minimum cost path from source to destination **do**
4:     **for each** $(v_1, v_2) \in \Pi$ **do**
5:         **if** $f(v_1, v_2) > 0$ **then**
6:             $f(v_1, v_2) \leftarrow 0$
7:             remove $-a(v_2, v_1)$ from E'
8:             add $a(v_1, v_2)$ to E'
9:         **else**
10:             $f(v_1, v_2) \leftarrow 1$
11:             remove $a(v_1, v_2)$ from E'
12:             add $-a(v_2, v_1)$ to E'
13:         **end if**
14:     **end for**
15: **end while**

The algorithm can be extended to accommodate more than one constraint but it should be noted that adding additional constraints could mean that an optimal team assignment ceases to exist.

3.3   Team Recommendation

At the end of Week 6, automated team assignments were formed using data from the reflection-feedback setup through Week 5 and then sent by the course instructor to the students who belonged to the same team over email. The email provided information to the students about how the teams were formed, what empirical evidence was used to form the teams and also served as their introduction to their teammates. Importantly, the email highlighted that the team assignments were only a recommendation and not a prescription from the course staff. An excerpt from the email is given below:

"At this point in the semester, it is time to get organized into teams for the course team project work. Up until now, your work has been entirely individual, though you have shared it with the class community, and have offered each other feedback. Research in online team-based learning suggests that some aspects of interactions in a public class space signal collaboration potential. In particular, these aspects relate to expression of ideas and ways of evaluating the ideas and perspectives of others. Based on observation of your participation in the online feedback activities in this class, that prior research suggests you would work well together. Please consider this recommendation as you make your official declaration of team commitment for this course."

Students were then asked to deliberate over these recommendations and their final team assignments were to be submitted on the TheProject.Zone. 35 total teams were formed with 23 teams in the Pittsburgh campus, 11 teams in the Silicon Valley campus and 1 team in the Rwanda campus. All suggested teams had 3 members each except the Rwanda team which had 2 members. Out of these 35 teams formed algorithmically, 5 teams took up our recommendation at least partially. A total of 27 teams survived till the end of the course with 7 teams of 2 members each and 20 teams of 3 members each.

At the end of the course, students filled out a post-course survey where they discussed their reasons for taking the recommendation or not.

4   Method

In this work we adopt a case study methodology to investigate how the Transactivity-Based team assignment paradigm plays out differently in a 16 week for-credit project course than in a 4 week MOOC, where it had been evaluated in the past. Here we discuss observations from the online discussion in the Reflection-Feedback Setup, the team formation processes that ensued after the Automated Team Assignment, and the subsequent team project work and set up for a quantitative analysis that is found in the Results section.

4.1   Measurement

Auto and Manual Project Grade. We measure the success of the teamwork in terms of the grade each team received on the final project. There were two aspects of the project, namely, an autograded portion of the software and a manually graded portion based on their report.

Post-course Survey. Students were given a post-course survey at the end of the semester. The survey contained three open response questions including: "What was most valuable to you and worked best in the team experience?", "What was least valuable to you and worked least well about the team experience?", "What criteria did you use to choose team members, and when did you begin that process?". From this data we coded three variables for each student, namely SelectionProcess, RelationalIssues, and DivisionOfLaborIssues. We coded SelectionProcess as a nominal variable with the following values: *Know* if students indicated selecting people they knew already, *Recommendation* if students indicated taking the recommendation, *Observation* if students indicated making a selection based on their observations on the course platform, and *Generic* if they did not indicate how they found their team. RelationalIssues was coded as a numeric variable with score 1 if they mentioned something positive about relationships in their group, -1 if they mentioned something negative about relationships in their group, and 0 otherwise. Similarly we coded DivisionOfLaborIssues as 1 if students mentioned something positive regarding division of labor, -1 if they mentioned something negative and 0 otherwise.

Transactivity Score. Each team was assigned a Transactivity score, which was the average of Pairwise Transactivity scores across each pair of students within the team. The team assignment used for this analysis was the final team students worked in for the project.

4.2   Online Discussion Quality

The automated team formation paradigm relies on data from the online reflective discussion that was requested of students after each individual project. If the students were not engaged in this process, the paradigm would have broken down from the beginning. One of the big successes we observed was student engagement in these discussions. In total, the students contributed approximately 200 posts to the discussion forum after each individual project. Up through the third individual project when teams recommendations were computed, a total of 1007 posts had been contributed. Out of these, 438 (43.5% altogether) were labeled as transactive in the automated analysis. This suggests that students were engaged in the initial portion of the intervention. Since transactivity is typically low in discussion forums of online courses [25], this finding suggests that uptake of the intervention was strong at the initial stage. The reflection-feedback setup led to substantive discussions between students. Discussion about the methods they used in their individual projects led to fruitful interactions between the students. Even though the teams were co-located and the students were also meeting outside of class, participation in the reflection-feedback setup remained high throughout the course. This was presumably because students found the feedback and interaction they had to be useful. Survey responses highlighted the value of different perspectives, approaches and suggestions that students were able to obtain from their interactions on the reflection-feedback setup. Students also reacted positively to the team suggestions.

4.3 Team Formation Processes

As mentioned above, most team recommendations were not taken up in this study. Thus, uptake of the intervention was low at this point. We found that if one team chooses not to take the team recommendation, it has a ripple effect where the students they choose to work with instead must then leave the teams they were assigned, and then their team-mates must also find alternative arrangements. The ripple effect in conjunction with some students desiring to pick their own team meant that the structure overall broke down. In the end, only 5 team recommendations were partially preserved in the teams that were eventually finalized.

The lack of uptake of the recommendations afforded the opportunity to test whether students of their own accord would choose team-mates that inadvertently maximized our estimate of collaboration potential. For this analysis we measured for each student the average Pairwise Transactivity score of the team they were assigned to as well as the average Pairwise Transactivity score of the team they eventually ended up on. The score for teams that were assigned was 1.14, while that of the final teams was .27. The pooled standard deviation was .89. We used a 2-tailed pairwise t-test to test the difference in scores, t(77) = 7.3, p < .0001 and the effect size was .98 s.d., thus indicating a large effect. For 63.38% of students who did not take the team assignment recommendation, the average transactivity of the self-selected teams was lesser than that of the teams we assigned them to. In 9.86% of the cases, the average transactivity was the greater and in 26.67% of the cases, the transactivity of the assigned and self-selected teams was the same.

4.4 Team Work

The final project grade, both the manual and autograded portions, provide an indication of how effectively teams were able to work together. Here the team is the unit of analysis. SelectionProcess is a quasi-experimental variable which we can use to obtain correlational evidence to evaluate the intervention. In this analysis, we investigate the role of Transactivity as an influence on group processes that affect how well teams produce joint work. For both team performance measures, we built an ANOVA model with project grade as the dependent variable, SelectionProcess as the independent variable, and Transactivity score as a covariate nested within the independent variable. We nested Transactivity score because it has different implications for team process if it was used in order to select teams or just happened to be the case. As a covariate, we also included the average grade the students per team scored on an individual assignment they did prior to the teamwork activity. There were no significant effects on the manual portion of the grade, which focused on the written report. However, there was a trend on the autograded portion for the SelectionProcess variable, which targets the actual software they produced, and a significant positive effect of the transactivity variable, $F(4, 7) = 3.3$, $p < .05$. The transactivity variable accounts for an additional 30% of total variance in team performance accounted for by the model. As for SelectionProcess, teams where selection was based on prior friendship performed worse than the other 3 approaches. The two highest scoring categories were Observation of behavior on the platform and Recommendation.

The post-course survey provides an indication of the subjective perception of teamwork within projects. Here the individual is the unit of analysis. In this analysis, we investigate the role of Transactivity as a criterion for team selection as well as implications of student response to the recommendations. We measure perception of teamwork experience using RelationalIssues and DivisionOfLaborIssues as outcome variables. First, we built an ANOVA model with DivisionOfLaborIssues as the dependent variable, SelectionProcess as the independent variable, and Transactivity score as a covariate nested within the independent variable. There was a significant effect of SelectionProcess, $F(3, 69) = 3.4$, $p < .05$. A student-t posthoc analysis indicated that students with SelectionProcess had significantly lower scores than all other students with an effect size of .83 s.d. The TransactivityScore variable showed a moderate positive correlation with DivisionOfLabor issues within the set of students coded as Recommendation suggesting that the recommendations may have been more effective to the extent that the algorithm was able to find a high criterion solution. Next, we built an ANOVA model with RelationalIssues as the dependent variable, SelectionProcess as the independent variable, and Transactivity score as a covariate nested within the independent variable. We nested Transactivity score because it has different implications for team process if it was used in order to select teams or just happened to be the case. In this case, there was no significant effect. However, comparing those students with SelectionProcess coded as Know with all other students showed a marginal negative effect, $F(1, 75) = 1.69$, $p < .1$, effect size of .52 s.d. Overall, this suggests that student tendency to select team-mates they were friends with worked out poorly for them. On the other hand, students who based their choice on their observation of other students' behavior, did not suffer the same fate.

5   Discussion and Recommendations

Because the data from this study does not include an experimental manipulation and because it is only a case study from one offering of a single course, no strong claims can be made. However, the case study does illustrate how factors that were not present in the earlier evaluations of the approach impact its success. In this study, the Transactivity-Based matching broke down once some students chose to form their own teams. In order to be successful, the recommendations must be taken by all. However, the fact that the students chose to ignore the recommendations in most cases suggests that forcing students to take a recommendation made without their involvement would not be appreciated by students. However, a policy of recommendations taken by all would not need to require students to be passive recipients of the recommendations. If we can actively engage their preferences in the constraint satisfaction process, we may be able to achieve the success observed in past evaluations of the approach. Consistent with prior work

[18], the data from this study suggests that allowing students to choose to work with their friends is counter-productive. In this course, students appear to be as successful in selection based on goal-directed observation as the algorithm is in transactivity-based assignment. Together these two observations suggest that in engaging the preferences of students in the constraint satisfaction process of team assignment should encourage application of wise criteria observed from behavior within the course rather than selecting friends.

6   Conclusions and Future Work

In this paper we have presented a case study evaluating a team assignment intervention that was successful in a 4 week project-based MOOC offered in the past. We described the intervention and how it played out in a 16 week course for credit. The analysis shows some signs of success and many opportunities for growth. In the next iteration of the study, our intention is to inform students up front that a recommendation is coming, engage their observations of behavior in the course in addition to automated observations of Transactive exchange, and use both forms of estimate of collaboration potential in the constraint satisfaction approach.

Acknowledgement. This work was funded in part by the NIH grant 5R01HL122639-03 and NSF grants IIS-1546393 and ACI-1443068. The research reported here was further enriched by being conducted in the context of the Program in Interdisciplinary Education Research (PIER), a training grant to Carnegie Mellon University funded by the Institute of Education Sciences (R305B150008). The opinions expressed are those of the authors and do not represent the views of the Institute, the U.S. Department of Education or other funding organizations that supported this work.

References

1. Ahuja, R.K., Orlin, J.B.: A fast and simple algorithm for the maximum flow problem. Oper. Res. **37**(5), 748–759 (1989)
2. Ai, H., Kumar, R., Nguyen, D., Nagasunder, A., Rosé, C.P.: Exploring the effectiveness of social capabilities and goal alignment in computer supported collaborative learning. In: Aleven, V., Kay, J., Mostow, J. (eds.) ITS 2010. LNCS, vol. 6095, pp. 134–143. Springer, Heidelberg (2010). https://doi.org/10.1007/978-3-642-13437-1_14
3. Azmitia, M., Montgomery, R.: Friendship, transactive dialogues, and the development of scientific reasoning. Soc. Dev. **2**(3), 202–221 (1993)
4. Berkowitz, M.W., Gibbs, J.C.: Measuring the developmental features of moral discussion. Merrill-Palmer Q. **29**, 399–410 (1983)
5. Coetzee, D., Fox, A., Hearst, M.A., Hartmann, B.: Chatrooms in MOOCs: all talk and no action. In: Proceedings of the first ACM Conference on Learning@ Scale Conference, pp. 127–136. ACM (2014)
6. Decker, R.: Management team formation for large scale simulations. Dev. Bus. Simul. Exp. Learn. **22**, 128–129 (1995)

7. Ferschke, O., Yang, D., Tomar, G., Rosé, C.P.: Positive impact of collaborative chat participation in an edX MOOC. In: Conati, C., Heffernan, N., Mitrovic, A., Verdejo, M.F. (eds.) AIED 2015. LNCS, vol. 9112, pp. 115–124. Springer, Cham (2015). https://doi.org/10.1007/978-3-319-19773-9_12
8. Ghadiri, K., Qayoumi, M.H., Junn, E., Hsu, P., Sujitparapitaya, S.: The transformative potential of blended learning using MIT edXs 6.002 X online MOOC content combined with student team-based learning in class. Environment 8(14), 14–29 (2013)
9. Graf, S., Bekele, R.: Forming heterogeneous groups for intelligent collaborative learning systems with ant colony optimization. In: Ikeda, M., Ashley, K.D., Chan, T.-W. (eds.) ITS 2006. LNCS, vol. 4053, pp. 217–226. Springer, Heidelberg (2006). https://doi.org/10.1007/11774303_22
10. Gweon, G.: Assessment and support of the idea co-construction process that influences collaboration. Ph.D. thesis, Carnegie Mellon University (2012)
11. Gweon, G., Jain, M., McDonough, J., Raj, B., Rosé, C.P.: Measuring prevalence of other-oriented transactive contributions using an automated measure of speech style accommodation. Int. J. Comput. Support. Collaborative Learn. 8(2), 245–265 (2013)
12. Ikeda, M., Go, S., Mizoguchi, R.: Opportunistic group formation. In: Artificial Intelligence and Education, Proceedings of AIED, vol. 97, pp. 167–174 (1997)
13. Joshi, M., Rosé, C.P.: Using transactivity in conversation for summarization of educational dialogue. In: Workshop on Speech and Language Technology in Education (2007)
14. Kirschner, F., Paas, F., Kirschner, P.A.: A cognitive load approach to collaborative learning: united brains for complex tasks. Educ. Psychol. Rev. 21(1), 31–42 (2009)
15. Kizilcec, R.F., Schneider, E.: Motivation as a lens to understand online learners: toward data-driven design with the OLEI scale. ACM Trans. Comput. Hum. Interac. (TOCHI) 22(2), 6 (2015)
16. Kotturi, Y., Kulkarni, C.E., Bernstein, M.S., Klemmer, S.: Structure and messaging techniques for online peer learning systems that increase stickiness. In: Proceedings of the Second (2015) ACM Conference on Learning@ Scale, pp. 31–38. ACM (2015)
17. MacNeil, S., Latulipe, C., Long, B., Yadav, A.: Exploring lightweight teams in a distributed learning environment. In: Proceedings of the 47th ACM Technical Symposium on Computing Science Education, pp. 193–198. ACM (2016)
18. Oakley, B., Felder, R.M., Brent, R., Elhajj, I.: Turning student groups into effective teams. J. Stud. Centered Learn. 2(1), 9–34 (2004)
19. Ounnas, A., Davis, H., Millard, D.: A framework for semantic group formation. In: Eighth IEEE International Conference on Advanced Learning Technologies, ICALT 2008, pp. 34–38. IEEE (2008)
20. Paredes, P., Ortigosa, A., Rodriguez, P.: A method for supporting heterogeneous-group formation through heuristics and visualization. J. UCS 16(19), 2882–2901 (2010)
21. Smith, M.K., Wood, W.B., Adams, W.K., Wieman, C., Knight, J.K., Guild, N., Su, T.T.: Why peer discussion improves student performance on in-class concept questions. Science 323(5910), 122–124 (2009)
22. Staubitz, T., Renz, J., Willems, C., Meinel, C.: Supporting social interaction and collaboration on an xMOOC platform. In: Proceedings of EDULEARN 2014, pp. 6667–6677 (2014)

23. Teasley, S.D., Fischer, F., Weinberger, A., Stegmann, K., Dillenbourg, P., Kapur, M., Chi, M.: Cognitive convergence in collaborative learning. In: Proceedings of the 8th International Conference on International Conference for the Learning Sciences, vol. 3, pp. 360–367. International Society of the Learning Sciences (2008)
24. Wang, X., Wen, M., Rosé, C.: Contrasting Explicit and Implicit Support for Transactive Exchange in Team Oriented Project Based Learning. International Society of the Learning Sciences, Philadelphia (2017)
25. Wang, X., Wen, M., Rosé, C.P.: Towards triggering higher-order thinking behaviors in MOOCS. In: Proceedings of the Sixth International Conference on Learning Analytics & Knowledge, LAK 2016, pp. 398–407. ACM, New York (2016)
26. Webb, N.M., Palincsar, A.S.: Group Processes in the Classroom. Prentice Hall International, New York (1996)
27. Wen, M.: Investigating virtual teams in massive open online courses: deliberation-based virtual team formation, discussion mining and support. Ph.D. thesis, Stanford University (2016)
28. Wen, M., Maki, K., Wang, X., Dow, S., Herbsleb, J.D., Rosé, C.P.: Transactivity as a predictor of future collaborative knowledge integration in team-based learning in online courses. In: EDM, pp. 533–538 (2016)
29. Zhan, Z., Fong, P.S., Mei, H., Liang, T.: Effects of gender grouping on students group performance, individual achievements and attitudes in computer-supported collaborative learning. Comput. Hum. Behav. **48**, 587–596 (2015)
30. Zheng, Z., Vogelsang, T., Pinkwart, N.: The impact of small learning group composition on student engagement and success in a MOOC. In: Proceedings of the 8th International Conference of Educational Data Mining, pp. 500–503 (2015)

Perseverance Is Crucial for Learning.
"OK! but Can I Take a Break?"

Annika Silvervarg[1], Magnus Haake[2(✉)], and Agneta Gulz[1,2]

[1] Department of Computer Science, Linköping University, Linköping, Sweden
{annika.silvervarg,agneta.gulz}@liu.se
[2] LUCS, Division of Cognitive Science, Lund University, Lund, Sweden
{magnus.haake,agneta.gulz}@lucs.lu.se

Abstract. In a study with 108 10- to 12-year-olds who used a digital educational game targeting history, we addressed the phenomenon of perseverance, that is, the tendency to stick with a task even when it is challenging. The educational game was designed to make all students encounter tasks they did not succeed to solve, at which point they were offered a set of choices corresponding to perseverance and non-perseverance. Methods used were behavioral log data, post-questionnaires, and an in-game questionnaire conducted by a game character, who asked the students about the reason for their choice. Overall, we found no differences between high and low-perseverance students as to their experiences of effort, difficulty, and learning, and neither in their self-reported motives for persevering – when doing so. With respect to performance, however, high-persevering students solved significantly more tasks at higher difficulty levels. Comparing high-perseverance students who tended to take a break directly after a failed test – before they continued with the same task – with those who did not take a break, we found no significant differences, indicating that taking a break is not detrimental to learning and perseverance.

Keywords: Perseverance · Challenge · Meaning-making · Pausing
Performance · Teachable agent · Educational software

1 Introduction

Without *perseverance* in a domain, i.e. a tendency to stick with tasks in the domain even if they are challenging, the likelihood that a learner will make progress in the domain is very low (or next to nothing). Development, growth, and progress presupposes that a learner engages in increasingly more difficult and complex tasks – and at some point, the mastering of a novel task or novel level of difficulty will not be immediate but require perseverance. In effect, perseverance is no guarantee for success, but conversely, non-perseverance is a guarantee for non-success.

The present study analyzes middle-school students who, during a series of lessons, used an educational game addressing history. The system was explicitly designed to enable data collection related to perseverance. Tasks were of an increasing degree of difficulty so that each student, at some point, would encounter a situation where they did not manage to accomplish the task. In that situation students were presented with a

© Springer International Publishing AG, part of Springer Nature 2018
C. Penstein Rosé et al. (Eds.): AIED 2018, LNAI 10947, pp. 532–544, 2018.
https://doi.org/10.1007/978-3-319-93843-1_39

set of choices that correspond to 'persevere' or to 'not persevere'. *Perseverance* was here defined and measured as 'choosing to continue working on a task after having failed at solving it'. This could be done in one of two ways: (i) continue working at once, or (ii) continue working on the failed task after a shorter break. *Non-perseverance* was defined as the choice of one of the other alternatives, that all involved that the student received another task than the one she had not managed to solve.

In this way, we use a behavioral measure of 'perseverance', aligning with the idea that perseverance is a choice of action. Specific for this study is that we also analyze two slightly different ways to persevere: 'get straight on'-perseverance (*strong perseverance*) and 'take a break and then get on'-perseverance' (*weak perseverance*).

The overall goal of the study was to learn more about the circumstances connected to students' perseverance. How does perseverance affect performance? How do students themselves reason about their choices to continue working on task they have failed on? How does perseverance affect their experiences of using the game?

1.1 Previous Related Studies

In a series of studies, Dweck [1, 2] identified the importance of what she calls a *growth mindset*, i.e. the belief that competence and intelligence is learnable, and that abilities can grow with effort. Attitudes and preferences that go along with a growth mindset are: seeing a failure as an opportunity to learn; focusing on learning rather than performing; and choosing more challenging activities before easier ones when given the choice. Students with a *fixed mindset*, on the other hand, see capabilities as more or less unchangeable and primarily something you have or have not. Consequently, there is no point in sticking to a difficult task, giving it a second, third, or even fourth try, in a domain that "one is not good at". Perseverance has been shown to relate to the presence of a *growth mindset* [3].

There is evidence that perseverance is domain related [4]. A student can be non-perseverant regarding math assignments but highly perseverant with respect to figure skating, have a high degree of perseverance for tasks in language classes but low for tasks in physics classes, or vice versa. (That said, it is possible or even likely that some students generate a high-level schema of "school subjects" and tend to be low – or high – in perseverance with respect to all school subjects).

Chase [5] conducted a study with adults who were experts in either English literature or in Mathematics and found differences in approaches towards challenging tasks in the participants' domain of expertise compared to the domain in which they were non-experts. (All tasks in both domains were both approachable and difficult, to ensure that while all participants could attempt to solve them, all were likely to fail). The participants were more perseverant in tasks in their domain of expertise in at least two ways. First, they were more inclined to make use of the maximum time allowed for the tasks in their domain of expertise (the maximum was 12 min for each task). Second, it turned out that participants tended to continue work on the tasks in their own domain of expertise also when the experiment was over – to a considerably higher degree than for the tasks in the other domain.

On the basis of these results, Chase [5] proposed a model that distills out what was involved in perseverance as reflected in the data. The model suggests that there are (at least) three motivational tools that underlie perseverance: (i) *having an ego-protective buffer*, i.e. not perceive a failure as a receipt that one is inept, thus not letting a failure get onto one's ego or identity; (ii) *taking personal responsibility* for overcoming whatever the obstacles were that influenced the non-success; and (iii) *having actionable tools*, i.e. have cognitive tools and resources to use for continued attempts to solve the task. Chase then applied the model to analyze a previous study where middle-school students studied the mechanisms of fever. Half of the students, the TA-group, used an educational game with a teachable agent included; their task was to teach the agent about the mechanisms of fever. The other half, the Self-group, used the same game without a teachable agent, to learn for themselves. In principle, a TA-system can, Chase argues, provide a novice learner with the three motivational tools listed above. Indeed, the TA-group showed more perseverance than the Self-group. They were more inclined to get back and revise a task that they had received feedback on, and they spent more time on revising than students from the Self-group.

Ventura and colleagues [6, 7] developed a measure of perseverance (persistence) of the following kind. Students get to work on a variety of hard and easy problems (e.g. picture comparison tasks) over a series of trials, with half of the problems being easy to solve and the other half impossible. For each task there was a maximum time allowed. Perseverance was measured as time spent on unsolved trials. The researchers used this measure of perseverance as a contextual variable to be analyzed against learning outcomes and other behavioral outcomes derived from use of digital learning resources. In other words, perseverance is here not measured within the actual learning domain but 'outside' of this domain, thus handled as a (general) off-domain variable for comparisons with different patterns of on-domain learning behaviors. In this way the approach of Ventura et al. [6, 7] differs from ours.

In our study, the participants had the choice to persevere after a shorter break. This means that we could distinguish between the two choices: (i) continue to work on the failed task right on (*strong perseverance*) and (ii) take a short break and then continue to work on the failed task (*weak perseverance*). We have not found any previous studies within the learning sciences (in a broad sense) on the topic of perseverance in relation to taking breaks.

1.2   Research Questions

Our aim was to explore potential differences between (i) students who showed a high degree versus a low degree of perseverance, and (ii) the two sub-groups of students with a high degree of perseverance, as described above: weak perseverance (taking a break) and strong perseverance (continue directly). Would there be any differences in the following: performance; motives provided by the students themselves on why they chose to continue work on a failed task; and views on how they experienced the learning activities? Our research questions were:

- *Research Question 1 (RQ.1).* Would there be differences in performance as to: (a) How many tasks they completed? and (b) The weighted value of the number of tasks they completed in combination with the degree of difficulty of the tasks?
- *Research Question 2 (RQ.2).* Would there be differences in the motives provided for the choice to continue with a task they had failed at, i.e. differences in their motives for perseverance?
- *Research Question 3 (RQ.3).* Would there be difference in the students' views on: (a) how difficult the tasks had been, (b) how much effort they had made during the sessions, (c) how much they had learnt during the sessions, and (d) how enjoyable they found the learning experience to be.

1.3   Predictions

The study had a pronouncedly explorative character and was not guided by hypotheses, yet we will comment on possible outcomes.

RQ.1. Prior research [5, 8] as well as everyday experience indicates that students that tend to stick to tasks also when it gets difficult, perform better than those who don't. We therefore expected high perseverance students to perform better than low perseverance students both in the number of completed tasks (RQ.1a) and in the weighted performance measure including the level of difficulty for the tasks (RQ.1b). For RQ.1a, however, it is possible that low-perseverance students as often as possible would choose an 'easier' task, and therefore score relatively higher on the total number of completed tasks. Turning to the weak vs. strong perseverance groups, we predicted that the latter would perform better than the former on both measurements.

RQ.2. We hypothesized that high-perseverance students might be more inclined to identify themselves as 'someone who does not give up', and therefore more likely motivate the choice in such terms. As for weak vs. strong perseverance students, we hypothesized that the strong perseverance group would motivate their answers more often in terms of perseverance, since they 'by definition' stay focused on the task.

RQ.3. The high-perseverance students, we hypothesized, would rank their experiences of 'learning' and 'effort' higher than the low-perseverance students. From an *objective* (or outsider) standpoint, the former *made* more effort in the sense of "continue working on a difficult task". If our prediction on RQ.1b would hold in that the high-perseverance students solved more difficult tasks, they would, from an objective standpoint, learn more. Yet, the relation of these facts to students' subjective views is still an open question. Next, we hypothesized that the low-perseverance students, on their part, would rank their experience of 'difficulty' higher in coherence with their possible weaker performance (cf. Predictions on RQ.1).

2   The Learning Environment

The learning environment used is called *The Guardian of History* (hence *GoH*) and targets history for 10- to 13-year-olds [9]. The narrative in GoH centers on securing the passage of time and history when the old *Guardian of History*, who is in charge of *the Castle of Time*, is about to step down at work. It will be necessary to have a splendid *'Castle of Time'-team* to support him. To quality for being a member of the team one must prove to have sufficient knowledge of and abilities to learn about history.

The software is based on the teachable agent (hence TA) paradigm [10, 11] and there is a *Self*-version and a *TA*-version of GoH. In the Self-version, the student learns about history by means of time-travels to historical setting and the completion of learning activities that involve concept maps, timelines, sorting tasks, etc. In doing so the student tries to complete the missions provided by The Guardian of History, also named *Chronos*. In the TA-version, the student learns about history in order to *teach* this to the time elf *Timy* (the TA), who eagerly wants to be on the new 'Castle of Time'-team. Alas, Timy suffers from 'time travelling'-sickness. Therefore, the student takes on the time-travels and returns from these to teach Timy by completing the learning activities described above.

A mission is completed when the student or time elf, in the two respective versions, gets pass from Chronos on her mission test. When one mission is completed, a new mission on a higher level of difficulty is automatically provided. Examples of missions are "*Who was Galileo Galilei and what did he do?*" (level 1), "*Present a timeline of scientific breakthroughs during the 17th and 18th centuries!*" (level 3), and "*What questions relating to the Great Plague of London can be answered by different historical sources?*" (level 5).

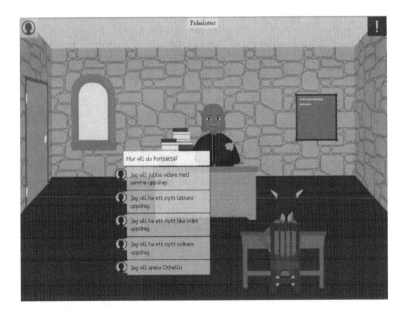

Fig. 1. If failing a mission test, the student is presented with five options.

When Timy (in the TA-version) fails on a mission test, Chronos asks how the student wants to proceed with her teaching the time-elf. When the student (in the Self-version) fails on a mission test, Chronos asks how she wants to proceed for herself.

In both cases, the student is provided with a set of choices: (i) continue work on the same mission; (ii) get a novel, less difficult mission; (iii) get another mission on a similar level of difficulty; (iv) get a more difficult mission; or (v) take a break to play Othello (Fig. 1). If the student chooses to take a break to play Othello, she returns after the break to once again be presented with the options (with the break option this time excluded).

After having made the choice on how to proceed after a failed mission test, the student exits from Chronos' office, and meets the helpful and curious archivist elf who asks the student about the reasons for her choice (Fig. 2). Half of the times the answers are collected as free text answers and half of the times as multiple-choice answers: (i) to show that the time-elf/I can do it; (ii) to show that the time-elf/I can learn this; or (iii) to not give up.

Fig. 2. Left: Three alternative answers (multiple-choice) to why the student chose to continue with the same mission: (i) to not give up (*perseverance*); (ii) to show that the time-elf/I can do it (*performance*); or (iii) to show that the time-elf/I can learn it (*mastery*). Right: The same situation as in the left panel, but with free text input format.

3   Method

3.1   Participants and Procedures

125 students (63 girls and 62 boys), 10- to 12-years-old, were recruited from six classes in three different Swedish schools in areas with median to low socio-economic status. Of these 125 students, a total of 17 students were excluded from the analysis due to scarce attendance resulting in too few data points, technical problems resulting in loss of log data; or diagnosed dyslexia or ADHD. The resulting dataset thus consisted of 108 students (57 girls and 51 boys). Another 8 students did not fill in the post-survey, which reduced the dataset to 100 students (54 girls, 46 boys) for analyzes addressing research question 3 (RQ.3).

The study consisted of four lessons over 2–3 weeks with all lessons held in the students' ordinary classroom with their ordinary teacher present and the students using their own laptops or tablets. At the first lesson, researchers briefly introduced the project, whereafter they were present during all lessons to help the students with technical issues. At the last lesson, the students filled out a post survey (questionnaire) regarding their experience of using the system: (i) How *difficult* did they think the missions had been? (ii) How much *effort* did they feel they had made? (iii) How much did they think that they had *learned*? and (iv) How *enjoyable* had it been to use the system?

For each student, we calculated how many times she had failed to pass a mission and thus been presented with alternatives for how to proceed. Next, we calculated the frequencies of how often after a failed test a student continued with the same mission without taking a break, and how often they continued with the same task after a break.

Based on these frequencies, we divided the students in three groups. The one third of students that most often (in more than 78% of the cases; $N = 36$) continued with the task directly or after taking a break to play Othello were classified as high-perseverance students. The one third of students that continued least often or never (in less than 43% of the cases; $N = 37$) were labelled as low-perseverance students. The remaining one third of students ($N = 35$) were labeled mid-perseverance students.

For the evaluation of weak versus strong perseverance students, the students were categorized according to a different schema. First the students that continued (with or without pause) in less than two thirds of the cases ($N = 52$) were removed. Of the remaining 56 students, the ones that continued directly in more than two thirds of the cases ($N = 30$) were categorized as 'strong perseverance' students with the rest ($N = 26$) categorized as 'weak perseverance' students.

As mentioned, the study involved a Self-group and a TA-group. However, as we found no differences in perseverance between these two groups we chose to collapse the data from the two groups. In the discussion we return to possible explanations of why the TA-group and Self-group did not differ with regard to perseverance.

3.2 Instrument and Measurements

Performance (RQ.1). We calculated two in-game performance measures based on the data logs for GoH. *Performance* reflects the number of tasks (missions) the student completed, regardless of their difficulty level. *Weighted Performance* takes the level of difficulty into account (a solved mission at difficulty level 3 counts thrice).

Motive for perseverance (RQ.2). When a student had chosen to continue on the same mission (after a failed mission test), she was asked by the archivist elf in the game: "*Why do you chose to continue with the same mission?*" The format for answering alternated between a free text answering option and a multiple-choice option with three alternatives presented in random order: "*To not give up*" (perseverance), "*To show that I/the time-elf can do it*" (performance), and "*So that I/the time-elf will learn it*" (mastery). The three alternatives had been pre-generated from a group of same-aged students.

On inspection of the free text format answers we found that most answers could be classified according to one of the three multiple-choice categories, i.e. as persistence, performance, or learning/mastery. Other free text answers (48% in total) did not fit in the categories, for example *"don't know"*, *"it's fun"*, and nonsense answers, e.g. "Rkxxy-ixyrjftkyv" and "☐☐☹☺☺,". For the analyzes, we counted the multiple-choice answers together with the free-text answers assigned to one of the three multiple-choice categories.

Questionnaire targeting experiences. At the end of the last lesson, a digital post-survey (questionnaire) was distributed, including four questions on the users experience of using and learning with the educational game (GoH). The questions, in the form of 5-level Likert items, were: *"How was it to use the Guardian of History?"* (1 = very boring, 5 = very fun; *"How was it to complete the missions?"* (1 = very difficult, 5 = very easy); *"How much effort did you put into completing the missions?"* (1 = none, 5 = very much); *"How much did you learn?"* (1 = none, 5 = very much).

4   Results

Statistical analysis used R version 3.4.3 (R Core Team, 2018) and an alpha level of 0.05. All effect sizes were interpreted using the guidelines from Cohen (1988). In the case of multiple comparisons, Holm corrections were used to adjust for family-wise error rates. Analyzes of performance (RQ.1) and motivations (RQ.2) used the full dataset of 108 participants. Analyzes of experience (RQ.3) used the reduced dataset of 100 participants due to missing questionnaire answers.

4.1   RQ.1: Performance

RQ.1 addressed performance as: (a) The number of completed tasks (b) The weighted value of the number of completed tasks in combination with task difficulty (Table 1).

Table 1. Medians (*Mdn*) and range (*Rng*) for performance and weighted performance, for the low, mid, and high perseverance groups plus the weak and strong perseverance groups.

Perseverance groups	N	Performance		Weighted Performance	
		Mdn	*Rng*	*Mdn*	*Rng*
Low	37	3	3–6	5	2–14
Mid	35	4	0–5	5	0–10
High	36	4	1–6	8	1–19
Weak	26	3.5	1–6	5.5	1–19
Strong	30	4	2–6	7.5	3–16

Evaluating RQ.1a (difference in performance between low, mid, and high perseverance groups), a Kruskal-Wallis test showed only a marginal significant effect of completed number of rounds on perseverance group ($\chi^2(2) = 5.03$, $p = .081$).

For RQ.1b (difference in weighted performance between low, mid, and high perseverance groups) a Kruskal-Wallis test displayed a significant effect of weighted performance on perseverance group ($\chi^2(2) = 12.1$, $p = .002$). A post-hoc test revealed that the significant effect on group stemmed from the differences in weighted performance between: (i) high vs. low-perseverance groups ($p = .0042$, $r = .37$) and (ii) high vs. mid-perseverance groups ($p = .022$, $r = .30$).

Comparing the strong and weak perseverance student groups indicated no significant effects (RQ.1a: $U = 334$, $p = .35$; RQ.1b: $U = 339$, $p = .40$).

In sum, we found a medium strength significant effect of weighted performance between the high vs. low-perseverance groups and a small to medium strength significant effect of weighted performance between the high vs. mid-perseverance groups.

4.2   RQ.2: Motives for Perseverance

RQ.2 addressed the motives provided for the choice to continue with a task they had failed at, in terms of perseverance, performance, and mastery (see Table 2).

The numbers presented are based on the relative frequencies for each of the three motives (summing up to 100% for each individual student).

Evaluating the difference in motives by means of Kruskal-Wallis tests showed no significant effects of motive on perseverance group (Perseverance: $\chi^2(2) = 0.880$, $p = .64$; Performance: $\chi^2(2) = 0.218$, $p = .90$; Mastery: $\chi^2(2) = 3.67$, $p = .16$). Comparing the strong and weak perseverance student groups, likewise, indicated no significant effects (Perseverance: $U = 270$, $p = .075$; Performance: $U = 456$, $p = .16$; Mastery: $U = 384$, $p = .87$).

Table 2. Medians (*Mdn*) for provided motives for perseverance in terms of perseverance, performance, and mastery for the low, mid, and high perseverance groups plus the weak and strong perseverance groups. (All measures ranging between 0% to 100%.)

Perseverance groups	N	Perseverance	Performance	Mastery
		Mdn	*Mdn*	*Mdn*
Low	37	58.5%	8.5%	0%
Mid	35	50%	14%	14%
High	36	63%	14%	0%
Weak	26	50%	25%	0%
Strong	30	53.5%	12.5%	5.5%

In sum, we found no significant effects between the different perseverance groups as to their motives for perseverance (the choice to continue with a task they had failed at) in terms of perseverance, performance, and mastery.

4.3   RQ.3: Experience

(RQ.3) addressed students' views on how difficult the tasks had been, how much effort they had made during the sessions, how much they had learnt during the sessions, and how enjoyable (fun) they found the learning experience to be (Table 3).

Table 3. Medians (*Mdn*) and range (*Rng*) for students' experiences of the game sessions in terms of effort, difficulty, learning, and fun for the low, mid, and high perseverance groups plus the weak and strong perseverance groups.

Perseverance groups	N	Difficulty	Effort	Learning	Fun
		Mdn (Rng)	*Mdn (Rng)*	*Mdn (Rng)*	*Mdn (Rng)*
Low	37	3 (1–5)	4 (1–5)	4 (1–5)	4 (1–5)
Mid	35	3 (1–5)	4 (1–5)	4 (1–5)	4 (1–5)
High	36	3 (2–5)	4 (2–5)	4 (2–5)	4 (2–5)
Weak	26	3 (1–5)	4 (2–5)	3 (1–5)	4 (1–5)
Strong	30	3 (1–4)	4 (2–5)	4 (3–5)	4 (2–5)

Evaluating potential differences in students' experiences by means of Kruskal-Wallis tests showed no significant effects of experience on perseverance group (Difficulty: $\chi^2(2) = 0.130$, $p = .94$; Effort: $\chi^2(2) = 1.22$, $p = .54$; Learning: $\chi^2(2) = 2.79$, $p = .25$; Fun: $\chi^2(2) = 0.516$, $p = .77$). Comparing the strong and weak perseverance student groups, likewise, indicated no significant effects (Difficulty: $U = 350$, $p = .38$; Effort: $U = 248$, $p = .21$; Learning: $U = 236$, $p = .13$; Fun: $U = 344$, $p = .50$).

In sum, we found no significant effects between the different perseverance groups as to their experience of the game sessions in terms of effort, difficulty, learning, and fun.

5   Discussion

We found, as predicted, a difference in performance between high-perseverance and low-perseverance students. The former performed significantly better than the latter in that they completed slightly more missions, and that the completed missions were of higher difficulty. This aligned with our prediction. On the other hand, we found no differences in performance when comparing the strong and weak perseverance student groups. A possible conclusion is, in view of the title of this paper, that perseverance in combination with "taking breaks" can be as productive as strict perseverance. This is interesting since the breaks imply that the weak perseverance students actually spend less time on the main tasks, but still perform as well. One can speculate that a break allows for cognitive rest so that one can return to the task with more focus after the break. A question to explore further is the reason to take a break; to what extent is it a planned strategy to rest between focusing on the learning task? It would also be interesting to investigate if taking a break influences the subsequent choice on whether to get on with the same (failed) task or not.

We speculated that compared to low-perseverance students, high-perseverance students, who per definition have perseverance in their standard behavioral repertoire, would be more likely to identify themselves as 'someone who is perseverant'. Consequently, we proposed, they would be more inclined to present motives for continuing on a failed task in such terms, e.g. *"Because I don't want to give up"*, *Because I want to complete what I start"*, *"Because I don't give up easily"*. However, no such difference was found. Low-perseverance students were as likely as high-perseverance students to reason in terms of perseverance – once they chose to persevere. A possible conclusion is that *the behavior of perseverance leads to self-attributions of perseverance*, i.e. a bottom-up process – not excluding the possibility of a top-down process as well. Indeed, there is collected evidence that behavior on the one hand and self-attributions on the other hand, mutually influence each other. Perseverance can be trained and learned – and most productively so, if the learning involves *two* legs: motivational tools such as self-attributions, and task-related tools that support actual working on a task or problem [4, 5]. For the purpose of this study, the system (GoH) was designed so that students after a failed test were presented with a set of alternatives to perseverance (a new easier task, a new task of same difficulty, a new more difficult task) or else had to continue with the same task on their own. To scaffold perseverance, the system can be implemented with supportive tools provided by game characters.

Our predictions that the high-perseverance students would rank their experiences of 'effort' and 'learning' higher than the low-perseverance students were not supported. This can be taken as an example of how an *objective* (or outsider) perspective says one thing, while the subjective perspective (here the students' subjective views on their experiences) says something else. Even though the high-perseverance students from an outside perspective *made* more effort in that they more often "continued working on a difficult task", the low-perseverance students rated their amount of effort just as highly. In addition, the low-perseverance students rated their learning as high as the high-perseverance students, even though the latter from an objective standpoint learned more. This might be explained in terms of high-perseverance students usually persevering and thus being more used to working on more challenging material and more motivated to do so. The baseline with respect to what counts as "effort" in a school setting is likely to differ between low- and high-perseverance students. When it comes to the experience of learning, it can be seen as a positive outcome that most students, regardless of degree of perseverance, experienced their learning as high (Median = 4). It can be noted that even though a student did not solve a task, he or she still worked on it and was exposed to the learning material.

Likewise, our speculation that low-perseverance students would score higher than high-perseverance students on the question on how difficult they thought the tasks were, was not supported. This could reflect that low-perseverance students may have exploited the system to avoid difficult tasks while high-perseverance students, by persevering, increased the likelihood of succeeding and by this the likelihood of encountering another (more) difficult task.

A major objective behind the study is to better understand when, how and why students persevere or not. This knowledge can in turn be utilized for the design and implementation of educational software that scaffolds – and nudges – students into productive perseverance. An intelligent adaptive system could identify different combinations of students' behavioral patterns of perseverance and their progress, and adapt accordingly. For students who are overall low on perseverance the system may increase scaffolds of the kinds proposed by Chase [5], not the least in the form of cognitive tools that make it meaningful to pursue the task – and at least temporarily shut doors for escaping or quitting. For persevering students, the system could keep track of whether they take breaks or not and if they increase or decrease perseverance over time. As long as a weak or strong perseverance student is making progress, there is likely no need to interfere. But if a strongly persevering student, with a pattern of generally keeping going without breaks, is dropping in performance, a way of nudging the student into taking a break would be appropriate.

An important factor of adaptivity is that we want to encourage and nudge rather than enforce a learning choice that the student is not considering herself, with the overall goal that the student herself develops good habits and makes productive choices in learning situations – also when no one is there to chose for them. But, in some cases it may also be beneficial for the system to more forcefully guide the student, in order to provide experiences of other types of choices and their consequences. Then the system can gradually retract the guidance and instead provide nudges.

Future work with the specific system we used in the present study, regarding supporting development of students' perseverance, also concerns strengthening the implementation of the teachable agent. In the study, we found no differences in perseverance between the TA- and Self-conditions. This is likely due to a weak implementation of the TA's role. One problem is that the TA in GoH competed with several other game characters, and another problem is that the TA provided practical interaction guidance to the student, which probably interfered with its role as tutee. Thus, this TA-version could not take full advantage of the motivational structures of *ego-protective buffer* and *taking personal responsibility* discussed by Chase [5].

In conclusion, some reflections on perseverance as the driving force to continue working on a challenging learning task. We saw that most students motivated their choice to continue work on a task after a failed test in the following kinds of terms: "*Because I don't give up that easily*", "*Because I just want to get this done*", or "*Because I want to complete a mission that I have started on*", rather than "*Because I want to learn more*" or "*In order to learn*". Could it be the case that we, as educators, overestimate the driving force of 'wanting to learn'? In the end, the outcome can be the same whether it originates from wanting to finish and not give up, wanting to solve a problem, or wanting to learn. Even if this may sound provoking, it is possible to learn a lot without being primarily driven by a desire to learn.

Acknowledgments. This research was financed by Marcus and Amalia Wallenberg Foundation.

References

1. Dweck, C.S.: Self-theories: their role in motivation, personality and development. Taylor and Francis/Psychology Press, Philadelphia (1999)
2. Dweck, C.S.: Mindset: The New Psychology of Success. Random house, New York (2006)
3. Duckworth, A.L., Peterson, C., Matthews, M.D., Kelly, D.R.: Grit: perseverance and passion for long-term goals. J. Pers. Soc. Psychol. **92**, 1087–1101 (2007)
4. Bass, H., Ball, D.L.: Beyond "you can do it!" developing mathematical perseverance in elementary school. Spencer Foundation, April 2015. http://www.spencer.org/resources/content/4/3/4/documents/bass_ball_mip_0415.pdf
5. Chase, C.C.: Motivating expertise: equipping novices with the motivational tools to move beyond failure. In: Staszewski, J.J. (ed.) Expertise and Skill Acquisition: the Impact of William G Chase. Psychology Press, New York (2013)
6. Ventura, M., Shute, V.J., Zhao, W.: The relationship between video game use and a performance-based measure of persistence. Comput. Educ. **60**, 52–58 (2012)
7. Ventura, M., Shute, V.J.: The validity of a game-based assessment of persistence. Comput. Hum. Behav. **29**, 2568–2572 (2013)
8. Scherer, R., Gustafsson, J.E.: The relations among openness, perseverance, and performance in creative problem solving: a substantive-methodological approach. Think. Skills Creat. **18**, 4–17 (2015)
9. Kirkegaard, C., Gulz, A., Silvervarg, A.: Introducing a challenging teachable agent. In: Zaphiris, P., Ioannou, A. (eds.) LCT 2014. LNCS, vol. 8523, pp. 53–62. Springer, Cham (2014). https://doi.org/10.1007/978-3-319-07482-5_6
10. Blair, K., Schwartz, D., Biswas, G., Leelawong, K.: Pedagogical agents for learning by teaching: teachable agents. Educ. Technol. Soc. Spec. Issue **47**, 56–61 (2007)
11. Biswas, G., Katzlberger, T., Brandford, J., Schwartz, D.: TAG-V: extending intelligent learning environments with TAs to enhance learning. In: Moore, J.D., Redfield, C.L., Johnson, W.L. (eds.) AIED 2001, pp. 389–397. IOS Press, Amsterdam (2001)

Connecting the Dots Towards Collaborative AIED: Linking Group Makeup to Process to Learning

Angela Stewart[(✉)] [iD] and Sidney K. D'Mello [iD]

University of Colorado Boulder, Boulder, CO 80309, USA
{angela.stewart,sidney.dmello}@colorado.edu

Abstract. We model collaborative problem solving outcomes using data from 37 triads who completed a challenging computer programming task. Participants individually rated their group's performance, communication, cooperation, and agreeableness after the session, which were aggregated to produce group-level measures of subjective outcomes. We scored teams on objective task outcomes and measured individual students' learning outcomes with a posttest. Groups with similar personalities performed better on the task and had higher ratings of communication, cooperation, and agreeableness. Importantly, greater deviation in teammates' perception of group performance and higher ratings of communication, cooperation, and agreeableness negatively predicted individual learning. We discuss findings from the perspective of group work norms and consider applications to intelligent systems that support collaborative problem solving.

Keywords: Collaborative problem solving · Collaborative learning
Group composition · Teamwork · Small group work

1 Introduction

Collaborative problem solving (CPS) is considered a core competency for the 21st century workforce [1]. Accordingly, modern curricula increasingly include tasks that require students to work together to achieve some goal [1]. But it is not enough for students to simply work together – they should also learn relevant content/skills [1, 2] as well as learn to collaborate effectively. Despite its importance to educators, small groups rarely achieve their full potential. They are often plagued by *process loss*, where the group does not achieve a level of performance compared to what is theoretically achievable [3]. Additionally, process gain, where group performance is better than any combination of individual members' performance, is difficult to achieve [3].

Can next-generation artificial intelligence in education (AIED) systems facilitate development of CPS skills similar to their success in promoting learning in more traditional domains [4]? An AIED-CPS system could monitor group CPS processes to create a *group model* and intervene when students are not collaborating effectively. Such systems could consider a variety of static factors related to group composition (e.g., gender, personality, motivation, prior knowledge) and dynamically monitor aspects of the collaboration process (e.g., level of frustration, individual member participation, number of ideas generated). The system could provide motivating feedback or offer hints

© Springer International Publishing AG, part of Springer Nature 2018
C. Penstein Rosé et al. (Eds.): AIED 2018, LNAI 10947, pp. 545–556, 2018.
https://doi.org/10.1007/978-3-319-93843-1_40

when problems are uncovered with the end goal of promoting successful task performance, satisfaction with the collaborative process, and individual learning.

What principles should guide the design of an AIED-CPS system? There has been considerable research in the fields of small group problem solving [5, 6], collaborative learning (CL) [2, 3] and computer-supported collaborative learning (CSCL) [7, 8]. However, these areas tend to be disjoint, either focusing on group makeup factors [9–11], the collaborative process itself [3], optimal group outcomes [12, 13], or learning as a result of the collaboration [2]. Our work aims to connect the dots –from group makeup to collaborative process to individual learning (Fig. 1) – by addressing the following questions: (1) How does group makeup affect subjective and objective collaboration outcomes? (2) How does subjective and objective collaborative outcomes affect individual learning?

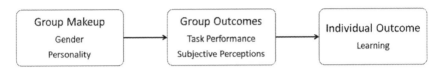

Fig. 1. In this work, we connect the dots of group makeup to group outcomes to individual learning outcomes.

We consider group makeup from the perspective of gender and personality as they are related to CPS outcomes (see Sect. 1.1). Further, both of these factors are fairly static and can be quickly measured through self-report, making them ideal candidates to incorporate into a group model (group equivalent of a student model in AIED).

We emphasize three types of collaborative outcomes: group-level objective task performance, group-level subjective perception of the collaboration, and individual-level learning. It is important to consider both group- and individual-level outcomes because they may depend on different factors and might even be negatively related. Furthermore, an AIED-CPS system cannot solely produce positive group or individual outcomes, but must balance the two. We also consider objective outcomes in the form of task performance and learning, as well as subjective perceptions of the CPS process as both are valued by individuals [3, 12, 14].

1.1 Related Work

The CPS literature is vast (see review by [3]). For example, researchers have investigated various factors related to CPS outcomes, such as social loafing [14], awareness and shared intentionality [15], information distribution [11], and problem solving approach [16]. CPS research in the learning sciences has mainly focused on online forums or massively open online courses [17, 18], CPS skill assessment [12, 13], automated support of collaborative discussions [19], and collaborative discourse [20]. To keep scope manageable, we focus on related work germane to our research questions, specifically group composition and cohesion, subjective perceptions of the CPS process, and group to individual transfer of learning [21].

There is a comprehensive literature on group composition and its relationship to collaborative processes and outcomes. Researchers have investigated group composition from the perspective of team familiarity [11], gender [9, 10, 22], ethnicity [22], team member ability [22], and group diversity [23].

Related research on group cohesion [3, 24–26] – the extent to which group members feel like they are part of the group and wish to remain in the group [24] – has indicated that cohesiveness can be affected by demographic factors (e.g. sex, race, age), attitudes or beliefs, and even task performance [3, 27]. Though research has generally found that more cohesive groups perform better [3, 24], Langfred [24] found that the relationship between cohesiveness and performance is moderated by the expectations of group member behavior, referred to as group work norms. When group work norms focused on behavior related to the task rather than social behavior (such as agreeableness or conflict minimization), high cohesiveness was predictive of group effectiveness.

Beyond performance on the collaborative task, it is also important to consider how teammates perceive the collaboration [28–30]. Attitudes and perceptions can be affected by process conflict [31], number of people collaborating (pairs versus multiple individuals) [28], or group affect [29]. Similarly, in the context of collaborative learning, students must also engage in transfer learning, where they apply knowledge gained in one context to a different context. Transfer in small group learning is achievable as indicated in a meta-analysis [32] of 38 studies where students learned independently or in a small groups The weighted average of the effect size (Hedges' g) across studies was .30 sigma. The authors concluded that small group learning promotes a deeper understanding of the content as students must coordinate differing viewpoints, an opportunity not present in individual learning [32].

In an effort to understand the factors that contribute to successful transfer, Olivera and Straus [21] compared transfer learning outcomes for individuals learning alone, students in a group, and students observing a group. They found that students learning either in a group or by observing a group outperformed students learning individually. They concluded that cognitive factors associated with the collaborative process were important for transfer learning. However, social factors related to the collaboration might not be as important for transfer learning because students who merely observed groups obtained the same benefits as working in a group.

1.2   Contribution

Our work contributes to basic research on collaborative problem solving with an eye towards developing AIED systems to facilitate CPS. We provide insights into the connection between group composition, group outcomes, and individual learning as a result of the collaboration. We focus on a combination of factors and outcomes because processes that lead to success on one type of outcome might not lead to success in the others (subjective vs. objective outcomes, group vs. individual outcomes).

Additionally, our context of inquiry is novel. We consider CPS in triads, which afford seven units of analysis (3 individuals, 3 dyads, and the triad), thereby providing a range of interesting interactions to explore. We focus on triad-level analysis to understand the group as a whole and individual-level analysis to understand how students situated within a group learn. We investigate CPS in the domain of computer programming where students used an interactive visual programming environment (see Sect. 2.3) to learn computer programming skills. Finally, we study CPS during virtual collaborations as an increasing amount of collaboration in the 21st century workplace is performed by teams communicating virtually [1].

2   Methods

2.1   Participants

Participants were 111 (63.1% female, average age = 19.4) undergraduate students from a medium-sized private Midwestern university, who were compensated with course credit. Students were 74.8% Caucasian, 9.9% Hispanic/Latino, 8.1% Asian, 2.7% Other, 0.9% Black, 0.9% American Indian/Native Alaskan, and 2.7% did not report ethnicity. Students were assigned groups of three based on scheduling constraints, with a total of 37 groups. Nineteen students from ten teams indicated they knew at least one person from their team prior to participation. Students had no prior computer programming experience.

2.2   Learning Environment

Students learned basic computer programming principles as a group using code.org's Minecraft-themed Hour of Code (Fig. 2) [33]. Hour of Code is an online resource for students of all ages to learn basic computer programming principles in an hour. It uses Blockly [34], a visual programming language that represents lines of code (such as if statements) as interlocking blocks. Blocks only interlock in a syntactically correct manner, allowing students to focus on the coding logic and programming principles, without considering syntax errors.

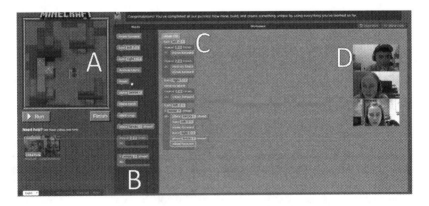

Fig. 2. Minecraft-themed Hour of Code from Code.org. Students could visualize the results of running their code (A), a code bank of possible blocks to use (B), the code they generated (C) and their team's faces (D).

2.3 Procedure

Students were each randomly assigned to one of three computer-enabled rooms with video-conferencing capabilities and screen sharing through Zoom (https://zoom.us). Each computer had a webcam with a microphone so students could see and hear each other. During the collaboration, one student's screen was shared so that everyone viewed the same content.

Surveys. Each student individually filled out demographic data including gender, age, major, and standardized test score (ACT and/or SAT). Students also completed the short version of Big Five Inventory (BFI) [35] to assess the following personality traits: extraversion, agreeableness, conscientiousness, emotional stability (previously neuroticism), and openness to experience.

Introductory Levels. After individually completing the surveys, students were asked to complete five levels and view three accompanying videos that taught basic computer programming principles, such as loops and if statements. Students were required to build structures within the game and navigate around obstacles. One randomly assigned student was tasked with controlling the group's actions in the environment. The other two students were tasked with contributing to the collaboration. Students were specifically instructed to collaborate as a team to complete the levels within 20 min.

Students then *individually* rated their satisfaction with their team's performance, communication, cooperation, and agreeableness using six point scales. Specifically, students rated the statements "I am satisfied with my team's performance at completing the lessons," "I am satisfied with how we communicated with each other," "I am satisfied with how we mutually cooperated to complete the lessons," and "I am satisfied with how agreeable my teammates are." They indicated whether they were very dissatisfied, somewhat dissatisfied, slightly dissatisfied, slightly satisfied, somewhat satisfied, or very satisfied for all items.

Challenge Levels. Teams were then tasked with working together to complete a challenging programming task in the same Hour of Code environment. The same team member who controlled interaction with the environment during the initial lessons also controlled the interaction during the coding challenge. In the challenge, teams were given 20 min to build a 4 × 4 brick building with the following constraints: use at least one if statement, use at least one repeat loop, build at least three bricks over water, and use 15 blocks of code or less. Students *individually* completed the same subjective measures of their team's performance, communication, cooperation, and agreeableness with the wording adapted for the challenge level.

Posttest. Students *individually* completed a ten-item researcher-created multiple choice test to assess their conceptual knowledge of coding concepts (such as repeat loops and if statements). Each posttest item had one correct answer out of four possible answers, and the possible range of scores was 0% to 100%. Figure 3 shows an example posttest question.

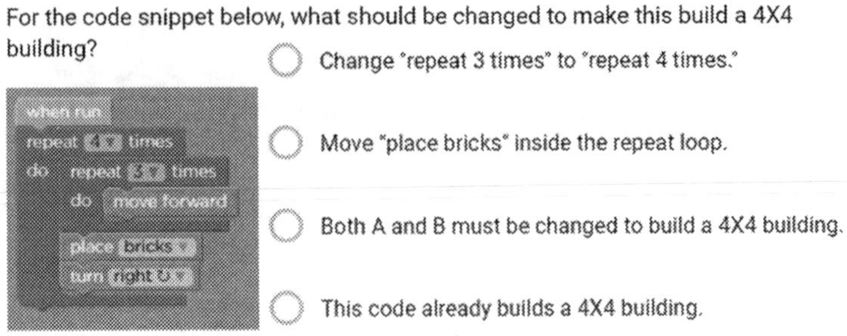

For the code snippet below, what should be changed to make this build a 4X4 building?

○ Change "repeat 3 times" to "repeat 4 times."

○ Move "place bricks" inside the repeat loop.

○ Both A and B must be changed to build a 4X4 building.

○ This code already builds a 4X4 building.

Fig. 3. An example posttest question.

2.4   Measures

We focus on team's performance during the challenge phase as this was the critical phase of the study; the introductory phase merely familiarized the teammates with each other and with the programming environment.

Subjective Perceptions. For each team, we computed the mean and standard deviation (SD) of the three students' performance ratings. The mean measured the overall assessment of the team's performance, and the SD measured divergence of assessments. Across all teams, students tended to rate the team's performance quite highly (performance mean, $M = 4.52$, $SD = .89$) with relatively little disparity (performance SD, $M = 1.03$, $SD = .67$).

We combined measures of communication, cooperation, and agreeableness (CCA) because ratings were highly correlated (Cronbach's alpha = .89). We first computed the mean and of the communication, cooperation, and agreeableness ratings for each team member, yielding three aggregated measures of CCA (one per team member). We took the mean of the CCA measure across the triad, to yield a single measure of CCA mean. Similarly, we took the SD of the CCA measure across the triad, to yield a single measure of CCA SD. The CCA SD was strongly correlated with the CCA mean ($r = -.76$), so we focused on the mean. Overall, students were quite satisfied with their team's CCA ($M = 5.45$, $SD = .56$).

Objective Task Score. Each team's final solution was scored by two independent raters on the five challenge criteria (see Sect. 2.3). The two raters reconciled any disagreements via discussion. Each criterion was worth a single point, so scores ranged from 0 to 5 with a mean of 2.86 ($SD = 1.06$).

Individual Learning (Posttest). We computed the average of the ten posttest items for each student ($M = 43.0\%$; $SD = 15.7$).

Group Makeup. We considered group makeup based on gender using two binary variables: whether all members of the group were the same gender (23%) and whether the group was female-dominated (71%). Group makeup based on personality was measured using dissimilarity scores of the BFI. Specifically, Euclidean distances between the 5-dimensional BFI vectors of each pair of participants in a team (three pairs in total) was computed and then averaged to obtain a single measure of personality dissimilarity.

A larger value indicated that participants had more disparate personalities ($M = 7.19$, $SD = 1.58$).

2.5 Data Treatment

Data was collected over two semesters, with a minor experimental change made between semesters, where we added a five minute warning before the end of the challenges. In order to prevent this change from influencing outcomes, we z-scored each of the following measures by semester: performance mean, performance SD, CCA mean, task score, and individual posttest score. Two teams were removed from the group-level analyses because students did not to report ACT scores (which was used as a covariate in several analyses – see Sect. 3.2).

3 Results

3.1 Relationship Between Group-Level Outcomes

At the group-level, task score was positively correlated with subjective perceptions of performance ($r = .56$, $p < .001$) as well as perceptions of the collaborative process (i.e., mean of communication, coordination, and agreeableness) ($r = .44$, $p = .01$), which were also correlated ($r = .57$, $p < .001$). Deviation in each individual's perception of group performance was not significantly correlated with task score ($r = -.26$, $p = .13$).

3.2 Predicting Group-Level Outcomes from Group Makeup

We used linear regression to predict subjective (performance mean, performance SD, and CCA mean) and objective (task score) group-level outcomes from group makeup (mixed gender, female dominated, and personality dissimilarity). We included the mean ACT score of the group and binary team member familiarity as covariates. Neither gender-based measure of group makeup was predictive of task performance or perception (see Table 1). However, teams with more disparate personalities performed significantly worse (task score) and were less satisfied with their team's communication, cooperation, and agreeableness, but not their team's performance. A follow-up analysis

Table 1. Results of predicting group-level outcomes from gender and personality variables. The standardized beta coefficients (with p-values in parenthesis) are shown.

			Outcome Variables	
	Task Score	Perf. Mean	Perf. SD	CCA Mean
Mixed Gender	.01 (.94)	.04 (.83)	.10 (.59)	-.10 (.59)
Female Dominated	.27 (.13)	.01 (.97)	-.23 (.20)	.14 (.47)
Personality Dissimilarity	-.36 (.03)	-.02 (.91)	-.04 (.83)	-.33 (.07)

Note, Perf. Mean and Perf. SD indicate the mean and SD of the subjective performance measure. CCA Mean indicates the mean of the subjective communication, cooperation, and agreeableness measure.

on individual dimensions of personality (obtained by including the standard deviation across the three team members as a predictor in five separate regression models) indicated that deviation in emotional stability predicted CCA mean ($B = -.40, p = .02$), but no individual dimensions of personality predicted task score.

3.3   Predicting Posttest Scores from Group Outcomes and Group Makeup

We used linear mixed effects models for individual posttest scores because participants were nested within groups. The fixed effects included group-level task scores, performance mean, performance SD, CCA mean, personality dissimilarity, mixed gender, and female dominated groups (each in separate models). Individual ACT scores, gender, teammate familiarity, and whether the student was controlling the interaction with the environment (see Sect. 2.3) were included as covariates. Group identity was a random factor (intercept only).

None of the group makeup variables were predictive of posttest score ($B = .03, p = .70$ for personality dissimilarity, $B = -.26, p = .33$ for mixed gender, and $B = .32, p = .36$ for female dominated).

Surprisingly, neither task score ($B = .08, p = .69$) nor performance mean ($B = .07$, $p = .72$) was predictive of individual posttest scores. However, participants' perceptions of the group's communication, cooperation, and agreeableness (CCA mean, $B = -.34$, $p = .05$), and variability in their perceptions of the group's performance (performance SD, $B = -.45, p = .06$) were negative predictors of posttest scores. These measures remained significant when included in a joint model ($B = -.75, p = .03$ for performance SD and $B = -.56, p < .001$ for CCA mean), demonstrating that they explain unique variance in posttest scores.

We also considered moderation of group-level outcomes by group makeup variables when predicting individual posttest score, but there were no significant interactions.

4   Discussion

4.1   Main Findings

It has long been known that composition of a group effects outcomes [9, 22, 23]. However, what group makeup variables should be measured is not clear. We found that personality dissimilarity negatively predicted how well a team did on the task and also negatively correlated with the team's perceptions of the collaborative process. This suggests that AIED systems that support collaboration should consider personality differences among teammates as part of the *group* model.

It is important that we do not imply causality between personality differences, task score, and perceptions of the collaboration. Teams that had similar personalities might have performed well on the task, and thus perceived their collaboration more positively. Alternatively, they could have perceived themselves as working well together, which might have resulted in enhanced task performance. There might even be a more tightly coupled relationship between task performance and subjective perceptions, where each boosts the other as teams sustain positive interactions and make progress towards the goal.

Gender-based group makeup measures were not predictive of any outcomes, despite some previous work suggesting a link [9]. It is possible that specific factors related to gender, such as expectations of social behavior [36], confidence in computing ability [37, 38], and perceptions of stereotype threat [39] might be more informative measures of group makeup than gender itself.

Prior research suggests teams should maintain common ground by constructing solutions jointly and working towards a shared goal, referred to as shared task alignment [40]. Thus, it is unsurprising that variability in students' perceptions of team performance negatively predicted individual posttest scores.

We additionally found that positive perceptions of the group's communication, cooperation, and agreeableness was negatively related to individual posttest scores. Although this finding might seem counterintuitive, it is possible that it could reflect group work norms, which should be task-oriented rather than social [24]. Groups with more socially-oriented group work norms, such as minimizing conflict and agreeability, might have achieved favorable subjective outcomes at the expense of learning.

Because objective task scores were unrelated to individual learning outcomes, it might not be enough to simply support successful task performance and subjective collaboration outcomes. Instead, a range of CPS goals (e.g. positive group perceptions, task performance, group to individual transfer of learning) should be considered when designing intelligent systems that support CPS.

4.2 Applications

This work can inform future AIED systems that aim to support CPS, with particular emphasis on virtual collaborations. For example, measurements of group makeup (specifically personality differences) could inform sensitivity to unproductive group interactions. Perhaps teams with highly dissimilar personalities should encounter interventions sooner and more often than teams with similar personalities.

Given the differences between group and individual learning outcomes, intelligent systems that support collaboration could be customizable to the outcome pertinent to the learning goals. For example, if successful task completion is the goal, an intelligent system might emphasize subjective outcomes by providing real-time feedback on how to improve collaborative processes if students are not communicating effectively or are being uncooperative and disagreeable. Alternatively, if individual learning is the goal, the intelligent system might encourage coordination amongst team members and task-oriented group work norms by prompting students to build on a particular idea or voice disagreements and discuss tradeoffs between competing solutions.

4.3 Limitations and Future Work

Like all studies, ours has limitations. First our sample size was modest and consisted of students from a private university with little age or ethnic diversity. Further, the data was collected in a laboratory context, thereby limiting broader claims of generalizability.

This should be addressed using more diverse and larger samples collected in more authentic context. Indeed, we are in the process of collecting data from more diverse samples both in the lab and in classrooms and with multiple CPS environments.

Our work considers a holistic view of the collaboration, and not how it unfolds over time. Analysis of the collaboration at more fine-grained intervals would provide insight into how perceptions, task performance, and learning change as students interact over time. We are also conducting expert coding of the collaborative process as a complement to the subjective assessments.

Finally, interventions based on our findings should be explored. We do not precisely know the most effective way to respond to unproductive teams. Research is needed to explore how to support aspects of the collaborative processes such as communication cooperation, and agreeableness, as well as instilling task-related group work norms.

4.4 Conclusion

Our work is an initial step in building AIED systems that intelligently support productive collaborative problem solving in groups. We found that group makeup with regards to personality dissimilarity influenced group-level task performance and subjective perception outcomes of the CPS process. Further, outcomes related to successful task performance were different from those related to individual learning, suggesting there might be different processes at play. Thus AIED systems that support CPS should consider both types of outcomes as well as the influence of group makeup in supporting effective collaborations.

Acknowledgements. We would like to thank David Blair, Eugene Choi, Mae Raab, and Samantha Scaglione for their invaluable help. This research was supported by the National Science Foundation (NSF DUE-1745442) and the Institute of Educational Sciences (IES R305A170432). Any opinions, findings and conclusions or recommendations expressed in this material are those of the authors and do not necessarily reflect the views of the funding agencies.

References

1. PISA 2015 Collaborative Problem Solving Framework (2015)
2. Dillenbourg, P.: What do you mean by collaborative learning? In: Collaborative-learning Cognitive and Computational Approaches, vol. 1, pp. 1–15 (1999)
3. Kerr, N.L., Tindale, R.S.: Group performance and decision making. Ann. Rev. Psychol. **55**, 623–655 (2004)
4. Du Boulay, B.: Artificial intelligence as an effective classroom assistant. IEEE Intell. Syst. **31**, 76–81 (2016)
5. Lou, Y., Abrami, P.C., D'Apollonia, S.: Small group and individual learning with technology: a meta-analysis. Rev. Educ. Res. **71**, 449–521 (2001)
6. Vijayaratnam, P.: Developing higher order thinking skills and team commitment via group problem solving: a bridge to the real world. Proc. Soc. Behav. Sci. **66**, 53–63 (2012)
7. Alavi, M.: Computer-mediated collaborative learning: an empirical evaluation. MIS Q. **18**, 159–174 (1994)

8. Borghoff, U.M., Schlichter, J.H.: Computer-supported cooperative work. Comput. Support. Coop. Work **27**, 87–141 (2000)
9. Fenwick, G.D., Neal, D.J.: Effect of gender composition on group performance. Gender Work Organ. **8**, 205–225 (2001)
10. Savicki, V., Kelley, M., Lingenfelter, D.: Gender and group composition in small task groups using computer-mediated communication. Comput. Hum. Behav. **12**, 209–224 (1996)
11. Gruenfeld, D.H., Mannix, E.A., Williams, K.Y., Neale, M.A.: Group composition and decision making: how member familiarity and information distribution affect process and performance. Organ. Behav. Hum. Decis. Process. **67**, 1–15 (1996)
12. McManus, M.M., Aiken, R.M.: Supporting effective collaboration: using a rearview mirror to look forward. Int. J. Artif. Intell. Educ. **26**, 365–377 (2016)
13. Rosen, Y.: Computer-based assessment of collaborative problem solving: exploring the feasibility of human-to-agent approach. Int. J. Artif. Intell. Educ. **25**, 380–406 (2015)
14. Linnenbrink-Garcia, L., Rogat, T.K., Koskey, K.L.K.K.: Affect and engagement during small group instruction. Contemp. Educ. Psychol. **36**, 13–24 (2011)
15. Tenenberg, J., Roth, W.-M., Socha, D.: From I-awareness to we-awareness in CSCW. Comput. Support. Coop. Work (CSCW) **25**, 235–278 (2016)
16. Chang, C.-J., Chang, M.-H., Chiu, B.-C., Liu, C.-C., Fan Chiang, S.-H., Wen, C.-T., Hwang, F.-K., Wu, Y.-T., Chao, P.-Y., Lai, C.-H., Wu, S.-W., Chang, C.-K., Chen, W.: An analysis of student collaborative problem solving activities mediated by collaborative simulations. Comput. Educ. **114**, 222–235 (2017)
17. Crossley, S., Dascalu, M., McNamara, D.S., Baker, R., Trausan-Matu, S.: Predicting success in massive open online courses (MOOCs) using cohesion network analysis. In: International Conference on Computer-Supported Collaborative Learning. International Society of the Learning Sciences, Philadelphia (2017)
18. Yoo, J., Kim, J.: Can online discussion participation predict group project performance? Investigating the roles of linguistic features and participation patterns. Int. J. Artif. Intell. Educ. **24**, 8–32 (2014)
19. Adamson, D., Dyke, G., Jang, H., Rosé, C.P.: Towards an agile approach to adapting dynamic collaboration support to student needs. Int. J. Artif. Intell. Educ. **24**, 92–124 (2014)
20. Hmelo-Silver, C.E., Barrows, H.S.: Facilitating collaborative knowledge building. Cogn. Instruc. **26**, 48–94 (2008)
21. Olivera, F., Straus, S.G.: Group-to-individual transfer of learning: cognitive and social factors. Small Group Res. **35**, 440–465 (2004)
22. Wilkinson, I.A.G.G., Fung, I.Y.Y.Y.: Small-group composition and peer effects. Int. J. Educ. Res. **37**, 425–447 (2002)
23. Cummings, J.N.: Work groups, structural diversity, and knowledge sharing in a global organization. Manag. Sci. **50**, 352–364 (2004)
24. Langfred, C.W.: Is group cohesiveness a double-edged sword? An investigation of the effects of cohesiveness on performance. Small Group Res. **29**, 124–143 (1998)
25. Gully, S.M., Devine, D.J., Whitney, D.J.: A meta-analysis of cohesion and performance: effects of level of analysis and task interdependence. Small Group Res. **26**, 497–520 (1995)
26. Evans, C.R., Dion, K.L.: Group cohesion and performance: a meta-analysis. Small Group Res. **22**, 175–186 (1991)
27. Harrison, D.A., Price, K.H., Bell, M.P.: Beyond relational demography: time and the effects of surface-and deep-level diversity on work group cohesion. Acad. Manag. J. **41**, 96–107 (1998)
28. Fernández Dobao, A., Blum, A., Dobao, A.F., Blum, A.: Collaborative writing in pairs and small groups: learners' attitudes and perceptions. System **41**, 365–378 (2013)

29. Barsade, S.G., Gibson, D.E.: Group affect: its influence on individual and group outcomes. Current Dir. Psychol. Sci. **21**, 119–123 (2012)
30. Ku, H.-Y.Y., Tseng, H.W., Akarasriworn, C.: Collaboration factors, teamwork satisfaction, and student attitudes toward online collaborative learning. Comput. Hum. Behav. **29**, 922–929 (2013)
31. Behfar, K.J., Mannix, E.A., Peterson, R.S., Trochim, W.M.: Conflict in small groups: the meaning and consequences of process conflict. Small Group Res. **42**, 127–176 (2011)
32. Pai, H.-H.H., Sears, D.A., Maeda, Y.: Effects of small-group learning on transfer: a meta-analysis. Educ. Psychol. Rev. **27**, 79–102 (2015)
33. Code Studio. https://studio.code.org/s/mc/stage/1/puzzle/1
34. Fraser, N.: Ten things we've learned from Blockly. In: Proceedings of the 2015 IEEE Blocks and Beyond Workshop, pp. 49–50 (2015)
35. Gosling, S.D., Rentfrow, P.J., Swann, W.B.: A very brief measure of the Big-Five personality domains. J. Res. Pers. **37**, 504–528 (2003)
36. Stake, J.E., Eisele, H.: Gender and personality. In: Chrisler, J., McCreary, D. (eds.) Handbook of Gender Research in Psychology, pp. 19–40. Springer, New York (2010)
37. Shashaani, L.: Gender differences in computer attitudes and use among college students. J. Educ. Comput. Res. **16**, 37–51 (1997)
38. Beyer, S., Rynes, K., Perrault, J., Hay, K., Haller, S.: Gender differences in computer science students. ACM SIGCSE Bull. **35**, 49–53 (2003)
39. Spencer, S.J., Steele, C.M., Quinn, D.M.: Stereotype threat and women's math performance. J. Exp. Soc. Psychol. **35**, 4–28 (1999)
40. Barron, B.: Achieving coordination in collaborative problem-solving groups. J. Learn. Sci. **9**, 403–436 (2000)

Do Preschoolers 'Game the System'? A Case Study of Children's Intelligent (Mis)Use of a Teachable Agent Based Play-&-Learn Game in Mathematics

Eva-Maria Ternblad[✉], Magnus Haake, Erik Anderberg, and Agneta Gulz

Cognitive Science, Lund University, Lund, Sweden
Eternblad@gmail.com,
{Magnus.Haake,Erik.Anderberg,Agneta.Gulz}@lucs.lu.se

Abstract. For learning to take place in digital learning environments, learners need to use educational software – more or less – as intended. However, previous studies show that some school children, instead of trying to learn and master a skill, choose to systematically exploit or outsmart the system to gain progress. But what about preschoolers? The present study explores the presence of this kind of behavioral patterns among preschoolers who use a teachable agent-based play-&-learn game in early math. We analyzed behavioral data logs together with interviews and observations. We also analyzed action patterns deviating from the pedagogical design intentions in terms of non-harmful gaming, harmful gaming, and wheel-spinning. Our results reveal that even if pedagogically not intended use of the game did occur, harmful gaming was rare. Interestingly, the results also indicate an unexpected awareness in children of what it means to learn and to teach. Finally, we present a series of possible adjustments of the used software in order to decrease gaming-like behavior or strategies that signalize insufficient skills or poor learning.

Keywords: Preschoolers · Gaming the system · Learning-by-teaching
Teachable agent · Wheel-spinning

1 Introduction

Educational software developers generally have ideas about the ways in which a certain digital learning resource is intended to support learning. Yet, it is obvious for anyone who has designed and developed educational software, and then studied its use in a real-world context, that pedagogical intentions and actual activities on the part of students do not always align that well. In other words, one will find certain mismatches between pedagogical intentions and students' behavioral and cognitive activities [1].

The starting point for the work presented in this paper was an intervention study in early math for preschoolers by means of a 'teachable agent'-based play-&-learn game. Teachable agents (hence TAs), are a form of educational technology based on the idea that a good way to learn is to teach someone else [2]. During this study, some teachers were concerned about an observation they made, namely that children 'fooled' the digital friend (the TA) they were supposed to instruct and guide. As reported by the teachers,

© Springer International Publishing AG, part of Springer Nature 2018
C. Penstein Rosé et al. (Eds.): AIED 2018, LNAI 10947, pp. 557–569, 2018.
https://doi.org/10.1007/978-3-319-93843-1_41

some children would – although they knew which alternative was correct – deliberately pick an incorrect alternative, or even wrongfully alter a correct suggestion from the digital tutee. That is, the teachers observed mismatches between (i) a pedagogical intention and expectation held by the game designers and teachers alike, and (ii) the children's behavior. The children were supposed to do their best in showing and guiding the digital friend how to solve the tasks, so that the digital friend would succeed, and thereby also learn for themselves. But – apparently – they did something else.

For us as game designers a worry arose, and we asked ourselves: *"How common were these and other kinds of mismatches between our pedagogical intentions and children's behavior?"* and *"What were the effects of such potential mismatches on children's learning?"* We decided to chart out the kind of behavior described by the teachers as well as potentially related kinds. As conceptual tools we decided to made use of the two behavioral categories *gaming* and *wheel-spinning* [3, 4] which both have been previously used to describe mismatches between pedagogical intentions and behavior in school children using educational software.

1.1   Related Previous Studies and Research Aims

The concept of *"gaming the system"* has been defined by Baker and collaborators [3, 5, 6] as a behavior aimed at advancing within instructional software by systematically taking advantage of regularities in the software's feedback and help. By performing a large number of studies on gaming in middle-school students, most of them targeting intelligent tutoring systems and some dealing with more open ended educational games [5, 6], the researchers have identified and modelled strategies whereby students, rather than learning the educational material, exploit properties of the system in order to succeed. Baker and colleagues [3, 5, 6] furthermore present two sub-categories of gaming behavior, proposing that: (i) *'non-harmful' gaming* typically occurs on problem steps the student already knows and is as such not associated with poor learning outcomes; (ii) *'harmful' gaming* occurs on the problem steps the student knows least well and is associated with poor learning outcomes. Since the consequences of 'harmful gaming' are far more severe, Baker et al. [3] suggests that designers of tutoring systems ought to deal with this kind of misuse.

Another related form of behavior in digital learning environments identified by Beck and Gong [4] refers to when students make unresolved attempts over and over again, to solve tasks that they really do not manage. This unsuccessful and meaningless 'wheel-spinning' could be due to insufficient skills, but also to boredom and frustration, and results in low scores, slow (or no) advancement, and inefficient learning.

The studies referred to above all concern school children. To our knowledge, no similar studies have been undertaken with respect to preschoolers' use – or misuse - of educational games. Neither have we found any previous research on possible systematic exploitations of TA-based systems. In the study presented in this paper, we therefore set out to explore and evaluate possible gaming and wheel-spinning strategies amongst 3- to 6-years-old preschool children using the early math game Magical Garden [7, 8]. In view of the observations that originally initiated the study, we broadened the concept of gaming in this particular case to include other strategic behaviors that do not align with the pedagogical design principles of the game – such as fooling or misusing the teachable agent. Data examined consisted of computer logged data from the children's interaction with the game, observations of children using the game, and conversations with children in relation to game-play. Our research questions were: (i) Would there be evidence for behavior resembling what for older children has been termed 'gaming behavior' and 'wheel-spinning'?; (ii) How frequently would these behaviors occur?; and (iii) How frequent was the behavior that teachers had pointed out to us?

In addition, we posed two more questions: (iv) Can we say anything about which children engage in these different kinds of behaviors? Specifically, can we illuminate reasons or motives behind the behavior, and are there differences in behavior between low- and high-performers? (v) What consequences do these kinds of behavior have for the way a child progresses in the game, and for the child's learning, respectively?

2   The Play-&-Learn Game Magical Garden

In brief, a teachable agent is a computer agent that is taught by a student, with AI techniques guiding the agent's behavior based on what it is taught. Students can revise their TA's knowledge (and consequently their own) based on the agent's behavior [2]. Numerous studies involving school children have shown that TA-based software can be beneficial for learning outcomes [9, 10]. Additionally, recent studies have shown that this applies also to preschoolers [11, 12].

Magical Garden (MG), the TA-based play-&-learn game used in this study, is developed by The Educational Technology Group at Lund and Linköping Universities with the collaboration of AAA-Lab, Stanford University. MG builds on work by Griffin, Case, and Siegler [13] and the main goal is to support an integration of multiple number concepts and ways of representing numbers. At the beginning, the child is presented with three characters (the TAs) – a mouse, a panda, and a hedgehog – whose garden is barren and needs water to flourish again. The child chooses one of the characters as their 'friend' with whom to collect water drops in order to bring the garden back to life (Fig. 1). While the explicit narrative presented to the child is about helping her friend taking care of the garden, the underlying purpose of each task is that the child learns and practices early numeracy.

Fig. 1. MG screenshots showing: (left) the initial garden; (mid) the three characters Panders the Panda, Mille the Mouse, and Igis the Hedgehog; (right) the later, gradually thriving garden.

At its core, MG is composed of a set of 60 *pedagogical scenarios* (or levels), ordered according to an increasing level of difficulty. In line with the approach by Griffin et al. [13], the first level in MG involve neither symbolic nor iconic representations. This initial level is followed by a stepwise linking of number words with both magnitude and a variety of different number representations, starting with iconic representations and progressing via semi-symbolic to fully symbolic representations. Since the game covers early math operations and as well as representations, the level of difficulty is a combination of number range, type of representation, and mathematical operation.

Furthermore, each of the 60 scenarios is repeated in three subsequent modes following a TA-paradigm. First (*Mode 1*), the child learns and practices on her own by playing the game. Next (*Mode 2*), the child shows her friend how to play. Third (*Mode 3*), the child monitors her friend who attempts to play on its own with opportunities to correct the friend if needed. After having completed these tasks, the child and her friend receive water drops for their garden.

As mode 3 is crucial for the analyzes in this paper, we present its structure in more detail: The friend (TA) proposes an answer by exposing it in the thought balloon (Fig. 2, lower right). Thereafter, the child presses either the green 'happy face'-button for 'correct' or the red 'non-happy face'-button for 'incorrect'. When the child choses 'correct', the action proposed by the digital friend is effectuated (in this case the elevator brings the baby bird to that tree branch in the tree). When the child choses 'incorrect' in response to the digital friend's proposal, she herself has to present a new answer. It should be pointed out that the TA's behavior in mode 3 reflects how the child has managed in modes 1 and 2; more correct answers prompts the TA to provide better

Fig. 2. Screenshots from MG showing the three subsequent pedagogical modes reflecting the teachable agent paradigm. *upper left:* overview of the sub-game Bird Hero where the task is to help the baby birds up in the tree to their mothers; *upper right:* the child practices; *lower left:* the child shows her friend (Panders); *lower right:* the child supervises her friend (Panders).

proposals in mode 3. The mapping is not 100% but has an element of chance. One reason for this is to provide also a child who herself only provides correct answers with the possibility to 'act as teacher' to her friend (TA).

3 Method

3.1 Participants, Procedure, and Instruments

The original study involved 43 children (20 girls, 23 boys) aged 3;9–6;1 recruited from four different Swedish preschools. All children were Swedish-speaking and came from socioeconomic middle-class families. The present study relies on the log data, observational data, and interviews from the original study. During the study, the children played MG in 20-min sessions 2–3 times a week during five consecutive weeks. Each session took place in a separate room and involved a smaller group of 2–4 children with one iPad each, together with a teacher or researcher. The children were only allowed to touch their own iPad, not their peers'. Depending on children's wishes, they could use headphones. Researchers were present at the first session and at two occasions during the third and fifth week respectively. At each occasion, they observed children playing and talked to them using a topics/question guide. Notably, many children talked spontaneously – both to game characters and researchers – while playing.

3.2 Defining Gaming-like Strategies

When playing Magical Garden there are four possible ways of acting that all can be considered as mismatches between pedagogical design principles and actual behavior, and thus also have some resemblance to gaming or wheel-spinning:

1. In modes 1 and 2, a child can systematically guess by choosing one button after the other (for instance by always starting with the first button (representing "1") and then continue all the way up to the last button until the answer is correct).
2. In mode 3, a child can use the TA as a trial-&-error machine by systematically 'avoiding to correct' the TA – whether its proposal is correct or incorrect.
3. In mode 3, a child can systematically 'correct' the TA – whether its proposal is incorrect or correct.
4. In all modes, a child can apply random guessing without paying attention towards previous performances or feedback (*wheel-spinning*).

Strategies 1 and 2 can both be categorized as harmful gaming. If the corresponding behavior is indeed systematic the child will not proceed to more advanced levels, that is, learning is not facilitated. Yet, there is the reward of water drops so that the child can water his or her garden and thereby use the software as an instrument for play and entertainment. The presence of any of these two strategies is an indication that the child has insufficient knowledge on the subject or that she does not fully grasp the meaning of the play-&-learn game. Strategy 3 however, differs from the strategy 2 since the child in this case does not seem to 'gain' anything at all. Even though this could be regarded as a kind of harmless misuse rather than exploitation, we have chosen to categorize this behavior as *non-harmful gaming*. Dismissing the TA's response may indicate a wish for testing the system, while learning and progress may still work out as intended. Nevertheless, it is worthwhile to look into this kind of events to learn more about what is going on.

Finally, children with insufficient skills could also lap into strategy 4 (non-systematic guessing with little or no progress at all). Even though this kind of wheel-spinning doesn't lead to easy-earned water drops, it could indicate that the child does not learn properly by playing the game, and perhaps needs other guidance or preparations.

3.3   Student Categories

During the sessions, the children progressed at their own pace and could choose to spend time on watering their garden or solve mathematical problems, all according to their own liking. They thereby reached different levels of difficulty. To be able to compare the students' performances, we used log data to plot progression curves and from these calculate performance coefficients by analyzing how many rounds (that is, how many complete series of modes 1, 2 and 3) that were necessary for advancing one level in the game (Fig. 3). Next, taking the lower and upper 25-percentile for all coefficients, the following performance categories were defined:

- Low performing students (25%; $N = 11$): > 1.3 rounds/level
- Medium performing students (50%; $N = 21$): 1.3 – 0.9 rounds/level
- High performing students (25%; $N = 11$): < 0.9 rounds/level

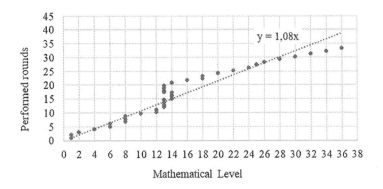

Fig. 3. Example (girl, 6 year) of a progression plot and the corresponding calculation of a performance coefficient.

4   Results

To answer the research questions presented in Sect. 1.1, behavioral data from game play (log data) was used together with teachers' verbal reports and notes from interviews and observations. By log data calculations, each of the four gaming strategies was identified, quantified, and analyzed in relation to the performance categories mentioned above. The results are presented in the passages below together with possible reasons and consequences of gaming and wheel-spinning tendencies.

4.1 Strategy 1: Systematic Guessing in Mode 1 and Mode 2

Here, we focused on behavioral patterns where the player systematically guesses the answer by following a stepwise procedure, e.g. starting with the highest or lowest number such as guessing number 1, 2, 3, and 4 when the correct answer is 4. For a mode to be classified as being 'gamed', the minimum number of trials before hitting the target was set to three. That is, if the correct answer was 4, the player had to start guessing at 1 or 2 (followed by 3 and 4), while if the correct answer was 1, the player had to start guessing at 4 or 3, (followed by 2 and 1). For a complete round to be categorized as gamed, the behavior had to be found in at least one of the modes 1 and 2.

The result reveals a quite small amount of systematic guessing. In total, 18 of the 43 players (42%) applied this strategy at some occasion while playing. However, only a handful of them (5 children) did it for more than one round. Looking at the three children that most often applied systematic guessing (20% of the rounds or more), all of them were classified as low performing. An analysis showed this behavior to be more common at levels where new mathematical concepts were introduced (such as when the number range was changed from 1–4 to 1–9 or at the introduction to proto-addition).

4.2 Strategy 2: Avoiding to Correct the TA Although It Is Sometimes Wrong

To apply systematic guessing in mode 3 is more difficult. As explained earlier, when the child corrects the TA (by telling the TA its proposal was incorrect), the TA will ask for help to choose the right answer. After such a correction, the child has one chance only to provide the correct answer before the TA guesses again. On the other hand, if the child does not correct the TA (by telling the TA its proposal was correct), the TA will act upon the suggestion. If the answer is accurate, the game progresses; if it isn't, the TA proposes another suggestion and the child has another chance to confirm or correct the TA. This repeats until the answer is correct.

A possible gaming strategy in this mode is to systematically avoid to correct the TA's answer (whether correct or not), and thereby use the TA as a trial-&-error machine. This amounts to exploiting a mindless 'click-&-wait strategy' instead of trying to reason and make an own effort. It is a strategy that does not inflict on working memory resources (which other systematic guessing might do), since the child does not need to attend to or remember previous guesses. Consequently, this can be regarded as a strategy that is simple to use. For a round to be classified as including gaming in this particular sense, one of two criteria had to be reached.

- Avoiding to correct the TA three times in a row (or more).
- Avoiding to correct the TA twice in a row at two (or more) separate occasions.

The log data revealed an even smaller amount of this kind of gaming compared to strategy 1 presented above. That is, only 11 of the 43 children actually behaved in this way at all, and only five of them did it more than once. None of these five children were classified as high-performing and one of them was, furthermore, identified as a systematic guesser according to Strategy 1 (above). An additional finding is also that when children refused to correct the TA's erroneous proposals for two or more times in a row, it was likely that the child actually never corrected the TA at all during that specific round. This could, in particular, be seen on higher levels of difficulty and in consistence with the previous analysis on Strategy 1, this strategy mainly occurred at levels where new mathematical concepts were introduced.

It is important to emphasize that the data log themselves do not reveal anything about the children's thoughts and reasons for behaving this way – that is, if the child actually is aware of the fact that the TA is mistaken or not when avoiding to correct it. Interestingly, when observing and listening to some of the children that applied this strategy, two of them revealed that they actually knew that the answer was wrong, but that they wanted the TA to learn from its own mistakes (*"get to see that this is wrong"*). This meta-level of teaching was not considered when designing the game in the first place. Also note that the two children that were caught in the act of 'teaching the TA a lesson' by letting it answer incorrectly, only did this occasionally. The qualitative and quantitative findings do therefore not match in this particular matter.

4.3   Strategy 3: Systematically Correcting the TA Although It Is Sometimes Right

A deliberate false disapproval of the TA's correct answer (where the student knows that the TA is right, claims that it is not, and then answers correctly) could be interpreted as consciously 'fooling' the TA, and this was also one of the behaviors originally reported by the teachers. Even if this behavior is classified as non-harmful, it could jeopardize the child's perception of the TA and its purpose and was therefore investigated. For a round to be categorized as 'systematic correction of the TA', we required that the player must have corrected the TA twice in mode 3, in spite of it being correct.

The logs tell us that this kind of gaming was quite rare, even if occasional unjust corrections of the TA did occur every now and then. In total, 11 children applied this systematic behavior – but only 3 children did it for more than one single round. The performance levels for these students were mixed, and the pattern was found at all difficulty levels. Why a child would choose to apply this kind of strategy can be discussed. Naturally, if the child tells the TA that it is 'wrong' when the TA has made a correct suggestion, the child 'gains' in the sense that the he or she gets in control. There are, however, other plausible reasons that could be of interest to investigate.

- Impatience and reluctance to wait for the TA to answer.
- Poor understanding of the purpose of the TA.
- Mistrust or irritation with the TA's presence.
- A wish for testing the system to see if the TA (the system) is smart enough to discover this kind of behavior.

During the observations and interviews, we found support for the second and third of the reasons stated above. Some of the children specifically stated that they would prefer to play themselves, without the TA present. The children's own reports were, however, not always consistent with their actual actions. Some patterns discovered in the log data could be due to simple mistakes or unconscious choices.

4.4   Strategy 4: Wheel-Spinning

If the student does not pay attention to what happens in a game, such as correcting previous incorrect responses and responding to formative feedback, she may neither progress in the game nor learn anything useful. For a round to be classified as involving 'wheel-spinning' in Magical Garden, some of the following patterns must have occurred more than once:

- Repeating identical incorrect responses during the same task (all modes).
- New (random) guesses that does not follow the presented formative feedback (mode 1 and 2).

The log data revealed that as many as 21 children (49%) occasionally lapsed into wheel-spinning, but only 8 of these did so for more than one round. Amongst these 8, three children revealed wheel-spinning tendencies during more than five rounds. The strategy was found at all levels of difficulty, but was more common at levels introducing new mathematical concepts. In contrast to the analyzes of Strategy 1 and 2, both low- and more high-performing children occasionally fell into this kind of 'wild guessing'.

4.5   Summary

In sum, all three kinds of behaviors (*harmful gaming*, *non-harmful gaming*, and *wheel-spinning*) were discovered in the log data, but none was commonly occurring. As reported above, the most frequent behavior was wheel-spinning, followed by systematic guessing in mode 1 and 2, whereas inappropriate corrections of the TA in mode 3 were substantially rarer.

Regarding harmful gaming, 11 out of 43 children lapsed into harmful gaming activities (strategy 1 and 2) more than once during their game play. The results also show that children who dedicated more than occasional rounds to harmful gaming strategies, and thus could be regarded as more notorious 'gamers', were low-performers.

Another finding was that both gaming and wheel-spinning often occurred when new mathematical concepts were introduced, and this also applied to the more high-performing learners. When a new mathematical concept is introduced – requiring more effort to progress – there is an obvious risk that a child will try some of the gaming strategies to be able to proceed. Some of the qualitative data indicated that this behavior also occurred when children were frustrated or bored.

Finally, the unexpected strategies noticed by the teachers (fooling or misleading the TA when knowing the correct answer) were quite uncommon and could be regarded as non-harmful behavioral patterns, sometimes with a surprisingly advanced meta-cognitive content. Observation data here indicated an unexpected capability of investigating the intelligence of their TA and, not the least, an unexpected awareness of what it means to learn and teach.

5   Discussion

A general conclusion drawn from the results above is that harmful gaming and wheel-spinning did occur, even if the behavior was rare, and that these strategies could be related to slow learning curves and low performance. These results are in line with the studies of Bakers et al. [3, 5, 6], who also point out that the majority of the students using intelligent tutoring systems do not apply harmful gaming strategies, but that the students who do are at risk for insufficient learning. The present study thereby shows that also very young children can be inclined to use systematic strategies to be able to (in some sense) progress in an instructional game. Even if it is impossible to verify the exact relationship between these patterns, since the performance level of the child could either affect – or be an effect of – said gaming strategies, we regard this to be an important finding. We will further discuss these conclusions in the passages below.

5.1   Investigating Cheating, Fooling, and Gaming Behavior in Young Children

The background of the study was the reports provided independently from some preschool teachers about children 'fooling' or 'misleading' their digital tutee. That is, intentionally not correcting the tutee although knowing it was wrong, or deliberately correcting the tutee although knowing it was right. Since three or four teachers had made the same observation, we expected the behavior to be common. The log data and our own recorded observations indicated otherwise. In effect, 'fooling' the digital tutee primarily occurred when someone else – a teacher or researcher – was around and watched. Hence, this behavior more seemed to be a social act, with the child being excited and eager to show that she had grasped something regarding the structure of the game, e.g. that the TA was a teachable, and thus foolable, being. Importantly, the concepts and ideas involved in these acts of 'misleading' are fundamental for the psychological development referred to as the development of a 'theory of mind'. That is, even if the cognitive and behavioral acts involved did not promote the child's under-standing of *early numeracy*, they are by no means meaningless.

On the other hand, some strategies with similarities to the ones defined by Baker et al. [3, 5, 6] and Beck and Gong [4] were, in fact, discovered during the analysis. They were all relatively unusual, still most children showed some tendencies to use these strategies when reaching more difficult levels that they didn't master. Behaviors of this kind can be due to poor learning skills, but they can also be due to boredom or frustration. Another possibility is that they reflect a disinterest in the game. As it is unlikely that preschoolers have much understanding of and thoughts about learning expectations, the forces that drive these kinds of behavior in children of this age are probably not as straight-forward and goal-oriented as for older children. It is more likely that these kinds of behavior stem from other sources, e.g. from an inclination to try something new, curiosity about constraints and affordances in the game, or a general wish for things to happen.

Another conclusion from the study is that strategic behaviors that foremost concern the testing of game constraints are not necessarily harmful – in particular not if they only happen occasionally. Equally important, as illustrated by the examples in 4.3 above, a behavior that on the surface indicates that a child 'has not fully grasped what the game is about' by avoiding to correct the TA, may turn out to be quite the opposite when investigated more thoroughly. Consider the children who actually showed a deeper understanding than the game was designed for, in proposing that he TA would have to see for herself and learn from her mistakes. To reveal this unpredicted understanding of what it means to learn and teach, the combination of log files with observational and conversational data was instrumental. Even though the qualitative data in this particular study was limited and partly anecdotal, such explorative analyzes and comparisons also revealed mismatches between observable behavior and verbal reports on performed actions. Consequently, a general lesson learnt from this study is that complementing data logs with qualitative inquiries is essential, not only for finding underlying cognitive reasons for interactive patterns, but also for revealing simple mistakes or unconscious choices. This paper advocates the use of 'qualitative' log data analyzes to track down important aspects of undesirable or unpredictable strategies used in instructional games. Such a mixed-method design also makes it possible to distinguish harmful from more harmless pedagogical use and promotes insights in children's understanding of and reasoning about playful learning applications.

In this regard, the present study would have benefitted from a more methodological and extensive qualitative data gathering. Since the research questions presented in this paper were raised and investigated after the original study was completed, the results have to be interpreted accordingly. Consequently, the study should be considered as an exploratory attempt to (with available data) find indications for the presence of gaming behavior amongst preschoolers in a TA-based game.

5.2 Preventing Gaming in an Instructional Game (Magical Garden)

Although harmful gaming was rare, the consequences of it should be addressed. When applying this strategy in Magical Garden, water drops are gained whilst advancement to more difficult levels is disrupted. This can possibly stress the children since the game might be seen as repetitive and less meaningful. Another risk is that the children mistake the rewarding water drops for successfully solving the mathematical tasks and that they believe themselves to be more skilled than they actually are. Children that turn to harmful gaming learn less and even if this could be harsh to find out, it is important that the children acquire an awareness of the downside of such strategies. Consequently, this study was followed by an inventory of possible adjustments and redesigns of MG to hamper further harmful gaming behaviors. Some of these have been implemented while others are being looked over, as discussed in the following passages.

Before discussing redesigns for the current software, it should be pointed out that Ryan Baker and colleagues [6, 14–16] have made substantial contributions on the topic. Analyzing and studying instructional software for middle-schoolers, these researchers have performed and compared a series of different redesigns intended to target harmful gaming. Specifically, they compared (i) an accompanying agent that expressed irritation when the system detected gaming behavior with (ii) the provision of additional tasks to cover the material the students had skipped via their gaming strategy [16]. The latter strategy turned out to be more successful in decreasing harmful gaming. This kind of adaptation is, however, not feasible in MG since the game doesn't comprise any 'material to be added'. In the view of the preschool children, MG is not perceived as schoolwork or learning material, but as a game to be played.

At present, we have implemented two novel features related to possible gaming: (i) positive reinforcement when the child 'instructs the TA correctly'; if the child guides the TA adequately three times in a row (mode 3), the TA will jump or dance happily and exclaim "What a good teacher you are!" (ii) demonstrating more 'awareness' in the TA; if the child first inadequately corrects the TA and then makes the same choice herself, the TA responds: *"But that is the same that I chose?!"* This version of MG has not yet been systematically tested in class, but the design seems promising.

Another possibility, not implemented but discussed, is if a child systematically avoids to correct the TA, including when it picks the wrong alternative. We could in this case make the TA respond by getting weary of this, for instance saying: *"I am tired, I need to get some rest/sleep."* The child would then have to be more active and make her own choices. It would be interesting to see if this could break the pattern of completely handing over the decisions to the TA. For children who have a hard time to get started and understand the gist of the game perhaps this would be of help.

A completely different approach, that could be introduced as a 'consequence' for all harmful gaming strategies (systematic guessing and avoidance to correct the TA) as well as wheel-spinning, is if the TA (or another character in the game) would question the child's understanding of the game by suggesting getting help; for instance, saying *"This seems to be a bit tricky. Perhaps we should ask the teacher for help so that we can figure this out together?"* Since both this study and others [3–6] have come to the conclusion that harmful gaming often is due to poor prior knowledge or insufficient skills, this could be a way to make the child to ask for much-needed assistance. Low-performing school children that avoid seeking help are especially at risk for not overcoming thresholds and achieving knew knowledge. This kind of guidance could serve as a push in the right direction.

Yet another point of discussion relates to the children at the other end of the performance spectrum, i.e. those who quickly grasp the game and its mathematical content. In the log files we can see that some of the children initially had a high success-rate with rapid advanced, only to suddenly fall into aimless and disengaged guessing. The peril of high-performing students finding the game unchallenging and getting tired of it was confirmed by both observations and conversations. To prevent this, it is important to let them advance at a rate that fits their skills and learning capabilities.

Acknowledgments. This research was financed by the Wallenberg Foundation.

References

1. Lindström, P., Gulz, A., Haake, M., Sjödén, B.: Matching and mismatching between the pedagogical design principles of a math game and the actual practices of play. J. Comput. Assist. Learn. **27**, 90–102 (2011)
2. Blair, K., Schwartz, D., Biswas, G., Leelawong, K.: Pedagogical agents for learning by teaching: teachable Agents. Educ. Technol. Soc. **47**, 56–61 (2007). Special Issue

3. Baker, R.S., Corbett, A.T., Koedinger, K.R.: Detecting student misuse of intelligent tutoring systems. In: Lester, J.C., Vicari, R.M., Paraguaçu, F. (eds.) ITS 2004. LNCS, vol. 3220, pp. 531–540. Springer, Heidelberg (2004). https://doi.org/10.1007/978-3-540-30139-4_50

4. Beck, J.E., Gong, Y.: Wheel-spinning: students who fail to master a skill. In: Lane, H.C., Yacef, K., Mostow, J., Pavlik, P. (eds.) AIED 2013. LNCS (LNAI), vol. 7926, pp. 431–440. Springer, Heidelberg (2013). https://doi.org/10.1007/978-3-642-39112-5_44

5. Baker, R.S.J.D., D'Mello, S.K., Rodrigo, M.M.T., Graesser, A.C.: Better to be frustrated than bored: the incidence, persistence, and impact of learners' cognitive-affective states during interactions with three different computer-based learning environments. Int. J. Hum Comput Stud. **68**(4), 223–241 (2010)

6. Baker, R., Walonoski, J., Heffernan, N., Roll, I., Corbett, A., Koedinger, K.: Why students engage in "gaming the system" behavior in interactive learning environments. J. Interact. Learn. Res. **19**(2), 185–224 (2008)

7. Husain, L., Gulz, A., Haake, M.: Supporting early math– rationales and requirements for high quality software. J. Comput. Mathe. Sci. Teach. **34**(4), 409–429 (2015)

8. Haake, M.: No child left behind, nor singled out – reasons for combining adaptive instruction and inclusive pedagogy in early math software (submitted)

9. Chase, C., Chin, D., Oppezzo, M., Schwartz, D.: Teachable agents and the protégé effect: increasing the effort towards learning. J. Sci. Educ. Technol. **18**, 334–352 (2009)

10. Wagster, J., Tan, J., Wu, Y., Biswas, G., Schwartz, D.: Do learning by teaching environments with metacognitive support help students develop better learning behaviors? In: Proceedings of the Annual Meeting of the Cognitive Science Society, vol. 29, pp. 695–700 (2007)

11. Haake, M., Axelsson, A., Clausen-Bruun, M., Gulz, A.: Scaffolding mentalizing via a play-&-learn game for preschoolers. Comput. Educ. **90**, 13–23 (2015)

12. Axelsson, A., Andersson, R., Gulz, A.: Scaffolding executive function capabilities via play-&-learn software for preschoolers. J. Educ. Psychol. **108**(7), 969–981 (2016)

13. Griffin, S., Case, R., Siegler, R.: Classroom lessons: integrating cognitive theory and classroom practice. In: McGilly, K. (ed.) Rightstart: Providing the Central Conceptual Prerequisites for First Formal Learning of Arithmetic to Students at Risk for School Failure. MIT Press, Cambridge, pp. 25–50 (1994)

14. Baker, R.S.J.D., de Carvalho, A.M.J.A., Raspat, J., Aleven, V., Corbett, A.T., Koedinger, K.R.: Educational software features that encourage and discourage "gaming the system". In: Proceedings of the 14th International Conference on Artificial Intelligence in Education, pp. 475–482 (2009)

15. Baker, R.S.J.D., Corbett, A.T., Koedinger, K.R.: The difficulty factors approach to the design of lessons in intelligent tutor curricula. Int. J. Artif. Intell. Educ. **17**(4), 341–369 (2007)

16. Baker, R.S.J.D., et al.: Adapting to when students game an intelligent tutoring system. In: Ikeda, M., Ashley, K.D., Chan, T.-W. (eds.) ITS 2006. LNCS, vol. 4053, pp. 392–401. Springer, Heidelberg (2006). https://doi.org/10.1007/11774303_39

Vygotsky Meets Backpropagation
Artificial Neural Models and the Development of Higher Forms of Thought

Ilkka Tuomi$^{(\boxtimes)}$ (ID)

Meaning Processing, Helsinki, Finland
ilkka.tuomi@meaningprocessing.com

Abstract. In this paper we revisit Vygotsky's developmental model of concept formation, and use it to discuss learning in artificial neural networks. We study learning in neural networks from a learning science point of view, asking whether it is possible to construct systems that have developmental patterns that align with empirical studies on concept formation. We put the state-of-the-art Inception-v3 image recognition architecture in an experimental setting that highlights differences and similarities in algorithmic and human cognitive processes.

The Vygotskian model of cognitive development reveals important limitations in currently popular neural algorithms, and puts neural AI in the context of post-behavioristic science of learning. At the same time, the Vygotskian model of development of thought suggests new architectural principles for developing AI, machine learning, and systems that support human learning. In this context we can ask what would it take for machines to learn, and what could they learn from research on learning.

Keywords: Development of cognition · Inception · Neural AI
Conceptual thinking · Abstraction · Generalization · Categorization

1 Introduction

In recent years, big data and the availability of low-cost parallel computation have led to rapidly growing interest in artificial neural networks. Although neural network models have been developed and studied since the 1930's [15] and many currently popular network models reflect ideas that have been well-established several decades ago [1], only in the recent years the convergence of computational capability, connectivity, and data have started to create visible breakthroughs in neural AI. The remarkable successes of "deep learning" now suggest that learning theorists may learn something important from neural network research and its algorithms.

For a learning scientist, an attempt to review research on neural AI can be quite confusing. More than superficial understanding of the domain requires competences in theoretical physics, computer programming, probability theory,

© Springer International Publishing AG, part of Springer Nature 2018
C. Penstein Rosé et al. (Eds.): AIED 2018, LNAI 10947, pp. 570–583, 2018.
https://doi.org/10.1007/978-3-319-93843-1_42

linear algebra, and neurobiology [5]. Successful application of neural AI methods requires experimentation with large numbers of model parameters, skills with exotic hardware and software platforms, as well as deep understanding of the available data. Somewhat surprisingly, very little knowledge about human learning is needed, however. From learning sciences point of view, "deep learning" verges on being an oxymoron. Often the implicit models of learning in neural AI resemble associationist, neo-behavioristic and reflexological models from the turn of the 19th century.

In this paper, we ask whether neural AI algorithms can learn concepts. We therefore start from learning theory, asking to what extent current neural AI algorithms can simulate different stages of development in conceptual thinking. In the venerable tradition of AI in education [10], we put the learner in focus; this time the learner, however, is a machine. As a starting point, we use the empirical and theoretical studies on concept formation by Vygotsky and his colleagues, conducted at the turn of 1920s. Vygotsky's main claim was that advanced forms of adult thought use culturally and historically developed conceptual systems. In the ontogenetic development of a child, different types of pre-conceptual thinking gradually evolve to a point where the child becomes able to internalize socioculturally accumulated word meanings and use these in his or her thinking. This, according to Vygotsky, leads to qualitatively new types of thought that are not available for animals or young children [8,12,27,30].

Although Vygotsky's stage model of conceptual development does not directly map to the developmental age of a child, using this conceptual framework we may roughly locate the capabilities of different learning algorithms among the various developmental stages. Using this approach, we may characterize the different types of conceptual thinking that current neural AI architectures use, and highlight those processes of concept formation that these architectures currently lack. A similar approach has previously been used to study concept formation and knowledge creation in groupware environments [23,24].

Due to space limitations, we focus in this paper on one influential neural architecture: feedforward convolutional network (CNN). CNNs use supervised learning, and they are now extensively used for various image recognition and pattern matching tasks. As a prototypical convolutional network we use the Inception-v3 network that currently represents state-of-the-art in object recognition and image classification [21,22]. A similar analysis could be extended to other network architectures, including recurrent networks that use sequential data for learning, unsupervised self-organized feature maps, adaptive resonance networks, or, for example, networks that use reinforcement learning.

The paper is organized as follows. In the next section, we briefly describe the empirical basis that informed Vygotsky's work on conceptual development in children, based on the experimental method developed by Leonid Sakharov in 1927 [18], and outline the resulting stages of conceptual development. The following section then describes results of testing Inception-v3 with a simplified Sakharov experiment. We then use this conceptual framework to discuss learning in neural AI systems. The paper ends with some concluding comments.

2   Vygotsky's Model of Conceptual Development

According to Vygotsky [28,29], advanced forms of conceptual thinking can not be explained as purely quantitative growth of associations. He criticized heavily the "associationist" model of concept formation that was reflected in Galton's attempt to generate composite "family portraits" of people by exposing the same plate many times and generating an "average" person. A simple overlay of pictures, according to Vygotsky, would never be able to get from concrete features to abstract concepts. Unlike the more primitive forms of thought, which are characterized by the immediacy of intellectual processes, conceptual thinking is mediated by signs. The structure of signification, which plays a formative role in all higher types of behavior, does not coincide with the associative structure of elementary processes. The quantitative growth of the associative connections, therefore, can never lead to those forms of higher intellectual activity that characterize adult human thinking [29, p. 109].

Vygotsky based his model of conceptual development on the empirical method devised by one of his collaborators, Leonid Sakharov [18]. The original Sakharov experiment in 1927 used wooden pieces varying in color, shape, height, and size. There were 5 different colors, 5–6 different shapes, tall and flat blocks, as well as large and small blocks. One of four nonsense words was written on the underside of each piece, invisible to the subject of experiment. Regardless of color or shape, *mup* was written on all tall large figures, *rots* on all flat large figures, *dek* of the tall small ones, and *bat* on the flat small ones.[1] In the original Sakharov experiment, the pieces were placed on a game board, and the child was told that they were toys that belonged to children from some foreign country. At the beginning of the experiment, the pieces were put in random order on the game board in front of the subject. The examiner then turned one of the blocks, read the word on its backside, put it on a special field on the board, and asked the subject to pick up all the blocks that were of the same kind. If the child successfully picked all the correct blocks, she or he got a prize such as a sweet or a pencil. After the subject had selected the blocks, the experimenter asked why the child had picked up these blocks and what are the toys that are called by the name written on the sample piece. He then turned around one of the "wrongly" chosen blocks and read the word that was written on it. The wrongly chosen piece was then put next to the original sample so that its text was visible to the child, the rest of the pieces placed back on the game board, and the child was asked to try again to get the prize.

Vygotsky and his collaborators studied more than three hundred children, adolescents, and adults using this experimental method. As Hanfmann and Kasanin [6, p. 30] state:

> Whether the subject actually uses conceptual thinking in trying to solve the problem... can be inferred from the nature of the groups he builds and

---

[1] Vygotsky [29] discusses experiments done with the words mur, cev, bik, and lag. We use these in training the Inception network.

from his procedure in building them: Nearly every step in his reasoning is reflected in his manipulations of the block. The first attack on the problem; the finding of the solution—all these stages of the experiment provide data that can serve as indicators of the subject's level of thinking.

Based on these studies, Vygotsky argued that there are three main phases in the development of conceptual thinking, each consisting of several sub-stages. Below, we focus on two of the first major phases: syncretic thinking and thinking in complexes. These characterize thinking both in pre-adolescent children and in "primitive" cultures. The third phase, fully developed conceptual thinking requires the use of socio-culturally accumulated conceptual systems. According to Vygotsky, these advanced forms of conceptual thinking are often acquired through systematic education, and thus only available in modern societies.

2.1 Syncretic Thinking

In the first major phase, a child clusters objects into unorganized congeries or heaps. At this stage, word meaning denotes nothing more to the child than a vague syncretic conglomeration of individual objects that have somehow coalesced into an image in the child's mind. During this stage of "syncretism" or "incoherent coherence," the child takes subjective bonds between an object and the child as dominant ones.

According to Vygotsky, this first major phase of development in concept formation consists of three distinctive sub-stages [29, p. 111]. The first stage manifests the "trial-and-error" stage in the development of thinking. During the next stage, the composition of the groups of the blocks in the experiment is determined largely by the spatial position of the objects. The clusters are formed based on the purely syncretic organization of the child's visual field. In the third stage, in turn, clusters are formed using a two-step procedure, by taking pieces from the clusters formed using the previous two approaches. The heaps are combinations of earlier heaps but the heaps still have the same "incoherent coherence" as in the previous stages.

2.2 Thinking in Complexes

In the syncretic phase of concept formation, the child adopts an "egocentric" view on objects and their characteristics. Categories of things are built based on what they mean to the builder and how they appear to her, from her idiosyncratic point of view. The second major phase of development, however, is characterized by clustering that is based on the bonds existing between the objects themselves. Vygotsky calls this phase "thinking in complexes":

When a child moves up to that level, he has partly overcome his egocentrism. He no longer mistakes connections between his own impressions for connections between things—a decisive step away from syncretism toward objective thinking. Thought in complexes is already *objective* thinking, although it does not reflect the relations between things in the same way as adult conceptual thinking [29, p. 112]. In complex thinking, bonds between objects are concrete and factual, instead of abstract of logical. A child at this phase forms concepts as "family names," and the universe becomes organized as separate and mutually related families. Whether a person belongs to the Petrov family is not because there would be some abstract or logical bond between the members of the family; instead, the question is settled by the facts. In complex thinking, a child uses the concrete bonds between the objects to form clusters. The bonds, in turn, are found through direct experience. Because the bonds are not generated by any abstract system of attributes or characteristics, any factual bonds can be used to link objects.

Vygotsky claimed that this second major phase of development consists of five sub-stages. The first type of complex is *associative*. In building an associative complex, a child may observe the sample block and pick up pieces that the child thinks belong to the same family. According to Vygotsky, to the child at that stage the word ceases to be the proper name of an individual object; it becomes the family name of a group of objects related to one another in many kinds of ways, just as the relationships in human families are many and different [29, p. 114].

In the second stage, a child clusters objects in *collections*. In this stage, association by contrast dominates over association by similarity. In the experiments, the child picked objects that were not similar but which complemented each other:

> This long, persistent stage in the development of the child's thinking is rooted in his practical experience, in which collections of complementary things often form a set or a whole. Experience teaches the child certain forms of functional grouping: cup, saucer, and spoon; a place setting of knife, fork, spoon, and plate; the set of clothes he wears [29, p. 115].

The third stage is dominated by *chain complexes*. These are characterized by sequential links of factual associations. When the sample block would be a yellow triangle, the child could, for example, pick up some triangular blocks until her attention is caught up by the blue color of the block; at that point she switches to blue blocks of any shape, until the criterion changes again.

Chain formation strikingly demonstrates the perceptually concrete, factual nature of thinking with complexes. An object included because of one of its attributes enters the complex not just as the carrier of that one trait but as an individual, with all its attributes. In a chain complex, there is no hierarchical organization of the different traits of the object, and all attributes seem to be equally important. The resulting cluster lacks stability as the types of bonds between its elements may change almost imperceptibly. This leads to the fourth type of complex, *diffuse complex*. They are marked by the fluidity of the very attribute that unites its single elements:

> To go with a yellow triangle, for example, a child would in our experiments pick out trapezoids as well as triangles, because they made him think of

triangles with their tops cut off. Trapezoids would lead to squares, squares to hexagons, hexagons to semicircles, and finally to circles. Color as the basis of selection is equally floating and changeable. Yellow objects are apt to be followed by green ones; then green may change to blue, and blue to black [29, pp. 117–118].

Finally, a bridge between conceptual thinking and thinking in complexes is provided by *pseudoconcepts*. Although they the look similar to concepts used by adults, they are formed differently from concepts. "Taken phenotypically, pseudoconcepts and concepts look alike, as a whale looks like a fish" [29, p. 121]. If we study their genetic origin, it becomes clear, however, that they are of a different species. Using pseudoconcepts, a child may generate clusters that are the same as those generated by an adult who uses fully-formed conceptual thinking. Pseudoconcepts, however, are provided by the speech of adults. At this stage, the child's and adults words coincide in their referents but differ in their meanings.

This similarity makes it possible for a child to share culturally accumulated word meanings, and gradually learn conceptual thinking. Beyond laboratory settings where artificial words are used, most world meanings are not invented by the child; instead, she grows in an environment that is already fully populated by words. Adults, therefore, supply the child with ready-made meanings, and the child builds her own complexes around these. For a child, the word represents a complex, a family name, as it were. At the same time the same word represents a fully formed concept to an adult. This dual nature of pseudoconcepts allows the child to operate in the world of adults and observe how concepts are used in adult thinking. Gradually, the child may internalize such concepts and start to use them in her thinking.

2.3   Abstraction

The development of conceptual thinking requires grouping of objects that are different. This, in turn, requires abstracting some features that make them similar. In general, abstraction is based on detecting observable features and constructing more complex configurations or mappings from them [16]. For adult humans, observation is often aided by culturally accumulated measurement instruments; for young children, abstraction relies on biological capabilities [25].

Vygotsky argued that the first step toward abstraction was made when a child grouped together maximally similar objects. An object thus does not appear anymore in its full perceptual complexity. Some of its characteristics are considered important and focal whereas others have become peripheral.

In the next stage of abstraction, grouping based on maximum similarity is superseded by grouping based on the basis of a single attribute. For example, the group may now consist only of round objects. Vygotsky calls such formations *potential concepts*. Potential concepts, according to Vygotsky, result from sequences of primitive isolating abstractions that may be found already in very young children and even in animals. Because of this, for example hens may be trained to respond to a distinct object attribute, such as color or shape. But as long as complex thinking dominates, Vygotsky points out, the abstracted trait is unstable and easily replaced by another trait. Only when concrete traits are synthesized anew and the resulting new abstraction becomes the main instrument of thought, fully formed conceptual thinking becomes possible.

Culturally shared word meanings, embodied in spoken language, thus become key factors in those forms of thinking that characterize the special capabilities of human cognition. The ontogenetic development of a child, therefore, cannot be understood as a maturation of individual; instead, it is a process where bottom-up maturation and top-down enculturation both play a crucial role.

3   Conceptual Thinking in Neural AI

Following Vygotsky, we define abstraction and generalization as the two key dimensions of pre-conceptual thinking. Learning, in this developmental context, can be understood as the movement from developmentally simpler forms of thinking toward fully formed conceptual thinking.

The Sakharov experiment has been used to observe thought processes in normal and mentally retarded children, adolescents, adults and also schizophrenics. In the spirit of Turing's simulation game, one might ask what level of thinking deep learning systems reflect. What types of abstractions and generalizations the different algorithms of neural AI can generate?

One way to address these questions is to program the Sakharov procedure and study neural architectures in this experimental setting. In the next section, we report some results along these lines, using the Inception-v3 model as a reference point. The idea is to look "under the hood" of neural AI models and see what they do with abstraction and generalization. We use a simplified form of the Sakharov experiment that illustrates the approach in this particular architectural context.

3.1   Abstraction and Generalization in Inception-V3

The Inception-v3 network [21,22] currently represents the state-of-the-art in computer vision. It is 42 layers deep, contains 25 million parameters, and each inference requires about 5 billion multiply-add operations. Inception-v3 has been widely used in various image processing tasks, including image labeling and classification. With the ImageNet Large Visual Recognition Challenge 2012 data set that consists of 1000 classes, Inception-v3 reaches "top-5" error rate 3.46%, achieving or exceeding the human recognition capabilities. The fully trained network model is available from Google's Tensorflow model repository[2], uses about 95 Megabytes of storage, and—although training from scratch may require days or weeks—the trained model can easily be run on portable computers.

---

[2] https://www.tensorflow.org/tutorials/image_recognition.

Inception-v3 is a feedforward convolutional neural network. Convolutional networks typically consist of convolutional layers, pooling layers, some fully connected layers, and classification layers. In image classification, the convolution layer that reads the input data applies convolutional filters to subregions of the image, sums the weighted inputs, and outputs "activations" to the following layers based on some non-linear transfer functions. Subsequent layers then use these outputs as their inputs, and apply their own convolution filters to generate further output. Pooling layers may be used to reduce computational complexity, and the final classification layer generates predictions about the image category. Input data, thus, "flows" through the network, each "neuron" adding inputs it receives and transforming the data for next layers to use.

Learning in deep convolutional networks occurs by gradual adaptation of "weights" between network layers. During the training phase, large numbers of training examples are used as input to the system, and the output of the system is compared with the correct classification. If the image is wrongly classified network weights are adjusted so that the error diminishes. In deep multi-layer convolutional networks, the adjustment is based on computing the relative contribution of the weights to the error, and using the chain rule of calculus to compute the contributions of the weights of earlier layers. This is known as "backpropagation".

After learning the training set—which in the case of ImageNet consists of about 1.2 million images—the different convolutional layers represent different "abstract" features of the input. In a simple network, the first "hidden" layer might, for example, have neurons that become active when the pixels in the input image form line segments in specific directions. The next layer, in turn, might contain neurons that become active when the segments form right angles. The next layer might have neurons that become active when four equidistant corners are detected. A classification network could then use the output from this layer to predict that the input image contains a square.

3.2   Sakharov Meets Inception

It is possible to modify the final classification layer of a pre-trained Inception-v3 model to reflect new object categories. We used this opportunity to categorize computationally generated block images that followed the categories in the Sakharov experiment. Using 1000 block images of each of the four categories ('lag', 'bik', 'mur', 'cev'), we re-trained the final layer of Inception-v3. This approach is known as "transfer learning". The full training of complex convolutional networks often takes hundreds of thousands of examples and several days but the final layer can easily be trained in less than an hour.

We varied the block size, height, color, and shape according to the original Sakharov experiment. Some example blocks are shown in Fig. 1.

Theoretically it is clear that a multi-layer convolutional network can learn to recognize images that it has been trained to recognize. A convolutional network is a mathematical mapping from one set of input data to another set of output data [11]. It is not very surprising that Inception-v3 is able to learn four types of

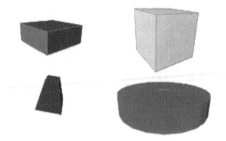

Fig. 1. Examples of training block images.

inputs. It may, therefore, appear that it is able to generate conceptual categories that are similar to fully developed concepts. But what does Inception-v3 actually think about?

A simple test is to run the computer generated Sakharov blocks through Inception-v3, and check what it thinks they are. For this, we generated a block shape that was not included in the training set. For the block parameters we used values (tall, big) that were used in generating blocks in the 'lag' category. The test block, the predicted full-model Inception-v3 categories, and the predicted Sakharov categories are show in Table 1. The size of the "block" is large as its base is 120 pixels (vs. 80 for small ones), and it is tall because its height is 200 pixels (vs 80 for small ones). The color or shape are not supposed to matter. For a human, the right way to put the block into the right class would be to note that it is tall and large, in relation to other blocks.

Table 1. Predicted categories for a test block.

Test block image	Predicted probabilities using full Inception-v3 model	Predicted probabilities using the Sakharov-trained model
	bucket: 0.594 ashcan: 0.107 pencil sharpener: 0.071 measuring cup: 0.041 pick: 0.009	mur: 0.802 lag: 0.169 (correct one) cev: 0.0264 bik: 0.00325

The predicted image class for the model that was retrained using the computer generated Sakharov block is 'mur', instead of 'lag', with probability of 80%. Although the blocks in the training set and the evaluation set that was generated using similar parameters were categorized with 100% accuracy, a change in the shape of the block is enough to confuse the AI. It is difficult to know what exactly it is thinking about without studying filters in the hidden layers, but it seems that it has not yet been able to abstract such features as "height" and "size". Although blocks with two different heights and two different sizes were provided as training inputs, the Inception-v3 model did not seem to use these aspects in classifying images. This, of course, may also depend on the fact that the image data that is used to train the Inception scales objects with varying sizes, such as oil tankers and ants, so that they nicely fit a standard sized image.

4   Discussion

It is clear that a CNN such as Inception-v3 can recognize a small set of image categories that have been included in the training set. Inception-v3 is a supervised CNN, and given enough time, its weights can be made to converge toward values that perfectly categorize its training inputs. Perhaps more surprisingly, Inception-v3 generalizes very badly what it learns from the Sakharov blocks.

The Sakharov experiment, indeed, illustrates interesting differences between the capabilities of CNNs and humans. First, the early syncretic stages of clustering rely on an egocentric view of the world. Two toys on a table may belong to the same heap because they are *my* toys, or because they are close to each other from *my* point of view. Such subjective associations do not seem to be available in feed-forward networks.

In the first stage of complex thinking, associations between objects are based on abstracting some aspects of the object and finding similarities. This, indeed, resembles the model built into CNNs. In these networks, each layer extracts a set of "features" that capture some aspects of the object. These are then "added up" to generate increasingly "abstract" features that in the final network layers are combined to generate predictions. In contrast to Galton's average portraits of people, convolutional networks, however, also induce separation between trained image classes.

The "collection" stage of complex thinking, however, requires more from CNNs. To generate a collection, complementary differences need to be used. Such information can not be found by observing the characteristics of an object in isolation. The same object may also be member of many different collections. Furthermore, as the Sakharov studies showed, collections are often based on practical information about the use of objects. Such information is deeply social, and there is no simple way to discover it without knowledge about pragmatic uses of objects in a specific historically and culturally situated setting [9].[3]

Feed-forward networks also seem to be unable to move to the chain complex stage of complex thinking. As Vygotsky pointed out, in object chains the objects enter the cluster "in their totality," with all their objective attributes. Because of this, objects can be linked using one attribute after another, and the end points of the chain may have no shared attributes. In chain complexes, earlier objects determine what later objects may be members of the complex. Chain complexes

---

[3] Relational information might, however, be captured using other network architectures, e.g., [3, 7, 13, 19].

thus require both episodic memory and relational knowledge. Although chain complexes might be implemented using recurrent network architectures [13], they remain beyond the capabilities of feed-forward networks.

Inception-v3 also has clear difficulties with adult conceptual thinking. It knows "buckets" and "ash trays" that have immediately observable characteristics that glue them into a group, but is not able to note that both have cylindrical shapes. Geometrical shapes require "theoretical" abstraction, or "scientific" concepts [4], instead of simple feature detection or observation of object qualities. Ecologically natural objects, such as buckets or ashtrays need to be perceived *as* geometric shapes, in a conceptual system that organizes different geometric concepts.

This, indeed, points to an important difference between Inception-v3 and human cognition. As Vygotsky emphasized, advanced forms of human thinking are based on meaning processing. The semiotic structure that underpins meaning processing, in turn, is a three-part relation [20], where perceived objects are not only represented but also simultaneously interpreted. When objects are perceived as meaningful objects they are perceived *as* something. For example, as cylinders. The appropriate way of abstracting the object depends on current context and action, and both are strongly influenced by existing cultural, historical and pragmatic context. Vygotsky also argued that during development, the cognition of a child makes a qualitative transition when language and concepts become tools for thinking. In the teaching of Inception-v3, only isolated labels are provided to the system, and the cultural and social context where they make sense remains known only to the humans that label the data. In contrast to a child who can move from pseudoconcepts to "higher forms of thinking" with the help of adults, Inception-v3 is left with a list of words. Strictly speaking, therefore, it is an error to call Inception-v3 AI, as both its inputs and outputs need to be interpreted using human cognition.

5   Conclusion

In this paper we have elaborated some key elements of Vygotsky's work on the development of conceptual thinking, using the resulting model to discuss learning in artificial neural networks. Much of neural AI literature focuses on learning; so far there has been little discussion about what learning means in this context, and how it relates to learning as understood in learning sciences. In many currently popular deep learning models, learning reduces to minimization of prediction error, and to the idea that association equals learning. Both ideas have been extensively criticized during the last century. Although one may well adopt a purely engineering approach, and argue that the intent of neural AI is only to generate systems that simulate associations in practically important domains of application, a theoretically more interesting question is to what extent neural algorithms can simulate real human learning processes. This is also important if we try and use neural AI systems as components in technology-enabled learning environments.

In this paper we focused only on one specific network architecture, Inception-v3, and it is clear that this architecture has not been designed to work in settings such as the Sakharov experiment. Using this intentionally contrived setting, we were, however, able to illustrate interesting questions about the similarities and differences between neural AI and human cognition. This approach allows us to nudge research on neural AI from the very practical and important questions about computational challenges towards the more theoretically important questions about the capabilities and functionalities of neural AI. Studies on human learning provide a new framing on discussions about computational architectures in neural AI, and link research on neural AI with research on learning. Recent developments in neural AI have to a large extent been about optimizing architectures from a computational point of view, and much remains to be done in developing models that can successfully be linked with processes that underpin human learning and teaching.

Learning in convolutional networks remain on a level that—using Bergson's distinction between instinctive and intellectual knowing—could be called instinctive. According to Bergson, a defining characteristic of human intelligence is its capacity to generate a mediated image of the reality, which frees it from the concrete observed reality, and makes novelty, creativity and creative learning possible [2]. A similar view was suggested by the Russian neurophysiologist A.A. Ukhtomsky at the beginning of the 20th century [31]. This mediated view on human reality has, of course, been shared by such pioneering thinkers as Peirce and Vygotsky, and Vygotsky, in fact, was influenced by the ground-breaking but now little-known neurophysiological studies of Ukhtomsky [26]. Such a mediational view naturally leads to a focus on the role of words and language in human thinking and cognition. Most probably, as Vygotsky suggested, the border between associations and concepts is qualitative and cannot be crossed simply by quantitative means.

This also means that new computational approaches may be needed to simulate conceptual thought processes. Cognition, as we know it, is fundamentally a biological phenomenon, and the species-specific human capabilities for learning and teaching have evolved during hundreds of millenia [14]. An essential characteristic of life is the self-referential nature of its processes [17], and this means that it may be impossible to generate algorithmic systems that accurately model or simulate human cognition [11]. Computers are not brains and brains are not computers; reflecting each against the other may, however, teach useful lessons about both. As neural AI now captures the attention of both policy-makers and the general public, it is also important to understand better to what extent the recent successes of AI, indeed, can inform our theories of learning and vice versa. In this paper, we aimed to suggest such a dialogue. As shown above, already a brief exploration shows that such a cross-disciplinary enterprise opens interesting new lines for future research.

References

1. Anderson, J.A., Rosenfeld, E. (eds.): Neurocomputing: Foundations for Research. The MIT Press, Cambridge (1988)
2. Bergson, H.: Creative Evolution (1st edn. 1907). University Press of America, Lanham (1983)
3. Carpenter, G., Grossberg, S.: A massively parallel architecture for self-organizing neural pattern recognition machine. Comput. Vis. Graph. Image Process. **37**, 54–115 (1987)
4. Davydov, V.V.: Types of Generalization in Instruction: Logical and Psychological Problems in the Structuring of School Curricula. National Council of Teachers of Mathematics, Reston (1990)
5. Hagan, M.T., Demuth, H.B., Beale, M.H., Jess, O.D.: Neural Network Design, 2nd edn. Martin Hagan, Boston (2014)
6. Hanfmann, E., Kasanin, J.: Conceptual Thinking in Schizophrenia. NMDM, New York (1942)
7. Kohonen, T.: The self-organizing map. Neurocomputing **21**(1), 1–6 (1998). https://doi.org/10.1016/S0925-2312(98)00030-7
8. Kozulin, A.: Vygotsky's Psychology: A Biography of Ideas. Harvard University Press, Cambridge (1990)
9. Lakoff, G.: Women, Fire, and Dangerous Things: What Categories Reveal About the Mind. University of Chicago Press, Chicago (1987)
10. Lane, H.C., McCalla, G., Looi, C.K., Bull, S.: Preface to the IJAIED 25th anniversary issue, part 2. Int. J. Artif. Intell. Educ. **26**(2), 539–543 (2016). https://doi.org/10.1007/s40593-016-0109-9
11. Louie, A.H.: The Reflection of Life: Functional Entailment and Imminence in Relational Biology. Springer, New York (2013). https://doi.org/10.1007/978-1-4614-6928-5
12. Luria, A., Vygotsky, L.: Ape, Primitive Man, and Child: Essays in the History of Behavior. Harvester Wheatsheaf, Hemel Hempstead (1992)
13. Mikolov, T., Karafiát, M., Burget, L., Černocký, J., Khudanpur, S.: Recurrent neural network based language model. In: Kobayashi, T., Hirose, K., Satoshi, N. (eds.) INTERSPEECH-2010. pp. 1045–1048. Makuhari, Chiba (2010). http://www.isca-speech-org/archive/interspeech_2010
14. Morrison, D.M., Miller, K.B.: Teaching and learning in the pleistocene: a biocultural account of human pedagogy and its implications for AIED. Int. J. Artif. Intell. Educ., 1–31 (2017). https://doi.org/10.1007/s40593-017-0153-0
15. Rashevsky, N.: Mathematical Biophysics: Physico-Mathematical Foundations of Biology, 3rd edn. Dover, New York (1960)
16. Rosen, R.: Fundamentals of Measurement and Representation of Natural Systems. North-Holland, New York (1978)
17. Rosen, R.: Life Itself: A Comprehensible Inquiry into the Nature, Origin and Fabrication of Life. Columbia University Press, New York (1991)
18. Sakharov, L.: Methods for investigating concepts. In: van der Veer, R., Valsiner, J. (eds.) The Vygotsky Reader, pp. 73–98. Blackwell, Oxford (1994)
19. Shimizu, H., Yamaguchi, Y.: Synergetic computer and holonics: information dynamics of a semantic computer. Phys. Scr. **36**(6), 970–985 (1987)
20. Short, T.L.: Peirce's Theory of Signs. Cambridge University Press, Cambridge (2009)

21. Szegedy, C., Vanhoucke, V., Ioffe, S., Shlens, J., Wojna, Z.: Rethinking the Inception architecture for computer vision. In: 2016 IEEE Conference on Computer Vision and Pattern Recognition (CVPR), pp. 2818–2826 (2016). https://doi.org/10.1109/CVPR.2016.308

22. Szegedy, C., Liu, W., Jia, Y., Sermanet, P., Reed, S., Anguelov, D., Erhan, D., Vanhoucke, V., Rabinovich, A.: Going deeper with convolutions (2014). arXiv:1409.4842

23. Tuomi, I.: Vygotsky in a TeamRoom: an exploratory study on collective concept formation in electronic environments. In: Nunamaker, J. (ed.) Proceedings of the 31st Annual Hawaii International Conference on System Sciences, vol. 1, pp. 68–75. IEEE Computer Society Press, Los Alamitos (1998). https://doi.org/10.1109/HICSS.1998.653085

24. Tuomi, I.: Corporate Knowledge: Theory and Practice of Intelligent Organizations. Metaxis, Helsinki (1999)

25. Tuomi, I.: Data is more than knowledge: implications of the reversed knowledge hierarchy to knowledge management and organizational memory. J. Manag. Inf. Syst. **6**(3), 103–117 (2000). https://doi.org/10.1080/07421222.1999.11518258

26. Tuomi, I.: Ontological expansion. In: Poli, R. (ed.) Handbook of Anticipation, pp. 1–35. Springer, Cham (2017). https://doi.org/10.1007/978-3-319-31737-3_4-1

27. van der Veer, R., Valsiner, J.: Understanding Vygotsky: A Quest for Synthesis. Blackwell Publishers, Cambridge (1994)

28. Vygotsky, L.: Mind in Society: The Development of Higher Psychological Processes. Harvard University Press, Cambridge (1978)

29. Vygotsky, L.: Thought and Language. The MIT Press, Cambridge (1986)

30. Wertsch, J.: Vygotsky and the Social Formation of Mind. Harvard University Press, Cambridge (1985)

31. Zueva, E.Y., Zuev, K.B.: The concept of dominance by A.A. Ukhtomsky and anticipation. In: Nadin, M. (ed.) Anticipation: Learning from the Past - The Russian/Soviet Contributions to the Science of Anticipation, pp. 13–35. Springer, Cham (2015). https://doi.org/10.1007/978-3-319-19446-2_2

Providing Automated Real-Time Technical Feedback for Virtual Reality Based Surgical Training: Is the Simpler the Better?

Sudanthi Wijewickrema[1(✉)], Xingjun Ma[1], Patorn Piromchai[1,2], Robert Briggs[1], James Bailey[1], Gregor Kennedy[1], and Stephen O'Leary[1]

[1] The University of Melbourne, Melbourne, Australia
{swijewickrem,ppiromchai,rjsb,baileyj,gek,sjoleary}@unimelb.edu.au,
xingjunm@student.unimelb.edu.au
[2] Khon Kaen University, Khon Kaen, Thailand
patorn@kku.ac.th

Abstract. In surgery, where mistakes have the potential for dire consequences, proper training plays a crucial role. Surgical training has traditionally relied upon experienced surgeons mentoring trainees through cadaveric dissection and operating theatre practice. However, with the growing demand for more surgeons and more efficient training programs, it has become necessary to employ supplementary forms of training such as virtual reality simulation. However, the use of such simulations as autonomous training platforms is limited by the extent to which they can provide automated performance feedback. Recent work has focused on overcoming this issue by developing algorithms to provide feedback that emulates the advice of human experts. These algorithms can mainly be categorized into rule-based and machine learning based methods, and they have typically been validated through user studies against controls that received no feedback. To our knowledge, no investigations into the performance of the two types of feedback generation methods in comparison to each other have so far been conducted. To this end, we introduce a rule-based method of providing technical feedback in virtual reality simulation-based temporal bone surgery, implement a machine learning based method that has been proven to outperform other similar methods, and compare their performance in teaching surgical skills in practice through a user study. We show that simpler rule-based methods can be equally or more effective in teaching surgical skills when compared to more complex methods of feedback generation.

Keywords: Virtual reality surgery · Automated real-time feedback
Simulation-based surgical education

1 Introduction

As surgeons' skill is often the determining factor between life and death during critical operations, it is important that they are properly trained. Traditionally,

© Springer International Publishing AG, part of Springer Nature 2018
C. Penstein Rosé et al. (Eds.): AIED 2018, LNAI 10947, pp. 584–598, 2018.
https://doi.org/10.1007/978-3-319-93843-1_43

surgical education has revolved around the apprenticeship model where experienced surgeons would mentor trainees during cadaveric dissection and later in the operating theatre. However, in the current climate, the sole use of this model of surgical training is not practical due to issues such as scarcity of cadavers and demand for better trained surgeons in less time.

With the advent of haptic technology, it has become possible to incorporate the sense of touch into virtual reality (VR) applications, thus leading to its wide spread use as a supplemental training technique in surgical education. VR offers a risk-free, repeatable, and accessible platform where surgeons can practice operations. It can be used to develop a standardized curriculum with the possibility of including rare pathologies that are difficult to come by in practice. As such, it is being employed in a wide range of surgical fields.

Although practice on a VR simulator has been proven to improve surgical skills [5,9], the sole availability of a simulator is not always adequate to offer a meaningful educational experience [30]. As such, understanding how surgical skills are acquired and designing a curriculum based on VR simulators accordingly is essential. One important aspect when designing an effective surgical curriculum is the provision of performance feedback [30,31]. Feedback is essential for effective skill acquisition, and must be both timely and contextually relevant [8,22]. Performance feedback in surgical training has typically been provided by human experts. However, if time-poor expert surgeons are solely relied upon to provide feedback during practice, the use of VR as an independent surgical training platform will be limited. Thus, in recent years, research has been conducted on how performance feedback can be automated in VR surgical simulation.

Both real-time and summative feedback are important for skill acquisition [13] and should considered when developing automated feedback systems that emulate human experts. Although there exist numerous examples of automated feedback systems that provide summative feedback at the end of a procedure [14,20,28], provision of real-time feedback in VR simulation is relatively rare.

Feedback is closely related to assessment [13]. Assessment is typically based on a set of performance goals, and thus, feedback should be provided so that it assists in achieving these goals. In surgery, there are standardized assessment scales that test different aspects of surgical skill [15,21]. These skills include knowledge of anatomy, use of correct instruments and settings such as magnification, knowledge of procedure (procedural skills), and technical/motor skills.

Performance feedback on the first three types of skills/knowledge is relatively straightforward to provide. For example, trainees can be assisted in locating anatomical structures or landmarks using verbal warnings [34]. Feedback on environmental settings can be provided by comparing against pre-defined value ranges [32]. Procedural guidance has typically been provided visually based on an expert procedure [1,6,16]. For example, Rhienmora et al. [24] presented a ghost drill that a trainee had to follow in a dental surgery simulation. Step-by-step guidance on how to perform temporal bone surgery was presented through visual cues such as highlighted overlays and instructions in Anderson et al. [1], Wijewickrema et al. [34], and Copson et al. [4].

In contrast, the quality of technical skills in surgery is harder to define and therefore, there has been no consensus on how best to provide feedback on technical skills. Work on real-time technical feedback can be broadly categorized into two types: rule-based and machine learning based methods.

Rule-based feedback methods typically work with fixed operation rules based on performance metrics identified by experts in the field. Operations that violate these rules are considered poor technique. The range of acceptable values for these performance metrics are either determined by experts or calculated through the analysis of pre-collected expert data. For example Fried et al. [10] introduced measures for evaluating performance in virtual endoscopic sinus surgery (such as violation of tissue, violation of instrument tolerances, force patterns etc.) and developed a database of expert performances, that they used to identify performance that deviates from these value ranges. In temporal bone surgery simulation, Sewell et al. [28] provided feedback on technique based on individual metrics selected by the user such as visibility, force, and region of bone removed.

Machine learning has also been applied to generate technical feedback in VR based training. Feedback generated via machine learning techniques is generally considered to be more flexible than that generated by checking fixed rules [19]. These methods learn characteristics of expert and novice behaviour using pre-collected data. The learned characteristics are then used to identify novice behaviour in real-time and generate feedback to improve technique.

Zhou et al. [36] introduced one such method that extracted expert and novice patterns by training a pattern mining algorithm on expert and novice data. Zhou et al. [35] further demonstrated that random forest prediction models can also be used to generate technical feedback. Cui et al. [7] showed how optimal performance feedback can be generated by transforming the random forest feedback problem to an integer programming problem. To overcome the issue of high processing time of this method, Ma et al. [19] introduced a near-optimal method that was more suitable for real-time feedback generation. Ma et al. [18] also introduced a less memory intensive, yet accurate and efficient method of providing feedback in temporal bone surgery simulation. Here, the adversarial concept [11] was used on a pre-trained neural network to generate minimal changes in behaviour (suggested feedback) that changes novice technique to expert technique.

An important consideration in providing technical feedback is the number of metric changes suggested by the feedback. As it is difficult to change more than one feature at a time in practice, some methods limit the feedback generation to the 'best' feature change [19,35,36]. However, there may be instances where changing one metric may not be sufficient to move from novice to expert technique, rendering these methods inaccurate in such instances. Other methods generate the optimal feedback irrespective of the number of metric changes suggested in the feedback [7]. Ma et al. [18] finds a balance between these two extremes, by introducing a penalty that ensures the best performance change (feedback) is returned with the least number of metrics involved in that change.

The feedback provided by these methods have been proven to improve surgical skill acquisition in comparison to the case where no feedback is provided [34]. However, to our knowledge, no investigations have yet been conducted to ascertain whether machine learning based methods of feedback generation are better in practice than their simpler counterparts: rule-based methods. In this paper, we undertake such an investigation with respect to the provision of technical feedback in VR temporal bone surgery simulation. To this end, we introduce a novel rule-based method for technical feedback generation in an existing VR simulator, implement a validated machine learning based generation technique for the same, integrate them with other types of automated feedback (procedural guidance, proximity warnings, and environmental settings feedback) and evaluate their effectiveness with respect to practical surgical skill acquisition.

2   Simulation Environment

The VR platform used in this research is a temporal bone surgery simulator (see Fig. 1). The virtual temporal bone comprises anatomical structures such as the dura, sigmoid sinus, and facial nerve. A virtual drill reflects the movements of a haptic device that provides tactile feedback to the user. The impression of depth is achieved through NVIDIA 3D vision technology. A MIDI controller is used as a convenient input device to change environment variables such as magnification level and burr size. Using the VR simulator, surgeons can perform middle and inner ear operations to remove diseased tissue and improve hearing.

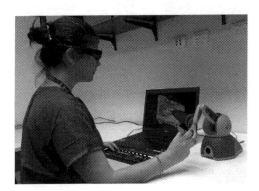

Fig. 1. The University of Melbourne VR temporal bone surgery simulator.

Our VR simulator provides different types of real-time feedback. Procedural guidance is presented using the method of Wijewickrema et al. [34]. Each step of a surgery is highlighted on the temporal bone (see Fig. 1) and the next step is only provided once the current step is completed. Following existing work [33], verbal proximity warnings are provided when drilling within a specified distance of an anatomical structure. Verbal feedback on environment settings such as magnification level and burr size is provided by comparing the current setting with preset ranges of acceptable values [32].

Technical skills, although usually related to instrument handling, may have different meanings in different application contexts. Our focus is on open surgeries such as temporal bone surgery, where technical skill is reliant on how drill 'strokes' are fashioned. A stroke represents a continuous motion of the drill with no abrupt changes in direction. To segment strokes from a surgical trajectory, we use the method introduced by Hall et al. [12]. The quality of a stroke can be determined by analyzing the characteristics, or stroke metrics, that define that stroke (stroke length, duration, speed, acceleration, force, straightness) [18,19].

Surgical technique varies according to the region being drilled. For example, long strokes and high force can be used when drilling in an open area, but more caution is warranted when drilling near an anatomical structure. Therefore, it is important to identify regions and define the quality of surgical technique for each region separately. We identify the regions of a temporal bone using the method discussed in Wijewickrema et al. [32]. Figure 2 illustrates these regions.

As a whole, the guidance/feedback provided by the system pertains to how a task is conducted and as such, can be placed in the task level of the feedback framework introduced by Hattie and Timperley [13].

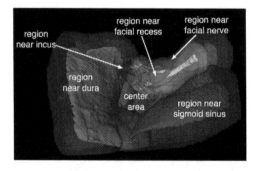

Fig. 2. Regions where surgical technique can be considered uniform.

3   Implementation of Surgical Technique Feedback

3.1   Rule-Based Technical Feedback

To develop our rule-based feedback generation method (RBFB), we first identified a set of rules that have to be satisfied (and their importance) for technique to be deemed acceptable for each region. This was done in consultation with two expert ear surgeons, based on the technical performance metrics (or stroke metrics) discussed in Ma et al. [18,19]. Table 1 illustrates the rules (in order of priority) along with the suggested action or feedback when a rule is violated.

In real-time, during a VR surgery, strokes are segmented from the surgical trajectory, and performance metrics calculated for each stroke. Depending on the

Table 1. Rules defined for surgical regions in decreasing order of priority.

Region	Priority	Rule	Feedback
Center area	1	Force too low	Use more force
	2	Strokes are too short	Use longer strokes
	3	Drilling too slow	Drill faster
Dura Sigmoid sinus Facial nerve	1	Force too high	Use less force
	2	Drilling too fast	Drill slower
	3	Strokes are too long	Use shorter strokes
	4	Strokes are too short	Use longer strokes
	5	Drilling too slow	Drill faster
	6	Force too low	Use more force
Incus	1	Strokes are too long	Use shorter strokes
	2	Drilling too fast	Drill slower
	3	Force too high	Use less force
	4	Strokes are too short	Use longer strokes
	5	Force too low	Use more force
	6	Drilling too slow	Drill faster
Facial recess	1	Force too high	Use less force
	2	Drilling too fast	Drill slower
	3	Strokes are too long	Use shorter strokes
	4	Force too low	Use more force
	5	Strokes are too short	Use longer strokes
	6	Drilling too slow	Drill faster

region that is being drilled, the individual stroke metrics are compared against pre-defined ranges determined from expert data (discussed next) according to the order of importance of the rules. For example, in the center area, the current force is first compared with the minimum recommended force value for the area. If the force is less than the minimum, feedback to increase force is provided. If the force is greater than the minimum, the next rule is checked (that is, if the stroke length is less than the pre-defined minimum).

The acceptable ranges for each stroke metric was calculated offline using 16 surgeries performed by 7 experts. Each expert trajectory was segmented into strokes and divided according to which region they belonged to. Then, for each region, and for each stroke metric, the acceptable range x_{range} was calculated as $x_{range} = [x_{mean} - 2 * x_{std}, x_{mean} + 2 * x_{std}]$, where, x_{mean} and x_{std} are the mean and standard deviation of the pre-collected expert values of a stroke metric for a given region respectively. Note that the full range of expert data was not used as the acceptable range because of the possible existence of outliers.

3.2   Machine Learning Based Technical Feedback

We chose the neural network feedback generation method (NNFB) of Ma et al.
[18] over other machine learning based methods due to a few reasons. First,
it has been evaluated on pre-collected simulator data in comparison with other
existing methods and found to be efficient and accurate. Second, it has an in-built
penalty term related to the number of metrics on which to provide feedback, and
as such, returns the best feedback that has the least number of metric changes.
Third, its memory footprint is low (especially when compared to random forest
based methods), thus making it ideal for implementation in a VR application
with substantial memory requirements. Figure 3 shows how NNFB can be used
to provide real-time technical feedback in VR surgical simulation.

Fig. 3. NNFB feedback generation method.

For the offline training of the neural network classifier, we used a dataset of
16 surgeries recorded by 7 experts (same data used in the RFBF range calculation above) and 34 surgeries from 18 novices. The surgical performances were
segmented into strokes with all strokes in expert and novice performances considered to be expert and novice strokes respectively. The strokes were separated
according to the region they were performed in and stroke metrics were calculated for each of these. Expert and novice strokes of each region were used to
train neural networks with one hidden layer. The number of hidden neurons for
each region was chosen using cross validation [18].

In real-time, strokes are segmented from the surgical trajectory, and the
neural network classifier for the relevant region is used to identify whether it is
an expert or novice stroke. In the case of a novice stroke, the change in metrics
that modifies it to an expert stroke that minimizes the distance between the
original novice stroke and the resulting expert stroke subject to a constraint
(the number of metrics that need to be changed) is calculated [18].

The resulting feedback consists of a change in one stroke metric (for example,
'decrease force') if this can be achieved at a minimum cost. If not, it will comprise
changes in multiple features (for example, 'decrease force' and 'decrease speed').
However, as higher numbers of metrics changes are penalized, the number of
metric changes in the suggested feedback remains low. This ensures that the
feedback is useful in practice where changing multiple aspects of performance

at once can be difficult. Performance results of NNFB in comparison with other machine learning based methods can be found in Ma et al. [18].

Although we assume that all expert strokes are indeed of high quality, this may not always be the case. Therefore, to ensure accuracy, exceptional behaviour (or outliers) in data has to be removed prior to training the classifiers in NNFB. We adopted a commonly used outlier removal method: isolation forests [17]. Unlike simpler methods (for example, that used in Sect. 3.1), isolation forests consider the interaction between the stroke metrics in multi-dimensional space. For example, a high force value may be detected as an outlier when considered by itself. However, when combined with a low speed value, a high force value may be acceptable. By considering all stroke metrics at the same time in relation to each other, outliers can be detected more accurately. Approximately 10% of our original dataset was removed as outliers using an isolation forest. Outlier removal was done separately for experts and novices and for each region and the resulting strokes were used to train the classifiers.

4 Presentation of Feedback

As mentioned above, surgical skills are multi-faceted and feedback on these have to be presented as a whole. Thus, we investigated how different types of feedback (procedural guidance, technical feedback, proximity warnings, and environment settings feedback) can be presented together based on existing work [2,23] and consultation with surgeons, education psychologists, and computer scientists. Presentation strategies thus implemented in the feedback system are as follows. Note that the same settings were used in presenting both RBFB and NNFB.

Presentation Medium: The presentation medium of feedback is important, specifically when there are multiple types of feedback being presented. The effectiveness of a feedback presentation medium depends on factors such as task complexity and skill level of the trainee [29]. Thus, it is not possible to define global rules relating to the effectiveness of a presentation medium. Studies have however, shown that multimodal feedback (such as visual and auditory) can be used effectively in teaching skills [3,29]. In view of this, we combined the use of verbal auditory and visual feedback following previous work in the field [32–34]. Technical feedback (along with environmental settings feedback and proximity warnings) was provided in the form of verbal auditory instructions [32,33]. Pre-recorded audio clips were saved for each type of feedback for each region, to be played when the relevant type of feedback is generated. For example, if a trainee is using too much force around the facial nerve, the presented feedback would be 'use less force near the facial nerve'. Procedural guidance was provided through a visual step-by-step process [34].

Priority of Different Types of Feedback: In our system, different types of feedback are generated in parallel by different algorithms. As such, it is important to determine the order of priority in case two or more types of feedback are generated at the same time. In consultation with expert surgeons, considering the level of skill of the novices being taught, it was decided that proximity warnings were to take first priority as they warn trainees when nearing anatomical structures so that damage could be minimized. The second most important was environment settings feedback, as use of magnification and burr size are critical to a successful surgery. Technical feedback was the last in order of priority. Therefore, for example, if a proximity warning and an instance of technical feedback (say 'reduce force') are generated at the same time, the proximity warning will be played by the system. As procedural guidance was being provided through a different medium (visual), there were no restrictions on its presentation.

Confidence of Presented Feedback: The temporal placement of concurrent (real-time) feedback can be immediate or delayed [26]. The choice of temporal placement depends on the task at hand and skill level of the trainee. We used immediate presentation for proximity warnings and environmental settings feedback as they are considered to be critical and immediate action should be taken to avoid damage. Also, these forms of feedback are more straightforward to define than technical feedback and therefore, deviations from the norm can easily be determined with a high level of confidence. In contrast, as surgical technique cannot be as clearly defined, it is prudent to delay the presentation of technical feedback until a high level of confidence in its accuracy is reached. This ensures that feedback is provided only when a certain aspect of surgical technique is consistently poor. We implemented this through a form of buffering. Technical feedback (a suggestion to increase or decrease a certain stroke metric) was added to a buffer every time the system generated one. A feedback item in the buffer could consist of one metric change (RBFB or NNFB) or several metric changes (NNFB). The latest generated feedback was checked against those already in the buffer, and considered to be a candidate for presentation only if it had a significant presence in the buffer. In our application, the buffer size was 10 and the confidence threshold for a feedback to be eligible for presentation was 60%.

Region Crossing: As we implemented separate feedback generation models for different regions to account for variations in surgical technique, we also employed strategies to maintain the confidence of feedback when regions are crossed. First, we cleared the feedback buffer when a region is crossed so that the integrity of the region-based feedback is maintained. Second, to account for situations where the boundaries of regions are being drilled, we kept track of the regions of the latest strokes and used this to ensure that the feedback provided is consistent. To this end, we saved the regions of the 100 latest strokes in a region buffer. The generated feedback in a region was considered for presentation only if the percentage of that region in the region buffer was more than a preset threshold. Lower threshold values were used for regions of higher importance so that more feedback can be provided. The threshold values were: center area - 30%, dura and sigmoid sinus - 20%, and incus, facial nerve, and facial recess - 10%.

Frequency of Presentation: The guidance hypothesis [27] predicts that the guiding properties of concurrent (or real-time) feedback are beneficial for learning motor skills (such as technical skills in surgery) when used to reduce error, but detrimental when relied upon. It also suggests that a reduced frequency of feedback may facilitate learning. Reducing the frequency of feedback also ensures that trainees do not face cognitive overload. In view of this, we implemented strategies to only present a subset of feedback that pass the conditions discussed above and are deemed eligible for presentation. First, we suppressed any feedback that is generated at the start of a surgery while trainees familiarize themselves with the procedure. This initial time period was set to 30 s for technical and environment settings feedback and 10 s for proximity warnings. Second, we suppressed the presentation of feedback generated immediately after another feedback was presented. The period of suppression for technical and environment settings feedback was 7 s while for proximity warnings, it was set to 30 s. Third, once a feedback has been presented, if the same feedback was generated within a given interval from its last presentation, it was not presented. This time interval was set to 15 s for all three types of auditory verbal feedback.

5 Experimental Results

We conducted a randomized trial of medical students to evaluate the effectiveness of the above two feedback methods in improving surgical technique. Ethics for this study was obtained from the Human Ethics Sub-Committee of the University of Anonymous (Ethic ID: 1647227). 26 students participated in this study. In previous studies, significant effects were seen with as little as 20 participants (10 per group) [34], thus ensuring that our study was sufficiently powered. Data from one participant was removed from the study due to an error in data collection. Participants were randomized into two groups: rule-based feedback (RBFB) and neural network based feedback (NNFB) using a block randomization technique.

After the consent procedure, all participants were shown a video tutorial on how to perform a simple ear surgery (i.e. cortical mastoidectomy). Then, they were given 5 min to familiarize themselves with the simulator. Next, they were asked to perform the same procedure without any guidance (pre-test), so that their initial skill level could be gauged. Then, they received two training sessions with automated guidance: technical feedback, procedural guidance, proximity warnings, and environment settings feedback as discussed in Sect. 2. Depending on which group the participant was in, technical feedback was provided using the two techniques RBFB or NNFB. After the completion of the two training sessions, the participants performed a mastoidectomy procedure without any guidance (post-test). Finally, they filled out a questionnaire on their experience of the technical feedback. Figure 4 illustrates the study design.

Non-parametric tests were used in the statistical analysis of the results due to the non-normal nature of the data and small sample sizes. Kruskal-Wallis and Mann-Whitney U tests were used to compare between groups and to compare pre and post behaviour within groups respectively. The effect sizes were calculated as $r = \sqrt{\frac{\chi^2}{N}}$ and $r = \frac{Z}{\sqrt{N}}$ for the two tests respectively, where χ^2 and Z are the outputs of the tests and N is the total sample size [25].

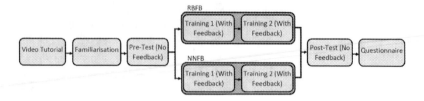

Fig. 4. Design of the user study. Note that all conditions other than the source of the technical feedback were the same for the two groups in the training sessions.

Comparison of Performance: As mentioned in Sect. 1, competency in surgery is typically evaluated against validated objective assessment scales that consider all aspects of surgical skill (procedural, technical etc.). Here, we used a scale developed specifically for cortical mastoidectomy [15]. It was shown to have high construct validity (accuracy in determining skill level) and inter-rater reliability (agreement between different assessors) and comprised two parts: checklist and global scores. Participant performance for the pre- and post-tests was determined by an expert surgeon via anonymized videos using this scale.

The checklist score (CS) of the cortical mastoidectomy assessment scale is based on the procedural steps emphasized in surgical course curricula and dissection manuals, with a total score of 110. The global score (GS) of the assessment tool measures technical as well as procedural competence, and has a total score of 50. The results based on both scores for within group (pre-post analysis) and between group (for performance improvement) are shown in Table 2.

Table 2. Results of the performance analysis.

Within groups	Pre: Median (IQR)	Post: Median (IQR)	p	r
CS - RBFB	29 (25 → 34)	46 (39.5 → 48)	**0.0001**	−0.7633
CS - NNFB	29 (26 → 36)	41 (32 → 44.25)	**0.0040**	−0.5757
GS - RBFB	14.5 (10.5 → 22)	30 (27 → 39)	**0.0003**	−0.7239
GS - NNFB	16 (10.75 → 18.25)	28 (21.75 → 30)	**0.0013**	−0.6426
Between groups	RBFB: Median (IQR)	NNFB: Median (IQR)	p	r
Improvement in CS	16.5 (9 → 20.5)	10 (0.25 → 15.75)	0.0906	0.3385
Improvement in GS	17 (13.5 → 21.5)	11 (2.75 → 13.75)	**0.0409**	0.4089

Assessment of Feedback Accuracy: The accuracy of the feedback generation methods was determined by an expert surgeon through the analysis of anonymized videos and calculated as $ACC = \frac{TF-FP-WC}{TF+FN} \times 100\%$, where, FP are false positives (feedback provided when stroke technique is acceptable), WC is wrong content (technique is accurately detected as poor, but the content of the feedback is inaccurate), FN are false negatives (feedback not provided when stroke technique is unacceptable) and TF is total feedback provided [33]. Table 3 shows the results of this analysis.

Table 3. Results of the expert analysis of accuracy.

	RBFB: Median (IQR)	NNFB: Median (IQR)	p	r
False positives (FP)	2 (0 → 2.75)	0 (0 → 1)	**0.0137**	0.3522
Wrong content (WC)	0 (0 → 0)	0 (0 → 1)	0.1637	0.1990
False negatives (FN)	0 (0 → 1)	0 (0 → 1)	0.3218	0.1416
Total feedback (TF)	17 (13 → 21.75)	15.5 (10 → 19)	0.2134	0.1778
Accuracy (ACC) %	84 (77.98 → 93.21)	87.5 (76.92 → 94.12)	0.7251	0.0502

Perception of Participants: A questionnaire based on a 5-point Likert scale was used to gather participants' impressions of the technical feedback. Table 4 shows the results of this qualitative analysis.

Table 4. Results of the user perception analysis.

	RBFB: Median (IQR)	NNFB: Median (IQR)	p	r
Q1: Usefulness	4 (4 → 4.5)	5 (4 → 5)	0.1495	0.2882
Q2: Clarity	4 (4 → 5)	4 (4 → 5)	0.1495	0.0244
Q3: Accuracy	4 (4 → 5)	4 (4 → 5)	0.6292	0.0966
Q4: Timeliness	4 (4 → 4.5)	4 (4 → 5)	0.3919	0.1712
Q5: Too much feedback	2 (2 → 3.5)	2 (2 → 3)	0.8131	0.0473
Q6: Too little feedback	2 (2 → 3.5)	3 (2 → 3)	0.6623	0.0874

6 Conclusion

The results of the performance analysis showed that both groups showed significant improvement with respect to the checklist and global scores of the assessment scale from pre- to post-tests. This indicates that the different types of feedback/guidance, along with the presentation strategies used, worked in concert to successfully improve different aspects of surgical skill.

A between-group comparison of the improvement in checklist scores showed no significant difference. This is not surprising as both groups received the same procedural guidance which is the sole purview of the checklist score. However, a significant difference was observed in the improvement in the global scores. This indicates that the technical aspects of the assessment scale was indeed affected by the different feedback generation methods leading us to the conclusion that the simpler RBFB method may be more effective in improving technical skills.

The accuracy of the two types of feedback generation methods, as assessed by an expert surgeon was not significantly different. It was seen that more false positives were observed in the RFBF method. These observations do not however explain the better performance seen in the RBFB group with respect to the global score of the assessment scale. Further analysis, for example, a breakdown of the feedback content provided by the two methods, may be required to uncover the reasons behind the difference in performance. Similarly, the analysis of user perception showed that both groups had equally positive experiences of the feedback, indicating that the system was seen to be usable and useful.

From these observations, it can be concluded that simpler rule-based methods of providing technical feedback in VR temporal bone surgery simulation can be equally or more effective than those that are based on methods that consider more complex interactions between performance metrics. It can also be inferred that a system that provides different types of automated feedback/guidance can be used to effectively train different aspects of surgical skill.

References

1. Andersen, S.A.W., Foghsgaard, S., Konge, L., Cayé-Thomasen, P., Sørensen, M.S.: The effect of self-directed virtual reality simulation on dissection training performance in mastoidectomy. Laryngoscope 126(8), 1883–1888 (2016)
2. Baddeley, A.: Working memory: looking back and looking forward. Nat. Rev. Neurosci. 4(10), 829 (2003)
3. Burke, J.L., Prewett, M.S., Gray, A.A., Yang, L., Stilson, F.R., Coovert, M.D., Elliot, L.R., Redden, E.: Comparing the effects of visual-auditory and visual-tactile feedback on user performance: a meta-analysis. In: ICMI, pp. 108–117 (2006)
4. Copson, B., Wijewickrema, S., Zhou, Y., Piromchai, P., Briggs, R., Bailey, J., Kennedy, G., O'Leary, S.: Supporting skill acquisition in cochlear implant surgery through virtual reality simulation. Cochlear Implants Int. 18(2), 89–96 (2017)
5. Crochet, P., Aggarwal, R., Dubb, S.S., Ziprin, P., Rajaretnam, N., Grantcharov, T., Ericsson, K.A., Darzi, A.: Deliberate practice on a virtual reality laparoscopic simulator enhances the quality of surgical technical skills. Ann. Surg. 253(6), 1216–1222 (2011)
6. Crossan, A., Brewster, S., Reid, S., Mellor, D.: Multimodal feedback cues to aid veterinary training simulations (2000)
7. Cui, Z., Chen, W., He, Y., Chen, Y.: Optimal action extraction for random forests and boosted trees. In: KDD, pp. 179–188 (2015)
8. Ericsson, K.A.: Deliberate practice and the acquisition and maintenance of expert performance in medicine and related domains. Acad. Med. 79(10), S70–S81 (2004)
9. Francis, H.W., Malik, M.U., Diaz Voss Varela, D.A., Barffour, M.A., Chien, W.W., Carey, J.P., Niparko, J.K., Bhatti, N.I.: Technical skills improve after practice on virtual-reality temporal bone simulator. Laryngoscope 122(6), 1385–1391 (2012)
10. Fried, M.P., Satava, R., Weghorst, S., Gallagher, A., Sasaki, C., Ross, D., Sinanan, M., Uribe, J., Zeltsan, M., Arora, H., et al.: Identifying and reducing errors with surgical simulation. Qual. Saf. Health Care 13(suppl 1), i19–i26 (2004)

11. Goodfellow, I.J., Shlens, J., Szegedy, C.: Explaining and harnessing adversarial examples. In: ICLR (2015)

12. Hall, R., Rathod, H., Maiorca, M., Ioannou, I., Kazmierczak, E., O'Leary, S., Harris, P.: Towards haptic performance analysis using k-metrics. In: Pirhonen, A., Brewster, S. (eds.) HAID 2008. LNCS, vol. 5270, pp. 50–59. Springer, Heidelberg (2008). https://doi.org/10.1007/978-3-540-87883-4_6

13. Hattie, J., Timperley, H.: The power of feedback. Rev. Educ. Res. 77(1), 81–112 (2007)

14. Kerwin, T., Wiet, G., Stredney, D., Shen, H.W.: Automatic scoring of virtual mastoidectomies using expert examples. Int. J. Comput. Assist. Radiol. Surg. 7(1), 1–11 (2012)

15. Laeeq, K., Bhatti, N.I., Carey, J.P., Della Santina, C.C., Limb, C.J., Niparko, J.K., Minor, L.B., Francis, H.W.: Pilot testing of an assessment tool for competency in mastoidectomy. Laryngoscope 119(12), 2402–2410 (2009)

16. Lamata, P., Gomez, E.J., Bello, F., Kneebone, R.L., Aggarwal, R., Lamata, F.: Conceptual framework for laparoscopic VR simulators. IEEE Comput. Graph. Appl. 26(6), 69–79 (2006)

17. Liu, F.T., Ting, K.M., Zhou, Z.H.: Isolation forest. In: ICDM, pp. 413–422 (2008)

18. Ma, X., Bailey, J., Wijewickrema, S., Zhou, S., Mhammedi, Z., Zhou, Y., OLeary, S.: Adversarial generation of real-time feedback with neural networks for simulation-based training. In: IJCAI, pp. 3763–3769 (2017)

19. Ma, X., Wijewickrema, S., Zhou, Y., Zhou, S., O'Leary, S., Bailey, J.: Providing effective real-time feedback in simulation-based surgical training. In: Descoteaux, M., Maier-Hein, L., Franz, A., Jannin, P., Collins, D.L., Duchesne, S. (eds.) MICCAI 2017. LNCS, vol. 10434, pp. 566–574. Springer, Cham (2017). https://doi.org/10.1007/978-3-319-66185-8_64

20. Mackel, T., Rosen, J., Pugh, C.: Data mining of the e-pelvis simulator database: a quest for a generalized algorithm for objectively assessing medical skill. Stud. Health Technol. Inf. 119, 355–360 (2006)

21. Martin, J., Regehr, G., Reznick, R., Macrae, H., Murnaghan, J., Hutchison, C., Brown, M.: Objective structured assessment of technical skill (OSATS) for surgical residents. Br. J. Surg. 84(2), 273–278 (1997)

22. McGaghie, W.C., Issenberg, S.B., Petrusa, E.R., Scalese, R.J.: A critical review of simulation-based medical education research: 2003–2009. Med. Educ. 44(1), 50–63 (2010)

23. Oviatt, S.: Human-centered design meets cognitive load theory: designing interfaces that help people think. In: ACMMM, pp. 871–880 (2006)

24. Rhienmora, P., Haddawy, P., Suebnukarn, S., Dailey, M.N.: Intelligent dental training simulator with objective skill assessment and feedback. Artif. Intell. Med. 52(2), 115–121 (2011)

25. Rosenthal, R., DiMatteo, M.R.: Meta-analysis: recent developments in quantitative methods for literature reviews. Annu. Rev. Psychol. 52(1), 59–82 (2001)

26. Schmidt, R.A., Lee, T.D., et al.: Motor control and learning: a behavioral emphasis, vol. 4 (2005)

27. Schmidt, R.A., Young, D.E., Swinnen, S., Shapiro, D.C.: Summary knowledge of results for skill acquisition: support for the guidance hypothesis. J. Exp. Psychol. Learn. Mem. Cogn. 15(2), 352 (1989)

28. Sewell, C., Morris, D., Blevins, N.H., Dutta, S., Agrawal, S., Barbagli, F., Salisbury, K.: Providing metrics and performance feedback in a surgical simulator. Comput. Aided Surg. 13(2), 63–81 (2008)

29. Sigrist, R., Rauter, G., Riener, R., Wolf, P.: Augmented visual, auditory, haptic, and multimodal feedback in motor learning: a review. Psychon. Bull. Rev. **20**(1), 21–53 (2013)
30. Stefanidis, D.: Optimal acquisition and assessment of proficiency on simulators in surgery. Surg. Clin. North Am. **90**(3), 475–489 (2010)
31. Stefanidis, D., Heniford, B.T.: The formula for a successful laparoscopic skills curriculum. Arch. Surg. **144**(1), 77–82 (2009)
32. Wijewickrema, S., Ioannou, I., Zhou, Y., Piromchai, P., Bailey, J., Kennedy, G., OLeary, S.: Region-specific automated feedback in temporal bone surgery simulation. In: CBMS, pp. 310–315 (2015)
33. Wijewickrema, S., Ioannou, I., Zhou, Y., Promchai, P., Bailey, J., Kennedy, G., OLeary, S.: A temporal bone surgery simulator with real-time feedback for surgical training. In: NextMed/MMVR21, pp. 462–468 (2014)
34. Wijewickrema, S., Zhou, Y., Bailey, J., Kennedy, G., O'Leary, S.: Provision of automated step-by-step procedural guidance in virtual reality surgery simulation. In: VRST, pp. 69–72 (2016)
35. Zhou, Y., Bailey, J., Ioannou, I., Wijewickrema, S., Kennedy, G., O'Leary, S.: Constructive real time feedback for a temporal bone simulator. In: Mori, K., Sakuma, I., Sato, Y., Barillot, C., Navab, N. (eds.) MICCAI 2013. LNCS, vol. 8151, pp. 315–322. Springer, Heidelberg (2013). https://doi.org/10.1007/978-3-642-40760-4_40
36. Zhou, Y., Bailey, J., Ioannou, I., Wijewickrema, S., O'Leary, S., Kennedy, G.: Pattern-based real-time feedback for a temporal bone simulator. In: VRST, pp. 7–16 (2013)

Reciprocal Kit-Building of Concept Map to Share Each Other's Understanding as Preparation for Collaboration

Warunya Wunnasri[✉], Jaruwat Pailai, Yusuke Hayashi,
and Tsukasa Hirashima

Graduate School of Engineering, Hiroshima University, Higashihiroshima, Japan
{warunya,jaruwat,hayashi,
tsukasa}@lel.hiroshima-u.ac.jp

Abstract. Collaborative learning is an active teaching and learning strategy, in which learners who give each other elaborated explanations can learn most. However, it is difficult for learners to explain their own understanding elaborately in collaborative learning. In this study, we propose a collaborative use of a Kit-Build concept map (KB map) called "Reciprocal KB map". In a Reciprocal KB map for a pair discussion, at first, the two participants make their own concept maps expressing their comprehension. Then, they exchange the components of their maps and request each other to reconstruct their maps by using the components. The differences between the original concept map and the reconstructed map are diagnosed automatically as an advantage of the KB map. Reciprocal KB map is expected to encourage pair discussion to recognize the understanding of each other and to create an effective discussion. In an experiment reported in this paper, Reciprocal KB map was used for supporting a pair discussion and was compared with a pair discussion which was supported by a traditional concept map. Nineteen pairs of university students were requested to use the traditional concept map in their discussion, while 20 pairs of university students used Reciprocal KB map for discussing the same topic. The results of the experiment were analyzed using three metrics: a discussion score, a similarity score, and questionnaires. The discussion score, which investigates the value of talk in discussion, demonstrates that Reciprocal KB map can promote more effective discussion between the partners compared to the traditional concept map. The similarity score, which evaluates the similarity of the concept maps, demonstrates that Reciprocal KB map can encourage the pair of partners to understand each other better compared to the traditional concept map. Last, the questionnaires illustrate that Reciprocal KB map can support the pair of partners to collaborate in the discussion smoothly and that the participants accepted this method for sharing their understanding with each other. These results suggest that Reciprocal KB map is a promising approach for encouraging pairs of partners to understand each other and to promote the effective discussions.

Keywords: Collaborative learning · Pair discussion · Kit-Build concept map
Shared understanding

© Springer International Publishing AG, part of Springer Nature 2018
C. Penstein Rosé et al. (Eds.): AIED 2018, LNAI 10947, pp. 599–612, 2018.
https://doi.org/10.1007/978-3-319-93843-1_44

1   Introduction

Collaborative learning is an active teaching and learning strategy, which has been utilized in elementary, secondary, and higher education. It can contribute many advantages that consist of an improving interpersonal skill, development of critical thinking, problem solving skill, content mastery and etc., and various studies can be used to confirm that the collaborative learning is beneficial [1–3]. Therefore, it is focused as an effective instructional medium and attracts many educators to utilize collaborative strategy in their classes and develop computer support system for increasing a learning achievement. A discussion is also one of the collaborative technique for communicating and sharing knowledge. Nunan [4] mentioned that "A good give-and-take discussion can produce unmatched learning experiences as students articulate their ideas, respond to their classmates' points, and develop skills in evaluating the evidence of their own and others' positions." This sentence demonstrates that the discussion can support people to improve their skills. From a reviewing of several studies, Slavin concluded that "students who give each other elaborated explanations are students who learn most in cooperative learning [5]."

Nevertheless, it is not common for a learner to give an explanation in an actual class. In Mercer's studies, he categorized talk in classroom discussion into three types, namely, exploratory talk, cumulative talk, and disputative talk [6]. He claimed that exploratory talk reveals the reasoning which is valuable for discussion. In addition to Mercer's research, the value of exploratory talk also was confirmed in terms of its ability to facilitate reasoning in social contexts and to lead to the generation of new knowledge and understanding [7–12]. However, from Mercer's observations [13], exploratory talk is rare in classroom discussion.

The Kit-Build concept map framework (KB map in short) is one of the automatic concept map assessment methods that uses a teacher-build map to compare with the learner-build map by using exact matching at the propositional level. It is utilized in the form of a learning task or exercise for checking learners' comprehension of a topic that they have already learned [14, 15]. Following results of a previous study [16, 17], KB map can be used to express understanding and the automatic concept map assessment method can attain the same reliability and validity level as a typical manual assessment. Hence, we assume that KB map can be an effective instructional medium for sharing understanding. In this paper, we propose a collaborative use of KB map called "Reciprocal KB map", which aims to encourage sharing understandings with each other in pair discussion. In Reciprocal KB map for pair discussion, at first, the two participants of the pair make their own concept maps expressing their comprehension. Then, they exchange the components of their maps and request each other to reconstruct their maps by using these components. The differences between the original map and the reconstructed map are diagnosed automatically, as an advantage of the KB map. Reciprocal KB map is expected to encourage pair discussion to promote shared understanding and to create effective discussion. In this paper, the results of an experiment where a pair discussion with Reciprocal KB map was used are compared with those of a pair discussion using a traditional concept map. The comparison is analyzed using the following three metrics: a discussion score, a similarity map score and questionnaires.

2   Related Work

2.1   Collaborative Learning in Classroom

In a collaborative knowledge-building process, a step where collaborators share others' understanding is very important [18]. We aim to apply KB map in the shared understanding step. Each collaborator has to adjust their perspectives and awareness of the others' understanding, even if they do not agree with the others' thinking. To make a shared understanding, several collaborative learning approaches were investigated. Advantages of collaborative learning are proposed in many researches, including increased measures of achievement, higher-level reasoning, increased frequency of new ideas, and situational transfer [19]. Additionally, a theory proposed by Resta and Laferriere [20], maintained that the social context can enhance creativity and learning.

Hence, to encourage the quality of discussion among collaborators, we focus on the collaborative approaches that emphasize shared understanding. Reciprocal teaching [21] is an approach which deals with a summarization of understanding. This collaborative approach requests collaborators to participate in four roles that contain summarizing, questioning, clarifying, and predicting. These four roles really suit the discussion situation which aims to share understanding. Summarizing is a way to help collaborators to reconsider their understanding, using for example, short-notes, mind maps, and concept maps. Hence, we can properly apply summarization with KB map because it uses the concept map as a representation of understanding. After summarizing, the next role of collaborators is questioning. This role requires collaborators to think about the topic and forces them to identify areas where they are confused and require clarification. Once collaborators have questions in their mind, the role of clarifying encourages them to point out confusing areas and to clarify these. The predicting role is a more advanced stage for contributing collaborative knowledge. The collaborators have to send out their idea regarding what can happen next in the comprehension that they have just learned. They have to utilize their imagination to think ahead. However, the last role, predicting, is not contained in our current approach, the aim of which is to encourage shared understanding. However, it is necessary for the next step which involves producing a creative idea from collaborative knowledge.

2.2   Kit-Build Concept Map and the Practical Use

The KB map is a framework to realize automatic concept map assessment [14, 15]. Instant and automatic assessment of a learner-build concept map, realized in this framework, is referred to as the "Kit-Build method" (KB method). In this framework, the set of components as the set "kit" are made by decomposing a concept map that is built by a responsible teacher. This map is called the "teacher-build map". The responsible teacher is requested to build the teacher-build map as a criterion to assess a learner's comprehension for a specific topic or teaching. Then, a learner is requested to build a concept map to express his/her comprehension for the same topic or teaching. Because all components of the learner-build map are the same as the teacher-build map, an automatic assessment of a learner-build map is realized by comparing the learner-build map with the teacher-build map. Because of a page limitation, the figure of KB map procedure is represented in [16, 17] additionally. KB map and assessment methods have already been practically used in classrooms in various schools, for example, in science learning in elementary schools [22, 23], geography in junior high schools [24], learning English as a second language [25], and university-level social science and computer science [26, 27]. Even the KB map assessment method is automated, and the validity of this for evaluating learners' understanding has been confirmed previously [16, 17]. This investigation suggests that KB map can support learners to effectively express their understanding. Moreover, the diagnostic results from KB map can be utilized as a formative assessment tool for supporting teachers in designing feedback in their class effectively [28].

3   Research Methodology

In line with the objective to show that KB map can be used to achieve a productive discussion, we designed the experimental procedure. Firstly, participants were required to summarize their understanding and represent it in the form of the concept map by using the provided components. In this experiment, 12 labeled concepts, which related to a reading article, were provided for all participants. This method, which provides a concept list to learners, is a regular strategy for limiting the scope of content [29, 30]. Next, the participants were required to formulate questions on the parts that they could not understand. Participants were then required to ask or find the answers to their questions during the pair discussion. Lastly, they were requested to think about the understanding that they got from asking questions and discussing. This experimental procedure was designed to answer two research questions:

1. Could KB map be utilized for sharing understanding with each other?
2. What is the difference between discussions that use a traditional concept map and those that use Reciprocal KB map?

3.1   Reciprocal Kit-Build Concept Map

In the usual KB map, teachers use it for checking learners' understanding about the topic that they have already learned. The teacher's expectation is constructed in the form of the teacher-build map, and then the system generates the kit. The kit is provided for the learner and they are requested to reconstruct it. After the learner-build maps are uploaded, the teacher gives feedback to learners based on the diagnosis results. However, procedure of Reciprocal KB map is different as Fig. 1. It is designed for encouraging pair discussion to aid understanding of each other. Two conversational partners have to summarize their understanding in the form of the concept map, and then their map is extracted as the kit. The kit is provided for their partner and they are requested to reconstruct it. Next, they have to discuss their understanding by using the comparison map that is generated by comparing the original concept map and the reconstructed map.

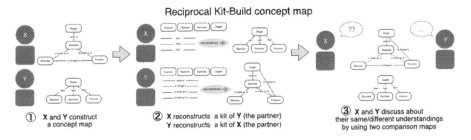

Reciprocal Kit-Build concept map

① X and Y construct
a concept map

② X reconstructs a kit of Y (the partner)
Y reconstructs a kit of X (the partner)

③ X and Y discuss about
their same/different understandings
by using two comparison maps

Fig. 1. Procedure of Reciprocal KB map

3.2 Participants

The participants in this study were university students who were categorized by language into three groups. These three groups contained 16 international students who possessed a good level of English, 14 Japanese students and 48 Thai students. The total number of participants was 78 students who were volunteers from engineering fields. The participants were paired and divided into two groups. Thus, four pairs of international students, three pairs of Japanese students and 12 pairs of Thai students were grouped in the Normal Concept Map (NCM) group to serve as a control group. The participants in the Reciprocal Kit-Build (RKB) group served as the experimental group and this contained four pairs of international students, four pairs of Japanese students and 12 pairs of Thai students. All of the participants were given introductory training in concept maps before participating in the experiment.

Three graduate students, who were familiar with the use of the concept map and understood the content of the experiment material well, were assigned as raters. They were responsible for scoring discussion and concept maps in their own expert/native language. Hence, one rater was assigned to scoring the concept map and analyzing the conversations of the learners for each of the language groups of English, Japanese, and Thai. The procedure of the concept map assessment method was explained to the raters and they were required to study the procedures carefully before scoring the discussion and concept maps. In this study, the English article "Hurricane" [31], which uses common explanatory words, was chosen for the learning process so the participants could understand it without bias. An English concept list, which contained 12 concepts, was prepared. These were translated into Japanese and Thai by native speakers that could use and understand English well.

3.3 Experiment Procedure

Even though the 78 university students used different languages, they participated in the experiment under the same conditions, using the same experiment procedure, content, and concept mapping tool. The concept mapping tool was developed based on an original KB map and new functions were added for supporting the pair discussion. An overview of the experimental procedure is illustrated in Fig. 2.

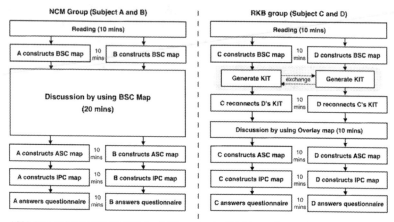

Fig. 2. Overview of the experimental procedure

The Experimental Procedure of the NCM Group

The participants received the paper based article and they were allowed to underline and take short notes on the paper. After reading for 10 min, they had to construct the concept map by using the provided concept list in 10 min. In this step, they could freely create the linking words for specifying meanings of the relationships. The concept map constructed in this step is called "Before Self-Comprehension Map" (BSC map) for the individual, and "Before Partner's Comprehension Map" (BPC map) for the partner's concept map. After the participants had uploaded the concept map to the server, they were paired with other students randomly. They were then requested to discuss their understandings between each other, including why they thought differently. The participants in the NCM group were given 20 min for discussion which they could terminate at any point.

After the discussion step, they had to construct a map from the concept list in 10 min, but this time they had to construct the concept map following their understanding after the discussion. The concept map in this step is called "After Self-Comprehension Map" (ASC map) for the individual, and "After Partner's Comprehension Map" (APC map) for the partner's concept map. When they had completed the second concept map, they were requested to construct the last concept map in 10 min, which had to be constructed following the individual's understanding of their partner's viewpoint, which they obtained from the discussion task. This map is called "Inference Partner's Comprehension Map" (IPC map). After they finished the last concept map, they were asked to complete the questionnaire.

The Experimental Procedure of the RKB Group

The experimental conditions for the RKB group were the same as the NCM group. The participants had 10 min for reading the article and they could also write on or underline the paper. They had to construct the concept map by using the provided concept list and they could create the label for each relationship freely in 10 min, in the same way as the

NCM group. After they completed their BSC Map, they were paired with other students randomly and their concept maps were decomposed to form the "kit", which contained a list of concepts and a list of relation lines with linking words. After the kits were generated, these decomposed components were sent to the partner of the kit's owner. The participants had to use the kit to construct the concept map following their understanding in 10 min. Then the participants had 10 min to discuss with their partner any points where they had the same or different understandings, as well as the reasons for any different understandings. In this discussion, they were provided an overlay of each other's maps for facilitating their discussion. The comparison map can represent the links that the pair connected both same and different connections.

As with the NCM group, after the discussion, they had to construct the ASC Map and the IPC Map, for which they were allowed only 10 min for each step. They then had to also complete the questionnaire.

3.4   Preparation Before Analysis

To evaluate the similarity between two concept maps, the relational concept map assessment method (the relational scoring) is applied. This is a well-known manual concept map assessment method was claimed to have the highest reliability compared to the other five manual methods among those considered reliable [32]. This method scores the concept map by checking the possible relationship between each proposition, the suitability of the label between concepts of the proposition and the compatibility between label and the direction of the arrow or hierarchy between two concept maps. Hence, it can illustrate the similarity between two maps [30]. The raters awarded scores between zero and three points for each proposition based on the suitability of the meaning of the proposition. The relational scoring is proper to use to compare how the same/different meaning of each proposition between two concept maps. Because the procedure of this scoring method pays the attention of scoring to the meaning of linking words in propositional level. So the relational scoring was selected to checked the similarity of concept map of two collaborators in this study.

In this experiment, the results of all participants which contained three languages, (English, Japanese, and Thai), were combined for analysis. To confirm that before discussion these three group of participants are not different, the relational scoring was used to evaluate the similarity between the BSC and BPC map of each participant. The average of relational score of each language was represented in Table 1. These relational scores of three language groups were examined using ANOVA and the results

Table 1. The average relational scores between the BSC and BPC maps

Language of group	The number of participants	Average score	Variance
International students	16	31.72	12.97
Japanese students	14	40.04	13.97
Thai students	48	30.87	21.23

Note: Calculated ANOVA are statistically _not_ significant difference (p-value = 0.2708)

showed the difference in the relational scores of these three language groups were not statistically significant, having a p-value = 0.2708. This means they had the same understanding in pairs not much different before discussion.

3.5   Questionnaires

The questionnaires were prepared for the NCM and RKB groups separately to examine their opinion about the discussions using the traditional concept mapping and Reciprocal KB map. These questionnaires also asked the participants about their activity during the discussion. These questions request the participants to evaluate both themselves and their partner. Lastly, they had to conclude their discussion by identifying where their understanding was the same and where it was different. If they had a different understanding, they had to give the reason, based on their discussion.

4   Experiment Results and Discussion

4.1   Discussion Score

The experimental results show that discussions with the traditional concept map and with Reciprocal KB map are different. The discussion score was evaluated from the BSC map and the content of discussions from each pair of participants. The raters had to match each proposition with the conversation in the discussion, and then categorize that conversation to each type of talk [6]. The raters had to consider each proposition of the concept maps and give a discussion score for each type of talk on the mentioned proposition. The raters counted a conversation as exploratory talk when the pair discussed cooperatively and shared the reasons for their statement/answer. For the cumulative talk, the raters counted conversations where the participants tried to share their understanding but they did not explain clearly or they did not give a reasonable answer. Conversations where the participants just made their own decisions, or which led to more competition than cooperation, were classified as disputative talk. Lastly, talk where the participants only read to their partner were scored as "Non-Contributed Discussion Talk." For these, the participants did not receive any critical discussion points.

Following these criteria, the results of the discussion score for each group are illustrated in Fig. 3. These graphs show the difference between the ratios of each type of talk from each participant group. In the experiment, most of the participants from the NCM group read their concept map for discussion. Their partner just checked the same and different parts and then asked a few questions and finished the discussion. Therefore, this process can produce all types of talk, but the Non-Contributed Discussion talk was more dominant than the others. This situation shows that the concept map can help participants to represent and organize their understanding, but it requires more features to encourage the participants to think about their propositions more deeply than just reading them. On the other hand, Reciprocal KB map requests that the participants reconstruct the kit of their partner, so they have to think deeply about their partner's understanding. Even if they cannot connect their partner's kit well, they can ask questions of their partner during the discussion. Because they have questions in their mind during the connecting of the kit, their questions have an inquiring charac-teristic regarding the form of the kit, such as "Why did you connect like this? Why can I not connect your proposition? How do you think about this proposition?" In addition, during the connection of the kit, participants can arrange their questions in order to clarify their confusion.

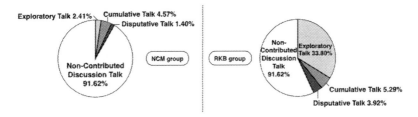

Fig. 3. The results of the discussion score

Table 2 suggests that Reciprocal KB can support the participants in discussing the topic more smoothly compared to the traditional concept map because during the construction of their partner's kit, they had to think about the kit and their partner's understanding before formulating questions in their mind. This behavior affected their discussion. The participants in the RKB group gave the questions to their partner regularly. They asked about the reason for their partner's proposition construction and answers were given in the form of an explanation. On the other hand, the participants in the NCM group tried to read the propositions to each other and they assumed that their partner could understand them. Since they used a short amount of time for choosing their proposition to discuss, it was rather difficult for them to achieve a smooth dis-cussion. In addition, there were a lot of different propositions which they could not notice and they could not articulate the reasons for different understandings between each other.

Table 2. The average relational score of each type of concept map

	NCM group	RKB group
The number of mentioned propositions (props)	255 props from 770 props (33.12%)	347 props from 860 props (40.35%)
Average time of discussion	6 min (S.D. = 3.30) from 10 min provided	8.7 min (S.D. = 1.59) from 20 min provided

From the different types of talk that the participants from the both groups produced, we can conclude that the Reciprocal KB map can encourage the participants to produce more exploratory talk, which is effective for discussion, compared to the use of the traditional concept map. This result corresponds to the second research question which was related to investigating the differences between discussions that used the traditional concept map and discussions that used Reciprocal KB map.

4.2   Similarity Map Score

During the experiment, the participants in the two groups were requested to construct the concept map three times. The first corresponded to the BSC map, which represents their understanding before discussion. The second was the ASC map, which represents their understanding after discussion. The last map was the IPC map, which was constructed following the understanding gained from their partner. These three maps were paired and were scored by the relational scoring. The average score from each paired map and each group is represented in Table 3.

Table 3. The average relational score of each type of concept map

Average score	NCM group	RKB group	
BSC map and BPC map	29.39 (S.D. = 16.69)	35.83 (S.D. = 20.30)	
ASC map and APC map	49.04 (S.D. = 32.08)	61.85 (S.D. = 26.56)	+
IPC map and APC map	46.57 (S.D. = 29.52)	61.15 (S.D. = 22.16)	*

+ Marginal difference between NCM and RKB groups (p-value < 0.1)
* Significant difference between NCM and RKB groups (p-value < 0.05)
BSC: Before Self-Comprehension, **BPC:** Before Partner-Comprehension,
ASC: After Self's Comprehension, **APC:** After Partner's Comprehension,
IPC: Inference Partner's Comprehension

From the relational scoring, all participants in both the NCM and RKB groups had the same understanding after reading the article with no significant differences. After discussion, the participants in the RKB group could construct the same concept maps as their partner more than the participants in the NCM group, with this difference close to being statistical significant. This shows that the discussion can change some parts of their understanding to achieve a joint viewpoint. In addition, the participants in the RKB group constructed their IPC map to be the same as the APC map more effectively than the participants in the NCM group, with a statistically significant difference. These similarity map scores correspond to the first research question. This illustrates that Reciprocal KB map can encourage the participants to recognize their partner's understanding better than the traditional concept map. This ability will be a strong advantage for the next step of creating collaborative knowledge, as partners that can understand each other can better generate collaborative knowledge.

4.3   Results of Questionnaire

Tools of Discussion
In this study, two types of concept mapping tools were provided for participants. The participants of both groups were provided the list of concepts and created linking words by themselves. The participants in the NCM group used their concept map as content for discussion. From the open-ended question that requested them to share their opinion on this discussion method, most participants noted that the concept map was a suitable tool for representing their understanding allowing them to further understand their

partner's viewpoint. Some participants said it was harder to understand their partner's concept map compared to reading text and the improper propositions made them confused. It was also noted that the experimental process took a long time.

The participants in the RKB group noted that Reciprocal KB map was a new and interesting thing for them. They stated that reconstructing the kit to concept map of their partner was fun and like playing a game, and that they could understand each other better from the discussion. Additionally, they stated that the 10 min provided was not enough for the discussion. Some people found that it took a long time to create the concept map when they were requested to construct the ASC and IPC maps. However, these two maps were used only to confirm the assumptions in the experiment and are not required in the general application of the approach.

Collaborating During Discussion

In the questionnaire, participants were also required to check the actions during the discussion of both themselves and their partner. A total of 31.25% of participants from the NCM group evaluated themselves and their partner in the same way as not breaking the interim silence by introducing a possible topic for consideration. This means that they did not discuss a topic continuously. In contrast, most of the participants from the RKB group identified that they and their partner tried to explain their understanding to each other clearly and tried to introduce their interesting or confusing topic as much as they could but the time provided was not enough. Moreover, in the part of the questionnaire which asks about identification of the same/different understanding, the participants from the NCM group recognized areas where they had the same understanding as their partner but they had some confusion about where their understandings differed. For example, the NCM group participants filled out the different understanding field in the questionnaire but their partner completed that topic in the same understanding field. Additionally, they could not give clear reasons for their different understanding. This situation may indicate that the participants were still confused after the discussion. In contrast, the RKB group participants could identify the same/different understanding and they could give reasons for this. In addition, the pairs of participants who changed their proposition on the map tried to explain the reason why they changed their understanding.

4.4   Summary of Experiment Results

From the experimental results, we can answer the two research questions posed in Sect. 3. The similarity score between the IPC and APC maps indicates that Reciprocal KB map can support the participants in understanding each other. Additionally, the difference between the ratios of each type of talk in the NCM and RKB groups can answer the second research question, related to the difference between discussions using the traditional concept map and Reciprocal KB map. The participants from the RKB group who had to reconstruct their partner's kit were encouraged to produce exploratory talk more than the participants from the NCM group. These advantages over the traditional concept map can contribute to generating high quality collaborative knowledge through better understanding of each other.

5 Conclusion and Future Work

Kit-Build concept map (KB map) is an automatic concept map assessment framework which is utilized in the form of a learning task or exercise for checking learners' comprehension of a topic that they have already learned. Usually, it is used for confirming understanding between a teacher and learners in a class and it has previously been investigated in terms of its ability to support learners in expressing their understanding. This research proposes the utilization of KB map with a collaborative approach for encouraging shared understanding in pair discussion. The experiment was designed to compare discussions using a traditional and Reciprocal KB concept map. The results are separated into three parts: (1) the discussion score, (2) the similarity map score, and (3) the questionnaire. For the similarity map score, the concept map of participants was evaluated for similarity using several viewpoints. The most important aspect is represented by the similarity between the IPC and APC maps, which showed that the participants from the RKB group could recognize their partner's understanding better than the participants from the NCM group. This was because during reconstruction of the concept map using the provided components from Reciprocal KB map, the participants had to consider their partner's understanding more deeply than just reading the concept map or just checking the same/different understanding, as was the case for most participants from the NCM group. The similarity map score and the results of the questionnaire correspond to the first research question. They indicate that the Reciprocal KB map can contribute to pair discussions for sharing understanding. Additionally, in the discussion score, the participants from the RKB group produced more exploratory talk, which is valuable for contributing to effective discussion, compared to the participants from the NCM group. Most of the participants in the NCM group just read their concept map to check their understanding with their partner. Therefore, the discussion score answers the second research question and indicates that Reciprocal KB map is useful for encouraging pair discussion and producing effective discussions which can contribute to creating high quality collaboration more effectively than the traditional concept map. However, because the topic of discussion is guided by the kit, the creative discussion might be reduced. Evaluation of Reciprocal KB map from viewpoint of creativity is our important future work.

The results of this experiment confirm that the Reciprocal KB map can encourage collaborators to engage in high quality discussion and to share their understanding. However, the relation between the quality of discussion and the method by which they changed and shared their comprehension after discussing was not be investigated in this study. A deeper analysis of this aspect is reserved for future work. Additionally, we will attempt to use Reciprocal KB map for practical applications in a classroom, and to evaluate the products of discussion. The use of different topics and ages of collaborators is also an interesting focus for future work, in order to confirm the efficiency of Reciprocal KB map. In addition, to expand this research, Reciprocal KB map will be designed for supporting group discussion. After completing the supporting aspects for sharing understanding within pairs, we plan to promote collaborators to create continuous creative discussion. This next step of Reciprocal KB map will support its use in various discussion tasks.

Acknowledgements. This work was partially supported by JSPS KAKENHI Grant Number 17H01839 and 15H02931.

References

1. Barkley, E.F., Cross, K.P., Major, C.H.: Collaborative Learning Techniques: A Handbook for College Faculty. Jossey-Bass, San Francisco (2005)
2. Johnson, D.W., Johnson, R.T., Smith, K.A.: Cooperative learning returns to college: what evidence is there that it works? Change Mag. High. Learn. **30**(4), 26–35 (1998)
3. Johnson, D.W., Johnson, R.T.: Learning Together and Alone: Cooperative, Competitive, and Individualistic Learning. Allyn and Bacon, Massachusetts (1999)
4. Nunan, D.: Collaborative Language Learning and Teaching. Press Syndicate of the University of Cambridge, New York (1993)
5. Slavin, R.: Research on cooperative learning and achievement: what we know, what we need to know. Contemp. Educ. Psychol. **21**(1), 43–69 (1996)
6. Mercer, N.: The quality of talk in children's collaborative activity in the classroom. Learn. Instr. **6**(4), 359–377 (1996)
7. Barnes, M.: Cumulative and exploratory talk in a collaborative learning classroom. In: Proceeding of 22nd Conference of the Mathematics Education Research Group of Australasia, pp. 53–59. MERGA, Sydney (1999)
8. Haiyan, X.: "When the water flows, a channel is formed": professional learning and practice innovation through district research lesson study in the context of China's new curriculum reform. Thesis submitted for the degree of Doctor of Philosophy at the University of Leicester (2015)
9. Mercer, N., Dawes, L.: The value of exploratory talk. In: Exploring Talk in School, pp. 55–71 (2008)
10. Rojas-Drummod, S., Perez, V., Velez, M., Gomez, L., Mendoza, A.: Talking for reasoning among Mexican primary school children. Learn. Instr. **13**(6), 653–670 (2003)
11. Webb, P., Treagust, D.F.: Using exploratory talk to enhance problem-solving and reasoning skills in grade-7 science classrooms. Res. Sci. Educ. **36**(4), 381–401 (2006)
12. Knight, S., Mercer, N.: The role of exploratory talk in classroom search engine tasks. Technol. Pedagogy Educ. **24**(3), 303–319 (2015)
13. Mercer, N.: Sociocultural discourse analysis: analysing classroom talk as a social mode of thinking. J. Apply Linguist. **1**, 137–168 (2004). https://doi.org/10.1558/japl.v1i2.137
14. Hirashima, T., Yamasaki, K., Fukuda, H., Funaoi, H.: Kit-Build concept map for automatic diagnosis. In: Biswas, G., Bull, S., Kay, J., Mitrovic, A. (eds.) AIED 2011. LNCS (LNAI), vol. 6738, pp. 466–468. Springer, Heidelberg (2011). https://doi.org/10.1007/978-3-642-21869-9_71
15. Hirashima, T., Yamasaki, K., Fukuda, H., Funaoi, H.: Framework of Kit-Build concept map for automatic diagnosis and its preliminary use. Res. Pract. Technol. Enhanced Learn. **10**(1), 1–21 (2015)
16. Wunnasri, W., Pailai, J., Hayashi, Y., Hirashima, T.: Reliability investigation of automatic assessment of learner-build concept map with Kit-Build method by comparing with manual methods. In: André, E., Baker, R., Hu, X., Rodrigo, M., du Boulay, B. (eds.) AIED 2017. LNCS, vol. 10331, pp. 418–429. Springer, Cham (2017)

17. Wunnasri, W., Pailai, J., Hayashi, Y., Hirashima, T.: Validity of Kit-Build method for assessment of learner-build map by comparing with manual methods. IEICE Trans. Inf. Syst. **E101**(4), 1141–1150 (2018)
18. Stahl, G.: A model of collaborative knowledge-building. In: Proceeding of 4th International Conference on the Learning Sciences, Mahwah, NJ, pp. 70–77 (2000)
19. Johnson, W., Mesch, D., Johnson, R.: Impact of positive interdependence and academic group contingencies on achievement. J. Soc. Psychol. **128**(3), 345–352 (1988)
20. Resta, P., Laferrière, T.: Technology in support of collaborative learning. Educ. Psychol. Rev. **19**(1), 65–83 (2007). https://doi.org/10.1007/s10648-007-9042-7
21. Palincsar, A.S., Ransom, K., Derber, S.: Collaborative research and development of reciprocal teaching. J. Educ. Leadersh. **46**(4), 37–40 (1988)
22. Sugihara, K., Osada, T., Nakata, S., Funaoi, H., Hirashima, T.: Experimental evaluation of Kit-Build concept map for science classes in an elementary school. In: Proceeding of Computers in Education, Singapore, pp. 17–24 (2012)
23. Yoshida, K., Sugihara, K., Nino, Y., Shida, M., Hirashima, T.: Practical use of Kit-Build concept map system for formative assessment of learners' comprehension in a lecture. In: Proceeding of Computers in Education, Bali, Indonesia, pp. 906–915 (2013)
24. Nomura, T., Hayashi, Y., Suzuki, T., Hirashima, T.: Knowledge propagation in practical use of Kit-Build concept map system in classroom group work for knowledge sharing. In: Proceeding of Computers in Education Workshop 2014, Nara, Japan, pp. 463–472 (2014)
25. Alkhateeb, M., Hayashi, Y., Hirashima, T.: Comparison between Kit-Build and Scratch-Build concept mapping methods in supporting EFL reading comprehension. J. Inf. Syst. Educ. **14**(1), 13–27 (2015)
26. Hayashi, Y., Hirashima, T.: Kit-Build concept mapping for being aware of the gap of exchanged information in collaborative reading of the literature. In: Proceeding of Human Interface and the Management of Information, Greece, pp. 31–41 (2014)
27. Hayashi, Y., Hirashima, T.: Analysis of the relationship between metacognitive ability and learning activity with Kit-Build concept map. In: Proceeding of Human Interface and the Management of Information, United States, pp. 304–312 (2015)
28. Pailai, J., Wunnasri, W., Yoshida, K., Hayashi, Y., Hirashima, T.: The practical use of Kit-Build concept map on formative assessment. Res. Pract. Technol. Enhanced Learn. **20** (12), 1–23 (2017)
29. Novak, J.D., Cañas, A.J.: Technical report IHMC CmapTools. Institute for Human and Machine Cognition (2008)
30. McClure, J.R., Bell, P.E.: Effects of an Environmental Education Related STS Approach Instruction on Cognitive Structures of Preservice Science Teachers. State University, Pennsylvania (1990)
31. ReadWorks: Earth Science: Hurricanes (2012). https://www.readworks.org/article/Earth-Science-Hurricanes/7bb94583-4566-48e4-98ce-a8a0a92a6724. Accessed 08 Jan 2018
32. McClure, J.R., Sonak, B., Suen, H.K.: Concept map assessment of classroom learning: reliability, validity, and logistical practicality. J. Res. Sci. Teach. **36**(4), 475–492 (1999)

Early Identification of At-Risk Students Using Iterative Logistic Regression

Li Zhang[✉] and Huzefa Rangwala

Department of Computer Science, George Mason University, Fairfax, VA, USA
lzhang18@gmu.edu, rangwala@cs.gmu.edu

Abstract. Higher education institutions are faced with the challenge of low student retention rates and high number of dropouts. 41% of college students in United States do not finish their undergraduate degree program in six years, and 60% of them drop out in their first two years of study. It is crucial for universities and colleges to develop data-driven artificial intelligence systems to identify students at-risk as early as possible and provide timely guidance and support for them. However, most of the current classification approaches on early dropout prediction are unable to utilize all the information from historical data from previous cohorts to predict dropouts of current students in a few semesters. In this paper, we develop an Iterative Logistic Regression (ILR) method to address the challenge of early prediction. The proposed framework is able to make full use of historical student record and effectively predict students at-risk of failing or dropping out in future semesters. Empirical results evaluated on a real-wold dataset show significant improvement with respect to the performance metrics in comparison to other existing methods. The application enabled by this proposed method provide additional support to students who are at risk of dropping out of college.

Keywords: Iterative Logistic Regression · Educational data mining Early dropout prediction

1 Introduction

According to the National Center for Education Statistics [17], more than 41% of students who began seeking an undergraduate degree at a four-year institution in Fall 2009 failed to graduate within six years. In 2008–2009, higher education institutions spent more than $263 billion on education and related expenses, delivering the equivalent of $487.5 million semester-credit hours of instruction. The spent amount has grown up to $536 billion in academic year 2014–2015. According to recent work by Schneider [20], US taxpayers spent more than $9 billion providing education to first year students who failed to return the following year. Schneider and Yin [21] further estimated the opportunity cost for college dropouts from just a single cohort of entering students lost is $3.8 billion in lifetime income, and the government loss is at $730 million in potential tax revenue.

© Springer International Publishing AG, part of Springer Nature 2018
C. Penstein Rosé et al. (Eds.): AIED 2018, LNAI 10947, pp. 613–626, 2018.
https://doi.org/10.1007/978-3-319-93843-1_45

Prior research work in this area has involved the analysis of student dropout data and identified the need for early determination and possible intervention and additional support from the institution [22]. Dynarski [9] provides several possible practical intervention ideas for secondary school dropouts which can be implemented at the university level. There is also evidence that summer bridge programs are helpful in learning and producing environments that can ultimately improve student performance and retention [5,16].

There are many different definitions that have been used for the term 'dropout' and 'retention' based on the count of returning next-year students and graduating in 6 years. Typically retention is staying at school until completion of a degree and dropping out is leaving school permanently without a degree. However, a student might leave the college to work a few years and come back to finish the degree. This is known as *stopout* [14]. More than three decades ago, Alexander Astin identified the dropout as a problematic concept [3]. According to Astin, "a 'perfect' classification of dropouts versus non-dropouts could be achieved only when all of the students had either died without ever finishing college or had finished college." Hagedorn [13] discussed this vague and complicated definition of retention/persistence and concluded there is not a consensus on the correct way to measure retention – it depends on the context. To accommodate both dropout and stopout, our study use a stricter definition: a *dropout student* is defined as a student who fails to register the next semester or has a GPA of 0.0 in the next semester. Our goal is to effectively predict and identify students who are at a high risk of dropping out. We propose an Iterative Logistic Regression (ILR) to predict student dropouts, which has interpretable coefficients and identifies at-risk students at an early stage.

Our paper has several main contributions. We propose a robust method with regularization to model the sequential effect of previous term performance. We are able to learn from all the semesters from historical data of the past cohorts of students and effectively generate important features for dropout prediction in future semesters. Our proposed model has the further advantage of easily interpreted predictions.

2   Literature Review

In recent years, research work has explored key features using classical statistical methods to identify students at risk of dropping out from their field of study and leaving college/university. Golding et al. [12] identified the relationship between students' overall academic performance (GPA) and matriculation chances in the first year based on enrollment information. Druzdzel and Glymour [8] were among the first researchers to apply machine learning algorithms to study the student retention problem. Campbell [6] used factor analysis and logistic regression on a set of student features derived from data extracted from Blackboard [4]. Pittman [19] compared several data mining techniques (logistic regression, decision tree, Bayesian classifiers and neural network) to predict student retention and concluded that logistic regression had the best performance. Logistic regression has also been used in different contexts for early dropout prediction [11,23].

Kovacic [15] explored the effect of demographic variables and study environment on the outcome of student enrollment with various tree-based methods and logistic regression. Nandeshwar et al. [18] analyzed retention records and concluded that focusing more resources on high-risk groups of students is helpful in improving their chances of completing a university degree. Baradwaj and Pal [4] applied decision tree to classification using features derived from attendance reports, class test scores and assignment submissions. Tanner [24] used the k-nearest neighbor method to predict student failure in an online course setting. Although these methods are able to predict student dropout, none of them are able to make full use of the extra semesters in the data from the previous student cohort for early dropout prediction. Ameri et al. [2] and Chen et al. [7] performed survival analysis, particularly cox regression, on the student performance datasets. Their analysis does not take into account the additional correlation in the data after the first dropout occurs and hence is not able to model student stopout. Our proposed method is able to work with the extra available semesters in the past student record and does not assume one-time dropout.

3   Methods

The primary objective of this study is to predict student dropouts in future semesters. A *dropout student* is defined as a student who fails to register a semester or has a zero GPA in the semester. Table 1 is a summary of notations which we use in this paper. Let n be the number of semesters a student is typically at a university. We have p_t students at the beginning of each semester, where p_t is different in each semester. Let $\boldsymbol{R}$ denote time invariant features of students (such as demographic information). We use $\boldsymbol{G}_t = [\boldsymbol{g}_1, \boldsymbol{g}_2, \cdots, \boldsymbol{g}_t]$ to represent semester GPA from 1 to t-th term. We also developed additional features including *Absence* denoted by $\boldsymbol{A}_t$; generated by GPA in t-th semester. $\boldsymbol{A}_t = [\boldsymbol{a}_1, \boldsymbol{a}_2, \cdots, \boldsymbol{a}_t]$ represents absence and is indicated by semester GPA $\boldsymbol{g}_t$. For Student j in t-th term,

$$a_{tj} = \begin{cases} 0 & g_{tj} \geq 0 \\ 1 & \text{Otherwise} \end{cases} \tag{1}$$

We use y_{tj} as labels for a dropout event in t-th term for student j. $y_{tj} = 1$ implies that student j is considered a dropout.

Logistic regression is a technique that has been widely used by researchers in the field of education data mining. Observing student performance in previous semesters usually has an impact on his future performance, we focus on using this fact to improve logistic regression.

Table 1. Glossary of symbols

Notation	Description
s	Number of students by semester t
m	Number of available semesters of new students available
n	Number of semesters of new student we predict up to
$\boldsymbol{x}_t$	All predictor variables for the set of students existing for prediction in semester t
$\boldsymbol{x}_{tj}$	Vector of predictor variables for Student j existing for prediction in semester t
$\boldsymbol{G}_t$	Matrix containing GPA record up to semester t
$\boldsymbol{g}_{tj}$	GPA record for semester t for student j
$\boldsymbol{A}_t$	Matrix containing feature of absence up to semester t
$\boldsymbol{a}_{tj}$	Record of absence for semester t for student j
$\boldsymbol{R}$	Matrix containing static features such as demographic feature
$\boldsymbol{\omega}_t$	The weight vector for semester t
λ	L_1 regularization parameter for over-fitting
$\boldsymbol{y}_t$	Set of labels for students by semester t
y_{tj}	The label for student j in semester t
$\boldsymbol{p}_t$	Predicted probability for dropout for semester t

Logistic Regression. Let m be the number of semesters that we have GPA for in the test set. $\boldsymbol{x}_{tj}$ denotes all features including static and time-dependent features for student j in the t-th semester. d_{tj} is the length of the feature vector $\boldsymbol{x}_{tj}$.

y_{tj} are class labels representing the event of dropout for student j in t-th semester (1 for dropout and 0 otherwise). Logistic regression computes the probability that student j dropouts in a semester by:

$$p(y_{tj}|\boldsymbol{x}_t; \boldsymbol{\omega}_t) = \sigma(y_{tj}\boldsymbol{\omega}_t^\mathsf{T}\boldsymbol{x}_{tj})$$
$$= \frac{1}{1 + \exp\left(-y_{tj}\boldsymbol{\omega}_{tj}^\mathsf{T}\boldsymbol{x}_{tj}\right)} \quad (2)$$

where $\boldsymbol{\omega}_t = [\omega_{i1}, \omega_{i2}, \cdots, \omega_{id_t}]^\mathsf{T}$ is the coefficient vector to be solved for.

We impose the L_1 constraint [25] to enforce sparsity. This estimator is known as lasso and its L_1-regularized log-likelihood is given by:

$$l(\boldsymbol{\omega}_t) = \sum_{j=1}^{s_t} \log(1 + \exp(y_{tj}\boldsymbol{\omega}_t^\mathsf{T}\boldsymbol{x}_{tj})) + \frac{\lambda}{2}|\boldsymbol{\omega}_t| \quad (3)$$

λ is a parameter that we need to tune. The L_1 penalty is used for both variable selection and shrinkage. A sufficiently large λ will cause some coefficients equal to 0 and hence not be included in the model. By setting appropriate λ value, we are able to eliminate misleading or unnecessary features and make the model easier to interpret. ω_i can be solved by the Proximal Newton method proposed by Friedman et al. [10].

Iterative Logistic Regression. The key idea behind the iterative logistic regression is to incorporate the predicted outputs that denote the probability of dropout in earlier semesters for future semesters in a cascaded manner. Given m semesters of historical data as a first step we use the LR model with lasso penalty to obtain dropout prediction for the $(m + 1)$-th semester. Besides the time-invariant features, we use this probabilistic value as an additional variable to include for training a new regularized LR model for identifying dropouts in the $(m + 2)$-th semester. Generalizing this further, the estimated probability $\hat{p}_k$ of dropout in a future semester k $(m < k \leq n)$ can be computed by the following equation:

$$\hat{p}(y_{jk}|\boldsymbol{x}_m) = \sigma\Big(\sum \omega_k \Big(\sum_{t=m+1}^{k-1} \hat{p}(y_{jt}|\boldsymbol{x}_{mj}) + \sum_{t=1}^{m}(\boldsymbol{A}_t + \boldsymbol{G}_t) + \boldsymbol{R} \Big) \Big) \qquad (4)$$

Algorithm 1. Algorithm for Iterative Logistic Regression (ILR).

Data: m, n, training data $\boldsymbol{x}_n$, testing $\boldsymbol{x}'_m$
Result: testing data $\boldsymbol{x}'[(m + 1) : n]$
parameter : λ_L, λ_U
1 Extract $\boldsymbol{G}_n$, $\boldsymbol{A}_n$, $\boldsymbol{R}$ from $\boldsymbol{x}_n$;
2 Extract $\boldsymbol{G}'_m$, $\boldsymbol{A}'_m$, $\boldsymbol{R}'$ from $\boldsymbol{x}'_m$;
3 $\boldsymbol{x} = [\boldsymbol{A}_n[1 : m], \boldsymbol{G}_n[1 : m], \boldsymbol{R}]$;
4 $\boldsymbol{x}' = [\boldsymbol{A}'_n[1 : m], \boldsymbol{G}'_n[1 : m], \boldsymbol{R}']$;
5 **for** $t = (m + 1)$ **to** n **do**
6 $\quad$ $\boldsymbol{y}_t = \boldsymbol{A}[t]$;
7 $\quad$ Learn ω_t by Eqs. (2) and (3);
8 $\quad$ Estimate $\boldsymbol{p}_t$ into Eq. (2);
9 $\quad$ $\boldsymbol{x} = [\boldsymbol{x}, \boldsymbol{p}_t]$;
10 $\quad$ Substitute ω_t into Eq. (2) to estimate $\boldsymbol{p}'_t$;
11 $\quad$ $\boldsymbol{x}' = [\boldsymbol{x}', \boldsymbol{p}'_t]$;
12 **end**

By Eq. 3, $p(y_k|\boldsymbol{x}_m)$ is the probability of dropout and m represents the available terms for testing data. A_t and G_t are the feature of absence and GPA of semester t. (i.e. if $G_j = 0$, $A_j = 1$.) R contains the non time-dependent feature including high school GPA, gender, race, school/department while admitted. We can then substitute ω_k iteratively to estimate the probability of dropout in the next few years.

4   Experimental Protocol

4.1   Dataset

We performed experiments on a dataset from George Mason University (GMU), a large public university in the United States, starting from Fall 2009 to Spring 2016. Since the record of transfer students have less data, we focus on first-time-entry students. The following information from the student grade database are obtained: id, cohort, age, the major they applied, high school GPA, ACT scores, Scholastic Assessment Test (SAT) scores, graduating term, SAT math score, duration, enrollment years and semester GPA.

For evaluation, we only use students who are in cohorts within the Fall 2009 to Spring 2013 ranges. This ensures we have full six semesters for validation. We have a total of 13643 records.

4.2   Experimental Protocol

Figure 1 shows our evaluation protocol. Assume we are at the end of Spring 2013 and would like to identify dropouts for the students first enrolled in Fall 2012, then there are only data available from Fall 2012 and Spring 2013 for this cohort. We use student enrolled first enrolled from Fall 2009 to Spring 2012 as training set, and the students enrolled from Fall 2012 to Fall 2013 as testing set. There are 7932 students in training set and 5690 students in the testing set. We compare our proposed method with six baseline methods: random guess (RD), Naive Bayes (NB), Random Forest (RF), Decision Tree (DT), k-Nearest-Neighbour (KNN) and Logistic Regression (LR).

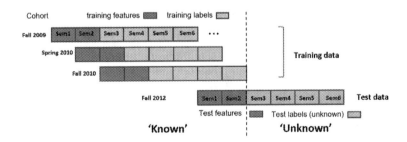

Fig. 1. Demonstration for using historical student records from Fall 2009 to Fall 2011 to predict Fall 2012 students dropout in the end of Spring 2013. 'Sem' is short for semester

4.3   Data Pre-processing

Figure 2 shows the student dropout rate from cohort Fall 2009–2013. The results shows that students enrolled in different years have similar distribution irrespective of their starting semester since they first enrolled. Under this assumption, we are allowed to use the data from the past cohorts of students to predict current students dropouts in the future semesters. We simply align the data by the term they first enrolled in the system. Tables 2 and 3 are the sample student data before and after alignment and cleaning. Student A first enrolled in Fall 2015 and obtained a GPA of 3.0 and student B first enrolled in Spring 2016 and obtained a GPA of 3.5. Then student A and student B have a GPA of 3.0 and 3.5 for their first semester, respectively. There are approximately 15–40% of missing data for the high school GPA, ACT scores and SAT score features. The missing values for high school GPA and SAT scores are imputed by the respective mean value. We also take the natural logarithm of SAT scores to avoid scaling issue on regression model.

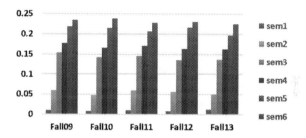

Fig. 2. Barchart on first 6 semesters of student dropout rate for cohort Fall 2009–2013 shows very similar distribution across different cohorts. 'Sem' is short for semester.

Table 2. Sample student data before aligning and cleaning.

Id	Cohort	Fall15	Spring16	Fall16	Spring17
1	Fall15	3.0	NA	2	?
2	Spring16	–	2	3.2	?
3	Fall16	–	–	4	?

Table 3. Sample student data after aligning and cleaning. G(t), A(t) denotes GPA and Attendance for semester t. (1 means dropout and 0 means retain).

Id	G(1)	G(2)	G(3)	G(4)	A(1)	A(2)	A(3)	A(4)
1	3.0	0	2	0	0	1	0	?
2	2	3.2	1.8	–	0	0	?	?
3	4	4	–	–	0	0	?	?

4.4   Metrics

Our goal is to evaluate the performance of various models on the task of predicting if a student is likely to enroll in the next semester; and hence predict whether the student will drop out or not. The outputs of logistic regression are in the form of probability. Since we are dealing with the prediction of a binary outcome, we apply True Positive (TP), False Negative (FN) and False Positive (FP) to measure the counts. We use 0.5 as the decision boundary. We also use *AUC*, *PRAUC* and *F1* to accommodate the imbalance issue. AUC is expressed as Area Under the Receiver Operating Characteristic (ROC) where the curve is created by plotting the true positive rate (TPR) against the False Positive rate (FPR) under various threshold values. PRAUC (Precision-Recall Curve) is the curve created by plotting Precision against Recall. This curve is more sensitive on positive class in general. Since we are more interested in positive prediction being correct (precision) without missing students at risk (recall), we pick PRAUC as our evaluation metrics.

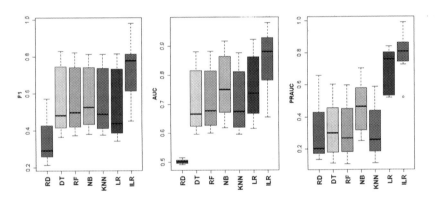

Fig. 3. Boxplots of F1 score, AUC and PRAUC on the next-4-semester dropout prediction after 2, 3, 4 semesters with different methods. The table shows ILR has a higher mean and lower variance across all metrics.

5   Experimental Results and Discussion

Figure 4 shows the F1 and PRAUC for ILR approach and comparative baselines. In the cases of predicting next term, ILR has similar performance to standard LR. After adding the first estimated probability feature $\hat{p}_3$, the F1 score improves by 34% and the PRAUC improves by 20% using only two semesters worth of data (Table 4).

After normalization, the coefficient of $\hat{p}_4$ is 9.25, which is more influential than the binary absence feature A_2 (-2.1). Most other methods show poor results given data for just two semesters and ILR perform the best. ILR shows almost identical performance in F1 score when predicting 4th and 5th semesters

Table 4. F1 and PRAUC generated by prediction for cohort Fall 2013 students after 2, 3, 4 semesters with different methods. Table results shows out of 12 experiments, ILR wins 9 and 10 times for F1 and PRAUC respectively.

Given	Predict	F1 Score						
		RD	DT	RF	NB	KNN	LR	ILR
2	3	0.213	0.517	0.525	**0.544**	0.511	0.474	0.473
	4	0.226	0.449	0.47	0.51	0.465	0.405	**0.813**
	5	0.29	0.437	0.423	0.473	0.432	0.386	**0.778**
	6	0.296	0.42	0.442	0.44	0.413	0.374	**0.744**
3	4	0.241	**0.83**	0.822	0.813	0.813	0.815	0.814
	5	0.276	0.728	0.726	0.733	0.72	0.714	**0.778**
	6	0.295	0.692	0.698	0.697	0.691	0.677	**0.747**
	7	0.551	0.363	0.372	0.379	0.375	0.341	**0.485**
4	5	0.283	**0.791**	0.785	0.781	0.788	0.785	0.785
	6	0.306	0.763	0.757	0.747	0.755	0.75	**0.869**
	7	**0.556**	0.415	0.405	0.422	0.401	0.386	**0.452**
	8	0.572	0.411	0.418	0.428	0.41	0.392	**0.98**
Wins		0	1	2	3	0	0	**9**

Given	Predict	PRAUC						
		RD	DT	RF	NB	KNN	LR	ILR
2	3	0.135	0.289	0.262	0.312	0.261	**0.525**	0.524
	4	0.155	0.316	0.276	0.328	0.256	0.521	**0.726**
	5	0.2	0.32	0.319	0.366	0.295	0.528	**0.749**
	6	0.218	0.344	0.324	0.378	0.295	0.539	**0.741**
3	4	0.153	0.114	0.108	0.568	0.114	**0.84**	0.839
	5	0.189	0.198	0.193	0.556	0.188	0.747	**0.802**
	6	0.209	0.232	0.212	0.554	0.214	0.733	**0.886**
	7	0.633	0.604	0.598	0.705	0.589	0.77	**0.807**
4	5	0.197	0.13	0.146	0.25	0.146	**0.82**	0.82
	6	0.225	0.164	0.172	0.28	0.183	0.802	**0.888**
	7	0.633	0.572	0.58	0.596	0.583	0.786	**0.81**
	8	0.66	0.589	0.583	0.615	0.587	0.801	**0.989**
Wins		0	0	0	0	0	3	**10**

dropouts with training sets of two and three semesters. Figure 3 is a boxplot of F1, AUC and PRAUC. ILR perform the best in all three evaluation metrics with a higher mean and a smaller variance. From Fig. 2, we notice that the dropout rates are all below 25%. This is a highly imbalanced dataset. Precision and recall do not consider true negatives and thus won't be affected by the relative imbalance. Hence, both F1 Score and PRAUC are good at imbalance data on

True Positive (TP), False Negative (FN) and False Positive (FP). PRAUC is more sensitive to False Positive than AUC. A low PRAUC prediction tends to identify a lot of students who are not going to dropout as target group.

We also report the counts of student across terms. Figure 4 is a stack barplot in predicting dropouts given two semesters of test sets. False negative (black), false positive (dark grey) and true positive (light grey) correspond to the number of students we missed dropping out, successfully caught, and false alarms, respectively. The plots show that ILR has significantly greater area in correctly prediction of dropout (light grey) and less misses (black) while not producing many false alarm (dark grey). Therefore, we conclude that ILR performs significantly better in predicting future dropout.

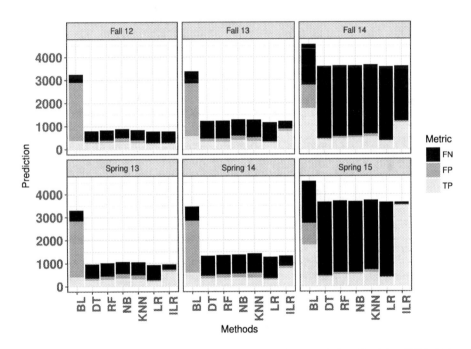

Fig. 4. Stacked barchart Given 2 terms dropout prediction of True Positive (TP), False Positive (FP) and False Negative (FN). For TP, the higher the better, FP and FN the lower the better.

5.1 Interpretation of Coefficient

Since our model is essentially a logistic regression model, the coefficient of our model has direct interpretation. Standardized coefficients are usually useful for comparing the relative influence of different predictors within an logistic regression model [1]. To compute standardized coefficients, we divide raw values of the coefficients ω_t by the standard deviation of their corresponding attributes.

Table 5. Raw and standardized coefficients of ILR for predicting dropout for 6th Semester with 2 (Early) and 4 (Late) semesters of data. ω_6^{Raw} is raw coefficient of ILR, where ω_6^{Norm} is standardized coefficient, which is not affected by scale of attributes. Attributes with '*' are generated by ILR.

Early prediction			Late prediction		
Variables	ω_6^{Raw}	ω_6^{Norm}	Variables	ω_6^{Raw}	ω_6^{Norm}
(Intercept)	-1.236	.	(Intercept)	-	-
A_2	-0.248	-0.980	A_2	0.46	1.34
G_1	-0.109	-0.107	A_3	0.34	0.94
G_2	-0.034	-0.015	A_4	.	.
log(SAT_Total_1600)	.	.	G_1	-0.042	-0.0412
HSGPA	-0.121	-0.14	G_2	.	.
log(ENTRY_AGE)	-0.0022	-0.0011	G_3	-0.102	-0.0766
log(SAT_Math)	.	.	G_4	-0.0188	-0.144
$\hat{p}_3*$	.	..	G_5	-0.677	-0.308
$\hat{p}_4*$	**4.789**	**17.0**	log(SAT_Total_1600)	.	.
$\hat{p}_5*$	.	.	HSGPA	.	.
			log(ENTRY_AGE)	.	.
			log(SAT_Math)	.	.
			$\hat{p}_5*$	**3.96**	**4.87**

Table 5 shows the raw and standardized regression coefficient of ILR for predicting dropout in semester 6 after 2nd and 4th semesters. The former is an early identification and the latter is a late identification. We are interested in understanding how relevant our latent probability p_t compare to other given predictors such as GPA and absence in previous semesters. In the table, the coefficient of p_4 and p_5 are 17.0 and 4.87, and the magnitudes are much greater than the all other attributes. This shows ILR generates dominant features from historical students records and successfully improved prediction greatly. That is why we have good performance of ILR in terms of F1 score, AUC and PRAUC.

5.2 Analysis on Correlation

To analyze the effect of adding the previous latent probability p_{t-1} is added as a regressor, which we present in Fig. 5, the correlation plot. Stronger correlated variables are shown in dark color. Our model applies lasso on top of the features to remove highly correlated or irrelevant features to get a robust and interpretable model. From the plot, *SAT_MATH* and *SAT_1600* are strongly correlated and have not been selected twice in the coefficient table. From the top row of both plots, the colored grids of p_t against y_6 shows that p_t are highly correlated with y_6. We also observe that later semester has greater correlation with the label y_6. The correlation plot agrees with our coefficient analysis and shows our features are relevant in the prediction.

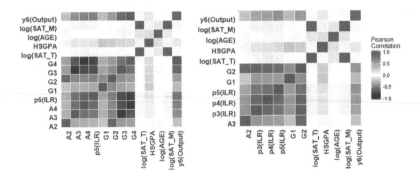

Fig. 5. Left Figure is the correlation between the regressors when predicting dropout in the 6-th semester given 2 semesters of data. Right Figure is the correlation plot for predicting dropout in the 6-th semester given 4 semesters of data (late). Darker color indicates higher correlation. $\hat{p}_t$ are generated by ILR given t terms. A_t and G_t are known features of Absence and GPA for semester t. Result shows that the latent features $\hat{p}_t$ have higher weights than given features both for early and late prediction.

6   Conclusion and Future Work

Predicting students at-risk is important for both, the institution and students. The event is rare and the timing is important. We propose an ILR model, learning from both the students' current semester-wise information as well as historical data from other students in the past with relatively small set of features. The coefficients of ILR can be normalized by dividing by standard deviation of the predictor variables to generate the variable importance for further interpretation. Our method has a few advantages compared to other methods.

First, it is an early prediction method which only requires a small amount of previous data from current students. Furthermore, because it uses the probability as a feature in the semester-wise trained model, we are able to take account of the previous "state" student performance and predict dropout for the next semester. The regularization of ILR features as well.

The proposed method will allow educational institutions to target student dropouts in a timely fashion and execute necessary actions accordingly. The model can be extended into coursework context with more available temporal information such as assignments, quiz and exams. This might lead to helpful interventions that help students and improve the overall educational quality and graduation rates.

Acknowledgement. This research work was supported by the National Science Foundation Grant 1447489. The experiments were running on ARGO, a research computing cluster provided by the office of research computing at George Mason University, VA (URL: http://orc.gmu.edu).

References

1. Agresti, A., Finlay, B.: Statistical models for the social sciences. Revascularization procedures after coronary angiography. J. Am. Med. Assoc. **269**, 2642–46 (1997)
2. Ameri, S., Fard, M.J., Chinnam, R.B., Reddy, C.K.: Survival analysis based framework for early prediction of student dropouts. In: Proceedings of the 25th ACM International on Conference on Information and Knowledge Management, pp. 903–912. ACM (2016)
3. Astin, A.W.: Predicting Academic Performance in College: Selectivity Data for 2300 American Colleges (1971)
4. Baradwaj, B.K., Pal, S.: Mining educational data to analyze students' performance. arXiv preprint arXiv:1201.3417 (2012)
5. Cabrera, N.L., Miner, D.D., Milem, J.F.: Can a summer bridge program impact first-year persistence and performance?: A case study of the new start summer program. Res. High. Educ. **54**(5), 481–498 (2013)
6. Campbell, J.P., DeBlois, P.B., Oblinger, D.G.: Academic analytics: a new tool for a new era. EDUCAUSE Rev. **42**(4), 40 (2007)
7. Chen, Y., Johri, A., Rangwala, H.: Running out of stem: a comparative study across stem majors of college students at-risk of dropping out early. In: Proceedings of the 8th International Conference on Learning Analytics and Knowledge, LAK 2018, pp. 270–279. ACM, New York (2018). https://doi.org/10.1145/3170358.3170410
8. Druzdzel, M., Glymour, C.: What do college ranking data tell us about student retention? (1994)
9. Dynarski, M., Clarke, L., Cobb, B., Finn, J., Rumberger, R., Smink, J.: Dropout prevention. IES practice guide. NCEE 2008-4025. National Center for Education Evaluation and Regional Assistance (2008)
10. Friedman, J., Hastie, T., Tibshirani, R.: Regularization paths for generalized linear models via coordinate descent. J. Stat. Softw. **33**(1), 1 (2010)
11. Glynn, J.G., Sauer, P.L., Miller, T.E.: A logistic regression model for the enhancement of student retention: the identification of at-risk freshmen. Int. Bus. Econ. Res. J. (IBER) **1**(8), 79–86 (2011)
12. Golding, P., Donaldson, O.: Predicting academic performance. In: 36th Annual Frontiers in Education Conference, pp. 21–26. IEEE (2006)
13. Hagedorn, L.S.: How to define retention. In: College Student Retention Formula for Student Success, pp. 90–105 (2005)
14. Horn, L., Carroll, C.D.: Stopouts or stayouts. In: Undergraduates Who Leave College in Their First Year (1999-087) (1998)
15. Kovacic, Z.: Predicting student success by mining enrolment data (2012)
16. Lonn, S., Aguilar, S.J., Teasley, S.D.: Investigating student motivation in the context of a learning analytics intervention during a summer bridge program. Comput. Hum. Behav. **47**, 90–97 (2015)
17. McFarland, J., Hussar, B., de Brey, C., Snyder, T., Wang, X., Wilkinson-Flicker, S., Gebrekristos, S., Zhang, J., Rathbun, A., Barmer, A., et al.: The condition of education 2017. NCES 2017-144. National Center for Education Statistics (2017)
18. Nandeshwar, A., Menzies, T., Nelson, A.: Learning patterns of university student retention. Expert Syst. Appl. **38**(12), 14984–14996 (2011)
19. Pittman, K.: Comparison of data mining techniques used to predict student retention. Nova Southeastern University (2008)
20. Schneider, M.: Finishing the first lap: the cost of first year student attrition in America's four year colleges and universities. American Institutes for Research (2010)

21. Schneider, M., Yin, L.: The hidden costs of community colleges. American Institutes for Research (2011)
22. Seidman, A.: College Student Retention: Formula for Student Success. Greenwood Publishing Group, Santa Barbara (2005)
23. Stage, F.K.: University attrition: LISREL with logistic regression for the persistence criterion. Res. High. Educ. **29**(4), 343–357 (1988)
24. Tanner, T., Toivonen, H.: Predicting and preventing student failure-using the k-nearest neighbour method to predict student performance in an online course environment. Int. J. Learn. Technol. **5**(4), 356–377 (2010)
25. Tibshirani, R.: Regression shrinkage and selection via the lasso. J. R. Stat. Soc. Ser. B (Methodol.), 267–288 (1996)

Author Index

Printed in the United States
By Bookmasters